W9-BTI-722

New Community Networks

Wired for Change

Douglas Schuler

Seattle Community Network

EMERSON COLLEGE LIBRARY

ACM Press
New York, New York

ADDISON-WESLEY PUBLISHING COMPANY

Reading, Massachusetts • Menlo Park, California • New York • Don Mills, Ontario
Harlow, United Kingdom • Amsterdam • Bonn • Sydney • Singapore • Tokyo
Madrid • San Juan • Milan • Paris

HM
131
.S3773
1996

In Praise of Study from "The Mother" by Bertolt Brecht. Copyright © 1957 by Suhrkamp Verlag, Berlin. Translation copyright © 1978 by Stefan S. Brecht. Reprinted by permission of Arcade Publishing, New York, NY.

"I'm the Slime" Words and music by Frank Zappa. Published by Munchkin Music © 1973. "I'm the Slime" is a musical composition that originally appeared on the Frank Zappa album "Over-Nite Sensation."

Photographs reproduced by permission of: Michelle Bates, pages 3, 39, and 40; Kit Galloway and Sherrie Rabinowitz, pages 44 and 45; Community Memory, page 59; Peter Miller, page 106; Felix Ruiz, page 159; Paper Tiger Television, page 245. Cover graphic courtesy of Seattle Community Network.

Sponsoring Editor: Thomas E. Stone
Assistant Editor: Kathleen Billus
Senior Production Supervisor: Nancy H. Fenton
Cover Designer: Meredith Nightingale
Senior Manufacturing Supervisor: Roy E. Logan
Composition: American Stratford Composition Company
Illustrations: Ryba Graphics

This book is published as part of ACM Press Books—a collaboration between the Association for Computing Machinery and Addison-Wesley Publishing Company. ACM is the oldest and largest educational and scientific society in the information technology field. Through its high-quality publications and services, ACM is a major force in advancing the skills and knowledge of IT professionals throughout the world. For further information about ACM, contact:

ACM Member Services
1515 Broadway, 17th Floor
New York, NY 10036-5701
Phone: 1-212-626-0500
Fax: 1-212-944-1318
E-mail: ACMHELP@ACM.org

ACM European Service Center
Avenue Marcel Thiry 204
1200 Brussels, Belgium
Phone: 32-2-774-9602
Fax: 32-2-774-9690
E-mail: ACM_Europe@ACM.org

Library of Congress Cataloging-in-Publication Data

Schuler, Douglas.
New community networks : wired for change / by Douglas Schuler.
p. cm.
Includes bibliographical references and index.
ISBN 0-201-59553-2
1. Community life—Technological innovations. 2. Community organization—Technological innovations. 3. Computer networks—Social aspects. 4. Technological innovations—Social aspects. 5. Community. 6. Social participation. I. Title.
HM131.S3773 1996
307—dc20   95-7271
                                        CIP

Many of the designations used by manufacturers and sellers to distinguish their products are claimed as trademarks. Where those designations appear in this book, and Addison-Wesley was aware of a trademark claim, the designations have been printed in initial caps or all caps.

Access the latest information about Addison-Wesley titles from our World Wide Web page:
        http://www.aw.com/

Copyright © 1996 by Addison-Wesley Publishing Company.

All rights reserved. No part of this publication may be reproduced, stored in a retrieval system, or transmitted, in any form or by any means, electronic, mechanical, photocopying, recording, or otherwise, without the prior written permission of the publisher. Printed in the United States of America.

1 2 3 4 5 6 7 8 9 10–MA–00 99 98 97 96

To

Flo Frankel and Donna Schuler

Contents

Preface

This book examines both community and technology but it is more concerned about community than it is about technology. It takes the position that technology is a tool that can serve humanity. Too frequently, however, humanity seems to be the servant of technology. We as concerned community members need to reassert ourselves into the design process, to reorient the focus appropriately. We should not think of technology as an end in itself or as an autonomous force; nor should we exalt the machine at the expense of the human and the humane. With those values and perspectives centermost, this book is concerned with designing technology that helps people work together more effectively and more creatively. It is about creating a future where human conviviality, ingenuity, and compassion can be encouraged to flower. Above all, it is about potential and possibilities.

Communication is at the core of almost all aspects of modern life. Education and health care rely upon it, as do everyday work and community life, and democratic governance. Since new communication technology does offer significant opportunities—as well as grave risks—and because the form of the communication infrastructure of tomorrow is being shaped today, it is critical that people from all walks of life play more active roles in this crucial transition period.

New computer-networking technology currently has many attributes that could undergird communication and technology that is truly democratic. Since it supports "many-to-many" communication, community, regional, national, and even international "conversations" on any topic are possible. This new media is unlike traditional media like newspapers and television that are "one-to-many" (broadcast) or telephones, and letter writing that are usually "one-to-one." These new systems can also dispense with traditional gatekeepers both corporate (who naturally and reflexively prioritize profit-making over the public good) or governmental (who may decide to supersede freedom of speech and expression for "national security," "decency," or a number of other ostensibly good reasons).

Although I argue for the development of democratic technology in general, this book is focused on the development of community computer networks, a concrete manifestation of democratic technology that demands our attention *right now*. These systems are not utopian pie in the sky. Five hundred thousand people currently use community networks and people have launched projects in *hundreds* of cities and regions in the United States and around the world. These are communication systems that can be developed *by* the community and *for* the community. They can be built and maintained inexpensively so access to them can be free. They can be designed so that "ordinary citizens" can use them to publish as well as to subscribe to a truly public media under local control. They can be part of an overall democratic renaissance and civic revitalization. Community networks can become important civic institutions that complement the public library and other community and civic assets. But they will not be created without determination and persistence. There is nothing inevitable about community network systems.

A Meliorist Stance

In this book, I take a *meliorist* stance. Meliorism assumes that things *can* get better, but *only* if people act to ensure that outcome. Meliorism is a pragmatic viewpoint, a problem-solving viewpoint. It does not ignore problems or explain them away with platitudes or ideology. The opposite of meliorism is fatalism, the doctrine that claims that the trajectory of human history is irrevocably set by powerful forces beyond human influence. Today there are fatalists of all kinds. Some feel that technology is intrinsically evil and is leading us ever closer to disaster. Others believe that technology is an unqualified boon, and that the newer, faster, shinier, and more powerful the technology is, the sooner we'll arrive at our utopian destination.

People, of course, do influence the course of the future in large and small ways through their actions. Increasingly, however, many critical decisions are made out of the public view and are oblivious of, and insensitive to, the public good. This need not be the case. Democracy is a tool of *public* deliberation and decision-making. It is a tool of meliorism. Today, unfortunately, we are finding that the tool of democracy is becoming increasingly misunderstood, underused, irrelevant, and blunt. It may also be the case that people have lost the skill and/or the desire to wield the tool. If there is to be a democratic revival in which people begin to increase their motivation and effectiveness, community computer networks and the struggle to develop them may play a major role.

Who Should Read This Book?

This book is intended for a wide audience of people who are interested in telecommunications technology as a tool to strengthen and reinvigorate community. This group of people may include librarians, educators (both K-12 and higher education); elected officials and other government employees; journalists; social change activists; students; business people; and people active in their communities; people in the computer or communications industry; minority and alternative-community members; doctors, nurses, and other health workers; people interested in computer networks, social change, the future of democracy, the revitalization of community or—as a matter of fact—just about anyone. I also hope that the book can introduce some critical issues, insight, or controversy into college and university courses. These courses may include computer science, architecture and urban planning, library and information sciences, sociology, public affairs and policy, public health and nursing, urban studies, political science, economics, communications and media studies, and science technology and society (STS) studies.

Historical Context

Historically, the most significant aspect of our era is the ending of the cold war. While this should be a cause for elation, this global realignment has seemingly left many people—including many in government—confused and with little sense of direction. And what could have been have been viewed as a unique opportunity to use the resources no longer required for war—the so-called peace dividend—in ways that benefit society such as improved schools, access to higher education, health promotion, economic development, and libraries—has apparently evaporated.

The other significant force is that of global economic competition and the concentration of economic power into multinational behemoths and trading blocs. In this post-cold war age, everyday citizens are increasingly becoming passive observers while huge global forces are changing, possibly irrevocably, communities and the lives of the people within them. This moment in time offers ample opportunities as well as powerful threats; it offers a compelling invitation for meliorists, to make a difference in this moment of historic transition.

Community Orientation

Communities are the right scale for many human endeavors. In this book I argue that community computer networks are an important community resource that should be built by the *community*. A global—or even national or state—scale is too large because there would be no allowance for particulars. Endeavors of that magnitude are too large, too distant, too inefficient, and too difficult to participate in.

Although we focus on community, the prototypical traditional—and static—community will play a limited role. Instead, a new type of community must be built that combines aspects of the old and the new. This new community must rest on a solid foundation of principles and values. It must be flexible and adaptable. It must be intelligent and creative. It must be wily. And it must be inclusive: Everybody must be allowed to participate.

While building the new community, we need to be pragmatic with respect to government and business. Both institutions are comprised of human beings—both have important functions and neither will go away in the near future. While building our new communities we will need to simultaneously engage both of these groups. Since both institutions ostensibly exist to provide services for people and communities, we must begin a serious and prolonged campaign to assert and improve this relationship. These institutions must be accountable to the people—rather than the reverse.

Organization of the Book

The first chapter introduces many of the main issues that will be explored in the rest of the book, including community and its relationship to technology. In this chapter I discuss the need for a "new community" that is built upon aspects of older, traditional communities, but is more "conscious" and is oriented toward flexibility, inclusivity, action, and sustainability. This chapter also introduces the six "core values" that form the foundation of this new community including (1) conviviality and culture; (2) education; (3) strong democracy; (4) health and human services; (5) economic equity, opportunity, and sustainability; and (6) information and communication. Finally, I introduce community computer networks as an appropriate technology for new communities and we take a short tour of the Cleveland Free-Net, the largest community network in the world.

Each of the next six chapters (2–7) is devoted to one of the six core values. In a sometimes roundabout way, each chapter presents four types of information: dysfunctional or declining aspects of the core value; prescriptive advice on stemming or reversing these trends; case studies of community networks or community-network projects that demonstrate interesting and/or successful approaches to the core value being examined; and, finally, an "agenda for action" for strengthening the community core value being discussed.

The next two chapters (8–9) take a slightly different approach by placing the existing or planned community network into a *context*, then examining the major entities in this context and discussing their relationship to community networks. Each chapter examines a special type of context—Chapter 8 examines the *social* context or architecture, while Chapter 9 examines the *technological* architecture of a community network. Two words of warning on Chapter 9: (1) It is the most technical of all the chapters and may safely be skipped by those not interested in this aspect; and (2) at the same time, it's not comprehensive enough to provide an unerring recipe (nor does one exist) for creating the perfect platform for hosting community networks. But hopefully the chapter has enough useful heuristics and insights to make it worth the read by technophiles and technophobes alike.

Chapter 10 is probably the most pragmatic of the chapters, as it describes the stages in the life-cycle of a community network. This includes establishing a group, running the network, implementing projects and programs, building strategic alliances within the community, organizing and planning, inaugurating the community network, evaluating the community network, and ensuring long-term impact and sustainability. The impact and sustainability section discusses some of the most important issues facing community networks today, including the critical question of funding.

Chapter 11, the book's concluding chapter, Directions and Implications, contains some glimpses of possible futures and how the university, the library, and the government (among others) could play a part in the movement towards democratic technology. The chapter concludes with a short section on why it's important to become active in the struggle to develop democratic technology and offers some suggestions. This book is *not* intended for armchair edification or amusement. The ideas discussed in the book have a chance to become realized only if there is a strong and sustained struggle.

Finally, I've provided a bibliography and numerous appendixes. The appendixes contain some useful pointers to organizations, electronic resources, community networks, hardware and software, and some documents from the Seattle Community Network project. There is also an appendix that describes the Sustainable Seattle project and the social contract ideas of Philadelphia activist Ed Schwartz as they relate to community participatory action research. All the appendixes are designed to provide useful information for the community activist, budding, lapsed, or current. Since this book is about using technology there is also a Web site (see Appendix B) that contains much of the information that can be found in the appendixes as well as some additional information. I'd like to thank the Morino Institute for support with the Web site.

Motivation and Purpose

This book is *not* intended to be a cookbook for community networks. The hardware, software, and development methodology are all indispensable, of course, to creating community networks, but the most important aspects of a community network, to my mind, are the involvement of community members and organizations in the process and the ability of the system to address *real* world problems using primarily *real* (nonprofessional) people to do it. Computer networks *can* be thought of as an important tool, but this is only a partial viewpoint, for it leaves many of the most critical questions unanswered. These questions center around *who* uses the tool and controls its use, *what* policies guide its use, and what is the *purpose* of the tool. The citizens of today and tomorrow can help determine the answers to these questions.

One of the most critical questions we can ask is whether we are building new communication technologies because we can or because they can actually provide some genuine use. I believe that the potential exists to craft demo-cratic technology, technology that can be actively used for actualization, not passively consumed out of boredom or because alternatives do not exist. I believe that these systems are sufficiently fluid and have enough "conceptual bandwidth" (as Free-Net founder Tom Grundner might say) to accommodate the commercial interests (that are dominating current development) as well as the community interests that are currently gaining strength. These community interests are vulnerable to being swamped in the coming months and years, if history is any guide.

I hope this book will be useful to you. I also hope that the dedication and vision of the developers will be as inspiring to you as they were to me. I apologize in advance for topics that I didn't cover or cover well enough and for those that received far too much ink. The field is immense—it is growing much too fast for me to capture all of it. I look forward to hearing your comments—both positive and negative—and advice. Most importantly, I look forward to working with you in the future in building a strong and effective community network movement.

Doug Schuler
douglas@scn.org
Seattle, Washington

Acknowledgments

I am very thankful for all the thoughtful comments and advice that I've received. Many people graciously reviewed sections of the book in progress. Their comments were invariably useful (in spite of the sometimes embarrassingly incomplete and muddied state of the sections that they reviewed). Phil Agre, Rita Altamore, Putnam Barber, Pat Barry, Phil Bereano, Ellen Bialo, Ann Bishop, Peter Blomquist, Alan Borning, Patricia Brennan, Amy Bruckman, Greg Byrd, Sylvia Caras, Marge Cargo, Gary Chapman, Jeff Chester, Steve Cisler, Richard Civille, Richard Conlin, Lucy Copass, Karen Coyle, Rick Crawford, Pavel Curtis, Lauren-Glen Davitian, Jim Davis, Bart Decrem, Linda Delzeit, Andreas Dieberger, Charles Ditzel, Jesse Drew, Janeane Dubuar, Stewart Dutfield, Mary Eaton, Michael Eisenmenger, Joan Fanning, Carl Farrington, Lee Felsenstein, Adam Feuer, John Finke, Stephanie Fowler, Steve Fram, Lew Friedland, David Friedlander, Batya Friedman, Kaye Gapen, Kit Galloway, Ben Gardiner, Ken Gillgren, Andy Gordon, Katherine Graham, Randy Groves, Tom Grundner, Kathleen Gygi, Peter Harter, Robert Hawkins, Tom Hicks, Kevin Higgins, Roberta Hinds, June Holley, Phil Hughes, Jon Jacky, Jeanette James, Hans Klein, Peter Kollock, Nancy Kunitsugo, Keith Kurtz, Richard Ladner, David Levinger, Roberta Lewis, Mike Lipson, Jamie Love, Richard Lowenberg, Philip Machanick, Chris Mays, Michael McCarthy, Joe McDonald, Ellen Meier, Jim Meinke, Peter Miller, Steve Miller, Lawrence Molloy, Mario Morino, Aki Namioka, Neil Oatley, Frank Odasz, Ken Phillips, Evelyn Pine, Steven Prest, Sherrie Rabinowitz, Pat Radin, Eric Raymond, Howard Rheingold, Eric Roberts, Scott Robinson, Marc Rotenberg, Gloria Rubio-Cortes, Richard Sclove, Ben Schneiderman, Ed Schwartz, Geoff Sears, Carmen Sirianni, Eric Smith, Tom Sparks, Kay Strauther, Dave Sutherland, Jim Taylor, Kallen Tsikalis, Jim Warren, Mark Wheeler, Rosslyn White, Terry Winograd, Press Winslow, Michele Wittig and Edward Woodhouse. And I thank those who have helped whose names were inadvertently omitted from this list.

Thanks to David Byrne for permission to print lines from his song, "In the Future." And thanks to the Fremont Arts Council for their permission to reprint an image of the Fremont Troll.

Finally, I'd like to thank Tom Stone, Kathleen Billus, Bob Donegan, Nancy Fenton, Marybeth Mooney, Tiffany Moore, Meredith Nightingale, and the others at Addison-Wesley who worked so patiently, diligently, and enthusiastically with me on this project.

Chapter 1

Community and Technology— A Marriage of Necessity

A community is a group of people united by the common objects of their love that incorporates three elements: shared values, unity, and intimacy.

Ed Schwartz (1991)

In moving society forward, many different communities may be destroyed or die, but for the survival of mankind we must not capitulate to the concept that the sense of community is dead. The most binding, vital, and healthy sense of community may be generated through this struggle.

Hannah Levin (1980)

THE PRIMACY OF COMMUNITY

Communities are the heart, the soul, the nervous system, and the lifeblood of human society. Communities provide mutual support and love in times of celebration and in times of crisis. There are also pragmatic reasons for banding together. Communities can help get things done: People are infinitely more capable when they work together than when they work on their own.

Communities are found all over the world—of course—and differ widely in the temperaments and diversity of their inhabitants and in their size and economic and political status. Some are bucolic, while others are dangerous. Some "bedroom communities" are empty by day, while some downtown areas are empty at night. Some communities are very well-off, the schools are good, and the streets safe. Some have a fast pace and everybody is in a hurry, while in others, no one seems to be going anywhere. Some communities are up and coming, while some are dying. Some communities are seen as boring and the children move away as soon as they're able. Some communities are open and have a diverse population, while others are exclusive and have strict membership rules based on religion, ethnicity, or economic class. Some have relatively stable populations, while some fluctuate wildly and have continual turnover. But even with such wide diversity, they all have one major point in common: Communities are the physical (and, to a large degree, mental and emotional) places where people do their living. As David Morris and Karl Hess remind us, "We all live someplace" (1975). *We are all members of communities.*

Interactions and relationships help create strong and vital communities. Greeting a neighbor on the street, having a coffee or beer at the corner bar with neighbors, attending a funeral or wedding, walking to school with your children and their friends, or simply buying the week's groceries are all important parts of everyday community life. A community, however, is more than a sum of its parts, much as a human body is more than a sum of its organs. To Robert MacIver, a community "is the common life of beings who are guided essentially from within, actively, spontaneously, and freely . . . relating themselves to one another, weaving for themselves the complex web of social unity" (1970).

While a community necessarily has boundaries or frontiers, those boundaries are fluid in many ways. Although a community is generally a mid-sized social grouping, the term is often applied to social groupings of greater and smaller magnitude. Seattle, for example, may be thought of as a single community, but it is composed of over 100 neighborhoods each of which could be considered as an individual community. Neighborhoods in turn can be broken up into smaller units such as blocks, which can be decomposed into still smaller units—apartment complexes, and families, for example—that can also be considered communities. Moving upwards in scale, people can be members of "regional," "national," or even "global" communities. As Robert MacIver (1970) points out, "even the poorest in social relationships is a member in a chain of social contacts which stretches to the world's end." Admission is not limited to one community; a person might be a member of a religious, ethnic, political, business, labor, professional, or a host of other "communities of interest" as well as a location-based community. Although 50th Avenue North may be thought of as separating the communities of Wallingford and Green Lake in Seattle, boundaries are not strictly fixed. A schoolgirl might play soccer in one community, but participate in Brownies in another and attend school in yet another. And community membership fluctuates. People move in and out of communities and play a wide variety of roles at various times within all of them.

People use the word "community" in at least three ways. The word may mean a group of people living in a contiguous geographical area, a group of like-minded people (the community of librarians, the self-help community, or a "virtual" community, for example) or it may mean a state of group communion, togetherness, and mutual concern. In this book, we use "community" to mean an integration of the three meanings: (1) A community can be comprised of people who *live* together. (2) They are "like-minded" to some degree, as they perform the ordinary as well as extraordinary human activities *together*, including working, playing, meeting, discussing, eating, relaxing, selling and buying, celebrating, commemorating, mourning, or just hanging around. Beyond these two definitions, there is also a "sense of community" (the third usage), in which community members have a sense of belonging to a greater social unity.

Scenes from "the Center of the Universe"

At the summer solstice each year, the Seattle neighborhood of Fremont that brashly proclaims itself to be the "center of the universe" sponsors a community parade (Fig. 1.1) in which anyone can participate. As could be expected, the quality varies considerably. A young boy dressed as a pirate may stroll by hauling his pet cat behind him in a wagon, followed by a group of elaborately costumed "sky people" holding clouds and rainbows aloft on sticks, succeeded by a troupe of primeval "mud people." There is always a

Figure 1.1 Fremont parade

variety of musical offerings, but the "Band from Hell," composed of minor demons dressed in scarlet, blowing brassy, somewhat discordant, but eminently suitable blues for the sultry first day of summer, stands out in my memory for creating an impressive and exhilarating atmosphere. The parade is a source of well-deserved pride for the community and is the prelude to a popular two-day arts and crafts festival.

The Fremont summer solstice parade is a natural product of the community, an event unshaped by the blare of mass culture and media. The acts, costumes, and person-powered floats are built in a nearby school basement. Since Fremont has an abundance of artists and musicians, this type of event is natural for that community. Every community need not have a solstice parade or an arts and crafts festival, but communities do need to convene their *own* events. The purpose may be religious, entertainment, cultural, reflective, or gustatory, but it should be fun, meaningful, and wide open to community participation and improvisation.

In addition to having their own events and rituals, communities have a continuous stream of history from their founding up to the present. History is an integral part of communities'—and hence its inhabitants'—identity and character. Without history, the inhabitants become like the character Chance in Jerzy Kosinski's *Being There* (1971) who was isolated from the continuum of human events, his awareness and consciousness defined instead by the schizophrenic superficiality of television. Rather than being reduced to caricatures like Chance, community members need to be aware of the past and be active creators of the future if their community is to remain alive.

Today's Communities—*Not* Like They Used To Be

In the mythic American elm-lined "Main Street" community, everybody knew everybody, there was time to hang out by the soda fountain and nobody locked their doors. This was an era where Homer Price worked at the doughnut machine and barbershop quartets serenaded from every corner. Although this picture of community has been scrubbed clean of any inconvenient inequities of the time (such as racial prejudice, unsanitary living conditions, or unsafe working conditions) and preserved as a specimen at various Disneylands around the world, it still serves as an idealized notion that people compare with the realities of today's communities. There is a growing view that the strands of community life are unraveling and that reversing this process may be beyond our control.

The modern world stresses and overwhelms communities by such pressures as population changes, communication technologies, pollution, urban "development," and global capitalism. Today, large groups of people live in close proximity to each other, but the groups are often atomized and cut off from one another. The recognition of shared aspirations and interdependence is missing. Inhabitants are clumped together according to economic class and ethnicity, but the clumps themselves often lack the vitality of a healthy community. The raw ingredients—people with their associated beliefs, interests, and values—exist for forming communities, but the catalytic spark to energize these ingredients into an organism we call community is missing in many ways. Why are so many communities impotent, incoherent, and dysfunctional?

Alarming Trends

In the United States, at least, there is ample evidence of community deterioration. The phenomenon of drive-by shootings might be the most graphic and extreme example. This particularly American phenomenon (combining two archetypically American artifacts—guns and cars) pits community members directly against each other in guerilla warfare, while creating an atmosphere of fear and helplessness even among the noncombatants. In the parts of the country away from the "free fire zones" of the inner city, violence—at least in its virtual sense—is never more than a click of the TV remote control away. According to George Gerbner and his associates, the average 15-year-old will have witnessed an average of 15 television killings (not counting cartoons or the news) per week for every week of his or her life (1994). In addition to this barrage of television violence and the high murder rate and overall violence, Americans seem to have an insatiable appetite for drugs both illicit and licit. Americans consume a large percentage of the world's illegal drugs, while alcohol consumption factors heavily in traffic fatalities, murder, robbery, divorce, and job loss (greatly outweighing the ill-effects of illegal drugs). Education is notoriously unequal. The richest 1 percent of the population continue to increase their holdings (estimated at nearly 50 percent of total U.S. wealth), but schools in the inner city continue their slide into disrepair and disgrace. Meanwhile, economic circumstances—created in large measure by powerful corporate and governmental bodies—have virtually eliminated most jobs in the inner city that provide a living wage (Davis, 1992; Kozol, 1991).

Harvard professor Robert Putnam has identified a large number of "civic indicators," all demonstrating a marked decline in "civic associations" in the United States over the past thirty years (1995). At the same time, participation in the political process, the traditional approach for addressing public problems democratically, is at an all-time low. The inner cities resemble war zones, while the suburban enclaves, formed largely as an escape from the realities of the city, have little sense of community within their boundaries.

With their movements defined largely by the demands of the automobile, suburbanites spend much of their time driving *through* their community to the grocery store, soccer field, video store, or gas station. As their less fortunate brethren in the inner cities, the suburbanites spend many of their waking hours absorbing the relentless programming of commercial television. Indeed, Putnam posits that increasing "privatization of leisure" may be one of the major factors that underlies the recent decline of community life.

Factors in Community Decline

What factors have led to the decline in communities? There are many partial answers to that question. Some people feel that the transitory nature of our communities is to blame. In America, for example, many families pick up their household every few years and start over in another location. In two years, 30 percent of the addresses on a mailing list will have changed (Shaffer and Anundsen, 1993). Moving to a new city often severs any relationships that were formed in the old neighborhood. A friend of mine described his previous neighborhood as "a bus stop" where people were always coming and going. When associations are fleeting, why bother to join forces to fight city hall or a strip mall developer? Why bother to preserve or develop community resources? The time is too short and most people will have moved anyway.

Fear is also a factor. People have become increasingly wary of each other. The next-door neighbor may turn out to be a devil worshipper, the driver in the next lane, a psychopath. Indeed, the media is so devoted to this message both as factual reportage and as entertainment that one may idly wonder if one of the purposes of television is to dismember communities. Although street violence is far from insignificant in the United States, its portrayal on television is vastly overplayed. In a given year, fewer than 1 percent of Americans will be the victim of a violent crime. The sad truth is that violence may be the easiest, most reliable way to ensnare the largest number of people into watching the programs (and commercials).

America's infatuation with extreme individualism is another enemy of community. Individualism—as it is practiced—is a myopic denial in which people believe (a) they *can*, (b) they *did*, or (c) they *should*, "make it on their own," that is, with no help from other people. This belief, which is epidemic in the United States, probably fulfills a variety of psychological needs, but it is fundamentally false, a holdover from days gone by when cowboys and trappers roamed the country. Whatever its origins, the concept of individualism ignores the current and historical realities while it distorts and degrades the potential of community life in the future.

Obsessive consumerism also leads to community disintegration, and America leads the world in consumption and preoccupation with products. If people's attention can be kept directed to commercial products and consumption, then the wheels of industry will keep turning and investments will be repaid. The incidental effects of this focus are more insidious. The main effect is diversionary—when one is considering products for individual consumption, one is not considering activities or ideas to support the community. There is an unspoken contract: "Here are some jeans, a new car, and a coke for you to desire, purchase, and enjoy. Don't worry, we'll spare you the messy details of living. We'll define a lifestyle that's right for *you*!" When pressed, some people may offer a corollary of Adam Smith's concept of the "hidden hand," claiming that social problems will somehow be addressed (or just go away) through the market mechanism. In other words, purchasing things is the only *proper* approach to address human suffering. A better tomorrow with no money down today!

External Factors

External factors—outside of the control of the community—also contribute to the demise of community. Many civic and social service institutions that traditionally sustained communities have become severely overtaxed. Their burden has grown while their resources have declined. Ups and downs in the economic system and heightened economic competition worldwide also help to ensure continuing disequilibrium in communities. In addition, multinational corporations are using advanced communication technology to create a mass culture that ignores and devalues local culture, depriving communities of a shared cultural base.

Against these profound challenges, the individual citizen is nearly helpless, insignificant when compared to the size, organization, and resources controlled by business and government, the two titans of modern society. Both institutions are ostensibly controlled by "the people." Business says "the customer is always right" and that business provides "what people want;" while the government is said to be "of the people, by the people, and for the people." Unfortunately, these concepts have become nearly meaningless slogans, as neither institution can be said to be under the "control" of the people in any meaningful way.

While government and big business both claim to know what's best for citizens, both institutions are steadily withdrawing from their social responsibilities. Many people in government claim that it can no longer afford education and social services; yet government spends billions on a bloated military budget that is larger than the rest of the world's put together. Business, for their part, is concerned exclusively with profits, and is feverishly "downsizing" its work forces to ensure this. (As I write this, Boeing, a major employer in the Puget Sound region of Washington State, is preparing to lay off 7,000 "surplus" employees, the third layoff in two years.) Ironically, corporate support for education, the arts, and social services has been declining for several years (Reich, 1995) at the same time that the corporate share of federal tax contributions has dropped dramatically.

Many people literally have *no* power. When they can find employment, they have little time for other things. When they're laid off or the plant in which they work closes, they have extra time, to be sure, but no money, credibility, or influence. And they have no forum to help express their ideas or channel their grievances. The citizen is alone—unorganized, divorced from a viable community—with little notion of solidarity. When individuals are disconnected, they are powerless. And, all too often, when "communities" move as one, they are often moving against others—African-Americans, Asians, immigrants, women, gays, or others not of their ethnic, religious, or sexual orientation.

Interestingly, the forces of public relations and the media may be more powerful than the economic ones. These forces are more subtle but ultimately more oppressive because they define the limits of acceptable thinking and action. These forces establish the vocabulary, structure the debate, and define the agenda of public discourse, which further undermines the imagination, power, and cohesiveness of today's communities.

Although modern forces have forever changed the circumstances of living, the need for mutual support and community remains unchanged. Although the unorganized citizenry is generally powerless against the forces of big business and government, the potential for creative transformation is staggering. If people, with their vast numerical superiority, could join together and consciously work to rebuild communities, while challenging and engaging the powers that be at the same time, little could stop them.

A CALL FOR A NEW COMMUNITY

I can't predict what kind of community it will be, but the new community will be in reaction to the crushing bigness of systems.

Theodore Roszak (Krasny, 1994)

Global forces—societal and technological—have shattered communities in many ways. On the one hand, citizens may feel like they're part of an undifferentiated crowd with no personal identity. On the other hand, they may feel isolated and alone, disconnected from the human community. Destroying the community was not part of anybody's master plan any more than degrading the environment was. Yet in many ways this is what has happened. Rebuilding the community—like cleaning up toxic dumps or reclaiming buried streams—will be a long process that will require diligence and patience. Rebuilding the community, however, is not optional, nor is it a luxury. It is at the core of our humanity; rebuilding it is our most pressing chore.

The Need for a New Community

Communities are a natural focus for addressing today's problems. For one thing, many current problems are community problems—poverty, crime, unemployment, drug use, and many others. These problems are manifest in the community and are best examined and dealt with by a community. Communities are also a familiar and *natural unit*. Smaller units can be clannish, unrepresentative, and powerless, while larger units are often too anonymous and unwieldy.

The old concept of community is obsolete in many ways and needs to be updated to meet today's challenges. The old or "traditional" community was often exclusive, inflexible, isolated, unchanging, monolithic, and homogeneous. A *new community*—one that is fundamentally devoted to democratic problem-solving—needs to be fashioned from the remnants of the old.

A new community is marked by several features that distinguish it from the old community. The most important one is that it is *conscious*. In other words, more than ever before, a community will need a high degree of awareness—both of itself (notably its capacities and needs) and of the milieu in which it exists (including the physical, political, economic, social, intellectual and other *environments*). Further, the consciousness of the new community is both intelligent and creative. The intelligence of a new community comes from its store of information, ideas, and hypotheses; its facility with negotiation, deliberation, and discussion; its knowledge of opportunities and circumstances; as well as its application of technology and other useful tools. The creativity of a new community comes from its ability to reassess situations and devise new, elegant, and sometimes unexpected methods for meeting community challenges.

In addition to consciousness, the new community has both *principles* and *purpose*. Its principles are based on equity—"no one is free when others are oppressed"—and sustainability, because a lifestyle based on overconsumption is illusory and ultimately self-defeating. Using these principles as a foundation, a new community also has goals and objectives that it strives to attain. Having purpose, the new community is oriented around *action*. This action must be consonant with its principles and it must be flexible. Projects and processes need continual reevaluation and adjustment, and projects and processes based solely on faith, tradition, or conventional wisdom will often be inequitable and ineffective.

As an inevitable consequence of its consciousness, principles, and purpose, the new community will have increased power. This power will be manifested in its ability to resist unwanted outside influences and to ensure designed outcomes. This new power could establish communities as rivals of government and business, or at least serve to mediate some of their vast power. This power is also a power that—like all power—could be abused. Hopefully, the power would be wielded according to the principles of the new community to the advantage of people everywhere.

It is clear that communities need to be responsible to a large degree for addressing their own problems and this is being done in many different ways by individuals and groups all over the United States and the world. Besides looking in—at their problems *and* at their resources—communities also need to be looking out. Sometimes the problem is *caused* by forces outside of the community, sometimes the problem must be shared by forces outside the community, sometimes it is necessary to communicate with others outside the community, and sometimes it is necessary to reach out because resources to deal with the problem aren't available locally.

The new community needs to contain elements of the old community. At the same time, many elements of the old society have outlived their usefulness. Modern circumstances have made change constant and new communities must learn to adapt. Modern circumstances have also made conflict likely so the new community must learn to discuss issues effectively. Finally, modern circumstances have created huge, inequitable chasms between economic classes so the new community must be built upon justice and compassion.

Architect Christopher Alexander and his colleagues have developed an intriguing "pattern language" (Alexander et al., 1994) for designing rooms, buildings, and towns. This "language" embodies a powerful *vocabulary* of over 250 architectural patterns that are life-affirming and convivial. Although we are just beginning a similar discussion, it is probably not too early to begin thinking about an analogous "pattern language" that knits together a collection of civic, social, political, economic, and environmental patterns into a coherent and compelling vocabulary or language through which people can conceive, discuss, and build new communities.

Who Will Create the New Community?

Government has often been called in to help solve problems in communities. As we shall see, it is unlikely, as well as ultimately undesirable, for government to attempt to solve—*by itself*—the problems of deteriorating communities. Government is often too big, paralyzed, and partisan to be able to respond effectively. Also government—at least in the United States—is manipulated to an uncomfortably large degree by powerful corporate interests. For one thing, corporations and the very rich contribute a large percentage of political campaign dollars, thereby becoming the constituency to whom politicians are beholden. For another thing, corporate lobbyists pore over every piece of possible legislation, looking for sections to support, change, or remove that might give them an advantage in some way. Needless to say, unaffiliated citizens play a minimal role in this important part of the political process. The best reason not to expect (or want) a government "bailout," however, is that real solutions to community problems need strong community participation, and the U.S. government has rarely shown itself capable of being an equal participant with citizens in community projects.

Is business then likely to play the leading role in rebuilding communities? Taking business' current practices and philosophy into account, the answer to this is a resounding no; in fact, business to a large degree has been one of the major forces behind community *deterioration*. Since business places profit-making as its highest priority, it necessarily favors "profits over people," as the slogan goes. If moving a factory out of a community means greater profit for the corporation, the factory will generally be moved. Perhaps more significant is the fact that business is increasingly not a part of the community even when it's physically located there. Business is rarely accountable to the community beyond making merchandise and services available for a price. Indeed, the actions of business often suggest independence from and indifference to the broader needs of the human community.

The world is looking for new approaches to community problem-solving, as many of the old institutions (including the church, government, business, academia, and the science and technology establishment) and their traditional methods are being stalemated by new—and old—problems that are becoming *global* problems. At the same time, it is becoming clear that the specialist or expert model is obsolete, and new approaches must be inclusive, discursive, participatory, and community-oriented. Increasingly, these new approaches may be idiosyncratic and vary from place-to-place. Interestingly, many signs are currently pointing to *democracy* as the public problem-solving approach it was originally intended to be.

Core Values of the New Community

A human body has a nervous system, a digestive system, and a skeletal system, among others, that work together to sustain life. A community, likewise, has systems or core values that maintain its "web of unity" (MacIver, 1970).

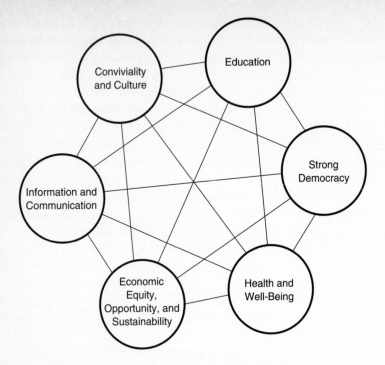

Figure 1.2 The core values of the new community

These six core values—conviviality and culture, education, strong democ-racy, health and well-being, economic equity, opportunity, and sustainability, and information and communication (Fig. 1.2) are all strongly interrelated: Each system strongly influences each of the others, and any deficiency in one results in a deficiency of the whole. Strengthening these community core val-ues, particularly along the lines suggested by the attributes listed in Fig. 1.3, will result in stronger, more coherent communities.

It is important to realize that addressing these core values is a dynamic and interdependent process that will necessarily change over time. Further-more, there is no static final state, a utopia, that we are striving for, that we would recognize if and when we ever arrived there. Instead, community members need to develop a range of small and large projects that strengthen these community core values. Some projects will help individuals, some will help larger groups. Some will be short-term, while others will be longer-term. If all of these projects, however, follow from the principles of the new community, they are likely to reinforce each other, forming a broad progres-sive movement that spreads broadly throughout society. Although the six core values are discussed in more detail later, a preliminary exploration of each system will be useful at this point.

Attributes of the Core Values

- *Conviviality and Culture:* belonging, being supportive, inclusive, active, conversational, affirming

- *Education:* equitable, empowering, effective, lifelong, inquiring, flexible, providing individual attention, creating communities of learning

- *Strong Democracy:* deliberative, equitable, proactive, functioning every day, voluntary, pluralistic

- *Health and Well-Being:* equitable, holistic, preventive, humane, community-oriented

- *Economic Equity, Opportunity, and Sustainability:* responsive, responsible, fair, cooperative, people-oriented

- *Information and Communication:* participative, trustworthy, affordable, universal, civic, pluralistic

---

Figure 1.3

Conviviality and Culture

Conviviality and culture are the invisible forces that help to sustain the community. Conviviality can be thought of as an animating spirit that helps organize people into a community that is infused with identity, purpose, and love. Culture is complementary; it is the shared memory—both tangible and intangible—of a community.

While this core value may sound mystical, vague, or amorphous, we know quite a lot about building it. A major part is the fostering of a *shared culture* through sporting events, parades, festivals, farmers' markets, literacy programs, fairs, dances, theater, or any of a number of community events. Community culture should focus on local events, local issues, local geography, local history and local destiny, and part of the process can be directed using "civic maps" (Kretzmann and McKnight, 1993) that depict promising linkages between people and organizations in the community. A community database of "community assets," the basis of civic maps, can be made available on-line using computer networks. Besides focusing on the local, communities must also build bridges to other communities and be aware of other events and forces beyond community boundaries.

Education

Education is the process by which a person learns fundamental as well as specialized skills. Minimally, this includes reading, writing, mathematics, and critical thinking. With a solid base, students are more capable of conducting individual quests for knowledge, instructing others, and participating in public discussion and deliberation. Note that education doesn't necessarily mean schools, teachers, or other aspects of traditional educational institutions. Some of these institutions may indeed be changing already, though the fundamental need for something analogous to them remains.

Without education, one's economic opportunities are diminished substantially; many jobs will be simply unattainable. On a community level, lack of overall education means that businesses would be unwilling to settle in the community—and those that did would probably offer dead-end, low-wage jobs. The community would also be less likely to initiate, sustain, or expand business ventures. Furthermore, when individuals do not have proper education, the political process itself is unfathomable, and decisions would tend to be relinquished to people who represent other interests.

Education can provide an effective foundation for a community: It can provide a lifelong grounding based on active learning. There are well-known educational approaches that promote working together as a community. These include students teaching other students and students working with community members on community issues and projects. Education needs to be reinvented as a dynamic force, within a social context, working for social change, instead of relying on its present conception as a passive indoctrination of skills, conventional values, and cultural dogma.

Strong Democracy

Democracy is the process of self-government in which the people that are affected by decisions take part in them. Without democracy, people are limited in their communities and in their own potential. Without democracy, the vast majority of people are forced into the roles of serfs, continually awaiting a scrap from their master, be it their allowance, paycheck, report card, or layoff notice. In a self-perpetuating cycle of disempowerment, one is forever governed—never governing. Democratic participation, on the other hand, can be educational as well as empowering. Carole Pateman and others have stressed the importance of learning through participation (1970). When the Soviet Union collapsed, many groups of people—coal miners and others—found themselves lacking the tools of democratic discourse and, hence, unable to play an effective role in a democratic reformulation of their society. Democratic participation leads to community spirit, a greater need and ability to communicate and seek information, and increased economic opportunity.

We need to reestablish democracy in communities by building new forums for discussion and genuine participation in the affairs of society. In some cases, government will welcome the participation. In many other cases, community participation will be fought, ignored, or begrudgingly suffered. In the longer term, citizens should move towards increased democratization of other community organizations including the schools, workplaces, and media outlets including genuine public radio and television.

Heath and Well-Being

"Health and well-being" is an overarching concept. Without health, very little else is achievable. When people in a community are healthy, the more likely it is that the community is healthy. Health in a community refers simultaneously to the physical, mental, and psychological state of the individual inhabitants and to the community itself. It refers to the relations *among* the inhabitants. How do they get along? Commiserate? Lend support? And health-and-well-being also refers to the general physical surroundings of the community. Are there trees or toxic dumps? Is there grass or broken glass and syringes? Song birds or rats?

Community health should be considered in a holistic sense, where emotional and psychological factors are as important as physical ones. The community can be the developer of neighborhood action programs and clinics, and can provide support for health and well-being programs within the community.

Economic Equity, Opportunity, and Sustainability

Economic equity, opportunity, and sustainability is indispensable to the well-being of a community. It's an unfortunate reality (in the United States and other places) that economic class is strongly tied to quality of education, employment opportunities, access to information, and health. Perhaps the most tragic addition to this list is that money is the de facto key to democratic participation in the United States. All aspects of political life—from voting to running for political office to lobbying and petitioning the government—are almost the exclusive domain of the corporations and the wealthiest Americans (Philips, 1990; Greider, 1993). Nor is this necessarily considered anything less than correct. A (liberal!) Seattle newspaper reporter was recently asked about the desirability of having hearings in places other than Olympia (the state capitol) or on evenings and weekends, to enable working people to participate. This would make it "too easy" she said, while other heads on the panel nodded in concurrence.

One of the roles of new communities is to fight against corrosive corporate policies that destroy communities. Part of this role will be to develop and support media that offer alternative viewpoints, such as those of labor or displaced workers. One need only look at traditional media coverage of a labor strike—usually pitched as an inconvenience to all concerned—to realize the inherent bias of the newspaper, radio, and television news coverage. The community can also work with corporations and labor to maintain employment in the community, help keep worker skills up-to-date, and promote labor-corporate-community dialogue. Finally, communities can go beyond the traditional corporate economic paradigms and play a role in the development of new economic institutions that support the community directly, not as a side effect.

Information and Communication

In a free society, information is widely available to its citizens. Although some information is proprietary, trade secret, private, or sensitive for national security reasons, most information should be available inexpensively. The public library—a relatively modern invention—is the best-known expression of that objective. Ready access to information coupled with the ability for citizens to communicate freely using that information undergirds a legitimate democracy. Freely available information promotes self-guided and self-motivated education while supporting traditional educational institutions as well. Freely available information also promotes health in a community because people can find the information they need about foods, prenatal care, hospitals, clinics, and prevention of illnesses and accidents.

Information and communication—what we commonly call "media"—could be redirected towards better meeting the needs of the new community. Community media could allow those whose voices have traditionally gone unheard to have an outlet. This access may lead to a clash of cultures that hopefully will lead to richer interactions and deeper understanding rather than to increased animosity and misunderstanding. The major challenge facing us in relation to this core value is the need to develop community media that strengthens communities—by providing increased access to minority and alternative opinion and by guaranteeing increased involvement in a productive way by *all* members of the community.

ACTIONS FOR THE NEW COMMUNITY

In the United States and in other places, community members have launched a wide variety of programs and institutions to address the needs of communities. These include civic, social, economic, political, religious, and environmental community projects. Earlier this century, the community-center movement was influential (Fisher, 1981), and in the years preceding World War I, a very ambitious program in Cincinnati (Melvin, 1981) established a revolutionary approach to neighborhood health care. Numerous "cooperative commonwealth" compaigns like the Nonpartisan League, the Farmer-Labor Parties of the Midwest, and the End Poverty in California (EPIC) movement were noteworthy efforts in the 1930s and 1940s (Boyte, 1989). In the 1960s in the United States and elsewhere, food and other types of co-ops were fairly common, and the War on Poverty program under Lyndon Johnson called for "maximal feasible participation" (Kramer, 1969). Currently there is a growing "Communitarianism" movement, and other civic renewal efforts as espoused in the writings of Amitai Etzioni (1993) and Robert Bellah and others (1985). Harry Boyte (1989), John Kretzmann and John McKnight (1993), Benjamin Barber et al. (1984), Francis Moore Lappé and Paul Du Bois (1994), David Mathews (1994), and countless others are involved in strengthening and working with local efforts while also developing a national agenda and building ties between various new community efforts.

There are many ways of approaching the problems in our society. These range from small kindnesses that relieve hunger for a day, to large system-wide changes in society. The next few sections discuss important types of actions for the new community.

Capacity Building

Historically, community activists and social service workers have developed responses to community *needs* or *problems*. Indeed, this seems entirely appropriate, as some community problems, such as unemployment during the Great Depression, reached epidemic proportions. Focusing on needs, however, leads to inadequate and inappropriate responses in two closely related ways.

Community *needs* are community *deficits*—aspects of society that are broken and need to be repaired. Thinking in terms of needs elevates negative aspects of the community above positive ones, and this thinking leads to certain unforeseen and unfortunate implications. For one thing, it casts the community as needy, implying that the community has nothing to offer, no assets or capacities of its own to draw on. For another thing, that perspective lays the groundwork for "solutions" to be imposed from the outside, from professionals, from the government, solutions requiring passivity from the "clients."

In recent years, Kretzmann and McKnight and others have begun reconceptualizing community development that focuses on community *assets*—not deficits—and of developing *community capacity*. Developing a community's capacity means building skill and knowledge bases, local institutions, local resources, and programs that empower a community to deal effectively with its own circumstances. It should be noted, that this focus on community capacity building should not be construed as a reason (or excuse) for the government, business organizations, or individuals to not be concerned about communities in trouble, to arbitrarily shut down programs, or to impose strict cut-off limits or otherwise make life more difficult for individuals and communities that are wrestling with serious problems. Instead, this new focus should suggest ways in which rethinking the situation can result in better programs for people in troubled communities and for society as a whole. Capacity building takes time; patience will be required. A change in focus from client to capacity-builder, however, is desirable as it will be ultimately more effective over the long-run.

Citizen Participation

The question of how well community residents understand the problems in their community and whether they're willing to participate in addressing them is critical to our inquiry. Perhaps residents are too uneducated, ill-informed, lazy, or just too busy to get involved. Perhaps they feel that business or government will take care of any problems that arise. Or perhaps—and this may be the predominant feeling—they feel that their participation is unwanted or would be ignored.

In the aftermath of the 1992 Rodney King riots, the infamous Los Angeles street gangs, the Bloods and Crips, jointly wrote a little-known document containing their thoughts on rebuilding the city (Bloods and Crips, 1992). Three facts are worth noting. First, it is remarkable that the document was produced at all. With middle-class citizens themselves feeling disenfranchised by the political process, the fact that street gang members, with presumed low levels of education and civic spirit, would undertake such an effort is notable. Second, the understanding of the situation and the breadth and creativity of their proposal is profound and subtle. Third, the reaction (or, more accurately, the lack of reaction) to the document by the press is also quite interesting—and distressing—to consider.

The first part of the proposal addresses a physical facelift for the community, with suggestions regarding burned and abandoned structures, lighting, repavement, landscaping (with special attention on trees), and sanitation. The second part deals with education. Along with refurbishing school structures and raising teachers' salaries, the Bloods and Crips asked for $200 million for computers and computer supplies, strongly suggesting that people in the economic underclass realize their relative disadvantage in this area and are interested in computers and communication technology. Recognizing the value and efficiency in having students help educate each other through "co-educating," their proposal stipulates that students will "receive bonus bonds for extra scholastic work towards assisting their fellow students." The third part of the proposal, "Human Welfare," addresses medical and recreation facilities. In this part, interestingly, the Bloods and Crips eschew welfare in most cases, and recommend "state work and product manufacturing plants that provide the city with certain supplies." In another part, "Law Enforcement," they call for "former gang members to be given a chance to be (unarmed) patrol buddies in assisting the protection of the neighborhoods," and the last part calls for low-income loans to minority entrepreneurs, with stipulations for hiring neighborhood residents. While this proposal was posed as a series of "demands" with—unfortunately—some implication of violence, it is also clearly a call for participation, self-help, and community awareness.

Strong citizen participation—from *all* sectors of the community—is more likely to result in better and more creative approaches to community problems than those approaches attempted without such participation. The indirect effects may be the most important, however. Citizen participation changes the relationship from a "client" receiving the expert (and unassailable) advice of a professional to that of an equal partner. This arena provides training in problem-solving, citizenship, and leadership and all these are indispensable tools in what Frances Moore Lappé and Paul Du Bois (1994) call the "arts of democracy."

Citizen-led Projects / Citizen Action

Whereas participation suggests a general acceptance of existing processes, the idea of citizen-led action transcends the status quo. While participation is basic to a functioning and vital community, citizen action is in some ways more important, for action implies leadership, and any sustained citizen movement necessarily includes the development and nurturing of leadership capabilities within its membership. Moreover, when community members establish their own projects, they set the agenda. When they participate in others' projects, the agenda is often set by someone else.

Citizen action should be directed towards strengthening the six community core values. This action will frequently be undertaken in conjunction with other groups; often it will involve integrating the works of disparate groups forming projects that cut across core-value boundaries—like setting up community computer networks. These projects should focus on goals, but always on community capacity-building as well. Several excellent books on organizing exist. *Organize! Organizing for Social Change*, written by Kim Bobo, Jackie Kendall, and Steve Max (Bobo et al., 1991) is particularly detailed and instructive. While much of this action will take place "within the system," other forms of unorthodox citizen action, including civil disobedience, can also play a role.

In Seattle, a citizens' group called Sustainable Seattle has begun developing a long-range program (discussed in more detail in Appendix F) that may eventually lead to a higher quality of living for Seattlites and help give rise to a variety of other community-related action projects. Their first project was to work with the community to identify a set of measurable "critical indicators" that can be used to show progress along certain measures that the group feels are both important in their own right and reflective of other important values. The group initially developed 20 indicators on a variety of important themes including wild salmon, water consumption, solid waste, population, energy consumption, air quality, vehicle-miles traveled, health-care expenditures, pedestrian-friendly streets, hours of work to meet basic needs, employment concentration, housing affordability, children in poverty, juvenile crime, low-birthweight infants, library and community center use, participation in the arts, voting rates, adult literacy, youth in community service. A citizen-led critical-indicators program can provide a versatile vehicle for a rich variety of volunteer activities that leads to extensive citizen involvement, projects, and political action.

Roles of Government and Business

As we have seen, a crisis in community currently exists in the United States and in other countries; significant breakdowns are occurring in all six community core values. To address these problems, government, business, and the citizenry all have important roles. Government has played a major role traditionally, while business provides products, services, and jobs for citizens. And although both institutions need to support community work, the lead will need to come from the community.

The government and business are the two largest institutions in American life today. The government is ostensibly controlled by the people, and business is ostensibly controlled by its stockholders. Both, however, have in the main become institutions that no longer address the needs of *all* people, particularly people in lower economic classes or those with other obstacles to overcome. One important task for the new community is to redirect government and business to facilitate, not supplant, citizen enterprise and initiative. It is crucial to establish the fact that communities don't exist for or at their pleasure.

It is important to have a broad base supporting these *community-led government* and *business reinventing initiatives* when they are actually helping the community. For one thing, larger groups of people are more difficult to ignore. For another thing, the accusation of "special interests" raised divisively (and effectively) in recent U.S. elections, will be more difficult to make stick on a truly broad-based movement. Lastly, and perhaps most importantly, the gains of one group shall not be made at the expense of another: The lower middle class, for example, shouldn't be made to bleed for those worse off than they.

The new community must strongly support positive steps made by either of those institutions. Let's look at a hypothetical example. Suppose Company One is a company that takes significant steps to support community revitalization work. On the other hand, suppose Company Two relocates its operations to a location where it can dump toxic waste in an unrestricted way and exploit child labor to manufacture its products. If the products of both companies are roughly equivalent but the product from the unenlightened, purely profit-driven company costs less, then the consumer's tendency is to buy that product. In this case, the new community has the obligation to support Company One and let other buyers (and both companies) know why!

Intercommunity Cooperation

Communities will need to work together—*synergistically*—to build interlacing communities of communities that can help address problems that transcend community boundaries. David Morris and Karl Hess (1975) refer to the "outward movement" that will interconnect communities throughout the world. For these communities of communities to thrive, it will be necessary to identify common concerns and build common agendas. At the same time, the pitfalls of exclusivity, parochialism, mean-spiritedness, and marginalization will need to be avoided.

A community that is truly healthy shouldn't take its sustenance at the expense of other communities. In fact, it should put more into the store of "social capital" (discussed in more detail in Chapter 2) than it takes out, and new communities will need to explore how their assets (social and otherwise) can be shared with less fortunate communities. Communities—rich and poor, healthy and ailing—will need to work together cooperatively if serious structural problems are to be addressed. Many communities have precious few resources to draw on and will need to work with others outside their boundaries to get back on their feet. Jonathan Kozol, writing in *Savage Inequalities* (1991), a devastating critique of educational inequities in the United States, discusses the plight of the people of East Saint Louis. Through little or no fault of the residents, their neighborhood is polluted, their schools deficient, their streets dangerous, and their wallets are empty. "Pulling themselves up by their own bootstraps" is not realistic. Cooperative ventures *between* two or more communities will be necessary, and they can be mutually beneficial and rewarding to people in both communities. It will be especially important to develop these types of win-win programs.

BUILDING COMMUNITY TECHNOLOGY

> *But how would you build it if you wanted to build it right?*
>
> Lee Felsenstein, Community Memory Co-founder

Technology profoundly affects the way we live, communicate, and think, yet these issues are rarely publicly discussed with any deep understanding. For some reason, technology criticism in the United States is often off limits, and those who try to engage in these discussions are swiftly disciplined for their allegedly "Luddite" views. This epithet is usually reserved for those who have been critical of technology in a general or particular way and are therefore judged to be "antitechnology," as if it makes sense to be "for" or "against" technology. The topic of technology—as any topic in a democratic society—is a suitable subject for discussion, debate, legislation, investment, and even, dare I say, regulation. These points are made well in the introduction to *Technology for the Common Good* edited by Michael Shuman and Julia Sweig (1993): "Responsible technology begins with the recognition that all technology is a human activity and like other human activities it can have both good and bad intentions and consequences, it can affect different people or different people in unequal ways, and it can be supported or regulated as much as the national government or communities want. Nothing about technology is preordained, unless we choose to do nothing about it."

Individuals and their communities can help shape the future—for good or ill. This realization, however, contradicts several highly popular prognostications. For example, futurists like Alan and Heidi Toffler (1980) sell millions of books filled with sweeping predictions of the coming "Third Wave" in which society has become totally transformed (by magic?) into a brave new age. With this viewpoint, it is easy to single out government as a "Second

Wave" proposition, a dead-end or "smoke stack" institution whose lingering existence serves merely as a hindrance for risk-taking "entrepreneurs" (as well as for vast corporations whose best-laid plans could in theory be thwarted by environmental or other laws imposed through democratic processes). And what does it suggest for a social activist? Readers of these grand millenarian visions might be moved to resolute inaction. Why should anyone participate in community work when their puny efforts will only be swept away by a gigantic historic "wave"?

Lee Felsenstein, a researcher at the Interval Corporation, and co-founder of the Berkeley, California, Community Memory computer system, is more interested in what technology can do and is doing, than in sweeping historical generalizations. He asks a simple yet provocative question (quoted at the beginning of this section) that challenges both designers and citizens to step back and consider the purpose and impact of new technology. Will it provide a useful service? Who will gain from its use? Who will lose? Will it promote community?

Technological systems, as technology scholar Langdon Winner (1986) has pointed out, result from conscious as well as subconscious design. "Artifacts are congealed ideology" according to Iain Boal (1995). They are necessarily infused with "politics," a politics that encourages certain actions, attitudes and values and discourages others. The advent of air conditioning, for example, in the American Southeast, has encouraged the growth of cities because it provides relief from the inhospitable weather. At the same time, air conditioning has helped to destroy many traditional, often community-oriented, activities like sitting on the front porch in the evening. On a much broader scale, the automobile and the national highway system have dramatically altered the physical and cultural landscape of the United States (Sclove and Scheuer, 1994).

When designing technological systems, decisions at early stages have a stronger and longer-lasting influence on the system than decisions made later on. As Winner explains (1986), "Because choices tend to become strongly fixed in material equipment, economic investment, and social habit, the original flexibility vanishes for all practical purposes once the initial commitments are made." He goes on to say that, "The same careful attention one would give to the rules, roles, and relationships of politics must also be given to such things as the building of highways, the creation of television networks, and the tailoring of seemingly insignificant features on new machines." And since the politics of new electronic communication systems have the potential to fundamentally alter the ways in which people communicate and obtain information, Winner's advice is especially important. Early participation in community (computer) network development—and in other information and communication infrastructure development—is absolutely critical.

Felsenstein's challenge points out the upside-down nature of current commercial development in the world of electronic communication. Rather than building on human capacities to help meet human needs, the emphasis is on producing whatever is necessary to yield the highest profit. Greed and the allure and novelty of technology often cloud our desire and ability to design, build, and use democratic technology. The media's adrenaline-packed gush over "500 channels" and "instant communication" also adds to the confusion by placing the focus and attention on all the wrong issues. The mergers and the huge financial expenditures of the "information superhighway" purveyors, for example, regularly provide the basis for blaring headlines.

There have been some critical voices. One of the pioneers of community networks, Tom Grundner, for example, warns, "When there's a stampede somebody always gets trampled. Always." When the stampede to deploy new technology is over, what will these systems be like? Will they be systems that real people can use to address real problems or will they be systems full of hype, fantasy, consumerism, and unfulfilled promise?

In the next section, we will introduce the idea of community networks. These systems will be difficult to build, yet have the potential to play a strong role in a broad effort to rebuild our communities. Communities must make their demands clear today if tomorrow's technology is going to make good on some of its promises. If technology is to be used to empower the disenfranchised; to solve problems democratically; to help care for those with illness and disability; to participate in the affairs of the community, the region, the state, and the world then these systems can be truly revolutionary. Future capabilities such as electronic home shopping and movies on demand, although much ballyhooed in the media, are banal and unimaginative in comparison.

WHAT IS A COMMUNITY NETWORK?

The associations in community are interdependent. To weaken one is to weaken all. If the local newspaper closes, the garden club and the township meeting will each diminish as they lose a voice. If the American Legion disbands, several community fundraising events and the maintenance of the ballpark will stop. If the Baptist Church closes, several self-help groups that meet in the basement will be without a home and folks in the old peoples' home will lose their weekly visitors. The interdependence of associations and the dependence of community upon their work is the vital center of an effective society.

John McKnight (1987)

Networks of civic engagement embody past success at collaboration which can serve as a cultural template for future collaboration.

Robert Putnam (1993)

Before computers took center stage, the term "community network" was a sociological concept that described the pattern of communications and relationships in a community. This was the web of community that described how news traveled and how social problems were addressed in the community. New computer-based "community networks" are a recent innovation that are intended to help revitalize, strengthen, and expand existing people-based community networks much in the same way that previous civic innovations have helped communities historically.

Currently, community members and activists all over the world are developing these new community-oriented computer services, often in conjunction with other local institutions including colleges and universities, K–12 schools, local governmental agencies, libraries, or nonprofit organizations. There are currently nearly 300 operational systems (with nearly 200 more in development) (Doctor and Ankem, 1995) and the number of registered users exceeds 500,000 people worldwide.[1] These *community networks* (sometimes called civic networks, Free-Nets, community computing-centers, or public access networks), some with user populations in the tens of thousands, are generally intended to advance social goals, such as building community awareness, encouraging involvement in local decision-making, or developing economic opportunities in disadvantaged communities. A community network accomplishes these goals by supporting smaller communities within the larger community and by facilitating the exchange of information between individuals and these smaller communities. Another community-network objective is to provide electronic "one-stop shopping" for community information and communication, by using discussion forums; question and answer forums; electronic access for government employees; information and access to social services; electronic mail; and in many cases, Internet services, including access to the World Wide Web (WWW). These networks are also beginning to integrate services and information found on existing electronic bulletin board systems (BBSs) and on other computer systems. The most important aspect of community networks, however, is their immense potential for increasing participation in community affairs, a potential far greater than that offered by traditional media such as newspapers, radio, or television.

Community members interact with community networks in various ways. Community-network terminals can be set up at public places like li-

---

[1] Usage figures from the National Public Telecomputing Network (Appendix A).

braries, bus stations, schools, laundromats, community and senior centers, social service agencies, public markets, and shopping malls. Community networks can also be accessible from home via computers and, increasingly, from the Internet. In recent years, activists have also been establishing community computing-centers where people, often those in low-income neighborhoods, can become comfortable and adept with computer applications and network services.

The actual services on a community network vary from system to system but there are some typical ones, such as providing access to information about nonprofit organizations and government agencies. Community networks also offer on-line discussion capabilities on a limitless number of topics. Possible topics include pets, homelessness, religion, gay activism, "ask the mayor," alternative education, cultural events and classes, public hearings, artists' and craftspersons' forum, dental clinic, public safety updates, international news, and neighborhood news.

Community networks are thus far local and independent projects. Many are affiliated with the National Public Telecomputing Network (NPTN), an umbrella organization that helps establish and sustain community networks—or, in NPTN's terminology, Free-Nets[2] (see Chapter 8)—but this affiliation is quite loose. In general, community-network developers have not explored just what the nature of a stronger or closer relationship between them would mean. Historically, community-network systems have had a difficult time financially, but increased public interest and some financial infusions from the government, businesses, and foundations have at least temporarily relieved some of the problems with some of the systems. Even so, very few of these systems have much in the way of paid staff. Whether or not community networks "implode," as Mario Morino of the Morino Institute has warned (1994), in the near or intermediate term, is an important concern that hinges on the question of whether or not community resources can coalesce around the idea of community computer-networks as a permanent institution in the community.

Community networks offer a new type of "public space" with similarities as well as major differences between other public spaces that our society currently offers. Steve Cisler, a senior scientist at the Apple Library forecasts (1993) that "just as electrical systems began to transform urban and small-town America a century ago, community computer networks will do so in the 1990s." Regardless of whether that forecast turns out to be true, community networks offer an important and rare opportunity for communities to develop and manage democratic technology.

---

[2] The term Free-Net is a service mark of the National Public Telecomputing Network.

The Cleveland Free-Net—A Whirlwind Tour

Community networks take different forms in different communities. Changes in computer technology (notably in graphical interfaces and World Wide Web technology, discussed in Chapter 9) will also undoubtedly influence the look and feel of future systems. Nevertheless, a very brief tour of the Cleveland Free-Net (CFN), one of the first community networks, should prove useful at this point.

Even though I could call the CFN from my home via computer and modem, I used the Internet Telnet capability to connect to CFN. Since I was not a registered user of the system, I was allowed to explore the system, but was not allowed to send or receive e-mail or post messages to on-line forums. After their logo (Fig. 1.4) and some introductory information scrolled by, the main menu (Fig. 1.5) displayed the main areas within the CFN.

The CFN, like many community networks around the world, is organized as a group of "buildings" in an electronic "city." When the user wants to begin working with a service or see a menu at a lower level, they type the corresponding number. Typing a 1, for example, brings up The Administration

Figure 1.4 Introductory screen for CFN

```
              Cleveland Free-Net directory
   1 The Administration Building
   2 The Post Office
   3 Public Square
   4 The Courthouse & Government Center
   5 The Arts Building
   6 Science and Technology Center
   7 The Medical Arts Building
   8 The Schoolhouse (Academy One)
   9 The Community Center & Recreation Area
  10 The Business and Industrial Park
  11 The Library

Your Choice ==>
```

Figure 1.5

Building menu that describes the purpose, technology, contents, policy, and other administrative information about CFN. If the user types a 2, the Post Office menu pops up that displays options for sending or receiving electronic mail (e-mail) or for performing other more specialized tasks such as filtering it (causing certain things to be done with the mail, depending on subject, sender, or other characteristics of the mail). Typing a 3 brings up the Public Square menu (Fig. 1.6) that brings together several services related to communication including The Cafe, where users can "chat" (where each line of text that a participating user types in is displayed to the other on-line users who are also using the "chat" program), vote, or participate in a number of forums.

The Courthouse and Government Center choice on the main menu provides access to government related information such as the U.S. budget, Internal Revenue Services, weather services, legal information, and historic documents (such as the U.S. Constitution), while the Arts Center contains information on video, photography, literature, visual arts, theater, and other arts related areas, and The Science and Technology Center contains information on museums, computers, a "skeptics corner," and technology organizations.

The Medical Arts Building (Fig. 1.7) contains a wide range of information and services related to health and medicine, including an HIV/AIDS forum where users can submit anonymous questions (Fig. 1.8) related to HIV or AIDS to a registered nurse who answers them on the forum for anybody who's interested in that topic.

The CFN also offers Academy One educational services that often involve kids from all over the world in science, art, or cultural projects. A list of KID-

```
                    Public Square
   1 About Public Square
   2 Announcements
   3 The Kiosk (aka "The Zone") (Open Board,
     Adults Only)
   4 The Cafe (Chat with Other Users)
   5 The Podium (Electronic Speeches, Adults Only)
   6 The Polling Place (All Voting Areas)
   7 The Kiosk Voting Booth (Kiosk Voting Area)
   8 The Speakeasy (General Discussion, Open)
   9 The Singles Partyline
  10 The Nonsexist SIG
  11 Boomers' Place
  12 The Mensa Forum
```

Figure 1.6

LIT poems, stories, or other compositions by young writers is shown in Fig. 1.9, and other Academy One projects are discussed in Chapter 3.

Several Community Services are featured (Fig. 1.10) as are other Free-Nets in the USA (Fig. 1.11).

The Cleveland Free-Net is probably both the oldest (launched in 1986) and largest community computer network. When I last logged on, there were 216 other users logged in (their literature says that the system can handle 406 si-

```
                 The Medical Arts building
   1 About the Medical Arts Building
   2 USA TODAY: Health Headline News
   3 St. Silicon's Hospital
   4 The Handicap Center
   5 Alzheimer's Disease Support Center
   6 Psychology and Mental Health
   7 The Byte Animal Clinic
   8 The Center for International Health
   9 Substance Abuse Education
  10 The Pediatric Information Resource Center
  11 Safety and the Environment
  12 Bioethics Network of Ohio
  13 Nursing Network of Northeast Ohio(3NEO)
```

Figure 1.7

```
Article #15 (49 is last):
Newsgroups: freenet.med.stsil.aids.questions
From: anonymous
Subject: Public Pool danger


Is it true that there is a high risk of getting
AIDS from a public swimming pool?


***answered by Stefan Ripich, RN

Absolutely not. The only way that you can get
exposed to the virus is if the virus has access to
your bodily fluids. The virus cannot live in pool
water.
```

Figure 1.8 Anonymous AIDS question

multaneous users) and there were over 160,000 registered users. New users continue to sign up at rates of over 10 percent per month, as they have been doing since it began. There are approximately 6 million user sessions per year, and the system consists of 18 interconnected Pentium, 486, and Sun computers running the UNIX operating system and the Free-Port community networking software. Each user session lasts 28 minutes on the average and costs Case

```
**R 1. A Scary Tale
    2. How the Rabbit Got Long Ears
    3. Re: How the Rabbit Got Long Ears
    4. Tiggers By: Christina Lynn Aust
    5. My Bird J. R., By: Christina Lynn Aust
    6. My Dad, By: Christina Lynn Aust
    7. Camping
    8. I'm a Little Mermaid
    9. About Christina's Poems
   10. Re: I'm a Little Mermaid
   11. An Elder Named Ron
   12. The Reading Song
   13. A Swordsman Named Fred
```

Figure 1.9 Kids-Lit submissions

```
                 Community Services
  1 Alcoholics Anonymous/Al-Anon
  2 Habitat for Humanity
  3 The Handicap Center
  4 Disabled and Proud
  5 Jobs Wanted/Jobs Available
  6 Lake Metroparks
  7 Lesbian/Gay Community Service Center
  8 Real Estate Exchange
  9 United Way Services
 10 Wanted and For Sale Boards
 11 The Scouting Center
```

Figure 1.10

```
                 Free-Nets in the USA
  1 Free-Nets in Ohio
  2 CIVITAS: The Electronic Home of NPTN
  3 Heartland Free-Net
  4 Tallahassee Free-Net(Tallahassee, Florida)
  5 The Big Sky Telegraph (Dillon, Montana)
  6 Buffalo Free-Net(Buffalo, New York)
  7 Denver Free-Net(Denver, Colorado)
  8 Traverse City Free-Net(Traverse City,
    Michigan)
  9 Prairienet(Illinois)
 10 Rio Grande Free-Net(El Paso, Texas)
 11 Sendit Free-Net(Sendit, North Dakota)
 12 The Columbia Online Information
    Network(Columbia, Missouri)
 13 The Greater Detroit Free-Net(Detroit,
    Michigan)
 14 The Los Angeles Free-Net(Los Angeles,
    California)
 15 The Seattle Community Network
```

Figure 1.11

Western Reserve University (the institution that oversees the Cleveland Free-Net) approximately five cents per session over the telephone and modem and one-tenth of a cent for a session over the Internet (Neff, 1995).

TOWARDS A MARRIAGE OF COMMUNITY AND TECHNOLOGY

People need not only to obtain things, they need above all the freedom to make things among which they can live, to give shape to them according to their own tastes, and to put them to use in caring for and about others.

Ivan Illich (1973)

Both community and technology are inseparable parts of the human condition. A community is a *web*, a web that is real yet intangible, a web of social relations. Ideally, the web of community is a unity, a cohesive force that is supportive, builds relationships, and encourages tolerance. Sadly, the web of community is growing weaker in many ways. Technology too is a web of sorts, for it also connects people in real and intangible ways. Technology mediates communication between people, changes social space, and alters roles and relationships in society. Humankind has fashioned and used technology for over a million years—to multiply force or shrink distance—and technology, like language, is a natural and inseparable extension to our world and our world view. Yet especially in recent years, technology has become out of balance and out of control in many ways. Increasingly, communities are at the mercy of a seemingly autonomous technological imperative.

There is an apparent tension between the concept of "community" and the concept of "technology" that needs to be addressed. The stereotypes persist that communities are warm and fuzzy, whereas technology is cold, unyielding, mysterious, and dangerous. Part of the reason for those generalizations can be found in history—the grim and merciless toil in the factories of the industrial revolution—and part can be found in our collective imagination of the idyllic and convivial communities that existed "once upon a time," in the "good old days" before the machine.

Technology is viewed as complex and incomprehensible. It is seen as larger in scope than the more familiar and comfortable spheres of the individual or community. Technology can be complex and it can be inhumanly vast. But if people don't demystify the technology, it will forever be daunting, and people will continue to be victimized. The truth is that the culture of humankind can't be separated from its tools or from its technology. Like communications, tool-making and tool-using are inseparable from our nature. For although technological systems may seem complex, incomprehensible, and overwhelming in size, they need not be. As we will show, existing systems can be tamed and new community-oriented systems can be devised. By reasserting our control of our technological systems, some of the tension between "community" and "technology" can be removed and technology can be made to better serve human needs.

Preferences of the New Community

In the following six "core value" chapters, we discuss ideas and projects—both computer-oriented and not—that could help support the aims of the new community. In general, those ideas and projects embody a set of value *preferences* (Fig. 1.12) that indicate the general *perspective* of the new commu-

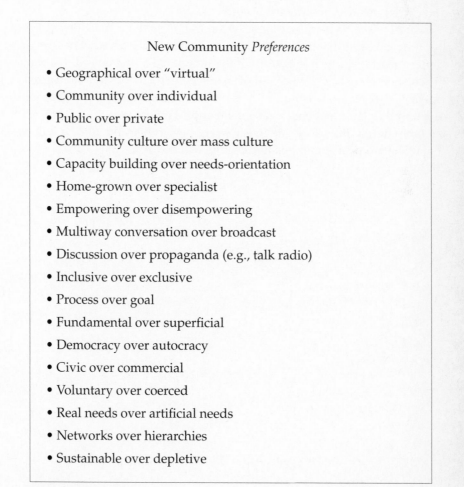

New Community *Preferences*

- Geographical over "virtual"
- Community over individual
- Public over private
- Community culture over mass culture
- Capacity building over needs-orientation
- Home-grown over specialist
- Empowering over disempowering
- Multiway conversation over broadcast
- Discussion over propaganda (e.g., talk radio)
- Inclusive over exclusive
- Process over goal
- Fundamental over superficial
- Democracy over autocracy
- Civic over commercial
- Voluntary over coerced
- Real needs over artificial needs
- Networks over hierarchies
- Sustainable over depletive

Figure 1.12

nity; they are not binary choices. The rights of individuals are not to be abrogated, for example, just because there is a focus on community. Nor, for example, does the figure imply that commercial interests are not important, only that the focus here is primarily noncommercial (except in the cases where a commercial focus is relevant for the new community).

Computer technology—in concert with other efforts—can play a positive role in rebuilding community by strengthening the six core values. Whether these aims are realized will depend on citizens from all walks of life. Truly democratic systems can only be developed through broad participation. This endeavor must not be a charitable good-works project of elites nor a rebellion of the underclasses. It should be open to citizens of all races, economic classes, ethnic origins, religions, genders, ages, and sexual preferences. It must be *global* in nature, because a confluence of perspectives, experiences, and skills is needed in order to succeed.

Saul Alinsky, the premier American community activist, says (Boyte, 1989) that "the radical is that unique person who actually believes what he says. He wants a world in which the worth of the individual is recognized. He wants the creation of a society where all of man's potentialities could be realized."

The vision of a new community is a radical one. Building it will require care and diligence, patience, and intelligence. The broader the effort is and the more tightly the efforts are interwoven, the stronger the force it will become. The momentum for positive change will be irresistible.

Chapter 2

Conviviality and Culture

People are looking for community in all the wrong places. It's not good-will and like-mindedness, it's daily experience in workplaces and neighborhoods and churches and civic groups.

Francis Moore Lappé (Krasny, 1994)

Members of Florentine choral societies participate because they like to sing, not because their participation strengthens the Tuscan social fabric. But it does.

Robert Putnam (1993)

THREADS OF COMMUNITY

"Conviviality and culture" might be the most important core value of the new community. Although conviviality is often viewed as being synonymous with the welcoming and cozy nature of the archetypal neighborhood tavern, its meaning embraces much more. Conviviality—"together with living"—embodies the idea that people are part of a greater association. It suggests that people derive strength and meaning through living together, not in the narrow sense of residing in the same place or "cohabiting" but by actually *living* together—working, playing, eating, communicating, and *being* together. Conviviality is something to which people make contributions, and at times, from which they take comfort. Conviviality includes joyousness and fun, but it is much more than that—it encompasses all aspects of life. A funeral or memorial service, for example, can help renew and strengthen community bonds, while reminding us of the universality and impermanence of life.

"Culture" also has popular connotations; it is vaguely reminiscent of opera, ballet, and old dark oil paintings. It also refers to more approachable (and affordable) elements of living. It need not be the exclusive domain of the wealthy or "cultured" classes. Culture is a thread running through society that removes people from their everyday existence while simultaneously placing them firmly in the universality of everyday existence. Culture is music, craft, dance, art, ritual, theater, and play. It provides texture and pattern—and meaning—to human existence.

In this chapter we'll discuss a wide range of ways to which community networks have and are being used to support conviviality and culture in the community.

Bowling Alone and the Decline of Social Capital

Society would run more smoothly if everybody cooperated better with each other and, in fact, societies in which people cooperate do run more smoothly and more equitably than those where people are less willing or able to work together. Why is it that some societies are more cooperative than others? Social scientists from many disciplines are beginning to look at a concept that they call *social capital*, which is analogous to other types of capital such as physical capital or human capital. According to Harvard University professor Robert Putnam, social capital "refers to features of social organization, such as networks, norms, and trust" (1993).

Social capital, like other concepts from the social sciences (or, for that matter, from our everyday discussions of social traits and behavior), is not a precise concept like weight, length or like other terms derived from the physical sciences. Yet, however imprecise the term, it is still possible to come to some conclusions based on various *indicators* that reflect some aspect of social capital. As it turns out, much of this analysis has been going on for the last 50 years or so. Researchers have collected data on attitudes, patterns of political participation, and organizational membership even though they were not explicitly interested in measuring social capital itself.

The measurements are now in—at least for the United States—and they almost uniformly indicate the same trend: a steady erosion of social capital (Putnam, 1995). To catalog all this evidence would be boring and depressing, but a quick glance would be useful as well as convincing. For starters, all types of political participation from party membership and campaigning to serving on a committee and voting are decreasing. Membership in associations is also down; PTA membership has dropped over 40 percent since 1964, while membership in church groups, unions, League of Women Voters, Boy Scouts, Red Cross, Lions, Elks, and Jaycees is also down. In a seemingly whimsical but nevertheless revealing indicator, Putnam cites the decrease in league bowling and the upsurge in the number of people who are doing their bowling *alone*. Concomitant with the statistical evidence is evidence from questionnaires that sample values and attitudes. For example, the number of people that said "that most people can be trusted" fell by more than a third since 1960.

To what changes can we ascribe these declines in social capital? Putnam discusses several possible factors including American's penchant to change residences (the "repotting" hypothesis) and womens' movement from the home into paid employment outside the home. Although joining the workforce is generally a matter of economic survival, women had previously played a larger role in civic engagement in the community. Membership in some organizations like the PTA, the League of Women Voters, and the Red Cross has been hit particularly hard in recent years. Putnam also reasons that recent demographic changes may also play a part, citing the decline in the number of marriages, the decline in the number of children, and the increased number of divorces. Although not mentioned specifically by Putnam, the "free time" of an employed American is declining. There is little time for anything but work or home life. Economist Juliet Schor has documented this "unexpected" development quite dramatically in her *The Overworked American* (1991). Community development takes time, and time, for a number of reasons, is becoming a scarce commodity.

Putnam also names several changes in the economic context including "the replacement of community-based enterprises by outposts of distant multinational firms" as additional likely culprits. Putnam's final hypothesis—and one that is particularly relevant here—is the "technological transformation of leisure." Putnam suspects that "technological trends are radically privatizing or individualizing our use of leisure time and thus disrupting many opportunities for social-capital formation." In other words, if people spend all their time watching television (or surfing the web), they'll have little time to contribute to the web of community life.

THE SOCIAL ATMOSPHERE

On a stroll through our neighborhood last year, we came upon an unfamiliar sight, a large plywood sign in somebody's front yard, hand painted with the words:

> *When I moved to Wallingford*
> *I thought it would be good.*
> *Now I know it's great!*
> *Thank you for returning my purse!*

On another street, other neighbors carved a bench from a tree trunk and placed it strategically so passerbys could sit on the bench and watch the chickens that are running loose in the backyard. These neighbors also put up a sign describing the breed and the habits of the chickens.

A couple of blocks away, on the grass of another neighbor's front yard, was an old dog, Sarge, well-known for his ability to sleep through his golden years. When Sarge finally died, neighbors brought over plastic bones, photos, and poems written in Sarge's honor. Sarge's owners arranged them into a small shrine on their front porch and they attached a short thank-you note to the neighbors for their kindness and sympathy.

These three vignettes—no single one particularly extraordinary—demonstrate individual efforts to do something positive for their community, to add to the neighborhood's social stock, and to maintain its conviviality. Each was personal and unexpected. Each was also radical in a small way because each was performed for the *collective* good, with no personal gain. Each was unusual because, increasingly, the public and the noncommercial are being sacrificed for the private and the commercial in modern society. These three acts of conviviality contributed in a small way to the web of community, which needs constant care and nurturing.

Back to Fremont

Fremont, the Seattle neighborhood just west of Wallingford, has a strong identity and is well-known for its creative community enterprises. The summer solstice parade mentioned in Chapter 1 is one example of a cohesive community event; there are countless others that can help bring communities together. Movie-going these days is not generally seen as an opportunity for community-building, but the Fremont Almost-Free Outdoor Cinema (Fig. 2.1) is billed as "an experiment in interactive community cinema." During the summer months, "B" movie classics, such as *The Mummy* or *Viva Las Vegas,* are shown outdoors in the U-Park parking lot against the wall, European style, with movie-goers furnishing their own lawn chair, couch, or beach-blanket seating.

Fremont also asserts its community identity with unique community landmarks. The Fremont Troll (shown with hapless Volkswagen in Fig. 2.2) that resides under the Aurora Avenue bridge is one such landmark. A more recent addition to Fremont's urban landscape is the large rocket that's affixed to the corner of the Aw Nuts store in downtown Fremont, where everything from vintage adding machines and used records to bat fetuses may be found. Every hour on the hour, the rocket's lights blink on and off; steam emanates from the exhaust nozzle, signaling an apparently imminent blast off.

In addition to community events and community landmarks, communities need institutions that are part of the community and support the community. In this regard, Fremont has its own First National Bank of Fremont, a very active Arts Council, the Fremont Public Association which coordinates

Figure 2.1 Fremont's Almost-Free Outdoor Cinema

over 20 social service programs all over Seattle, and more recently, the Fremont Neighborhood area in the Seattle Community Network.

The on-line presence complements Fremont's other community institutions, landmarks, and events. Neighborhood activist Tom Sparks, with the help of Greg Byrd and others on the SCN services committee, has started a Fremont Neighborhood section, which branches off the Community Life and Culture menu on the Seattle Community Network. In an attempt to set up a model for the other 100+ Seattle neighborhoods, developers are creating a template containing both dynamic information (such as community discussion forums) and static information (semipermanent information that is not conversational in nature).

Seven forums were initially established on the system (Fig. 2.3) and each forum was complemented by static information that presented some of the data, background, and lore that makes Fremont Fremont. This includes information that may be unknown to younger or new residents or to visitors or the merely curious.

Since the network was still new and the number of users still relatively

Figure 2.2 The Fremont troll

Fremont Talk

For Sale/Trade/Wanted

Garage Sales

Volunteer Opportunities

Politics

Fremont Vital Issues

Events

Figure 2.3 Fremont forums

Geography and Demographics (including map and transportation routes)

Community Histories

Landmarks

Events

Schools, Organizations, and Services

Programs and Projects

Community Businesses

Figure 2.4 Community template information

small, the forums were used infrequently, and Sparks scaled back to two, the Fremont Talk and the For Sale/Trade/Wanted forums. Since the talk forum was used to discuss anything, the other five categories were not really lost and with this approach, the omitted forums (and others) could be added as needed. Ultimately, the Fremont section could be expanded to include community information like that pictured in Fig. 2.4, and this approach could be adopted and used in other Seattle neighborhoods.

Sparks is currently taking the project into the community. He and fellow SCN volunteer Greg Byrd recently developed a poster that was posted in several Fremont hang-outs. When he visits businesses in Fremont, Sparks also plans to drop off a form with business owners on which they can easily submit information about their business to the Fremont neighborhood community business section.

FIRST STEP: THE GREAT GOOD PLACE

The environment in which we live out our lives is not a cafeteria containing an endless variety of passively arrayed settings and experiences. It is an active, dictatorial force that adds experiences or subtracts them according to the ways it has been shaped. When Americans begin to grasp that lesson, the path to the planners' offices will be more heavily trod than to the psychiatrists' couches. And when that lesson is learned, community may again be possible and celebrated each day in a rich new spawning of third places.

Ray Oldenberg (1991)

Roy Oldenberg's delightful book *The Great Good Place*—subtitled *Cafes, Coffee Shops, Community Centers, Beauty Parlors, General Stores, Bars, Hangouts, and How They Get You Through the Day* (1991) provides much of the inspiration for this chapter. Oldenberg argues that people need a "third place" where they can go and feel part of a community, away from their home (the "first place") and away from their place of work (the "second place"). Oldenberg's list of "common and essential features" of "third places" (Fig. 2.5) is important for community-network developers that are trying to foster the creation of convivial electronic spaces in which people might choose to spend time "hanging out" with other community members.

As shown in Figure 2.5, third places are characterized by their location on "neutral ground," a "leveling" tendency where social and economic standings (as well as physical characteristics) are greatly diminished, and as places where "conversation is the main activity." Although Oldenberg's "third place" refers to a physical location such as a coffee house or a tavern, it is useful to keep in mind the comfort, utility, and timelessness of third places. Although the systems do not provide a physical space, they do provide an opportunity for *interaction;* hence some people have used the term "virtual space" to describe the new arena for communication. In the sections that follow, we consider each of the attributes listed in Figure 2.5. The new community reaches beyond this important—yet partial—approach to community, and so we will discuss those more extensive issues in the latter part of this chapter, in the section called Beyond the Great Good Place.

Common and Essential Features

- Conversation is the main activity
- A low profile
- Accessibility and accommodation
- The third place is a leveler
- On neutral ground
- The regulars
- A home away from home
- The mood is playful

Figure 2.5

Conversation Is the Main Activity

Although talk is ubiquitous and somewhat prosaic—after all, it's something that we all do—Oldenberg celebrates its commonality. He explains that Paris, Rome, London, and other cities have built much of their greatness on the foundation of talk. According to Oldenberg (1991), conversation is the "cardinal and sustaining activity of third places everywhere." Talk in a community network is the main form of transaction. Words are the principal medium of exchange.

Although conversation is, in fact, the *fundamental activity* in a community network, the conversations may differ in profound ways from traditional ones. For example, conversations in Oldenberg's third places occur *synchronously*, so that the contributions of the participants are interwoven with each other in "real time." One person will stop talking, taper off, or even continue talking, and one or more people will begin talking. Telephone conversations are also synchronous in that participants don't wander off in search of sandwiches or clean socks while the other person is still talking. With a community network, however, a conversation using either e-mail or forums plays itself out *asynchronously*—over the course of hours, days, or even months—much like traditional mail with paper, stamps, and envelopes. E-mail, of course, lacks the ornate floridness, indecipherable scrawl, or other individual touches that are often found in handwritten letters. Lacking an ASCII equivalent, scent or tearstains are also virtually untranslatable.

While the simultaneity of conversations isn't central for community networks (except for the "chat" capability), an interesting variant emerges: There is a capability of engaging in several asynchronous conversations synchronously. An example will make this clearer. Typically, a person will log-on to a community network, read his or her mail, and read the postings in some forums. Each piece of mail and each forum posting offers, in fact, an opportunity to respond, to participate in the conversation. If a person is involved in many conversations using e-mail and participates in many forums, his or her "conversation" can be more schizophrenic, like an extreme sort of mingling at a cocktail party where a party-goer goes from person to person or group of people, listens, then either says something or doesn't, then leaves the person or group without waiting for a reply, going instead to join another conversation in progress.

In face-to-face conversations, speech characteristics (such as loudness, hesitation, timbre) body language and eye-contact all play a role in the overall message that's conveyed. With the telephone we lose the visual but retain the audio—the words and nonverbal utterances like sighs and laughs, and sounds in the background, for example, the sounds of tinkling glasses, music, or a crying baby. When messages are composed solely of text—as in most current e-mail systems—communication is squeezed into a list of alphanumeric symbols arranged in row after tidy row.

A Third Place: The Electronic Cafe International

Artists Kit Galloway and Sherrie Rabinowitz experimented for years with "virtual spaces," using telecommunications technology (including their 1980 Hole In Space project and their collaborations with NASA using communications satellites). In 1984 they launched a "third place," the Electronic Cafe International, based on their successful cultural and technological project, the Electronic Cafe, that incorporated the diverse cultures of Los Angeles, California in a unique experiment. Now from their Santa Monica, California nerve center, the Electronic Cafe International hosts a multitude of live multimedia cultural events with participants at sites all over the world. Cafe visitors encounter, in roughly equal measures, high-tech communications and computing paraphernalia of all stripes, chairs, tables, and other cafe-like accoutrements, and a diverse collection of decidedly low-tech and funky knick-knacks (Fig. 2.6). Using a wide range of available and state-of-the-art technology including audio links, slow-scan television over voice-grade telephone lines, real-time video conferencing, and collaborative Internet technology (among many others), Galloway and Rabinowitz have hosted a wide variety of real-time encounters that they see as a way to explore and develop alternatives to corporate mass culture.

The original 1984 Electronic Cafe project linked five diverse locations in

Figure 2.6   Inside the Electronic Cafe, 1995

Figure 2.7 Inside Anna Maria's, 1984

the Los Angeles area, including the Los Angeles Museum of Contemporary Art with family-owned restaurants in Korean (8th Street Restaurant), Hispanic (Anna Maria's—see Fig. 2.7), African American (The Gumbo House), and "artsy" beach communities (Gunter's) together into one shared virtual space. Within this space participants "could send each other slow-scan images, draw or write together with an electronic writing tablet, print pictures with the video printer, enter and retrieve information (including graphics) and ideas in the computer database, and store or retrieve images on a videodisk recorder that held 20,000 images" (Galloway and Rabinowitz, 1992). This cultural exploration was widely enjoyed by community residents at the same time that it was a pioneer groupware application.

Spread out over hundreds of square miles, home to over 80 languages, lacerated by freeways, and, in 1992, the scene of a devastating "multiethnic eruption" (Navarro, 1993), Los Angeles (being more of a "chunky stew" than a "melting pot" according to Galloway) served both as a global model and as an intercity urban model for the original Electronic Cafe project. Galloway and Rabinowitz consciously chose centers of various ethnic communities within Los Angeles for the project (10 sites had originally been planned but budget restraints forced them to scale back) and worked with community members for six months before the project was launched. They deliberately avoided selecting an establishment-approved cultural icon for the position of artist-in-residence, selecting instead strongly indigenous voices that more closely represented the community.

It would be impossible to describe the 7-week project exhaustively. "There are hundreds of stories," according to Rabinowitz, "and over 9,000 images were generated and saved on disk." The most interesting aspect of the project might have been how the behavior of the participants changed over time. Initially participants at the various sites engaged in "community definition" by broadcasting images that offset their stereotypes to the other sites and by having community poets and artists come forward and read their poetry or display their art on-line. After this period subsided, a less formal period began, where people at different sites worked in collaborative 1-to-1 experiments that were increasingly well-executed (as they mastered the technology) and experimental.

Based on their Electronic Cafe experience, Galloway and Rabinowitz declared that they had "reached the limits of models" and they began setting up a more permanent institution that could support itself and grow. This institution, dubbed the Electronic Cafe International was based on the idea of a cafe as an informal, community-gathering area "that exists in all communities and in all cultures." As of this writing other cafes have been established in New York City, Tokyo, Vancouver, Toronto, Dublin, Jerusalem, Paris, Barcelona, Copenhagen, Austin, Woodstock, Managua, Seoul, and many other locations, including several at sea.

While most of the systems discussed in this book are asynchronous and text-based, Galloway's and Rabinowitz's focus on real-time audio and video connections is complementary in many ways. The Electronic Cafe International's explorations into multimedia, cultural diversity, international communications, and aesthetics serve as important reminders of creative opportunities that transcend conventional text and discussion-based approaches. Galloway and Rabinowitz have been collaborating for 20 years and they now speak of their cultural explorations with "recombinant telecommunications" in which both low-end and high-end technology is employed in different ways depending on the resources, skills, interests, and wishes of the participants. Galloway's and Rabinowitz's focus on community, both local and global; their involving people in poor neighborhoods, less developed countries, disabled people, and children among others; and their commitment to experimentation with new models and encounters, all serve as important social experiments that can help people understand developing technologies while developing a consciousness for community-oriented modes of communication. Since cafes exist in all cultures as community meeting points the recent upsurge in cyber-cafes around the world reaffirms their vision of an Electronic Cafe.

A Low Profile

To Oldenberg a third place is not ostentatious or glitzy; it's serviceable but plain, a place that Thoreau or Emerson would approve of. The reason for this spareness is more likely to be economic necessity rather than a vow of simplicity. A more expensive place means a higher tab for the customers. It also means that more paying customers are needed and their stays must be limited to accommodate this greater number: "Hanging around" without consuming doesn't help pay off the loan and is discouraged. Moreover, an expensive, elegantly appointed establishment means that people of lesser means won't feel comfortable and even well-to-do people may not dress and act naturally. While a low profile is an important attribute of a third place, today's commercialism generally exalts the newest, shiniest, fastest in everything. It's difficult these days to find proponents of anything less than "the best."

Accessibility and Accommodation

In Oldenberg's view, "third places that render the best and fullest service are those to which one may go alone at almost any time of the day or evening with assurances that acquaintances will be there." Again the parallels with community networks are strong. First, community networks *are* open all the time—one can "go there" literally any time. But many factors including technology limitations and policies do interfere with this ideal. For example, at any given time, the telephone lines may be busy or the system may be unavailable. This occurrence would be like going to the corner bar and finding it locked when it's usually open. Accessibility also raises a wide range of economic and policy questions. It is true that "anybody with a computer, telephone line, and modem" can connect to a community network, but not everybody has the required technology. While over 90 percent of the homes in the United States have telephones, only about 27 percent (in 1993) have personal computers and only 11 percent of individuals use computer network services (RAND, 1995). And some people have no residence or workplace at all. Unless there is free or very low-cost public access from libraries, schools, community or senior centers, shopping malls, or other public locations, these people are effectively barred from using community networks.

There are other important issues that must be addressed if full accessibility is to become a reality. One of these is access for people who cannot read or write in the language presented on the screen (or in any language). Still another barrier to access is the wide range of physical disabilities that participants may have. In general, there are many computer applications, such as text-to-speech synthesizers, that can help bridge the gap that makes using the system possible. Those adaptive technologies will have to be inexpensive and widespread and exist on the public systems, however, to bring "universal access" closer to reality. Ironically, window-based and other more technologically advanced approaches to user interfaces have historically been less amenable to adaptive technology for disabled people than their more prosaic text-based predecessors.

The Third Place Is a Leveler

The term "leveler" comes from a seventeenth century English political party that sought to abolish all positions of rank or position that were used to divide people into categories. Oldenberg uses the term to mean anything that acts to reduce differences between people, especially those distinctions based on economic class. In London coffeehouses of the 1600s and 1700s, a commonly accepted "Rules and Orders" stated that everybody was welcome and had equal status (Oldenberg, 1991). Community networks, and many other forms of electronic communication share this leveling tendency with the coffeehouses and other third places that Oldenberg describes. That this tendency exists is well illustrated by the well-known New Yorker cartoon in which one dog is explaining to another dog, that "On the Internet nobody knows you're a dog." Although electronic interaction is currently limited to humans, physical characteristics such as gender, race, attractiveness, and physical capabilities are not visible using text-based systems. The species of participant on the other end, be it extraterrestrial, software agent, or quadruped can't be known with absolute certainty. Moreover, personal wealth, an important nonleveling factor in our era, is invisible and, like other characteristics, difficult to infer from text alone. As Oldenberg says, "Even poverty loses much of its sting when communities can offer the settings and occasions where the disadvantaged can be accepted as equals." Current systems generally serve as levelers (a much ballyhooed "feature" of the new medium), but many observers including community network pioneer Lee Felsenstein feel that leveling is *not* an inherent aspect of electronic forums and "de-leveling" is already occurring in many places (1995). In the three sections that follow, several nonmainstream or marginalized communities and their extensions into the electronic realm are discussed.

The LGBT Neighborhood

Idyllic communities of yesteryear seem to have had more solid existence in the American popular imagination than they have had in historical reality. These idealized communities are generally depicted as friendly, ethnically homogeneous, and economically autonomous. Financially, everybody had enough to get by. These romanticized communities, epitomized by Disney-

land's Main Street, may actually have existed in some areas for brief historical moments. There is no modern-day equivalent, however, in the city, the
suburbs, the town, or the country.

When people move from one place to another, when populations grow,
and trading occurs, people from disparate cultures must interact. Just as ur-
banization forced people of widely disparate beliefs, attitudes, and habits
into close proximity, the new community networks may bring people into
closer virtual proximity. Gays and lesbians have throughout history served
as scapegoats for all manners of social ills and dissatisfactions. Thus gays
have been persecuted in a variety of ways, most systematically by the Nazis
in the Second World War. America's mistreatment of sexual minorities has
historically included everything from verbal derision to physical violence
but, in general, the approach has been an attitude of "don't ask—don't tell."
Unfortunately, hostility seems to be growing in the United States, fomented
to a large degree by the religious right. It will be interesting, and possibly dis-
heartening, to observe how Americans conduct public electronic discourse
when gay and lesbian citizens and their supporters have information and
conversations available for all to see on new community networks.

As I write this, beginning salvos in the name of "on-line decency" are being loosed on the legislative front by Senators Exon, Gorton, and others in the
U.S. legislature and at the state level in various locations. Although these
very real threats are discussed in Chapter 11, it should be noted that they are
already having a chilling effect on minority populations who fear stepped-
up persecution from the authoritarian wing of the conservatives. Defending
the on-line rights of minority and alternative users will be an important and
perennial responsibility for community networks.

In the Seattle Community Network, there is a LGBT (lesbian-gay-bisexual-
transgender) neighborhood that "deals with local and global issues of queer
interest." The founders, Tom Hicks and Richard Isaac, take a militant stance:
"Fight Back with Technology" is the rallying cry that appears at the end of
the About the LGBT Neighborhood section, their Action Alerts, and other
messages. Their use of the word "queer," historically a taunting and pejorative epithet, indicates a willingness to reclaim the offensive. So too does their
posting of LGBT material in a public, community network where various enemies from the unaffiliated homophobe to the organized machinery of the
new radical right are likely to be lurking.

The LGBT Neighborhood on SCN also features Action Alerts on gay-
related events, issues, or legislative work. The Welcome Home area features
LGBT Library Archive News from the gay press locally, nationally, and internationally, and includes information from LGBT not-for-profit as well as
other nonprofit groups.

CyberQueers@cyberzine.org

Figure 2.8   CyberQueers electronic logo

On Sparky, the machine run by Hicks and Isaac, the new Cyber Queer Lounge has been opened. The Cyber Queer Lounge offers more complete Internet access than does the Seattle Community Network, including Internet Relay Chat (IRC), FTP, and Telnet (see Chapter 9 for more discussion on these capabilities). A critical part of their mission is "cyber instruction," in which people can learn how to use technology more effectively. Hicks and Isaac offer on-line help and off-line tutoring on all cyberspace topics and they offer the on-line and hard-copy publication "Cyber Queers" (Fig. 2.8). They will also be promoting the use of global chats in which gay people from around the world can talk with each other. In many countries and regions of the world, sexual minorities are persecuted to a higher degree than in the United States and some, according to the write-up, "have never talked to other queers."

Sistah Space

In January of 1993, three black women students, Toyia Taylor, Sumir Brown, and Dawn Hampton, at the University of Washington, started Sisterhood, an informal group that was formed to "foster a sense of belonging and under-standing" among all black women associated with the university. Sisterhood's "continuing goals are to embrace ourselves and others through education, participation, and elevation." Two years after Sisterhood's creation, Jeanette James, a graduate student in the Communications Department of the University conceived of "Sistah Space," a Web site for Sisterhood (Fig. 2.9).

James was concerned that the mainstream media did not portray "realistic and positive representations of black women" and she explored several ways of electronically publishing their own perspectives, basically because of the low costs associated with electronic distribution.[1] James considered

---

[1] Art McGee has been involving the African American community in network activities for many years and his Web site (see Appendix B) contains hundreds of pointers to relevant electronic resources.

Welcome To Sistah Space

Browse through the selected items in Sistah Space and discover the mysteries of Sister Power!

- All about Sisterhood's <u>history</u> and <u>members</u>.
- All about the Home Page <u>creator</u>.
- Check out original <u>poetry</u> in the Poet's Corner.
- Sisterhood choices for <u>best books</u> authored by Black Women.
- Project <u>rationale</u>--included is a brief summary of why this space was created, methods for data collection, suggestions for future creators and other social science type information.

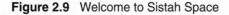

Figure 2.9 Welcome to Sistah Space

various approaches, including electronic list serves, forums, or even pressing a CD, before she settled on the World Wide Web approach, primarily for its ability to show graphics, a critical aspect of the project. In addition to gaining some measure of control over the media, James also uses the Web site to help people (especially women and minorities) gain understanding of the technology.

James involved the Sisterhood group in all decisions regarding the Web site and asked each member what issues should be conveyed, what a reader/viewer should learn about Sisterhood, and how the page should look. Based on the feedback, James designed an outreach page containing a photograph of the Sisterhood members visiting a home for homeless teen mothers and news about other Sisterhood events. She developed pages that recounted Sisterhood's history and described its members, a list of "best books" by black women, and original poetry and artwork by Sisterhood members.

The Oneida Indian Nation

The Oneida Indian Nation was one of the original members of the Iroquois Confederacy and also one of only two tribes to support the American colonies in the War of Independence from England, delivering 600 bushels of corn to starving American troops at Valley Forge. In recent history, the Oneida Indian Nation was the first to put a home page on the World Wide Web, even predating another sovereign political unit, the United States government, the "White House Tribe," as an Oneida spokesman stated at the 1995 Ties That Bind conference.

The Oneida Web site (Fig. 2.10) contains a short audio welcome message in the native language; some historical narratives, including that of the Valley Forge incident; the Shako:Wi Cultural Center (featuring on-line photographs of a kostaweh, the traditional headdress of the Iroquois, a war club, and the traditional woman's outfit); press releases from the nation's leadership; a calendar of events, and information about the Oneida economic venture, the Turning Stone Casino, and "The Villages" RV Park.

The Oneida People, through their electronic presence are looking back as well as toward the future. There are links to various historical documents, including the text of six treaties dating from 1784 to 1838 (Fig. 2.11) as well as descriptions of the Oneida plan for the Villages-on-the-White-Pine housing complex that includes fiber optic cables to each house. They are also making plans to link 21 Indian nations via the Internet in a project supported by Apple computer.[2]

According to Internet Coordinator Daniel Umstead (1995), the most important part of their Web site development is "that it provides the Oneida People with the means to tell their own story, using their own words and ideas, not those of an outsider." Umstead also relates how the electronic presence helps link Oneida people who don't live in Oneida territory and how people in other countries (he mentions Germany and China) can obtain

---

[2] The U.S. Office of Technology Assessment maintains a Native American resource page (OTA, 1995) as part of a study requested by the Senate Committee on Indian Affairs. Included are a wide variety of pointers, including an Aboriginal Art Gallery, an Indian Pueblo Cultural Center, and the Fourth World Documentation Project, whose archive contains over 300 documents pertaining to indigenous people.

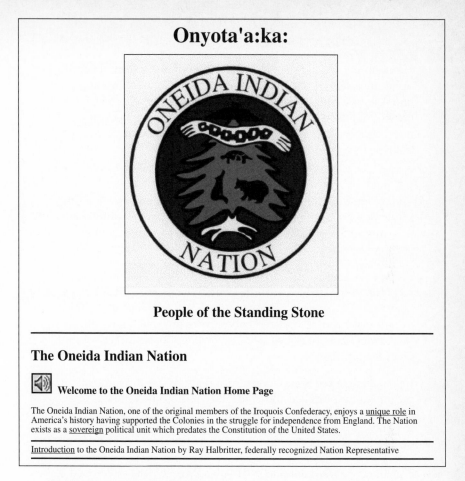

People of the Standing Stone

The Oneida Indian Nation

🔊 **Welcome to the Oneida Indian Nation Home Page**

The Oneida Indian Nation, one of the original members of the Iroquois Confederacy, enjoys a <u>unique role</u> in America's history having supported the Colonies in the struggle for independence from England. The Nation exists as a <u>sovereign</u> political unit which predates the Constitution of the United States.

<u>Introduction</u> to the Oneida Indian Nation by Ray Halbritter, federally recognized Nation Representative

Figure 2.10 Oneida Web site

Oneida information and thus "develop an appreciation for the culture and history of the United States' first ally, the Oneida People."

On Neutral Ground

A "third place" is a place where everybody is welcome and nobody has the responsibility of being the host nor the burden of being the guest. If all space is owned by somebody, then no neutral space exists, and encounters that depend on neutral space will be denied. A community network provides ample neutral ground, particularly in its unmoderated forums. Beyond providing this feature, the neutrality of a community network must be fiercely maintained and no policy, written or de facto, should undermine this crucial feature.

"TREATIES PROJECT"—INTRODUCTION

"I remember when I was 10 or 11 years old and my aunt coming up to me and saying, 'Do you know your treaties? You must know your treaties.' Well, I did not know my treaties and I did not know where to look. Her statements led me to become actively involved with my Nation. If I did not know my own treaties, how could I expect anyone else to?"

—Brian Patterson, Bear Clan, Men's Council Member

The concept of an Indian Nation's sovereign status is often misunderstood, and the true answers sometimes are misinterpreted. Sovereignty means self-determination as a separate distinct governmental entity.

President Clinton, in addressing the 500 or more tribal leaders of recognized Indian Tribes in the United States in April '94, reaffirmed that the Indian Nations of the United States, where they exist as federally recognized tribes, have the sovereign authority to interact on a government-to-government basis directly with federal agencies.

Just as the United States Constitution still bears the same uncompromising importance and credibility it did when the ink was still wet on its pages, so do the treaties that were made between a fledgling United States and its first ally and steadfast friend, the Oneida Indian Nation.

The Oneida Indian Nation's "Treaties Project" was developed to provide easy access for native and non-native people alike to important treaties. The first treaties presented in the project will focus on Oneida treaties. As the project grows, significant treaties from other Indian nations will be added.

We hope you will find this project to be helpful.

```
http://nyser.org/oneida/treaties/introduction.html/
```

Figure 2.11 From the Oneida Indian Nation Web site.

A Day in the Global *Life*

Traditional communities, as we have seen, are increasingly becoming arti-facts of history. Modern circumstances dismember societies in which mono-lithic rules and customs dictate acceptable behavior. The emergence of cyberspace as a new medium for inexpensive communication that blithely ignores old community boundaries propels society even further from his-tory's everyday stasis. At the same time cyberspace offers opportunities for understanding and communication as well as for conflict and upheaval.

Although the circumstances of people's lives vary greatly from place to place, there is also much that people have in common. Sheldon Smith, a ju-nior high school English teacher in Atascadero, California, has designed a networking project that highlights both these differences and similarities in a form that is interesting and useful for students. For the last few years, Smith has invited "tele-educators" and their students from around the world to participate in the yearly Day in the Life project in which students chronicle their experiences over a single school day. In the October 1994 event, 5000 students from over 120 schools worldwide took part. Each participating stu-dent carried a pad of paper throughout the day and transcribed the events and their thoughts. After describing the entire day from wake-up to bedtime, each chronicle was then typed into a computer and sent electronically to an electronic "listserve," which automatically sent the message to each of the other participating schools. "We can't all be in Japan or any other place on a given day, but we can be there *virtually*—and in many places at the same time," Smith reports.

The average day is usually ordinary (Fig. 2.12), by definition, but the per-sonalities and cultural milieu of the individual participants are revealing enough to make us reflect on the diversity as well as the commonality of the world's inhabitants. And the events of the particular day chosen for the proj-ect aren't necessarily ordinary. In the case of the 10th and 11th grade Israeli students, the day was marred by a terrorist bombing in Tel Aviv and through their writings we can gain an increased understanding of how people and communities respond to traumatic events (Fig. 2.13).

Smith feels that the Day in the Life project is a good learning vehicle for students. For one thing, it's an event that is limited to a single day. The "high-tech, low-tech" ratio is a good combination, he explains, because students can be involved with high-tech computers and networking technology through the use of low-tech equipment, namely paper and pencil. Interdisci-plinary educational follow-ups to the project are being used. Students in English class are writing essays on cultural similarities and differences. In math class they are using data analysis techniques to conduct scientific re-search on the most watched television show or the most disliked school sub-

Sleeping and Waking
    6:00 AM In Dream World (Japan)
    6:00 AM I wake up to the annoying but useful sound of the alarm clock. (US)

School
    7:00 AM We have the first subject—it's gym, we do nothing because we do not have equipment. (Slovenia)
    10:00 AM I'm taking a history test. I hope I do good and pass. (US)
    2:00 PM I had a social studies class in the fifth period. We watched the video about Hiroshima. I realized that the atomic bomb is cruel. (Japan)
    5:00 PM Damn, damn. I have to make my homeworks. (Finland)

Meals
    7:00 AM The menu was cheese toast and consomme soup. (Japan)
    7:00 AM I am eating breakfast, the usual cereal toast and O.J. (US)
    8:00 AM I had vegemite on toast for breakfast. (Australia)
    12:00 PM For pudding I had sponge with syrup on it. (UK)
    5:00 PM We had spaghetti and beef gravy. It was good. (Finland)

Family
    7:00 AM I got in a fight with my brother. I won! (US)
    2:00 PM I'm feeding the baby. His face is all dirty. He sure likes to eat a lot. (US)
    3:00 PM I changed Jorge's diaper and clothes. (US)

Games and Entertainment
    11:00 AM I was playing monkeys and lions with my friends. (UK)
    12:00 PM We played Tutti Frutti until it was time to go to eat. (South America)
    8:00 PM I watched "Australia's Most Wanted." (Australia)

Figure 2.12 A Day in the Life—Global excerpts

7:00AM	I woke up and got ready for school.
8:00AM	A regular day at school—the next lesson was Hebrew Grammar.
9:00AM	I had a quiz, and I kept thinking about how difficult the quiz had been.
10:00AM	During the break, I see a lot of students standing in the middle of the school listening to the radio. I'm beginning to think that something bad happened. From what I hear, I understand that there was a terrorist attack in the middle of Tel Aviv, a bus explosion, and many people were killed and others were injured.
11:00AM	I got into the class, and I could not concentrate. I kept thinking how could I be so worried about my quiz when people were murdered.
12:00PM	I opened the television and watched the news. I saw the pictures from the incident, it was horrifying. I felt very sad and confused.
1:00PM	I got back home. Listening to the radio I became horrified by the descriptions of the horrors.

Figure 2.13 A Day in the Life—Excerpts from Israel

ject, for example. Smith also uses the chronicles to help students devise a character that they then use in fictional narratives in their social studies classes. As the Day in the Life project has shown, communication technology can provide intriguing new possibilities for increasing cultural understanding and community networks can provide similar opportunities on the community level.

The Regulars and the Home Away from Home

People are not attracted to third places "by management but by fellow customers," according to Oldenberg. This is what separates a public forum or conversation from a "product" like a newspaper. In a forum or on e-mail list, one becomes accustomed to certain people through their mail or postings. These people become, in effect, the "regulars" of the system. It is true that some large commercial network providers pay people to make forums interesting or useful by contributing to the discussion, much as a social director is employed on an ocean cruise to create fun on the voyage. However, unlike an ocean voyage whose "community" dissolves upon the cruise's end, an on-line community needs to sustain *itself*.

Community Memory—A Virtual People's Park

Community Memory of Berkeley, California, created by Efrem Lipkin, Lee Felsenstein, and Ken Colstad, was the world's first community network (Levy, 1984; Farrington and Pine, 1992). Initially begun in the mid-70s as a follow up to experiments conducted in 1972 and 1973 on unmediated two-way access to a message database through public computer terminals, the Community Memory effort was intended to develop and distribute a technology supporting the free exchange of information to communities all over the world, according to long-time Community Memory volunteer Carl Farrington.[3] The Community Memory brochure reflects this idea, making the point that "strong, free, nonhierarchical channels of communication—whether by computer and modem, pen and ink, telephone, or face-to-face—are the front line of reclaiming and revitalizing our communities." Their commitment to reducing the barriers to information technology was demonstrated by the simplicity of the system (described in a five-page users' manual), numerous training programs, and the insistence that all Community Memory terminals be located in public places: Terminals could be found in libraries and in laundromats (Fig. 2.14) but could *not* be reached via modem or from the Internet. Community Memory adopted a creative approach to funding: They offered coin-operated terminals through which forums were free to read, but required 25 cents to post an opinion and a dollar to start a new forum.

The Community Memory developers pushed the community-network principles to their logical limits. Users, for example, were not required to use their own name or register to use the system. Thus it was possible to use the system anonymously. Former Community Memory executive director Evelyn Pine remarked that it was *possible* that the moderator of the Women forum (who requested that men not contribute) was a man! The anonymity made it very easy to use the system and gave users almost complete freedom to write what they wanted. Perhaps the most noteworthy of the developers' convictions was that all of the information on the system was community generated. This had several important consequences, some of which were different from those pursued by later generations of community-network developers. For one thing, there was no central authority that determined who the information providers were. For another thing, information from outside the immediate area such as Internet newsgroups was not brought into the system.

---

[3] Personal correspondence.

Figure 2.14 Community Memory terminal

Although community-network developers divided the system into categories such as New/Alerts, Ideas, Discussions, Jobs, Housing, Graffiti, and Assistance, the forum titles within each category as well as the contents of the forum were provided by the users. Thus many of the forums had a distinctly Berkeley flavor, while many others would be appropriate anywhere. Some of the forums included "<Peoples' Park> discussion around Peoples' Park," "<Hacking> confessions of programming addicts," "<VDC Reunion> Vietnam Day Committee," "<Military Life-Facts> Look before you Join," "<Poetry>," "<Senior Cuisine> Senior Centers' Lunch Menu," "<Help Wanted>," "<Help offered>," and "<an estimated terrapin> Grateful Dead information," and more.

Although Lee Felsenstein is planning to make the Community Memory source code publicly available, the Community Memory system is no longer available for the Berkeley community. Evelyn Pine feels that there are so many communication outlets for cultural and community activities in Berkeley that in some sense Berkeley organizations have less need for such a system than organizations in other cities. Felsenstein, on the other hand, feels that community organizations and service providers never had a good opportunity to become partners—or co-owners—of the system. To make this point, Felsenstein mentions that organizations and other community information providers did not put their own information on the system but, rather, handed it off to Community Memory staff or volunteers, who entered it for them. This lack of involvement or investment on the part of the community members not only created a bottleneck for Community Memory staff and volunteers but it helped prevent the type of community *ownership* that is key to Cleveland Free-Net founder Tom Grundner's vision and is demonstrated by volunteers at community networks all over the world.

The Community Memory insistence on an exclusive street-level community focus also may have diminished their chances for success. For one thing, being able to communicate with the system from fewer than 10 locations almost guaranteed a minimal community involvement, and not providing access to the outside world (via news groups or e-mail) may have reduced community interest and created a vision of the system as being unnecessarily parochial and exclusive. Despite its relatively short life (which could yet experience a rebirth), the concepts and services that Community Memory pioneered have had and will have lasting impact on the design of future systems.

The Mood Is Playful

Words are the raw material of many creative forms of language, both spoken and written. Examples abound from all cultures (including nonliterate ones) and include riddles, rap, epigrams, haikus, and verbal duels (Farb, 1974) among many others, and new forms can be invented indefinitely.

Joan Coate, formerly of the WELL on-line system states that "The all-text display that still dominates on-line systems appeals to people who love word play, language, and writing. And it appeals to people with active minds" (1992). Along these lines, Philip Wohlstetter, posting on the IN.S.OMNIA, BBS established by the Invisible Seattle group, reported that "Art is an activity always available, attracts abundant aspirants among Americans and aliens alike" (Wohlstetter, 1985). That sentence was the first sentence of Chapter A in a never completed text entitled *Art A to Z*. Chapter A contained words that began with the letter A, while Chapter A, B contained words beginning with letters A or B. The text was to continue in that vein until the 26th chapter, which could contain words beginning with any letter. Chapters 27–52 would reverse the process, gradually eradicating the alphabet until the letter A again abided alone. The IN.S.OMNIA originators realized (in the early 1980s) that a BBS could be used as a creative vehicle for interactive literature in which "every reader is a writer, and new forms appear, a new writing that is at once literature, grafitti, conversation, and word game." The IN.S.OMNIA BBS (now disbanded) was open to anybody, but in reality was used by a small, basically self-selected group of adventurous literary cognoscenti (who would routinely quote Derrida, for example). Nevertheless, IN.S.OMNIA provided a good experimental station for performing communication collaborations that were at once both playful and intellectually ground-breaking (Wittig, 1994).

According to Oldenberg "The persistent mood of the third place is a playful one." He goes on to say, "Those who would keep conversation serious for more than a minute are almost certainly doomed to failure." While there are exceptions, one would not characterize the mood of many current community networks as *playful*. Perhaps it's because these networks don't really support "traditional" conversations. The computer-based conversations don't take place in real-time and typing text is slower and more labor intensive than speaking. People often can effortlessly utter 90 words per minute, while the casual typist types around 30 words in one minute (Hiltz and Turoff, 1993). In Usenet newsgroups, there are often established conversation topics or "threads," and undirected conversation is frowned upon by other participants as "noise." Moreover, participants often don't know the people with whom they're conversing, so they're less likely to make jokes or make wry comments. Also, as frequently noted, many aspects of conversation including timing, facial cues, and body language are nearly untranslatable in the text-only medium. A broad range of conventions and ad hoc methods are used to circumvent this limitation, including the typographical "smiley face" : -) [4] used to indicate that the comment was intended to be funny or issued in jest, or "stage directions," such as "Doug steps onto his soap box," that indicate a deviation from ordinary protocol.

Discussion areas in the Santa Monica PEN system are more reminiscent of "real" conversations than many other systems I've used. In the discussion "item" (equivalent to a forum or newsgroup) with the provocative title "Pen is dead," there were many one-liner conversational responses, such as "if unread." Why is this? For one thing, PEN messages are displayed one after another without clearing the screen in between. For another, the header, showing "envelope" information (such as who sent the letter and when) is short (unlike my current UNIX mail reader that displays some 20 lines of headers). Although current community networks aren't often noted for their great spirit of fun, increasing this playful aspect is an important goal. If these systems are perceived as strictly "serious" and if using them is a purely civic chore, then usage will likely deteriorate and "playfulness," an important aspect of community life will be lacking.

---

[4] These can get quite elaborate. For example, LL*8;-) stands for a lesbian librarian with tiara winking and smiling. It is doubtful that this is used much in practice. (Turn the page 90° clockwise to view these "faces.")

BEYOND THE GREAT GOOD PLACE

What the tavern offered long before television or newspapers was a source of news along with the opportunity to question, protest, sound out, supplement and form opinion locally and collectively.

Ray Oldenburg (1991)

Community members need great good places such as those Oldenberg discussed to help them be a part of their community. Those locations, whether physical or virtual, provide natural forums for dialog, cushions against hardship, and outlets for frustration. As history has shown, they can also provide the backdrop or setting for political or social activism. In the latter half of the seventeenth century, for example, King Charles II issued "A Proclamation for the Suppression of Coffeehouses," which was ostensibly created to prevent idleness but was more deeply connected to fears of "Defamation of His Majestie's Government" (Oldenberg, 1991). The resistance to this proclamation was so strong that it was retracted by another proclamation several months later. Oldenberg provides other interesting examples from history, including the underlying organizational support that meetings in colonial taverns in America furnished in the times preceding the American War of Independence. Thus, while great good places are indispensable to communities, their existence supplies only a part of the struggle for community. In the sections ahead, we briefly discuss some of the ways in which community members can build on the lessons and foundation of the great good place and how they can strengthen communities—by making them more deeply connected to each other by being more aware and more effective in dealing with current and anticipated issues.

The Built Environment

Eighty percent of everything ever built in America has been built in the last fifty years, and most of it is depressing, brutal, ugly, unhealthy, and spiritually degrading.

James Kunstler (1993)

The designed or built environment is the part of the environment that is neither the natural environment, the cultural environment, nor the environment of cyberspace. Because it is intimately related to the state of the community, it's necessary to discuss briefly the "built environment" here.

There are implications for today's communities and for tomorrow's in how we build our cities and towns and in the technology we employ to sustain these built environments. A highway that makes suburban living more convenient could have deleterious effects ranging from the physical and psychic dismemberment of the community that the highway bisects (with its accompanying noise and air pollution) to increased geographical isolation between economic classes. On a larger level, spending public money on the highway means that the money was not spent in other possible ways, such as public art, housing, or recreation. The highway, therefore, could hasten urban decay while simultaneously placing those of greater economic means even further both psychologically and geographically from the older inner city neighborhoods.

The physical space in which our physical selves must navigate has such a strong influence on us that it could profitably be thought of as a technology or a tool. However, as the Kunstler quote at the beginning of this section indicates, this physical space, the space that we as a people have consciously *constructed* over the past few decades, is a depressing mish-mash. While possibly addressing the short-range exigencies and needs of developers, the built environment falls terribly short of our needs as individuals and as members of communities.

Ceremony and Memory

Some cursory words are in order because the concepts of ceremony and memory both underlie the web of community life in important ways. Everyday life is by its very nature ordinary. And the living that takes place everyday, similarly, takes place *now*, in the present. In other words, everyday life is ordinary and current. If life is *only* ordinary and current, it is unpunctuated; it has no connection to the greater mysteries and wonders of life, nor to the historic linkages between the past, the present, and the future. Without meaningful *punctuation* through ceremony and memory, life loses its meaning through its loss of meaningful connections to the web of community.

When "ceremony" becomes too opaque, too resistant to change, or exclusive, it becomes sterile and counterproductive for new communities. If it becomes too self-conscious or too up-to-date, it becomes a superficial and useless fad. The idea of "memory" also needs balance and temperance. *What* should we remember, how should it be remembered, and for what purpose is it being remembered? I can't presume to answer these questions because they're part of a community web of which I'm just one aspect. The perspectives of ceremony and memory are critical, however, to the new community. The Alameda County War Memorial is an example of ceremony and memory in a community network.

Electronic Memorial

Joe McDonald, the leader of the 60s rock band, Country Joe and the Fish, is the unlikely instigator of a unique experiment in the early days of community-network development. Although McDonald's song "I Feel Like I'm Fixing to Die Rag" was a devastating antiwar anthem in the Vietnam era, McDonald, a veteran of the U.S. Navy, feels a strong kinship with soldiers. In fact, he describes himself as a person obsessed with soldiers, war, and war's aftermath.

McDonald was inspired by the stark black memorial wall in Washington, D.C., that is covered with the names of the U.S. Vietnam war dead, and he then began to carefully examine the idea of memorials. He began corresponding with the U.S. Department of Defense and ultimately collected the names of all the veterans from Alameda County (which includes Berkeley and Oakland, California) who had died in World War I, World War II, the Korean war, the Vietnam war, and the Persian Gulf war. The Vietnam war names were supplied on long rolls of computer paper, while the World War I names were supplied on two-inch microfilm. The microfilm contained photos of the deceased along with full-page tributes to individual Red Cross workers and military nurses, and also contained decorative borders and stylized layouts.

While reflecting on *physical* war memorials—like the one in Washington, D.C.—McDonald was struck by two things. One was the cost of a physical memorial (the Washington memorial cost seven million dollars) and, the second, was that people had to make a physical pilgrimage to experience it. McDonald realized that if a war memorial were stored electronically on a networked computer, the issues of cost and distance could be circumvented. Additionally, because cyberspace is cheaper than physical space, he reasoned that "if the war memorial existed in a computer, then anybody in the world should be able to interface with it" and that it should be possible to add names from any war and any time and place.

The Alameda county names, nearly two thousand in all, were loaded into the Community Memory system by McDonald, Gert Chiarito, YaVette Holts, and many other volunteers (including people from various political persuasions) and these names became the Community Memory Alameda County War Memorial. The belief of the volunteers, according to the literature on the on-line memorial was that "in remembering, we can promote understanding." Since people left gifts or offerings at the war memorial in Washington, D.C., it was decided that community memory participants should be able to leave their comments on the system, to gain closure on the death of a loved one by electronically "leaving flowers." Phil Elwood, a Bay area journalist who had lost a relative in World War II, for example, looked up his relative's name and typed in his reminiscences. This venue also allowed people to express other comments and thoughts on war, including comments of those opposed to war, an option that is unavailable with traditional war memorials. Thus people representing many viewpoints could contribute to the dynamic, living community memorial.

Although McDonald was not familiar with the technology, he also suggested that a wounded Vietnam veteran (or a veteran from any other war) who was confined to a hospital bed for a protracted period of time would ultimately be able to add graphics or music beside the electronic entry of a comrade who had been killed.

Although there was a lot of local interest, the Alameda County War Memorial existed for just a "hot minute," according to McDonald. The Community Memory system's revenue hit rock-bottom around that time and the system itself suffered many glitches. Although Country Joe remembers the experience as "almost a dream," it's clear that network services have the potential, if not the obligation, to serve the convivial needs of the community as well as the merely informational. Although the original system is unavailable, McDonald is working with the city of Berkeley to memorialize their Vietnam war fatalities and welcomes inquiries from interested people (see Appendix B).

Local Identity and Culture

Many communities now have concocted official slogans to artificially improve their image: "City Middletown, Where People Say Hi!," "Fun in the Sun in Smogville!," "Best Darn Town in the Whole Darn World," or "Low Murder Rate in Sleepy Acreage." Contrived slogans notwithstanding, communities need landmarks, both physical and conceptual, that distinguish that community, provide identity and awareness, and generally help to build shared perspectives.

These landmarks—particularly the conceptual ones—can be part of the terrain supplied by the community network. Some of these landmarks include homegrown poetry, interviews, or oral histories involving local celebrities known citywide or throughout the neighborhood. They might consist of high or low culture, involving both civic betterment or civic mischief. All of these can be presented on a community network.

As we have seen, cultural issues are becoming increasingly dominated by corporate concerns. At the same time, many contemporary artists are producing work that is highly individualized, inaccessible, and of little relevance to people in communities. Although introspective, individual, alternative, and even "deviant" art is valid—if not critical—in our society, it is also important to realize that visual art and other artistic forms can provide a fundamental integrating factor in the web of community (Gablik, 1991). Increasingly, community cultural planning is being advocated as a way to address these issues.

Although there are now several efforts nationwide to institute cultural planning, the Community Cultural Plan (Bainbridge Island Arts and Humanities Council, 1995) from Bainbridge Island, an island community of 17,000, 15 minutes from Seattle by ferry boat, will serve as a useful example. The Bainbridge Island Arts and Humanities Council spent approximately one year in a planning process with maximal community involvement. The first step in their process was to assess their cultural needs and capacities through extensive interviews, through over 20 focus groups (involving a wide variety of cultural, ethnic, youth, and business groups) and through surveys, which were mailed to over 300 island residents chosen at random. Interestingly, the survey revealed strong cultural *capacities* in the community: 54 percent of the respondents reported that at least one member of their family was an artist of amateur or professional status. The data also revealed that in 25 percent of the households, individuals earned an income in the arts. After the initial assessment and surveys, the results were distilled into a draft of a cultural plan that was discussed at a public meeting. A detailed plan was then developed involving vision, goals, and strategies in several major interrelated areas (arts, education, economic vitality, the arts, facility development, financial resources, history and heritage, the humanities, individual artists, marketing and communications, public art and community design, and services to cultural organizations). Whether or not the cultural plan is ever instituted in its entirety, the process is still useful in terms of identifying actions and in terms of building community relationships, both actual and intellectual.

Culture can be an authentic expression of community life and it can be produced by ordinary people. Culture can also be a mass-produced commodity, a creation of committees and "creative directors" in corporations with little, if any, interest in the well-being of individuals and communities. Culture is increasingly the by-product of the corporate drive to maximize profits. The corporate cultural product often is the lowest common denominator of possible choices. Since this cultural product did not evolve organically within a real community, it is unlikely to address real cultural needs of the community. Moreover, any community *use* of the cultural product is generally forbidden. If cartoon characters such as Mickey Mouse or Donald Duck were to find their way into community murals, theater, or stories, Disney corporation lawyers would quickly exercise their considerable legal clout to prevent the use of that creation. Barbies, GI Joes, and Cabbage Patch dolls are all ersatz manifestations of culture, as they are developed, distributed, marketed, and controlled by noncommunity interests. Just as authentic nonmanufactured culture is rapidly becoming an alien concept in the U.S., the drive to mass production and commodification also takes its toll on other cultures as well. For example, the impact on other cultures can be seen when native American stories are packaged into books and audio tapes and sold on the mass market, or when violent action movies are marketed worldwide.

Hawaii Immersion

I ka 'ōlelo nō ke ola, i ka 'ōlelo nōka make. (In the language there is life, in the language there is death.)

Hawaii 'ōlelo no'eau (wise saying)

'Ōlelo Hawai'i, the Hawaiian language, once perilously close to extinction, is now showing strong vital signs in many ways, including through community networking (Donaghy, 1994). Until 1820, when a written form was created by Christian missionaries, Hawaiian had existed only as a spoken language. By the mid 1850s, Hawaiians were among the most literate people in the world, and Hawaiian was the language of choice of business, education, and government. Shortly after the United States overthrew Hawaii in the 1890s, the language was made illegal as a medium of instruction. In 1978 at the state's constitutional convention, with fewer than 50 speakers under the age of 10 left, Hawaiian was made the legal equivalent of English. And in 1985, after extensive lobbying, it became legal again to teach school using the Hawaiian language. Now over one thousand children are enrolled in Hawaiian immersion programs.

Keola Donaghy, whose ethnicity is Irish, Dutch, and American Indian, can trace his interest in "Hawaiian things" back to the 1970s, around the same time as the Hawaiian Renaissance (a time at which the interest in the Hawaiian tradition, culture, and language began to increase). He was "hanai," informally adopted as an Hawaiian, by a Hawaiian couple who lived on his parents' property. In his late teens, Donaghy began to be interested in telecommunications and launched his first BBS, MauiLink, in 1989 or 1990. Soon after that Donaghy started to learn the Hawaiian language and, shortly after, modified the fonts of his BBS software so that he could exchange e-mail in Hawaiian with his instructors.

According to Donaghy, "the premise of the Hawaiian language immersion program is to educate the children completely in Hawaiian," and he asked the question, "Why should that stop when they turn on the computer?" Accordingly, Donaghy started to modify the operating system on his Macintosh so the menus and dialog boxes would be displayed in Hawaiian, an effort that involved the creation of hundreds of new Hawaiian words for words such as "modem," "font," "bulletin board," and the like. After that, he modified other programs including Claris Works, Kid Pix, and FirstClass. He uses the modified software for his BBS, using Hawaiian rather than English for the user interface. Donaghy now has Hawaiian-only systems set up at all of the eight Hawaiian immersion schools, the Leoki BBS, and a Hawaiian Web site that includes pointers to Kualono, a Hawaiian language Web server (Fig. 2.15).

Darker Sides of Community

Americans felt a strong sense of community when they put Japanese-Americans in concentration camps in the 1940s and persecuted suspected communists in the 1950s.

Michael D'Antonio (1994)

Communities rarely have a coherent agenda, shared goals, or political will. In fact, they often have no seat at the table for important issues that affect them. When communities are aligned together over an issue, it is often crisis-oriented and typically labeled, in a pejorative sense, as a NIMBY ("Not In My Backyard") response. Although neighborhoods have a very important role to play in local, regional and other issues, all too often community groups choose to organize *against* something. In my neighborhood, for example, a small daycare was the subject of an effort to prevent its opening. In another Seattle neighborhood, the citizens rebelled because their new manhole covers were inadvertently manufactured without their neighborhood emblem.

Once in a presentation after I had replied to a question about community

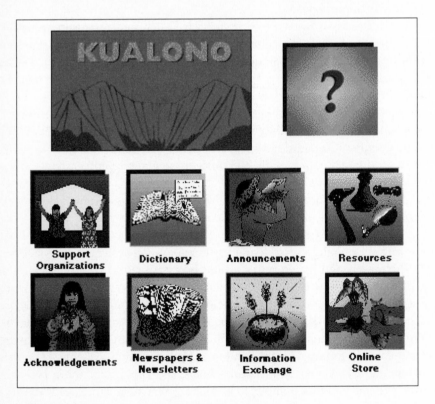

Figure 2.15 Hawaiin Language Web server

	Cooperative	*Competitive*
Community focus	New community	"Balkanized" community
No community	"World citizen"	Mass society (Consumer)

Figure 2.16 Visions of Future Society

networks in which I had stated that I thought that Seattle needed its own network, and that the Eastside (including Bellevue, Kirkland, Redmond, and other cities, towns, and rural areas), Tacoma, and other regions of the state needed theirs too, somebody in the audience muttered that I advocated "balkanizing" the state or the country. Although I didn't realize it at the time, he expressed a common fear, one that recognizes the dark side of community, one that is exclusive and competitive and fiercely chauvinistic. Unfortunately, this fear is not entirely groundless. For example, the Citizen's Council in New Orleans, Louisiana, that formed earlier this century to keep African-Americans in segregated institutions and organizations (McMillen, 1981), is a kind of community and the various organized crime families are also communities. How can new communities avoid becoming pathological like those above? Although there is no guarantee, one way to avoid these possibilities is to pay close attention to the idea of "ties" and "norms." When the membership requirements ("ties") are based on racist, religious, or economic grounds, the civic engagement will be incomplete and have a natural predilection towards corruption. In the same vein, the "norms" of the organization will be continually reflected in the actions that the organization takes over the years.

On the other hand, there is another view that indigenous community is disappearing entirely. Perhaps all local identity and conviviality will recede, and anonymous, asocial, and alienated creatures will take its place. One side of this view, a cooperative society without a community focus is benign if unrealistic. In this view, local differences will fade over time and we'll all be much the same type of person—a "world citizen"—in the future. These varying viewpoints showing four visions of community are presented in Fig. 2.16 above. While all of these visions may be relevant at various times in the past and in the future, a new community that is cooperative yet maintains local differences, is possible and well worth striving for.

AGENDA FOR ACTION

A man has only one life and if during it he has no great environment, no community, he has been irreparably robbed of a human right.

Paul Goodman (1960)

Communities today often lack a discernible identity. People are *from* a community but they often don't *belong to* a community. This is a problem of identity that translates into a need for community-specific events, places, landmarks, institutions, and people that can be distinguished from those in other communities and can be a source of pride for community members. Additionally, communities will need power. This is not power in an absolute sense, nor should whatever power is developed be wielded capriciously or selfishly. But without power, without the ability to compete with larger and better organized institutions, nearly all the aspirations of the new community will go unrealized.

In order to begin to rebuild communities as important social organizations, we need to begin to rebuild trust between individuals that has eroded over time. Community-network developers will need to work with community activists and community-development organizations to design new projects. They will need to support and extend existing services electronically, to help repair broken links in the community, while building social capital. In Seattle, for example, an electronic pen-pals project to promote communication between school children in diverse neighborhoods has been proposed.

To truly support community conviviality and culture, access must be universal. The barriers of cost, availability, literacy, and physical disabilities must be bridged. Connecting to community-network services must be inexpensive and easy. Free or minimal cost use from the home and public access points at existing community locations such as libraries, schools, community and senior centers, and parks are required. Other candidate locations include all places where people traditionally congregate such as bars, coffee houses, laundromats, bus stations, and shopping malls. Additionally, access points for community networks will need to become as ubiquitous as telephones (and at least as inexpensive) if community network use is to become a natural, everyday occurrence.

Finally, as communities begin to rebuild and reinvent themselves, community activists will need to assert their interests and needs into the larger picture. They will need successes in this area to build confidence. They will also need vision, wisdom, and humility to avoid the pettiness of NIMBYism and the tunnel vision of avarice.

Although community members must sometimes take action on their own behalf to sustain their communities, they are far from being masters of their own fate. Exterior forces, often of an economic nature, can be the cause of major disruptive changes. South Central Los Angeles, the scene of 1992 riots, for example, had lost tens of thousands of jobs when the defense industry imploded and unemployment skyrocketed (Davis, 1992). Between 1979 and 1992 the United States lost nearly three million manufacturing jobs (Judis, 1994). Camden, New Jersey, discussed in Jonathan Kozol's devastating critique of America's educational system, recently lost Campbells, General Electric, and RCA manufacturing plants. In spite of very high tax relief, Camden can't attract new business (Kozol, 1991). The jobs are going overseas where unprotected workers earn a dollar or less per hour. Communities, especially disadvantaged ones, also have little influence upon major construction projects such as highways (New York City), sports stadiums (Los Angeles, California), bridges (Massachusetts), or sewage treatment plants (Camden, New Jersey), which can devastate communities by displacing its inhabitants, severing social as well as geographically-based ties.

The damage wrought by these disruptions goes beyond the harm done to individuals. "Because social capital is a public good, the costs of closing factories goes beyond the personal traumas borne by individuals" (Putnam, 1993). Putnam also cautions that programs that are ostensibly devised to help disadvantaged communities can backfire: "American slum-clearance policy of 1950s and 1960s, for example, renovated physical capital, but at a very high cost to existing social capital." Unfortunately it will take time to repair the damage done by these powerful forces.

However, as sociologist Craig Calhoun reminds us, "It is misleading to try to understand, and potentially pernicious to foster, community life, without paying attention to the nature of its incorporation into structures of large-scale social integration" (1986). It might be tempting, in other words, to think of *community* as being independent from other forces. For better or worse, communities are *embedded* in the external world to a large degree, and this knowledge can be used both reactively and proactively in dealing with external forces.

At both the superficial and the deepest level of analysis, a community network must offer community members a cheerful and unpretentious venue—where admission is free and open to all. It must also support community culture and community activism. The challenges that communities are facing are deadly serious. Only a sustained and widespread effort has a chance to slow down or stop the trend toward community deterioration.

Chapter 3

Education

Give people some significant power and they will quickly appreciate the need for knowledge, but foist knowledge on them without giving them responsibility and they will display only indifference.

Benjamin Barber (1984)

In the future, technology will have eliminated the need for education of any kind.

Anonymous

WHAT IS EDUCATION FOR?

Education ideally provides perspectives and tools for participating in society, for understanding society, and for shaping society. Education thought of in that way is fundamental to any society—not just Western or literate societies. Education in the general sense is a systematic and rigorous approach towards perceiving and learning in the individual *and* society, and it has very little to do with the gathering of information, the stockpiling of knowledge, or the institutionalizing of education for its own sake. The broad aim of education should be to help make individuals more competent, thus indirectly benefiting the larger society. It should also instil a social ethic; it should allow us to engage in discourse with others, help us to accept and appreciate different viewpoints, and urge us to take action that benefits society and the natural world.

Note that the above views of education do not explicitly specify the need for teachers, schools, books, classes, or formal education. The widespread availability of electronic networks may propel substantial transformations in education in the near future. However, the need for facilitators of education traditionally called "teachers," educational material ("books"), physical and virtual places where learning is the chief enterprise ("schools"), coordinated events that facilitate learning ("classes"), and courses of studies ("formal education" and "curricula") will remain.

People are beginning to think about how computer-network technology might transform education, and pundits are beginning to make revolutionary pronouncements and extravagant claims about the future of education which, however woolly, may be influential. If citizens are going to play any part in these discussions and important decisions about the future, they will need to begin articulating issues and discussing concerns about possible new modes of learning—how these modes could evolve from today's institutions; how effective could they be; who might reap the rewards; who might be penalized; and how, could, or should the system be paid for.

Society is constantly changing. Modern transportation systems and communication technology accelerate change, as do other upheavals, both social and environmental. For those reasons determining concrete educational goals is an uncertain and ambiguous enterprise: How can we educate for the twenty-first century when we can't realistically expect to know what it will be like? Our approach to education must therefore be flexible and somewhat open-ended. Education should help produce citizens that are just and prudent as well as intelligent and effective. Society can adapt to changing times if its citizens are able to help themselves and others, have strongly developed civic and social ethics, and can intelligently and creatively face challenges. Indeed, education's main role is shaping the world of the future. Unfortunately, current approaches to education often fail in this role.

INSTITUTIONALIZED EDUCATION

School reserves instruction to those whose every step in learning fits previously approved measures of social control.

Ivan Illich (1972)

There are two broad criticisms that can be made against current educational programs in the United States and around the world. For our purposes, the shorthand expressions of "equity" and "empowerment," as expressed by Jonathan Kozol (1991) and by Ivan Illich (1972), respectively, will suffice. While Kozol focuses on the extreme inequity in *funding* and public investment for education, Illich focuses on the more insidious problem of intellectual straitjacketing, the systematic constraining of thought that occurs in many schools. While children of all income levels are garrisoned in schools for large portions of their lives, the children of higher income families have friendlier surroundings and more expensive diversions.

Perhaps the best way to reconcile the apparently unrelated arguments of Kozol and Illich is to look at them from the point of view of a "job" metaphor. The kids from rich backgrounds get "good jobs," while those without economic means get the "bad jobs." If you had to have a job, you'd probably want a "good one," but perhaps it isn't a job that you're looking for at all. How is education like a job? For one thing, students report to the same boss at the same place every day at the same time. The boss (their teacher) hands them out assignments that are due at some set time. When the whistle blows, the factory gates swing open and the workers—students—are free for the time being. Their services are not required until the next day. If a student does well at this job, then he or she can get a better job (say, an admission to Harvard) and, from there, a still better job, say, a partnership in a big law firm. But the job metaphor is inappropriate for education: Society needs citizens, not wage slaves.

Institutionalized Education Is Intellectually Stultifying

Relying on drills and memorization, teachers, often with too few resources and too many students, often end up lecturing to the mythical average student. This style of teaching rarely addresses the individual student: The lesson is out of reach for some, while being maddeningly obvious and boring to others. The teacher rolls through the lesson until a bell rings and the cycle is repeated with another batch of hapless students.

Added to this assembly-line approach is the imperious "canon" that determines *what* ought to be taught. The canon is often boring and irrelevant to middle-class whites, and it is alien if not totally meaningless to others. Another way to promote intellectual conformity is to simply declare everything that is "political" to be off-limits. This dictum, implicit and generally unchallenged, helps keep a wide range of issues off the table for public discussion. This approach, along with stringent pigeon-holing into academic disciplines, is often effective in keeping any discussion of the social context or implications out of the sciences, engineering, literature, the arts, and the educational process itself. As African author, Chinua Achebe (Graff, 1992) has pointed out, taking this stance implicitly endorses the status quo: Its hidden lesson is that everything is as it should be. In the United States there is also an effort to maintain a pro-American perspective in all texts that are used in American classrooms. This effectively means that lynchings, repression of organized labor, native American genocide, and other unsavory motifs of American history must be sanitized or excised entirely from the textbooks. Certainly this treatment is dishonest and disrespectful to the learner, but there are even more insidious consequences. A learner who doesn't understand shortcomings or flaws in society is far less likely to grapple positively with social issues than someone who can see the problems as well as the promise.

Institutionalized Education Is Nondemocratic and Coercive

Although American society ostensibly values democracy, our schools seemingly prepare us for a passive and powerless existence. How is this accomplished?

In the first place, the schools provide little exposure to genuine democratic discourse and decision making. People can hardly be expected to participate in public affairs without this grounding. Grappling with complex issues—especially doing so collaboratively—is not reflexive, like eating or breathing. It is a hard-won and difficult-to-master skill that can be honed only through training and practice.

In the second place, students in an institutionalized environment do not govern, they are governed. People unaccustomed to active involvement will habitually shrink back from engagement and action. Unfortunately, people will generally live up (or down) to the general expectation that they are incapable of leadership, thus helping to perpetuate the problem. Moreover, people who make a practice of participation possess a more active control of their life and have a more positive outlook. The democratic theorist Carole Pateman (1970) and others point out that the experience of participation leaves the individual better equipped psychologically for dealing with future events.

In the third place, lessons in such an environment tend to be orthodox and sterile. When a teacher leads students down a preordained path, spontaneity and the joys of new discovery are lost—lively intellectual pursuit can degenerate into dismal and pointless toil. Institutes of higher learning unfortunately offer more of the same: required courses, huge classes, and an assembly-line approach to education that often restricts independence and power still further. The "participatory education" ideas that surfaced in the 1960s and 1970s focused on an equal partnership between students and teachers.

Institutionalized Education Is Like a Prison Sentence

If education consisted of learning a set number of facts and figures, then it would make sense to call an abrupt halt to the learning process at some magical cut-off point (after memorizing the "cultural literacy" books, for example). But education is a process, not a goal, and life-long learning is critical. In order to open up a multitude of other educational possibilities—including adult literacy, peer-to-peer teaching, foreign language immersion, counseling, and discussion groups—society must jettison the idea of education as a jail sentence that one must suffer through before one can attain freedom.

Institutionalized Higher Education Is Divorced from Reality

Benjamin Barber describes two models of the university that many professors and administrators are advancing: "One model is scholastic and calls for refurbishing the ivory tower and reinforcing its splendid monastic isolation, while the other apes the marketplace and calls for tearing down the tower and overcoming isolation by forging new associations with—and a new servitude to—the market's whim and fashions, which pass as its aims and purposes" (1992). Neither of these models—especially when seen against the backdrop of a factory-like "diploma mill"—displays any interest in the community at large, which is seen as lurking irrelevantly outside the ivied walls.

With few exceptions, the modern university has partitioned knowledge into a bewildering number of departments, schools, institutes, and the like. The result of this is an uneasy pluralism that lacks interdisciplinary degrees, interdepartmental cooperation, or common vocabularies. Like animals that cannot breed, academic institutions that cannot engage in intellectual discourse beyond their own discipline are sterile.

Institutionalized Education Is Inequitable

Education is key to economic survival. On the individual level, economic success is strongly tied to formal higher education. College graduates in the United States earn substantially more than high school graduates. Political participation is also largely determined by the amount of formal education, as is the ability to obtain information about health or other important concerns, and the ability to communicate with others. On a national or international level, education or lack of it may help or hinder our ability to make peace with our neighbors and with our environment.

Students from upper-class backgrounds have access to a wide array of educational resources and, in general, far more options open to them than do those of more modest means. Those students are less likely to be subjected to repetitive drill and practice and are much more likely to be encouraged to be entrepreneurial (stage their own plays or design their own curriculum and lesson plans, for example), have modern technology available to them (computers connected to the Internet, for example), or participate in civic activities outside the classroom.

As in other important aspects of modern life, educational opportunity is heavily weighted in favor of the economically advantaged and the disparity is growing. Jonathan Kozol writing in *Savage Inequalities* (1991), provides numerous examples from the United States. Students in East Saint Louis,

Missouri; Camden, New Jersey; and the South Bronx, New York (among countless other locations) face a daily grind of overheated or underheated classrooms; bathrooms with no toilet paper; overcrowded classes; damaged, outdated, and inadequate supplies of books and other materials; no theater, music, sports, computers, or other "frills"; broken glass, poor ventilation, unlit stairs, and general violence. At Goudy Senior High School in Chicago, for example, Kozol reports that "Slow readers in an eighth grade history class are taught from 15-year-old textbooks in which Richard Nixon is still president. There are no science labs, no art or music teachers. Soap, paper towels, and toilet paper are in short supply. There are two working bathrooms for some 700 children." Highland Park High School in a wealthy suburb of Dallas, by way of contrast, has a planetarium, indoor swimming pool, and a closed-circuit television studio for its students. While education offers the best opportunities for economic advancement, the environment provided for poor children in the United States is a cruel travesty.

Kozol is concerned about *inequities* and he lays them before us in grim and devastating detail. This testament, however, is not his only issue. He also discusses how many of us deny, explain away, or otherwise disassociate ourselves from the problem. There is, for example, one popular rationalization that states money *by itself* cannot solve the problem. Although there may be a germ of truth in this view, it is difficult to imagine a solution to this problem in which money cannot help. Money, in simple terms, can't guarantee excellence—it can only improve the chances. Kozol makes this point in concrete terms:

> If the New York City schools were funded, for example, at the level of the highest-spending suburbs of Long Island, a fourth grade class of 36 children such as those I visited in District 10 would have had $200,000 *more* invested in their education during 1987. Although a portion of this extra money would have gone into administrative costs, the remainder would have been enough to hire two extraordinary teachers at enticing salaries of $50,000 each, divide the class into *two classes* of some 18 children each, provide them with computers, carpets, air conditioning, new texts and reference books and learning games—indeed, with everything available today in the most affluent school districts— and also pay the costs of extra counseling to help those children cope with the dilemmas they face at home. Even the most skeptical detractor of "the worth of spending further money in the public schools" would hesitate, I think, to face a grade-school principal in the South Bronx and try to tell her that this "wouldn't make much of a difference."

However glaring these inadequacies may be, the harsh realities seem to elude many Americans. The lesson for community-network developers is that any community network that is intended to support the community must help address the crisis in equity and access in education. While computer technology has much to offer in educational realms, much of the current evidence suggests that computer technology has helped exacerbate the problems of inequality. Community-network developers risk becoming part of the problem if they focus on the technology or if they believe that computer-network technology is a substitute for adequate funding.

INDIVIDUALIZED EDUCATION

. . . everyone can learn at every age and ability, and there are many ways to help everyone to do so.

Dee Dickinson (1988)

We need to create an educational system to help *every individual* develop intellectual independence and a sense of empowerment. Its purpose must be to help form active, awake, and questioning citizens who can participate fully in society. If education helps the individual, it helps, by extension, the community, industry, and government.

Respect for the Student

An educational environment that respects the student means a more effective educational environment. For one thing, respect for the student implies that there is a relatively high ratio of teachers to students. If there are too many students, the teacher cannot provide adequate individual attention, and the student will participate less and skip class more (Lindsay, 1982; Ornstein, 1991). Along the same lines, there should be continuity of teachers to allow genuine personal relationships to develop. Learning can occur more naturally when trust exists and suitable role models are present. Unfortunately, some classes in poorer school districts are presided over by a succession of substitutes, temporaries, or administrators, sometimes numbering 15 or more in a given school year, according to Kozol.

Just as bedside manner may be the most important aspect of medical care, a "hands-on" teacher may be the most important element in education. People need the "human touch," direct contact with teachers and fellow students. This is particularly true in cases where home life is dysfunctional, through abuse, lack of security or love, or when the caregiver is working and must leave the child alone in the house. In some cases, the teacher may be the only dependable and caring adult in a student's life and may offer the only hope for the student's success at school. This need for human contact seriously challenges the idea that electronic delivery of education through teaching machines, television, or computer networks can *replace* the in-person student-teacher setting.

Reading, Writing, Arithmetic, and Beyond

The traditional 3-Rs of education are cornerstones for learning. One must read and write and be able to respond using various media including speech. Reading might mean *listening* and writing might mean *speaking*. One must be able to communicate with fellow human beings directly and indirectly, sometimes in conversations that span thousands of miles and years. Arithmetic provides another language, a language of abstractions and algorithms, which complements the "natural" language modes of speaking, listening, reading, and writing.

Using these fundamental skills allows people to sample and employ a wide range of disciplines, or *perspectives*, including philosophy, anthropology, economics, political science, physics, and biology, among many others. When a student reads the literature within the perspective—reviews the data, evidence, and theoretical propositions—he or she shares a body of co-operatively developed knowledge and thinking and can contribute to the ongoing growth of that perspective.

As if to complement the perspectives listed above, humankind has also developed a wide range of other modes of expression—like dance, music, and the visual arts—that are also essential to education. These expressive languages provide meaning and raise issues that may be inexpressible in words or numbers alone. Unfortunately, since it's difficult to directly link these skills to commercial achievement or technological development, conventional wisdom often portrays them as inessential, especially in poorer communities. In affluent communities, on the other hand, not offering these "frills" would, of course, be unthinkable.

However valuable these traditional perspectives are, we need to be aware of their confining as well as their enabling nature, for a perspective can be a straitjacket of the mind: All major scientific advances, for example, have come from *rejection* of the conventional perspectives of the time. Educational policy and educational processes—especially with support from communication technology—must be fluid enough to encourage the exploration and development of new syntheses, paradigms, and perspectives. Arriving at a new interpretation using a fresh perspective is often very valuable. Brenda Laurel, for example, uses metaphors from the world of the theater to create new conceptualizations of the computer "user interface" (1991), while the Evergreen State College in Olympia, Washington, uses coordinated studies to encourage educational exploration from multiple perspectives. One such coordinated study, for example, entitled "Harmony in the Universe," combined the perspectives of art and music with those of physics and astronomy.

Finally, there is the inescapable fact that many cultures inhabit the globe and a monocultural planet is neither likely nor desirable. However strong one's belief in their own cultural superiority may be, one cannot reject the usefulness of broad multicultural respect and understanding. Beyond just getting along, people need to have some understanding in order to communicate—and to do business—with people from other cultures. At a deeper level, multicultural perspectives provide alternative ways of seeing and understanding the world. As people from different cultures come together to address common concerns, elements or viewpoints from various cultures will fuse together in new patterns that help establish new habits and techniques for working together.

Critical Thinking

Our intellectual history is a chronicle of the anguish and suffering of men who tried to help their contemporaries see that some part of their fondest beliefs were misconceptions, faulty assumptions, superstitions and outright lies."
                                        Neil Postman and Charles Weingartner (1969)

Traditional education stresses the importance of finding the right and final answer—not an incomplete, flawed, or provisional answer. Yet moving forward, learning, and expanding one's understanding requires a constant *questioning* of the status quo, the conventional viewpoint, and the traditional answers. This freedom of thought gives rise to technological invention, paradigm shifts in science, and new directions in the arts. It ensures intellectual vitality and prevents stagnation. Questioning—or penetrating beyond what appears on the surface—is fundamental to science and, indeed, to all learning. This skill need not be limited to scientists, scholars, and artists. It can be practiced on the more prosaic plane of daily life as well.

Sometimes the misleading messages that we receive are the result of a conscious effort or campaign to color our perception, shift our attention, or to simply deceive us. Neil Postman and Charles Weingartner, writing in *Teaching as a Subversive Activity* (1969), call the ability to spot these propagandizing efforts "crap detection." Effective "crap-detectors" can detect and dissect why and how consciously or subconsciously constructed messages deviate from the truth or how they color or pollute the intellectual landscape.

Although we will be looking into media issues more extensively in Chapter 6, it is important to realize that a solid media education is critical if students are to become clear and critical thinkers. The mass media as the primary creator and purveyor of images and ideas in modern society is an excellent place to start. One can start with an observation, then focus by asking probing questions. Why do the people in beer commercials wear cowboy hats? Don't accountants, engineers, or barbers drink beer? Where were the bodies of dead Iraqi soldiers in all the Gulf War footage? There were plenty of bodies to be seen in the coverage of the Vietnam war. Why might a commercial for a convenience store use the American flag so prominently? Are war dead buried there? Why might *Time* or *Newsweek* run a photo of a smiling Ronald Reagan or a tired Jimmy Carter? Was only one photo available? Why is government fraud news and corporate fraud not? Who's making these decisions and at what level?

Unfortunately, as Postman suggests in his book (1969), critical thinkers and other active "crap-detectors" run the risk of being shunned by others, those more obeisant to the sanctity of the status quo: "In the land of the blind, the one-eyed man would be killed." Of course, children from the upper and upper-middle classes are relatively free to criticize (within bounds), while children from the lower economic classes often do not gain these skills or are encouraged not to complain too vocally. Our society needs to offer children tools with which to develop critical perspectives, the courage to do so, and an environment where it is acceptable to articulate them.

COMPUTER NETWORKS AND EDUCATION

> *Technology is available to develop either independence and learning or bureaucracy and teaching.*
>
> Ivan Illich (1972)

Computer networks offer two basic capabilities to education. The first is that information can be disseminated over a distance and to select or diffuse groups of people easily. The second is that new forms of collaboration are now possible. This area is being explored in depth in many places (e.g., Soloway, 1993), so only a few examples are described in this section.

The Exploratorium and the ExploraNet

The Exploratorium, located in the beautiful Palace of Fine Arts in the Marina district of San Francisco, is one of the world's premiere hands-on science museums, featuring a rich assortment of over 650 interactive exhibits that illustrate principles and concepts of anatomy, hearing, sound, electricity, genetics, vision, astronomy, and motion to name a few. Each year, more than 660,000 people visit the Exploratorium and over 500 teachers train there each year.

The Exploratorium is currently extending their place-based approach into cyberspace through The Learning Studio, an experimental multimedia and communications lab. For one thing, they have on-site terminals that are equipped with a wide variety of Internet access software as well as CU-SeeMe video-conferencing software. They have also made much of the information about their programs available on the Web. There are also pointers to other science-based Web sites (Fig. 3.1) and several "on-line exhibits" on their Web site that deliver some of the Exploratorium's exhibits, including "Mutant Fruit Flies" (showing altered shapes and colors in fruit flies), "Vocal Vowels" (where

---

The Learning Studio's Top Ten Web Sites

Check out the Learning Studio's favorite sites to visit this month. Remember to check back next month to see 10 more!

- UC Berkeley Museum of Paleontology Public Exhibits—A fascinating exploration into the past. The "Web Lift to any Taxon" is especially interesting. Follow the path of evolution!

- Virtual Frog Dissection Kit Info Page—Dissect a frog without the mess! Save a frog's life, virtually dissect one instead.

- HST Greatest Hits 1990-1995 Gallery—Spectacular images from space taken by the Hubble Space Telescope.

- Mars Multiscale Map—An interactive look at the Martian surface.

- The Visible Human Project—Navigate through a human cadaver using the "Caltech Interactive Volume Browser," fascinating but a bit gross.

- Welcome to the Rainforest Action Network Home Page— Loads of information on the rainforest and what we can do to save it. Includes a section just for kids.

- Maine Solar House—An informative look at a solar house in Maine. Check out the floor plans, view pictures, and learn more about renewable energy.

- Aurora Page—Get information about the northern lights.

- Volcano World Home Page—Learn all about volcanoes. A great site for teachers and students.

- Weather World General Menu—Satellite photos, animations, and all sorts of weather maps.

Figure 3.1

"hollow plastic models of the human vocal tract turn the squawk of a duck into vowel sounds") and several optical illusions that produce nonexistent colors, disappearing dots, and perceptual peculiarities with an upside-down image of the Mona Lisa. (The Mona Lisa on-line exhibit also offers a "Mona Movie," which is an MPEG format "movie" that Web-browsing software downloads. It displays the rotating images similar to the way it's done at the nonvirtual—i.e., the actual physical—Exploratorium). ExploraNet is a program that is exploring a wide range of on-line resources to support science education. These include "virtual field trips" to the Exploratorium in San Francisco by students in Chicago High Schools using videoconferencing. Students at remote sites can also experience exhibits that would be very difficult or unpleasant to experience directly, such as being in the eye of a hurricane!

The Exploratorium is enmeshed in several educational communities including science educators worldwide, other science education organizations, projects through the Science Learning Network (SLN), and activities with teachers and schools nationwide as well as in the San Francisco region. One of these projects, the Science Learning Network, is a collaborative alliance between six U.S. science education participants: Franklin Institute, Philadelphia; Miami Museum of Science; the Museum of Science, Boston; the Oregon Museum of Science and Industry; the Science Museum of Minnesota; and the Unisys Corporation, which together support teacher development in science education. The Exploratorium also works with the San Francisco United School District (SFUSD) and three Marin County school districts to develop strong hands-on science education in the schools in those districts. The project includes school teachers and principals, Exploratorium staff, and pilot hands-on, discovery-based workshops for students and their families from a local elementary school. The project exemplifies a flexible model focusing on school-based change with multiethnic urban schools, decentralized suburban schools, and a regional public science resource center.

Academy One—A Miscellany of Educational Projects

A wide variety of computer-network-based educational programs are now becoming available to students. Academy One, an international program of the National Public Telecomputing Network (NPTN), the umbrella organization of "Free-Nets" and other community networks (Delzeit, 1995; NPTN, 1993a) helps make a wide-ranging collection of ongoing projects, special events, programs, and information services available to classrooms all over the world via the Internet.

Currently NPTN Director of Education Linda Delzeit runs the Academy One program from her office in Buena Park, California. In addition to the programs that it develops, Academy One facilitates a steady and straightforward use of existing services. In this case, Academy One helps refine existing services to make them more suitable for network use, provides training for participants, and markets the services. Delzeit initially started by developing programs for her own children and volunteered for three years before taking the Academy One reins as its director. Delzeit's vision is of a values-oriented curriculum-centered approach that strives to include everybody with an interest and stake in K–12 education, including students, teachers, parents, community members, businesses, and organizations. The Academy One programs place an emphasis on "student safety" and every posting in an Academy One program is screened prior to distribution to other networks. Academy One uses U.S. Federal Communication Commission (FCC) standards as the screening criteria for all its messages, implicitly subscribing to the idea that networks are a type of public broadcast communication medium. While community networks need fewer restrictions on free speech guarantees, the Academy One "safety" measures offer a straightforward way to ensure that the programs remain focused on their objectives. Although the services in some cases consist of static information, most use novel modes of interaction with students and teachers that exploit the medium in creative ways. There are currently over 50 Academy One projects and more than 12,000 students at 70 schools participated in a single project, the TeleOlympics project. Many of these projects are listed below in Fig. 3.2 and two literature projects are described in the sections that follow. (The Day in the Life project was discussed in Chapter 2 and the Co-Laboratory is discussed later in this chapter.)

Sonnet-Writing Contest

Marge Cargo, a librarian and media specialist from Troy High School in Fullerton, California, launched a sonnet-writing contest a few years ago under the auspices of the Academy One program. Cargo chose the sonnet because she wanted to give students the challenge of writing using structured form and to keep the number of entries to a manageable level. Even so, she received nearly 300 entries last year, including those from the United States, Canada, and Czechoslovakia. Judges publish the winning sonnets in the "Student Author" newsgroup at NPTN sites as well as in a hard-copy booklet (a 1994 honorably mentioned sonnet is shown in Fig. 3.3). A panel of teachers judges all sonnets and some cash prizes are awarded to the winners. The quality of some of the entries has been rewarding to Cargo; she's also pleased with the personal contacts she's made during the project. In fact, she corresponds regularly with the student who submitted the first sonnet via e-mail in the first contest.

Some Academy One Offerings

Literature
    Sonnet-Writing Contest
    Star Trek RPG

Science
    Co-Laboratory
    Space Mission
    Forest Day
    Structures: Technology and Science for Young Children

Art and Culture
    A Day in the Life
    International Holiday Exchange
    Project Ecology Art Exchange
    Student Artist
    Jewish Education Project

Simulations
    TeleOlympics (A "virtual track meet")
    Space Simulation

Democracy, Civics, and Current Events
    Project Common Ground
    Institute for Democracy in Education

The Environment
    Save the Beaches

Other
    Teacher Education
    Parent Discussion

Figure 3.2

Star Trek RPG—Commanding Star Ships from Willoughby Hills

Steven Prest, a 14-year-old from Willoughby Hills, a suburb of Cleveland, Ohio is an unlikely Star Ship commander. Yet he commands the (virtual) Star Ship Olympus in the cyberspace world of the Star Trek RPG ("Role Playing Game") that he created and has made available through Academy One. Approximately 50 others (including other teenagers, several adults, and a fifth

Why Do I Write Sonnets?

Perhaps I merely feel the inner need
To write in stricter forms of late, you see,
It gives me inner pleasure, quenches greed
To write in sonnets, for when I'm less free
To overuse the words with which I write,
I find more meaning in the ones
I use. When writing sonnets, I must often fight
To make words fit, but when I finally choose
The perfect word, it's great. Perhaps I'm wrong
To be so strict, to limit my own form
When I could write Haiku, quatrain, or song,
Or make up styles which violate the norm
Of poetry and prose, but I'm no lamb.
My motto's this: I think, therefore iamb.

Honorable Mention

Nate Barksdale
Grade 12
Sunny Hills High School
Fullerton, CA

Figure 3.3

grader who's being coached along) take part in the various imaginary missions (to distribute vaccine to a planet beset with disease or to help repel an enemy attack on a friendly outpost, for example) in roles of characters that they've created and described according to rules and procedures devised by Prest and described in detail in a comprehensive on-line guide.

When a person first signs on as a participant in the Star Trek RPG, they must create their character's biography, which is then distributed to all the other participants on the ship (approximately 10), added to a forum, and placed on their Web site. They must also undergo the necessary "training" in order to participate in the upcoming missions. The participants on the ship take turns fulfilling the objectives of the mission, writing down what they think happens next.

Why is this an educational endeavor? The primary reason is that all participants are involved in a *writing process,* in this case the writing of a fictional account of a mission in space. Each participant tells the story from his or her own point-of-view, at the same time trying to keep other people's personalities and behavior consistent with the written biography and the story as it has thus far developed. This task is no different from other types of fiction writing where the author must juggle a cast of characters. Steven has noted definite improvements in the writing of the Star Trek RPG participants. He's noticed, for example, that he gives more thought to his writing, particularly to how it's structured. He also noticed that his spelling has improved as has the spelling of many other participants. Since it is now much more fun, and since it is important to communicate effectively to the other participants, Steven and the others are approaching the act of writing with more enthusiasm and care. These are exactly the characteristics a teacher strives to instill in young writers.

A COMMUNITY OF LEARNING

> *And if little learning is taking place in American schools and colleges, it may be because there is too much solitude among the learners (and teachers, too).*
>
> —Benjamin Barber (1992)

Although Steven probably would not use this exact verbage, it is clear that the Star Trek RPG helps promote a "community of learning." The concept of a community of learning is a powerful one that contains at least two important ideas for the development of new communities. The first is that education and communities need to be interlinked into one community, where the community helps support education (through information, tours, volunteering, and financial support, for example) and the educational system helps the community (through civic action, job training, and resource sharing, for example). The second idea is that classrooms—virtual or otherwise—need to become communities (of learning) where students and teachers alike work cooperatively to ensure that everybody's educational experience is as useful and rewarding as it can be.

In the next two sections, ways in which classrooms can become communities of learning are discussed. Those sections are followed by descriptions of some on-line systems that have begun to address some of these issues.

Diverse and Conflicting Viewpoints

Dealing with conflicting and diverse viewpoints is no longer optional—it has become a survival skill of the individual and society and will probably become even more critical in the future. Conflict, as Harvard Negotiation Project researcher Roger Fisher has noted, "is a growth industry." Indeed, conflict is something we experience as individuals, families, clans, geographical groupings, economic classes, communities, nations, political parties, races, religions, or as members of an almost infinite number of groupings in which human beings place themselves. What is the best way to address conflict? Can or should it be forbidden, or should it simply be ignored in the vague hope that it will go away? Unfortunately or fortunately, depending on how you look at it, we cannot explicitly or implicitly banish conflict from the human arena. Should we ignore conflicts—including what has become known as the culture wars in higher education in which multiculturalism advocates are pitted against advocates of "the canon"? Or should we follow the advice of Gerald Graff, who advances the case that conflict can help enrich, engage, and extend education? In other words, Graff believes that educational practice should naturally embrace conflict as a vehicle for understanding or resolving issues. Not only would this be powerful and relevant to students, but it would help equip students for conflict and help instill an appreciation of the importance of conflict in discourse. Beyond the need for engaging in reasoned debate and the importance of *training* in debate, dialogue, and discussion, arguing over timely issues can be a very good way to inject relevance into the educational process (Graff, 1992). As Patricia Bizzel (1982) states:

> Students often complain that they have nothing to say, whereas "real-world" writers almost never do, precisely because real-world writers are writing for discourse communities in which they know their work can matter, whereas students can see little purpose for their own attempts . . . other than to get a grade.

Note Bizzel's focus on the concept of "community of discourse," which reformulates the idea of writing into an extended discussion containing many voices. The "conversation" becomes a single collaborative unity. If students are writing for others—in addition to the teacher—writing becomes more meaningful. Electronic community networks can provide a natural medium for collaborative writing as well as for providing a backdrop for communities of discourse.

Cooperative Learning—Working with Other People

While virtually every conceivable post-school occupation involves working with other people to achieve some objective, schools are remarkably deficient in the area of cooperative group work. Classrooms rely heavily on the "broadcast mode" of teaching, conspiring—along with the mass media—to produce an "audience" of passive consumers.

The standard model of the classroom dictates that students must work alone—not in groups—and they are admonished not to "share their work," a euphemism for cheating. When students are aware of each other, it is often in the context of trying to outperform one another. According to Roger and David Johnson (1988), "The research indicates that a vast majority of students in the United States view school as a competitive enterprise where you try to do better than the other students." Ironically, this attitude is not even useful in most business situations. Although competition is a much-heralded hallmark of capitalism, too much competition *within* a company makes work less productive and less enjoyable for everybody.

If students do not learn how to work together, they will be deprived of valuable learning experiences, and will not make use of a valuable untapped resource for teaching in the classroom—other students. Roger and David Johnson define cooperative learning situations as having positive goal interdependence with individual accountability. In other words, each student must gain mastery or perform at a certain level but obtain additional rewards if the group does well. Thus students don't just work in groups—they work cooperatively in groups toward shared goals. Johnson and Johnson draw the following four conclusions about cooperative interaction from data from over 500 studies:

1. Students achieve more.

2. Students are more positive about school, subject areas, and teachers or professors.

3. Students are more positive about each other.

4. Students are more effective interpersonally.

Johnson and Johnson offer several pieces of advice on setting up tasks that help ensure successful outcomes in cooperative learning situations, including advice on choosing the task, explaining the task and the cooperative goal structure to the students, dividing students into groups and monitoring tasks. They sum up the indispensable nature of cooperative learning as follows, "Being able to perform technical skills such as reading, speaking, listening, writing, computing, problem solving, etc. are valuable but of little use if the person cannot apply those skills in cooperative fashion with other people in career, family, and community settings."

As seen in the projects described below, computer networks can be used advantageously in a wide variety of collaborative education programs. "Student Author" projects, for example, encourage students to post poems, short stories, and other works to the rest of the subscribers, and community networks are natural hosts for "progressive stories" in which each chapter is written by a different author or group of authors.

The Co-Laboratory

Academy One also offers several science-oriented projects that build on collaboration and participation. The Co-Laboratory, a "school-owned experiment and database" project developed by Lakewood (Ohio) High School science teacher James Meinke, invites schools to describe an experiment and to solicit other schools to perform the experiment and to contribute their results to a shared repository. As more schools perform the experiment, the larger the database grows and the more data that is available for analysis. Previous collaboratory projects have included information gathering on dating practices and on ozone levels across the United States. In one Co-Laboratory experiment (Meinke, 1995) students measured the length of the shadows that were cast at the solar noon in order to calculate the circumference of Earth just as the Greek geographer Eratosthenes did in the second century B.C. Meinke's on-line solicitation is shown in Figs. 3.4 and 3.5. Students from a variety of locations participated in the experiment to calculate Earth's circumference including schools in Kent, Washington; Lakewood, Ohio; Dripping Springs, Texas; Paradise, California; Kendall, Florida; and Delta Junction, Alaska; as well as schools in Finland, Germany, Canada, Ecuador, Brazil, Denmark, Germany, Bahrain, Romania, and Slovenia.

Meinke is a fount of ideas for these types of experiments, having created 77 courses and events that fostered global awareness, including meteor-shower observation and analysis, mapping the earth's magnetic field, and many other experiments.

Equitable Access

> *[poor] Children, of course, don't understand at first that they are being cheated. They come to school with a degree of faith of optimism and they often seem to thrive during the first few years. It is sometimes not until the third grade that their teachers start to see warning signs of failure. By the fourth grade many children see it too.*
>
> Jonathan Kozol (1991)

As we discussed earlier in this chapter, traditional education—which has changed little in the last 100 years—has its share of problems. That is not to say that some of its offerings are not valuable; in some cases it is the method of providing the offerings that is wanting. While improving the traditional model, we also need to simultaneously improve *access* to existing processes

Eratosthenes Experiment

ATTENTION—MARCH 21, 1995 IS THE EQUINOX
A WORLDWIDE SCIENCE AND MATH EXPERIMENT

Eratosthenes, a Greek geographer (about 276 to 194 B.C.), made a surprisingly accurate estimate of the earth's circumference. In the great library in Alexandria he read that a deep vertical well near Syene, in southern Egypt, was entirely lit up by the sun at noon once a year. Eratosthenes reasoned that at this time sun must be directly overhead, with its rays shining directly into the well. In Alexandria, almost due north of Syene, he knew that the sun was not directly overhead at noon on the same day because a vertical object cast a shadow. Eratosthenes could now measure the circumference of the earth (sorry Columbus) by making two assumptions—that the earth is round and that the sun's rays are essentially parallel. He set up a vertical post at Alexandria and measured the angle of its shadow when the well at Syene was completely sunlit. Eratosthenes knew from geometry that the size of the measured angle equaled the size of the angle at the earth's center between Syene and Alexandria. Knowing also that the arc of an angle this size was 1/50 of a circle, and that the distance between Syene and Alexandria was 5000 stadia, he multiplied 5000 by 50 to find the earth's circumference. His result, 250,000 stadia (about 46,250 km) is quite close to modern measurements. Investigating the Earth, AGI, 1970, Chapter 3, p. 66.

The formula Eratosthenes used is:

$$\frac{D}{d} = \frac{A}{a}$$

d = distance between Syene and Alexandria
A = 360 degrees assumption of round earth
a = shadow angle of vertical stick
D = to be determined (cirucmference)

Figure 3.4

```
         Are you interested in participating?

All you need to do is place a vertical stick
(shaft) into the ground at your school and when
the sun reaches its highest vertical ascent for
the day (solar noon—therefore, the shadow length
will be the shortest), measure the angle of the
shadow of the stick (a).

                        -\
                        - \
            stick -> -  \
                        - a \     a = shadow angle
                        -     \
                        -      \
ground _____ -_____\shadow_____
```

By doing this experiment on the equinox we all know
that the vertical rays of the sun are directly over
the equator, like the well at Syene. By using a
globe or an atlas, the distance between your
location and the equator (d in equation) can be
determined and the circumference can be calculated.
****
But how about sharing your shadow angle
measurement with others around the real globe?
****
Send your measurement of the shadow angle_____
_____degrees

Send your location city _____

Send your location country _____

Send your latitude _____

Send your longitude _____

To: Lakewood High School bd765@cleveland.freenet.edu

We will compile all the data and send you a copy
to use in your classroom to compare the various
locations and angles.

If you're interested, send us your data. We will
compile and return it to you by March 31, 1995.

Figure 3.5

```
Chances are your lesson plans will not be able to
fit this in on Tuesday, (?) March 21, 1995 (the
equinox). Most any day plus or minus 2 days of the
equinox will give fairly good data (like Monday or
Wednesday or Thursday or Friday).

Jim Meinke—Lakewood High School bd765@cleveland.
         freenet.edu Learning Link h906109e
         @llohio.ll.pbs.org
```

Figure 3.5

and knowledge (which, as Jonathan Kozol has eloquently shown, is profoundly unbalanced). To do otherwise would be like denying food to a starving person because it was poor in quality.

The question of access to education and educational technology is complex. Access can be understood somewhat as a chain that reaches from learner to an appropriate educational resource. If any link in the chain is missing or broken, the opportunity is lost. In the next section we explore ways in which new links can be forged by use of communication technologies.

Telephone Homework Assistance

In a report entitled "Using Computer-Based, Telecommunications Services to Serve Educational Purposes at Home," Jay P. Sivin-Kachala and Ellen R. Bialo (1992) discuss the use of telephone homework hotlines. Although telephone-based, these hotlines could serve as a model for similar services on community networks. Using the telephone allows immediate feedback and the opportunity for a more interactive Socratic-style dialogue between teacher and learner than asynchronous approaches such as e-mail. In fact, the telephone to a large degree offers a more natural interface than a community network whose sole interface generally is a keyboard. On the other hand, text-based community networks offer the ability for both learner and teacher to see the question being asked, the issue being posed, or the writing being analyzed. In other words, a text-based system is extremely well-suited for text-based homework. Homework that relies on maps, figures, drawings, photographs, mathematical symbols, or other graphical information will be underserved on either network or telephone-based services—at least until technology is readily available that handles this information more easily.

Sivin-Kachala and Bialo's report provides useful information on many basic issues of homework hotlines based on in-depth analyses of services in Baton Rouge, LA; Bridgeport, CT; Indianapolis, IN; Los Angeles, CA; New York, NY; Rochester, MN (serving the entire state of Minnesota); and Trumbull-Shelton-Stratford, CT. Five of the services fielded phone calls from elementary, middle (junior high), and senior high schools, while two services concentrated on elementary and middle school students. The services typically operated three to four hours per day within the after-school time slot. Interestingly, more than half of the phone calls were on math questions, and a high percentage of the math questions involved the notorious "story problem," in which the problem was described in words rather than mathematical symbols.

The services at every site in the report relied on "paid, licensed, practicing teachers" as the homework helpers. Some of the services required additional qualifications for the staff positions, such as a master's degree. All sites required some teacher training, such as how to engage students in thinking through a problem to avoid merely supplying them with an answer. Reference material—including teacher's editions of all relevant textbooks, encyclopedia, dictionary, almanac, maps, contact information, answers to frequently asked questions, and other materials—were furnished at each site.

As with many other on-line services, the telephone homework assistance service has largely depended on adequate funding, although volunteers could certainly play a significant role. The service in small Connecticut towns receives about 35 calls per day, while the service based in New York City receives about 550 calls per day. The staffing ratios vary from 2 to 15 teachers per 100 student calls, while the average is 8 teachers per 100 calls. The report concludes that an average helper costs $7,560 (and varies across regions) for 120 days of 3½ hour sessions. Other costs include costs of computer equipment, telephone lines, reference material, as well as administrator's salary, clerical support, and publicity.

The homework helpers generally worked at a central location. Interestingly, a service in Arizona that routed calls to teachers at home who answered questions on a voluntary basis was shut down after a year due to lack of interest on the part of the teachers. While this probably indicates that the teachers were too busy or too tired to continue their teaching on into the night, it also suggests that a social context for the helpers is important. Whatever the reason, community-network developers will need to seriously consider what the limits and limitations of volunteers will be if they plan to offer homework assistance electronically.

Big Sky Telegraph—Supporting Rural Long-Distance Education

In 1988, Frank Odasz of Western Montana University in Dillon, an ex-dude-ranch operator with a degree in Educational Technology, started the Big Sky Telegraph (BST) community-network system (Odasz, 1991) with the idea that computer technology could help tame the vast distances of the American West (Fig. 3.6). His first task was to electronically link more than 40 one- and two-room schoolhouses and 12 rural libraries across Montana with microcomputers and modems. Linking these schoolrooms provided a low-cost way for teachers to share information such as subject curricula, to ask questions and discuss concerns with other teachers, and to "check out" educational software in order to evaluate it before purchasing it.

Odasz describes Big Sky Telegraph as an "action-oriented rural telecomputing testbed," which is intended to overcome some of the problems of the rural American West associated with its sparse population and the long distances between communities. Big Sky's epicenter, Dillon, has 4000 souls; approximately 10 percent of the households own computers. From this location, Big Sky Telegraph uses "appropriate technology" to demonstrate "low-cost, low-tech, high-imagination, scaleable networking models." Big Sky Telegraph is now replicated in various "Big Skies" and "Little Skies" located across Montana and other Western locations and is in daily use by hundreds of people, many of whom are in rural locations.

Figure 3.6 The Big Sky Telegraph "Patch"

Education is the focus, and economic opportunity and individual and regional self-sufficiency are the goals of the Big Sky Telegraph. The system offers 600 K–12 lesson plans serving as a "telecurricular clearinghouse" for K–12 projects running on networks all over the world. The system also offers on-line courses on how to use network and bulletin-board services (Fig. 3.7). Odasz uses the telegraph as a metaphor for all aspects of BST, reflecting the communication technology of the last century that was influential in the rural American West. As their "Homesteading the Educational Frontier" brochure (BST, 1993) states, "Teachers in rural Montana serving as Circuit Riders, Community Telegraphers, and Teletutors have used modems to overcome time, distance, and economic limitations to empower rural education and community survival through the Big Sky Telegraph network." Although technology is central to the program, Odasz advises us not to lose sight of the real objective, developing "communities of purpose," which address "caring, commitment and cause," and he is quick to point out that he'd prefer 50 pages a week of high-quality material (over a 1200-baud modem) to 500 channels of high-band-width tripe. Odasz is particularly concerned about building an infrastructure that is self-sustaining. For several years Big Sky Telegraph has offered an on-line course in Microcomputer Telecommunications that covers the basics of telecomputing and modem use. Other courses covering free self-study and teacher in-service training for recertification are available, thus supporting self-directed and economical educational opportunities both within and outside of the educational institutions.

EDUCATION FOR HUMAN NEEDS

> *It is possible to view the "school". . . more of a* process *than as a structure . . . the process could be structured around 1) identifying community problems, 2) planning possible solutions on a variety of levels, and 3) carrying out a plan, the objective of which is to produce some immediate and palpable amelioration of problems.*
>
> Neil Postman and Charles Weingartner (1969)

Education is not just a set of skills—education must also impart an outlook or perspective that prepares individuals for the future. When education helps to actually address this need, it becomes an active institution for community development. When education fails in this task, it becomes an impediment, a vestige of days gone by.

```
   Big Sky Telegraphy—Lessons and Essays for the
                    On-line Class

CLASS FILES

Quickstart   3730  Dec-91  Quick Reference Guide to
                           Getting Started.
Startup     15190  Dec-91  Step-by-Step Guide for
                           Beginners.
BeginClass   1666  Sep-90  How to Begin the On-line
                           Class.
Syllabus     6598  Nov-88  The On-line Course
                           Syllabus.
Lesson1      8926  Jan-92  Sending and Receiving
                           Messages.
Lesson2      6797  Jan-92  Capturing and Printing
                           Text.
Lesson3     11368  Feb-92  Conferencing and Sharing
                           Resources.
Lesson4      6219  Oct-91  Word Processing and
                           Telecommunications.
Lesson5     11605  Feb-92  Accessing On-line Library
                           Services.
Lesson6      9777  Oct-91  Calling Other On-line
                           Services.
Lesson7     10369  Oct-91  Receiving On-line Text
                           Files and Using
                           Databases.
Lesson8     10438  Mar-91  Contributing On-line Text
                           Files.
Lesson9      9984  Aug-91  Becoming a Community
                           Telegrapher.
Lesson10    14504  Oct-91  Teleliteracy:
                           Understanding Instruct.
                           Telecom.
Acropmsg    82603  Aug-90  Collection of Messages
                           from the Acropolis Conf.
ProfTest     1469  Feb-92  Proficiency Test for the
                           Advanced Class.
LessonTasks  2311  Aug-90  Homework Required for
                           Credit.
DemoTips    15479  Aug-90  Tips for Your
                           Community/School Board
                           Demos.
```

```
BBSLecture   8055  Aug-90   A Discussion on Using and
                            Running BBS's.
Unixtour     7008  Aug-92   A Walking Tour for Unix.
                            Unix Id's Needed.
Akcstour     4041  Feb 4    WalkingTour for Global
                            AKCS. Unix ID's Required.
```

Figure 3.7

Teachers, Students, and the Community

Postman and Weingartner (1969) point out the pervasive nature of pretense within the schools (which are often contrasted with "real life").

> Let's pretend that you are not what you are and that this sort of work makes a difference to your lives; let's pretend that what bores you is important and that the more you are bored, the more important it is; let's pretend that there are certain things everyone must know, and that both the questions and answers about them have been fixed for all time; let's pretend that your intellectual competence can be judged on the basis of how well you play Let's Pretend.

Students need to feel that their education has some relevance or value or many will reject it as boring, artificial, and meaningless. Therefore, it is critical that the educational program be useful to individuals, families, and to the community. When students are actively engaged with problems or issues that concern them, a stronger and deeper respect between teacher and students emerges. Solving problems individually and in groups through planning and acting is also indispensable to education. Techniques may include hypothesizing and experimenting, tracking down information, interviewing people, understanding issues through dialogue and argumentation, and developing good work habits and discipline. Becoming fluent with a variety of these approaches and knowing when and how to employ them will remain important no matter how much technology may change.

There is no end to the number of problem-solving projects that are educational as well as being useful and relevant to the community. Some of these include neighborhood mapping, community histories, interest or opinion surveys, or developing catalogs of information, organizations, services, and other "community assets." Many schools from middle school to universities are now requiring or otherwise encouraging students to take part in community activities, often through awarding credits. Rutgers University in New

Jersey, for example, has an extensive civic participation program in which students are expected to volunteer for community activities for 12 months. For their part, community members should also be willing to help in the schools. Their role can vary from providing general assistance in the classroom to taking advantage of their individual expertise—by teaching about computers, describing their jobs, or discussing aspects of their places of origin or culture, for example. Community networks can play a role in developing and strengthening projects along these lines.

Entrepreneurial Spirit

Although the expression may be somewhat debased from its close association with the unregulated capitalism of the Reagan years and with the American "can-do" boosterism of earlier this century, entrepreneurial spirit, or perhaps what my neighbor Press Winslow calls "social entrepreneurism," needs to become a central element of the educational process. The idea of entrepreneurial spirit could help motivate the whole educational process while breathing new life and meaning into it. When students have an entrepreneurial attitude, they have the confidence to tackle problems by recognizing, diagnosing, and responding to them—rather than ignoring them, explaining them away, or being paralyzed by them.

The development of entrepreneurial spirit comes largely from education and experience. When a person has the ability to perceive the world as being somewhat organized and knowable, and couples that perception with an entrepreneurial spirit, that individual can proactively engage the world. Entrepreneurial spirit requires both ability and a positive psychological outlook; it complements the idea of "empowerment." People without this feeling can only react—not initiate—and participating in the world can only be chaotic, arbitrary, and confused, not developmental, integrative, or learning-directed. The open-ended aspect of the entrepreneurial spirit has helped keep it an unpopular and untried approach within most school systems. It may generate more work for the teacher and more trouble for the administrator. The change in consciousness that is required may be the largest hurdle, however, as students are elevated to the role of co-teacher.

Self-Directed Learning at Virtual High

The Virtual High is a learning center for 14–18 year olds in Vancouver, British Columbia in Canada. Self-directed learning is the overriding philosophy of the Virtual High. Both students and their families are involved in the process of curriculum design. There are no teachers per se—they've been replaced by "learning consultants" whose role is asking students what they want to do and asking students how they—the learning consultant—might help. The students are encouraged to launch ambitious real-world projects, like starting businesses. These projects generally motivate a train of other supporting learning activities such as writing proposals or developing budgets using a spreadsheet in a more natural needs-driven mode, rather than in the usual agenda-driven mode of traditional education.

Virtual High's founders Michael Maser and Brent Cameron are consciously trying to reinvent the institution of schooling from an industrial-age model into one that fosters "social evolution and adaptation in the face of increasing change" (Maser, 1994). Their perspective is similar to the philosophy of the Institute for Learning Technology at Columbia (Reibel, 1994) that acknowledges the superiority of smaller classes, a collaborative relationship between teacher and learner, increased flexibility, and the adoption of more sophisticated communication technology, especially that of the computer. Some of the Virtual High's projects include Blue Fish Magazine, Village Quest, and the Power Smart Game. The Power Smart Game, which uses a model of a "virtual house" (Fig. 3.8) to help students to better understand household energy usage, is an excellent example of the type of project that the Virtual High produces. It was produced by students at the Wondertree Education Society (a precursor to Virtual High) in 1991, has subsequently been distributed throughout British Columbia's public schools, and is currently being sold to utility companies around the world.

Most students at Virtual High have a personal Macintosh PowerBook and connect to each other using the WonderNet Educational Telecommunity computer network system. Clearly computer networks can help facilitate learning between teachers (or "learning consultants") and motivated and technologically literate students (and between fellow students). At the same time it is important to realize that electronic access to each other is not a substitute for face-to-face contact. Also, as we shall learn in the next section, there is still the critical question of "Education for what?" that needs addressing.

COMMITMENT FOR THE FUTURE—LINKING HOPE AND STRUGGLE

All our children ought to be allowed a stake in the enormous richness of America.
Jonathan Kozol (1991)

Education can give rise to great flights of imagination and creativity. It can be a source of freedom and joy and inspiration while providing meaning to individuals and to communities. Education can actively engage citizens

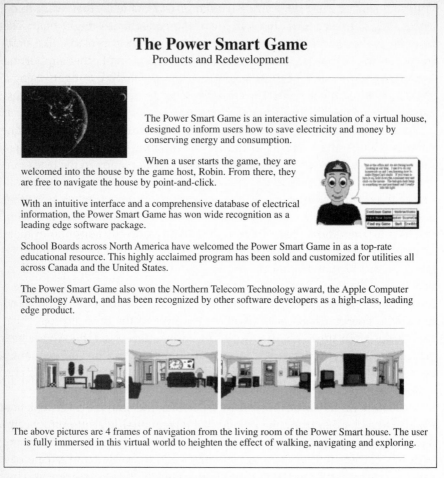

Figure 3.8 The Power Smart Game

into the broader sphere and thus be an effective integrating force in the future.

For education to be *equitable* as well as enlightened and humane, society must open opportunities to *all* its members. Education cannot address these noble goals without commitment from both individuals and institutions. Individuals should be willing to invest something of themselves in order to achieve this goal, and to create proper role models. Schools, government, and business all need to help in this process. Society needs to make the necessary investments of time, thought, and struggle, as well as money.

More than anything else, education offers hope for the future. If it doesn't offer this hope, it offers nothing. Especially for the downtrodden, education must have the potential to liberate intellectually and spiritually as well as tangibly through economic advancement. Ultimately, education needs to have the transformative potential to change society, as the poem by Bertolt Brecht (on the next page) expresses.

Education activist Herbert Kohl (Karp, 1994) stresses that "the trick is to link effective education with hope and struggle." Students must come away from an educational experience with knowledge and analytical skills, but also with a sense that they can—need—to change the world and that some real possibility exists to do so. Kohl also stresses that education needs to be integrative: Just as education must be part of the community, the community must be part of education. In the same interview Kohl mentions that a "recent innovation is creating educational institutions in partnership with other community institutions" and points to recent partnerships with labor unions. An integration or partnership between community-network organizations and the schools naturally fits well with this approach.

Community Computing-Centers

A community computing-center is an actual place in the community where people can go and feel comfortable. This center, of course, can offer more than access to computers. Besides traditional community-center services, it can serve as a center for a wide range of democratic technological issues. In his article "Democratizing Technology" (1994) Richard Sclove describes similar centers around the world. "Dutch Universities, for example, have evolved a vigorous network of public 'science shops' to respond to the concerns of citizens, trade unions, and community groups about technological issues." He goes on to say that "Each shop's paid staff, student interns, and faculty volunteers answer questions and refer challenging questions to other university faculty members." Sclove cites cases where science shop-oriented programs "have helped workers evaluate the employment consequences of new production processes and helped environmental groups document sources of industrial pollution." Clearly centers of this type are examples of community empowerment where citizens gain skills and knowledge to become researchers and advocates as well as learners.

The organization, Playing to Win (PTW), discussed in the next section, places its focus on supporting a "center" that is an actual physical location in the community equipped with computing facilities. This approach has both social and economic advantages. From the social point of view, a community computing-center promotes conviviality and a community orientation. For a homeless person or a person whose home is abusive, a center can serve as a safe haven. PTW is committed to strengthening communities in a way that of-

PRAISE OF LEARNING

Learn the simplest things. For you
whose time has already come
it is never too late!
Learn your A B C's, it is not enough,
but learn them! Do not let it discourage you,
begin! You must know everything!
You must take over the leadership!

Learn, man in the asylum!
Learn, man in prison!
Learn, wife in the kitchen!
Learn, man of sixty!
Seek out the school, you who are homeless!
Sharpen your wits, you who shiver!
Hungry man, reach for the book: it is a weapon.
You must take over the leadership.

Don't be afraid of asking, brother!
Don't be won over,
see for yourself!
What you don't know yourself,
you don't know.
Add up the reckoning.
It's you who must pay it.
Put your finger on each item,
ask: how did this get here?
You must take over the leadership.

Bertolt Brecht

ten takes the form of empowering individuals. The center can be an example of what Ray Oldenberg calls a "third place," a place in the community where people are welcome to just "hang out" if desired. Moreover, the possibility of co-teaching and collaborative project opportunities is much higher when a physical location as well as a virtual location for such activity exists.

The centers also make sense economically. Although connections of sufficiently high bandwidth may someday reach every home, the cost of wiring the "last mile" may ultimately cost tens of billions of dollars in the United States alone. People in economically disadvantaged and rural areas are especially skeptical of claims that their community will be included in corporate or government plans because they know that the expected return on investment is low in these areas. Thus even those who believe that wiring public places is only an interim step should support the concept of community-based computer centers as a step in the right direction for providing universal access.

Playing to Win—The Learner's Needs Come First

"The community computing-center movement," writes Peter Miller (1993) is "guided by radical democratic principles, resting upon the conviction that basic tools of daily life need to be accessible to everyone." The Playing to Win organization, now at the heart of the community computing-center movement, first opened its operation in the basement of a Harlem housing project in 1981 with 20 Atari 400s. There are now over 50 PTW affiliates in the United States, and there are plans to establish a national, self-sustaining, self-governing network of 300–350 centers with support from the National Science Foundation.

Playing to Win is a technical assistance program that generally focuses on the community computing-center model, in which computers are placed in community centers, such as settlement houses, YMCAs, libraries, museums, or other places (Fig. 3.9). PTW also ensures that related assistance such as training is also available. The focus on actual centers in the community complements the work of other social activists (as well as some commercial vendors) who are striving to bring electronic access to the home.

I spoke with Peter Miller at the United South End settlements community-computing lab after he finished teaching a class to some of Boston's homeless population. Miller's educational philosophy is similar to that of Paolo Friere: The needs of the student must drive the education process, not the needs of the teacher or any other outside force. There are lots of anecdotes supporting this notion. Antonia Stone, PTW's founder, tells the story of a Hispanic woman who came into one of the New York centers just "wanting to look at the computers." She gradually became more fluent with the technology as she used it to meet her own needs. She organized a number of home remedies or nostrums that were used in her community and entered them into the computer. She ultimately printed, bound, and distributed the booklet of home remedies, thus contributing to the accumulated knowledge and wisdom of the community.

At the Somerville (Massachusetts) Community Computer Center, low-income residents can obtain access to equipment, training, and technical assistance. Furthermore, neighborhood schools, organizations (such as the Council

Figure 3.9 Playing to Win center, Boston, Massachusetts

on Aging, The Mystic Learning Center Teen Program, and the Short Stop Youth Center, for example), and programs (such as Head Start and Early Start) are all beginning to obtain computer equipment, which can accelerate the *integration* of literacy and computer literacy with other community programs.

Miller reports that when the types of literacy are integrated the task is much less daunting. For example, literacy and computer literacy are integrated while one is preparing resumes on a word processor, improving language skills through on-line chat, or working on collaborative projects involving graphics and desktop publishing. PTW's founder, Antonia Stone, has collected a wide variety of techniques that PTW has developed over the years into a book entitled "Keystrokes to Literacy" (1991). One technique, for example, involves using a word-processing system to remove letters that don't spell words—as in the following example:

```
cornx xx xbeans xxx xxbaconxx xpizzax xxx xxcake.
Erase the letters that don't belong.
```

Although there are several PTW models, one approach requests a two-dollar donation to use the facilities, but doesn't turn away anyone for lack of funds. One facility that offers free admission is the Computer Clubhouse at the Boston Computer Museum for low-income 10- to 16-year-olds. The Clubhouse provides an array of special resources for exploring multimedia, virtual reality, robotics, music, desktop publishing, game design, and other computer applications that are often out of reach of low-income people.

AGENDA FOR ACTION

Our challenge now is to make this kind of learning more readily available to the hundreds of millions of students who will soon be deciding the fate of the earth. Surely their decisions will be more intelligent, humane and foresighted if they are given better opportunities now to develop as whole people.

Dee Dickinson (1988)

There is accumulating evidence that many unfortunate trends in education are continuing—often under the banner of the ongoing computer revolution or the impending "information superhighway." For example, many people seem to believe that both lessons and tests can be delivered electronically. This would obviate the need for teachers, who, along with other professional service providers, are seen as increasingly unnecessary in the posthuman future. With this perspective, delivering the multimedia equivalent of a multiple-choice test over the cable television system is heralded as a revolutionary innovation in education when, in fact, it's generally more expensive, more isolating, and less effective than its old-fashioned equivalent.

Although technologically advanced and superficially more engaging, electronic delivery of education is often debased and isolating. One of the reasons for this is that large software companies with little or no appropriate experience or knowledge are busily cranking out "educational" software. Computer programmers and graphic artists rather than educators are often responsible for the software development. While education can be entertaining, software vendors sometimes sacrifice the love and discipline of learning for the enticement and detachment of flashy graphics.

In addition to the short-circuiting of the learning process with poor quality software, commercial involvement in the educational process introduces other dangers. The forecasted reliance on computer technology for the electronic delivery of services also provides an increased opportunity for corporate control and influence of the educational milieu much in the same way that corporations dominate the news that Americans receive daily. The controversy surrounding the Whittle Communication Corporation's development and distribution of news and feature videotapes containing advertisements which are aired to captivate sixth through twelfth graders in over 10,000 U.S. schools illustrates this point. When educational content is merely "window dressing" that surrounds advertisements, the chief source of income for the producer, educational content will suffer (Templeton, 1994). Views, also, that are controversial, nonmainstream, or unsympathetic to corporate interests may be quietly and unceremoniously removed from the curriculum.

As we have seen, computer and communications technology could be applied toward improving educational processes and our educational systems by making them more open, empowering, and equitable. Unfortunately, adopting these technologies may actually increase inequality in many ways. For one thing, school districts with ample resources tend to have more technological resources than those who are lacking in these resources. Also school districts with smaller budgets might spend a larger share of their resources on technology when the money could be better spent on other more basic and important needs. Moreover, there is ample evidence that these technologies—bowing to strong social and economic pressures—may further trivialize education by reducing its transformative potential. This can be done by (1) restricting the field of inquiry, (2) reducing education to entertainment or repetitive drill, and (3) further isolating the learner and decoupling the teacher from the process. Community networks offer alternatives to these trends, but much work will be required to realize those alternatives.

Community networks offer an opportunity for reinventing education by suggesting modifications of older methods and new methods of conducting education (Fig. 3.10). They can promote education in unstructured and structured ways. Providing access to community information and network re-

---

New On-line Educational Modes

- Virtual study-group or seminar
- Co-education
- Hybrid electronic/traditional courses such as homework helping
- Correspondence or distance-learning courses
- Collaborative "distributed" projects, such as the measuring of the earth
- Educational contracts between teachers and learners
- Access points at schools and at educational centers in the community

Figure 3.10

sources—with no structure imposed—allows people to pursue their own education. More structured approaches involving professional educators, schedules, and guidelines are also possible. MIT professor George Johnston, for example, offered a distance-learning course on chaos theory using the Big Sky Telegraph system that students accessed over the Internet. Lakewood, Ohio, science teacher James Meinke used the Cleveland Free-Net and the Academy One program to coordinate large collaborative science and math experiments with participants who were located all over the world. Other educational hybrids are also possible. A student could set up an agreement or "contract" with a teacher or facilitator to study some topic for some period of time using any methods agreed to by both the learner and the facilitator.

Community networks can provide a variety of educational material on-line, bringing both the library and the educational archive into the home (see Fig. 3.11). Community networks also offer conversational capabilities that are more significant than providing another way to access static information. The conversational capabilities (in theory) provide an opportunity for all "players" in the educational arena—students, teachers, parents, policymakers, and other community members—to enter into conversations regarding educational policy, consider the rights and responsibilities of each of the players, and to participate in both the content and process of education. Community-network systems can play a part in this metamorphosis toward what educational consultant Edward Fiske calls "learning communities" by providing a living forum for the interplay of these new ideas.

Ironically, as Lauren-Glen Davitian, Executive Director of Chittenden Community Television (CCTV), has pointed out, "Education is one of the

---

On-line Educational Material

- Lesson plans
- Bibliographies
- Databases
- Famous speeches
- Digital libraries
- Curriculum
- Reference material
- Pro/con essays
- Worked problems
- Student newspapers (see Chapter 7)

Figure 3.11

least democratic institutions in this country."[1] Also education may now have the strongest claim on the title of "most-maligned institution," and many people are wondering how it might be elevated from its abyss. Fortunately, the germs of a democratic educational system do exist. Many teachers and administrators want to expand the dialogue to involve students, their families, and the rest of the community. At the same time, many students, family, and community members also want to enrich and extend and breathe new life into existing educational programs as well as develop new ones. Clearly, we can go farther in the direction of establishing an educational system that is responsive to people's needs: a university that is universal—education for everyone, everywhere.

---

[1] Remarks made in presentation at The Directions and Implications of Advanced Computing (DIAC-94) conference, Cambridge, Massachusetts, April 23, 1994.

Chapter 4

Strong Democracy

Democracy is the worst system devised by the wit of man, except for all the others.

Winston Churchill

Democracy is the art of running the circus from the monkey cage.

H. L. Mencken

In the future, political and other decisions will be based completely on opinion polls.

David Byrne, "In the Future"

DEMOCRACY IN DECLINE

As the above quotations suggest, the idea of democracy evokes a spectrum of reactions, each highlighting one aspect. Since there is no formula for two people to solve their problems satisfactorily, there is little hope of discovering a formula for solving problems involving thousands, millions, or billions of people. Thus, democracy will always be messy, uncertain, tentative, and experimental. Democracy is a tool of *the people*—not of the elite like a guardianship—or of the unaffiliated masses, like anarchy. And since democracy is a tool—one might even call it conceptual technology—individuals, communities, and societies can become more adept at using it, by thinking about it and by using it.

Very broadly defined, democracy is the equitable participation in the affairs of the state at various levels from the neighborhood to the planetary. Although participants in the "affairs of the state" are often motivated by self-interest, democracy is inherently a social endeavor that begins with the individual and extends outwards until it encompasses all of society.

Although generally acknowledged to be indispensable to a modern democracy, political participation is at a low ebb at least in the United States. Many people now speak of a "crisis in democracy." In Benjamin Barber's words, "thin democracy"—a pale substitute for the rich potential, largely un-realized, of "strong democracy," the subject of his influential book (1984)—is endemic. The waning of democratic life is bemoaned by those of a variety of political persuasions. Paul Weyrich, for example, a conservative with the Free Congress Foundation, says, "We're perilously close to not having demo-cracy" (Greider, 1993).

The number of people voting in the United States has been declining steadily for years and is now hovering around 50 percent of those of eligible voting age (United States, 1994). Note also that the 50-percent figure is for a presidential-election year; figures for off-year, nonpresidential-election years are below 40%. It's been pointed out that nonvoters now form a larger bloc than either of the two major American political parties. The number of people who have written a letter or made a telephone call to an elected official is even lower. The number of people signing a petition, testifying for or against legislation, or speaking at a public meeting is lower still. The number of people who have served on a committee, worked on a political campaign, or demonstrated to bring about so-cial change is minuscule. Sadly, with the sometime exception of voting, these varieties of participation, when engaged in at all, are often done for individual or corporate pecuniary gain, rarely for the enrichment of the community.

Coupled with this pathetically low degree of political participation are widespread attitudes that further cripple the prospects for democracy. One such attitude equates political participation with voting, so that participation becomes something that one does in private on an occasional basis at a time and place determined by somebody else. With this view, participation is lim-ited to ratification and, even then, is confined to a small number of decisions. This view of the tip of the iceberg as the iceberg itself effectively cedes power to those few who realize and take advantage of the fact that there is more to political participation and influence than voting.

The other public attitude that limits public participation is the belief that the system is irredeemable. This belief takes two main forms: The first is that all politicians are corrupt and the second is that big money completely controls politics. If *all* politicians are corrupt and if the situation *is* hopeless, the only sensible recourse might be to stay uninvolved. While some politi-cians *are* corrupt—or unprincipled in large or small ways—and political impact *is* skewed in favor of those with more economic clout, people hold-ing these views about politicians and the political system are often seeking a rationale to validate their lack of involvement. Unfortunately, those views in themselves are damaging to a democratic society. The attitude that politicians are invariably corrupt paralyzes efforts of democratic reform and ethical maintenance of the system. If a politician or agency is found to be corrupt and there is no public outcry, no efforts will be made to clean house and there will be little deterrent to discourage future wrongdoing. And if those with little or no economic clout choose to keep out of politics because it's dominated by money, then who is left to set agendas and to make decisions?

In an essay on "Conventional Political Participation" (1980), Goel identifies three dimensions of political alienation. The first, "political powerlessness," comes from a feeling that "one cannot affect or influence what goes on in politics." The second, "political normlessness," reflects the view that "the rules governing society are either fraudulent or broken often by the powerful groups and individuals for private gain." The third, "political distrust and cynicism," suggests the attitude that politicians are corrupt, self-serving, and manipulative. While these feelings of political alienation may be rationalizations offered to explain nonparticipation, any approach to strengthening or extending democratic participation through community networks or other means must address these issues of alienation.

William Greider in his "Who Will Tell the People?" (1993) unfortunately confirms many, if not most, of people's nagging suspicions that the process is stacked against them, that it's out of control and corrupt. Greider feels that "the self-correcting mechanisms of politics are no longer working." Thus the poor get poorer and the rich get tax breaks. And the person of average means grows more cynical. Greider feels that elections and political work have become empty, ritualistic charades that are increasingly orchestrated by powerful economic elites. According to Greider, "by the 1980s there were 7,000 interest organizations active in Washington politics, and business's share of this pressure system was overwhelming." He points out that five of Washington's suburban neighborhoods, home to Washington's lobbyists and lawyers, are in the Commerce Department's list of the 10 richest counties in the country. And elections themselves are often "purchased"—in 1994, for example, 86 percent of the House of Representatives victories went to the candidates who had spent the most money (NVRI, 1995).

Without effective *two-way* communication between people and government, politicians and the media can determine the agendas and the style of political discourse, which increasingly consists of sound-bites and empty rhetoric. Greider provides an illuminating example of this chasm by comparing priorities of ordinary citizens to campaign rhetoric. He cites a 1988 Washington poll in which people were asked what issues *they* wanted the next president to pursue. High on the people's list was "having large companies pay their fair share of taxes, imposing stricter environment regulations on toxic waste products, and helping the poor and homeless find jobs." Instead nonissues like flag-burning took center stage.

REBUILDING THE DEMOCRATIC PROCESS

Democracy is not an alternative to other principles of associated life. It is the idea of community life itself . . . [It is] a name for a life of free and enriching communion.

John Dewey (Barber, 1984)

Criteria for Democratic Process

Democracy, like mom and apple pie, has few public critics. Even dictators of the most brutal regime claim that they support democracy or that they intend to move towards democracy. But what constitutes a democracy: How do we know when a government is a democracy and when it isn't? If we can identify the ingredients of a democracy, then we can improve our ability to evaluate how democratic a particular process is. Moreover, identifying democratic criteria will help us in our development of democratic technology. Robert Dahl, writing in *Democracy and Its Critics* (1989), presents five basic criteria for a democratic process that community network developers should keep in mind while developing services that support democratic participation.

Effective Participation

The criterion of *effective participation*—often lacking or poorly exercised in practice—states that all citizens that may participate in the democratic process do so on an equal footing. This simple criterion has many important and far-reaching implications, which we'll explore further in the next section. Poverty, as we shall see, presents a formidable barrier to effective participation. "If cost is a permanent barrier to democratic expression," Greider maintains, "then democracy becomes a contest merely for organized economic interests, not for citizens." To help ensure effective participation, we need to examine (and change if necessary) the location, method, and timing through which political participation occurs.

Voting Equality at Decision Stage

This one criterion—*voting*—is often mistaken for the democratic process as a whole. If one were to take this one criterion to extremes, one might sanction occasional voting on issues of little importance, say, in establishing an official song or motto, as evidence of a democratic society. Voting is a necessary, but far from sufficient, aspect of a democratic society.

The criterion of voting is, however, crucial, as it states that all decisions are ultimately in the hands of the citizens. Note that in many workplace settings where "Total Quality Management" or other similar approaches are being used that purport to empower the worker, the other criteria for a democratic process are often achieved, while this one alone is denied to workers. Worker participation (or any type of citizen participation) without voting equality at the decision stage is not a democratic process.

Enlightened Understanding

Dahl's third criterion, *enlightened understanding*, is, by his own admission, described by "words that are rich in meaning and correspondingly ambiguous." Meeting this criterion is both difficult to assess and difficult to attain. The intent is clear, nevertheless: Citizens who are aware of the facts, players, precedents, related situations, history, and any other relevant information of a given political matter are in a better position to contribute to the democratic deliberation and decision-making in the matter. While enlightened understanding can't guarantee better laws or policies, most people would agree that it helps remove arbitrariness from participation. When people can't achieve "substantive consensus," it is still important to achieve "procedural consensus." In other words, people will still disagree, but they're more likely to agree on where they disagree.

The main implication of this criterion is, of course, in the realm of education. Groups like the League of Women Voters focus on this approach. People need understanding of facts, history, patterns of reasoning, and the political process to effectively participate in the process. A strong general education is certainly important, but *civic education* is also necessary. This criterion can be used in two ways— (1) proactively in improving quality and equity of education, and (2) defensively, in holding the line against cutbacks in educational funding.

Control of the Agenda

Citizens, in Dahl's words, "must have exclusive opportunity to decide how matters are to be placed on the agenda of matters that are to be decided by means of democratic process." This criterion—control of the agenda—gives citizens the power to establish and to modify their own decision-making process. This criterion, for example, allows citizens to establish a representative democracy if they want. They could also later replace it with something else. As Dahl makes clear: Any decision regarding "control of the agenda" must be "revocable" in the future. So citizens cannot permanently sign away—even voluntarily—fundamental democratic rights.

Inclusiveness

This criterion states that "all adult members of the association except transients and those mentally deficient must have all the rights of citizenship." This criterion is based on the experience that "any group of adults excluded ... will be lethally weakened in defending its own interests." Thus this criterion is one of *inclusion*, although Dahl feels that the process should deny access to children, transients, and the "mentally defective." Although the trend is towards increased inclusiveness, children and teenagers under 18 cannot vote. Lowering the minimum age still further would help provide useful civic training while helping younger citizens to increase their political clout in an era where their well-being is declining.

Beyond Minimal Democracy

Although Dahl's five criteria do, in fact, perform the important job of sketching the outlines of a more equitable and active democracy than we currently have, they still represent the *minimum*—almost mechanical—requirements for a democracy. How do we build on these requirements to conceptualize an enriched democracy, a strong democracy, a democracy that not only performs its perfunctory chores but inspires, enlightens, and empowers?

COMMUNITY NETWORKS AND STRONG DEMOCRACY

> *Masses make noise, citizens deliberate; masses behave, citizens act; masses collide and intersect, citizens engage, share, and contribute.*
>
> Benjamin Barber (1984)

Benjamin Barber's response is that we need "strong democracy," a modern form of participatory democracy, which rests on new definitions of public talk, public action, citizen, and community (1984). These four concepts, Barber believes, can form the basis of new institutions and "public talk," the first of the four concepts, is most relevant to our focus on community networks.

The Functions of Strong Democratic Talk

Strong democratic talk provides the original impetus on which strong democracy is built. Strong democratic talk is talk in which people discuss issues in a way that spawns ideas, builds community, and develops new rela-

---

The Functions of Democratic Talk

1. The articulation of interests; bargaining and exchange

2. Persuasion

3. Agenda-setting

4. Exploring mutuality

5. Affiliation and affection

6. Maintaining autonomy

7. Witness and self-expression

8. Reformulation and reconceptualization

9. Community-building as the creation of public interests, common goods, and active citizens.

Figure 4.1

tionships. It is a rich concept that "always involves listening as well as speaking, feeling as well as thinking, and acting as well as reflecting." That Barber wishes to transcend traditional uses of talk in "thin democracies" is obvious in his description of the nine functions which underlie democratic talk (Fig. 4.1). While the first two are quite familiar, the next six are "muted and undervalued" in weak democracies. The last function, community-building, is the overall function of talk, according to Barber. To the extent that community networks can address these nine functions, they can help in the development of a strong democracy.

Whither Electronic Democracy?

As we move closer to the twenty-first century, the specter of "electronic democracy," "electronic town halls," and other new forms of technology-mediated practices seem to loom ever more expectantly over us. The 1992 presidential candidate Ross Perot has hosted events on national television with these grandiose taglines, while radio and television programs with listener or viewer call-ins are copious. Do these new formats warrant optimism, or should we approach them with caution? Will they help foster public talk? Or will experiments in electronic democracy prove to be antithetical to democracy and help usher in new authoritarian or chaotic regimes?

There are numerous signs that the public is interested in pursuing new forms of democratic participation using computer networks. For example, we see electronic open meetings, electronic mail to elected officials, government Web pages, and increasing calls for making government information available easily and inexpensively in electronic form. A recent *MacWorld* poll (Piller, 1994) showed that people strongly desired the ability to participate electronically in the political process. One of the ways in which community networks can promote strong democracy is by providing another point of access to elected officials and agency employees through e-mail and electronic forums. They can also improve access to government information and services and be the home of dozens of community-created forums on local issues. The technology by itself, however, cannot ensure a more strongly democratic culture. The *policies* and *processes* that we develop are crucial to that goal and therefore deserve our critical attention.

As we begin to investigate new ways of supporting democratic processes with communications technology, we must be aware that the process itself is open to change and experimentation. It is far from obvious what models of participation are best for what types of issues, constituencies, and technological support systems. Computer networks, it should be noted, could introduce qualitative changes in the process, and these changes could come about through the increased speed of information transmission and through the increased number of participants that are likely to become involved. Since due deliberateness is critical to the democratic process, changes wrought by electronic technology may further reduce the chances for equitable and just democratic governance. Technological advances may be occurring faster than our ability to assimilate them. Moreover, the current rapid changes in technology and the still-developing social conventions may make adoption of any particular model ill-advised and premature.

Since community networks and other computer-mediated systems *do* offer real promise and raise expectations as to their potential, there will undoubtedly be calls for new approaches to democratic discourse, including calls for "direct democracy" (in which citizens actually propose and pass legislation). The scale and seriousness of the undertaking, however, requires some caution and direct democracy is unlikely to be workable. With each proposed change, we need to assess how well the change would meet democratic criteria and principles.

The Public Electronic Network (PEN) in Santa Monica

In 1987, Ken Phillips, Director of the Information Systems Department of Santa Monica, California, and Joseph Schmitz of the U.S.C. Annenberg School of Communications began looking into ways that computer technology could help promote community-oriented, participatory democracy in their city. In 1989, with guidance from Phillips and Schmitz, the Public Electronic Network, or PEN, the first city-sponsored public-access computer system in the United States was established in the affluent, Southern California city on the Pacific Ocean. Drawing from a population of 95,000, the system now has over 7000 users and over 4000 user log-ons per month. Since its launch PEN has served as one of the most important prototypes for understanding issues of electronic democracy as it is played out in the real world. In addition to providing service of genuine value, PEN has also provided cautionary tales (discussed later) as a result of being used regularly by a variety of Santa Monicans.

PEN is designed to promote community-oriented participatory democracy. Based on Hewlett-Packard hardware, running the UNIX operating system and Caucus conferencing software donated by Meta Systems Design, PEN provides access to city government information (such as city council agendas, reports, public safety tips, and the library's on-line catalog) and to government services (such as the granting of permits or the reporting of petty thefts). Citizens can converse with public officials and city servants as well as with each other using e-mail and electronic conferences that cover a wide variety of local civic issues. According to Phillips,[1] council members used PEN to collect input from citizens and citizens used the system to gather information and forward it to the city.

The objectives of the PEN system are shown in Fig. 4.2. Because one of the most important objectives of the PEN system is increasing participation in government and since PEN is run by the city of Santa Monica, city government functions are the most prominent of PEN's offerings.

When a resident contacts the PEN system, he or she first sees the opening screen of PEN (Fig. 4.3) followed by the MAIN MENU (Fig. 4.4), which lists the major categories of service. If a user types a 1 to investigate City Hall, another screen (Fig. 4.5) appears, which lists 11 major city-oriented issue categories. If the user types a 2 at that screen, a City Agendas screen is displayed (Fig. 4.6), which is further subdivided into 17 organizations, including commissions, boards, corporations, task forces, and the Santa Monica City Council.

Each city organization in Santa Monica is on-line, and because of this high degree of participation, PEN users can *assume* that they'll be able to obtain the information they need electronically. If users can't locate what they're looking for in the listings that already exist on the system, they can send electronic mail containing their query to *any* city organization. Each city organization has one designated contact person who has pledged to answer all e-mail within 48 hours. This lag allows enough time to frame an appropriate response without the strict demands of a telephone call. Interestingly, this role has often gone to

---

[1] Personal correspondence, 1995.

PEN Objectives

1. To provide easy electronic access to public information for use by city residents.

2. To provide an alternative means of communication for residents to convey their needs, preferences, and intentions to their local government and to other residents.

3. To enhance delivery and awareness of public services available to residents, and to facilitate the public service inquiry process.

4. To provide an electronic forum for participation in discussions of issues and concerns of residents in order to promote an enhanced sense of community.

5. To extend to all members of the community the opportunity to understand computer technology, and to provide access to the hardware and software needed to learn to communicate via an electronic network.

Figure 4.2

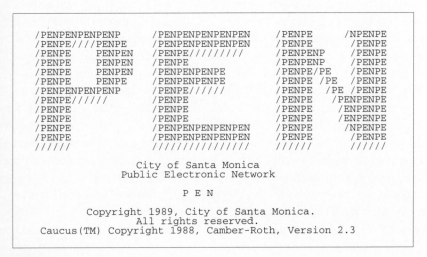

```
/PENPENPENPENP       /PENPENPENPENPEN     /PENPE        /NPENPE
/PENPE////PENPE      /PENPENPENPENPEN     /PENPE         /PENPE
/PENPE      PENPEN   /PENPE////////       /PENPENP       /PENPE
/PENPE      PENPEN   /PENPE               /PENPENP       /PENPE
/PENPE      PENPEN   /PENPENPENPE         /PENPE/PE      /PENPE
/PENPE      PENPE    /PENPENPENPE         /PENPE /PE     /PENPE
/PENPENPENPENP       /PENPE//////         /PENPE  /PE /PENPE
/PENPE//////         /PENPE               /PENPE   /PENPENPE
/PENPE               /PENPE               /PENPE    /ENPENPE
/PENPE               /PENPE               /PENPE    /ENPENPE
/PENPE               /PENPENPENPENPEN     /PENPE    /NPENPE
/PENPE               /PENPENPENPENPEN     /PENPE     /PENPE
//////               ////////////////    //////     //////
             City of Santa Monica
          Public Electronic Network

                   P E N

       Copyright 1989, City of Santa Monica.
             All rights reserved.
   Caucus(TM) Copyright 1988, Camber-Roth, Version 2.3
```

Figure 4.3

```
                City of Santa Monica

             Public Electronic Network

                    Main Menu

  1. CITY HALL
  2. COMMUNITY CENTER
  3. MAILROOM
  4. CONFERENCES
  5. ON-LINE FORMS
  6. CURRENT EVENTS

  Bye Type bye to exit PEN
```

Figure 4.4

those with high positions in the organizations, people who can in most cases speak *for* the organization. This reduces the bureaucratic process of filtering of every piece of e-mail through large numbers of people in the organization just to get a response. On the other hand, answering e-mail might not be the wisest (or most economical) use of senior people in an organization. Yet these electronic queries have nearly eliminated the commonplace (and frustrating) experience of a caller being led through a seemingly endless succession of phone

```
                City of Santa Monica

             Public Electronic Network

                    City Hall

   1. Information Desk
   2. Agendas, Schedules, Notices, and Reports
   3. City Government
   4. Public Works
   5. Planning and Building
   6. City Attorney
   7. Public Safety
   8. Transportation
   9. Rent Control
  10. Environmental Programs
  11. Parking and Traffic
```

Figure 4.5

```
                    City of Santa Monica

                Public Electronic Network

                      City Agendas

   1. City Council              9. Personnel Board
   2. Planning Commission      10. Airport Commission
   3. Commission on the Status 11. Arts Commission
      of Women                 12. Library Board
   4. Rent Control Board       13. Bayside District Corp.
   5. Commission on Older      14. Pier Restoration Corp.
      Americans                15. Task Force on the
   6. Recreation and Parks         Environment
      Commission               16. Landmarks Commission
   7. Social Services          17. Architectural Review
      Commisssion                  Board
   8. Housing Commisssion
```

Figure 4.6

calls while attempting to locate information or conduct business with the government. If a PEN user sends a query electronically to the wrong office, the person who has received the mail redirects the response to the correct office. Interestingly, only 5 percent of PEN e-mail was resident-to-government; the remaining 95 percent is sent between nongovernmental users.

Supporting Political Action: The SHWASHLOCK Experience

Besides obtaining basic government and community information and discussing community issues, Santa Monicans also discovered that a community network can support purposeful political action. Michele Wittig a professor at California State University, Northridge (1991) has described how the PEN Action Group, a diverse group of community members and some homeless residents organized themselves electronically using PEN, when they realized the potential for the local system to be a catalyst. In this case, the network provided a convenient medium for group discussion, deliberation, strategizing, and action. In August of 1989, Bruria Finkel, a Santa Monica resident posted an idea to the Homeless Conference on PEN based on discussions she had had with homeless residents. The concept, dubbed SHWASHLOCK (for SHowers,

WASHers, and LOCKers) was intended to help homeless people find, and maintain jobs by providing them with morning showers, laundry facilities, and lockers for their belongings.

It is instructive to examine the process that the group followed. First, the PEN Action Group identified a problem. This first identification was followed by a period of self-education in which the group investigated local service organizations and resources. The group identified gaps in service that weren't provided by other local organizations; closing those gaps became the focus of the PEN Action Group. Other concerns surfaced during the process: Philosophical disputes arose as to whether SHWASHLOCK services ought to be provided at all. There were political concerns as well. At one point local social-service providers "expressed unease over the threat that the new group would be competing with them for scarce social service dollars" (Wittig, 1991). This fear was allayed by cooperating with existing agencies rather than starting a new one. Other sectors such as the business community also played a part. A locker manufacturer agreed to provide 30 lockers for seven months without charge. The Santa Monica City Council ultimately allocated $150,000 for lockers, showers, and a laundry facility, demonstrating that using on-line resources for *community organizing* can work.

Although PEN's SHWASHLOCK experience appears to be a success in electronic grass-roots organizing, it is critical not to underestimate the hurdles that must be circumvented nor think that the magic of community networking will make the job trivial. Commitment, hard work, intelligence, planning, creativity, and luck will still be needed. Being aware of the potential pitfalls and possible misunderstandings as well as the opportunities afforded by the new medium is also strongly advised: Knowing when a face-to-face meeting is necessary can save a committee or group hours of frustrating and useless electronic communication that could jeopardize the entire project.

Also, as the SHWASHLOCK experience suggests, there are always other players involved. In this relatively small example, there were no less than six "stakeholder" groups—the homeless residents, the on-line PEN Action Group, the social service agencies, various businesses, the City Council, and other residents of Santa Monica. The success of any project will often hinge on the relationships among and within various groups such as these.

Sobering Thoughts

Experiences with the PEN system experience also highlight possible shortcomings of the medium. When people use a computer as an intermediary—when people relate to each other only through a keyboard and a computer screen—the quality of political talk can sometimes plummet. Ideally, electronic discussions provide a civil forum of reason, respect, and reflection, but sometimes retort, recalcitrance, and rancor can dominate. Pamela Varley who has extensively observed and written about the Santa Monica system has some sobering thoughts for idealistic community-network developers. In her reports she notes widespread problems and, as a result, "Santa Monica's political movers and shakers have, for the most part, stayed clear of PEN's crucible" because "PENners tend to pounce on any officeholder bold enough to make accusations and demand a response" (1991). On the other hand, according to Wittig[2] several Santa Monica elected officials were unwilling "to participate in written debate on an equal footing with residents," preferring city council meetings "during which residents are strictly forbidden from directing any comment to an individual council member."

Several elected officials who had originally participated using PEN ultimately rejected its use. In Varley's account, Chris Reed, a city council member, quit PEN stating that she was tired of continued abuse: "If people would have been the least bit polite, or respectful of the need for people in democracy to differ, I would have stuck it out." Another Santa Monica council member, Judy Abdo, also stopped using the system after differing with colleagues on the council and with PEN participants. When a government employee or politician takes part in a conference, it may be impossible to participate on an equal and relatively anonymous basis. In the PEN experience the person was unable to blend in, to be just another citizen casually conversing; he or she was apparently marked as an *official representative*, at least by some people, and became a target for attack. While most of us have made poor suggestions or unwarranted conclusions on occasion, we're usually able to escape without undue damage. The public servant on a PEN-like system may not have the same privilege.

Other officeholders and staff also complained about the heavy time commitment that PEN participation incurred. Mel Levine, Santa Monica's congressman, agreed to sponsor on-line forums, and since Levine did not participate directly, his staff took on the extra burden. Unfortunately, replies sometimes took several weeks, a delay that was unsatisfactory to many PEN participants. Even though increasing access to the political process through access to officeholders is important, these experiences highlight the obvious tradeoffs. If the time spent communicating with constituents goes up due to increased electronic access, more staff people will be needed or time must be redirected from other activities, including time spent with other constituencies using other forms of communication such as the telephone, written correspondence and face-to-face meetings.

Since the medium is new—and still in flux—and people's attitudes and behaviors are still being formed, it is too early to come to definitive conclusions about the relative magnitude of these problems. The apparent vulnera-

---

[2] Personal correspondence, 1995.

bility of the medium to "flaming" (sending harsh and abusive electronic mail or forum postings) and other antisocial behavior is well established. Perhaps this just demonstrates the vulnerability of those people who "play by the rules" in any social setting to those who don't or can't. Perhaps these problems are inevitable. A medium can only reflect, albeit imperfectly, the thoughts and actions of the people who use it. Like democracy itself, a medium that supports democracy will have its shortcomings. These systems, however, provide a vital laboratory for research into democratic talk, processes, and technology, and ignoring the hypotheses and observations of these early experiments would be an unfortunate mistake.

The discussion of PEN and PEN-like systems does not end here. PEN is a government-run community network and, hence, is subject to a host of major questions. These questions hinge on one main issue: What is the proper role (or roles) for the various branches of government in this area? Then, based on that answer (or answers) the important questions regarding how money is raised and spent, and how systems are administered and regulated can be taken up. These questions are discussed in some detail in Chapter 8— the social architecture of community networks.

On-line Democracy: NCF in Ottawa

Community networks offer excellent opportunities to experiment with and learn about new forms of democratic processes. Electronic communication can be used to mediate or augment some of democracy's fundamental aspects: education, discussion, decision, and implementation.

In early 1994, the National Capital Free-Net (NCF), one of the largest of the Free-Net NPTN affiliates (described in Chapter 10) in Ottawa, Canada, conducted one of these early experiments when it hosted an extended on-line meeting. The process was divided into a month of resolution-proposing and discussion followed by two weeks of voting. Every NCF user was considered a "member" and was entitled to vote in the meeting. Each time the users logged on, they were presented with a message exhorting them to participate in the process. If they hadn't yet voted during the two-week election voting period, another message would remind them to vote the next time they logged on. Although member users also elect people (to the NCF Board of Directors), this "meeting" only dealt with resolutions—electronic motions from the floor. These resolutions were nonbinding and were considered to be recommendations to the elected board, which had the ultimate authority and responsibility for the system.

The NCF staff created one general discussion forum and one information-only forum for each new resolution using the standard FreePort forum software. The NCF staff and board used the additional forum to inform the users about relevant NCF objectives, technology, and organizational practices. The staff and board also placed documents such as financial statements in the organizational forum as the need arose.

In addition to the forum software, NCF also used the FreePort voting module, which presented a ballot to the user for voting. Interestingly, voters could revisit the ballot any number of times during the voting period. In other words, they could change their votes as often as they liked, and the pro and con votes could—in theory—fluctuate wildly until the voting period ended, whereupon the software automatically would tabulate the results based on the tally at that moment. Since electronic voting is still a rarity and because it introduces new opportunities for fraud (as well as risks from software bugs), the NCF system administrators kept an archive of all the final votes as a safeguard in case the results of an election were challenged.

As mentioned before, the member-user resolutions were advisory and not legally binding upon the board. That was actually beneficial, according to Dave Sutherland, chairman of the NCF. For one reason, some motions could not be implemented because of limited resources. Interestingly, some board members could not in good conscience implement some of the resolutions because they contradicted the platforms on which they were elected. In Sutherland's opinion, the statements of the candidates were very thoughtful and the best people were chosen by the membership for board positions. Thus, in Sutherland's views, the on-line voting for *people* was successful while voting for on-line resolutions was less so.

The 17 motions (shown in Fig. 4.7) generally represented users' desires for expanded computing capability (beyond the limitations imposed by the FreePort menuing software) such as UNIX shells, full Internet access, and the like. While expanded service is generally a good thing, demands for resource expenditure need to be considered in the aggregate, and this is the province of the NCF board. For example, full Internet access for all NCF users (14,000 at the time of the meeting; 24,000 at the time of my writing; and an estimated 40,000 or more by the time of your reading) was judged by the board to be too expensive. Although nonbinding, advisory measures are still useful as they provide a guage of users' needs and concerns.

Toward an Electronic Town Hall:
The OTA/NPTN Teleforum Project

Along with the "information superhighway" and "electronic democracy," the other new metaphorical cliché that many people use but fewer understand is that of an "electronic town hall," which takes its name from the

```
              National Capital Free-Net

        1994 On-line Annual Meeting Resolutions

                 Motions From Members

    1 Setting Board Priorities
    2 Binary Gopher Transfers
    3 International IRC
    4 IRC 24 hours per day
    5 User Names
    6 Display of NCF Logo Be Optional
    7 Make the Logo Small
    8 High Speed Modems
    9 Announce Newsgroup Be Moderated
   10 Public Discussion of Free-Net Business
   11 Second Elected Board
   12 Sell Internet Services to Local
      Companies
   13 Group Accounts for Teachers and
      Classrooms
   14 Thanking the Board of Directors
   15 UNIX Shell Access and Full Internet
      Services
   16 A Standard Date Format
   17 Make the MOTD Short
```

Figure 4.7

much romanticized New England town meeting in which any citizen can attend and participate in determining how to manage the town's affairs.

The National Public Telecomputing Network (discussed in more detail in Chapter 8) conducted one of the first examples of an electronic town hall in 1992 for the Office of Technology Assessment (OTA) in what they labeled an OTA Teleforum. The purpose of the first teleforum was to help the OTA get an initial feeling for the feasibility and desirability of using networked communications to enable the OTA to perform its role (Beasley, 1994). That teleforum involved three sites representing urban, suburban, and rural populations. It lasted for six weeks and hundreds of people participated.

The second teleforum took place at five NPTN affiliate sites in January 1994 on four issues related to the U.S. Social Security Administration (SSA), particularly pertaining to customer relations and the use of telecommunications technology to conduct Social Security business. Each issue was accompanied by one general question and several suggestions that were intended to provoke additional thinking on the issue. A USENET newsgroup was started on each topic, and any responses posted at one site were propagated to each of the other sites (within minutes of original input). Thus the teleforum content was identical at each site, effectively making physical distance irrelevant in this experiment.

The four issues were "social security and customer interaction," "network access to benefit filing services," "distribution of benefits," and "general satisfaction with the SSA" and there were over 240 responses to the four issues during the three-week period. Although the people that participated were not representative of the population as a whole, there was widespread agreement that the SSA should begin exploring the idea of using telecommunications technology to conduct its programs, especially routine business where privacy issues are not likely to come up.

In this case, the results of the teleforum were generally encouraging. It is, however, necessary to point out the aspects of this project which were *not* addressed. Although the teleforum was not designed to be anything more than what it was, looking at it critically from the standpoint of electronic democracy is a useful exercise. One of the first things to observe is that the issues placed on the agenda were placed there by the teleforum convenors, *not* the participants. This in no way invalidates the teleforum, but it places it nearer to a focus group than to a New England town meeting. Beyond that, there was no ability for participants to make decisions—one of Dahl's criteria. Participants were free to offer opinions, but there was no guarantee that the SSA would *do anything* with the information. A final observation—one for anybody that wants to use electronic forums in this way—is that people are capable of generating quite a lot of text, and more people can generate a colossal amount more. Sifting through hundreds or thousands of pages of opinion is an onerous task, and getting the sense of the writings, with their broad and subtle differences, can be extremely challenging.

Future Directions

The SHWASHLOCK project, NCF on-line annual meeting and the OTA Teleforum examples mentioned have been the work of electronic pioneers with uncommon industriousness and ingenuity. However useful, their work—like others who have done similar work—is basically ad hoc. These impromptu experiments in democracy have been largely outside the realm of academia, government, or business and—thus far—have been anomalies that are outside the everyday experience of most people. Since their efforts lack rigorous scientific methodology, "respectable" origins, or widespread familiarity, it may be difficult to capitalize on their trailblazing work.

COMMUNITY NETWORKS AND CITIZEN PARTICIPATION

All the ills of democracy can be cured by more democracy.

Alfred E. Smith

Citizen participation in government can be roughly divided into passive and active modes of participation, and both modes suggest new roles for computer technology and community networks.

Passive participation itself can be subdivided into three areas: civic education, doing business with the government, and public talk. For individuals to meaningfully participate in the political process, civic education is vital. One needs knowledge of context, history, and process in order to be involved in addressing issues democratically. Part of the context of a U.S. style democracy is an appreciation of the source documents that help form the conceptual underpinnings of the country. The National Public Telecomputing Network's (NPTN) TeleDemocracy program offers a collection of 30 documents of relevance to U.S. democracy, including the Magna Carta,[2] the Constitution, and the Bill of Rights, as well as important modern statements such as Martin Luther King's "I Have a Dream" speech. The Oneida nation in New York state has made treaties and other historical documents available electronically for similar reasons (see Chapter 2).

In recent years the government—especially at the federal level—has been producing a steady flow of information available electronically, including the full text of all major press releases, executive orders, press briefings, and other presidential documents. U.S. Supreme Court decisions and dissenting opinions are available within minutes of judgment. The full text of representative's bills, floor statements, the Congressional Record, contact information, committee assignments, as well as other legislative information is now available through the Thomas system (http://thomas.loc.gov). The Internet site, fedworld.gov (telnet fedworld.gov, or http://www.fedworld.gov) is also available through dial-up; this is essentially a one-stop shopping center for a staggering amount of government information from 130 federal bulletin-board systems (BBSs) and 60 federal agencies.

The Library of Congress operates the gopher-based Marvel system, which

---

[2] The *original* "Magna Carta" that is—*not* the libertarian manifesto issued by the Privacy and Freedom Foundation.

provides access to the House, Senate, C-SPAN, and Congressional Quarterly gophers, and contains information about committee assignments, Congressional directories, house legislation, and status, e-mail addresses, and voting records. There is also a large amount of legislative, executive, military, and other information such as the Catalog of Federal Domestic Assistance Programs, containing information on over one thousand federal programs. The Government Printing Office (GPO), through their WAIS GPO Access system, offers the full text of recent (103rd and 104th sessions) House and Senate bills, the Federal Register, and the History of Bills. GPO Access is available free to the public through various public library systems such as the Seattle Public Library. Additionally, virtually every state government, as well as many county and city governments, are now making information available in electronic form. The Library of Congress Marvel system even supplies links to goverment information in many countries outside the United States.

Other basic information such as how to register to vote and how to contact elected officials is becoming available electronically. The League of Women Voters of Seattle, for example, has posted on the Seattle Community Network an electronic version of their "They Represent You" brochure, an up-to-date collection of information on how to contact elected officials. In preparation for the 1994 election, the League also posted answers to questions that it had asked the candidates, as well as briefing papers that the League had prepared on issues facing the Washington electorate. The national League of Women Voters through their Education Fund has also supported other projects with their "Wired for Democracy: Using Emerging Technology to Educate Voters" program.

The creation and maintenance of the gigantic body of government information has been paid for by American taxpayers, yet a citizen that needs access to this information sometimes finds that it's available from a private vendor or not at all. When the information is available from the government, it is often in some unusable format or has a high user fee attached, even though electronic distribution costs are lower than traditional paper-based methods.

While there are many signs that government is releasing more and more information electronically to the general public, there are still great strides to be made. For one thing, there is no overarching policy or commitment for all departments to provide this service. Consequently, key pieces of government information may be unavailable or available at a price above the reach of many individuals. Moreover, withdrawal of services could come at any time with changes in agency policy or in selected areas of government if we should return to an administration less inclined to public access.

The Taxpayer's Assets Project (TAP), originated by Ralph Nader in 1988 to play a watchdog role for various government assets including land, other property, and patents, is now focusing its attention on securing "better access to the federal government's extensive electronic collections of documents, statistics and technical data." James Love of TAP has identified the "crown jewels" (Love, 1992) of government information and is working to make these freely available in electronic form. Love has been concentrating on information residing in the Securities and Exchange Commission's (SEC) Electronic Data Gathering Analysis and Retrieval (EDGAR) system, The Department of Justice JURIS system, and the Federal Acquisition Regulations (FAR) system. Other people have been pushing for more open electronic access. Microcomputer pioneer Jim Warren, for example, has concentrated his efforts at the state level in California. Warren is currently supporting some changes in the California Public Records Act to make all disclosable state information available electronically for incremental costs. Chris Mays, a student at San Francisco State College, in an effort to make government information more widely available to activists and others has created a California Electronic Government Information Web page (Fig. 4.8) on the World Wide Web that contains pointers to important government information caches such as the City of Palo Alto's Web page (Fig. 4.9) and a wide variety of bulletin-board systems (Fig. 4.10).

California Electronic Government Information

 Hypertext links & resource descriptions for over 200 California state, regional & municipal databases available over the Internet or through dial-up bulletin board systems. Entries grouped by source & listed by title. Links to other compilations & search engines. Entire file available for downloading.

Title: California Electronic Government Information
Archived as text via anonymous ftp:
ftp.cpsr.org/cpsr/states/california/cegi.txt
URL: http://cpsr.org/dox/cegi.html
Version: 19960215
Edition: 14th
Udpate Frequency: Varies, one to two months.

The date of last revision is February 15, 1996. Copyright 1996 Chris Mays. This document may be freely distributed in its entirety provided that this copyright notice is not removed. It may not be sold for profit or incorporated in commercial documents without the written permission of the copyright holder.

Table of Contents

Figure 4.8   California Electronic Government Information

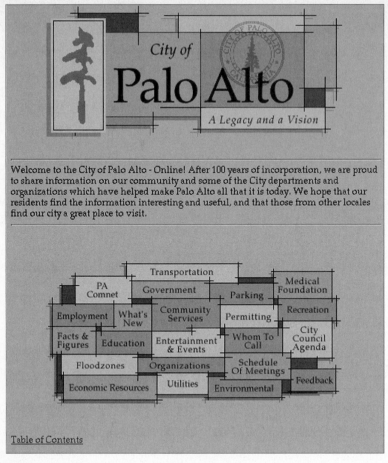

Figure 4.9 City of Palo Alto Web Page

The availability of pertinent information is critical to a sound democratic system. Without access to the necessary information, participation in the political process is inequitable and ineffective. Of course "availability" is itself a catchall for various other concepts, including cost, timeliness, and usefulness of the information. If the cost is too high, the waiting time too protracted, or the format of the information too indecipherable, the information can be effectively unavailable.

Doing Business with the Government

The government does other things besides collecting and distributing information. In many cases the government is an entity with whom we conduct business. Sometimes this is at our own instigation—obtaining a building per-

---

CEGI: 2.6 Municipal

Entries operated by city governments are alphabetized by city. Asterisks (*) identify keywords for other services by which the list is alphabetized. There are many cities in California with home pages that are not included here. City pages must offer current minutes and agendas for council meetings as a minimum criterion for inclusion. Unofficial pages that meet the criterion are encouraged.

- TITLE: City of Alameda.
- SOURCE: City of Alameda & ABAG.
- PATH: WWW: http://www.ci.alameda.ca.us/alameda.htm
- ABSTRACT: Currently, only the City of Alameda's Bureau of Electricity has an active page.
- ENTRY COMPILED: 960210

- TITLE: Belmont Access for the Community.
- SOURCE: City of Belmont & Aimnet.
- PATH: http://www.belmont.gov
- ABSTRACT: The Belmont Access page has links for:
  - ○ Business Information; the Chamber of Commerce
  - ○ Education and Library
  - ○ Local Government: Your Link to City Hall
  - ○ Metropolitan area: S.F. Bay Area links and beyond
  - ○ Organizations, Clubs and Groups
  - ○ News and activities
  - ○ Technology Plan and Partnerships
- FEEDBACK: Belmont Webmaster <bacadmin@belmont.gov>
- ENTRY COMPILED: 950515

- TITLE: inBerkeley: City of Berkeley Home Page.
- SOURCE: City of Berkeley.
- PATH: WWW: http://www.ci.berkeley.ca.us/
- ABSTRACT: Resources include:
  - ○ Government and City Agencies
  - ○ Internet E-Mail Addresses for City Officials & Departments
  - ○ Berkeley Libraries (including the Berkeley Information Network)
  - ○ Berkeley Businesses and Organizations
  - ○ Information about the City of Berkeley
- CONTACT: Malcolm Humes <mah2@ci.berkeley.ca.us>

Figure 4.10   Some California Government Bulletin-Board Systems

mit, for example—and sometimes at the government's—paying taxes, getting drafted, or getting arrested, for example. Community networks and other on-line services can be used to conduct some of these transactions. In Santa Monica, for example, residents can use the PEN system to conduct several types of city businesses from home or from public terminals. These services include submitting petty theft reports with the Santa Monica Police Department and gaining information on how to transact other government business. The U.S. Office of Technology Assessment has produced a report devoted to the "electronic delivery of federal services" in which many important issues in this area are brought out and discussed (U.S. Congress, 1993).

While electronic transactions between citizens and government may be less expensive and more convenient in some ways for both citizen and government (through 'round-the-clock service, fewer car trips to city hall, and less time spent processing forms), there are other important concerns that arise with this style of interaction. The first concern is that of access to the service. If a computer and a modem are required to use the service, then those without ready access to the technology will be forced to use the traditional methods. Faced with this situation the government must now provide *at least* two methods—electronic and paper-based—by which to access the service, and the cost, necessarily passed on to the taxpayer, may rise. Perhaps more significantly, clients of the new, state-of-the-art electronic service may experience improving service, while people without access to the technology may experience deteriorating service.

There are many related concerns that arise when computers and communication technology are used. While privacy (of personal information), fraud (in vote counting, for example), and security (especially in financial transactions) are foremost among these, the change in the way in which people perceive and interact with the government might also be problematic. Based on their observations of electronic delivery of services in Europe, researchers Ignatius Snellen and Sally Wyatt have noted that "The citizen tends to become more of an outsider for whom the organization is impenetrable" (1993). This bodes ill for those with dreams of reinventing government along more humane lines. Since many people already regard the government as faceless and bureaucratic, an increased reliance on filling out forms at a computer would undoubtedly exacerbate that perception. Furthermore, at a time when government is expected to become more of a partner, it is less likely to be perceived as an organization that needs or could accommodate partners.

Public Talk

The last method of "passive" political participation is "talk." Talk, while fundamental to a democracy, is still "cheap." If people engage in talk—no matter how enlightened—without acting on it, it is useless in the political sense. Talk, however, straddles the line between passive and active participation. When one learns of a situation or important information through talk and is compelled to take action, talk becomes a catalyst for active democracy. An electronic forum can serve as a sounding board and is one way to get a fairly quick feel for a range of opinions. Of course, a forum is nothing more than a straw poll that has very little real validity. There is often no way of knowing just who's participating in the discussion or how representative the responses are to the larger population. Although subject to the same caveats, there are several software packages that are designed to conduct electronic surveys, making it easier to collect and manage large amounts of semistructured information.

A community network should minimally provide discussion on the major issues in the region. In the Seattle area, for example, these issues would include youth violence, growth management, urban villages, the "Commons" issue, the city's information highway plan, and the proposed Seattle-Tacoma airport third runway, among many others. Some issues are short-lived like specific ballot measures, while some topics are perennial: education, recreation, and public health, for example. Since topics are often locally relevant, discussion areas should be associated with that particular region, be it state, county, region, city, or neighborhood. The threatened closing of the Wallingford Library, for example, is probably more important to a citizen of Wallingford than to a citizen of Leschi.

Active Participation

Ralph Nader has said that daily democracy depends on daily citizenship. Hopefully community networks can play a role in that daily citizenship. Community networks and electronic communication have been used in active forms of citizen participation such as in developing or influencing legislation, electing candidates, or passing citizen initiatives. James Love of the Taxpayer Assets Project, for example, has been particularly successful at mobilizing people using the Internet. His remarkable story "Internet Community KO's Anti-FOIA Provision" (Love, 1995) relates how Internet activism helped prevent a special interest provision that would allow private companies (in this case West Publishing) to control access to public information. At the same time, efforts have been made to provide electronic connections between candidates and the citizenry. Both the Center for Civic Networking in Cambridge, Massachusetts, and the State of Minnesota have been establishing e-mail accounts for all political candidates in their region.

Voting Electronically

Voting (using Dahl's criterion of "equal participation at the decision stage") is the most obvious form of active participation in a democratic process, and voting could certainly be facilitated electronically. As we saw in the National Capital Free-Net section, the FreePort software used by many NPTN affiliates has a "voting module" that allows users to electronically cast ballots on issues of interest. Use of this electronic balloting is generally confined to straw polls that are not legally binding. Electronic voting could, however, be legally binding for an organization if the legal requirements for voting, for a quorum, and for "meetings" were specified in the by-laws of the association. The Computer Professionals for Social Responsibility (CPSR) board of directors, for example, has voted electronically for several years. An amendment to the by-laws specifies how board members without electronic mail can participate, the length of discussion period preceding the voting, and outlines other aspects of the process. No national, state, or other governmental entities have allowed electronic voting, but with proper certification the process could ultimately be legally binding, in the same way that absentee voting is today.

However appealing electronic voting may appear, the concept raises some troubling concerns. The first, of course, is the opportunity for fraud. Current election systems are prone to a variety of errors, including software-design flaws, program bugs, security holes, and failure of management controls. The current situation is a "can of worms" according to computer scientist Erik Nilsson who has studied the issue extensively. Nilsson reports that increased reliance on automated systems may exacerbate existing problems (1988). Another concern is that electronic voting may actually *increase* political disparity while simultaneously providing an additional avenue for participation. This potential for increase in political disparity is due to the extremely unequal distribution of computers and telecommunications capabilities in homes. The wealthier a family is, the more likely it is to have the technology to access a voting service electronically from their homes. Although this problem could be somewhat mitigated by free-access terminals in public places, this new capability would, in effect, make it easier for the well-to-do to participate. While the well-to-do have every right to participate, the barriers to participation generally affect lower income people, and electronic voting from home without universal access would exacerbate an already profound inequity.

The most troubling aspect to on-line voting, however, is its secondary effects. As Richard Sclove, Langdon Winner, and others have elucidated, technologies affect social relations and structures far beyond their nominally intended purposes. The introduction of the automobile, as we know, brought forth vast changes in virtually all aspects of society, including work patterns, leisure activities, and sexual behavior. Since voting already occupies the preeminent position in the public's perception of the political process, an intensified preoccupation with voting would push the focus farther from agenda building and deliberation more toward the direction of judgment. To direct the focus to decisions rather than deliberation is the heart of the problem according to Lloyd Morriset writing in the president's essay in the 1993 Markle

Foundation annual report. Furthermore, voting electronically could help create an "electronic lynch mob," where people could come to a decision within minutes of first hearing about an issue. In an exaggerated scenario—but certainly within the realm of technological possibility—a person could be "tried" on television before an audience seated on couches across America. This jury of couch-potato peers could listen to eloquent testimony from both sides, render a quick judgment, flip to another channel, then return to the "Democracy Channel" for another go at democratic participation.

Although the effects are less obvious and dramatic, a concentration on voting at the expense of other aspects of the democratic process, such as discussion and deliberation, has other more insidious implications. As mentioned earlier, voting is but one aspect of a rich and dynamic process of political engagement. Voting without strong participation relegates citizens to mere ratifiers, reinforcing the presumption of citizen ignorance and sloth, while leaving the texture, subtlety, and ultimate power of the democratic process in the hands of the few.

Finally, it should be noted that we've used the expression "active participation" in political processes to mean active *conventional* participation. Americans have the right, as well as the responsibility, to resort to unconventional political processes when circumstances dictate. American history is replete with examples of individuals and groups using civil disobedience to fight against the status quo. Without undue extrapolation, we shouldn't be surprised if the future "net" becomes the scene of new varieties of civic cyber-disobedience.

Voluntary Associations and Everyday Democracy

Alexis de Toqueville, the French observer of American democracy, was so profoundly impressed by the numbers and types of voluntary associations in America that he placed the phenomena at the core of American civic life (1945).

> Americans of all ages, all stations in life, and all types of disposition, are forever forming associations. There are not only commercial and industrial associations in which all take part, but others of a thousand different types—religious, moral, serious, futile, very general and very limited, immensely large and very minute . . . Nothing, in my view, deserves more attention than the intellectual and moral associations in America.

Everyday life is punctuated sporadically with glimpses into the guts of the American democratic process. These glimpses often consist of partisan squabbling or scandals involving sex, money, or both. During an election year the media coverage always escalates, but somehow the *quality* rarely does. The citizen becomes a spectator to a constant barrage of claims and counterclaims, charges and countercharges. Then, on election day, many Americans vote, discharging in private their sole democratic obligation. It should come as no surprise that so many have opted out of this nearly empty, ritualistic process—the superficial spectacle that politics in America has become.

With the intermittent and nearly meaningless act of voting forming the mainstay of American elections, one wonders where and how Americans might get *training* or experience in democratic decision making. In the schools? Certainly not. It would be heretical to let students decide where, when and what they'll learn, or who will teach them. And as we discussed in Chapter 3, the broadcast mode of teaching is dominant; students almost invariably are expected to work *alone*. How about on the job? Nope. The same answer goes for privately owned and publicly owned firms (with a handful of exceptions) and, ironically, for government jobs. In church? With few exceptions—Quakers and Mennonites among them—churches are run like a hierarchy; sermons, not discussions, are the rule. Nor does the family provide fertile ground for growing democratic awareness. Everyday life—from birth to death—in an ostensibly democratic country like the United States is almost devoid of democratic experiences. Sadly, the idea of developing democratic skills with authoritarianism reigning in almost all aspects of everyday life is unlikely.

New communities, however, will *depend* on democratic principle and democratic skills. As part of this push for new communities we must put pressure—from both the outside and from the inside—on nondemocratic institutions to become more democratic. We must also concentrate on the one institution that does routinely rely on democratic processes to get things done—the voluntary association.

As community activists and others have long acknowledged, voluntary associations in the United States have extensive influence and reach. In Washington State alone there are nearly 33,000 nonprofit organizations (Barber, 1994). These include colleges, churches, day-care centers, libraries, trade associations, social service organizations, museums and many others. The annual payroll is nearly four billion dollars, a sum approximately equal to that of another Washington employer, The Boeing Company. Although not all of these associations are paragons of democratic discourse, there is a strong thrust in that direction. The boards of directors are often elected by the membership, and general meetings are held at regular intervals. Additionally, these associations often address the issues that government has overlooked or cannot address fully, and those that for-profit corporations will not touch. Clearly, voluntary associations are key to the development of the new community and community networks.

Voluntary associations have an additional role to play in the revitalization of democratic participation—that of the *mediating institution* that Greider and many others have recommended. A mediating institution is one that plays a role in linking two institutions—communities and their government, in this case. Ideally, the mediating institution can articulate needs and demands, promote discussion and awareness on an issue, and present a more coherent, more compelling, and a more feasible case than community members individually could develop.

Since the aims of voluntary associations coincide significantly with the aims of the new community movement, a special effort should be made to develop support of voluntary associations by means of community networks. Strengthening voluntary associations should strengthen the community-network movement and vice versa. Community-network developers should seriously examine the needs of voluntary associations when they are designing new systems for democratic processes. These organizations need support for discussion, for deliberation, and for decision-making that will help them effectively take action on issues that are important to them. These support systems need to be easy to use, and their functions (discussion and decision-making, for example) should be integrated together.[4] Voluntary associations need the new systems and will use the new systems. Furthermore, they will help to uncover any major problems before the systems are used with large populations for significant decisions. Untested "democracy-in-a-box" systems could further degrade America's already ailing political process; voluntary associations could provide the "beta-test" for the new systems.

Additionally, new democratic support systems need to be parameterized so that the features of the particular organization (number of people constituting a quorum, for example) can be changed to match specific needs. Some of the new systems like eVote developed by Marilyn Davis (1994) allow vote changing, voter visibility, proportional voting and other variations. The next section continues this discussion by looking at computer support for on-line meetings.

New Algorithms for Democratic Technology

In 1922, French Strother, writing in *The Unfolding Marvel of Wireless*, wrote that "Broadcasting has turned the nation into a town meeting. But there is no chairman, and no parliamentary law. This will bring anarchy in the ether" (Czitrom, 1982). Now, over 70 years later, we face a similar situation with cyberspace. What can be done to tame the anarchy that exists there?

[4] Putnam Barber, private corespondence, 1994.

Five decades before the problems with "anarchy in the ether" surfaced steps were being taken to curb the anarchy of face-to-face meetings. In 1876, Major Henry Robert of the U.S. Army Engineers first published his set of rules for running orderly meetings in which everybody would have an opportunity to express their own opinions but no one could prevent a deliberative majority from coming to a decision. This seemingly simple requirement occupied Henry Robert for nearly 40 years, demonstrating the inherent complexity of such a goal. His work, which culminated in a relatively thin book called *Robert's Rules of Order, Revised* (1971) is in daily use by tens of thousands of organizations around the world from the smallest neighborhood organizations to the United Nations, from groups whose members you can count on two hands, to those with membership numbering in the thousands.

If meetings are going to be *mediated* by computers in any way (allowing impromptu meetings, that are not face-to-face, for example) then *something* like Robert's Rules of Order (revised again, this time for the electronic age) will be necessary. Since community networks can be used—at least in theory—to support both synchronous communication (like a telephone conversation or a face-to-face meeting) and asynchronous communication (like using letters) as well as to support hybrid modes containing elements of both, modifications to Robert's Rules that address the basic requirement need to be developed.

Software can be used to mediate human communication in many ways; a whole body of work has grown up that addresses this topic. The discipline of Computer Supported Cooperative Work (CSCW) has emerged in which computer systems are built to support groups rather than individuals who are working together on shared tasks (see Greif, 1988, for example). These systems are notoriously difficult to design, however, and software that imposes too strict, unnatural, or inflexible structure on the interactions has been labeled "naziware" by those who found its constraining features untenable.

Developing "democracyware" will be challenging. If meeting participants were all available at the same time but at different locations, a close approximation to Robert's Rules could be used using "chat" technology similar to that used in America Online and other commercial services. Without the constraint of all users being stationed at their respective computers at the same time, a variation on Robert's Rules could be used if participants agreed to log on for some minimal number of hours per week or month. An on-going meeting, for example, could be held using electronic mail. It should be noted, however, that these new approaches give rise to new issues and challenges, some of which are quite subtle. A person who was quite adroit in face-to-face meetings might find the situation far different if all input was typed in at the keyboard. In an electronically supported meeting with distributed participants, for example, what happens if one network connection goes down? And without a password or audio or video authentication, how can one guarantee that a remote participant is really who he or she says?

The prospect of electronic support suggests interesting new possibilities for democracy-in-the-small processes. Computer software could, for example, guide, record, and instruct during the course of the on-line meeting. A menu showing the options that were available at any given time (and an on-line help facility to explain each option) could also be incorporated into the system. With this type of computer support, those less familiar with the rules could participate on a more equal footing. The software, for example, might only allow a participant to second a motion after a motion had been made. It could also be "tunable," allowing groups to change parameters to suit their situation and preferences. During a voting period, for example, the software might always make the *current* tally available. On the other hand, the count could be kept hidden until after the voting period had closed, preventing voters from making their votes based on the likely outcome, as representatives in the U.S. House of Representatives sometimes do.

Government Accountability

Democratic societies require governments. The shape that the government takes depends on the rules and habits that guide it, the people involved in it, and the perseverance and persuasiveness of the people who are trying to influence it. Government accountability is of primary importance to the new community: The government must be made to be increasingly receptive to the people that it both serves and is constituted of. Used this way, government accountability is a catch-all term for the community's "conspiracy" to encourage the government to do its job and to ensure that there is an honest and straightforward connection between government principles and goals to its actions.

Community networks can be part of the campaign for government accountability that proceeds along the two avenues of confrontation and cooperation. The new community needs to *confront* the government when it is failing—when it's wasteful, unresponsive, secretive or corrupt—and to *cooperate* with the government when it is succeeding—when it's prudent, responsive, open to public discussion and direction, and honest.

Community networks can play important roles in opening up the governmental process to public view. The new community needs to know what an agency's mission is and how its issues are being addressed. Its activities must be monitored continually, perhaps through associations created specifically to monitor individual agencies. The process of engagement can be initiated through face-to-face meetings. The goal is the creation of mechanisms that facilitate two-way communication, sharing of information, and that facilitate the development, implementation, and evaluation of joint projects.

It may be difficult for people in government—elected or otherwise—to accept a peer-to-peer relationship with citizens. It may also be difficult for citizens to feel equal to people in government. Yet a balanced relationship is required. The size, prestige, available resources, or other characteristics that the government possesses need to be disregarded—by both the governmental and the non-governmental parties—if a meaningful relationship is to develop.

Government needs to be monitored and engaged, but the new community needs to also set its sights on business—particularly big business—to make it more responsive and accountable. Although engagement should not be construed as an attack, it should be construed as a serious *challenge*. Although the government is unquestionably mighty in terms of resources, influence, and in innumerable other ways, an allegiance of principled new communities can also be enormously tenacious and powerful.

AGENDA FOR ACTION

> *Democracy is the most humane, the most advanced, and in the end the most unconquerable of all forms of human society.*
>
> Franklin Delano Roosevelt

The challenge of revitalizing the ailing political process in the United States and in other countries around the world is a daunting task, but the consequences of ignoring the challenge could be catastrophic. Community-network developers and new community activists need to work towards opening up the system by "lowering the cost" of political participation. Simultaneously, they need to work with individuals and organizations to develop and implement political strategies that will increase political participation, particularly among those who currently have little or no influence.

While improving access is important, other critical concerns that strike into the core of our national consciousness must also be faced. The first is economic. Since political participation is related to and constrained by wealth or lack of it, improving economic equity and opportunities is required if an equitable and genuine democracy is to be attained. On the other hand, since the political determination to address these issues is currently lacking, it is not practical to wait for economic reforms before developing projects in democratic and other core-value areas. As Robert Putnam has observed, economic vigor is often built on a base of civic associations.

Community networks offer the potential to shift the balance towards democratic participation and away from the powerful government and corporate sectors, yet the balance could very easily move towards increased government and corporate control. Democratic renewal will depend on a transformation of powerful economic forces, and this will require the cooperation of the rich, the poor, and those in between. Unfortunately, the more well-off may not feel the desire nor the need to work together to address this schism. As Robert Reich explains, "Increasingly the fortunate fifth are selling their expertise on the global market and are able to maintain and enhance their standard of living and that of their children even as that of other Americans declines" (Reich, 1992). It is important that we develop programs that engage *all* sectors of society and create a shared consciousness that makes it important to do so.

While we are improving access to democratic processes, it is also important to provide opportunities and the means by which people can conduct their own civic education. People need to feel inspired to participate. The alienation described by Goel earlier in this chapter will need to be replaced by hope and confidence. The key to this is increased power. Community residents need to have a genuine voice in the affairs of their community and in the broader community. Since people naturally avoid political activities that they feel are fraudulent or exclusionary, working towards legitimate and inclusionary processes will increase political participation. Furthermore, fundamental belief in the viability of the political system will only come after there have been some successes in the political arena. For this reason, working with the disenfranchised for political successes at the neighborhood, community, regional, and international levels will help build both expertise and confidence, as well as help restore the critical "mediating structures" whose absence William Greider has noted.

Alexander Meiklejohn says that "democracy is the art of thinking independently together." At a minimum, this means that a modern democratic society has the responsibility to uphold Robert Dahl's criteria. Working with the new community, it should be possible to create a *strong democracy,* a democracy that's inclusive and just, a democracy that is greater than the sum of its parts.

Chapter 5

Health and Well-Being

Medicine is a social science and politics nothing else but medicine on a larger scale.

Rudolf Virchow (Miller, 1973)

In the future half of us will be "mentally ill."

David Byrne, "In the Future"

HEALTHY COMMUNITIES

The health of a community is determined by the health of its citizens and by the well-being of the community as a whole. If the physical, mental, or emotional health of citizens is poor or is declining, the health of the entire community suffers. On the other hand, if the community itself is not healthy—if health care is inadequate or not affordable, if physical conditions are unsafe, polluted, or ugly, and if basic emotional support among citizens is lacking—the health of its citizens will be diminished. Community health and individual health cannot be separated.

There is now a growing realization among health-care professionals, especially among public health nurses, that health is not just the absence of disease in individuals; the concept of "health" must be considered in a more holistic way so that health is directly linked to "broader social, political, economic, and physical environmental components" (World Health Organization document, 1986) that must be addressed if the goal of a healthy society is to be realistically addressed. In other words, the concept of *health* care must include and expand upon the traditional focus on *medical* care. Whereas *medical* care is primarily concerned with curing the sick, health care is additionally concerned with issues such as poverty, nutrition, the environment, public safety, education, and mental health, to name just a few. "Health" is a broad, proactive perspective that links numerous other aspects of life into a whole. Thus health—or wellness—is best thought of as a holistic amalgam of physical, mental, and emotional well-being that exists in individuals as well as communities.

Health and Wealth

Victor and Ruth Sidel, writing in *Reforming Medicine* (1984) state that "it is difficult to believe" that in the late 1950s "there existed a feeling that medicine in the United States could be effectively reformed bit by bit, piece by piece, to meet human needs." Now, approximately 10 years after that statement, the optimism has faded even further. The price of medical care has skyrocketed while the number of Americans with adequate and affordable health care has declined. Along with trends in other areas, the health gap between rich and poor has been expanding, and children, frequently, are the victims of this widening gap. People without economic means often must wait until a disease turns deadly in order to obtain professional assistance in an emergency ward. A 1990 report in the *New England Journal of Medicine* (McCord and Freeman, 1990) reveals that men in Bangladesh, one of the poorest countries in the world, have a better chance of reaching 65 than a man in Harlem. Forty percent of men in Harlem reach the age of 65 while nearly 80 percent of white men in the United States do. Also, pollution of various varieties finds its way into poorer communities, which lack the resources to change its destination, rally against the source, or defend itself from the pollution. With poor communities weakened in several ways, it becomes increasingly costly to treat problems, and health resources are often withdrawn, resulting in an implicit triage operation.

While children, the aged, the poor, and minorities in both urban concentration and rural isolation are the usual victims, increasingly the middle class is vulnerable to treatable diseases that may kill or merely bankrupt. Other troubling health statistics about middle-class people are emerging. For example, more than one out of every three children in the United States is overweight, highlighting the poor nutrition habits of children who increasingly feed on salty, sugary, and starchy junk food. Lack of exercise also contributes to this problem. The long hours spent watching television apparently can cause physical as well as mental weakening.

There is an implicit assumption that the rich can disassociate and distance themselves from the poor, both physically and emotionally, by moving to the suburbs, away from the turmoil and conflicts of the city. Television—and possibly computer-based entertainment of the future—also establish artificial environments divorced from the vexing realities of life. From the health perspective, running away from problems doesn't seem to work. From a strictly selfish viewpoint, ignoring the health issues of some segments of the population may be penny-wise and pound-foolish. Examples abound in this area, and include the renaissance of "extinct" diseases like smallpox or tuberculosis, the return of old diseases in deadly new forms, the diminished power of antibiotics through overprescription and overuse, and the possibilities of new epidemics rising from diseases spawned in poverty-stricken and polluted neighborhoods.

Money, as we have seen, plays an inordinate and unconscionable part in people's health and well-being. Although out of the scope of this book, it is worthwhile to call into question what role that the free market should actually play in the health process. Victor Fuchs (1983) raises these issues cogently.

> Health is the outcome of a process that involves patients and health professionals working together; mutual trust and confidence contribute greatly to the effectiveness of that process. However desirable it might be in other markets, an arms-length, adversarial relationship between buyer and seller should not be the goal of health-care policy. It is one thing for a healthy individual to choose among competing health plans, and another to expect a sick patient to shop among competing physicians and hospitals. Not only is cooperation between patient and physician often essential in the production of health, but cooperation among physicians is also valuable. Thus, the atomistic competition that economists set as the ideal market structure for producing and distributing most goods and services is far from ideal for health care.

American health care (and research money) is skewed towards expensive, high-tech, heroic-measure, hospital-oriented, highly specialized treatments rather than less expensive, prevention-oriented, primary care, and community-centered treatment. Changing this orientation would reduce the overall national health-care expenditures while significantly improving the health care of the disadvantaged. However, those in the broader community—at least in the United States—have shown through their antagonism to health-care legislation their apparent indifference to any shift in emphasis.

Health and Culture

According to Victor and Ruth Sidel (1983) "A particular kind of depersonalization concerns patients with a set of cultural beliefs that are not shared or understood by the health worker." This depersonalization may offend or make the patient uncomfortable, but may also lead "to failure in diagnosis and treatment as well."

The Sidels present a picture of some Puerto Rican patients that illustrates this issue. Many of these patients "classify illnesses, medicines, and foods according to an etiological and therapeutic system derived from the ancient Hippocratic humoral theory of disease." This theory states that a healthy person should have a "moderately wet, moderately warm body" and the four humors—dry, wet, cold, and hot must be in a state of balance. In this system, "cold" diseases are treated with "hot" medications, and so on. Thus some "pregnant women may be reluctant to take iron supplements or vitamins, which are considered hot, because they believe that hot foods and medications will cause the baby to be born with a rash." This lack of knowledge—or lack of respect—on the part of health practitioners regarding various non-Western cultures (including Asian cultures and native American cultures) breeds distrust between patient and the health practitioner. If the web of community is well-integrated, the culture of the community and the "culture" of the health care in the community will complement each other.

Health and Food

Food and water are prerequisites for survival. Beyond mere survival, the type and quality of food can help promote a longer and healthier life, or dictate a shorter and less healthy one. In many rural areas and in low-income urban areas residents must contend with food that is less fresh, less nutritious, and more expensive than the food found in upper-income, urban, and suburban areas, as information from several sources indicates. A team from The University of California Graduate School of Architecture and Urban Planning, for example, discussed their findings in a 1993 report (Nauer, 1994). They demonstrated, for example, that a family of four from South Central Los Angeles using the government's "thrifty food plan" would spend more than a family of four shopping at a nearby middle-class suburb. The report also reveals that South Central Los Angeles has nearly 25 percent fewer supermarkets per capita than other areas in the county. As pointed out by Kim Nauer in *The Neighborhood Works,* a highly recommended community-oriented magazine, "Neighborhood supermarkets are particularly important because some 38 percent of the households surveyed did not have a car" (1994).

Community-Based Food Systems

The Los Angeles group took an interesting community-based rather than individual-based look at basic questions of food and hunger. According to Nauer, "the study concluded that a strong food system feeds a community in the same way that nutritious meals feed an individual. Conversely, an inadequate food system starves a community and directly contributes to the fraying and deterioration seen in many of today's inner-city neighborhoods." To help understand basic inequities and hardships related to food, Ken Meter profiled the neighborhood of Phillips, a poor, ethnically diverse neighborhood in Minnesota's Twin Cities metropolitan area (Nauer, 1994). Using data from a variety of sources, Meter paints a picture of urban poverty, no food cooperatives or farmers' markets, and severely limited access to supermarkets. (Supermarkets tend to have fresher and more abundant food than corner food stores, which tend to have higher priced and non-perishable processed and canned food.) This unenviable situation is compounded by the fact that there is little or no mass transit, although nearly half of the households do not own a vehicle, a situation that is echoed in poorer neighborhoods all over America.

Meter is to be applauded for his diligence in assembling this information, for it is a side of the story that is seldom heard. It is a story that community members—possibly with the assistance of academics or social activists—all over the world need to develop and use as a tool for social awareness and change. This "snapshot" of "food access" can be used to help a community understand its situation and begin to address its concerns, much the same as the "critical indicators" were developed and used by the Sustainable Seattle project, discussed in Appendix F.

Health and Education

The relationship between health and education is close. When people are ill or undernourished, they lack the attentiveness and energy to perform well at school. While this relationship is obvious, Jonathan Kozol (1991) provides many unforgettable examples of this link, such as the situation in a Chicago elementary school he describes:

> The school nurse, who walks me through the building while the principal is on the phone, speaks of the emergencies and illnesses that she contends with. "Children come into school with rotting teeth," she says. "They sit in class, leaning on their elbows, in discomfort. Many kids have chronic and untreated illnesses. I had a child in here yesterday with diabetes. Her blood sugar level was over 700. Close to coma level . . ."

When situations like this are commonplace in a community, the health or well-being of the community itself is obviously threatened. Community-network developers need to help develop "snapshots" of education and other community concerns. New community advocates need to work with individuals and community groups to ensure that these snapshots improve rather than deteriorate as time goes on.

TECHNOLOGY'S ROLE IN HEALTH CARE

Better understanding and use of these empowering tools and networks will both promote a new form of community and can accelerate the natural cycle of social and health change—helping people to move quickly and readily network, organize, educate, or advocate to meet their needs.

                                                          Ed Madara (1993)

It is important to develop approaches that overcome the limitations imposed by the impersonal, expensive, incomprehensible, and inflexible system of medicine that exists today. It is also important to develop approaches that improve the quality of health care for individuals and their loved ones who may be faced with illness or injury today and to change the system for improved effectiveness and deeper compassion for individuals and their loved ones tomorrow.

Part of the Problem

While medical practice is already geared toward the high tech and impersonal, researchers, supported by the U.S. Advanced Research Projects Agency (ARPA), are currently hawking a bizarre approach for the future. In the medical field, researchers look towards "teleoperating" or "on-line surgery," in which doctors in downtown or suburban compounds "operate" on someone located miles away. While viewing the subject on a video monitor (or—even more technologically bewitching—through a head-mounted virtual reality display), the surgeon cuts, sews, drills, sucks, and removes material from the "virtual" patient, while robot arms flawlessly mimic the surgeon's motions from a distance, directly interacting with the patient of actual (that is to say nonvirtual) flesh and fluid. That software bugs, miscalibration, transmission blackouts or delays could bring fatal results is not of primary concern at this point. Nor is the fact that expensive high-tech equipment is rarely—if ever—employed equitably, a fact that considerably undercuts the part of the sales pitch that claims that the technology will somehow address the health needs of the poor. Continued funding and the desire to push technology are more important concerns, and here the influence of cold-war infatuation with esoteric technology is clear: "We are closing the loop on the digital physician ... we can put a doctor in every foxhole" (Flower, 1994). The desire to substitute technology for services that people provide is rarely demonstrated more clearly than in a gee-whiz telemedicine article in *Wired* magazine (never noted for its subtlety). The subtitle of the article suggests that people should "leave Bill and Hillary" out of it and their pursuit of equitable health-care legislation—because of virtual reality, artificial intelligence appliances (with whom kids can "have a discussion about puberty and sex"), expert systems "that can learn," and telemedicine applications to battle zones, rural areas, inner cities, prisons, and mental hospitals.

Part of the Solution

While technology is not an answer by itself, it *can* be an element of the answer. The designers of CHESS (Comprehensive Health Enhancement Support System), a computer-based system, discussed below, have developed a list of six interrelated criteria for effective health information and communication, which can help in the evaluation of health-care-related computer systems. Each criterion is listed below, followed by a brief discussion of its implications.

Accessible

Health-care information and communication with others about health issues must be accessible to everybody. The most important barrier to accessibility is cost; to be truly accessible, costs should be very low. If technology of any sort is part of a system that provides information, it must be readily available and easy to use. This is one reason why telephones are often the cheapest route to health information.

Convenient

Although abundant medical information exists in medical libraries, this information is not readily available to nonprofessionals. The information is available in few locations—in big city medical schools, for example—and only then during certain hours. Telecommunications technology, obviously, could be used to overcome these constraints of time and distance.

Comprehensible

Once information is obtained, what good is it? What does it mean? How should it be interpreted? Information targeted at people who have been studying or practicing medicine for years will have little relevance to people outside this cognoscenti. Clearly this information must be significantly reorganized and restructured if it is to be truly useful to the average citizen.

Although people aren't incapable of penetrating the polysyllabic haze of medical-speak, the average person—particularly one under stress due to a medical emergency and the necessity of making major life decisions quickly—won't undertake or will give up prematurely in the search for knowledge from the traditional medical literature. Viewed from this perspective, a substantial amount of work and financial resources would be necessary for the transformation and general democratization of health-care information.

Timely

Needless to say, information, especially health-care information, is extremely time-critical. People need information when *they* need it, not when a doctor is available to tell them. They may come up with questions at 2:00 A.M. Additionally, people often have many questions, and they may not feel comfortable or calm enough to ask them all when talking to a health-care professional.

Nonthreatening

Although health-care workers generally strive to be unintimidating, their knowledge, prestige, or matter-of-fact demeanor can seem threatening, uncaring, or could act to cloud peoples' ability to think clearly and come to their own conclusions. Similarly, the physical surroundings of the clinic or hospital may be alien to the patient and may prevent independent and well-reasoned decisions.

Anonymous

Health-care discussions offer many situations where anonymity is appropriate. People are often embarrassed by their problems, which they don't want shared with the world. People are also embarrassed by their ignorance: They don't want to admit to not knowing about something that, presumably, everybody else knows about. Moreover, diseases involving sexuality or social stigmas are difficult to address in a public way. Finally, there are important concerns over privacy of data, insurability, and other insurance-related concerns. Computer systems *can* be designed in ways that preserve anonymity where appropriate, as well as preserve privacy of confidential information generally.

Controlled by the User

According to the developers of CHESS, "people understand more and make better decisions, when the information and support environment allows them to control how they receive and assimilate information" (Gustavson et al., 1992). In contrast many aspects of today's health-care systems make it difficult for a patient to have any control of the process. When that happens, people become demoralized and, consequently have reduced confidence and ability to take care of themselves and their family.

Improving Community Health

Ultimately what effects might we anticipate if we develop community-network services based on the criteria listed above? Several computer-based services are beginning to offer integrated, wide-ranging, health-related services to nonprofessionals. While the lessons are still being learned, the questions rephrased, and the projects revised, there are some useful insights that we can gain from current efforts.

The developers of the CHESS system suggest three major outcomes that network health-based systems should help bring about: (1) improved health status, (2) improved health behavior, and (3) cost-effective service utilization. These are useful goals for any system that strives to support health care in the community. Let's turn our attention to the CHESS and ComputerLink systems to see how these goals were addressed in two computer-based systems.

CHESS

The Comprehensive Health Enhancement Support System (CHESS), (Gustavson, 1992; Gustavson, 1993) developed at the University of Wisconsin in Madison and Indiana University in Bloomington, is a good example of an integrated computer-based health information system. CHESS program goals include increasingly involving persons in relevant health-care decisions, discussion, and knowledge. In the words of CHESS's developers, overcoming traditional barriers such as "limited accessibility, complex material that is difficult to understand, need for confidentiality, and limited financial resources" are the major goals. The developers assert that: "A computer-based support system can overcome or reduce many of these barriers, providing information and support that is convenient, comprehensible, timely, non-threatening, anonymous, and controlled by the user." Additionally, CHESS addresses communication and information needs through an integrated set of services that allow users to "anonymously talk with peers, question experts, learn where to get help and how to effectively use it, read stories of people who have endured similar crises, read relevant articles, examine their risks, think through difficult decisions, and plan how to regain control over their lives" (Gustavson et al., 1992). Furthermore, the researchers have evidence that shows (in the case of CHESS-HIV) reduced medical costs based on fewer or shorter hospitalizations that more than pay the costs of providing the system.

The chief researchers have developed content in six areas: (1) breast cancer, (2) AIDS/HIV infection, (3) sexual assault, (4) substance abuse, (5) stress, and (6) academic crisis. The researchers developed the information in each area after extensive assessment (including surveys, focus groups, and interviews) of the needs of people in each content area. The information was then organized into electronic form by an interdisciplinary team.

The CHESS system itself ran in the patients' homes on personal computers that were connected via modems to a central host computer. CHESS was conceived of as a "shell" or modular system that connected different types of services under one roof. There are currently nine generic services, including Questions and Answers, Instant Library, Getting Help/Support, Personal Stories, Expert Mail, Discussion Group, Decision Aid, Action Plan, and Assessments, that can be used for a wide range of health-care information and support needs. The Expert Mail and Discussion Group services support *anonymous* communication, so that the confidentiality of the user is guaranteed. The Action Plan component is geared toward helping those affected by a health crisis come to a decision and determine a realistic way for them to carry it out.

Users of CHESS rated its usefulness very high, and most indicated that they had very positive reactions to it. With the users of the AIDS/HIV services, several encouraging results were found, including decreased negative emotions, decreased interference of AIDS in their daily lives, and increased perceived control over their health care. An HIV-positive patient left the following message in the on-line Discussion Group that eloquently describes those feelings:

> I'm proud to say I've gotten as far as I have in the past couple of months because of this CHESS program. I feel as if I've grown by giant leaps and bounds, as if a whole new person has come out from inside me, it was always there but never came out, something like a spring flower. Thanks for all your great support and advice.

The underlying complexity of some modules raises some important issues. The Decision Aid module, for example, uses multiattribute utility models, and the Assessments module uses a Bayesian model of probabilities. Robert

Hawkins, one of the project researchers, reports that these modules are not difficult to use, and that patients with low levels of education actually used them more than those who had completed higher levels of education. Complex software, nevertheless, carries greater inherent risks than simple software. Complex software, for example, is more likely to have undetected bugs that produce inaccurate results under certain conditions. Complex software is also less likely to show a direct relationship from user inputs to software output, which could be confusing to a user that wanted a cause and effect explanation.

Another major issue, of course, for our litigious society is the legal issue: What legal responsibilities are involved when health information is supplied *indirectly* over computer networks? In the case of offering advice in a public forum (e.g., using a community network) where no doctor/patient relationship has been established, the advice giver must make it clear that any "advice" is taken from standard medical references and that it should not be construed as a directive—thou shalt do this or thou shalt not do that—for individual patients. Thus the "advice" comes from the realm of information-providing, not from the realm of doctor prescribing actions to a patient. In the case of CHESS, developers have placed more attention on the decision *process* than on the *decision*. According to Hawkins, "The most valuable part of these decision aids is not the math, but instead the path of being led to consider what one's options are, and which considerations matter more than others."[1]

ComputerLink

Another computer-based medical information system, ComputerLink (Brennan, 1992), was developed in conjunction with the Cleveland Free-Net, one of the earliest community networks. The system is intended to promote collaboration between Alzheimer's disease caregivers and health-care professionals and between caregivers themselves who use the system to exchange information, advice, and emotional support. To this end, ComputerLink provides three services: information, communication, and decision support.

Information in ComputerLink is provided via an Electronic Encyclopedia containing over 200 pages of relevant information that has been organized around four major topics. These topics can be browsed screen-by-screen, selected via key words, or found through a computer search of specific words or phrases. The communication component provides private e-mail among

---

[1] Personal correspondence.

participants; an unrestricted bulletin board called The Forum, in which all users can read the others' messages and post their own comments or questions; and a Q&A area, in which the nurse moderator answers questions submitted anonymously on the system for others to see.

Early evidence from the ComputerLink project suggests that the *indirectness* and anonymity provided by computer-based systems, may make computer-based systems more popular than telephone-based services offering similar capabilities. Although privacy of records is an important concern that networked computer systems tend to make more problematical, the issues that arise in the health context are of special concern. While the Code of Fair Information Practices discussed in Chapter 8 provides general guidelines for privacy, computer-based systems like the ones above raise vexing questions about what is being done with the information, especially when the information is sensitive. Is it stored for future use or distributed to other sites? If the data are used in scientific analysis, how is the information about specific—yet anonymous—individuals maintained without being linked to *specific* identities? Answering these questions is particularly important when the effectiveness and usefulness of the system depends on the (guaranteed) anonymity of the users. The experience strongly suggests that privacy must be *designed into* these systems at the onset and must remain an important consideration through the life-cycle of the system. Privacy can't be patched onto a system after the fact, nor can it be added on after a haphazard or minimal effort. For these reasons, privacy advocates will need to scrutinize the development, as well as the use, of these health-related systems carefully.

These new computer-based health services also raise the specter of health care with no human contact, just as the computer-networks phenomenon raises the specter of "communities" of people that never encounter each other face to face and education without teachers. While computer-based aids and—especially—computer-mediated conversations can be of great value, they must be regarded as intriguing possibilities that *may* play some role in human-centered community health care in the new community. Reinvigorating the human side of community health is more important than merely injecting technology into it.

HEALTH IS A COMMUNITY CONCERN

The welfare system is being dismantled at the moment whenever more helpless human beings are being generated. Child welfare agencies, with all their contradictions, are being devastated as more abused and neglected children are forced upon them. We are laying off teachers and closing schools while we open more prisons. This is the legacy a society in decline leaves to its children: the disruption of the gossamer network of mutual responsibilities we call "community."

Matthew Dumont (1994)

Howard Rheingold, in his highly original book on *The Virtual Community* (1993) relates several stories about how the health problems of an individual acted as catalysts that helped draw people together into communities of shared concerns, interests, and goals using computer networks. In one example, a frequent contributor to the WELL's parenting conference informed the other participants that his seven-year-old son had been diagnosed with leukemia. Rheingold reports that many people sent supportive messages and several others—including two doctors—also started contributing to the discussion. Other people began to provide firsthand information based on their experiences as patients with blood disorders. The participants became increasingly knowledgeable in a multitude of health issues from the physiological to the political to the practical. Since health is a central issue to every individual as well as to the entire community, bonding and organizing around health and well-being is a natural outgrowth of these discussions. The shared experience recounted by Rheingold—including the happy news that the boy's leukemia yielded to chemotherapy—illustrates the power of health concerns in a community.

Ray Oldenberg, author of the *Great Good Place,* also develops persuasive arguments for a strong connection between community and health. He argues that Americans' love affair with self-help programs, prescription-drug treatments, and other individualistic approaches to mental, physical, and emotional health show how the retreat from community has eroded collective health. The deterioration of community health from stress-related symptoms is also suggested by statistics of America's prescription-drug consumption. Oldenberg (1991) quotes researcher Claudia Wallis to make this point, "It is a sorry sign of the times that the three best-selling drugs in the country are an ulcer medication (Tagamet), a hypertension drug (Inderal), and a tranquilizer (Valium)." According to Oldenberg, belonging to a community generally diminishes the need for drugs and therapy.

By focusing on the individual, society has built an environment that degrades the community. "Our cities frequently make us sick," as Oldenberg points out (1991). As a society we've let public places become ugly, hostile, dirty, and dangerous, while commercial establishments and malls with sculpture, fountains, and private security forces become increasingly elaborate and expensive. Mike Davis, in his book *City of Quartz* (1992) and in other articles, has written persuasively on this topic as it applies to Los Angeles. He describes the virtual Balkanization of Los Angeles into sectors of luxury malls, walled neighborhoods, and "free fire zones." In Los Angeles' Skid

Row, home to thousands of homeless people, Davis reports, there are *no* public toilets. The last one was bulldozed down several years ago by the Community Redevelopment Agency.

While Davis describes *conscious* efforts to segregate people by income and race, contrary to all hopes for a "civil society," James Howard Kunstler writing in *The Geography of Nowhere* (1993), has chronicled the steady, largely unconscious, erosion of public space accompanied by the individualistic suburbanization that has occurred throughout the United States, segregating people into enclaves according to economic class. The rich shop in luxurious stores and travel to Europe and Asia, while the poor languish in dangerous and depressing squalor, and those in the middle class spend their nonworking hours in sterile strip malls and television torpor.

HELPING COMMUNITIES WITHIN COMMUNITIES

> *To whom do most people turn for help with their day-to-day problems? Social workers? Physicians? Psychologists? Nurses? Counselors? Therapists? These professionals are part of the picture, but they are not the primary or first-line sources of assistance for most people most of the time. Research by community psychologists and others has shown that most people usually turn for help to friends, relatives, neighbors, co-workers, and even acquaintances. When professional assistance is sought, clergy, teachers, and physicians rank highest on the list; however beauticians, bartenders, and the like also rank high.*
>
> Garbarino (1983)

Health is more than physical health; it includes mental, emotional, and psychological well-being and connections to the community. In particular, community-computer networks can help support the ad hoc development of human networks that undergird community health.

The New York Youth Network

The New York Youth Network is a computer-based network that first came on-line in 1987 and is devoted to serving the needs of disadvantaged urban youth (Fig. 5.1). Rather than focus on information or educational resources, this network focuses primarily on critical areas in the psychological development of young people. These areas (which are often neglected and misunderstood) include communication skills and self-esteem. In addition, NYYN's users increase their familiarity and comfort with computers, as a

Figure 5.1 Using the New York Youth Network

useful side-effect of using the computer to communicate. Their reading and writing skills are improved through communicating with each other, commenting on issues, and sharing their experiences. The founders of the NYYN feel that users' confidence in themselves and in their ability to communicate is bolstered through using the network.

NYYN is a text-based system with an extremely simple and intuitive user interface. It's currently running on an old 286 computer and accessed through eight dial-in ports. The system is accessible at no cost through a number of community-based organizations (CBO) in New York, including Playing to Win sites (discussed in Chapter 3) and the Door, a large multiservice center for youths that includes an alternative high school. At any given time, 8–25 CBOs have access to NYYN and between 250 and 800 youths have accounts on the system. The CBO generally picks up the costs for telephone usage. NYYN executive director Ellen Meier and NYYN co-founder Orlanda Brugnola believe that there is virtually no limit to the number of youths who'd like to use it: Finances are the only limiting factor.

Brugnola, NYYN's on-line counselor, notes that the network provides alternatives to traditional writing venues: "Kids that have trouble writing *for school* may not have the same trouble writing for the network."[2]

---

[2] Presentation at Computers for Social Change Conference, New York. June 11, 1994.

From the NYYN Poetry Corner

The stench of confusion lingers in the air,
Causing misunderstanding and argument—beware.
I think no one understands themselves,
And therefore, they can't anyone else.
I have seen the problems from misplacement.
I have felt the wars brewed from argument.
There is no love if there's none for ourselves,
There's no peace in a world so disheveled.

Jessica Ortiz

Figure 5.2

There is a poetry corner on the NYYN (Fig. 5.2) as well as several discussion forums on relevant topics. Parenting, for example, is an important topic because teenagers are often unprepared for responsibility of this magnitude.

Over the years, members have helped each other with personal problems and have communicated to the whole membership in times of distress—to everyone's benefit. For example, when one young woman mentioned that she lost her boyfriend in an accident resulting from a foolish stunt, she was answered by another young woman who had lost her boyfriend, who had been killed in an argument over a car. The messages of both of these grieving young women were in a public discussion group, and both had words of concern and caution for all the readers on NYYN. The opportunity for such interactions is part of what makes NYYN unique in these young people's lives.

Providing an "arena for rehearsing" is one of the most important needs met by the network. Because peers often have a greater impact than adults in young peoples' decision-making (see, for instance, Rice and Atkin, 1989), NYYN has written scenarios for young people to "role-play" on-line. Role-playing in this way provides an environment in which individual young people can "practice," in private, responses to classic teen issues. NYYN believes that when young people rehearse their behavior, they may find it easier to make responsible decisions in actual situations. Several scenarios for dating have been written for network use.

Meier believes that networks offer three intrinsic attractions to the population that NYYN serves. "Young people really love to use computers and these young people rarely have access either at home or school. A second motivation is the opportunity to communicate with others in the relative anonymity of an on-line environment. Bypassing the traditional cues of race, ethnicity, even gender, NYYN members can move beyond stereotypical interactions. Finally, by creating an environment based on their interests, the network becomes a 'place' that is theirs. This sense of security helps even those with literacy problems persevere within our communications environment."[3]

Meier believes that the information that NYYN should provide is also of personal nature—information that is not readily available elsewhere. This stems from a need to counter the misleading or inaccurate information that the media or peer groups dispense, some of which may have come electronically. Although peer-to-peer communication is of primary importance, Meier and Brugnola are planning to develop a "Dear Abby"-like service in which youths can submit questions to the NYYN counselor and other social-service professionals to augment or clarify information obtained elsewhere.

Electronic Mutual Help

People helping people, providing mutual assistance, has always been a cornerstone of the American tradition. Alcoholics Anonymous groups, for example, currently meet in thousands of locations across the United States to help provide understanding, support, and conviviality for recovering alcoholics who are struggling to remain sober.

While not a substitute for face-to-face contact, electronic discussion groups centered around mutual-help topics offer an increasingly popular and convenient way for large numbers of people to communicate with each other. These discussion groups allow people who are in remote locations, who work long or awkward hours, or who find travel difficult, to participate in conversations on topics of concern. Also, people suffering from uncommon conditions or ailments will generally have fewer people close at hand who are in similar situations with whom to discuss common concerns.

Ed Madara of the American Self-Help Clearinghouse recounts the important implications of the development of these electronic mutual help groups in the passage quoted at length below:

> Networking has often been the first activity leading to the early identification of new or growing health/social problems, the organization of actual mutual aid self-help groups, and the development of more formal health and social service organization. The seeds of many long-standing health foundations, societies, and agencies dealing with

---

[3] Personal correspondence. June 17, 1995.

various health and social problems have generally first taken the form of mutual-aid self-help groups or networks. These community support services were often created by individuals and/or families as they networked with one another and became aware of both their common needs and their abilities to help one another through group support and action. These small informal networks are often the first to provide support, information, skills sharing, education of professionals, and needed advocacy.

Madara goes on to say that, "The increased use of such computer networks could therefore help promote the more rapid and increased development of new self-help organizations that provide needed support, education, and advocacy for new or developing health issues or problems" and that more people will be participating in mutual-aid efforts and self-help communities as the technology becomes more widely available.

The opportunities afforded by computers have not gone unnoticed or underutilized. Ed Del Grosso who operates the Black Bag BBS in Wilmington, Delaware has an on-line listing of over 300 BBSs on health-oriented topics including addictions, disabilities, and health issues. Some of these BBSs include: Health Source BBS in Florida; Health Wisdom BBS in Nevada; HEX, Handicapped Users Exchange in Maryland; the Recovery BBS in Virginia, which has a special focus on adult children of alcoholics; the Friends of Bill W. BBS in California; Doc in the Box in Missouri, the Neuropsychology-Bound BBS in Ohio for head injury and stroke; several AIDS information BBSs; an OASIS BBS for overeaters, and many others for chronic fatigue syndrome.

Similar services are offered via Fidonet, an international network of message store-and-forward home computers, which hosts a variety of "echoes" or "conferences" on health-related concerns, according to Madara (1993). These Fidonet "echoes" include: Holistic Health, Grand Rounds Medical, AIDS, Alcoholism and Drug Abuse, Child Abuse, Diabetes, Disabled Interests, Nurses Network, Public Psychiatry, Overeaters, Social Services, Spinal Injury, Stroke/CVA, Visually Impaired, Deaf Users, Stress Management, and more. Forums also exist on SeniorNet, Compuserve, Prodigy, America Online, Delphi, and other networks. The Tallahassee Free-Net contains disabilities information, while the Denver Free-Net provides the Colorado Health Care Building and The Heartland Free-Net provides a Medical Center. Usenet, the large Internet-based "news" network has literally hundreds of newsgroups including sci.med.aids, sci.med.nursing, sci.med.telemedicine, sci.med.occupational, sci.med.nutrition, sci.med.diseases.cancer, alt.support.mult-sclerosis, alt.food.fat-free, alt.infertility, talk.politics.medicine, sci.psychology, and misc.kids.pregnancy. The Institute for Global Communications (IGC) system offers a wide variety of on-line periodicals and discussion groups including those devoted to global and third world health issues, news regarding children's health, bulletins from Physicians for Social Responsibility and discussions of repetitive strain injury and health-care reform. Many new Web sites are also cropping up. The NPTN site, for example, has pointers to The Clinic, which, in turn, contains pointers to other health-related sites, including sites of the United Nation's World Health Organization (WHO) and the U.S. National Library of Medicine.

AIDS Info BBS

One block off Market Street in the heart of San Francisco's Castro Valley, one of the most AIDS-devastated communities in the world, 73-year-old advocate for People with AIDS (PWA) Ben Gardiner has been operating the AIDS Info BBS system (Fig. 5.3 and 5.4) since 1985.[4] When he started the system, the only available information on AIDS was found "on telephone poles" and in the growing number of public meetings and articles in the gay press. It was within this information-scarce environment that Gardener launched the system. Much of "the information was simply not available anywhere else." Using BBS software developed by Mark Pearson in the year preceding his death from AIDS, the AIDS Info BBS soon attracted callers from all over the United States.

There were two main objectives for AIDS Info BBS: providing information—including newspaper and magazine articles and essays—and providing an Open Forum for discussions on all issues regarding AIDS. Although Gardiner excised a small number of postings that were inappropriate, all of the approximately 7,500 postings are still available on-line, forming an important historic community archive. Gardiner characterized the postings as varying from very rational to highly emotional: "People's anger was important." In his view, the first 5000 postings are "more interesting," reflecting community interest, concern, and outrage with the AIDS epidemic, than the subsequent 2500 or so postings. This change is probably a result of an increase in the amount of information available on AIDS, but it also could be because the BBS "was being swallowed by the Internet." The system used to get 25–40 calls a day, but is now down to between 3–10 a day. At the same time, the gopher site at San Francisco State University that contains the entire Open Forum archive, "Ben Gardiner's AIDS Database" has been receiving 400–2000 reads per day, demonstrating some interesting patterns of electronic use within communities of interest.

Many of the 8000 registered users on the AIDS Info BBS are now dead.

[4] Information in this section is based on telephone conversations and personal correspondence.

```
=========================================
               AIDS Info BBS

        Copyright Ben Gardiner 1994

        Free since July 25, 1985.

       Over [ 12564 ] items to view.
     Educated opinions and information.
     Suggestions for AIDS patient care.
        No medical advice given here.

    Please delete E-mail after reading.

=========================================
  1> Articles          : [4640 items] News, Articles,
                          Book Reviews
  2> Q & A             : Commonly Asked Questions
  3> OPEN FORUM        : [6750+ items] Public Message
                          area
  4> Resources         : Names & Phones lists
  5> Library Files     : Statistics, Stored Daily
                          Summaries
  6> Daily news items  : summarized from publications
                          everywhere
  7> Therapies         : Discussions, Threads, &
                          Reports
  8> Periodicals       : [521 items] Newsletters
  9> Calendar          : Scheduled Events on AIDS
 10> About this System : Information, Help and History
 11> Utilities         : Change User Settings
 12> What, Index, Who  : What's new, who called; word
                          research
 21> KEYWORD(s) SEARCH : one or two words
 22> ITEM COUNT        : prints the actual count
 23> PROTOCOL DOWNLOAD : via XMODEM
  h> Help.
  e> E-Mail.
  d> Directory of topics.
  g> Goodbye. Terminate session.

Top Level: Enter selection (or ?): 1
```

Figure 5.3   AIDS Info BBS — First Screen and Top-Level Menu

```
 0> Return to top-level menu.
 1> Wall St. Journal          : [3396 items] 1984 to
                                present
 2> AIDS -- How?              : Speculative Articles
 3> John Lauritsen            : on AIDS & Treatment
 4> Peter Duesberg            : on the HIV virus
                                theory
 5> U.S. Government Papers, Work : 1986-1993: Koop, and
                                now CDC
 6> Reviews: Books,Plays,Videos : and publication
                                lists
 7> News                      : Coverage of events,
                                conferences,
                                references
 8> Healing Ways              : alternative healing
                                treatments
 9> sci.med.aids              : from 100 to [200
                                items]
10> Miscellaneous             : Additional materials
11> Books now available       : [67 items]
12> Rethinking AIDS           : [ 1362 items] on two
                                lower levels
13> Holonet discussion group  : [ 107 items]
14> Rethinking AIDS discussion : [ 518 items] on two
                                lower levels
21> KEYWORD(s) SEARCH         : one or two words
22> ITEM COUNT                : prints the actual
                                count
23> PROTOCOL DOWNLOAD          : via XMODEM
```

Figure 5.4 AIDS Info BBS — News, Articles, Book Reviews Menu

Gardiner keeps no record of those, but assumes that a person that has used the system actively and stops for a year or two is probably dead. Nor does he reuse login names—every name on the system is unique and along with the archive itself is part of a living memorial, like the Alameda County War Memorial in Chapter 2. As a 73-year-old, Gardiner has survived a devastating epidemic from which most of his friends have died. Running the BBS is a "healthy response to the problems in his community" in Gardiner's view.

The system contains a wide variety of essays and articles of interest to PWA and a calendar of upcoming events. Circumstances have forced the

AIDS community into a crash course in a number of areas that are nearly incomprehensible to the average person. These include esoteric descriptions of how various drugs work, the life-cycle of diseases, and the minutiae of insurance, of government processes, and of bureaucracy. Most important, the educational process is collaborative—people ask questions and others will answer them as best as they can. There is little cause for competition or flaming—as there is a shared sense of struggle against a life-threatening enemy.

Health information including "cures" and therapies have historically been popular topics with new (unregulated and nonmonopolized) media. The fascinating book on *Border Radio* (Fowler and Crawford, 1990) describes in detail the wide range of medical misinformation that beamed across the American border from various powerful radio station outposts in rural Mexico. With products ranging from "Crazy Water Crystals" to goat-gland transplants, the electronic pitchmen used the airwaves to sell pills, salves, and cures for a profit, sometimes becoming rich and/or politically powerful in the process.

While Gardiner abhors censorship and considers it generally more odious than the information being censored, it is obvious that conditions are ripe for misinformation. The major problematic aspect, of course, is the literal life-and-death importance of such information. In addition there is a growing impatience with medical, insurance, and government approaches to the situation, and there is the seeming indifference of the "straight" community to come to terms with the epidemic.

Although conditions exist for electronic quackery, the AIDS Info BBS community is apparently taking a philosophical approach to the situation. Every posting that I saw that described a therapy (or "cure") was accompanied by a disclaimer that explicitly or implicitly acknowledged the very real possibility that it might not work as advertised or even that it might be a fraudulent solicitation. Although it is still possible that a reader of the information may be duped into false hopes, the free exchange of this information is the recommended course. Other forums, sci.med.aids on Usenet, for example, ask posters of "unusual or unorthodox" information to back it up by providing reference information. In any case, deliberate fraud, whether conducted in person, over the phone, or on a community network system is illegal and the perpetrators (*not* the community network organization) should be prosecuted.

MADNESS Listserv

MADNESS is a communication and information service for "people who experience mood swings, fright, voices, and visions." It is an electronic distribution list—or listserv—that allows anybody with an e-mail account to easily send messages to and receive messages from the entire group. In the words of Sylvia Caras, "The list is used to further low-cost exchange of information to serve cohesion and mutuality, and support increased power for 'people who' [experience mood swings, fright, voices, and visions]."

According to Caras, who started the listserv, "There is an intention to involve users of mental health services in their services and to have users directing their own care." This intention is much in keeping with other "rights movements" such as the civil rights and women's movements in that people are requesting equal consideration under the law as well as the right—as citizens in a democratic state—to participate with respect and dignity in the decisions that influence their lives.

Participants in this listserv are often participants in the C/S/X movement, for consumers, survivors, and ex-patients. The discussion on the list ranges from the immediately pragmatic to broad philosophic and political visions. Although the listserv discussion is unmoderated and uncoordinated, there is a strong coherent foundation of shared experience, values, and respect.

There are questions on the list about specific drugs: One participant wanted to know, for example, whether Ritalin is ever prescribed for children. A list of all medications was posted along with the ironic comment, "Certainly takes a lot to keep us in line.<g>"[5] One participant asked why medical patients have telephones and psychiatric patients usually don't. Besides asking questions and raising issues, many people offer their own "war stories" of actual situations. One participant had investigated the use of "seclusion orders" at a state hospital and found that their use was specifically forbidden by the Joint Hospital Accreditation Manual for Psychiatric Hospitals. This participant pointed out that knowing the rules and regulations that govern hospitals can be very useful to a patient in protecting him or herself.

Although it has not been universally so, mental patients have historically been incarcerated, shackled, drugged, operated upon, and shocked. Even with today's greater emphasis on rights, self-help, and respect, "almost all current activity and advocacy . . . is supported by local and national mental health systems and associations, and by grants," according to Caras. Caras and others believe that this approach is too indirect and "dulls the philosophic edge of the grass-roots user movement" and has high administrative costs. In addition, electronic distribution is more immediate and far less costly: "There is no postage, no envelopes, no address labels, no folding" (or copying)! Some participants have introduced the idea of coordinating efforts to address common concerns. One participant suggested a demonstration project in which policies and procedures would be rewritten to replace the concept of involuntary treatment.

---

[5] <g> is the typographical notation for "grin."

Although Caras is enthusiastic about this media, she realizes there may be some resistance to the technology. Some of the audience that she is trying to reach feel that radio and television may send "targeted messages" or speak directly to them. Caras feels that the nature of computers is interactive and "at the control of the operator" and hence "the medium may be acceptable."

Judi Chamberlin, an active participant on MADNESS, and an associate at the National Empowerment Center in Lawrence, Massachusetts, posted an eloquent case for psychiatric survivors that appear in her speech "The Right to be Wrong" (1994).

> For all the people confined in psychiatric institutions against their will, for all the people confined in group homes and congregate living facilities, for all the people confined by the internal walls of forced drugging, for all the people confined by the lost memories and broken brains of electroshock, I say: We will not wait! Our struggle is being fought today, on many fronts, by many brave people, who want nothing more than the chance to live our potentials, to take chances, to succeed, to fail, to try, to have opportunities, to make mistakes, to achieve, to change our minds, to be foolish, to pursue our dreams.

ENVIRONMENTAL JUSTICE AND INJUSTICE

I had experienced a miscarriage that same year, along with a neighbor. But we did not think anything of that. It was just coincidence. We made no connection to the children's health problems, or with the odor in the water.

Cathy Hinds (1992)

Increasingly, people are making the case that environmental degradation contributes to community degradation and is a key motivating factor for social and political activism and organization (Mann, 1991; Highlander, 1993). Environmentalism needs to be concerned with inhabited areas and the built environment as well as with the largely uninhabited and natural environment. Toxins and other pollution in the community contribute to disease and shortened life spans, and less obvious factors such as noise pollution and an ugly, repressive, and unsafe manmade environment take their toll as well. A liquor store specializing in cheap, fortified wine or an unsafe park, seen in this light, becomes an "environmental hazard" for an entire community.

Lower-income groups use fewer resources and consequently cause less environmental damage than people with higher incomes; at the same time they are forced to bear a larger share of the consequences because of their relative inability to resist. In many cases environmental injustice is strongly related to economic injustice.

Environment and Health in the South Bronx

In the South Bronx community in New York City, the archetypal benighted urban neighborhood in New York City, one finds grim proof of the tight interconnection between economics, health, community, and the media. In one of the most devastated areas of the country, where debris, broken glass, abandoned cars, and buildings dominate the landscape for literally hundreds of blocks, there is one beguiling artifact that beckons from thousands of locations: billboards. As Michael Kamber has written "On nearly every corner, on the sides of abandoned buildings, and in empty lots the shiny, slick billboards are plastered. The bus stops and subway entrances and building tops, everywhere you look, there's an ad staring back at you" (1990).

In a neighborhood of oppressive poverty and massive unemployment, what products would warrant such exposure? Sadly, the answers are alcoholic beverages and cigarettes, which, according to the Centers for Disease Control are the first and second most-advertised products in the black community and Latino community, where 90 percent of all alcohol and cigarette billboard advertising is located. In these communities the ratio of alcohol and cigarette ads to food ads is approximately 80 to 1. And while fresh food may be nearly impossible to obtain, liquor stores are ubiquitous. In South Central Los Angeles, the site of the massive 1992 civil unrest, liquor stores are over 10 times more prevalent than in the rest of the city (Nakano, 1994).

Dr. Charles Schade of the American Public Health Association sheds some grisly light on the consequences of *legal* drug use on low-income communities (summarized in Fig. 5.5) based on (pre-AIDS) mortality statistics

Cause of Death Related to Alcohol and/or Tobacco		
Rank	*Cause of death*	*Related to alcohol and/or tobacco?*
1	Cardiovascular disease	yes
2	Cirrhosis	yes
3	Homicide	yes[1]
4	Cancer	yes[2]
5	Drugs (illegal)	no
6	Diabetes	yes
7	Alcohol use	yes

[1] 50% of all homicides are related to alcohol.
[2] Lung cancer is the most common cancer.

Figure 5.5

from the Harlem district of New York City, clearly showing the lethal link between alcohol and cigarettes and mortality in poor communities. While cigarettes are responsible for 350,000 deaths per year, deaths from illegal drugs are roughly 1/70 of that. Ironically, the "war on drugs" costs $9 billion a year, dwarfing by a factor of over 200 the money spent on tobacco education.[6]

Public Safety and Violence

In 1969, seven years before the bicentennial of the United States, Graham and Gurr (1969) wrote an 822-page comprehensive and authoritative study, the *History of Violence in America*. That study provides details of some of America's more unseemly proclivities, including lynchings, vigilantism, race riots, labor violence, political assassinations, police oppression, as well as criminal violence. The drive-by shootings, teenage suicides, and domestic violence that have erupted since the book's publication could undoubtedly provide material for another chapter or two.

Violence is expensive and everybody helps pay the bill. In the United States, costs due to violence run to approximately $34 billion per year in direct medical costs (Mercy et al., 1993) and the medical costs of a single bullet wound are estimated at $30,000. Richard Blow, reporting on violence as a community health issue stated that, "In 1986 and in 1987 the most recent years for which statistics are available, 66,182 Americans died from gunshot wounds, more than died in nearly nine years of fighting in Vietnam." It is becoming increasingly common to view violence as a breach in public health (Mercy et al., 1993), a "disease" that afflicts communities, sometimes in epidemic proportions. The U.S. Centers for Disease Control in Atlanta is funding 15 experimental antiviolence projects across the country.

There are also costs to communities that go far beyond direct medical costs. The costs of security guards and sophisticated security systems are the fastest growing sectors in the U.S. economy, and the U.S. taxpayer must also bear the brunt of the staggering costs of incarcerating 1.3 *million* people (United States, 1994). Like other threats to our community lifeblood, violence—particularly the fear and isolation that comes from the perception and expectation of violence—results in *indirect* health care costs. These include therapist or psychiatrist fees, and the costs stemming from the use of prescription drugs, drugs for hypertension, anxiety, and other nervous disorders. The threat of violence also takes its toll in profound ways that can't be calculated in terms of dollar expenditures. Feelings of insecurity, unease, and apprehension act to diminish

---

[6] Some recent data suggests that smoking by African American youths may be declining. It has been conjectured that *community* pressure may be the main factor for this change.

the imagination, willingness to cooperate, and ultimate effectiveness of community endeavors. Thus violence erodes the health of a community by dampening its possibilities and its spirit, resulting in lost opportunities of incalculable proportions. All these costs—economic and psychic—are due at least in part to inattention and neglect of *community health*.

Although the flames of violence are often fanned by outside forces—cheap and plentiful hand guns, non-stop violence on television, and an economy that offers a very bleak future for many—the solution to the problem of community violence can't be dictated solely from the outside, any more than solutions to other community problems can. Violence is a community problem and must be addressed at the community level by community members who may or may not be working with outside institutions of the church, government or business.

Community Safety and PEN

In recent years, public safety concerns have begun to be addressed in more community-oriented and participatory ways. One of the most visible of these trends is the community-policing movement, where police take a more holistic approach to public safety by stationing officers in specific communities for relatively long assignments. This approach is used instead of assigning police to large territories (to traverse almost exclusively by car) or bumping them randomly from neighborhood to neighborhood while simultaneously liberating them from the burden of "harvesting numbers" (number of arrests, for example). Rather, police are granted the authority and flexibility to work with community members and organizations, to address community concerns in ways that are well-suited to the community. Inherent in this idea is the realization that public safety is a *community job* that can't be delegated in its entirety to a professional group. Community policing has its risks, such as favoritism and inconsistency, as well as promises. The biggest challenges come from the police bureaucracy itself (a paramilitary, hierarchically arranged organization) and from the community, who must be willing to put in the long hours that true participation requires while reconceptualizing the idea of police, and urging them to reconceptualize their own idea.

While a community network can't solve a problem like community violence, it can help facilitate the transfer of information that can be put to good use in the community. This might include information services that help support community policing, such as meeting notices, documents, and on-line submission of citizen complaints. The PEN system, for example, discussed in Chapter 4, provides several good examples of this material. Although PEN has public safety information on earthquake preparedness, emergency 911

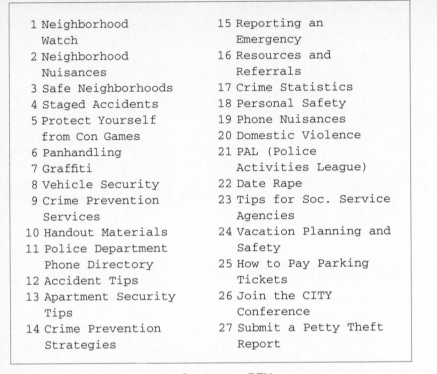

1 Neighborhood Watch
2 Neighborhood Nuisances
3 Safe Neighborhoods
4 Staged Accidents
5 Protect Yourself from Con Games
6 Panhandling
7 Graffiti
8 Vehicle Security
9 Crime Prevention Services
10 Handout Materials
11 Police Department Phone Directory
12 Accident Tips
13 Apartment Security Tips
14 Crime Prevention Strategies
15 Reporting an Emergency
16 Resources and Referrals
17 Crime Statistics
18 Personal Safety
19 Phone Nuisances
20 Domestic Violence
21 PAL (Police Activities League)
22 Date Rape
23 Tips for Soc. Service Agencies
24 Vacation Planning and Safety
25 How to Pay Parking Tickets
26 Join the CITY Conference
27 Submit a Petty Theft Report

Figure 5.6 Police Department Services on PEN

information, and information from the fire department, we will only look at the police department's collection of electronic services shown in Fig. 5.6.

PEN services include how to avoid problems, including "Protect yourself from con games" (Fig. 5.7) and "Apartment Security Tips", what to do if problems occur, including "Accident Tips" and "Phone Nuisances", how to work with the police ("Phone Directory," "How to Report an Accident," "How to pay parking tickets," and even how to "Submit a petty theft report" electronically), community information ("Crime Statistics"), and how to get additional "handout" materials (including "The ABCs of Self Protection," "30 Ways to Prevent Crime" (in Spanish), and "Senior Citizens Against Crime").

The Police Department also promotes community approaches to public safety. One way is by advocating on-line public discussion ("Join the CITY Conference") of community concerns. Another way is by offering tips on how to start and sustain a neighborhood watch. Although crime prevention is probably higher than community building on the police department's list of priorities, their suggestions of neighborhood block parties, housewarmings, picnics, and progressive dinners as part of the neighborhood watch

---

How to protect yourself from con games

Every year unsuspecting citizens are swindled out of their savings by con artists; smooth talking, often convincing criminals who seek by various schemes to separate honest people from their money.

  While these criminals prey primarily on the elderly, every one of us is susceptible; men and women, the successful and the unemployed, working people and the retired. You could be approached by a con artist almost anywhere, outside a bank or savings and loan, at a bus stop, at a Senior Citizens meeting, while you're shopping, or at your home.

  While approaches may vary, and the con artist may appear perfectly normal and friendly, there inevitably comes a time when you will be asked to withdraw money from your savings. The reason for this may seem logical; to show your "good faith". . . to help in the investigation of a "dishonest employee." BE ON YOUR GUARD. If you do turn over money to one of these people, even for a moment, you will never see it again.

Figure 5.7 Public Safety Information on PEN

program to prevent crime help to build community as well, which may ultimately be the best preventive medicine.

Other Network Responses

While we are discussing systems that provide information for empowering individuals and communities, three others deserve attention. The first, the Crisis Resource Directory on the Seattle Community Network, was developed by the Peace Heathens organization to provide survival information for street youths. The guide, originally produced as a printed booklet, contains information on social services as well as on emergency food, shelter, and medical resources. Advice is given on how to respond in dangerous situations that may arise when living on the street, such as being menaced by skinheads or other racist groups.

The thoughtful and innovative Center for Neighborhood Technology in Chicago has developed a Neighborhood Early Warning System (NEWS) that combines statistics from a number of municipal and county government sources to help illuminate warning signs of possible community decay by using seven problem indicators. These indicators (including building code violations, property tax delinquencies, fire records and others) are obtained from a variety of incompatible databases and combined as part of "an affirmative neighborhood-information strategy" to "more effectively counteract housing abandonment, commercial decline, and financial disinvestment in Chicago's inner city neighborhoods" (CNT, 1995). The NEWS system is available to people at various public access terminals and also provides electronic conferencing facilities and e-mail for people to discuss neighborhood issues. The Center has also made some NEWS information available on their Web site (see Appendix B).

RTK Net, originally suggested by Patricia Bauman and currently administered by OMB Watch, a Washington-based public interest group, was made possible through a 1986 law that requires the U.S. Environmental Protection Agency to make data publicly available by computer telecommunications and other means. RTK Net, (named for the people's "right to know") provides information on quantities of emissions of toxic chemicals by manufacturer in a community or zip-code area. RTK Net has already proved valuable in several community struggles. A construction union in West Virginia, for example, discovered information that was useful in helping to block legislation that would have allowed increased dumping of carcinogens into the state's rivers. The system has also been used by activists in Utah to help them limit toxic waste dumping in that state (Leslie, 1995).

These three examples illustrate the importance of information to communities. With thought, education, advocacy, and activism, community-network approaches such as these can be effective weapons in the battle for community health and well-being.

AGENDA FOR ACTION

Health care can become a force for social change that is not always universally desired. The medical care system has as much vested interest in maintaining the status quo as do the political and economic systems. Health care is intricately tied to social and economic status, to access and control over resources. If one seeks change in health status, through community participation and control, then one will certainly alter the existing economic and political systems.

John Hatch and Eugenia Eng (1983)

Although community health and well-being is deteriorating in many ways, there are also some hopeful signs. One is that there is a renewed interest in *community* health in contrast to *individual* health. The other is that a more holistic view of health is emerging, one with an increasing emphasis on *health care* rather than *medical care,* in which public safety, nutrition, housing concerns, environmental, economic vitality, and psychological well-being are all central issues.

The entire community needs to participate if community health is to be improved. Individuals and their families need to be aware of health issues and do what they can to ensure a healthy life for themselves. Groups in the community organized around health concerns and issues—be they Alcoholics Anonymous, groups of walking seniors, or bicycling enthusiasts—need to raise consciousness and to lend mutual support. Health-care professionals also have a role to play. They can provide the community with useful, timely, and comprehensible information. This information can help people and their community make informed decisions in times of relative well-being as well as in times of individual or community crisis or natural disaster.

The dialogue among the community participants and health care professionals should be used to develop a community consciousness on its relative well-being and to develop a community agenda for health that can be used proactively in the formulation of public policy. Community networks can help engender this dialogue.

Chapter 6

Economic Equity, Opportunity, and Sustainability

If I had the choice of being rich or poor, I'd choose being rich . . . I'm not stupid.[1]

Dottie Stevens, Welfare Rights League

In the future there will be a classless society, no one will be richer than anyone else.

David Byrne, "In the Future"

THE IMPACT OF TECHNOLOGY

Human existence is a complex tapestry of activity, so distributed yet so densely interwoven that it might be considered as a single organism or giant brain. In an organism or brain, however, the smallest units are usually considered reflexive and *non*thinking. Humans—the smallest unit of the social sphere—are sentient beings capable of *independent* thought. For that reason, the actions of individuals or communities are somewhat autonomous and somewhat subservient to the collective: Every person plays a role in the ongoing evolution of the entire system.

The complex rhythm of human life has dramatic differences between it and that of other organisms. For one thing, our adaptation is largely in reaction to *social* changes—not in reaction to *environmental* changes. Thus people are both master and slave to the social conditions they create. Another difference is humankind's domination over the environment of the earth itself which dramatically dwarfs the effects of all other animal species. While the ever-increasing numbers of people and their habits of consumption coupled with their disposition towards travel, agriculture, and war may not be cata-

---

[1] Statement made at Directions and Implications of Advanced Computing Symposium. Cambridge, MA. April 23, 1994.

strophic in the short run, the effects in the longer run may be so sudden, profound, and unanticipated that humankind may be unable to adapt quickly enough. Even though humankind has the power to make substantial changes to its own social sphere and to the physical environment within which people live, many changes are occurring at rates higher than at any other time in humankind's existence. It is possible to create conditions under which humans cannot survive.

The case of the automobile is particularly relevant here, for it shows the way in which a technology can completely, and unexpectedly, come to dominate the social, economic, and environmental patterns of communities and nations if not ultimately the entire world. The world has been essentially redesigned for the convenience and pleasure of the automobile with little or no *conscious* citizen participation in this process. The case of the automobile also illustrates the naive faith that some elements of humankind—particularly in the American sector—have when it comes to technology. People have been guinea pigs, often willingly, in a massive global experiment. Almost the entire fabric of American life has been modified for the automobile. It has dictated where people live, work, and shop. Neighborhoods have been destroyed, replaced to a large degree by highways and strip malls. But can the car last? Geologists believe that there may be fewer than 50 years of oil in the earth from which to refine gasoline. The average American, however, believes that a new fuel source *will* be found. A technological deus ex machina will arrive just in time to enable the suburban family of the future to drive to the shopping mall. People aren't quite sure what this new fuel will consist of. Perhaps it will be an elixir concocted from moonbeams and cucumbers.

Looking back on the impact of the automobile over the last 70 years should provide ample reasons for somber reflection. It's conceivable that people might learn the biggest and most lamentable lesson last, however. That's the possibility that we can create problems that are too big for us to solve. Humankind might be like the paradoxical God that was so powerful that He could create a rock that He couldn't lift.

The Need for a Sustainable Future

The effect that humankind's collective patterns of production, distribution, and consumption will likely have on the physical environment and the associated social relations are difficult to understand and perhaps more difficult to avoid. Many scenarios are grim. As Thomas Homer-Dixon and his colleagues have reported in their ominous *Scientific American* article, "Environmental Change and Violent Conflict" (1993), scarcities of renewable re-

yardsticks, they restrict humankind's capacity for creativity while denying its convivial instincts and values. Benjamin Barber, whose thoughts figured prominently in Chapter 4, believes that the main problem with focusing on economic thinking, "is not that it asks men to be greedy or competitive, but that it asks them to be *unimaginative*."

The reduction of all human action to economic transactions is apparently aesthetically and psychologically satisfying to some people. It allows the messy "flesh and blood" aspects of the human experience—life, death, unemployment, poverty, etc.—to be represented abstractly as numbers and equations. Searching for the elusive and accurate numbers becomes a game that takes precedence over addressing real problems. It provides a set of prepackaged rationales for the status quo. Thus a "natural rate" of unemployment, poverty, or malnutrition, for example, can be hypothesized from statistical data and become a part of the conceptual infrastructure that shapes the way that people view economic reality.

While the desire to simplify and therefore "understand" a complex phenomenon like an economic system with equations and/or platitudes is very strong and altogether human, there are several dangers to this approach. The first danger is that people believe the simplifications and act as though they accurately and comprehensively reflect reality. The second danger is that people defend the simplifications and act as though they cogently and compellingly reflect a reality that ought to be. The latter danger is demonstrated by the strong forces that strive to keep the slogans and ideological perspectives of American free-market capitalism as sacrosanct. Thus the wealthiest classes who feel they have the most to lose generally strive (and usually succeed) in shielding the system from scrutiny, analysis, and democratic adjustment. To accomplish this, the system must appear scientifically derived, harmoniously self-regulating, morally correct, technically incomprehensible, and so perfectly tuned as to defy adjustment. Furthermore, it must be *dominant*—all the popular notions of equity, democracy, and freedom must be subservient to it.

The dominance of economic thinking also helps to place a focus on money *itself* rather than its *uses*. Thus the millionaires and billionaires of the world generally have few ideas what to do *with* their money except to buy more things. While the media scoffed at Imelda Marcos's shoe-buying mania, the money-spending habits of many of the world's wealthy citizens are no less self-indulgent. While Andrew Carnegie may have amassed his fortune in nefarious ways, his funding of hundreds of libraries in the United States has gone unmatched by the newly minted megarich whose public contribution is generally limited to optimistic prognostications. Undoubtedly their entourage of lawyers and accountants would prevent them from expansive public investment even if they were inclined in this direction.

A CRITIQUE OF CONTEMPORARY ECONOMIC PRACTICE

The animal spirits of business are being released. Risk will bring its own rewards.

Business Week, October 17, 1994

Mellon pulled the whistle
Hoover rang the bell
Wall Street gave the signal
And the country went to hell.

—Song sung at march on Washington by the unemployed,
1932 (Piven and Cloward, 1979)

Current economic practices are so widespread and pervasive that neither their fundamental assumptions nor the consequences of their actions are challenged in a meaningful way. As we shall see in the sections ahead, ignoring this ubiquitous force in the vague hope that everything will come out OK may be a very big mistake.

The Inherent Bias of the "Free Market"

With the demise of planned economies in the former Soviet Union and other places, it is clear to some that the capitalistic system has won, and with that, its obvious economic—and moral—superiority has been established, much in the same way that a football match determines the superiority of one team over another. Of course, the idea that *exactly* two possible economic systems exist is a fantastically constraining and simplistic belief. In truth, there are any number of ways in which economic systems could be established. Given all these possibilities, the challenge is to establish an economic system (and to modify existing ones) in such a way that it creates and distributes goods and services in an equitable and sustainable manner. Unfortunately, the current system falls short in both equity and sustainability.

People seem quite willing to ascribe a mechanistic or autonomous power to the "hidden hand" of capitalism. Yet a universe of focus groups, marketeers, advertising firms, real estate agents, trade associations, stock brokers, tax lawyers, corporate lobbyists, business reporters, regulatory bodies, chambers of commerce, banks and other individuals, organizations, and business-oriented periodicals (like *Forbes, Business Week,* and *Fortune* to name just three) is devoted nearly full-time to maintenance and manipulation of the system itself. The "invisible" and nonmanipulated hand that Adam Smith described two centuries ago is largely irrelevant today in the face of the vast capitalistic machine.

The most obvious shortcoming of this vast system—so staunchly and absolutely defended against all breaches—is its profound and unrelenting bias toward the wealthy. Unbelievably, this obvious fact is somehow controversial and is not as readily acknowledged as the fact that humans need air, food, and water to survive. This intrinsic bias shows itself in two ways—both absolutely and fundamentally obvious. The first such bias follows naturally from the rules of the capitalist imperative alone: "There is one and only one social responsibility of business—to use its resources and engage in activities designed to increase its profits." (Friedman, 1962) People with little or no money have no existence in such a system. Without the tokens, they cannot play. Moreover, if the profit is greater on a luxury item than on a staple like food, the "logic" of capitalism decrees that the luxury item should be produced, satisfying the "needs" of the wealthy before the needs of the poor. "Commerce between master and slave," as Thomas Jefferson pointed out, "is despotism." Interestingly, the idea that extreme differences between economic classes may be inimical to democracy is shared by many thinkers on the right as well as those on the left.

The second bias is only slightly less obvious, though its truth and power generally do not escape those on the lower economic rungs. The bias is succinctly captured in the populist rewording of the "Golden Rule," which states that "the ones with the gold rule." Companies and individuals with ample resources to draw from are better equipped to exert their influence than those who aren't. Lobbyists from corporations don't need to take a day off from work to convince senators that additional corporate tax breaks are necessary. That *is* their work! Again, a short survey of the educational opportunities, health care, quality of life, safety, economic opportunity, democratic participation, and representation in governmental decisions, that are available to the poor versus those available to the rich, confirms this simple yet critical fact. This overarching bias must factor into any discussion of community networks if the new medium is to promote economic equity and opportunity, rather than reflecting or even accelerating the built-in biases of the current system. Computer networks—including community computer networks—will probably come to be dominated by the rich, as are almost all other aspects of society. Strong activism, solidarity, and perseverance will be necessary if this trend is to be checked even slightly.

Fundamental Economic Inequities

In the United States and elsewhere, children learn the beauty and the truth about capitalism from a variety of sources. Parker Brothers, the American game manufacturer that sells the "Monopoly" board game in which players buy, sell, and improve properties in an effort to drive the other players to bankruptcy, is one such source. In this game, each player begins the game with the same amount of money ($2000) and with equal holdings of property (none). No property is "inherited" from previous games. This "monopoly" is quite "fair" since everyone has an equal chance at the beginning of the game. A new revision of Monopoly—a reality-infused edition—could be easily devised to portray a more accurate situation. Only two changes are necessary. In the revised game, *all* the properties are owned *before the game begins* but *not* in a random distribution: 90 percent of the properties will be owned by 5 percent of the players. In the obsolete, inaccurate version, each player received $200 each time their marker moved across the space marked "Go." In our updated version, those without property must *pay* $200 when they pass "Go," and those with property receive a share commensurate with the property they own. To make the new game even more realistic, property-owning players would be able to change the rules as they deemed necessary to ensure their continued good fortune. If this change were made, it would boost the reality quotient still further. But why bother? Why not just play the real game? Although the revised game hasn't been test-marketed, my sense is that some players might find the game very satisfying while the majority would somehow feel that the odds are staked against them. Of course, if the winners can dominate the press . . .

Some hard facts: In 1973, one out of nine Americans was classified as poor by the U.S. Census Bureau, and by 1991, one out of every seven Americans was considered poor. One of every five *children* was considered poor. (Poverty is closely linked to educational and health problems, and the United States has one of the highest degrees of inequality in distribution in the developed world.) The United States also has the highest proportion of single-parent families (mostly female-headed) in the world, and the poverty rate among the children in female-headed households was 55 percent in 1991. While food, housing, and energy costs rise, jobs are becoming scarcer and the wages of the jobs that are left are dropping. New York City lost nearly a half million jobs between 1970 and 1984 (Schwartz, 1994a), while Philadelphia is currently losing about 1,000 jobs a month (Schwartz, 1994b). These staggering job losses may also have more ominous implications for the future. South Central Los Angeles, the scene of the 1992 riots that left 51 people dead and over a billion dollars in property damage, lost 75,000 blue-collar jobs between 1978 and 1982. The devastation of virtually all community safety nets, in employment, education, and recreation, as well as the "government betrayal" of the community is brilliantly portrayed by Mike Davis in *City of Quartz* (1992), his social and political history of Los Angeles.

"Downsizing," corporate newspeak for reducing the workforce through large layoffs, is currently taking its toll. In 1994, record job losses were tallied up in the telecommunications industry (itself a high-tech industry that is *still* touted as an engine of employment). The irony of this was not lost on 5,000 Bell-Atlantic workers who were slated to be sacked: 1200 employees came to work sporting "Road Kill of the Information Superhighway" T-shirts, much to the annoyance of their supervisors who told them to remove the shirts. Much to the displeasure of the company, this face-off over the road-kill T-shirts was prominently featured on the local television news that evening.

There is compelling evidence that economic inequities of alarming proportions, already commonplace throughout the world, are becoming increasingly unbalanced. We can get a broad understanding of this in both relative and absolute terms. In relative terms, we need to examine the differences between some fraction (say one-half, one-third, one fourth, or one-fifth) of the families at the economic top and that same fraction of families at the economic bottom, according to various economic indicators. In absolute terms, we need to look carefully at the lives of those at the bottom in terms of their health, amenities, living conditions, and overall outlook.

As Republican political analyst Kevin Philips has comprehensively documented, a profound upward transfer of wealth from the economic lower classes to the upper classes has occurred in the United States since the 1980s. From 1977 to 1988, the bottom four-fifths of families experienced income losses while the upper one-fifth's income increased. The changes at the extremes were the most pronounced. While the average family in the lowest one-tenth lost approximately $610 a year of income, for a drop of minus 14.8 percent, the upper one percent saw their average family income rise $134,513, for a gain of nearly 50 percent! The tax code in the United States has also undergone fundamental changes, mostly to favor corporations and wealthy Americans. As William Greider has pointed out (1993), leaving the tax code unchanged since 1977 would have resulted in a simpler and less expensive tax burden for nine out of ten American families. Tireless tinkering by corporations through their Washington lobbyists (now numbering over 90,000) coupled with steady congressional compliance has steadily shifted the tax burden from corporations to individuals. Based on this evidence, it is easy to conclude that corporate lobbyists are far more numerous and successful than people's lobbyists, an asymmetry that was clearly unforeseen by the framers of the U.S. Constitution.

Not only is there vast inequity in terms of economic well-being, there is increasing evidence that suggests that joblessness, homelessness, poverty, and other current signs of a dysfunctional economic system may become a *per-*

manent feature of global international capitalism. Robert Reich in *The Work of Nations* (1992) suggests that the economic fate of the "fortunate fifth" and the "unfortunate fifth" are becoming *decreasingly* co-dependent: "As the economic fates of Americans diverge, the top may be losing the long-held sense of connectedness with the bottom fifth, or even the bottom four-fifths." This economic segregation makes it increasingly difficult to use resources controlled by the "fortunate fifth" in any program, including community networks, that is designed to aid the "unfortunate fifth."

The "Logic" of Global Capitalism

When the worldwide depression hit in the late twenties, there was no shortage of factories, workers, or natural resources. As reflected in the 1932 song lyrics at the beginning of this section, the average person on the street appreciated that fact and realized that it was the *system* itself that had collapsed. Today communities are even more dependent on the "system" whose connection to community life is increasingly mysterious. U.S. currencies, for example, have had to be propped by emergency interventions involving billions of dollars, while banks and multinational corporations transfer trillions of dollars every day electronically.

In the years since the Great Depression, recessions of varying severity have cropped up regularly. Some were expected—many were not. Some had classic symptoms and many did not. Communities bore the brunt of these economic traumas unequally: Some prospered while others floundered. Many communities have been unable to get back on their feet from economic hard times that hit several years ago. High unemployment has often led to decreasing investment in education and health care, and to increasing social ills—street crime and drug use, for example.

The Great Depression is the most jarring and violent demonstration of an economic system that self-destructed, leaving communities and individuals without opportunities or the means to support themselves and their families. Unfortunately, global depressions on the same order of magnitude as the Great Depression are still possible in the future. Just as the Great Depression resulted from conditions that the economics of the time forced into being, society could be plunged into another worldwide economic catastrophe. Yet conventional wisdom insists that we accept this situation as a given.

As these depressions and recessions underscore, modern capitalism shows a capricious, unmerciful, and unwavering disregard for community and individual life. We *should* be surprised (as Thorstein Veblen was) at the everyday sanctity of capitalism. However, if we use the concept of *sanctity* as our point of departure, it is easy to see capitalism as a new force of nature that people can neither comprehend nor influence, in other words like a new God. With this perspective we begin to see a gigantic network of priests extending from Wall Street (the Vatican?) down to local talk radio show personalities and chambers of commerce (parish priests?). While the argument that portrays capitalism as a new God may be farfetched, the argument that says it is perceived as a "force of nature" is not. The average person sees capitalism as a natural force that exerts constant pressure, but can also cause sudden dislocations, like lightning or earthquakes, that strike suddenly and without warning. In general, capitalism to the average person is something that can be suffered through by keeping one's head down, not rocking the boat, and "looking out for number one"—not questioning the precepts, altering the conditions, or designing alternative systems. To continuously and unquestionably subject ourselves, however, to the potentially jarring and seemingly immutable "logic" of present day capitalism may be a formula for disaster.

The Death of the Job

Jobs—when they exist at all—are increasingly seen in one of two ways: as those for symbol pushers who intellectualize and work with abstractions (stock brokers, computer programmers, and lawyers, for example) and those for other pushers (hamburger pushers, cart pushers, automobile accelerator pushers, data input pushers, and assembly line pushers, for example). Symbol pushers get paid more than other pushers and the number of symbol-pushing jobs is growing slowly. The number of nonsymbol-pushing jobs, on the other hand, is declining rapidly and the wages are dropping just as quickly. It's getting more difficult to support a family on a nonsymbolic job wage. As corporate strategists have made perfectly clear, any job that can be automated *should* be. And any job that can be made simpler through automation *should* be. De-skilling—the process of simplifying jobs—will result in fewer jobs and less well educated—and therefore cheaper—employees to do the jobs that remain. Unfortunately, attempting to make individual companies more profitable in this way impoverishes the rest of society in many ways.

Apostles of the information age in general, and the electronic networked age in particular, are ballyhooing many of these trends. Thus they champion libraries without librarians, education without educators, and factories without factory workers. Indeed, as the cover story of the September 1994 issue of *Forbes* magazine proclaims, "The job itself is now 'dead'—jobs are being replaced with job searches." Downsizing all of these institutions so that they no longer need anybody to run them will likely result in increased numbers of "surplus" people, human beings for whom the system has no immediate need. In line with their general faith and trust in machines and systems over people, some of these information-age apostles are arguing that society should no longer attempt to educate these "surplus" people—for doesn't that just follow "logically" from economic principles?

COMMUNITY NETWORKS—A PLATFORM FOR CHANGE

Past

New people coming from many places. Settle in little neighborhoods with people of their kind. They stick together and name those areas, "uptown," Chinatown, skid row, Pilsen, "Little Italy," . . .

Present

People are still coming to settle but they are more scattered, more mixing, mixing names, ancestors, colors, but sharing the same problems.

    Down the road people begin to understand that time brings a change.

    Change comes in stages and struggle and each stage brings on a new way of life.

Kay Strauther (written during Chicago "Jobtech" conference)

Information can help people in communities. People who have need of goods or services or have something to offer may place a "want ad" in a newspaper, neighborhood message-board, or community computer network. People may need information related to employment, such as job listings, job counseling, and training, information on job searches, and information about unemployment benefits and other programs. This information could easily be made available electronically; applying for unemployment assistance or other programs could also be handled electronically. Richard Civille, for example, in his study on "The Internet and the Poor" (1995) believes that civic and community networks could provide valuable "job bank" services.

    Unemployed people may also need training or access to other educational opportunities. They may want or need to meet with other unemployed people to discuss their feelings, job-seeking strategies, or even ideas about starting their own businesses. When there are large layoffs in the community, workers, their families, and other people in the community need a forum for discussing these issues or for raising concerns with the management of the company doing the layoffs. Workers, whether employed or not, are often isolated and powerless, and community networks could help provide a new platform for a public voice, organization, and solidarity.

Community members also need information and support on other economic issues such as how to start small businesses. They need information on available programs, legal requirements and regulations, banking and loans, marketing ideas, model business plans, and on alternative organizations like cooperatives. Organizations like the Better Business Bureau, the Chamber of Commerce, and the Small Business Association all have useful information on these topics that they can make available electronically. Kretzmann's and McKnight's book *Building Communities from the Inside Out* (1993) contains an invaluable section on "Rebuilding the Community Economy" and the Center for Neighborhood Technology also offers a useful guide (CNT, 1992).

Jobs and Computer Technology

Coincidentally, on March 2–4, 1995, in Chicago and in New York City, two conferences on nearly identical themes were convened. People at both conferences—"The Midwest Conference on Technology, Employment, and Community," (Alkalimat et al., 1995) and "The Wages of Cybernation—A Working Conference on the Future of Work"—discussed the ruptures that global capitalism and technology are causing in many local communities and appropriate ways to respond. By the time the conference organizers discovered the double booking of the weekend, it was too late to reschedule either event, to avoid competing for attendees. Each conference, however, was successful and had several hundred attendees. Each conference maintained a regional focus while simultaneously addressing the global issues that were intertwined with the local ones. Electronic network communication played an interesting role, however, in enabling both groups to overcome some of the barriers that the venues of the same time and different place had created.

Network technology has already helped various conference organizers to extend the reach of a conference beyond the conference adjournment and beyond the number of actual conference attendees by making papers, abstracts, and notes available electronically through FTP, gopher, or the World Wide Web (see Morgan, 1995, and SFC, 1995, for example). Both the Chicago and the New York City conference organizers did this also, by making the program, workshop notes, plenary speeches, reading lists, and relevant essays available on the Web (Jobtech, 1995). Beyond this, however, the new networking technology allowed the organizers of the conferences to exploit the simultaneity of the two conferences by facilitating active sharing of information and communication between the participants *during* the two conferences. This "virtual attendance" took several forms. For one thing, workshop notes were posted during or immediately after the workshop. For another thing, participants could electronically make comments on events or start conversations on other issues that concerned them (Fig. 6.1). Finally, Chicago organizers, Robin Burke and Kate Williams recorded scenes from the Chicago Conference with a digital camera which were also "published" on the Web sites. (Fig. 6.2).

Figure 6.1   JobTech Topics

Both conferences explored "work" in its present and emerging forms. The treatment of that subject was turned on its head from the conventional treatment offered by the news media. Instead of examining work from the corporate perspective—markets, data, downsizing, investments, and mergers—the view was from the individual and community perspective. Instead of viewing the current trends as being inevitable, pre-ordained, and "natural," the future of work and future economic systems were conceived of as mutable, human systems in which people could make a difference.

The "Let Us Proclaim!" workshop, conducted by Anne Schultz (Jobtech, 1995) at the Midwest Conference on Technology, Employment, and Community in Chicago, provides an excellent example of the future as a canvas or medium in which we can actively design and develop. The workshop used Carl Sandburg's poem about Chicago that begins, "Hog butcher for the world, tool maker, stacker of wheat, player with railroads and the nation's freight handler" to open the workshop, encouraging people to envision and write about a future of Chicago. Like the workshop attendees (some of whose poems are now on the Web site), we as a society need to envision a future that is compelling to us as individuals, families, and communities. Without vision—and planning—society is reactive, never creative.

Liberty Net

Liberty Net, the Web-based system in Philadelphia, Pennsylvania has one of the most comprehensive economic development sections of any community network (Fig. 6.3). It contains information on businesses and organizations, opportunities and economic programs. The Philadelphia programs include the Greater Philadelphia Chamber of Commerce, the University City Science Center, and the Philadelphia Unemployment Project. The University City Science Center (UCSC), a consortium of 28 academic and scientific institutions in the Northeast United States, is a self-described "business incubator" that has launched more than 215 start-up organizations, which now employ more than 4,500 people. UCSC provides office and laboratory space, business development services, and research management assistance to science and technology-based companies and is linked to similar enterprises in Europe, Japan, and the former Soviet Union. At the lower-tech end of the scale, the Philadelphia Unemployment Project (PUP), also has a presence on Liberty Net. According to the online information PUP is dedicated to "educating and organizing unemployed and low-wage people around services, issues and policies affecting their lives," and offers job readiness, résumé building,

Photo Gallery

Abdul Alkalimat, conference chair

Panel #1

Panel #2

Panel #3

Figure 6.2   JobTech Scenes on the Web

Economic Development and Opportunity

Economic Opportunity: News and Updates

- Delaware Valley Business Events
- White House Releases on the Economy
- White House Releases on the Economy
- Federal Reserve Board: Tracking the Economy (Includes Beige Book)
- White House Releases on Jobs and Labor
- Department of Labor: Employment and Training Media Releases
- AFL-CIO News Online
- White House Releases on Welfare Reform
- Welfare Reform Watch and Alerts: Handsnet
- Summary of Current Economic Indicators

Philadelphia Organizations:

- Philadelphia Marketplace: Online Directory of Business
- The Greater Philadelphia Chamber of Commerce
- Philadelphia Business Journal
- The University City Science Center
- PECO Energy Economic Development
- Community Opportunity Program, Institute for the Study of Civic Values
- Jewish Employment Vocational Services
- Impact Services
- The Philadelphia Unemployment Project

Local and State Government Organizations:

- Philadelphia Commercial Development Corporation
- Pennsylvania Small Business Development Center
- Philadelphia Industrial Development Corporation
- Ben Franklin Technology Center
- Licenses and Inspections
- Philadelphia-Camden Empowerment Zone

Figure 6.3 Community Development Information on LibertyNet

and client representation services. Access to these services is increasingly possible electronically, and all PUP staff project coordinators have Liberty Net e-mail addresses.

The local government (anywhere, not just in Philadelphia) can also involve the community in local economic decisions to a greater extent. Thus local tax, fees, income, expenditures, and budget information could be made available. Unfortunately, this could easily provide the catalyst for a "tax-payer's revolt" in which the goal of *reducing* the government takes ideological priority over *improving* the government or serving the community. In addition to engaging the community in discussions about the government's use of public money, the government can be proactive on other community economic issues. The local government could sponsor local forums on employment issues in the community, for example. The local government could also work with community members to design programs to retrain laid-off workers and hone their job-searching skills.

Community Voice Mail

People without access to communication technology—including telephones—are disconnected from the rest of society in many ways. Sometimes the implications are quite profound. Imagine a homeless parent whose child is ill, calling a clinic or information service for medical advice from a pay phone. In many cases, he or she may be told that somebody will call them back. But they have no telephone! Another common situation might involve a prospective employer who'd like to ask an additional question or even offer a job to a homeless person. In either case, the person without access to a telephone could find himself or herself seriously inconvenienced.

It has been noted that when people lose their residence, they often lose other connections with the rest of the community. Family, neighbors, friends, and social service agencies lose the ability to easily and reliably communicate with them. It has also been shown that without social links, shared physical spaces, and other accessible and dependable relationships, it is common for a homeless person to feel adrift and rootless, thus compounding the problem.

In Seattle, community activists, Pat Barry and Rich Feldman developed the Community Voice Mail (CVM) program which takes advantage of the fact that a person can "own" a phone number without owning a residence. Barry's colleague, David Harrison, asks, "Why should we tolerate human suffering that is easily avoidable?" The Community Voice Mail project provides free voice mail accounts to those in need, particularly homeless people, to help reduce human suffering. Barry suggests that we think of the project as a giant telephone answering machine for the homeless community. Working with dozens of social service agencies and a custom voice mail system (including computer, modems, special hardware and software that is made available at cost by the system vendors), CVM works towards providing a "stepping stone out of poverty." When a social service agency provides a client with voice mail, he or she is not given a physical telephone but a voice-mail *account*. When a person has a voice-mail account, he or she has a telephone number that potential employers, health-care providers, landlords, family members, or friends can call and leave messages. When the client dials the telephone number (from any telephone) of the voice-mail system and enters the password, he or she can listen to the recorded messages.

CVM is showing dramatic results. For one thing, the time that it took for clients to achieve their goals went from more than 30 days in over 75 percent of the cases, to under 30 days in over 50 percent of the cases. CVM also serves an integrating function. Generally one social service agency specializes in providing one type of service, yet homeless people rarely have just one problem. The voice-mail system provides a convenient way to coordinate information from multiple agencies as well as providing a tool to the homeless person for managing his or her own life in his or her own voice and language. The cost is now less than $2.50 per month per client, and economies of scale could drive this cost down even further.

Barry and Feldman started the Community Technology Institute (CTI) to promote the use of technology to help solve human problems and improve delivery of social services. To this end CTI promotes "in-house" technologies that are owned and operated by the community. The institute has articulated a "best practices manifesto" that includes (1) interagency collaboration; (2) accessibility; (3) ethics (including dignity, self-esteem, and privacy of the client) and (4) maximal use of technological resources. CTI's core work is replicating the Seattle experience in other locations. San Diego and San Jose, California; Portland, Oregon; Waltham, Massachusetts; and Raleigh, North Carolina; Madison, Wisconsin; Minneapolis, St. Paul, Minnesota; New York City and Schenectady, New York; and Aberdeen, Washington are among these sites, with some 10–20 others in operation or planned. The Institute offers a variety of useful publications, and Barry has been traveling across the United States to set up programs and the actual voice-mail systems. There are many possibilities for collaboration between voice-mail service providers and other types of "community technology" providers.

Organized Labor and Community Development

Organized labor has long acknowledged the global scope of its issues and is organized into "international brotherhoods." Of course, "international capital" is stronger in nearly every way than "international labor," and its worldwide influence is broader and more powerful. This asymmetry of power has become more profound in recent years with treaties such as the North American Free Trade Agreement (NAFTA). Interestingly, this loosening of bounds on international corporations may help to usher in a new age of labor activism that is truly international (Alexander and Gilmore, 1994; Browne and Sims, 1993). Certainly, international networks will make it easier for labor activists to keep in touch with others and share information and ideas. Also, using computer networks could enable the coordination of global labor responses to global corporate actions at employers' sites around the world. (Recently a strike was held in South Africa in support of a strike in New Jersey.) There is some evidence that organized labor is learning to use new telecommunications technology. There was widespread labor opposition to the NAFTA treaty, for example, and computer networks were used to a greater extent than ever before (Frederick, 1993a).

Organized labor—at least in the United States—has been losing strength steadily for several decades. This is due to some degree to the media that portrays it unsympathetically by concentrating generally on negatives: scandals or people inconvenienced by strikes, for example. Since 1947 when the U.S. Congress made many of labor's most effective weapons—including "secondary boycotts"—illegal, the law has been turned against labor in significant ways. (In Washington State, for example, it is illegal for any public employee—including school teachers—to strike.) The negative view of the majority of Americans toward organized labor is important to consider. Labor has been used in many ways as a scapegoat for batches of economic bad news in recent years, notably a downturn in American competitiveness. This downturn has played well into the hands of the owners of large corporations who would enjoy nothing more than unburdening themselves from the constraints that organized labor attempts to place on them. The "average man— or woman—on the street" who is becoming increasingly less likely to be employed in a union job is generally inclined—with persistent nudges from the press (with its probusiness bias) and politicians (whose main source of campaign contributions is from corporate interests)—to be turned off by organized labor. Ironically, spurning labor in the name of "independence" and "rugged individualism" has isolated the worker, leaving him or her powerless to resist the aggregated forces of government and corporate capital who feel no similar desire for "rugged individualism."

With labor on the defensive—or "flat on its back," according to some (Geoghegan, 1992)—it is difficult to conceive of an overarching strategy or organizing tactic to revive it. It is necessary, however, to revive the solidarity of working people as a critical element of the new community, because the overwhelming proportion of people in the United States and in the world are *working* people—or unemployed people who want to work. The labor community must strive to become more inclusive and to reach out to the rest of the community and to workers internationally. This is being explored in many ways, often tentative and experimental. Organizing has always been the by-word of the labor movement and the new information and communication technologies have the potential to play a significant role in the reorganization of workers and others. Labor today faces massive challenges as corporations reduce the number of employees by downsizing and by relocating plants and offices to places with lower wages, worker protections, and environmental standards. While dialogue about work and work-related issues must be carried on in the community, this dialogue also needs to cross community and national borders. Spurred on in part by organizing against the NAFTA agreement, there has been an increase in "cross-border organizing"; indeed Jesse Drew at the University of Texas has started a Web page on that topic (Drew, 1995). Large software programming projects have taken place over the Internet. Why not distributed organizing projects? By the same token the rest of the community should reach out to those in organized labor. Community networks should include information on unions and union events, labor laws (and which ones were being violated in which country by what companies) and historical information and recommendations for the future. Labor activists could also greatly benefit from knowing the positions that multinational corporations take at the bargaining table in North America and around the world. Economic justice is unlikely if working people are not organized and community networks and new communities are essential to the organizing of the future.

Recently there have been some notable examples of organized labor becoming involved with related issues including community and environmentalism. These include the Labor/Community Strategy Center in Los Angeles that links labor issues, environmentalism, and social justice together, and has issued reports on "Reconstructing Los Angeles from the Bottom UP" (1992), "LA's Lethal Air" (Mann, 1991), and projects of the Center for Community Economic Research in Berkeley (See Appendix A).

LaborNet

There are many labor related resources available electronically. LaborNet, a rich source of information and a forum for discussion on labor issues, is one of the services provided by The Institute for Global Communication (IGC) which also runs PeaceNet and EcoNet. According to IGC's on-line description, "LaborNet is a community of labor unions, activists and organizations using computer networks for information sharing and collaboration on a global basis with the intent of increasing the human rights and economic justice of workers."[2] To this end LaborNet offers a wide variety of electronic conferences on topics relating to worker issues in Asia and in the Commonwealth of Independent States, worker education issues, articles in the labor press, hazards in the workplace, and many others.

In addition to LaborNet, there are also many other labor-oriented services, including the LABOR-L listserve and the LaborLine BBS. Richard Rose, a student at American University, has compiled a list of electronic resources that is intended for use by labor reporters. The list contains a wealth of information on labor issues including how to get statistics from the government and how to get resources on unemployment and downsizing, unions, worker education, compensation, part-time work, disabilities, labor law, and work and family. There are also several Usenet newsgroups such as clari.news.labor and misc.jobs.contract (see Appendix B for specifics).

Rural Community Development

On the Big Sky Telegraph FTP and BBS site, a 1994 essay by the pseudononymous author "Rough Writer" (whose prose bears a striking resemblance to Frank Odasz's) catalogs a list of economic opportunities offered by community networks. Although these are written with rural communities in mind, the ideas are also relevant to urban inner-city communities whose physical distance from "the rest of the world" is not large but whose economic and other distances are just as great.

The first benefit according to Rough Writer is derived from putting the community "in better touch with itself." If information on both goods and services that were either needed or offered were made more consistently and easily available, then the "inefficiency" or cost of making a transaction would be minimized while the number of opportunities that were lost for want of a seller or buyer would also be minimized. Rough Writer notes that informal, neighborly, social needs could be part of this system. For this strategy of improving the efficiency of the market within the community to work, a community-network system must be widely used by both buyers and sellers, and the cost (in both time and money) of using the community network must be lower than the savings it provides.

Rough Writer also describes how the educational opportunities made available by the community network could help strengthen local economies. For one thing, education—particularly education on how to use the computer—makes it easier to participate in the local marketplace. For another

[2] Send e-mail to labornet@igc.org or contact IGC. See Appendix A.

thing, the community networks can provide opportunities to create more so-phisticated economic enterprises. "Aluminum can collectors could start a comprehensive recycling project," for example.

Rural or "placebound" residents are separated by large distances from the higher density clumps of human existence found in the cities and suburbs. Thus there is economic potential for rural people in telecommuting, that is, having a job away from your home that's accessible via "the wire" instead of being dependent upon the highway or air travel. Another aspect, telemarketing, or identifying and developing markets at-a-distance via "the wire," is also possible. Telecommuting, however, carries risks along with opportunities (Howard, 1985). Although telecommuters currently may not be exploited in what Barbara Garson might label the "Cybernetic Sweatshop"—after her *Electronic Sweatshop* (1989) that the computer has made possible—the possibilities clearly exist. With workers "just a modem away," some exploitive labor practices including child labor become viable, including electronic piecework. It would also become more difficult to ensure that workers did their electronic job under safe conditions. Older video-display systems can be particularly bad for users' eyes, particularly after long uninterrupted hours of use. Repetitive strain injury might also be more difficult to prevent, diagnose, and treat (Pascarelli and Quilter, 1994). Finally, although networks can provide remote work for people, they may cause additional alienation by dissolving whatever workplace community or solidarity existed before. As Craig Calhoun and others have pointed out (1986), the "edge cities" where much of this work will be (physically) done are noticeably lacking in civic and cultural amenities.

As a recent *Business Week* article mentioned, telecommunicating possibilities allow people who *already* telecommute to move into rural areas if adequate telecommunications infrastructure exists. Finally, rural community networks allow for better communication in general with "the outside world." Thus, for example, information about "little known tourism sites and experiences" (Rough Writer, 1994) could be made more widely available.

ACEnet

Ed Schwartz, longtime community activist and coordinator of the Liberty Net community network in Philadelphia presents two diametrically opposed visions of "economic development"—one of personal independence and one of community interdependence (1994a). To illustrate the first concept, he draws on the study of Western Eye Press of Telluride, Colorado, presented by John Naisbitt and Patricia Aburdene in their book, *Megatrends 2000* (1991) as an example of liberation that technology can bring about: "They edit and design their books on a Macintosh computer, create camera-ready art on their own laser printer, have the books printed in Seoul, Korea, and in Hong Kong, and sell to the world."

But if the Western Eye story is a "megatrend," then communities may be in deep trouble. Communities hold together and thrive through interdependence, *not* through independence. I am not picking on the Western Eye Press: I suspect that the Western Eye books are good and the owners are good Telluride citizens. However, the idea that "liberation" from the rest of humanity is a *solution* to current large-scale economic problems is misbegotten. What percentage of the population could be entrepreneurial enough to run their own publishing company? How big is the market for products produced from "home-crafted" industries? And what about the rest of Telluride? Do they benefit from Western Eye's presence? What do they owe to Western Eye, if Western Eye fell on hard times, for example?

Schwartz argues that economics—at the core—is built on relationships "between investors and managers, between managers and workers, between producers and consumers" (1994a) and he sees a greatly expanded role for telecommunications in the process of establishing and strengthening these relationships. Thus Schwartz believes that the community-interdependence model, in which economics is a web of relationships, needs more attention. Harvard Professor Robert Putnam supplies interesting corroborative information when he points to the new "network economics" in Asia and in Silicon Valley, where densely connected networks of relationships are partially responsible for the economic success of those regions (1993). He goes on to say, "These communities did not become civic because they were rich. The historical record strongly suggests precisely the opposite: They have become rich because they were civic." Focusing on the relationships—the network or web of community life—will have more impact, therefore, on improving the local economy than importing telecommuters.

The Appalachian Center for Economic Networks (or ACEnet) in Southern Ohio is adapting a network-based approach to flexible manufacturing that originated and has been highly successful in Italy to suit conditions in rural southeastern Ohio. ACEnet operates in eight counties there and is "committed to the development of a healthy and viable regional economy which empowers low-income people through participation in innovative, collaborative economic development strategies" (Holley, 1993). Their primary role is assisting small firms (see Fig. 6.4) to aggregate into larger flexible manufacturing networks (FMNs) that can quickly organize together to produce a specialized product (that they couldn't produce *individually*) that meets an unmet or emerging need. When the product is no longer profitable, the FMN disassociates.

Currently ACEnet has two major project areas—an accessible products

Ohio Manufacturers of Accessible Products
Flexible Manufacturing Project

Firm	Location	Capabilities
Stirling Technology	Athens	Manufacturing and mfg process development
AD•AS	Athens	Product design, mech. & electronic assembly development
BJ Hardy and Associates	Lancaster	Stainless steel and metal fabrication
LMP Machine	Zaleski	Metalworking and machining
Runge Machine	Logan	Metalworking and machining
Amanda Bent Bolt Co.	Logan	Bolt manufacturing to specifications
Industrial Technology Services	Athens	Electronic control and design
Alchemical Electronics	Amesville	Electronic control and design
Harry Dewar	Amesville	Graphic design, illustrations, renderings

Figure 6.4

FMN and a food ventures FMN. The accessible products project is based on the emerging needs of a population that is living longer but is also more likely to be confined to a wheelchair or be disabled in some way. This FMN has initially focused on manufacturing housing components that promote accessibility, including adjustable counters and cabinets, but it also produces tools that make other aspects of everyday life easier for people with disabilities, such as The Appalachian Easy Weeder, whose handle makes gardening easier for those with limited gripping strength. The food ventures FMN has identified niche markets in the food industry such as reaching people with severe allergies or people with specific ethnic or gourmet food needs. Since these FMNs are both community-oriented and collaborative, the enterprises can expand in interesting ways. The food ventures FMN can work with farmers' markets, buying clubs, restaurants, community colleges, agricultural extensions, and so on.

In her essay "Growing Sustainable Communities," (1994) ACEnet director June Holley lists seven *network* features which, although they ostensibly describe the noncomputer variety, are pertinent to computer networks as well. Networks, for example, "provide forums for discussions of mutual interest" and "provide the opportunity to 'map' people, resources, and ideas in order to better access them when needed." The ACEnet organizers are well aware of the potential of community telecommunications technology and are already working within The Southeastern Ohio Regional Free-Net (SEORF) on joint projects.

NEW AND IMPROVED ECONOMIC INSTITUTIONS

At the very core of the building challenge is the effort to revitalize the community's economic life.

John Kretzmann and John McKnight (1993)

Money—or property—often loses the taint of its sometimes unsavory origins as time goes on. Much of the land in the United States was taken by force from the native peoples that lived there, for example. Yesterday's drug lord or robber baron may become today's philanthropist or respected art collector. This process is also reflected in the everyday transformation of raw material into commodity. The bottle of wine, pair of sneakers, or child's toy doesn't betray its ancestry, which could include unsafe working conditions, environmental destruction, political corruption, or other ills. A network of community networks, however, could make this previously invisible information visible. If a company in one community is exploiting workers in order to lower the price of their goods in another community, the citizens in the consuming community are linked—generally unwillingly and unknowingly—to the hardship in the producing community. And since all communities produce *and* consume, the cultural and economic impacts of a given product have the potential to do harm to everybody. The new community can acknowledge this fact by acting in solidarity with other communities by judging products and services on more than the amount that appears on a price tag.

Information is the key to this type of accountability, because information forges the link from the raw material to the manufacturing and discussion as well as to the quality of the finished product. And this information can move quickly—faster than the product itself can be moved—and to several locations at once. As I write this, two prominent Seattle companies are under fire for conducting business with companies outside the United States that exploit their workers or have unsafe working conditions. After this type of public controversy, those two companies, and others, are more likely to be concerned about questionable practices that occur as a result of their business.

If there were no downside to corporate engagement, most businesses would strive to be good citizens in the community and in the world. Competitive pressures, however, and the lack of accountability linking corporate actions to public review can prod even the most public-minded company into engaging in unsavory practices. By citizens exposing the worst offenders, those companies that are acting responsively are protected and encouraged. Thus this type of information belongs on community networks, and individuals in the community have the responsibility to develop and disseminate this type of information.

Reinventing the Corporation

Corporations, as the dominant economic force in the world, play a significant role in the social web. For that reason they could also play a significant role in helping to alleviate some of society's problems—poverty, illiteracy, drug use, or violence, for example. Rather than acknowledge that they are *part* of the social web, corporations often assume that they are independent from the rest of the world, implicitly assuming that the world exists for them to profit from. A set of accountability principles (Fig. 6.5) that corporations could adopt would help integrate them into the new community. Corporations have historically been a major source of creativity, bringing new products, technology, and services to the world. These same corporations could also be agents for change. Corporations could, presumably, harness this creative energy to help develop projects (working with the community at large and within the business community) that could strengthen the core values of the community. Community networks could help provide valuable support for the design, implementation, and evaluation of these corporate-community programs.

Democratizing the Workplace

For a society to be democratic, its institutions must be democratic. In this regard the United States falls short in a fundamental way. Although many Americans hold democratic principles like free speech in high regard, these same Americans quite passively shed them every morning at the beginning of the workday and adopt them again when the whistle blows at day's end. Interestingly, the modern corporation turns out to be surprisingly feudal when inspected more closely than browsing its annual reports. In the U.S.

Community Accountability Principles

A company should consider its social responsibilities in addition to its profit-making responsibilities.

A company should support the community and support employee involvement in community life.

A company should provide safe working conditions for its employees.

A company should treat employees fairly.

A company should engage its employees in decision-making and other important aspects of the company: employees should be as much a part of this process as stockholders.

A company should strive to keep the ratio of highest salary to lowest salary as low as possible.

A company should promote social justice and not lend support to repressive regimes.

A company should not pollute the physical, moral, or intellectual environment.

A company should make prudent financial decisions and make money for stockholders.

A company should make its "community accountability" information readily available to the public via community networks and other means.

Figure 6.5

fiefdoms, the CEO may earn from a hundred to a thousand times the wage of the lowest paid worker. And as if to make the situation even more distasteful, management routinely uses computers to monitor employee's work and to snoop on them in other ways (Piller, 1993).

A democratic workplace is a far cry from the majority of today's workplaces. In a democratic workplace, employees are more like partners, peers, and collaborators. Employees would also be able to place issues on the agenda, instead of just sleepwalking through management's agenda. They would also participate in *decision-making*, where their votes counted equally with those of other employees. Needless to say, employees would be more likely to be working in a decent and healthy work setting with dignity, respect, and privacy under such an arrangement. Management would be less likely to spy on them or use computers to monitor their activities.

Frank Adams and Gary Hansen present the wide range that workplace democracy could encompass in their book *Putting Democracy to Work* (1992). Their presentation starts at the smallest unit with "shop floor or work-group decision-making" and proceeds up through "management level decision-making," "board room decision-making," "profit/surplus/gain sharing," up to and including "ownership of equity in stock," noting that participation at each level can be judged to be none, partial, or complete. This matrix of possibilities can be used to evaluate the extent of workplace democracy in a given site, or company, or to determine a direction or objective in a struggle to attain workplace democracy.

Many companies are currently involved in a broad conceptual makeover in which they intend to "reinvent" themselves to make the company become more competitive, flexible, and efficient by increasing employee participation. These companies understand that people are not machines, that people are capable of proactive and creative action, and that workers probably understand their job better than anybody else does. Besides integrating the employee into a general forward-looking framework where problems are analyzed, identified, anticipated, and addressed on an everyday basis, the employee is much more likely to improve his or her productivity and have higher morale and dedication for the company. Of course, companies that shed large numbers of their employees through downsizing seriously limit their ability to garner the requisite employee support for the process.

Most of these efforts at democratizing the workplace, however, stop short of allowing employees to make decisions. We only need to review the principles outlined by Dahl in Chapter 4 to see that a critical criterion, that of "voting equality at the decision-making stage," is missing and, hence, the programs are *not* democratic. Additionally, the domain of legitimate discussion is often arbitrarily circumscribed by management to exclude contract issues and managerial policies and procedures. These shortcomings are not of academic interest alone. They are likely to cause the deterioration of the participative programs, according to researchers William Foote Whyte and others (Whyte et al., 1991) who have studied those programs at Xerox and other corporations.

Democratizing the workplace offers a host of benefits—many of them indirect—to the community. The major benefit is that the company could become more connected to the community, increasing the likelihood of mutual support. A company's problem becomes a community's problem, and vice versa, and both will be more likely to search for solutions together. A company that is connected to a community will be less likely to pick up its stakes and relocate. It would be less likely to lay off large numbers of workers. Ultimately, democratizing the workplace will help to democratize society; an unbroken democratic fabric is more effective and more durable than one that is threadbare in key areas.

The Power of Your Money

According to Jeffrey Hollender, "There is a direct and tangible connection between every investment or financial transaction you make and the values that are promoted throughout the world" (1990). Just as products will not reflect any environmental destruction or social injustice that accompanied their creation, economic opportunities rarely reflect the implications that an investment in them may provoke. In a more concrete example, money deposited in a bank account may—within minutes—be put to use by its new guardians in a way that is objectionable to the depositor.

The key to understanding the power of your money lies in realizing that where money is spent and invested has social and environmental implications and that there are decisions and choices that are more important than maximizing "return on investment" or "purchasing power" or other slogans of the free-market fundamentalists. In Jeffrey Hollender's words, each purchase is an implicit endorsement: "When a dollar passes out of your hand to purchase a product, acquire a service, make an investment, contribute to a worthy cause, or even to be parked briefly in your checking account—you are casting a vote." Information, again, is the key to making these types of decisions and community networks could help make this information more widely available.

Eric Smith, a certified Financial Planner in Seattle, has developed on-line services on the Seattle Community Network that offer information on socially responsible investing, as shown in Fig. 6.6. Smith has a wide range of other information available on socially responsible investing, including relevant books and periodicals, on recycling companies, and on community-based investing.

CDCUs and CLTs

To help in making the transition to a more equitable and sustainable society, new communities will need to work with existing economic institutions while simultaneously developing new ones. It is imperative to begin developing alternative institutions as these may be better suited for future conditions and future community requirements. With these institutions in place and with newly acquired knowledge about their effectiveness and their lim-

```
                Socially Responsible Investing

 1 About Socially Responsible Investing
 2 Books and Periodicals List
 3 Responsible Banks and Credit Unions
 4 Community Based Investing
 5 Recycling Companies
_____

Your Choice ==> 1

About the Socially Responsible Investing area.

Investing and spending our money has, in modern
times, become so complex and abstract that people
no longer feel a personal connection to what their
money is actually doing in society.

Socially responsible investing (SRI) is the
allocation of financial resources, after the
consideration of both economic and social
criteria, with the goals of maximizing the
potential financial and social returns to both the
investor and society at large.

The purpose of the SRI area in the SCN Business
Center is to share ideas and tools that can be
used to understand and begin to practice a more
satisfying investment approach. It is possible to
support companies and activities that more closely
reflect one's own social and environmental values
and objectives.

This area is sponsored by The Social Investment
Forum—Pacific Northwest Chapter and Wall Street
Northwest, Socially Responsible Financial
Services.

Your constructive comments and contributions are
welcome.

Contact Eric A. Smith, CFP:->
    E-Mail  easmith@scn.org
    Voice   (206) 448-7737
```

Figure 6.6

itations, new communities will be in better shape to weather changes in the economic conditions that might otherwise prove damaging.

Some of these alternative institutions are discussed in Jeffrey Hollender's 1990 book, *How to Make the World a Better Place*, which lists 124 specific "actions" that a citizen can take. Hollender describes several new community-oriented economic institutions and also discusses some existing financial institutions that have prioritized community development as a part of their charter. The Neighborhood Works (August–September, 1993) also has a good summary of "Community Development Financial Institutions."

The first institution is a community-development credit-union or CDCU. CDCUs are designed to serve low-income neighborhoods and they are owned entirely by their depositors. Unlike traditional banks, which typically invest 10 percent or less into local low-income neighborhoods, these financial cooperatives reinvest 80 percent or more into housing rehabilitation and acquisition, small and minority businesses, cooperatives, and lending for family needs, according to Hollender. CDCUs are gaining popularity. As of 1990 there were over 300 of these credit unions with total combined assets over $500 million.

Another institution is the Community Development Loan Fund or CLDF. This is a vehicle that is specifically designed to let investors lend money directly to community-development projects, institutions, and individuals with poor or no credit rating. Although these loans are not insured, as of 1990 all money was repaid and in January 1989, $50 million was being managed in this way.

Hollender also describes the Community Land Trust, or CLT, which is a nonprofit corporation that acquires and holds land for the benefit of the community. Since low-income people pay three to four times more money (in rent) in proportion to the value of their (generally substandard) housing than that paid by middle and upper income people, they *could* have purchased their house or apartment several times over if their rent payments had gone to a down payment. The CLT helps address this by buying rundown homes and bringing them up to acceptable standards through volunteer effort. Then the CLT *sells* the housing units to families that meet certain criteria, while *retaining* the deed to the land. This new economic institution is also gaining popularity. There are now over 65 community land trusts, each owning 100 to 150 housing units, in the United States.

Socially Responsible Institutions

Finally, traditional banks *could* be more responsive to community needs, although most choose not to. The South Shore Bank in Chicago, an exception to the rule, has been making investments for nearly 20 years in some of the poorer neighborhoods on Chicago's South Side. They now have over $100

```
Socially Responsible Banks, Credit Unions, and
              Money Market Funds

        Name of Institution                    Contact

South Shore Bank, Chicago              your advisor
Community Capital Bank, New York       800-827-6699
Calvert Social Investment Money
  Market                               your advisor
Working Assets Money Fund              your advisor
Vermont National Bank                  800-544-7108
Local revolving funds (for info
  call)                                215-923-4754
Your credit union                      community
Local banks                            community

(This list submitted by Eric Smith, CFP of Wall Street North-
west, a branch of KMS Financial Services, Inc, Seattle.)
```

Figure 6.7

million in outstanding loans to local residents, businesses, and community groups. The South Shore Bank (see Fig. 6.7) has many accomplishments to its credit, including renovation of 25 percent of the local housing and financing of 250 small businesses, among others. They have racked up these achievements with loan losses that were one-tenth the national average and have returned 18 percent on the equity.

However successful these new institutions have been in their communities, their effects are localized. Community networks can increase the influence of these new institutions in two ways. The first is informational—people need to find out about these institutions, how they can themselves invest, or how they can even look into establishing ones of their own (see Fig. 6.8). The second is conversational—people need to discuss these issues, what's needed, what's worked in the past and what hasn't.

Red de Información Rural

While many people in the United States are yearning for a return to communities that are more convivial and caring than today's cities and towns, many other people, particularly those outside the United States, live in those types of communities already. These communities, often poor in material terms,

Socially Responsible Investing Reading List

Selected Books

Investing for Good: Making Money While Being Socially
  Responsible, Peter Kinder, 1993, Harper.

Jews, Money & Social Responsibility: A "Torah of Money"...,
  Lawrence Bush, 1993, Shefa Fund.

Social Investment Almanac,
  Kinder, Lydenberg, Domini, 1992, Henry Holt and Company.

Investing From the Heart,
  Jack Brill and Alan Reder, 1992, Crown Publishers.

Investing With Your Conscience,
  John Harrington, 1992, John Wiley & Sons.

Investing with a Social Conscience,
  Elizabeth Judd, 1991, Pharos Books.

Socially Responsible Investing: How to Invest with
  Your Conscience, Alan Miller, 1991, NYIF.

Good Money: A Guide to Profitable Social Investing in the '90s,
  R. Lowry, 1991, WW Norton & Co.

The Better World Investment Guide,
  Alperson, 1991, Prentice Hall Press.

Shopping for a Better World,
  Council on Economic Priorities and Ballantine Books,
  annually revised.

Companies that Care,
  Morgan and Tucker, 1991, Simon & Schuster.

Everybody's Business,
  Milton Moskowitz, Levering, Katz, 1990, Doubleday-
  Currency.

Economics as If the Earth Really Mattered,
  Susan Meeker-Lowry, 1988, New Society Publishers.

Ethical Investing,
  Amy Domini & Peter Kinder, 1984, Addison-Wesley.

Honest Business,
  Michael Phillips and Salli Rasberry, 1981, Random
  House.

(This reading list submitted by Eric Smith, CFP of Wall Street
Northwest, a branch of KMS Financial Services, Inc, Seattle.)

Figure 6.8

are facing enormous challenges to their way-of-life, including economic strangulation and the onslaught of mass culture.

In Mexico there are currently over 28,000 Ejidos, communities of small land holders. Their primary enterprise is farming, but fishers or other people who work the land, sea, forest, and other natural resources, also live in Ejidos. These Ejidos, whose three million plus members are called *Ejidatorios*, have traditionally been the backbone of Mexico, both economically and culturally, and they have been vital to the very identity of Mexico. Currently in Mexico, there are policy makers who believe that the Ejidos are an inefficient anachronism that should die, much as the family farm in the midwestern United States was greatly diminished after the onslaught of large-scale agribusiness in recent decades.

Scott Robinson, an anthropologist at Mexico's Metropolitan University Iztapalapa campus and Director of the Red de Información Rural (REIR), the Rural Information Net, thinks that the Ejidos *are* worth fighting for. They represent communities who must adapt to the global economy and computer-network technology may be an effective weapon in this struggle. While the Ejidatorio may be the soul of Mexico, he or she is now competing on an economic playing ground that is extraordinarily unequal. For the small farmer is pitted against vast capital-intensive agribusiness with advanced technology, access to global distribution networks, up-to-the-minute knowledge about prices, markets, costs, modern methods of growing and of controlling pests, legal acumen, and resources. Robinson and representatives from national and regional Ejido organizations believe that the key to competitiveness that is also consonant with the existing way of life is to increase timely access to important information, and to improve strategic planning as well as communication among themselves and distributors, brokers, government bodies, and potential buyers of their product through appropriate, often low-tech computer-network technology.

The system (Fig. 6.9) was launched in November 1994 with funding for the first cycle provided by the Ford Foundation of Mexico. The initial information service consisted of bulletins from the National Market Information Service (SNIM) available via dial-up or via gopher. Since the Mexican government has no tradition of making agricultural information freely available (no equivalent of the USDA or extension services), REIR had to buy a subscription to this service from the government. It is important to note that the Mexican government knows that the information is going to be *freely* distributed electronically and has apparently decided not to prevent that. In fact, the REIR inaugurated government agencies' information on-line.

Robinson's ultimate dream is that REIR will help give form to a "cyber-extension service" among Ejidatorios in Mexico's widely diverse regions including Chiapas, Oaxaca, the Yucatan, and others. Although Ejidadorios may

Figure 6.9   Red de Información Rural

have to adapt in many ways if they're to survive as small farmers, Robinson's working hypothesis is that a network of community networks will add a needed patch to the colorful and complex quilt that is rural Mexico.

AGENDA FOR ACTION

> *But can the proposition that democracy should take precedence over economics really be taken seriously? Absolutely. After all, was not one lesson of Eastern Europe's anti-Communist revolutions in 1989 that an economy unsupervised by democracy is bad not only because it is undemocratic (bad as that may be) but also because it risks injustice, ecological spoilation, and gross economic inefficiency?*
>
> Richard Sclove (1993)

Global capitalism is vigorously defended by those who have benefited most greatly by it, but it is currently a force that can overwhelm the individual and the community. At the same time it is largely independent and unanswerable to the individual and the community. In other words, the (not so) "hidden hand"—the omniscient director of our affairs first described by Adam Smith, then deified by Milton Friedman and others—may be sweeping us into oblivion. Global capitalism is a juggernaut of unparalleled proportions that is marked by two tendencies. The first is the unwavering predisposition of its defenders to enforce its tenets as the only acceptable way to think and act. The second is its seemingly unstoppable drive toward exploitation of people and the environment.

Economics can't be ignored while developing community networks because economics has a major influence on all the other core values. Those with more money receive better education, their health is better, and their voice is more influential in politics. At the same time, we realize that we all can't be rich, at least not at the unconscionably high levels that rich people and rich countries enjoy today. We need to develop new patterns of production, distribution, and consumption that raise people out of poverty to adequate and dignified standards of living. At the same time, this must be accomplished without seriously depleting the resources of the earth.

What do all the issues and concerns in this chapter add up to? Although radical treatment may be in order to cure the patient, it is unclear that any particular new ideology or philosophy offers the appropriate treatment. One of the chapters of *The Quickening*, Francis Moore Lappé's and Paul Martin Du Bois' excellent book about the renewal of citizen participation (1994), is prefaced with the query, "What, No Manifesto?" that described why they're making no specific demands. The solution will have to be community-based—both community as neighborhood and community as global community. It must be based on the principles of respect, dialogue, and inclusivity; it could include civil disobedience but never violent action.

The economic system is a system that binds the entire human race. Its policies, rules, local customs, and other factors, are all of human invention. It's a dynamic, social system that touches people's lives continually as it largely determines who gets what and under what conditions. Unfortunately, people tend to view it as a "force of nature," while many exploit its special characteristics for increased control of resources and people. The rules—both legal and those of everyday practice—have been developed largely *for* the wealthy individual and *for* the corporate, and often *against* the community. Orthodoxy and obedience to authority, particularly of the moneyed and credentialed interests, are at least partially to blame for current predicaments, and it will become increasingly important not to accept outcomes based on conventional wisdom as sacrosanct or immutable.

The opportunity exists now for all people to begin to seriously explore the modifications of existing economic prerogatives and the invention of new economic institutions. It behoves us as a society to explore a wide range of actions. As Sally Lerner (1994) points out, the failure to examine "seemingly 'far-out' ideas" would "limit our ability to identify emergent issues and to address them effectively." Sustainable mechanisms for meeting human needs and shared principles of equity and inclusiveness must form the basis of new economic systems. For this reason, workers and poor people need to participate in ongoing discussions and deliberations. Economic data that is clear and understandable (including that on taxation, employment, profits, stock ownership, corporate holdings, and investments) are needed to support this process. Ironically, there is a wide range of data—including U.S. census data—that is often available to everybody except the people to whom it pertains! Citizens of the new community need to take the lead in reinventing and inventing economic institutions—including corporations—in their communities and replicating successes in other communities.

Chapter 7

Information and Communication

*A popular government without popular information, or the means of ac-
quiring it, is but a prologue to a farce or a tragedy, or perhaps both. Knowledge will forever govern ignorance, and a people who mean to be their own
governors must arm themselves with the power which knowledge gives.*

James Madison

*In the future there will be so much going on that no one will be able to
keep track of it.*

David Byrne, "In the Future"

COMMUNICATION AND TECHNOLOGY

For thousands of years the complex symbolic code known as language has
allowed humans to share thoughts with one another. Even before written
language, humankind communicated orally and pictorially, through paintings on cave walls, for example. Communication—including state news,
sports reports, and gossip—helped hold the Roman Empire together for five
hundred years (Stephens, 1989). Communication can also help hold a mar-
riage or community together as well. As modern technology is radically
transforming the reach and speed and methods by which individuals and organizations communicate, it is useful to inquire whether this new global web
can be used to hold communities together or whether it is serving the needs
of modern day empires exclusively.

We use technology every day to inform and to be informed. We watch television or listen to the radio for entertainment and for information. We talk
and listen to people across town or around the world using the telephone. Increasingly we send and receive faxes, use e-mail, and use electronic bulletin-
board systems or commercial network services. Some of us may even use
video conferencing systems or correspond with others using electronic mail
that contains graphics or video clips.

Humankind's thirst for communication and information is seemingly un-
quenchable, and technology is playing an increasing role. The speed by

215

which these new technologies are advancing should cause many of us to pause and ponder some fundamental questions about new communications technology. The means with which we communicate and the policies that guide their use may not be as neutral or as beneficent as we think. Besides allowing us to *share* our thoughts, our media systems may be *shaping* them.

Shaping Consciousness

The commonplace nature of familiar modes of communication prevents us from looking at them objectively and, often, from thinking about them at all. The simplest question we can ask about them is "What does the technology allow us to do?" In other words, when the technology is operating correctly, "What do we use it for?" In the case of the telephone in its conventional use, two people communicate with each other *synchronously* using sounds—usually voice. A television, on the other hand (in its conventional use) allows people in one location to watch and listen to moving pictures and sound that are broadcast from a different location. The converse of the previous question, "What *doesn't* it allow?" is rarely asked, although it's a very useful question to consider. We can't smile at a person whom we're talking with on the telephone, for example, and expect to receive a smile in return. And although the rare television program allows viewers to telephone in to a live show to express an opinion or ask a question, television is generally used for broadcasting, and viewers are never *participants* in any real way. People have been known to talk back, yell, or, even, shoot their television set, but these attempts at feedback fall on deaf ears. Television is a one-way street.

Although we're not accustomed to thinking along these lines, technological systems (and modern mass-media systems are certainly technological systems) affect us in many ways. Don Norman writing in *Things That Make Us Smart* (1993) describes this phenomenon quite clearly:

> Technology is not neutral. Each technology has properties—affordances—that make it easier to do some activities, harder to do others: The easier ones get done, the harder ones neglected. Each has constraints, preconditions, and side effects that impose requirements and changes on the things with which it interacts, be they other technology, people, or human society at large. Finally, each technology poses a mind-set, a way of thinking about it and the activities to which it is relevant, a mind-set that soon pervades those touched by it, often unwillingly. The more successful and widespread the technology, the greater its impact upon the patterns of those who use it, and consequently, the greater impact upon all of society. Technology is not neutral; it dominates.

Although Norman describes constraints imposed by the technology itself, the actual technology is just one aspect of mass-media communications systems we generally take for granted. To understand the system as a whole it is necessary to examine political, social, and economic aspects as well as the technological aspects. In this light, much of the irrelevance, vulgarity, commercialism, and lack of balance of the mass media can be viewed as a natural by-product of the pattern of near monopoly ownership and commercial dominance. While the prospect offered by community networks for overturning corporate dominance is small, it may be possible to develop alternative media systems that are community-oriented, open, accessible, and democratic that co-exist—however precariously—with the traditional closed media systems.

The Influence of Television

The birth of mass communication systems has made radical changes in our consciousness that we're just beginning to contemplate. As the prospectus from the Cultural Environment (CEM) explains, "For the first time in human history, most children are born into homes where most of the stories do not come from their parents, schools, churches, communities, and in many places, not even from their native countries, but from a handful of conglomerates who have something to sell" (CEM, 1995). This passage notes the relatively recent appropriation and overwhelming control of cultural symbols and messages by what former University of California at San Diego Professor Herbert Schiller calls the "global cultural factories." University of Pennsylvania professor George Gerbner, the founder and chair of the Cultural Environment Movement organization has conducted extensive research that reveals how far the effects of media extend. For one thing, the constant barrage of television, print ads, and billboards has helped to stamp product mottos, jingles, and images in our consciousness. Ninety percent of all U.S. six-year-olds, for example, can identify the Joe Camel character and most 10-year-olds can name more beer brands than U.S. presidents. Gerbner has been studying the effects of television on our collective consciousness for over 25 years. At the core of his research is exhaustive analysis of thousands of prime time television shows involving tens of thousands of characters; his analysis revealed patterns that are wildly inconsistent with reality. The incidence of crime and violence, for example, is 55 times more likely to occur on television than in real life, while elderly people, a rapidly growing and powerful age group in the United States, are shown infrequently and in stereotypical roles that are often silly, impotent, or irrelevant (Waters, 1982). That television helps to promulgate these views throughout society is strongly implied by Gerbner's research. In one experiment, Gerbner and his assistants devised a multiple-choice questionnaire designed to learn how close the world view of the test-taker matched actual real-world statistics. The conclusions were clear—and cut across *all* age, income, level of education, and ethnicity distinctions: The more television a person watched, the more his or her world view matched the phony world view that beams continuously into the minds of hundreds of millions of viewers.

Funding for the Media

While some may quibble at some of Gerbner's conclusions, the actual and potential effect that the consciousness industries have on what we think about and how we think about it is staggering. Thus Gerbner recommends that we think both about what the current media *is doing* to us, and what the media *could do*, both *to* us and *for* us. He believes (1994) that cultural policy that addresses these issues explicitly belongs on "center stage . . . where it has long been in most other democracies." Although the idea is absent from public consideration in the United States, countries in Europe and especially in Scandinavia often levy taxes on theater admissions, videotapes, and other cultural events and artifacts (such as commercials!) which are paid into a fund that loans money for independent productions. Community computer networks would obviously be good candidates for such public funding and there would be scores of other viable candidates. Talk of public funding along these lines is not currently fashionable. Politicians, corporate media moguls, and right-wing radio talk show hosts uniformly denounce public funding options of any type. Rejection of this option, however, virtually guarantees that global corporate fare will increasingly shape the images, symbols, and messages that people see, and as a consequence, the parameters of acceptable thinking.

A VIEW OF TODAY'S MEDIA

> *The trouble with newspapers is that they don't know the difference between a bicycle accident and the death of a civilization.*
>
> George Bernard Shaw

> *I'm the slime oozin' out from your TV set.*
>
> Frank Zappa, "I'm the Slime"

Many of us read, listen to, or watch the news as part of our regular schedule. While the companies and organizations that produce this news are undoubtedly proficient at what they do—gathering information from around the world, organizing and packaging it, maintaining a worldwide organization, employing advanced technology, soliciting advertisers, and presenting annual reports to stockholders or owners—it is less clear *why* they're doing it. The ubiquitous nature of the mass media generally prevents people from posing important questions, and the owners of mass media systems are unlikely to provide forums that could challenge their modus operandi. Nevertheless, the question should be asked: What *use* is the news?

Let's begin this query by looking at the product itself—the news and the system that produces it. Is the reportage accurate? Is it biased? And why is one story newsworthy while others are not? Who makes those determinations and by what criteria? And, finally, if we could redefine or reorient "information and communication"—the media—to enhance the role of the citizen and community, what would this new medium look like? To begin to answer this question, let's first examine some of the deficiencies of the existing mass media systems.

A Black Box

The first thing we notice about the mass media is that it's a "black box." A black box performs a function, but since it is black, the mechanism inside it can't be viewed and how it works remains a mystery. The media industry, exemplified by the medium of television, gathers information, determines its entertainment-worthiness, and packages it behind the scenes. News production is their business while news consumption is ours. When we consume "the news," we assume that what we see is accurate and, less obviously, that it *is* news. Conversely, what we don't see *isn't* news. These black boxes are extremely powerful, as they play a large part in defining public consciousness. And since the box is opaque, the community neither understands nor participates in the process.

Profits over Value

Commercial media has to make a profit in order to stay in business. This is, of course, an economic truism of capitalistic society. A stronger statement, but an element of conventional wisdom nonetheless, is that a company's primary—if not sole—obligation is to *maximize* profits. This stronger form has serious implications for an industry that in theory carries the responsibility of providing citizens with the information they need to actively participate in a democratic society. If a violent television program, for example, on the average can deliver more viewers and hence more advertising revenue than say, a science program for kids, the violent program will be aired. And since advertisers financially underwrite television programming, their influence over what gets aired will be far greater than that of community members with special communication and information needs.

Disjointed Offerings

Sometimes television stations or networks broadcast documentaries or "specials" on some vexing problem of society. The topic might be homelessness, drive-by shootings, youth violence, substandard education, or some other popular tragedy. Although these shows are often intended to entertain— rather than engage—they are generally more honest and useful than much of television's usual fare. However valid these documentaries might be, their context can only be described as arbitrary and schizophrenic. For example, a special on the short life-expectancy of homeless children might pop up on a Wednesday at 9:00 P.M., preceded by an hour of situation comedies and followed by half an hour of Wall Street news. The audience was not prepared for the show in any way (except possibly for a few sensationalistic teasers) and no discussion, update, or sequel followed it. It was a unique and unrelated event in history, lost in a series of other unique and unrelated events.

Finally, as alluded to earlier, there is literally no use to the news. While there are sporadic exceptions, news is generally useless in that there are no reasonable ways to follow up on a story, get more information, or to become involved in some positive action. As we will see in the next section, there are *useful* alternatives.

A VIEW OF NEW MEDIA

> *What is needed . . . is a new media "movement"—a consumer consciousness not unlike the recent nutrition movement that has revolutionized not only the way people eat, but ultimately the food industry itself.*
>
> Elizabeth Thoman (1989)

Media *can* be useful. It need not be disconnected from society like a hallucinogenic dream world on the other side of the looking glass. It can be integrated into society and into community life, in a genuine and meaningful way. Today, the standard forms of media, however, are largely disconnected from everyday community spheres. They are largely disconnected from the people they serve, and from any community program or goal, outside organizations, or activities; or with other media forms that can provide complementary approaches. Schools generally have proscribed series of events within a class (a lesson plan), across several years (a curriculum), or within a degree program (a sequence of classes including required and optional classes). With very few exceptions, the media has no analogs to this type of analysis, planning, coordination, or purpose.

Integrative Media

When a form of medium begins to *connect* to community activities, it becomes *integrative*. Fortunately, there are many ways for television, radio, or newspapers to become better integrated and enmeshed in community and civic responsibilities, and community networks can play a strong role.

Let's say that Channel 6 is showing a program on the hundreds of tons of hazardous waste that the U.S. Department of Defense has strewn over the State of Washington over the last few decades. Channel 6 could make the transcript and program notes available on-line. The program notes could contain bibliographies, addresses of organizations, lists of whom to contact in the government, and other information that would help people explore the issue in more depth or become active in dealing with the issue. Channel 6 could also tell people when the show would be repeated and how to order the videotape. It could announce upcoming shows on similar topics, even if they were being shown on other channels.

Contribution-based Networks

The media integration could go further than providing information, however. By using the community network's electronic forums, discussions could precede the airing of the show and be integrated into the show itself. Similarly, there could also be on-line discussions after the show, and people who appeared on the show could also be available on-line to answer questions and to facilitate discussion. In this scenario, a television show could be augmented by introducing an additional medium—that of an on-line community network system. By incorporating additional media—including newspapers, radio, and a variety of face-to-face meetings—interesting, exploratory public experiments could be implemented. These experiments have been tried in some locations: "We the People," in Wisconsin, is one example. The "Puget Soundings" project in Seattle, which combines community television, radio, and community networks, is another.

Discussion forums on computer-based systems encourage *conversations* in which public dialog is constructed in ways unlike that encountered with other information and communication technology. Forums—both moderated and unmoderated—are based on contributions from participants, and each contribution is captured and becomes a permanent part of the forum itself, a record that can be printed or distributed and may contain seeds upon which additional discussion is spawned.

Unmoderated computer-based discussions (and moderated ones to a lesser degree) reject the producer-consumer model. Any potential "consumer" of information, commentary, issues, or questions in an electronic forum is a potential "producer" as well. Compare this to television news programs, where an organization numbering in the hundreds dispenses its version of news to people numbering in the tens of millions. In the United States this consumer-producer ratio has been steadily shrinking in recent years. According to Ben Bagdikian, former dean of the School of Journalism at the University of California at Berkeley (1992), "twenty-three corporations control most of the business in daily newspapers, magazines, television, books and motion pictures."

The current Internet model seriously undermines the "information as commodity" world view. Millions of people routinely supply information—facts and opinions—into a shared and increasingly global knowledge resource. Additionally, new tools such as Mosaic, gopher, MUD software (see Chapter 9), and the like are being distributed without charge. Without direct financial reward, millions of people are making available information, services, and technology that is not only cheaper, but is often of higher quality than the commercial competitors (Schickele, 1993). Whether this model will endure is a matter of speculation, however, as there are strong efforts underway to commercialize many of these services.

The Public Journalism Movement

In the last few years the concept of public journalism has been raised as an alternative approach that could circumvent some of the problems with current mass media (Rosen and Merritt, 1994; Miller, 1994; Austin, 1994). Public journalism promotes a more participatory approach to journalism in which the media acts as an agent to help citizens develop their own agenda and address their own problems. NYU journalism professor, Jay Rosen explains that "the newspaper's willingness to intervene, its concern for the resolution and not just the existence of the dispute, its determination to create discussion where none existed, its aggressive style of proactive neutrality—are all signs of a public journalism approach."

Public journalism strives to be professional and neutral while shifting the focus to solution-driven from problem-driven journalism. For example, when potentially divisive disputes arose in Charlotte, South Carolina between users of a popular city park, the journalists at the *Charlotte Observer* worked with community members to develop an op-ed page that carried suggestions for solutions and commentaries that reflected the points of views of all the concerned parties. People in the area credit the newspaper with averting a confrontation. The park was reopened the following weekend and a panel was initiated to study the park situation and develop new youth programs.

The *Charlotte Observer* also launched inquiries into some of Charlotte's systematic problems, such as the city's crime rate, which had risen to nineteenth in the country although its population ranking was thirty-fourth. The city's six-month "Taking Back Our Neighborhoods" initiative combined newspaper and radio coverage, town meetings, and efforts of neighborhood organizations to help understand Charlotte's crime problem and begin devising community solutions.

Two newspapers, the *Wichita* (Kansas) *Eagle* and the *Charlotte Observer* are in the forefront of the public journalism movement, but the effort is spreading to many other locations including Seattle, San Francisco, Dallas, and Boston. Many newspapers are active in election issues, in which citizens are being encouraged to develop a political agenda that suits their needs rather than the politicians'.

Although these efforts are far from being commonplace, there are indications that wide-ranging experimentation in new forms of public journalism are happening at the same time that newspapers and other information purveyors like radio stations are "reinventing" themselves. One interesting aspect of this change is that different types of media organizations often collaborate on a project—two rival newspapers, or radio and television stations and a newspaper, for example. Newer electronic forms like e-mail and collaborations with community networks are being explored, and "old-fashioned" venues such as salons and neighborhood parties are being revived as forums for public discussion of civic issues. In Spokane, Washington, the *Spokesman Review* newspaper purchased pizza for 500 groups that met in local homes and backyards to discuss concerns, hopes, and suggestions for the future of the region. The newspaper published summaries of these meetings and sent the comments to elected officials.

While public journalism is just one aspect of the solution, it is an important one. But public journalism is not without disadvantages and risks. For one thing it may be costlier in some ways because preparing information for use rather than consumption takes more time and demands critical skills. Preparing graphic presentations of statistical information that help convey complex information requires artistic, mathematic, and communication expertise. A more serious danger, however, could come from a media that adopted the mantle of neutrality and public interest while practicing flawed public journalism by presenting information based on false consensus, bias, exclusionary participation, or sloppy reporting. There is no solution to this problem except a new community that expects and demands excellence from the media.

Cooperative Media Explorations

In Seattle, KCTS/9, the local Public Broadcasting System (PBS) affiliate, has initiated a variety of telecommunications activities as part of their "Puget Soundings" project, funded by the Corporation for Public Broadcasting (CPB) and USWest as part of CPB's Community Wide Education and Information Services (CWEIS) initiative. The Puget Soundings projects are centered around local community-affairs programming. Broadcasts used in the first year have included "TeenTalk," "State Budget 101," "Ask the Governor," and "Act Against Violence: Volunteer." The Seattle Community Network (SCN) will be hosting forums on each, with television program participants agreeing to take part in these forums. Bibliographies and other information will be made available on-line as well. KUOW-FM, the National Public Radio (NPR) station on the University of Washington campus, will also host a series of short shows on the topics. Print media like the *Seattle Times* newspaper, as well as community newspapers, television stations KCPQ-TV and KYVE-TV, local schools, and libraries are also involved with the project.

The National Capital Free-Net in Ottawa offers another connection to traditional media forums by providing an on-line "Letters to the Editor" section on their community network. Readers send their responses to articles appearing in *The Ottawa Citizen, Le Droit, The Hill Times, The Ottawa Xtra!* or several others to the community network, which doesn't have the severe space limitations that plague traditional newspapers. Also, the letters can provide a more persistent record on a community network than their print-based counterparts can provide.

This intermedia approach is interesting on several counts. The first, of course, is the heightened public knowledge and engagement over an issue. The second interesting point is that the people themselves will be aware that an important civic experiment is taking place in which they are both observers and observed. Since the issues will be taken up in several different ways by several different media, the public will be in a position to think about how various media presentations—using different technology and reflecting different policies and political persuasions—meet their individual needs.

MISANET: Independent News on a Budget for Southern Africa

People throughout the world are mounting efforts that attempt to reclaim some local control of the news that their community creates and receives. Southern Africa, home to some of the poorest people in the world, is also isolated from the rest of the world, due at least partially to very high communication costs. A three-minute telephone call from Dar es Salaam to Johannesburg, for example, costs $18.75. A subscription to an international magazine could cost more than half of a journalist's salary. From the perspective of information and communication, citizens of that region are being held hostage to a concentration of newspaper ownership within the region and a handful of news services outside the region. According to their prospectus, "It is a harsh reality that Africa's concept of Africa is mediated by the news agendas of London, New York, and Atlanta, Georgia" (Cohen, 1994).

The Media Institute of South Africa or MISA is a collective of seven independent African newspapers, including the MISA head office (Namibia), the *Namibian* (Namibia), *Nmegi* (Botswana), *Weekly Post* (Zambia), *Savana* (Mozambique), *Weekly Mail* (South Africa), and *SJA* (Angola), that is working to reduce the concentration of media control. Each of these newspapers is struggling financially. Their very low operating budget has forced them into low-tech, low-cost "desktop publishing." The *Weekly Mail* (now the *Weekly Mail and Guardian)*, for example, was completely typeset on Apple Macintoshes and printed on LaserWriters in 1985. The low cost and relative mobility of this approach helped the paper survive despite several government attempts at closing the paper because of its antiapartheid stance. Building on their experience with home-grown technology, MISA is currently developing an ambitious large-scale, low-cost information and communication infrastructure using network technology to serve independent journalists in Southern Africa.

A wide-range of on-line services has been planned by the collective (Fig. 7.1). These include the standard capabilities like a news photo service of current event photographs and a news wire service with selected articles, to more comprehensive and general capabilities that would help undergird an entire alternative press infrastructure for the region. These projects include a forum on press freedom, a job forum for journalists, and a training forum containing information on education and training opportunities for journalists. Although the primary intention is to strengthen independent media, it is interesting to note that the planned services address almost all the core values of a community network.

Planned Services for MISANET

1. An electronic newsletter

2. A general information exchange forum

3. A contact list of independent media and important institutions in Southern Africa

4. A press freedom forum

5. A job forum for journalists

6. A training forum with information relating to Southern Africa

7. An archive of key media information relating to Southern Africa

8. A photo archive containing current-events photos

9. A news photo service containing current-events photos

10. A news wire service with selected articles from the Southern African independent press

---

Figure 7.1

Although strong political and economic pressures continually nag their efforts, they currently now have some e-mail capability and they publish an on-line "MISA FREE PRESS" (see Appendix B), which carries news of the continuing struggle for freedom of press in South African countries. Their vision—as underscored by the planned services listed in Fig. 7.1— transcends their current technological achievement and continues to motivate their own labors, while at the same time providing an inspiration to other communities, both rich and poor, large and small.

IMAGES AND EFFECTS

Children would probably watch public torture if it occurred on their way home from school, but that does not make public torture in the public interest.

Ben Bagdikian (1992)

We've noted how unresponsive and inattentive the mass media is to community needs. Unfortunately, the situation is often much worse: In many cases the mass media actively battles against civil life and community values. Often the media will place the focus on some aspects of a situation, artificially elevating those aspects while ignoring other possibly more important aspects. National Public Radio senior editor Daniel Schor describes the focus that CBS television executives chose to place on the issue of poverty in the United States when he worked for them: "When I offered stories on abject conditions, news executives came back with demands for stories on welfare cheating and misappropriation of poverty funds" (Schor, 1995). Nowhere is this misplaced focus more obvious than in the media's grotesque fascination with death and violence.

Amusing Ourselves to Death

When a person is murdered, especially if the person was rich or famous or the method itself was particularly gruesome or novel, the gory details are disseminated quickly and easily through the media and, more importantly, into our consciousness. This act of violence becomes central to the lives of many, and society's resources are marshaled toward its reportage, discussion, and judicial and penal ramifications. While the details of one crime are forgotten until the next one occurs, the lingering mood is one of fear and suspicion. The incessant barrage of violence in the media has taken its toll. While crime has actually *decreased* somewhat in recent years in the United States, people perceive increased danger and hence experience fear and mistrust. Unfortunately, there is no analogous chain reaction or fanning out of influence accompanying the good or humane act. In the words of social critic Neil Postman, we Americans seem to prefer "amusing ourselves to death." Bad news makes good news, but good news is no news at all.

As Bagdikian has pointed out, people *will* view graphic violence if it's made readily available. It is also known that some people in certain age groups are more likely to gravitate towards violent entertainment than do people in others. According to George Gerbner's research (1994), the ratings of nonviolent television shows are—on the average—higher than of those violent shows *and* that difference *increases* as the amount and severity of the violence increases. But *younger* viewers (who are more desirable to advertisers) seem to prefer the more violent fare, and this provides the financial incentive for continued bloodletting on the screen. Gerbner quotes the producer of the megadeath movie *Die Hard 2* as stating that "violence travels well around the world." Jokes might not translate well and sexual themes can run into trouble with local censors, but violence is apparently universal. Exporting boosts the profitability of any television show and violent shows are more likely to be exported. Gerbner's findings reveal that crime/action shows comprise only 17 percent of domestically shown programs but 46 percent of the exported ones. Violent American shows can now be regularly seen throughout the world. Thus, the consciousness of non-Americans is now being altered according to unhealthy stereotypes and distorted views of reality manufactured in the cultural factories of America.

Mass Media as Diversion

Carl Jensen of Project Censored (discussed later in this chapter) and others use the expression "junk news" for the wide variety of entertainment (whose subject might include Lady Di, "new" Coca-Cola, or the O.J. Simpson murder trial) that goes under the guise of news. This was anticipated, of course, in *1984*, George Orwell's distopian treatise on totalitarian possibilities. In *1984*, the production and distribution of cultural material was based on the existence of two distinct social tiers. For party members, the ostensible citizens, the Ministry of Truth supplied "the citizens of Oceania with newspapers, films, textbooks, telescreen programs, plays, novels—with every conceivable kind of information, instruction, or entertainment, from a statue to a slogan, from a lyric poem to a biological treatise, and from a child's spelling book to a Newspeak dictionary." The party member of *1984* corresponds most closely to the intellectual and political elite whose opinions *do* matter and whose high positions and power make them indispensable allies in maintaining the status quo. For the rest of the people, the masses or proletarians in *1984*:

> There was a whole chain of separate departments dealing with proletarian literature, music, drama, and entertainment generally. Here were produced rubbishy newspapers, containing almost nothing except sport, crime, and astrology, sensational five-cent novelettes, films oozing with sex, and sentimental songs which were composed entirely by mechanical means on a special kind of kaleidoscope known as a versificator. There was even a whole subsection—Pornosec, it was called in Newspeak—engaged in producing the lowest kind of pornography, which was sent out in sealed packets and which no Party member, other than those who worked on it, was permitted to look at.

Although private corporations—rather than the state—orchestrate and define current "proletarian culture," the results are remarkably similar to those in *1984*. Graphic violence—sometimes coupled with sexuality—is apparently the pornography of choice in present-day America. (The action movie *Die Hard 2* featured over one thousand on-screen murders!) Violence and sex can provide a fleeting "sugar high" that removes the person—at least for the moment—from a life of deprivation, boredom, and lack of purpose or meaning. Unfortunately, this approach rarely offers even a glimpse of any social problem or a *community* response to a *community* problem. At the same time, it helps breed an entire class of apathetic, uninformed, and disconnected people who are singularly unprepared to deal with community problems.

Beyond Text

While discussion is at the base of a democratic society, new forms of electronic network involving film, video, audio, and computer-manipulated images are becoming increasingly widespread. It is important to consider what effects these new media will have on society and whether they can be used to support the new community. One of the first questions to ask is: Who can participate? Words—both spoken and written—are easily produced by commoners as well as kings. The written form, moreover, is particularly amenable to replication and distribution in books, newspapers, pamphlets, and on community networks.

It should be noted that although text is in itself easily produced and replicated, the average person's access to an audience of potential readers has traditionally been severely limited. This is expressed in the adage about the freedom of the press being limited to those who could afford one. It is this barrier—the distribution barrier—that has been breached by computer-mediated communications. Electronic BBSs, Fidonet echoes, conferences on Usenet, and community networks all provide nearly unlimited forums for the free exchange of ideas using text.

Multimedia information, however, changes the equation. Each aspect of the media system—its form, content, production, distribution, and access—is changed with the increased emphasis on non-textual information in the on-line world, altering the "affordances" in various ways. The first consideration is what can be portrayed by the medium. Postman (1986) argues persuasively that text is ideally suited for ideas and dialogue, while dynamic images (like movies and television) are better suited for entertainment. In terms of production, multimedia artifacts such as movies or television shows have been produced for *broadcast* by teams of people working together with ample resources. Historically, at least, the more complicated the artifact is, the more expensive it is to produce and distribute, and the more likely it is to be a well-funded corporate effort designed for profitable mass consumption.

It's true that multimedia technology is becoming increasingly available. Prices are dropping rapidly and tools are proliferating that make tasks such as editing video much easier. It's estimated that one in six households in the United States now owns a camcorder, an estimated 16 million having been sold. Since many households do not even own telephones, it seems unlikely that every household will be able to mount its own video productions any time soon. The availability of increasingly affordable and usable technology does mean that community centers, schools, libraries, and public access television centers could lend equipment and provide inexpensive or free training to community members of varying income levels.

A Video Revolution?

Availability is just one part of the picture, however. Another aspect is use. Will people use video technology for democratic and community ends? While there are some examples of that community orientation, much of the evidence suggests that today's camcorder users record "family documentation and ritualistic leisure practices, just as they did with the home movie camera and the Brown Box Brownie," according to media critic Laurie Oulette (1994). Oulette points out that the "video revolution" was hailed as a tool for democracy in other countries such as China and Czechoslovakia, while both the professional media and the video technology producers themselves stress more prosaic use within the United States.

Lastly, there are questions of distribution and demand. While independent video producers have been active for years, their work has been largely ignored. The first problem is distribution: What good is access to the means of production if distribution fails? The other problem is demand. Although it's relatively difficult to see independent and alternative productions, they can be viewed if people are persistent in their efforts. But if the large majority of people would rather "amuse themselves to death," as Neil Postman suggests, then neither increased access nor distribution would make any difference.

RECLAIMING MEDIA FOR COMMUNITIES

> . . . *newspapers are rapidly eliminating their place names. For example, in California, which has more daily papers than any other state, two thirds of all the daily papers have no city name showing on page one of their title.*
>
> Ben Bagdikian (1992)

Community-network participants have aspirations, needs, and issues in common. When the community owns the community network, it naturally will reflect these shared values and concerns, promoting creative and useful interaction within the community. As Boston area activists Paul Resnick and Mel King explained in their "Rainbow Pages" telephone-based community-network system essay (Agre and Schuler, 1996).

There is no such thing as a poor community. Even neighborhoods without much money have substantial human resources. Often, however, the human resources are not appreciated or utilized, partly because people do not have information about each other and about what their neighborhood has to offer. For example, a family whose oil heater is broken may go cold for lack of knowledge that someone just down the block knows how to fix it.

Community-oriented information such as "want-ads" on the community network could help address these basic needs. Other useful information includes calendars of events that are searchable by topic and date; bus schedules and routes; disaster preparation advice; carpool information; question and answer forums conducted by doctors, nurses, lawyers, recycling experts, master gardeners, weavers, and automotive mechanics; community maps; and community resources including social services, job banks, and after-school and summer activities for kids and families. Of course, community-networks systems must be readily accessible from public as well as private locations, and they must be free to use or have very low usage fees in order to serve all community members.

People also provide input in subtle ways that makes itself known over time as well. François Bar of the Communications Department at the University of California at San Diego tells an insightful story about how important these effects can be.[1] Earlier this century—almost impossible to believe in retrospect—the corporate view was that the telephone would play the role now held by phonographs, and phonographs would play the role now held by telephones. In other words, people would record messages in their homes as a type of "audio letter," which they would mail to their friends or relatives. After that they might ring up a number on the telephone and listen to a live concert. According to Bar, it is users who shape the ultimate use of a service or technology, and any attempt by companies to dictate uses in advance would be misguided and financially ruinous.

Bar further believes that the larger the number of users on a future information superhighway, the more services will be developed and enhanced *by users*. For this reason, network providers should embrace interconnection of their systems to avoid fragmentation of network services that would limit access to these services. Furthermore, Bar explains, telephone companies and other providers should push for universal access as an opportunity that will help them immensely to understand the media, rather than a threat that could hurt their bottom line in the short term.

---

[1] Keynote address. Annual Meeting of Computer Professionals for Social Responsibility, October, 1994.

Communities require community media for a variety of reasons. Ben Bagdikian (1992) has pointed out that national newspapers and television stations cannot adequately report on issues and candidates in each of the 65,000 local voting districts in the United States. Without local community media, people in these districts must rely on political advertisements or no information at all.

The InfoZone

Located high in the Rocky Mountains of Colorado, Telluride, with just over 1500 permanent residents, seems to be an unlikely hub for sophisticated telecommunication use, yet the combination of a high degree of computer ownership and literacy, relatively high income and educational attainment, coupled with a strong interest in the "ecology of the information environment," seems to be providing the necessary ingredients for an ambitious and imaginative project. This project, the Telluride InfoZone, is a community-network system that "intends to be a site-specific pragmatic response to Telluride's needs and desires," according to program director Richard Lowenberg (1995). The community in this case is actually a "community of communities" that includes a wide diversity of people from Montrose, the most populous city in the region (15,000 people), to tiny towns like Placerville and Sawpit. As Lowenberg explains, the Tellurcentric orientation is slowly diminishing as the InfoZone expands to serve the entire region.

Located in a spectacular setting, Telluride is a former mining boom and bust town now embarking on a potentially similar course through skiing and development. Telluride's economy is driven primarily by real estate development. The hope is to become economically more diverse without bringing in pollution or other deleterious side-effects at the same time. A November 1993 *Business Week* article on telecommuting explains that "the trend is making Telluride, along with other out-of-the-way places, into unofficial testing grounds for the new technology."

The InfoZone offers several telecommunication technologies to the residents of the region. For one thing, it offers a community-network system with free dial-up access. This aspect of the system (which uses the First Class BBS software) is currently used by over 1,000 people (including over 500 Telluride residents—approximately one-third of the city's population) for e-mail, forums, and access to local and Internet information caches. There is also extensive local information that would be useful in a number of different ways, including town council meeting agendas, land-use codes, as well as educational and health-oriented services. Local media have a strong presence on the network as well. Telluride's weekly and daily newspapers both accept letters to the editor on-line and publish articles on-line on an occasional basis. The entire *Anonymous Underground Newspaper,* an alternative newspaper from Telluride High School, is published on-line (and in hard copy) using the system's only anonymous account, and KOTO, the public radio station in Telluride, has published the transcript of its daily local news program on-line every day since July, 1994.

The InfoZone also offers an Internet point of presence to local residents (through Colorado Supernet) and provides support for Web pages (such as the one containing the town map shown in Fig. 7.2) on its Linux (public domain UNIX operating system look-alike) server. Those pages contain information about the Telluride and the regional community and geographic environment, and about the InfoZone's future plans ("conspiracies"). It should also be noted that the InfoZone has established Tetherless Access, Ltd., a TCP/IP spread spectrum wireless system which connects six community public access systems at up to 160 KB to the Internet point of presence.

Lowenberg and his associates are concerned with the physical and community "ecologies" as well as the information "ecology" of the region. Lowenberg explains that he is "a true believer in ecology" who is "interested in our interactive place in the larger environment." Applying this philosophy has many consequences. One example of this is the proposed project to the National Telecommunications Information Agency (NTIA) to provide citizens of the region with critical geographic (GIS) information that will be made available in a variety of formats including tabular and map-based graphical ones. The spatial data will be used for long-term economic and demographic analyses, for growth-management decision-making (which uses watershed, air quality, natural resources, and animal and plant inventory information), as well as for comprehensive regional planning. In addition, they're currently developing a regional cultural master plan on-line.

The Telluride Institute is concerned with research as well as action. Lowenberg stresses that *learning* is a key aspect of the project that can and must occur through experience. Ecology is a science of interrelationships. Information affects both the internal and external environments, and community networks may help to determine in the future whether these ecologies are harmonious or out of balance.

Plugged In in East Palo Alto

Like many other projects described in this book, Plugged In, located in East Palo Alto, California, is difficult to pigeon-hole. Like other community networks described here, Plugged In uses computer technology to help address its primary mission of supporting the community. Their work is grounded in

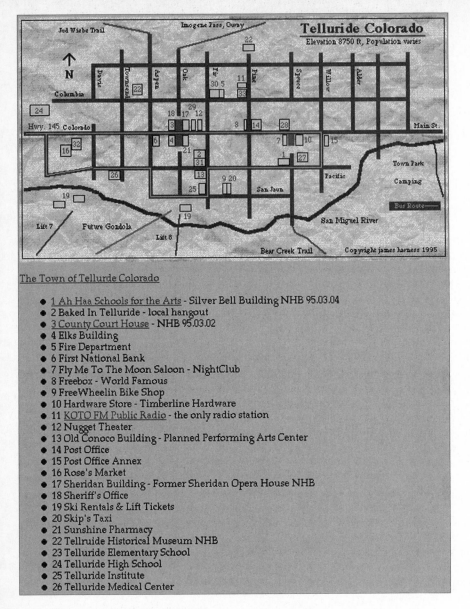

Figure 7.2 Telluride Colorado

the belief that low-income communities are at a grave risk of being cut off from economic and other opportunities as new technologies increasingly become key to economic success and political participation. It helps develop educational programs and helps community residents develop their own stories, which are distributed electronically.

East Palo Alto has very little in common with its more affluent neighbor, Palo Alto, the home of Stanford University and one of the wealthiest cities in the United States. East Palo Alto's average family income is approximately one-third of Palo Alto's and its unemployment rate is 31 percent. Eighty-seven percent of children growing up in East Palo Alto qualify for free or re-duced-cost school meals. Plugged In offers residents of the East Palo Alto Community a way to become comfortable and adept with the modern and often expensive high-technology equipment that they are unlikely to en-counter ordinarily. Plugged In offers access to the technology through intro-ductory workshops and on a drop-in basis.

Plugged In also develops and offers a variety of after-school team programs for children, teenagers, and families. The projects are remarkably congruent with the educational values discussed in Chapter 3. These projects, including Alien Cows, Community Kids Storybook, and Sand Castle Kingdom, are done in groups, are multidisciplinary, help develop critical thinking skills, and facilitate the expansion of the students' world view. The student projects generally engage the "real world" in a critical way. For example, their Propo-sition 187 Slide Show, available on the Web (Fig. 7.3), presents arguments that

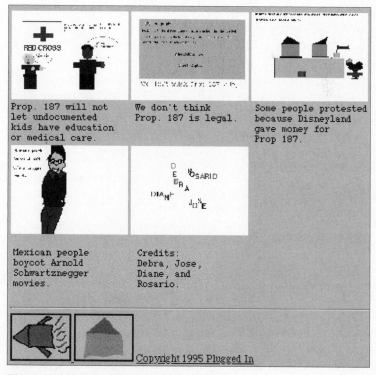

Figure 7.3 Proposition 187 Slide Show

show a wide range of negative implications of the restrictive illegal alien bill that was recently passed by California voters. Participants in these programs also developed a critique of how the mass media—particularly the commercial media—portray and target low-income people.

MEDIA CONTROL / MEDIA MESSAGES

> *Every culture has its official folklore. In ancient times medicine men transformed tribal legends to enhance their own status. The twentieth century is no different, but the high priests who communicate mythic dogmas now do so through great centralized machines of communication—newspaper chains, broadcast networks, magazine groups, conglomerate book publishers, and movie studios.*
>
> Ben Bagdikian (1992)

Before widespread communication technology, news was much more likely to be informal and community-oriented. A ferry disaster in the North Sea or a bus plunge in Bolivia now are more likely to take center stage. Why do we have the media we do? The answer centers around the issues of who controls the media, how this control is manifested, and how it operates. When these issues are better understood, community members will be in a better position to wrest away some of this control and shape a media that educates, encourages participation, and supports the community.

Ben Bagdikian has probably done more work than anyone else in sounding the alarm on the ever-increasing concentration of ownership of the nation's mass-media systems. Bagdikian documents the trend and describes the danger in the passage below from the 1992 edition of *The Media Monopoly.*

> The highest levels of world finance have become intertwined with the highest levels of mass media ownership, with the result of tighter control over the systems on which most of the public depends for its news and information.

While Bagdikian is immensely concerned about the effects of concentrated ownership on public discourse (charging that "public information" has been reduced to "industrial by-product"), Edward Herman and Noam Chomsky go one step further by asserting that "size, ownership, and profit orientation of the mass media" is but one "filter" of five that together define a model of systematic propaganda, which they feel is required "in a world of concentrated wealth and major conflicts of class interest" (1988). Although explicit government censorship is lacking, in the United States the dominant role of the mass media today is, in their view, "manufacturing consent."

The model proposed by Herman and Chomsky is as simple as it is chilling. They propose the existence of five major filters that act in powerful ways to define what is news and what isn't and that help ensure that the right "spin" is put on what does get reported.

> The essential ingredients of our propaganda model, or set of news "filters," fall under the following headings: (1) the size, concentrated ownership, owner wealth, and profit orientation of the dominant mass-media firms; (2) advertising as the primary income source of the mass media; (3) the reliance of the media on information provided by government, business, and "experts" funded and approved by these primary sources and agents of power; (4) "flak" as a means of disciplining the media; and (5) "anticommunism" as a national religion and control mechanism.

Herman and Chomsky make it clear that their model is qualitative, not quantitative, and that it isn't *total*. Individual books, articles, and periodicals attacking government or corporate wrong-doing do get published, but these are exceptions. Chomsky, himself, is booked several years in advance to standing-room-only audiences, yet rarely is noted in the mass media. The fifth point, "anticommunism" as a primary orienting force has recently lost the force that it's had for the last fifty years. Is there a new ideological orientation that will step in to fill this "void" or will the model survive without one?

There is not room for an exhaustive study of the propaganda model here and so readers are invited to investigate the model on their own. Some of the evidence is stunning. One example, the extent to which the U.S. Air Force contributed to shaping opinions and consciousness in a single year, is listed below.

140 newspapers, 690,000 copies per week

Airman magazine, monthly circulation 125,000

34 radio and 17 TV stations, primarily overseas

45,000 headquarters and unit news releases

615,000 hometown news releases

6,600 interviews with news media

3,200 news conferences

500 news media orientation flights

50 meetings with editorial boards

11,000 speeches

Note that the United States has three other branches of armed forces, each with their own public relations programs. In 1971, the Pentagon was publishing a total of 371 magazines at an annual cost of $57 million. Herman and Chomsky add that in 1968 the Air Force had 1,305 full-time public relations employees in addition to thousands with "public functions collateral to other duties." They note by way of contrast that the American Friends Service Committee, a humanitarian and pacifistic organization of the Quakers, in 1984–1985 ran a national office of 11 staff people. It will be interesting to see how the military's vast public relations machine changes in the years following the collapse of communism. Until their media budget is decreased, they will probably continue to be influential, at least in the foreseeable future.

The concept of "flak," the fourth filter of the propaganda model, is an important item to consider. According to Herman and Chomsky it is an attempt to "condition" or shape the media. Flak refers to negative responses to a program or negative statement in the media and is often generated by institutes established for this very purpose. Flak can be a very powerful tool. Faced with it, advertisers can be persuaded to drop their sponsorship or politicians to abandon their political support. Telecommunications technology can greatly aid in flak proliferation and talk radio hosts are well-known for their ability to mobilize their troops to produce flak on demand.

Interestingly, computer networks such as Usenet have historically been somewhat resistant to flak because of two basic factors. The first is the decentralized nature and prevailing attitudes on the net; the second is the lack of experience of corporations and public relations experts regarding the use of computer communication technology.

We may learn, to our dismay, sometime in the near future that the net is not invulnerable to flak. Indeed, it may be particularly susceptible, as many factors work in favor of flak purveyors. Institutions with deep pockets could easily pay people to surf the networks looking for objectionable information. When this information was located, it could be called in question or marginalized in some way by way of a response. More drastic measures might include contacting the poster's employer or school (assuming the person was not posting from a private account or public network). Or a flak purveyor could be under the employ of a large corporation but posing and posting as a private citizen. In this way, the response would probably be interpreted by others as one from a free agent, unfettered by corporate allegiances.

According to the *Wall Street Journal* (WSJ, 1994) some corporate monitoring of computer networks is already happening. Dell Computer Company and others pay employees to cyberspace-surf electronic bulletin board systems, Usenet newsgroups, and commercial computer networks. They are looking for references to their employer's products in order to help solve customer problems, change negative perceptions, protect the company's reputation, or just to "get bits and pieces" (of relevant information) from a vast, free-floating electronic focus group.

Herman and Chomsky's model effectively destroys the objectivity myth of the media. If the media were somehow neutral, then we should expect an equal number of pundits and hosts and guests from the political left as well as the political right, much as if darts had been used and most choices clustered around the political middle. If that were true, then it might be possible to have a "Rush Limbaugh of the left" with his or her own radio or television show. Surely somebody from the left could be found that could articulate progressive perspectives as well as Limbaugh does for the political right. Historically, popular commentators on the left have been forced out for one reason or another, sometimes to make room for less popular and less knowledgeable ones on the right (Jackson, 1993). Commentators on the right generally support corporate interests and spend their time going after "soft" targets. The targets for attack are rarely corporations or government—business joint interests, but can be immigrants, gays, feminists, environmentalists, African Americans, the poor, the homeless, gang members, or liberals of any stripe. Texas journalist Molly Ivins points out that "Rush [Limbaugh] consistently targets dead people, little girls and the homeless—none of whom can fight back" (Ivins, 1995).

Increasingly, the target of these commentators is government. This is because a weakening of government is seen as a strengthening of business. (Note that the current rallying cry is *less* government—not *better* government!) Not only can government's role as regulator (when it does act in that role) be reduced, but government occasionally intercedes, however imperfectly, on the behalf of the poor or the disenfranchised. Bagdikian's research (1992) reveals this tendency:

> The pattern is clear in American journalism: In general, items are more likely to be pursued in depth if they portray flaws in the public, tax-supported sector of American life, and less-likely to be pursued if they portray flaws in the private corporate sector.

Accordingly, a local television station in Seattle regularly exposes "waste, fraud, and abuse" in government (offering financial rewards for "tips"), while turning a blind eye to similar problems in the private sector. While pointing out government shortcomings is essential in a democratic society, subjecting the same scrutiny to corporations is also essential. Corporations exert enormous influence on almost all aspects of living and ignoring this powerful force invites tyranny.

Uncivic Discourse

While the traditional media, including daily newspapers, broadcast television, and radio, have intrinsic conservative biases, as Herman, Chomsky, and many others have demonstrated, most politicians and media pundits on the right still prefer to incant the idea that the media is "liberal," possibly because some newspapers or other venues are less right-wing than they are. The large upsurge in popularity of right-wing radio stars, including Rush Limbaugh (on 650 stations nationwide) and scores of other lesser-knowns who boast millions of regular listeners, has succeeded in shifting the fulcrum of political discourse in the United States further to the right. In all major cities, and in many suburban and rural areas as well, one can hear an unbroken chain of radio talk show hosts representing variations on the right-wing point of view.

Rush Limbaugh has helped to transform home-grown, knee-jerk mean-spiritedness into a political movement. Ironically, Limbaugh trumpets the "democratic" aspects of his show. After all, *some* citizens' voices are *heard* by other citizens. Since all callers are screened for (right-wing) political correctness, before they're allowed to talk and Limbaugh can hang up at will, there is little question that the agenda is controlled almost entirely by Limbaugh himself. (The format has been called "guestless confrontation.") It is risky placing political faith and judgment in that of a single person—especially one with neither accuracy, objectivity, or empathy to recommend him as a journalist. (See *The Way Things Aren't: Rush Limbaugh's Reign of Errors,* Rendell, Naureckas and Cohen, 1995, for a good compendium of Limbaugh's preposterous inaccuracies and misstatements.) It is particularly dangerous if any significant percentage of the population subscribes uncritically to the mindset of another person, as do Limbaugh's followers, proudly self-proclaiming themselves as "dittoheads."

Limbaugh himself has been outflanked by others more to the right than he is. John Schlosser, "commander" of the Colorado Free Militia, interviewed by Peter Boyles on Denver's KNUS, thinks that Limbaugh is too much an "insider," and many talk-show hosts go well beyond Limbaugh's jocular derision. Chuck Baker, host of Colorado Springs, Colorado, radio station KVOR, regularly mimics the sound of a pistol's firing pin while he rails against the government or discusses shooting members of Congress (Jorgensen, 1995). On "Hot Talk" radio station, KSFO in San Francisco, "General" Michael Savage argues against hiring people with disabilities, while another host, Ken Hamblin, refers to James Brady, who was permanently disabled in the assassination attempt on Ronald Reagan, as "the cripple guy" (Smith, 1995). Although hate talk is protected under the first amendment, there are some things that could be done to improve the situation. However unlikely the current Congress is to enact this type of legislation, something akin to the old "Fairness Doctrine" (in which citizens could demand equal time for rebuttal) could be brought into play again. Barring that, citizens could exert pressure on those stations in various ways, for example by writing letters to station managers and program sponsors.

In addition to the lack of access to the agenda, the complete lack of balance, the day-in and day-out saturation bombing of the nation's consciousness, the talk-show commentators (most are right-wing politically) offer little or nothing that is constructive. When anger, derision, and hate are the operative themes, there is literally nothing to build with. A genuine dialogue on health care, crime, education, the family, or the environment, where citizens rationally discuss programs or ideas, will not be found on "Hot Talk" radio.

Censorship Comes in Many Flavors

A democracy depends on the free flow of information for its survival, and most Americans take vague pride in this freedom without giving the matter much real thought. While overt government censorship surfaces only intermittently (but regularly, the gagging of the press during the Gulf War, for example), other more subtle forms of censorship are more frequent—and just as dangerous—to a democratic society. These include censorship to please a sponsor, a perceived audience, the corporate owners, a political party, or elected officials. When a journalist kills a story or aspects of a story because of *anticipated* censorship, that is a form of self-censorship. When an audience refuses to hear one side of a story, that is also self-censorship. When a society allows a full rein of censorship activities to cut across all aspects of their media—as described in the Herman/Chomsky model—that too, is self-censorship.

The influence of advertisers on the "free press" should not be overlooked or underestimated. A study published in the journal *Editor and Publisher* (Kerwin, 1993) reveals the extent of this phenomenon. Of the 150 editors surveyed, 93 percent stated that advertisers tried to influence the content of newspaper stories and 71 percent reported that advertisers had tried to kill some stories entirely. Thirty-seven percent of the editors admitted that on occasion they themselves had succumbed to the pressure. Interestingly, the pressure used did not always come *directly* from the advertiser. Fifty-five percent of the editors acknowledged that there was pressure from *within* their own organizations to tailor stories to better suit the (presumed) needs of the advertisers.

Why are these forms of censorship dangerous? For one reason, those acts of censorship often are directly related to miscarriages of democracy. For example, one of the "most censored" stories (Jensen, 1993) involves the tracking of big donors of George Bush's 1992 election campaign. Not only were many of the donations over the legal limit, but many were tied to direct favors in the form of appointments to ambassadorships and federal advisory appointments, high-level intervention on regulatory matters, and import-export assistance. Censoring this type of news for any reason is detrimental to the democratic process, as it shields offenders from the necessary scrutiny that citizens and media must focus on our government.

In 1976, Bantam Books published *Inside the Company* (Agee, 1976), a book on the United States Central Intelligence Agency (CIA), which the United States government reviewed prior to publication. Governmental censors prevailed and the book was published with many blank sections sprinkled throughout (the entire unexpurgated book was available in Canada). The lawyers for Bantam persisted in ongoing efforts to have excised text replaced and each legal challenge resulted in the appearance of more text, which the publisher usefully printed in boldface to make it easier to find.

Since 1976, Carl Jensen, of Sonoma State University in California, has located those bits of text that the American mass media purveyors have chosen to leave blank, and published them in a form of boldface. His book, *Censored! The News That Didn't Make the News and Why* (1993), not surprisingly, was rejected by over fifty publishers. Every year Jensen solicits nominations for the "top-ten" stories, which are then voted on by a panel of judges. (Incidentally, they decide on the top-ten "junk-food news stories" as well—those news stories that had received high visibility while providing little or no value.) In addition to providing a small "oversight committee" to the gigantic media industry by showcasing important forgotten stories, Project Censored provides support to fledgling reporters by disseminating "hot tips." Since the distribution of censored news stories, the "hot tips," and other information is a major problem, low-cost access to networks could play a major role. Jensen has begun to explore various approaches and has recently made some of this material available on the World Wide Web (see Appendix B).

Increasingly, cyberspace is becoming the battleground of new censorship issues. In the Washington State legislature, for example, a "decency" bill that would make it virtually impossible to run any on-line service that allowed unscrutinized conversation among adults and minors is being pushed. It is fueled by fears of largely imaginary enemies, especially a legion of "pedophiles" that presumably haunt cyberspace. Prodigy and the other major commercial services have already wrestled with this issue and the First Amendment apparently lost the match. All messages intended for forums are screened first by in-house censors. This is why users can only post in English on some commercial networks!

Commercial Networks

Apple Computer and Microsoft each have recently begun network services of their own. Microsoft will be bundling client software that communicates with its on-line Microsoft Network into its new operating system (OS) Windows 95. This will enable users of the new OS to nearly effortlessly communicate with Microsoft Network *only*, which is much like buying a television set or radio that only receives signals from stations that are licensed or otherwise approved by the television or radio manufacturer. Whether Apple or Microsoft uses censors to police the language of its users (or to determine whether their "cyberspace citizenship" should be revoked) will depend to some degree on whether "anti-decency" legislation similar to that originally proposed by Senators Exon (of Nebraska) and Gorton (of Washington) becomes a reality, on the policies established by the owners (the "new lords of cyberspace"), and also by the users themselves, who have vast potential, though typically somnambulant, clout.

The Microsoft Network developers are carefully blending a collection of special interest providers—including Christians, martial arts aficionados, womens' rights activists, New Age spokespeople, animal lovers, magicians and on-line merchandisers (including both QVC and Home Shopping Network) into a cybernetic brew that they hope will entice the public onto *their* information super-tollroad. Commercial services typically return a percentage of the money that they've earned from users at home to the service providers who've successfully lured the user to their neck of the cyberspacial woods. Whether or not a service provider is allowed to set up shop on the network will largely depend on how much revenue that service will bring in. Thus in the new commercial on-line services, as with television and other mass media, the ability to derive income (along with ideological preferences of the owners) will determine the shape of the "on-line community" in a commercial network. Because the bottom line is the dominant criteria for the on-line content and the mix of offerings is being assembled at corporate offices, the commercial network is as close to an on-line community as a shopping mall is to a real community.

In the conclusion to his chapter "Public Information as Industrial By-Product" in his book, *The Media Monopoly* (1992), Ben Bagdikian explains the main problem with media monopoly (of which the commercial on-line networks might ultimately be part). "The deeper social loss of giantism in the media is not in its unfair advantage in profits and power; this is real and serious. But the gravest loss is in the self-serving censorship of political and social ideas in news, magazine articles, books, broadcasting and movies." A democratic society demands open communication of ideas. Censorship—through either government or corporate imperative—invites fear and ignorance, both strong enemies of a civil society.

NEW AND ALTERNATIVE VOICES

As important and powerful as private capital and the state are, there is a third, potentially more decisive force. It has been called "people power." It is the American people, ultimately, who will have to decide.

—Herbert Schiller (1989)

Many people believe that community networks can help increase the strength of "people power" and that community networks can provide a much needed participatory media that is relatively free of government or corporate control. People power should also address and support diversity of opinion. Any idea at odds with conventional wisdom—enforced by either custom or by law—is a dissenting idea. Dissenting ideas have included Galileo's belief that the earth rotated around the sun; that women should be allowed to vote; or that African Americans should be able to ride at the front, middle, *or* back of the bus, at *their* discretion. Any current dominant belief was once a dissenting belief.

Paper Tiger Television

Developing a critical consciousness about the communications industry is a necessary first step towards democratic control of information resources.

The power of mass culture rests on the trust of the public. This legitimacy is a paper tiger.

—The Paper Tiger Collective (1991)

In the evenings, viewers of New York City's public access television stations in all five boroughs can flip to the weekly Paper Tiger Television (PTTV) show and see a welcome and unpredictable exception to the corporately controlled product that generally defines television in the United States. PTTV is the product of a collective of media activists whose specialty is producing Alice in Wonderlandlike "media about media." Hence their programs are often about other programs or other aspects of mass media, including television soap operas, talk shows, the portrayal of primates in *National Geographic*, the media packaging of the Gulf War, a seven-part dissection of the *New York Times* (by Herbert Schiller, who calls the *Times* "the steering mechanism of the ruling class"), race relations in "Star Trek," or high school students' reaction to the television program "Beverly Hills 90210." Their programs on cyberspace (in which they ask various New Yorkers on the street for directions to the information superhighway) raise many important issues about access and use of telecommunications technology. PTTV programs generally begin with the rhetorical, "It's 8:30 P.M. (or whatever time it happens to be). Do you know where your brains are?" and end with a blackboard that shows the episode's budget (Fig. 7.4), a ridiculously minuscule amount, especially when compared with other media offerings.

"Professionalism in broadcasting" states NYU journalism professor Jay Rosen, "systematically spoils the audience for anything other than the current level of slickness" (1994). PTTV helps to reverse this by throwing away the book on how to create professional television shows: Their titles are often

Figure 7.4 Inexpensive Television Is Possible!

hand-printed, cues can be heard, and the crew can be seen. Instead, they've written their own book: *ROAR!* provocatively subtitled "Rarely Organized, Always Radical" (Paper Tiger Collective, 1991), an invaluable guide to television media activism that is now available on Paper Tiger's Web site. *ROAR!* contains essays on media activism as well as helpful hints on using camcorders, building backdrops, and developing programs that aren't cut from a corporate cookie-cutter.

Although PTTV may have a limited impact, there are some valuable lessons for community-network developers. The first is that it is possible, and sometimes desirable, to do things *inexpensively.* A community network can't compete with blockbuster motion pictures of George Lucas or Steven Spielberg costing tens of millions of dollars. The second lesson is that *professionalism* and its accompanying high costs can actually be damaging to the "third places" that Oldenberg describes, whether electronic or actual. A third lesson is that media work can be alternative, creative, and *fun.* The PTTV collective has been following their principles and making programs that aren't cut from the mainstream cloth for nearly 15 years. The last lesson is that perseverance is important; it will always be a struggle to develop alternative media.

SF Free Press, SHRED, and the Vocal Point

The Internet has long offered the potential for new types of publishing enterprises. In recent years, the World Wide Web has helped to realize that potential by providing a simple way to access information on remote computers without passwords or knowledge of arcane UNIX commands. The information also is more accessible since it now can include graphics and, increasingly, sound or video. As the following three examples demonstrate, the World Wide Web can allow people and groups who traditionally have not been able to reach a wide audience to make their stories broadly available (without guaranteeing delivery, of course) to millions of people that point Web-browsing software in the direction of their site.

In early 1995, the workers at the *San Francisco Chronicle* newspaper went on strike. Normally, when newspaper employees are on strike the newspaper isn't published until the strike is over or the striking workers are replaced. This time, however, the striking newspaper employees took advantage of the World Wide Web capabilities on the Internet and published an abbreviated "Strike Special Edition" of the *San Francisco Free Press*, which was available to anyone in the world with a Web browser on the Internet (Fig. 7.5).

Gay skateboard-riding political activists living in San Francisco's Skid

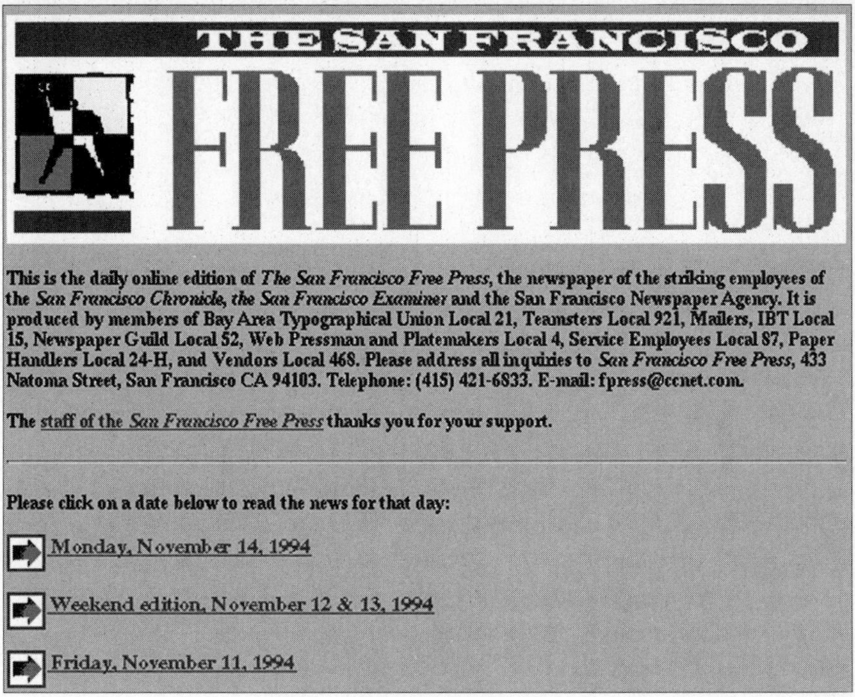

THE SAN FRANCISCO

FREE PRESS

This is the daily online edition of *The San Francisco Free Press*, the newspaper of the striking employees of the *San Francisco Chronicle*, the *San Francisco Examiner* and the San Francisco Newspaper Agency. It is produced by members of Bay Area Typographical Union Local 21, Teamsters Local 921, Mailers, IBT Local 15, Newspaper Guild Local 52, Web Pressman and Platemakers Local 4, Service Employees Local 87, Paper Handlers Local 24-H, and Vendors Local 468. Please address all inquiries to *San Francisco Free Press*, 433 Natoma Street, San Francisco CA 94103. Telephone: (415) 421-6833. E-mail: fpress@ccnet.com.

The staff of the *San Francisco Free Press* thanks you for your support.

Please click on a date below to read the news for that day:

➡ Monday, November 14, 1994

➡ Weekend edition, November 12 & 13, 1994

➡ Friday, November 11, 1994

Figure 7.5 *San Francisco Free Press* Home Page

Row rarely have a platform from which they can expound their views on politics, living in the city, or on anything else, for that matter. However, SHRED, a "general purpose skaters' (as in skateboard) union," using the World Wide Web, told the story of the rough and tumble neighborhood in which they live and gave their advice on political activism and working the media (as it related to their urban squatting actions in a derelict absentee-owned warehouse in the Yerba Buena area of San Francisco). Also, in a report replete with photographs, they described their ill-fated visit to an "incredibly stupid" Skin Heads' picnic in Napa Valley.

High school newspapers are rarely noted for high circulation or relevance. The K-12 students of the Boulder Valley school district, however, seem to have succeeded at both with the electronic edition of *The Vocal Point* (Fig. 7.6) that's available on the World Wide Web. According to their home page on the Web, "The newspaper creates a forum in which the youth of Boulder can express their ideas and be heard . . . throughout the world." The monthly *Vocal Point* covers topics of immediate and looming importance to high school kids, including reflections on violence, racism, and employment after high school. The October 1994 edition that I perused contained articles such as

October Vocal Point

Help

Vocal Point is a unique monthly newspaper created by the K-12 students of the Boulder Valley School District. The newspaper creates a forum in which the youth of Boulder can express their ideas and be heard... throughout the world.

Every issue, Vocal Point covers a significant local or national topic from the diverse perspectives of Boulder's youth. This month, that topic is violence.

Sections:

Click on the photograph or click here to learn more about the Vocal Point staff:

Centennial Video (283k)

- **Violence**

    Drugs and Alcohol: Do They Lead to Violence?
        Do drugs and alcohol increase violent acts among people?
    Big Screen Violence Hits the Real World
        Violence in Hollywood is Affecting the Level of Violence in the Streets of America.

Figure 7.6

"White Supremacy on the Rise," "Do computers and violence mix?," and "Is TV too violent?"

As a medium of communication, the World Wide Web is more like television than e-mail could ever be. The Web provides the electronic ocean for "Web surfing" just as television provides the opportunity for channel surfing as a way to idly (and often passively) wend your way through a wide range of attractive choices. (Television, we are told, will have 500 channels, while the World Wide Web is currently orders of magnitude more complex and growing more so every day.) The World Wide Web is changing quite rapidly; new versions of the software will go beyond the book-page metaphor, and developers are exploring new modes of interactivity between the Web page owners and the Web page users.

There are, finally, two major issues that relate to the efficacy of Web "publishing" for small, independent, and alternative publishers. The first is the question of quality of information and interactivity. To what degree is the Web turning into a new type of television? The second issue is visibility. Because the amount of information available on the World Wide Web is increasing exponentially, the current visibility enjoyed by publishers such as the three examples just mentioned will probably decline. Although independent and alternative information will probably still exist, the staggering quantity of other information, often of a commercial nature, will probably make it increasingly marginal and invisible as time goes on.

AGENDA FOR ACTION

Don't hate the media. Become the media.

Jello Biafra

Current information and communication systems suffer from problems that are profoundly disturbing to those concerned about a "free press" in the United States and around the world. Modern media systems (including television, radio, newspapers, and magazines) have been—until very recently—almost entirely distributed through broadcast. They are one-way channels in which citizens are *consumers*—consumers of a melange of information including realistic murder, rape, and robbery dramatizations, insipid situation comedies, game shows, deodorant and cat food and automobile commercials, and—sometimes—useful information, worthwhile dramatic fare, or educational programming. At the same time, this broadcast stream is owned by fewer (private) companies than ever before. There is virtually no two-way conversation nor community influence or input. While telephones *are* used by individuals, their use in nearly all cases is limited to a two-person conversation. Until recently, there has been very little in the way of many-to-many communication. Until the advent of "Cyberspace" there has been virtually no "public space" in the vastness of the media galaxy.

Tom Grundner, the originator of the Cleveland Free-Net and the National Public Telecomputing Network (NPTN) describes community networking as a "fourth media." "It's not radio, It's not television, It's not print, but it has characteristics of all three"(NPTN, 1992). He explains that the main difference is that community networks are interactive and that "People can interact with each other and with the issues of the day." Community networks, as Grundner explains, can provide an opportunity to help redefine media, to make it more responsive to individuals and their communities, and to allow more people to participate. This means free or very inexpensive fees and it means free public terminals—in bus stations, homeless shelters, schools, cafes, and retirement homes. From the policy side, it means that forums should exist where anybody can post, and that forums should be relatively easy to establish. Special attention should be paid to marginal voices, alternative voices, and voices not generally heard, so that they can be heard in an unfettered way. While community computer networks may serve as a good focus for new community media, it is clear that "ordinary" citizens need to involve themselves in all facets of the media world if it ever is to become more responsive and democratic.

Opening up communications and information along these radical lines poses threats to civil and community well-being in addition to providing promise. (Theodore Roszak has said that computers are now a "mature technology" in that they provide as much negative potential as positive potential![2]) In the "good old days" before computer-network technology, newspapers (such as the *New York Times*) could be trusted to publish a collection of written reports *every day* that had some degree of accuracy, using words that were spelled correctly and sentences that generally followed the grammatical guidelines of Strunk and White. There is a danger that information might be less accurate, less reliable (in terms of regularity and timeliness) and less "objective" when every information consumer can also be an information provider. It will become increasingly important (as if life wasn't complicated enough already!) for citizens to sift through conflicting reports, weigh evidence, entertain tentative hypotheses while maintaining a healthy media awareness and skepticism, without becoming stubborn and reflexive. Citizens also will need to learn how to become "good media citizens" by learning how to behave in new information commons.

But a community network is more than a sounding board for individuals (although it *is* that). A community network can be a tool for the community as a whole and can be used to address community needs using community assets. The community must "own" the community network both legally and psychologically. The community network should be a *part* of the community, like a park, public market, or familiar landmark. At the

[2]Computers Freedom and Privacy Conference, 1995.

same time, the network's communication and information base can be *integrated* with other media to encourage more public and responsible journalism and politics.

Minimum Community Media Requirements

While super high bandwidth networks, video on-demand, and telemedicine are grabbing the headlines, a wide phalanx of what Community Technology Institute Pat Barry call "rearguard technology" (Fig. 7.7) now exists. Government and business spokespeople, as well as some representatives of public interest organizations, are inclined to focus on the allure of the newest technology to articulate their vision. At the lower end, the "rearguard" are a variety of developers who are working to develop the *minimum* set of services that could be provided at very low cost to all. This road is ultimately the most difficult, the least glamorous, and the most radical, for its beneficiaries are

Varieties of Community Technology	
Model	*Example*
Universal Voice-Mail	Community Voice-Mail
Community Computing Centers	Playing to Win
Community Networks	Seattle Community Network
Homemade Television	Paper Tiger TV
Community Television	Davis (California) Community Television
Community Radio	KBIA (New York City)
Non-commercial Wire Service	Interpress (headquartered in Rome)
Community Network Services Sharing	NPTN Cybercasting
Public Ownership of Delivery Channels	———

Figure 7.7

often the least advantaged. Unfortunately, this approach has precious few effective spokespeople. With this perspective, tasks are grounded in *real life*— not in some ambiguous future where fancy technology (with no apparent human intervention) magically vanquishes societal ills. These visions—all motivated by similar dreams—form the basic infrastructure for what might be deemed universal access in the electronic age. These visions, as a unifying and collective vision, form a technologically viable and relatively inexpensive base for the media of new communities.

History is littered with failed and flawed prognostications of new community-based democratic eras ushered in by communications technology. Walt Whitman in 1856 wrote about the "electric telegraphs of the earth" and "the filaments of the news" (Czitrom, 1982), while years later both radio and television were touted as harbingers of a golden age. Communications technology can be used to help build a platform for human aspirations, but if history is any guide and if current players prove anywhere as powerful as they appear, the success of this vision is far from guaranteed.

Chapter 8

Social Architecture

Networks are empty without content; content is inaccessible without networks; networks and content are useless without computer systems, information specialists, and users; research is meaningless without systems for instantiating and disseminating the results; government funds, policies, and regulations have no impact unless they result in innovation; information specialists and users are isolated without systems to satisfy their needs for information. And so it goes.

John Garrett (1993)

The system is the people.

TWICS on-line greeting (Rheingold, 1993)

SOCIAL RELATIONSHIPS

The community network provides a "social space" for the community, a place where community members can interact with each other, a place to learn, discuss, persuade, or just have fun. The community network is also a *community institution*, an organization that is supported by the community, helps support the community, and is situated within the community. The community-network *organization* provides the framework and the *institutionalization* that helps create, administer, and promote continuing development of the community network. Both the community-network system and the community-network organization exist within a social and political context that helps shape the community-network *system* and *organization* and, in turn, is shaped by them.

We have attempted to show the social relationships (including political and economic) that influence a community network in Fig. 8.1. The figure shows major types of "players" that help determine the shape, direction, and philosophy that individual community networks might take, as well as the community-network movement as a whole. This figure is a very broad characterization of the social and political model, and developers in local communities must take the specifics of their local environment into account when building and maintaining a community network. The model includes (1) individual and organizational participants, (2) nonparticipants, (3) other

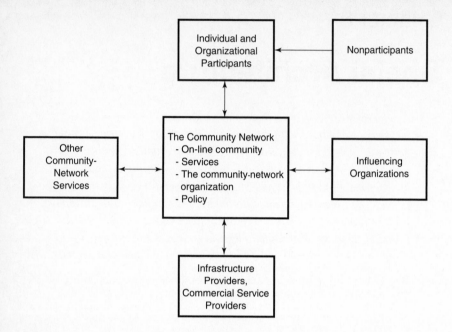

Figure 8.1 Social and Political Model

community networks (including BBSs), (4) influencing organizations, (5) infrastructure providers and other commercial service providers; and (6) the community network itself. We'll discuss each one in turn, starting with the community network.

THE COMMUNITY NETWORK

Just as electrical systems began to transform urban and small-town America a century ago, community computer networks will do so in the 1990s.

Steve Cisler (1993)

At the center of the model is the community network. The community network must be an integral part of the larger community—not autonomous and isolated—if the community network is to be truly a *community* network. Nestled within the community-network box are its essential attributes, including the on-line community, the community-network services, the community-network organization, and the information-usage policy that guides it.

On-line Community

The on-line community is the group of people who participate in the community network by offering their opinions, by reading those of others, and by using and providing information and services. The on-line community is at the center of the social and political architecture. If this community is inactive or dysfunctional, the entire community network is deficient.

The character of the on-line community is influenced in three basic ways: by the system itself, the users, and the culture. The first influence, the system itself, makes its presence felt through its user interface, capabilities, and content. The user interface should make the system easy to use and be free of surprises, and the system should do what users expect it to do. The system capabilities include various ways in which users communicate with other users, including the use of static files of information, forums, real time "chat," or e-mail, as well as by other available capabilities that could include file transfer capabilities or access to other community networks and the World Wide Web. The system content describes what's on the system. Is the information useful? Lively? Up-to-date? Are the conversations scintillating? Exasperating? Engaging? The second major influence is the user population, including its numbers, interests, and formal and informal roles. The third influence is the culture of the on-line community or society, with its interaction patterns, themes, conventions, folkways, and cast of characters that has evolved and will continue to evolve over time. Community-network developers and participants alike should keep these influences in mind as they work on the system. Although it is neither possible nor desirable to precisely mold the on-line community according to specific requirements, it is both possible *and* desirable to attempt to steer the system in ways that best advance community goals.

Technology as Mediator

In a community network—as in all other communications technology—technology plays a mediating role. The manner in which people use the system is circumscribed and partially shaped by the system. At a general level, the technology allows or *affords* certain activities. A telephone affords voice communication, whereas community networks afford text and sometimes graphics and other information. At a more subtle level, the technology also mediates. Usenet newsgroups, consisting of "postings" contributed by readers, are dedicated to a topic following a fairly rigid naming convention. They're often read using a "news reader" that displays computer paths, message-identifying numbers, and other generally technical (and largely irrelevant) information. On the other hand, the Caucus interface—used, for example, in the Santa Monica PEN system—displays virtually no header information except for the identification of the person who wrote the entry and the forums can have any name whatsoever. One PEN forum, for example, is entitled "Is PEN dead?" A Usenet newsgroup on a similar theme might be called `soc.comnets.pen` (where "soc" stands for "social" and "comnets" stands for community networks). The topic or general discussion area of an electronic forum sometimes sets the tone for the discussion—the "weird" discussions on the WELL, or the `rec.pets.cats` or `alt.tasteless` Usenet newsgroups, for example. Some forum topics, on the other hand, are so general—`seattle.general`, for example—that about the only thing a reader can expect is disconnected and heated disagreement.

Network Citizenship

There is a growing body of literature on the sociology of cyberspace (Kollock and Smith, 1994) that reflects the growing number of participants and the emerging diversity of forms of on-line communication. Although much of this is relevant and should be studied by developers, we will not include an extended discussion here, but instead turn to the concept of community network "citizenship." This concept helps define the responsibility that individuals should have for the on-line community and the responsibility that the on-line community should have for individuals. The community that is made possible by a community network is in actuality a multitude of smaller communities, each with an individual style and level of intimacy and purpose, much as a geographical community is comprised of neighborhoods, families, and associations, each with their own distinct characteristics.

Forums and e-mail distribution lists can support information sharing solely. They can be used to share feelings or opinions through conversation, or they can be used to accomplish specific tasks—planning a conference, or writing a proposal, for example. Shared purpose is an important way of unifying electronic communities. Confusion over the purpose of a mailing list or a forum is a common situation and can result in a disjointed electronic conversation, as can happen in a more traditional conversation in which participants have diverse expectations.

While passive participation ("lurking") will take place in all types of forums, it is far less disturbing than the aggressive antisocial behavior that seems to crop up all too frequently in electronic forums. Unfortunately, there are endless variations of these behaviors, varying from simple sarcasm to violent and sexual threats to "virtual rapes" (Dibbell, 1993). While a single person can fairly easily turn a pleasant (nonvirtual) social scene into an un-pleasant one through loudness, vulgarity, or threatening behavior, the elec-tronic venue seems exceedingly vulnerable to many types of abuse, probably because of the fact that people are not interacting face-to-face.

Design of "Virtual Communities"

Mike Godwin of the Electronic Frontier Foundation is concerned that new cyberspace visitors will be "left wholly alienated, isolated, without any sense of belonging" if there is inadequate planning and there is no "deliberate architectural vision" in mind when creating new systems (Godwin, 1994). With that in mind, he offers nine principles for *virtual* communities (Fig. 8.2). These principles play a role in but are not identical to those needed for com-munity networks (which are designed around *geographical* communities).

Although I'd suggest additional features such as the need to meet in per-son (in addition to *virtual* meetings) and the need for discussion modelling (discussed below), Godwin's principles are worth considering, especially as they compare and contrast with other principles sketched out in this book that are designed to support geographical communities. Note particularly Godwin's front-loading suggestion: Too often people feel that putting up the standard fare on the community network is sufficient. There is a vast number of other activities competing for people's time and attention and providing excitement and diversity in the community-network offerings is critical.

Nine Principles for Virtual Communities

- Use software that promotes good discussions.
- Don't impose a length limitation on postings.
- Front-load your system with talkative, diverse people.
- Let the users resolve their own disputes.
- Provide institutional memory.
- Promote continuity.
- Be host to a particular interest group.
- Provide places for children.
- Most important: Confront the users with a crisis.

Figure 8.2

Community-network organizers and volunteers need to think competitively in terms of market share, for example, to create a compelling culture by providing lively forums and esoteric information not readily found elsewhere.

Godwin's last point—confronting the users with a crisis—suggests that fabricating controversy (right here in CyberCity!) is acceptable. While beating the drum capriciously to whip up interest in the system is not acceptable, confronting and grappling with legitimate crises is fine. In Seattle, for example, Seattle Community Network users from all locations in the political galaxy rallied against a "mini Exon/Gorton" bill in Washington State that would have paralyzed Washington's community networks with unrealistic and unconstitutional restrictions and fines. Rheingold's book (1993) offers instructive anecdotes on how virtual communities on the WELL used electronic networking to deal with emergencies such as life-threatening diseases or natural disasters while incidentally strengthening their sense of community.

UCLA researchers Peter Kollock and Marc Smith have been concentrating on the problems and guidelines for managing the new "virtual commons" and have raised intriguing issues for community-network developers. The virtual commons, according to Kollock and Smith has many features that are shared with other commons, especially the temptation for individuals to behave selfishly, partaking of the results of others' benevolence without adding anything to the community assets in any way. They've researched the concept of cooperation in a virtual environment primarily by studying behavior and norms in Usenet newsgroup electronic forums.

In their analysis Kollock and Smith list seven design principles uncovered by researcher Elinor Ostrom who has studied a wide range of communities that have succesfully developed and maintained "collective goods" (Ostrom, 1990). Although not conclusive, these principles (shown in Fig. 8.3) could prove useful in setting up and maintaining new community commons, both virtual and actual. Many of these principles will be best addressed through a combination of democratic principles and clear policies that follow these guidelines. (The SCN policy, for example, clearly addresses the sixth and seventh points by specifying a range of penalties and for establishing a low-cost procedure for dealing with conflicts that arise on SCN.)

Discussion Modelling

While open computer-based discussions seem to be *generally* immune to outright rigging or controlling by those that established the system or by other participants, there is a strong need to preclude or curb some of the potential for antisocial behavior that the systems seem to allow or even to promote. Ken Phillips, the originator of the Santa Monica PEN system, feels that many

Ostrom's Design Principles for Collective Goods
(from Kollock and Smith, 1994)

1. Group boundaries are clearly defined

2. Rules governing the use of collective goods are well matched to local needs and conditions.

3. Most individuals affected by these rules can participate in modifying the rules.

4. The rights of the community members to devise these rules is respected by external authorities.

5. A system for monitoring member's behavior exists; this monitoring is undertaken by the community members themselves.

6. A graduated system of sanctions is used

7. Community members have access to low-cost conflict-resolution mechanisms.

Figure 8.3

of the forums on PEN became overly contentious. When such a situation arises, those with less aggressive natures are likely to lose interest in the forum and drop out. While monitoring forums or policing them in other ways represents reactive approaches, positive proactive approaches are also possible. Evelyn Pine, former executive director of Community Memory in Berkeley, says that "discussion modelling is critical but notoriously difficult." By definition, "modelling" a discussion forum is a conscious attempt to guide the conversational flow, primarily by providing good examples by engaging in exemplary on-line behavior. Pine says that the writers' group on the WELL is a good example of a cordial and convivial environment. When a new writer posts a short story to the group, the other participants are very supportive. Since the discussion actually creates a microculture, behavior is shaped by the sum of the participants—not by a moderator or discussion leader alone. For that reason, the mores and attitudes need to be shared and enforced by the whole group—or at least a large percentage of it—for the shaping to be effective. People must have the right to disagree and to offer dissenting opinions or the forum will become lifeless. On the other hand, a forum must have standards of conduct if it is to be useful. Contrary to the views of some people, the beauty of cyberspace is *not* that it's easy, or acceptable, to be a jerk.

> Retaining . . . the habit of expressing myself in terms of modest diffi-
> dence; . . . never using, when I advanced anything that may possibly be
> disputed, the words *certainly, undoubtedly,* or any others that give the
> air of positiveness to an opinion; but rather say, *I conceive or apprehend a*
> *thing to be so and so; it appears to me, I should think it so or so, for such and*
> *such reasons;* or *I imagine it to be so;* or *it is so, if I am not mistaken.* This
> habit, I believe, has been of great advantage to me when I have had oc-
> casion to inculcate my opinions, and persuade men into measures that
> I have been from time to time engaged in promoting.
>
> Benjamin Franklin (Rottenberg, 1985)

There are many ways to make the same point as the Franklin quote above indicates, and a message that follows the guidelines of the prevailing culture is
more likely to persuade than one that doesn't.

Limits and Restrictions

Although rarely used in practice, software could, in theory, prevent some
types of antisocial postings, such as messages that were too long or messages
that were going to too many recipients. This type of software protection
could have prevented the recent incident in which a religious enthusiast dis-
patched his apocalyptic warning to over one hundred Usenet newsgroups
on a single day. Current technology would not prevent this person from electronic proselytizing in this way on a daily if not hourly basis.

A more common phenomenon is that of a frequent poster dominating a
discussion: "The one who posts the most wins." Suppose Jane works fifty
hours a week as a nurse and barely has time to check in on her favorite discussions once every couple of weeks. John, on the other hand, does not have
a job and apparently does not have a life outside of posting to forums. Obviously, John can more easily influence others—all other things being equal—
than can Jane, who barely has time to read and post at all. System-imposed
limitations on size, number, and frequency of postings could be employed to
dampen this brand of built-in bias. An artificially low limit could, on the
other hand, act against people who are less succinct in their postings, or have
more ideas, or who provide more detailed analysis. People with less popular
ideas would also need latitude to adequately defend their position. In those
situations, posting limits would act as an electronic "gag rule," preventing a
person from exercising the right to speak.

Realistically, there are times when time limits or other restrictions must be
imposed on discussion in the non-cyberworld. This is particularly important
in decision-making bodies, which are discussed in more detail in Chapter 10.
Clearly there is a need to strike a balance between unlimited freedom and

overly restrictive constraints when designing and evaluating computer-mediated discussions.

Administrators need to have authority to warn, then later to suspend or ban a user from the system. Some possible abuses include sending e-mail to a person who has requested that he or she not receive e-mail from that person. Other offenses may include some malicious use like broadcasting to all users ("spamming") or sending chain letters. Advertising or using the system for financial gain could also be inappropriate in some cases. Using the system to gain illegal access to other machines needs also to be expressly prohibited.

Much has been written about proper on-line interactions or "netiquette," but Henry Sedgwick's seven rules on the art of conversation written in 1930 (Fig. 8.4) may be the most timely and succinct (Sedgwick, 1930; Oldenberg, 1991).

Services

Although services on the community network will vary to reflect the needs, interests, and assets of particular communities, the services need to support all six community core values. A set of core services derived from the core values for a generic community network is shown in Fig. 8.5. This set is not an exhaustive list, but it is representative of the types of needed services, and could be useful in identifying potential organizational participants as well as for determining locations for public access terminals.

The Art of Conversation

1. Remain silent your share of the time (more rather than less).
2. Be attentive while others are talking.
3. Say what you think but be careful not to hurt other's feelings.
4. Avoid topics not of general interest.
5. Say little or nothing about yourself personally but talk about others there assembled.
6. Avoid trying to instruct.
7. Speak in as low a voice as will allow others to hear.

Figure 8.4

Core Services for a Community Network

Conviviality and Culture

- Forums for ethnic, religious, neighborhood interest groups
- Recreation and parks information
- Arts events
- Community calendar

Education

- On-line homework help
- Forums for educators, students
- Q&A on major topics
- Distributed projects
- Pen pals

Strong Democracy

- How to contact elected officials
- E-mail to elected officials
- E-mail to government agencies
- Forums on major issues
- On-line versions of legislation, regulations, and other government information

Health and Well-Being

- Q&A on medical information
- Access to health-care information
- Self-help forums

Economic Equity, Opportunity, and Sustainability

- Want ads
- Job listings
- Labor news
- Ethical investing
- Community-development projects
- Unemployed, laid-off, and striking worker discussion forums

Information and Communication

- Access to alternative news and opinion
- E-mail to all Internet addresses
- Cooperation with community radio, etc.
- Access to library information and services
- Access to on-line databases
- On-line "Quick Information"
- Access to on-line periodicals, wire services

Figure 8.5

THE COMMUNITY-NETWORK ORGANIZATION

Leaders lead people but organizers organize organizations. Word play? Hardly! The role of an organizer is to build an organization that lasts.

Kim Bobo, Jackie Kendall, and Steve Max (1991)

The community-network organization is the organized body whose primary responsibility it is to ensure that the community network is as effective as possible. Some of its tasks include the actual administration of the system, financing, and other organizational duties. Most importantly, the organization must ensure that the system helps support the core values discussed in earlier chapters. The organization must be involved with day-to-day operations, including system maintenance and administration, as well as community outreach, fundraising, and participation in the political process at the local, state, and federal levels. The organization itself may be a nonprofit organization, a public development authority, a nonprofit/government cooperative venture, a governmental organization, or (if certain guidelines are met) a for-profit organization. The organization could also be allied in coalitions, cooperatives, or associations with other organizations. Chapter 10 is devoted to discussing the community-network organization in more depth. Although the community-network organization is a key element in the social architecture, we'll postpone an extensive discussion until then.

Information-Usage Policy

At its basic level, all information on a computer looks the same—a parade of bits, each holding the value of one or zero, in patterns no human eye can discern. Viewed from higher levels, however, the bits become *information*. And information is an important, highly scrutinized, and valuable commodity indeed.

Information policy determines the "rules of the road" for what information can be conveyed, by whom, and to whom, and under what conditions. The information policy will also cover what happens to an alleged or actual transgressor and specify who's liable in illegal communications. Unfortunately, the legal frontier in many areas has not been settled, and costly duels are being waged with lawyers, lobbyists, and politicians, leaving community-network participants and organizers in uncertain territory. The community-network movement (like the BBS community) is singularly underfunded and underorganized among the players weighing into the networked arena.

A community network's policy statement is the explicit attempt to formulate the guidelines by which the principles or goals are addressed. It can set up conditions under which an effective on-line society can grow, promoting successful use of the system to meet the needs of the new community. The policy statement also establishes the rules—or procedures—that will be followed when problems arise involving the use of the system.

A sound information policy is critical to a community network, for it must address the wide range of issues that undoubtedly will arise. An information policy must anticipate and address questions and issues like the following:

- How private is my e-mail?
- Can I be denied access to the community network?
- Can I post "adult" material?
- Do I have to use my real name?
- How can I register a complaint against a moderator?
- I'm receiving abusive e-mail. Can you put an end to it?
- I'd like to use the network to advertise my product. Is that OK?
- I have a commercial database service. Can you let your users access it?
- The doctor in your question and answer forum gave me bad advice. I'm suing you!
- Someone reprinted my posting in a magazine without my permission! What should I do?
- Somebody on your network posted stolen credit card numbers (or indecent material). We're confiscating your equipment (and sending you to jail). Please excuse the inconvenience . . .

These types of issues reflect in large part the tension that exists between individual and community rights. This conflict isn't unique to community networks, but since these networks are a new medium, many of the related issues are currently unresolved.

We can begin to devise policies based on other media, but the analogy is often strained. Community networks are like libraries, and like libraries, they must be champions of free speech. But disagreements in libraries usually arise between library users and contents of books—not usually between two (or more) library users. Furthermore, even though libraries don't officially disallow material, the space limitations on their shelves provide implicit constraints, unlike the essentially boundlessness of cyberspace. Community networks are also like telephones in some ways. Both provide a medium for discourse—discourse that is sometimes acrimonious. Phone calls, however, are fleeting, private, and have a limited number of participants. Some "discussions" in public electronic forums are more like public fist fights than private discussions. An on-line discussion involves potentially large numbers of participants and spectators, and every spectator optionally can record the session, which can be disseminated still further.

Privacy and Fair Information Practices

Privacy on the network is an important, yet not widely considered, aspect of community networks. Since the electronic media exacerbates many concerns over privacy, it is vitally important to consider these issues in the *design* of the system—not as an afterthought. The most important aspect of privacy probably has to do with e-mail. It is important that the contents of any private e-mail remain as private as the system administrators can possibly ensure. Just as telephones can be tapped, there are ways that computer-network communication can be intercepted with no indication to sender or recipient that the message has been inspected. For this reason, privacy cannot be totally guaranteed, but the system's administrators must consciously and conscientiously strive to ensure a high degree of privacy. Besides the contents of e-mail, all peripheral information must be kept secure. This certainly includes registration data, which could include address, phone numbers, and other information that the registrant regards as private. If it is necessary to collect other peripheral information such as records of to whom a user sent e-mail, from whom a user received e-mail, what forums he or she visited, and what files were downloaded by the user, then this information should be deleted regularly and subject to the same high standards of privacy as e-mail, private files, and user records.

It is not difficult to imagine ways in which electronic records could be used in ways that the user did not envision, intend, or expect, for legal, economic, or political reasons. Law enforcement officials and others, for example, sometimes attempt to find out what books people have checked out from the public library, while telephone companies have expressed the desire to sell telephone-call records to clients to aid in their marketing activities.

Although circumstances will undoubtedly vary from community to community and from system to system, the "Code of Fair Information Practices" (Fig. 8.6) adopted by the U.S. Department of Health, Education, and Welfare in 1973 offers a very good set of principles that can serve as a framework for privacy considerations of community networks (as well as other electronic systems may contain records on individuals). The code, based on five principles, contains simple and straightforward suggestions for protecting privacy.

The Code of Fair Information Practices

There must be no personal data record-keeping system whose very existence is secret;

There must be a way for a person to find out what information about the person is in a record and how it is used;

There must be a way for a person to prevent information about the person that was obtained for one purpose from being used or made available for other purposes without the person's consent;

There must be a way for a person to correct or amend a record of identifiable information about the person;

Any organization creating, maintaining, using, or disseminating records of identifiable personal data must assure the reliability of the data for their intended use and must take precaution to prevent misuses of the data.

Figure 8.6

Who's Who?

Computer systems don't know whether a user's identity is real or manufactured. But the value of knowing or not knowing the true identity of a user varies according to context. User anonymity is important, for example, when users ask sensitive questions about sexually transmitted diseases in an on-line forum or submit such questions on-line to a doctor or nurse who's volunteered to field such questions. On the other hand, delivering anonymous e-mail is *not* the main responsibility of a community network. It should not necessarily be trivial for people to send anonymous threatening letters to the president, their neighbor, or anybody else that's reachable via e-mail.

Beyond the idea of anonymity is that of a false or even intentionally misleading user ID. As *Newsday* writer Jonathan Quitner (1994) has pointed out, this can apply to login name but also to the domain name, which is to say the computer and the organization that hosts the user. Quitner, for example, registered the domain name "mcdonalds" with the Internet Information Center and began receiving e-mail at the address `Ronald@McDonalds.com`, a direct reference to the clown image and character that the McDonald's hamburger chain has made famous. The information center—swamped with applications for new domain names—basically just checks to see if the name is taken, not to see if the requester has a right to the name. Likewise, the Seattle Community Network will assign any login name that's not been spoken for. The assigned name will appear on any e-mail that is sent from that account. A "real name" will also appear unless the user has requested anonymity. Thus a user can send e-mail that has been basically purged of identifying information (except for the domain `"scn.org"`). If an e-mail message is objectionable in any way, the SCN administrators can make a *reasonable* attempt to establish the person's identity based on the original registration form that was filled out. Since SCN does not actively check registration identities, there is no way, of course, to know with certainty if individuals are really who they claim to be. Similarly, a new telephone subscriber is not fingerprinted or checked for identity by the telephone company, either. In any case, the *carrier* of the content should not be liable for the content. Telephone companies are not charged as accessories if thieves use their telephone wires to plan robberies. Unfortunately legislators in many states and at the national level seem to be pushing in the wrong direction.

Network Etiquette

In addition to the policy statement (see Appendix D), the Seattle Community Network has a netiquette (a portmanteau word from "network etiquette") guide to help promote good cyberspace citizenry among network users. Since the electronic medium is new, the use conventions are not established and there is a tendency for some people to use it in ways that seem rude to others. While the U.S. Constitution doesn't exclude *rude* speech as a protected form of speech, it's clear that many people would rather not receive sarcastic, insulting, insinuating, lewd, obscene, violent, or accusatory messages from other users.

The SCN "Netiquette Guide," is an attempt to anticipate these potential problems with the hope of preventing them from occurring in some cases and dealing with them effectively in other cases. Although the vast majority of people do want to be civil and realize that civil arguments are more likely to influence than uncivil ones, there are those people who will not and cannot be civil. Since it doesn't take too many of these people to spoil an electronic commons, we need to develop methods that will preserve civility without stifling free speech or introducing arbitrary and parochial restrictions.

In addition to community initiated influence—either positive or negative— it is necessary for some rules of conduct to be formalized and well-publicized to all users. This need is prompted by practical and legal considerations and is especially important in a moderated discussion where a moderator may exercise his or her power to excise postings or portions of postings from a forum.

The SCN Code of Etiquette

All registered users of the SCN MUST agree to the following Code of Etiquette while using SCN:

1. I will not knowingly engage in illegal distribution practices when posting information. Some examples of illegal distribution are: posting large portions of copyrighted material; posting libelous material; posting material that knowingly aids in a crime; posting credit card number; posting passwords.

2. I will not attempt to gain unauthorized access to SCN nor use SCN to gain unauthorized access to other systems.

3. I have read the SCN disclaimer.

4. I have read and understand the SCN policy statement and agree to abide by it as the governing policy of the SCN.

5. I will read the description of the forum to which I am posting and post only material relevant to its purpose and theme.

6. I will not use the SCN to harass individuals or organizations.

7. I understand that all public material on SCN may be redistributed, subject to copyright laws.

8. Private e-mail may not be redistributed without permission from the originator of the message.

Figure 8.7

In addition to its overall policy statement, the Seattle Community Network uses a code of ethics (Fig. 8.7) based on a similar document from the Victoria Free-Net organization. Forum moderators must also make their policies explicit. When situations arise, the moderator, community-network user and community-network administrators all have rights and responsibilities that should be well-defined and well-known. Although Mike Godwin (1994) would presumably disagree, the moderator should be able to censor postings for length, relevance, or unnecessary accusations and personal attacks. On the other hand, a user should be able to appeal a moderator's decision. The system administration should also be protected legally from controversies that erupt on their system much as the telephone company is not held liable for activities—legal and otherwise—that are accomplished or planned using the telephone system.

What are the appropriate responses to uncivil behavior? There is a fairly wide range of responses—some are informal, while others are more legalistic and formal; some are social, while others are technological. All have analogs in the "real world."

One response is to send a message back to the sender asking him or her to desist. This can be done in a private note—or via "cc" ("carbon copies" or duplicate messages) to a group of people. Sometimes the group "outing" approach backfires and the "offender" will redouble his or her efforts. Another approach is not to "take the bait"; ignoring unfounded accusations, attacks, and the like may be most successful. The offender often becomes bored and may seek other targets. If a user gets unwanted personal mail from somebody, he or she can ask the person not to send them any more personal mail. If the sender persists in sending them messages, this can be grounds for that person's temporary or permanent removal from the system. On a more unilateral level, the user can set up a "bozo filter" or "kill filter" that intercepts any e-mail or forum posting from any sender who is listed in the filter, effectively removing it *before* it can appear in the user's incoming mail or forum queue.

There are slightly different considerations in a moderated forum. The moderator can reject a posting if it doesn't pass the criteria established by the moderator—for example, if it is off the subject, too lengthy, if there are too many postings per day, or if it contains ad hominem attacks. Note that these criteria need to be explicit and as unambiguous as possible. The moderator can't reject a posting because he or she doesn't like the poster or doesn't agree with the posted argument. The posting can't be rejected because the poster doesn't meet some criteria—height, weight, race, religion, gender, IQ, and so forth. The poster also must have the right to appeal if he or she feels that the postings are being excluded unfairly. The SCN policy statement explicitly describes an appeal process for this eventuality.

INDIVIDUAL AND ORGANIZATIONAL PARTICIPANTS

> *What if you built a community network and nobody came?*
>
> Anonymous

Of course there would be no on-line community without contributors. The people and organizations that add information, opinions, issues, and questions to the system while noting what others have added are the life blood of the system. These contributors can best be thought of as belonging to one of two categories—individuals (who may assume the role of forum moderators as well) or organizational contributors.

Moderators and Other Individuals

As in a geographical community, people who participate in a community network do so for a variety of reasons. Some will use the system to find information, while others want to find conversation. Some will use the system to communicate on a one-to-one basis, others will be interested in forums—as active participants or passive "lurkers"—while others will want to assume even more active public roles in the on-line culture.

People who assume the responsibility for running an on-line forum are called "moderators." A moderator generally has strong interest, experience, or knowledge in a particular topic and wants to communicate with others on that topic. A moderator of a forum is like the host of a party, but how strenuously this role is assumed varies widely from moderator to moderator just as it does among party hosts. A moderator can also be seen as a discussion facilitator. If this role is assumed, it becomes a moderator's responsibility for ensuring that lively conversation occurs and that the conversation keeps on track if, indeed, keeping on track is important. While some types of forums—question and answer forums, for example—are less likely to be troubled, others may boil over with controversy and a moderator may need to wield some of the power of the role. If postings are too long or too numerous or if they contravene other established guidelines by being irrelevant, abusive, or libelous, the moderator is obliged to prune or excise the posting. As mentioned previously, guidelines should be established so that the moderator does not act capriciously or is viewed as acting capriciously. Since this area is among the most potentially hazardous realms for community-network developers and participants, these guidelines are critical.

John Coate, described by Howard Rheingold (1993) as the erstwhile "innkeeper, bartender, bouncer, matchmaker, mediator, and community-maker for the WELL" (the "Whole Earth 'Lectronic Link"), an on-line system run by the Whole Earth Catalog people, compares an on-line system to an inn (Coate, 1992). While staying at an inn, people converse with people they know and with people they encounter by chance. To Coate, facilitating an on-line community is like innkeeping; that is, the innkeeper encourages interchange between patrons but sometimes problems arise and order has to be restored.

Organizations

Many community organizations are interested in exploring opportunities offered by community networks. These opportunities range from e-mail use to large programs that use network facilities extensively. The League of Women Voters, for example, could distribute electronically some of the vast amount of information they collect on issues and candidates. They could also devise more ambitious projects as well, such as "electronic townhalls" in which citizens could question candidates directly on issues.

Virtually all organizations have information that they'd like to distribute electronically. Initially this effort may duplicate what they already distribute on paper: newsletters, briefing papers, and contact information, for example. Lack of resources or technical expertise may inhibit their desire to participate in a community network, although the promise of increased visibility in their community, reduced communication costs, and the desire to "modernize" their operations often helps to overcome these obstacles. Furthermore, organizations that are thinking about making their information or services available electronically may reduce their costs considerably by foregoing the development of an independent BBS system that they would have to purchase and maintain themselves. Using an existing community-network system also makes it easier for potential clients to use by providing a common access point—the "one-stop shopping" advantage.

A few of the possible organizational participants are listed in Fig. 8.8. *All* community organizations might feel the need to participate and none *should* be excluded. While some organizations may have exclusionary, undemocratic, or anticommunity principles, there is no valid reason for preventing them from using the system. As a matter of fact, *denying* them access to the system would be seen—justifiably—as exclusionary. While organizations should not be denied the right to participate, it is possible to argue that some types of electronic postings should be barred because of the content of the posting, such as the nature of an event being advertised. An analogous situation exists within the public library in regard to their meeting-rooms policy and their public-notices policy. A group is barred from using the facilities of the public library for meetings that deny participation on the basis of age, race, religion, sexual orientation, and the like. The public library also permits the posting of announcements for events that have no admission charge and are open to all. Whether or not policies like this are adopted for *public* postings (in forums, and so on) these restrictions would not apply to private e-mail correspondence.

Cooperative Projects

An "information provider" (IP) is defined as an individual or organization that uses the network to post information electronically or to convene on-line forums. An organization with whom the community-network organization has entered into a strategic alliance can be called a "partner." Somewhere between "information providing" and "strategic alliances" (discussed in Chapter 10), lies a myriad of possibilities for cooperative projects between organizational participants and the community-network organization. These projects are generally

---

Possible Organizational Participants

Culture and Conviviality

- Arts organizations
- Churches
- Boys and Girls Clubs
- Homeless shelters
- Activist groups
- Hobby groups

Education

- Public and private schools
- ESL and adult literacy organizations
- Drop-out programs

Strong Democracy

- League of Women Voters
- Political parties
- Government agencies
- Municipal research centers

Health and Well-Being

- Free clinics
- Referral services
- Hospitals
- Self-help groups

Economic Equity, Opportunity and Sustainability

- Labor unions
- Employment office
- Welfare rights organizations
- Community development groups
- Co-ops

Information and Communication

- Cable-access organizations
- Public TV and radio stations
- Libraries

Figure 8.8

less formal than strategic alliances, but they may require written agreements, as money, staff time, or other important resources may be involved.

A cooperative project is an endeavor that reflects the character and objectives of all participating groups and frequently will depend on the terms of specific project proposals. Some cooperative projects have included: placing terminals at organizational offices; obtaining, formatting, and distributing information of special interest; connecting particular BBSs, databases, or other systems to community networks; bringing in telephone lines to additional sites; producing printed materials; providing specialized training; developing new software; and enhancing the existing community-network software.

In addition to traditional community groups, like the YMCA, community centers, and the Camp Fire Girls that are evolving to meet changing needs in the community, there are scores of new organizations and informal groups, alliances, and coalitions of more recent vintage. These newer groups—described in more detail in the civic renaissance section of Chapter 11—are also worthy of attention. In many cases, these newer groups may be more politically aggressive, better tuned to the era, and more participatory. In other words, the values of these newer groups may be more consonant with the values of the new community and are likely to become valued partners in the development of community networks along with the more established groups.

NONPARTICIPANTS

Most community networks are more communities of networkers than networked communities.

Frank Odasz (1995)

Currently the largest group of players in the social architecture that encompasses the community-network universe doesn't even play. This is the large group of "nonusers" whose presence as a potential voice in the discussion of future technology is largely nonexistent. Users of electronic information and communication systems tend to be white, middle-class males between the ages of 20 and 50. They tend to be employed, have greater than average incomes, speak English, and have few disabilities. As the list in Fig. 8.9 indicates, there are large numbers of people that fall outside these categories. If community-network developers are serious about making systems that are used by a broad spectrum of people and provide genuine community benefit, then understanding the reasons why current systems aren't used is essential.

OTHER COMMUNITY-NETWORK
SERVICE PROVIDERS

The inter-organizational work involved may seem like it consumes more time than the project, and it may, depending on existing commonalities in the organizational mission and policy, and on the participant's interaction skills.

Clark Rogers and Brian Vidic (1995)

It is extremely unlikely that a community network will be the only computer-based resource that the community uses. It is far more likely that some combination of independent bulletin-board, referral, special-purpose, commercial, library, and government-based systems will be used to meet a community's diverse needs. The existence of this network stew has advantages

---

Not as Likely to be Community Network Participants

- Women
- Children and youth
- Elderly and retired people
- People in the lower and lower-middle economic classes
- Illiterate people
- Unemployed people
- Homeless people
- Disabled people—vision or mobility impaired
- Rural people
- Gay/lesbian
- Computer-illiterate/ computer-phobic/ computer-averse people
- Mentally or physically ill people
- Drug users

- Institutionalized people—prisoners, hospital patients
- People whose job or school doesn't provide connections
- People who are too busy (single moms) or too tired (those working two jobs)
- Ethnic minorities
- People who don't speak English or who use non-ASCII alphabets
- Indigenous people
- Immigrants (legal or otherwise)
- People in the (second and) third world
- Combinations of the above

Figure 8.9

and disadvantages. Among the advantages is the higher likelihood that the desired information would exist and that organizations would *compete* with each other, working harder to provide valuable services to the community. And competition would help ensure that rates were relatively low for access to useful community information. Competition also has its disadvantages. Competing networks might fight each other, squandering resources while missing important opportunities to cooperate; they might both concentrate on enlisting certain high-prestige or high-popularity information providers while neglecting others. They might compete for funds from the same sources. In addition to unproductive competition, the existence of many networks could present a daunting "user interface" (writ large) to the public: If every system had its own telephone number, user interface, registration procedure, policies, mail system, and so on, the public would be more likely to be puzzled than charmed.

Cooperation and Competition

Fortunately, there are many cooperative approaches that can strengthen community-network organizations while keeping community concerns uppermost. One approach is to provide reciprocal access to each others' machines. This means that the user would need to memorize one less phone number and make one less telephone call. Community networks could also cooperate on a registration system that would give users accounts on *both* machines, while going through one process. In a similar vein, it would be useful to provide e-mail access from both systems. Although this could result in more accounting and policy work, the benefits to the community are significant. With BBS systems, it makes sense for a larger community-network system to act as an e-mail gateway between the BBS and the Internet. The BBS system and the community network could also arrange for certain newsgroups and forums to be shared or "echoed," just like the Usenet community does with its newsgroups.

While it is technologically feasible to maintain the facade of a single community network by connecting multiple smaller systems together, this approach may also have its drawbacks. One danger is that the individual components of a "mega-network" might lose their individual identities. Without a discernible identity it might be difficult to find the necessary funding. And a community network with no discernible identity might offer no coherent theme or approach to the community. Additionally, a distinct identity may be irrelevant or overwhelmed if one of the network components is much larger and more conspicuous than the others.

Ultimately, many of these concerns boil down to questions of "turf": Who has the right and the responsibility to run what parts of what systems? And, furthermore, who is recompensed for their efforts and through what mechanism? Government, for example, should have the responsibility to provide government information, and information-referral agencies (such as crisis clinics and suicide-prevention hotlines) should probably retain their responsibility. While the government has the responsibility to engage the citizenry on current civic issues, should it have sole responsibility for running civic forums? Probably not. Moreover, there may not be global answers to these questions. One community may want government to provide a service and be willing to pay for it, while another community may rely on a nongovernmental organization for the same services.

There are many other ways in which geographically-based community networks can cooperate. At a minimum, it should be possible to send e-mail between them, over the Internet or via a variety of lower-tech ways, and community networks should be able to share forums that cross geographical lines. Community networks could share principles, policies—even user interfaces—and they could collaborate on fundraising and information-sharing on how best to run a system. It will probably be necessary to negotiate roles and responsibilities (based on new definitions of "turf") for improved cooperation to take root. An important form of collaboration could come from citizens who gain an increased understanding of people in adjoining communities and who work on projects for the benefit of both communities.

As time progresses and network usage becomes more widespread, one thing is quite clear. If access to e-mail and other network services is to become universal, joint planning, and cooperative ventures between many types of organizations—public, private, and nonprofit—will be required.

INFLUENCING ORGANIZATIONS

> *It can honestly be called a movement. In many people's minds the model of a citizens-based, geographically delimited community information system has taken hold.*
>
> Steve Cisler (1992)

A wide range of organizations influence community-network development and coordination. These include government agencies, nonprofit organizations, and for-profit companies. Advocacy groups, including library and educational groups as well as nonprofit groups such as the National Public Telecomputing Network (NPTN), the Morino Institute, the Center for Civic Networking (CNN), and Computer Professionals for Social Responsibility (CPSR), are also strongly involved and have produced influential documents and reports (CPSR, 1993; CCN, 1993; Morino, 1994 and 1995). Other organizations offer competitive services, including telephone companies, cable television companies, and various other media and communication companies. These companies are well-positioned to address community needs, but have not prioritized it because of the perceived lack of strong financial return on investment.

Government

The government's historical and current influence as well as its potential for future involvement, in its roles as both supporter and regulator, is very strong. Historically, the U.S. government is responsible for the existence of the Internet, and the tab for both the necessary research and the implementation has been picked up by U.S. taxpayers. More recently, the government, through then Senator (now Vice President) Gore's NREN (National Research and Educational Network) legislation, effectively subsidized the ubiquitous and free Internet connections that many university students enjoy.

In recent years, there has been an astounding amount of federal government information made available electronically, from impending legislation in the House of Representatives (via Thomas) to the Office of Technology Assessment (OTA) reports (via Fedworld) to Supreme Court decisions (via Juris). While much of this was done voluntarily, sustained political pressure by people like Jamie Love of the Taxpayer's Assets Project and entrepreneur Jim Warren has helped to make federal and state government information easily available electronically and to end commercial strangleholds on some government information (Love, 1995).

There has also been a great deal of activity at state, county, and municipal levels of government as well. Many elected officials are getting on the Net with an e-mail address, some on their own, using a commercial account or a community network and an increasing number on government-sponsored systems. Nearly all state governments and a large number of county and city governments have recently put information up on the World Wide Web. Some states are developing ambitious public computer systems such as Maryland's Sailor Project, slated to cost 87¢ per Maryland taxpayer after the initial seed money provided by the federal government has been spent (Powledge, 1995). In Washington State, numerous agencies are devising policies and seeking public input on how government services could be delivered more effectively. In the city of Seattle, the data processing Department of Administrative Services has set up the PAN (Public Access Network) system that is providing government information and is planning to provide many of the services that are currently found on community networks. Although the information in this area is exploding rapidly, we have provided some pointers in Appendix B that will continue to have relevance.

Government is showing a great deal of interest in electronic access to information and services, and generally this activity should be encouraged. Many concerns still remain, however, that we need to recognize as citizens and as proponents of the new community. The first is that these efforts are often very disorganized and spring from a desire to join the stampede. Often there is little understanding or experience of either the technology and its implications (both positive and negative) nor the principles and policies that should guide its development. The second is that there is often little effort to truly involve the public in a meaningful way. The third concern is that government law makers—who are essentially "clueless," according to Electronic Frontier Foundation (EFF) spokesperson John Perry Barlow—will pass unsound laws. Working more through ignorance (and political posturing) than malice, they might embrace measures like the Exon Bill that would address "decency" in the electronic realm by throwing the baby out with the bathwater.

Clearly the government can be a strong ally of community networks. Like the citizenry it ostensibly serves, it must be informed. If the legislators lack understanding or serve other masters than the people, democratic community networks are in for an uncertain ride ahead. Ready access to information and communication services, for example, is critical to a democracy, but government officials and agencies are generally unwilling to explore innovative concepts such as providing free e-mail accounts to all citizens. Although this could be provided inexpensively, corporate interests are likely to obstruct projects of this type. Since this medium may very well be the dominant medium in the twenty-first century, citizens can ill afford to let important government decisions go unmonitored. Without public outcry, government may—wittingly or unwittingly—leave citizens entirely out of the process.

The Commercial Sector

As we've mentioned throughout this book, corporations are the dominant structure of the modern age for organizing resources to attain goals. We've argued that these corporate goals—and the processes by which these goals are realized—have frequently gone unchecked, often to the detriment of communities. This caveat, however, is very general and is useful largely as a reminder not to rely *entirely* on the commercial sector for community networks or other public goods. The commercial sector will not do it. Corporations' priorities are elsewhere.

As consumers and as citizens, we need to work with corporations as independent groups of consumers and citizens in a give-and-take manner to ensure that citizens and communities get what they need. Unfortunately, as mentioned before, citizens are generally unorganized and rarely speak with authority or power. Citizen deference would need to change as some corporations are truly thinking big and are apparently poised to take multi-billion-dollar leaps into the network frontier. While their plans are certainly interesting and will undoubtedly expand the opportunities for entertainment (creating, for example, *Mortal Kombat XXIV* as interactive virtual reality), the concerns of ordinary people in ordinary communities may be the last thing on the minds of the developers of those new services.

Corporate Scenarios

In various places in the United States and all over the world, corporations are developing pilot programs, such as wiring homes for interactive television using fiber-optic cable. On top of that there is already a bevy of commercial-network providers that supply services (such as chat lines, on-line support groups, and hobbyist forums) in addition to or instead of standard Internet services like Telnet and e-mail and access to the World Wide Web through Lynx and graphical browsers. By now the software behemoth Microsoft has also weighed in with its Microsoft Network, which has already sparked harsh criticism based on its bundling of the network client software in with its Windows 95 operating system. Microsoft Network has been carefully crafted to appeal to a large spectrum of interests and features with, for example, a large section on women's issues. While Microsoft and others may be able to cultivate a large user base, the future of democracy and community building solely within the confines of a corporately owned "cyber-mall" is unlikely. There is also a push to build consumer expectations in ways that echo corporate direction. AT&T, for example, has launched a series of ads both testing the waters and painting a future for a series of (AT&T) products: "Have you ever gotten a call on your TV? Ordered tickets from a bank machine?" Et cetera, et cetera. "You will," they state confidently. Stay tuned . . .

In addition to the expensive and ubiquitous public relations campaign that companies are waging for the hearts, minds, and wallets of the next generation of media consumers, corporate lobbyists are also waging a behind-the-scenes struggle for legislation that favors their particular enterprise. Gary Chapman of the 21st Century Project in Austin, reports, for example, that Southwestern Bell had 129 registered lobbyists working in Austin (the Texas state capitol) to ensure passage of a telecommunications "reform" bill that was favorable to Southwestern Bell. In order to begin to appreciate the magnitude of this lobbying work done in the corporate behest versus a public-interest agenda (however defined) one need only consider the salaries *alone* of the people involved in the lobbying in this single state (albeit a large one) of the 50 American states. Clearly, outspending the corporate sector is not an option.

Corporations come in all shapes and sizes and do not speak with a single voice. Some have supported community networks. For example, U.S. West, a regional telephone company in the Northwest and West, has given Frank Odasz's Big Sky Telegraph project substantial financial support. At the same time, U.S. West has developed a Community Link system that provides low-cost access to community information, a system that would compete with community networks. Companies building new community products need to have a strategy that works for them, but the field before them is very dynamic, uncertain, and competitive, making long-term strategizing difficult. If U.S. West or other telephone companies can develop the content, then people might be willing to pay for it. On the other hand, if content exists, people may be willing to pay for the delivery—over the telephone line or other "channel," be it cable, wireless, or some other form. Since corporate interests clearly dominate many aspects of modern life, it will be impossible to ignore them. Developing and defining a new and balanced relationship between community and corporate interests is a critical goal and is one in which community networks can play a strong role.

Academia

Academic institutions have also influenced the development of community networks in various communities and could conceivably play a larger role in the future. (This topic is discussed in more detail in Chapter 11.) Universities have often provided the site and resources for a Free-Net or community network. Case Western Reserve University in Cleveland, Ohio was and is the home of the Cleveland Free-Net while Carleton University in Ottawa, Canada is the home of the National Capital Free-Net in Ontario, Canada. For every successful collaboration, however, there have been scores of non-starters. Many large universities seemingly have bigger fish to fry and appear to be relatively uninterested in the community in which they happen to be physically located. For that reason it may be more fruitful to work with community colleges or smaller schools. Other universities have cited the "appropriate use" and other restrictions (now largely historic) placed on them by their Internet provider to support their decision not to work with community-network developers. In other communities, universities that perceive declining support for their activities may now be willing to explore a range of community projects including community networks.

Advocacy Groups and the Community-Network Movement

The early community networks such as Community Memory, PEN, and the Cleveland Free-Net reflected the inclinations, idiosyncrasies, and best guesses of their originators. These systems were constrained by the relative unsophistication—yet high cost—of the available technology, insufficient financial resources, and a public that wasn't quite sure what to do with them. These pioneering systems were running on the energy and instinct of their developers without the benefits of market research, adequate funding, public understanding, or communication among developers. Currently, there are vibrant and healthy community-network projects in most states with over 250 public-access networks in the United States (Morino, Institute 1995a) and many others around the world. Tom Grundner of the National Public Telecommunications Network reports that the number of users on their affiliate "Free-Nets" is approaching 400,000[1] and the National Capital Free-Net in Ottawa, Ontario, Canada has over 50,000 registered users. The technical sophistication, community involvement, and communication among developers is very strong. Whether the momentum continues or whether the movement "implodes" (Morino, 1994), however, will depend on many factors and the next few years will be critical for the movement's survival.

Free-Net Roots—From St. Silicon's to NPTN

In the mid 1980s, Tom Grundner, working at the Case Western Reserve University Medical School in Cleveland, Ohio, started St. Silicon's Hospital, an Apple II based on-line question-and-answer forum that people could reach with their modems. Doctors were on-hand electronically to answer questions on a wide range of medical issues. The system proved to be very popular, and Grundner launched a more ambitious system, the Cleveland Free-Net in 1986 (Neff, 1995) whose basic features defined the canonical Free-Net or community-network system. Students and faculty members at U.S. universities had long had their Internet access subsidized by taxpayers but Case-Western was the first university (and still only one of a handful) that allowed some of its computer resources to be used by the community at large. After the success of the Cleveland system, people from all over the United States and from many other countries began to inquire as to how they might replicate the system. In response, Grundner started a new organization, the National Public Telecommunications Network (NPTN), to help facilitate these requests. Initially an "organizing committee" is formed and, later, for a small fee or an agreement to "cybercast" (distribute over the Internet) information to other Free-Nets, a community network becomes an NPTN affiliate. Each NPTN affiliate (now numbering over 70 and growing) has an exclusive franchise over its local calling region, precluding the existence of two NPTN affiliates in the city of Seattle, for example. Although NPTN does not play a major role in the development of the Free-Net or community network in the affiliate's community, NPTN provides useful services, particularly through their "blue book," which describes both organizational and technical advice on setting up community networks. Incidentally, NPTN has no desire to force community networks to develop according to a Free-Net "party line."

In recent years, Grundner's attention has been focused on ways in which community networks can be institutionalized. One such approach involves the creation of a "Corporation for Public Cybercasting," modelled somewhat

---

[1] Personal correspondence. July, 1995.

along the lines of the U.S. Public Broadcasting System, that would help develop and maintain community networks by leveraging community resources with federal support (Grundner, 1993a). Grundner has very strong feelings in this area: The first is that the U.S. taxpayer paid for development of the Internet and subsidized its use for many years and, consequently, should reap some of the benefits. Another is that Free-Net community networks should have *no* fees associated with their use—they must be *free* to use, much as public libraries are free to use. Grundner believes that free public computer networks will be as important to the twenty-first century as free public libraries are to the twentieth century.

The Rest of the Movement

In addition to the organizations working within communities, there are many organizations working outside communities that are nevertheless very important to the community-network movement. To build strong communities we must focus on communities as well as the context that surrounds the communities; we must look and work simultaneously inside the communities and outside the communities.

Although NPTN's influence has been significant, it is not the only player in town. A largely unrealized but potentially powerful alliance of librarians, educators, network and bulletin-board systems users, community activists, social service providers, government agencies, and concerned computer professionals has been growing that helps develop community networks, but is involved in all aspects of democratic communications technology as well. Several electronic distribution lists for discussion now exist on the Internet (Appendix B) that provide active forums on these issues. There are also an increasing number of conferences and workshops on these topics. Two early and influential workshops were organized in the early 1990s by Richard Civille for Computer Professionals for Social Responsibility and for the Center for Civic Networking. Steve Cisler of Apple Computer has hosted two well-attended "Ties that Bind" conferences (Cisler, 1994b and 1995b) with support from the Morino Institute in which many pioneering community-network advocates including Frank Odasz, Dave Hughes, Lauren Glen-Davitian, Andrew Blau, Tom Grundner, Jane Polly, Doug Carmichael, George Baldwin, and many others participated.

There are many organizations helping to shape issues and represent concerns of nascent community enterprises in larger contexts—in government, in media, and in the general consciousness of the citizenry. Many of these organizations are specifically interested in computer-network issues: the Center for Civic Networking, Computer Professionals for Social Responsibility, the Institute for Global Communication, the Morino Institute, and the National Public Telecommunications Network. Many others have expanded their roles as electronic information and communication technologies have become more prevalent. Groups in this category include the American Library Association, the Alliance for Community Media, the American Society of Information Scientists, the Taxpayers Assets Project the American Council of the Blind, the American Civil Liberties Union, OMB Watch, the Benton Foundation, and many other organizations and foundations. Participating in these organizations is an excellent way to help build an ameliorative environment for community networks; a list of many of these organizations can be found in Appendix A.

In early 1994, a number of nonprofit groups headquartered in Washington DC, started the Telecommunication Policy Roundtable (TPR, 1994), an informal coalition that meets monthly to present information and proposals. The TPR group and many other advocacy organizations have published numerous white papers on their recommendations for telecommunications such as "A Vision of Change" (CCN, 1993) by the Center for Civic Networking. Contact and other information on those organizations is also available in Appendix A and on the Web site for this book. In 1995, a regional version of TPR, TPR-NE was launched in the Boston area (Klein, 1995), and several others, including ones in Seattle and Chicago, are planned or are under development. Also, in 1994, the Corporation for Public Broadcasting (CPB) launched the CWEIS (Community-Wide Educational and Information Systems) Initiative to help develop community networks in conjunction with CPB radio and television affiliates.

INFRASTRUCTURE PROVIDERS AND OTHER COMMERCIAL SERVICE PROVIDERS

Don't let telecom politics leave you in the dark
   bell-com
      GOPHER <gopher://bell.com>
      FTP <ftp://bell.com/pub>
      WWW <http://www.bell.com>
      email <info@bell.com>

Ad in Wired, October, 1994

Infrastructure providers including Internet providers, telephone companies, and cable television companies influence individual community networks directly through their rates and policies. Their influence is much broader than that, however, largely because of their strong role in the creation of public policy through lobbying and public relations work as Bell's two-page, four-color advertisement in the October, 1994 *Wired* magazine exemplifies. The magnitude of actions of such companies has the potential to swamp issues of access and participation that are so critical to the development of community-oriented, democratic technology.

Since community networks will depend increasingly on these providers (which may ultimately involve Public Utility Districts) for their technological infrastructure, it is important to secure the best relationship possible. This generally means negotiating the best possible rate, but it sometimes means securing bandwidth for the network, especially when resources are limited. Historically, in order to win community presence on the cable television spectrum, it was necessary that political pressure be brought to bear. Community-access activists applied pressure on the government and the cable industry to provide channels and funding for access centers in exchange for local franchises according to public, educational and government (PEG) guidelines established by federal legislation. Although seldom realized, it may also be possible for the community network—by itself or as a member of a cooperative (Feuer, 1993)—to become an Internet provider, possibly attaining both better prices and peace of mind.

CONCLUSIONS

> *Whether you are a technical expert, information professional, government official, businessperson, or interested citizen, there is a role for you to play in incubating, growing, maintaining, and using these systems.*
>
> Steve Cisler (1993)

As this chapter shows, there is a rich and diverse set of players comprising a social web of a community network. Integrating the community network with this web is one of the fundamental challenges facing network developers and their supporters. Although the structure and the roles and responsibilities of the participants will necessarily vary from community to community, the nature of the challenge is identical: The community network must become part of the community in order to serve it.

Chapter 9

Technological Architecture

Lo! Men have become the tools of their tools.

Henry David Thoreau

Since the Industrial Revolution, society and culture have been sub-servient to technology. One of the compelling tasks today is to reverse the process and make technology serve culture and society.

Ben Bagdikian (1992)

BASIC COMPONENTS OF A COMMUNITY NETWORK

Until now we have said very little about the technology that supports the community network. In this chapter we discuss technological architecture that complements the social and political architecture described in the last chapter. The basic technological architecture (Fig. 9.1) consists of four main components: (1) *users* (including developers, participants, administrators, information providers, visitors, and others) and *user interfaces*, (2) the community-network *software*, (3) the computer *hardware* (including the various CPUs, memory, disk drives, interface drivers, and so on), and (4) the *delivery channels* through which users can access the services on the system. In the remainder of this chapter we discuss each component and related issues.

COMMUNITY-NETWORK USERS

As computer use becomes more commonplace, people who happen to spend more time working with computers are less likely to identify themselves naturally as "users."

Jonathan Grudin (1990)

A community network offers a multitude of capabilities to the community. Accordingly, there is a broad set of users of such a system and, ideally, the

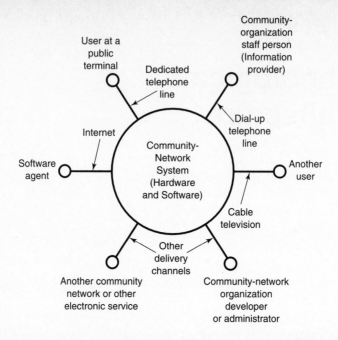

Figure 9.1 A Community-Network System Surrounded by Users

users are provided with an interface to the system that matches their needs, skill level, and temperament as closely as possible. Additionally, there will be a wide range of ways by which to access the system such as dial-up telephone lines, the Internet, and other ways. "Users" fall into four main groups— administrators and developers, information providers, basic system users, and "visitors" (nonregistered users). Each group has particular needs in relation to the community network and each group has different levels of access to the network software and hardware. Other computer applications available over the network can also be viewed as a fifth type of user, one lacking flesh and bones to be sure, but a user with distinct, usually precise needs.

A sometimes implicit, but nevertheless critical concept of the community network (pioneered by the Free-Nets) is the decentralization of administration. In a community network, the system is maintained by many people assuming many roles and accessed through a variety of means (Fig. 9.1). Information providers, for example, must be able to add, delete, edit information, or change the menu structure in areas in which they have jurisdiction. On the other hand, they shouldn't be able to modify information in other areas, nor should other information providers or users be able to modify information in theirs. Administrators and developers need, in general, more access to the computers and devices than the basic user. They will often need special privileges to add new users, install new software, reboot machines, etc. With the decentralized approach, the community network takes on the characteristics of the new community by supporting a network of peers, in contrast to a hierarchy, where rules and system content are developed at the top and "marching orders" flow downwards.

Community-Network User Interfaces

The user interface into the community network is what the user sees that allows him or her to use the services. It's the intermediary between the user and the computer and is responsible for displaying information to the user and conveying the user's input back to the computer. A powerful yet easy-to-use interface can help ensure the success of a community network, while a difficult-to-use, nonintuitive user interface can dampen interest rapidly. To be effective, the user interface must have several attributes. The most important one is that it must quickly and accurately *convey the capabilities* offered by the community-network system to the user. In other words, the user interface must convey the community network's information and services in an economical way and respond to user input in the way the user expects. When the user is dealing with e-mail, all available actions must be clear; when the user is looking for information on senior centers in a particular location, the information should be found under a category that makes sense to the user—senior services, community services, information about seniors, for example. The user interface should also be easy to use, consistent, and resistant to user input errors.

One important function of the user interface is to *integrate* different information and services into a package that looks and feels like one community-network system. On the one hand, the system software must allow software services to be easily integrated or plugged into the rest of the system. This is accomplished primarily through the technical design of the software. The FreePort software, for example, allows any resident Unix program to be launched with a menu choice. On the other hand, the system—with several new constituent parts grafted into one—should still appear to be *one* system rather than several distinct ones. In other words, if a user enters similar input on one subsystem, it should cause similar actions to take place when he or she enters it into another. Returning to the main program, for example, should not be caused by typing Q (for Quit), from one subsystem and E (for Exit) from another subsystem. It is presumptuous to expect a computer-naive user to know when he or she is working with one type of software rather than with another. Attaining this consistency is not trivial; different vendors do not share the same user interface philosophy and in some cases are legally prohibited from doing so. Some community-network developers supply their information providers with user-interface guidelines that help promote consistency within the system. These guidelines can also supply information providers (who may be relatively unskilled at presenting information electronically) with useful advice on effective presentation.

Special-Purpose User Interfaces

Some users (including, but not limited to, the estimated 49 million disabled people in the United States and the 750 million disabled people worldwide [NIST, 1994]) will find the traditional ASCII text-based interfaces difficult to use. User difficulties might include having limited sight or being unfamiliar with English (or other supported languages). Some users may be most comfortable using a language with non-Roman characters. For those used to non-English languages that primarily use Roman characters (such as Spanish), limitations are not as severe, though in practice users who use these non-English languages have generally seen their special needs ignored. Although the necessary effort would be substantial, instructions and menus of system functions (such as the mail reader) should be available in the languages most used within the community. Additionally, registration information and other important system documents (both on-line and paper versions) should also be available in a variety of languages.

Providing access to *all* members of the community is an important objective of community networks. The nontechnological aspect of this commitment means providing education and outreach as well as the actual infrastructure such as public terminals. From the technological standpoint considered in this chapter, there are many design decisions that must be made. The main principle is that the system be modular: It must be easy to swap out one piece of software and use another. For example, this principle allows the community-network developer—at least in theory—to provide different "shells" (user agents) to different users. This idea will be discussed in more detail later, but these shells could include a menu-based system, or a Mosaic or Netscape-like Web browser system. Modularity also allows a user to choose his or her favorite text editor, mail reader, news reader, or other generic tool where alternatives exist.

Although different software shells might make certain types of services easier to provide, it is important not to build separate community networks for different classes of users. It is also important to prevent duplication of effort wherever possible. In the discussion on World Wide Web browsers later on in this chapter, we see how it's possible to make the same community-network information available from the FreePort text-based software and the graphic-based (and text-based) Web browser with virtually no extra work.

Another important consideration is the issue of where customization should take place—at the information level, the system level, the shell level, or in the users' environment?

Ideally *all* information would be comprehensible as well as accessible to *all* people, but in the case of presenting information in other languages, this goal is very difficult to attain in practice. Accommodating every language is impossible, and accommodating just a few is difficult. As mentioned before, all on-line information and software prompts should be available in various languages, especially those most prevalent in the community. The main system software could check if an "environmental variable" USER-LANGUAGE had a value (such as "Spanish," "Laotian," or "Swahili") and display the text in that language, if it existed, to the user when available.

Another way that support for other languages could be done is at the menu level. As shown in Fig. 9.2, this approach would provide a very simple way to offer material in different languages (but with "Arabic" being written with Arabic characters, "Chinese" with Chinese characters, etc.). The National Capital Free-Net in Ottawa, Ontario, Canada has duplicate systems available in French and English.

Since automatic translation by computer is not a reality (and probably will never be!), supporting a multilingual community on a community network may result in separate community networks, each in a different language. For example, the opening screen could say "typez 1 pour français; type 2 for English." Of course we hope that information intended for the entire community will be translated into many languages, but this can't be required. Multilingual forums should also be promoted where people could converse about language differences as both an aspect of individual culture and as a barrier to effective communication between cultures.

While we are discussing language it is important to note that standards exist (ISO UNICODE, for example) for encoding hundreds of written languages. By means of the standard ASCII character set, various languages can be sent across the Internet and displayed on standard terminals. Software is available to perform both sides of the translation process. The first side (and this software is harder to find) allows users to input text in their own lan-

```
1 Arabic        5 Español
2 Chinese       6 Français
3 Deutsch       7 Swahili
4 English       8 Vietnamese
```

Figure 9.2 Language Options

guage. It is awkward but doable to use the common English-style keyboard as a way to input text in, say, Chinese, whose characters are composed of individual glyphs. The software then encodes the original language message into a coded message using only ASCII characters. At the other end, the display side, software is used that decodes the encoded message, and displays it in an acceptable original language form. This process presupposes that the terminal is capable of displaying arbitrary pixels on the screen rather than ASCII text only. With a terminal of this sort (known as a "bit-mapped display") it is possible to "paint" any pattern onto the display. Older terminals can only "type"; they're constrained to displaying the letters on a keyboard.

A community network can't assume that all users have bit-mapped displays or that they're running the same software suite at their local site. For that reason, community networks must support the lowest common denominator—text. As we've mentioned, the basic approach to supplying different interfaces is by using different shells as the primary system software that the user will use while on the system.

Blind people and others with limited sight have special requirements for interfaces that will work well for them. Traditionally, they have employed software that intercepts the text stream. Ironically, visually based approaches like Microsoft Windows and those of some network providers like American Online and Prodigy actually make it more difficult for users with limited eyesight who rely on the software assistants. If a text stream can be intercepted by software, text-to-speech software (that "reads" the text and "speaks" aloud through speakers or headphones) can be used. If the text stream can be intercepted, then users may be able to make the text larger or change the font or color of the text to make it more readable. While this aspect of user configurability is usually done on the user's display device, the host computer should be able to adapt and produce different output for different terminal devices at a minimum, and should be able to provide output for other user interfaces as well (such as the Tcl/Tk approach described later in this chapter).

There is a new software standard in the software grab-bag that may help in the struggle to support different users with different user interfaces. The MIME (for Multipurpose Internet Mail Extensions) standard defines a very convenient intermediate form for both multiple languages and for multiple types of information (including graphic, audio, and video). MIME allows messages written in non-ASCII languages to be sent electronically in their encoded form. This standard thus allows a person to read the message as it was meant to be read. Unfortunately, few public access terminals are capable of reading MIME messages. Nor are most terminal programs that people use at home to call network applications using a computer and modem. Until

MIME-compliant clients and MIME-compliant community-network shells are available, community-network users will have to download the encoded text in order to display it on their local computer using display software that understands and can decode the message.

The City as a Model for a Community Network

A community network offers a large amount of data and services. Since users must navigate through all these options, the organization is critically important. Many systems use a metaphorical approach where "real world" physical characteristics are used to help orient the user through the computer's artificial landscape. The Taos Telecommunity, for example, divides their system into a North Plaza (Fig. 9.3) and a South Plaza to convey a sense of place.

Figure 9.3 The Taos Telecommunity South Plaza

The right metaphor will successfully convey the range of information available to the users and suggest the best way to obtain the information or use the services they require.

Since the computer system is exceptionally pliable, there is a huge range of approaches to organizing the community network. Just as a desktop interface on a personal computer is meant to suggest an actual, physical desktop where people perform certain tasks, community networks (and other network systems) employ a city-with-buildings metaphor to provide a useful organizational scheme. Disparate systems use the metaphor, such as FreePort (used in the various Free-Net systems), InterLink, The Virtual City, and Apple's on-line eWorld service. The city metaphor implies that the information and services available in the community network are organized in "buildings." E-mail, for example, is received and sent at the "post office," whereas city council agendas may be found in a "townhall" or other government "building." Connecting to a community network in another location is accomplished via the "teleport." The main menu and some subsidiary menus from the fictitious Erewhon Community Network are shown in Fig. 9.4.

Placing the information into buildings is usually straightforward, and users generally know where to look. One question is, How far can or should the metaphor be taken? As the amount of information grows larger, say, in the case of legal decisions, one might want to divide the buildings into "floors" and the floors into "rooms." As the system grows larger and larger, the metaphor tends to break down, making other searching and navigating techniques necessary. However, the city metaphor is eminently serviceable and offers a sort of user portability. If users are familiar with the city metaphor in their own community, they should be reasonably comfortable with it in another. Since the number of community networks using a city metaphor is increasing rapidly, adopting it as a standard seems quite reasonable.

InterLink's Virtual City

The InterLink software (see Appendix D), developed by Eric Raymond as an alternative to traditional (generally FreePort) community-networking software, goes beyond the current community-network city metaphor in many ways. For one thing, it extends the metaphor to include other city amenities: Conveyances include elevators and monorails, while buildings may have desks, drawers, brochure racks, and other "real world" artifacts "inside" them. The InterLink approach as well as a view of how a system might look is shown in Fig. 9.5.

Information and services are found in likely city places. On Tech Street, for

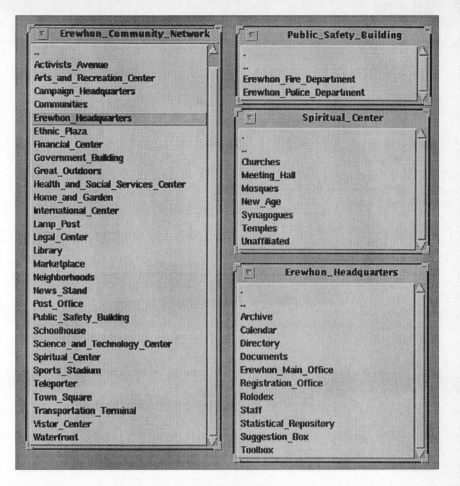

Figure 9.4 Erewhon Community Network

example, one can find technical libraries, computer user groups, and other technology-oriented information and discussion, as described below.

```
You are on a street lined with about equal proportions of
low-rent hacker crash pads and gleaming, futuristic
buildings (among the latter are the immense flying-saucer
shape of the Tech Library and the offices of Frobozz
Construction). A moving sidewalk in the center of the
street offers easy transportation to either end. The Town
Square is visible at the north end, and the Plaza to the
south. There is room for new construction here.
```

One could find business information in the Business Resource Center:

You enter a four story building and walk across the
marble floor of the Center's Lobby to the building directory
located next to the indoor pond. The directory lists the

The City is in virtual reality, not real space. It
doesn't really have a layout yet, in the sense of a set of
fixed geometrical relationships between places. But here is
a model that may help you think about it.

Imagine a beachball. The Town Square is one pole; the
Plaza is the other. The major streets (Random Avenue, Tech
Street, Commerce Place, Academy Lane, and Service
Boulevard) stretch from pole to pole, like the seams of
that beachball.

The City's geometry is subject to change without notice --
- this will help keep your life interesting :-). But the
routes between the major landmarks (the Square, the Plaza,
and the four main streets) won't be altered, at least not
without a lot of public notice and discussion beforehand.

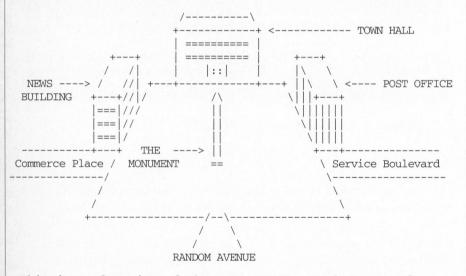

This is a plan view of the Town Square. Tech Street also
abuts on the square, but your view of it is blocked by the
Town Hall.

Figure 9.5   Interlink—"How The City Is Actually Laid Out"

```
current resources available and their locations within the
Center. You are standing in front of the directory. To your
left you notice a rack of brochures and pamphlets.
```

Here the Virtual City takes the building metaphor one step further by offering virtual elevator rides to more services:

```
a = Take elevator to On-Line Referral Library Area (1)
b = Take elevator to Direct Assistance Programs (2)
c = Take elevator to Self-Help Oriented Programs (3)
e = Take elevator to Business Events Calendar (4)
```

De Digitale Stad

Influenced by U.S. politicians Ross Perot and Bill Clinton and the existence of community networks in the United States like Santa Monica's PEN and the Cleveland Free-Net, the Dutch political/cultural party De Babe, XS4ALL ("Access for All"), and a handful of imaginative hackers launched "De Digitale Stad"—the Digital City—in Amsterdam in 1993.

The Amsterdam Digital Town was electronically visited by 15,000 people (or 2 percent of Amsterdam's 750,000 population) in its first eight months. Developers have found that users particularly like having access to job and housing information and that there is a large number of independent political groups and civic noncommercial activities represented on the system. There are similar projects in other European cities such as Berlin, Budapest, and Vienna, including some projects employing virtual reality (VR) techniques where users may ultimately be able to view 3-D scenes of the actual city (Dieberger, 1993).

COMMUNITY-NETWORK SOFTWARE

> *Procedures for software acquisition are similar to those for hardware acquisition, but with the unique guidelines and precautions. A demonstration of a software package provides certainty of what it can do, and quick verification with present users provides adequate confirmation.*
>
> Clark Rogers and Brian Vidic (1995)

From a technological standpoint, a community network provides an orienting framework and a collection of software services. On this level it is similar to an electronic bulletin board system, except that it can accommodate hundreds of simultaneous users with specialized needs and a user base of tens of thousands. As previously mentioned, the orienting framework often uses a city metaphor, but this particular approach is not required. FreePort software is often used, but BBS software such as First-Class or Galacticomm is also used, as are WWW browsers or specially developed software. The basic software services that community networks generally provide are: forums or discussions (moderated and unmoderated), access to static information contained in files, e-mail, and file download–upload capabilities. Other possible services include: chat (or "real-time" conferencing), remote login (to other computers), search capabilities, World Wide Web access, and database facilities. There is no real limit to the types of services. Community networks of the future could contain MUDs (discussed later in this chapter), and audio and video services. In addition, a simple menu structure with which to navigate information and services is often used. The system must also easily incorporate new capabilities as they become available, such as new search techniques, multimedia applications, or wide-area information servers.

E-Mail

Sending and receiving electronic mail (e-mail) is an essential feature of a community network; this capability allows users to send and receive private messages to and from other users. E-mail users might include people using the community network as well as users of other systems throughout the world including Internet sites, commercial networks like Compuserve and Delphi, and, in many cases, to homegrown, hobbyist networks such as Fidonet, which serves thousands of PCs around the world. Tens of millions of people around the world currently use e-mail, and this figure is growing rapidly (RAND, 1995).

Electronic mail implies an ability to send and receive messages over a network (Fig. 9.6). Those messages nearly always contain text only, but voice or graphic messages are becoming more common. In addition to sending and receiving e-mail, *mail readers* provide the ability to *manage* e-mail (Fig. 9.7). A user can view a list of e-mail messages (sorted by date, author, or by subject, for example) and is able to act on them. A user might respond to a message, include it in another letter, or save it as a file on the computer. Mail readers and mail systems also allow messages to be sent to lists of people as easily as they might be sent to individuals, thus making committee or other group work more viable electronically. Thus people often maintain mailing (or distribution) lists that contain e-mail addresses of people concerned about a particular issue.

```
                    Post Office
                    (go post)

1 About the Post Office.
2 Read Your Mail.
3 Send Mail.
4 Check the Size of Your Mailbox.
5 See Who Your New Mail Is From.
6 Edit Your Signature File.
7 Edit Your Personal Aliases File (Address Book).
8 Have Your Mail Forwarded.
9 Directory Services.
```

Figure 9.6 SCN Post Office Menu

Listservs and Mail Lists

Listservs and mail lists offer similar approaches to electronic discussions on community networks and on the Internet in general. A mail list is basically just a type of e-mail alias. For example, there might be an alias called "outreach-volunteers" that includes the e-mail addresses of all the members of the outreach committee, and any mail sent to "outreach-volunteers" will be forwarded to every address on the list. A listserv (such as majordomo), on the other hand, is more powerful, as users (including the list administrator

```
Current message is #3 (3 is last)

  R     1 maggadu!ben@queernet.org () (692 chars)
            Thu, 30 Jun -- Possibly a duplicate response
  R     2 ABRUNGER@TrentU.ca () (772 chars)
            Wed, 13 Jul -- Re: testing
 *R     3 bb140@scn.org (Barbara Weismann) (378 chars)
            Wed, 13 Jul -- Proposal
   n = Read next unread message
   d = Delete this message
   p = Back to previous screen
   h = Help, list of additional commands
```

Figure 9.7 Reading E-Mail

who oversees maintenance on the list) can send a variety of commands to the listserv via e-mail, to get the names of all listservs at a particular site, or the names and e-mail addresses of all subscribers, for example.

Listservs exist on thousands of topics. (See Appendix B for several listservs on topics related to community networks.) To participate in a specific listserv, one must "subscribe" to it. To begin a subscription to a listserv, one sends e-mail with the proper command in the body or the subject line of the message to the electronic address of the listserv software. To join the communet list-serv on community networks I would send a message "`subscribe communet Doug Schuler`" to `listproc@list.uvm.edu`, for example. Once a person has subscribed to the listserv, the person can also "post" to the listserv, also by sending electronic mail. (There is usually one address for sending articles or postings and another for subscribing, unsubscribing, and performing other administrative functions.) When the listserv software receives the posting, it automatically distributes it to all the other subscribers of that particular listserv.

Electronic Forums

Electronic forums are essential to community networks. A forum—sometimes called a "room" or "board" or "newsgroup"—enables a group of people to participate in an extended conversation on any topic. The conversation can be tightly focused or extremely broad, loosely conversational or concentrating on specific goals. The tone can be encouraging and welcoming or contentious and abusive. There are two main types of forums: a moderated forum that employs a moderator and an unmoderated forum that does not.

A user that wants to read forum postings will usually select the desired forum with a menu choice or by indicating that he or she wants to bring up a "news reader," which is functionally similar to a mail reader. The main distinction is that a user reads e-mail that is "owned" by that user, while a user reads news (or a forum) that is available to anybody who wants to participate in that particular forum. Many important policy issues associated with public forums were discussed in Chapter 8.

A message sent to an unmoderated forum is automatically posted to the forum. A message sent to a moderated forum is sent to the forum's moderator. The moderator then reads the posting and determines its suitability to the forum according to whatever criteria are relevant to the forum. Ideally, these criteria have been explicitly defined by the moderator and usually include relevance to the topic at hand (including clarity) and respect for other participants. Sarcasm and ad hominem attacks (universally referred to as "flaming") are often screened out, along with profanity and other strong language.

The moderator has several choices after receiving an intended posting. The first is to send the posting unchanged to the forum. The second is to post portions of the posting, omitting irrelevant or inflammatory remarks. If parts of the posting are deleted, it's customary to indicate where the deleted material had appeared and why the material was deleted. If the moderator interjects his or her comments into the posting, the changed portions must be made obvious to avoid any confusion as to authorship of the various sections. The third option is to not post the article and send it back to the author along with the reasons why the article was rejected and what would be needed to make it acceptable. In some cases, aspects of the posting might be unclear or confusing to the moderator. In those situations, the moderator will raise the issues with the author, who can then rewrite the posting and try submitting it again. It is generally recognized that moderated forums have higher-quality material—called a "high signal-to-noise ratio" in techno-slang—than unmoderated ones and have fewer digressions and flaming. The responsibilities of a moderator can be very demanding as the moderator must read every posting that is submitted to the forum. Moderators have the sometimes difficult chore of justifying their decisions to users whose contributions have been rejected. For that reason, and for the integrity of the entire community network, it is the responsibility of the moderator to articulate a clear policy for forum submissions.

Structured Forms of Moderated Forums

Since conversations in forums (even moderated ones) tend to stray or become fractious, participants often suggest approaches to structuring the conversation in various ways. These approaches ultimately must rely on the participants themselves abiding by a set of agreed-upon conventions, such as the use of key words in the subject line to indicate the conversational "thread" or subtopic within the forum that the posting addresses. The second approach is to let the moderator structure the conversation by guiding the conversation, asking questions, and even annotating postings from other users. Although this approach adds to the workload of the moderator, the result is more likely to be satisfactory. A third way to add structure is again to rely heavily on the good offices of the moderator. A common form of moderated structure is found in the "Question and Answer" (Q&A) forum. In this venue, users submit questions electronically to "experts" or whomever has agreed to find answers. The expert might be the moderator, or a group of people, who then researches the question. When the expert has devised a suitable answer, both question and answer are posted to the forum. Experts have included doctors and lawyers (in the Cleveland Free-Net) as well as automotive specialists (Heartland Free-Net) or ethical investment advisors (Seattle Community Network). The possibilities are endless for this electronic variation on the "Dear Abby" model found in daily newspapers. Scientists, nurses, gardeners, home-repair specialists, educators, policymakers, hobbyists, artists, musicians, craft people, farmers, and so on are all very good candidates for Q&A forum moderators.

Once a structured approach is known, it seems reasonable to develop software that enforces the desired interaction model. The trouble with this approach is that software developers aren't capable of second-guessing the ways in which people want software to mediate their electronic communication. Users in the past have balked at attempts to impose unyielding communication structure on their communication. Researchers at Bellcore damned this approach as "Naziware" when they were asked to use software that classified all their e-mail communication according to a rigid set of conventional conversational types.

While structuring electronic conversation has been generally unsuccessful, it seems likely that useful structuring conventions will be developed in the future. Jeff Conklin devised a structured communication tool called gIBIS (1988) (for graphical Issue-Based Information System) based on German researcher Horst Rittel's approach for dealing with "wicked problems." Rittel's "wicked problems" (Rittel and Kunz, 1970) are precisely the type of problems that modern society has in abundance, the types of problems that must be faced together by the new community. These problems can't be solved like mathematics problems, or solved by "professionals" in academia, government, or business. Solutions to Rittel's "wicked problems" can only emerge after extended dialogue with all participants and stakeholders. Rittel's approach to structuring this public dialogue is to categorize all comments into one of three conversational components (issues, positions, or arguments) and to build hypertext-style linkages between related comments. Other software like Lotus Notes, which provides the environment for developing structured communications programs, could be used to support systems of this nature but would probably not be useful in a community network due to the high costs of providing the client software to large numbers of people.

Chat and IRC

While e-mail or posting notes to electronic forums is analogous to sending letters to individuals or to a newspaper, the "chat" capability offered on many community networks is more like a telephone conversation, with the keyboard serving as a mouthpiece. With chat, a user can type at the keyboard and the text is displayed on the terminals of all people who are also currently chatting. The capability often exists on community networks as well as on commercial systems like America Online, where it is frequently used as a social-opportunity on-line singles bar. Internet Relay Chat or IRC (Reid, 1994) is the equivalent of chat except that anybody on the Internet with the IRC software can participate over any number of "channels," generally named for the topic to which the channel is dedicated. Although IRC, like chat, is often used for "idle" conversation, it has also been used as a way to rapidly disseminate information on a current events. For example, the #gulf channel was used to send late-breaking news from the Gulf War to participants all over the world.

Because chat is often used for conversation (as opposed to directed topical conversation in forums) and has been used for flirtatious conversation, it is sometimes considered frivolous by developers or not worth overcoming its costs and hence not instituted or even removed from the system after being in operation for some time. However idle or potentially problematical the chat capabilities are for the community-network organization (because of minors and adults flirting on-line, for example) chat systems offer informal conversational capabilities that are needed in convivial, community settings.

Navigating and Searching

When the amount of information increases to the extent that there is information of interest to everybody, it will necessarily contain more and more information *not* of interest for an individual person. As the community network becomes larger, the issue of finding information of specific interest becomes simultaneously more important and more difficult. The related issue of *navigating* through the system as quickly and as effectively as possible also becomes more important, and more difficult.

In the traditional community network, users navigate through the system via a series of menus. At each menu, there are one or more choices that a user can make. Some choices will cause information to be displayed, some choices initiate actions like opening a mail or forum reader, while other choices bring up additional menus. This series of menus can be arbitrarily deep. Navigation through menus is a serviceable method of locating the desired information or service on a community network. It is a method that new users can readily comprehend and use. It's not without drawbacks, however. Many times it is not clear what menu heading should be used, and where specific information belongs. Additionally, when there is a large body of information, a user might have to go through several levels (possibly 5, 10, or more) of menus to find the information they need or the forum they want to read. The FreePort system has go commands that short-circuit the lengthy menu traversal. An SCN user, for example, can type go senior at the prompt and skip immediately to the main senior menu. Using the go commands is like leaving bookmarks in a book to mark particular locations. One can immediately open the book to the marked page without skipping through the book page by page. The

Mosaic program (and Netscape and other World Wide Web browsers) has the equivalent of the bookmark idea with its "hot list" concept. When a user reaches a location via Mosaic that they plan on visiting again, they can add the location to their hot list. When the user wants to revisit that location at a later time, the hot-list menu is pulled down and that location chosen from the list of previously chosen locations. When the user indicates which location is wanted, Mosaic establishes a connection with the host computer and downloads the Mosaic "page." Thus, from any location, a user can go *directly* to a hot-list location, bypassing all the intermediate locations that the user had originally visited.

Ideally, a community network should support browsing as well as searching. Although a FreePort user can get a list of all the go commands which provides some type of global view of the system, there is very little support for a *directed* search, in which a user is looking for specific information. A community network should have at least one type of search capability. This capability would allow a user to focus in immediately on information in the system even though the location is unknown. Generally a user indicates that he or she wants to search for information and then must provide some indication on *what* is being sought. Sometimes the user also indicates the *range* of the search. For example, should the software search through all files on the local system, document files only, information on other systems, or use other specifications? Providing searching capabilities can have some interesting indirect consequences because information may be brought forth from unexpected sources. For example, a libertarian might find some traditional conservative writings that bear on an issue; a community-oriented person on the left might find community-oriented literature from the right, and vice versa.

The user interface to a community network ideally supports many ways for users to accomplish their goals. Terse or complex ways to find and manipulate information may be ideal for experts, whereas menus may be sufficient for inexperienced users. The user interface should also support the complementary modes of searching and browsing: Sometimes a user is looking for something precise—the time and location of the neighborhood Alcoholics Anonymous meeting, for example. Sometimes the user is just curious about the system and wants to casually amble around, heading down paths that happen to be appealing at the moment.

File Transfer (Upload and Download) Services

Users will also need an assortment of other services related to communication. The SCN Communications and User Services menu (Fig. 9.8) shows the

```
1 About Communications and User Services
2 The Post Office...
3 Read Usenet News
4 Offline News Reader...
5 Directory Services...
6 User Services...
7 File Transfer Services...
8 World Wide Web
9 Other Freenets and Community Computer Networks


- - - - - - - - - - - - - - - - - - - - - - - - - - - - - - - - - - - -
h=Help, ?=List of Commands, "go help"=Extended Help
m=Main Menu, p=Previous Menu, x=Exit SCN
```

Figure 9.8 Communications and User Services Menu

variety of these services. The first menu choice describes the general services, while the second is for sending and receiving e-mail. The third is for reading any Usenet news groups that are available on the local system. An off-line news reader allows users to download Usenet news articles to their home computer so that they can read them locally without being logged on to SCN (this is more important to users who are paying by the minute). Directory Services allows users to get user information or to access the user database, while File Transfer Services (Fig. 9.9) helps provide users with information and facilities for dealing with computer files that are stored on the community network and the user's personal computer. These facilities include sending files as part of e-mail messages and transferring files between the system and the personal computer using Kermit, Xmodem, Zmodem or other file

```
1 Using Files on SCN
2 Help with file transfers
3 Send a file from SCN to your PC
4 Send a file from your PC to SCN
5 Check for files sent to you by other users
6 Retrieve files sent to you by other users
7 Send a file to another user
8 Manipulate files in your 'work' directory
```

Figure 9.9 File Transfer Services

transfer programs. Finally, the last two capabilities can be used if I-Comm or Lynx Web browsers (described later in this chapter) are desired or if a user wants to login to another Free-Net or community network.

Lynx and Other Web Browsers

The Mosaic program, developed at the University of Illinois based on work pioneered at CERN, a physics laboratory in Geneva, Switzerland, is probably the most prominent of the second-generation Internet programs. Mosaic established as a reality world-wide hypertext (sometimes called "nonlinear" text because information can contain "links" to other information, providing a portal by which a user can "navigate" readily to the other information). It simultaneously made the Internet more approachable and accessible to the nonspecialist. The Mosaic program (and other Web browsers such as Netscape) enable users on the Internet to build multimedia "pages" that contain links to other pages, which themselves can contain still more links, forming an increasingly vast collection of interlinked documents known as the World Wide Web. Each page is identified with a URL (Uniform Resource Locator) that uniquely specifies its location on the Internet. When the Mosaic client (or browser) on the local machine is aimed at another page's URL, it connects to the other machine, fetches a copy of the page to the local computer, and then displays it on the local machine. Establishing a "home-page" using HTML (Hypertext Mark-up Language) is becoming an extremely popular way to "hang your shingle" on the Internet, and some community networks are providing that capability to their information providers (see Sustainable Seattle page in Fig. 9.13). Since browser software can obtain copies of the HTML version of Web pages, anyone who is new to HTML (or to computer "markup" languages in general) can easily learn by example from existing pages.

Although graphical Web browsers make fairly high-resolution graphic information widely and easily available, some people lack the requisite display devices, while others don't have the desire or patience to wait for the graphics to come streaming in. (Some graphics seem to take forever to load and supply little or no added information.) Enter Lynx, an extremely hardy, public-domain text-only Web browser (Lavender et al., 1995). Providing text-only access to the world of WWW via Lynx is an elegant solution to the dilemma posed by (1) the existence of a wealth of material available on the web, (2) the desire to provide comparable service to *all* users (especially those with older and less sophisticated equipment); and (3) finite resources. The SCN Webmaster's committee identified several issues that should be considered before providing Lynx to all users. These concerns included: the effects on disk space if Lynx users began transferring large files to SCN, policy implications of having "objectionable" information on the Web, support issues, processing and bandwidth resource issues, and, finally, the effect of this service (which might accentuate nonlocal characteristics of the system) on the community aspects that provided the initial motivation for the system. Currently Lynx is offered to all SCN users.

Other types of lower-tech browsers are also becoming available. The I-Comm browser (see Appendix D), for example, is a relatively inexpensive shareware graphical Web browser ($29.95 or $19.95 to students) that runs on Windows machines over ordinary telephone lines (those not running SLIP, PPP, or other protocols). The Seattle Community Network currently supports I-Comm as an alternative to the text-only Lynx browser, which is also supported. I-Comm finesses some of the issues that Lynx introduces. If users want to download a document with Lynx, for example, they usually must save it to a local file (on the community-network machine) and download it from there to their home or office machine. I-Comm, on the other hand, already downloads the remote files onto the user's machine as temporary files that can be readily saved without the additional step that is required with Lynx. Since I-Comm is shareware, it is perfectly legitimate to allow its downloading from the community network to a user's machine. Moreover, since it employs the public HTTP protocol, this approach does not force users into using I-Comm. Macintosh, DOS, and other non-Windows users, unfortunately, do not currently have an I-Comm equivalent and, as of this writing, must use Lynx or a non-SCN account for access to the Web.

The newer browsers are extending beyond mere information distribution. A new form of browser has emerged that will allow cross-platform (PC, Macintosh, Unix, and so on) information and application distribution. One of these is Sun's HotJava browser that permits distribution of "active content." Conceivably, in the future users would be able to use browsers to participate in virtual forums in which participants could see and hear each other "live." Delivery of application software via browsers may become increasingly common and could ultimately completely change the nature of software distribution.

FTP, Telnet, Gopher, and Other Internet Tools

FTP and Telnet are the two applications that have traditionally formed the backbone of intensive Internet applications. FTP, which stands for File Transfer Protocol, allows a user to connect to another computer on the Internet, list or retrieve files on the remote computer, or transfer files from the local computer to the remote computer. People often set up extensive FTP "sites" where information can be made more widely available to other users. It is common practice to set up public FTP sites where "anonymous" is the login name and the user's e-mail address is the password. The Telnet program enables a user with an account on another computer to connect to the other computer and interact with it as if directly connected. Many community-network systems allow users to Telnet to them and login as "visitor." Some community networks also allow users to Telnet out of the community-network system, but this is often limited to a pre-selected number of other community-network sites.

A wide range of other Internet tools that were developed for the most part by universities are becoming available; these have the potential to be used with community-network systems (Engst, 1994; Liu et al., 1994). Many of these tools have names from the Archie comics family: Archie (for locating files on the Internet), Veronica (a searching agent that's used with Gopher), and Jughead (which is similar to Veronica). Gopher is a network retrieval tool that provides access to files, on-line phone books, library catalogs, information stored in WAIS databases, Usenet news, e-mail directories, and Archie servers, all contained in one easy to use interface.

On-line Services

There is already a profusion of for-profit and not-for-profit on-line interactive services devoted to general and specific topics. CompuServe, America Online, Prodigy, Delphi, and GEnie are major commercial networks for general topics, while there are scads of special-purpose on-line systems devoted to special topics such as the law, health information, and computer games. The software giant Microsoft has just launched its Microsoft Network, while rival Apple Corporation has eWorld, and AT&T has Imagination Network. In the world of free on-line services, there are a number of special public access networks ranging from on-line public library catalogs to those supporting, for example, one community core value such as on-line health information. The World Wide Web is also serving as an amazingly fertile medium for new on-line services. Issues involving access *from* community networks to other networks and *to* community networks from other networks will become more important as more people become network users and community networks become increasingly important to community life.

MUDs

A MUD (standing nominally for Multi-User Dungeon or Multi-User Dimension) is software that allows multiple users to connect over a network to a shared "text-based virtual reality" (Curtis, 1992), creating a social setting that Howard Rheingold characterizes as a "virtual water cooler" (1993). This type of computer-mediated communication (CMC) allows users to communicate with each other and also to add and modify "objects" (such as "rooms," "notices," or other programmable "things"), which other users can then interact with.

MUDs are text-based and users interact with each other using a simple language (Fig. 9.10) that is reminiscent of older text-based computer games like Adventure. For example, a user can type in look and the system will print out the text description of the "location" of the person. If the description of the location contains a sign, the user might choose to type in the com-

```
@help communication

There are several commands available to allow you
to communicate with your fellow MOOers. Help is
available on the following communication-related
topics:

say        -- talking to the other connected players
              in the room
whisper    -- talking privately to someone in the
              same room
page       -- yelling to someone anywhere in the MOO
emote      -- non-verbal communication with others
              in the same room
gagging    -- screening out noise generated by
              certain other players
news       -- reading the wizards' most recent set
              of general announcements
@gripe     -- sending complaints to the wizards
@typo @bug @idea @suggest
           -- sending complaints/ideas to the owner
               of the current room
whereis    -- locating other players
@who       -- finding out who is currently logged in
@whois     -- finding out a non-anonymous player's
              real name & email address
@char      -- finding character names belonging to a
              given real name
mail       -- the MOO email system
email      -- email addresses for mailing lists
security   -- the facilities for detecting forged
              messages and eavesdropping
```

Figure 9.10 Available Communication Commands in MediaMOO

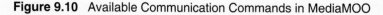

mand read sign. Based on the sign's text (printed on the screen) the user might type go east, go up, or other commands, to change locations within the MUD.

As Pavel Curtis (1992) and others have noted, a variety of social phenomena have arisen in MUDs. But are MUDs little more than a form of entertainment, a diversion for computer technologists and social misfits who are unable to communicate in traditional ways? Curtis of the Xerox Palo Alto Research Center (PARC) and others have been developing MUDs that can accommodate the requirements, skill levels, and tastes of communities with specialized needs. Curtis and David Nichols, for example, have built the Jupiter MUD for Astronomers (1993) and MIT student Amy Bruckman is developing a "MOOSE Crossing" (1994c) MUD for children.

As InterLink creator Eric Raymond (and others) have pointed out, a community network could be a type of virtual reality in which the objects—buildings and the like—could be given certain "real life" attributes like appearance and geographical locations. In fact these virtual cities could incorporate graphic virtual-reality technology over a network to provide graphic images as well as textual descriptions of the city's buildings and other resources. From this insight, it is but a short stretch to envision a community network as a specialized type of MUD.

From a technical point-of-view, merging MUDs and community networks is not overly daunting. One approach would be just to use the MUD software, with minor modifications, as the community-network software. The rooms of the MUD world would become buildings in the community network. Moving from one location to another with FreePort software is accomplished with go, same as with many MUDs. A MUD "note" could be the FreePort menu, containing a list of other locations. This note would serve as the location description that MUDs usually employ. All the MUD commands would be operational, so somebody in the Public Safety Building could communicate with other people that were in the building. If there were no other occupants, the person could leave a "note" there for others to read later, asking a question, making a comment, or suggesting a time when people could "meet" in the room and communicate. It would be interesting to build special-purpose MUDs for community use that incorporated democratic protocols (such as Robert's Rules) or new objects that would be useful in supporting the new community—for example, agendas, resolutions, petitions, or soapboxes.

Network Exotica—Filters, Agents, and Live Mail

Developers are currently designing new types of software that may permanently demolish the notion that network media is analogous to non-network media. These new types of software will enable users to develop environments and applications that are more capable of being tailored to the user's own needs; this effort might include setting up new and idiosyncratic services that will act in the user's behalf. Thus a user could receive a regular electronic "magazine" that contained only articles on preselected topics. At the same time, commercial vendors will be spending large amounts of resources on environments and applications that meet *their* needs with the citizen or user as the intended target.

Filters, especially mail filters, are at the low end of technological sophistication. Mail filters allow the e-mail recipient to set up *rules* to deal with his or her e-mail. At the simplest level, this takes the form of a "bozo filter" to delete upon receipt any e-mail received from anybody on the user's list of "bozos," generally people that have flamed, threatened, berated, or otherwise earned the wrath of the intended recipient. A more extreme version of the bozo filter is also possible. With this approach, the intended recipient makes a list of people that he or she *will* accept mail from, and *all* other mail is deleted. For example, the recipient could accept all mail emanating from specified companies, networks, or machines. Note that in this version, it is entirely possible to disallow a lot of e-mail that a user might really want to receive, such as e-mail from a friend or relative who just established a new e-mail account. In many—but not all—cases, the sender of a rejected message would receive an electronic reply stating that the mail filter rejected the message.

Moving slightly up the technological ladder are e-mail filters that process the contents of the e-mail in some way, generally to automate routine tasks like sorting the mail into appropriate mail folders. Mail from relatives might go into a personal folder and mail from the boss into an urgent folder, for example. A full discussion of processing e-mail is beyond the scope of this book, but the idea does have implications for the community network because collecting e-mail testimony, tabulating votes from an on-line meeting, tabulating survey results, and many other e-mail processing activities are directly related to community networks. Message-enabled e-mail or computational e-mail hold similar potential for structuring communication and for building interactivity into e-mail messages.

"Agents" are a still more unusual software technology. At their most exotic, they're envisioned as being as competent as humans that serve as round-the-clock, unpaid, artificially intelligent assistants. Although many people blithely assume that agents will exist in a few years or so, their existence in this most advanced form depends on developers solving many of the problems that the field of artificial intelligence has largely abandoned (for the second time), such as how to automatically extract "meaning" from text. In a more prosaic form, an agent could be employed to scan an on-line newspaper every day for news on a given topic, say, Romania, and the excerpts then could be e-mailed to the agent's owner. While this would provide handy assistance, it is by no means intelligent (as it just searches character-by-character for words such as "Romania" and "Romanian") and shouldn't be considered in any way as a substitute for a trained—human—librarian or researcher. Such an agent might constrain its results too much so that potentially interesting information is not returned. On the other hand, an under-constrained search might produce a mountain of unwanted information (such as this presumably irrelevant paragraph).

Agents can also search through archives of material in many ways as well as range through a wide variety of archives. One example of current agent technology is Perl or Tcl/Tk-based Web agents that navigate through the World Wide Web examining Web pages for "damage" such as nonexistent locations. At some point in the not-too-distant future agents may even negotiate with other agents for certain pieces of information, acting on the user's behalf. Future users of such agents will be well-advised to temper the zeal of the information ravenous infobot that has access to your credit-card number!

Integration of Services

A critical question is how these software services are organized into a unified, coherent community network. There are two general answers to this question and each one has several advantages and disadvantages: You can buy a system "off the shelf" (see Appendix D for more information) or you can "roll your own" using software components that will need to be integrated, adapted, or developed as necessary. FreePort is the original Free-Net menu-based text-only software available from Case-Western Reserve University in Cleveland and is used in many of the Free-Nets. The software costs $850 and is available only to NPTN affiliates (see Chapter 8). The FreePort software is written in C and must be compiled to run on your (Unix) machine. It is available only on an "as-is" basis and modifications may be necessary to get it running properly on your equipment. The nptn-admin mailing list (see Appendix B) provides a good forum if any questions or comments arise about FreePort (as well as other community-network issues). Additionally, the developers at National Capital Free-Net in Ottawa, Ontario, Canada, have developed several software additions and modifications that enhance FreePort considerably. CIX, which is modeled after FreePort, provides additional functionality and is another option. InterLink (discussed earlier in this chapter) offers yet another off-the-shelf solution and is used in the Chester County Inter-Link community network (see Appendix C). Although large-scale, multi-user network systems have traditionally been hosted on Unix machines, platforms (such as Macintoshes and PC clones) and available networking software have increased in power and flexibility in recent years. First-Class (BBS) software, available from SoftArc in Ontario, Canada, has been used extensively in Macintosh-based rural Free-Nets, while Worldgroup, a multifeatured BBS system for the PC platform is used all over the world, including the city of Seattle's PAN (Public Access Network) system (See Appendix D.). FirstClass and Worldgroup are client-server-based software and both use a proprietary protocol for "conversations" between the "client" software (on the user's machine) and the "server" software (on the community-network machine). Client software of either system can be distributed at no cost (although FirstClass does charge for use licenses). Moreover, both systems will work correctly (but not ideally) in a text-only mode if a user's machine does not have the appropriate client software.

Finally, the roll-your-own approach exists as an option for community-network organizers who meet any of the following characteristics: (1) they demand a certain style or functionality that can't be found elsewhere; (2) they prefer this approach; or (3) they're on a very tight budget. "Rolling your own" consists of adapting or integrating existing components or developing your own software (a daunting task that can be tempting—sometimes irresistibly—to software developers). Adapting or integrating software from various sources has other problems besides technical complexity, however. Each piece of software carries its own distribution constraint, from being strictly in the "public domain" (do anything you like with it) to GNU's "copyleft" approach to being "publicly available" (Lynx Web browsers) or being shareware (for which users are requested to send a fee to the developer).

Using the Web is a fairly good way of making community-network resources available on the Internet and other network tools such as Gopher and Archie can provide additional useful functionality. Community-network developers will need to integrate a variety of tools to provide the maximum utility. In other words, a Web-based interface to community-network services should provide as much functionality as FreePort or other interface. Designing and formatting information for a variety of accessing approaches, however, takes time and effort on the part of the information providers and developers. Preferably, one shouldn't have a different group of people working on each different interface. Nor should some services and information be available when using one interface while different services and information are available when using other interfaces. This would result in a schizophrenic community network as well as diluting the volunteer and staff effort.

To avoid the problem of disjoint services and information on the network, some developers might end up maintaining information in multiple formats.

```
                    Environment Menu
                      (go enviro)

   1 About This Area
   2 EarthSave Seattle
   3 The Mountaineers
   4 MPSFEG-Salmon Enhancement
   5 North Seattle Community College, ENV Forum
   6 Overpopulation
   7 Sustainable Seattle
   8 Washington Toxics Coalition
   ------------------------------------------------------------------
   h=Help, ?=List of Commands, "go help"=Extended Help
   m=Main Menu, p=Previous Menu, x=Exit SCN
   Your Choice ==>
```

Figure 9.11 FreePort Menu

Although avoiding duplication of information—as well as effort—may not always be possible, it is certainly worth some advance planning to achieve a functional approach. In Seattle, for example, the original SCN system used the FreePort menu-based software (Fig. 9.11). Using FreePort requires that developers and information providers "build menus." They must create formatted text files (see Fig. 9.12) that describe what the menu looks like and what happens when items are selected. It turns out that Mosaic, Netscape, or Lynx can provide alternative interfaces to the same functionality (Fig. 9.13) using "HTML" files (Fig. 9.14) instead of FreePort "menu" files. An HTML file, like a FreePort menu file, is a specially formatted text file. The SCN developers found that the same information could be made available both ways if an HTML file could be created that duplicated the functionality of the FreePort menu file. With that aim in mind, SCN volunteer Bob Kennewick created a small software tool using the Perl program that automatically generates an HTML file based on a FreePort menu file whenever a Web browser accesses the URL of the FreePort menu file.

Lynx as Community-Network Framework

Many community-network developers are currently suggesting that the Lynx browser could form the basis of a community-network shell or skeleton on which to build the entire community network. Lynx can fairly easily be made

```
# environment menu, community/environ/menu
# 5/13/94 tonyb@scn.org
#
%l
%L ENVIRONMENT MENU
%L (go enviro)
%l

%e About This Area
# %p p about.the
%p p not.ready
%l

%e Overpopulation
%t Overpopulation
%p $o/overpop/menu
%l

%e MPSFEG-Salmon Enhancement
%p $m/mpsfeg/menu
%l

%e Sustainable Seattle
%p $envtech/sustainable/Sustainable.menu
%l

%e Washington Toxics Coalition
%p $w/wtc/wtc.menu
%l

%e EarthSave Seattle
%p $e/earthsave/ESmenu.txt
%l

%e North Seattle Community College, ENV 150 Forum
%p nr scn.environment.nscc
```

Figure 9.12   A FreePort Menu File

to provide the same functionality as menu-based approaches while making community-network information and communication services available to outside users with Web browsers as well. Since HTML is becoming a de facto standard for publishing on the Internet, this approach seems quite reasonable.

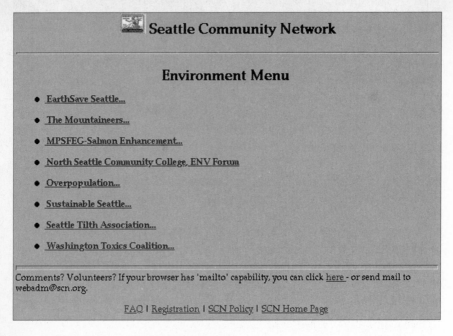

Figure 9.13 Comparable Web Page

This approach is not trivial, however, and it does raise some issues. For example, Lynx may not be as easy to use for a beginning user and the Web may not support interaction as readily. Moreover, if Lynx is used to access nonlocal URLs, the distinction between local community information and information on remote sites will become increasingly blurred in the minds of the users. This eventually could raise some support issue, and it could make the identity of the community network as a *community* network less distinct.

Security Issues

Since the early days of computer systems, the protection of resources and information from unwanted access and control has been a perplexing issue. With the advent of networked computers for which physical isolation is no longer possible (or desirable), the problem has become more acute. Community networks offer a number of challenging concerns to developers, as their very purpose is to provide access to very large numbers of people. Also, during at least part of the time, most community networks will be administered by volunteers, thus introducing some risks due to a possibly transient, uncertain, and inconsistently skilled work force.

```
<H2>  ENVIRONMENT MENU</H2>
<H2>  (go enviro) </H2><OL>
<LI><A HREF = "not.ready.text"> About This
Area</A></LI>
<LI><A HREF = "o/overpop/menu.html">
Overpopulation</A></LI>
<LI><A HREF = "m/mpsfeg/menu.html"> MPSFEG-Salmon
Enhancement</A></LI>
<LI><A HREF = "envtech/sustainable/Sustainable.
menu.html"> Sustainable Seattle</A></LI>
<LI><A HREF = "w/wtc/wtc.menu.html"> Washington
Toxics Coalition</A></LI>
<LI><A HREF = "e/earthsave/ESmenu.txt.html">
EarthSave Seattle</A></LI>
<LI><A HREF = "r.html"> North Seattle Community
College, ENV 150
Forum</A></LI>
</OL>
```

Figure 9.14 Equivalent HTML

While a deep analysis of security issues is beyond the scope of this book, a few observations are in order. The first is that 100-percent safety is impossible to attain. As they back away from the idea of total security, community-network developers need to face the important task of defining the appropriate level of security for their systems. AT&T senior researchers William Cheswick and Steven Bellovin have written a useful (and entertaining) book on Internet security that is subtitled "Repelling the Wily Hacker" (1994). In their book they stress the importance of a security policy that "determines an organization's posture towards security." This policy should describe the limits of acceptable behavior and the responses to violations.

User education is critical in community networks, for users are likely to be unaware of security risks and the precautions they should take. This education should include how to choose good passwords and keep them private. Users should also have a sense of how secure the system is, so they can make appropriate decisions regarding how much they can trust the system. This type of education needs to be ongoing: It can be conducted via several routes, including log-in banners, policy statements, informational and alerting e-mail notices, and newsletter articles.

COMMUNITY-NETWORK HARDWARE

*Common wisdom states that hardware decisions are secondary to software de-
cisions. This means that hardware purchases must be based on application objectives and end-user needs.*

Clark Rogers and Brian Vidic (1995)

The hardware may be the least complicated aspect of developing a community network. At the heart of the community-network system is a computer
(or group of computers) that needs to be an extremely reliable, multiprocess-
ing machine. Its main role will be gathering input from large numbers
of simultaneous users (from various delivery channels), running programs, accessing data from disk, and presenting output back to users. The
community-network computer must also be configured to communicate
with a potentially large number of devices. Since participants will want to
save e-mail and other documents (possibly including graphic or audio information), disk drives with gigabytes (or terabytes) of storage will also be required. The community network can be hosted on any number of platforms.
As the number of users increases and the services become more sophisticated, the platform must become correspondingly more powerful.

To adequately address hardware concerns developers must analyze
needs, select hardware, connect the hardware to the system, monitor the system, and repeat this sequence . . . forever. There is a basic sequence of four
questions that can be used to guide much of the process. The first question is
"What are the services that the community network will provide?" The second question is "What access methods will be used?" The third is "What type
of performance is desired?" (relating to the type of service and number of
users that will use the system) and the fourth is "How will the components
be assembled in a way that meets current needs and that can evolve to meet
future needs?"

As Table 9.1 shows, community networks can be characterized as either
low-end, mid-range, or high-end systems based on what services are available and how many simultaneous users the system will support. Note that
high-end services such as graphical Web browsers can stress the system, particularly in the delivery of the information over delivery channels, while
these systems can handle much higher numbers of users that are using only
text. A system that offers Internet capabilities such as FTP or Telnet makes
some type of Internet connection mandatory, while a system that simply provides Internet e-mail to its users can accomplish this goal in many lower-tech
ways such as by e-mail transfers over the telephone using UUCP (UNIX to
UNIX copy) or other protocols.

Table 9.1 Community-Network Hardware Classification

Computer-System Type	Capabilities
High-End	Multiple CPUs, 128–256-MB RAM per CPU Example: SPARCserver 1000 with 8 CPUs, RAID storage, multiple T1, multiple network interfaces
Mid-Range	Fast, single or multiple CPUs, 64-MB RAM, large storage Example: SPARCstation 20 with 2 HyperSPARC 125-Mhz CPUs, T1
Low-End	Single CPU, 16–64-MB RAM Example: SPARCstation 4 or 133-Mhz Pentium, ISDN or partial T1

Some SCN Hardware Anatomy

In early 1994, the Seattle Community Network first went on-line. It used a donated 386 clone and donated BSDI Unix operating system. The FreePort software was modified slightly ("ported") to run under this system. The modest system did surprisingly well—up to 10 simultaneous users could use it and the response was slow, but tolerable. The developers felt that it was important to have an operational system, but stressed that the system was only in "prototype mode." In December of 1994, the SCN organization bought a Sun SPARCstation 5, a fairly high-powered work station for approximately $5000. Plummeting computer prices have made grass-roots community-network projects more viable—a comparable machine would have cost tens of thousands more a few years earlier. In fact, the SPARCstation 4 that is now available is less expensive and faster than the SPARCstation 5 that SCN currently uses.

According to the classification scheme in Table 9.2, SCN is a low-end system. It is not, however, a toy system, and examining its architecture in some detail (Fig. 9.15) would be useful. Most SCN users access SCN from home using a personal computer, modem, and text-only terminal-emulation software. Approximately 20 percent use the 16 modem lines, which attach to the SCN main machine through a terminal server. Forty percent of SCN users reach SCN via the Seattle Public Library, King County Library, and Seattle Public Access Network (PAN) dial-in lines. Fourteen percent of SCN users are logging in from public terminals in the Seattle City and King County libraries. The rest reach SCN over the Internet via Telnet or the World Wide Web.

Table 9.2   Types of Hardware Needed

		Services	
Number of simultaneous users	Text only	Internet nongraphical capabilities	Internet graphical capabilities
High (500+)	Mid-range	High-end	High-end
Med (50–499)	Low-end	Mid-range	High-end
Low (1–49)	Low-end	Low-end	Low-mid-range

The SCN main computer (a Sun SPARCstation 5) is attached to the two other SCN machines—the 386 machine (now an adminstration machine) and a Sun SPARC SLC (the News/Web server)—and to the Seattle Public Library machines via a local area network (LAN). The LAN is attached to the Internet through a router. The SCN main computer has 64 MB of main memory and 4.5 GB of disk space. As of August, 1995, the system has over 5400 registered users and supports over 56,000 log-ins a month with up to 45 simultaneous users. Additionally, the SCN Web server is currently servicing over 4000 "hits" (or individual Web page accesses) a day.

Hardware Heuristics

To accommodate large numbers of simultaneous users, it is important to have as much memory as possible because the more memory there is, the less disk swapping and the better the performance will be. The SCN machine currently has 64 MB of memory, and NPTN recommends at least 32 MB of real memory, although 64 MB is better still (1993b).

Disk storage is cheap (now below $300 a gigabyte) and important. The system will need a lot of storage for information-provider areas and user space (allowing 1+ megabyte per user). The operating system requires about 300 MB and FreePort software uses an additional 80 MB. SCSI disks are currently increasing in capacity and becoming faster. In addition, newer storage systems provide high-capacity and redundancy by using RAID (redundant array of inexpensive disks) technology. RAID storage allows for single disk

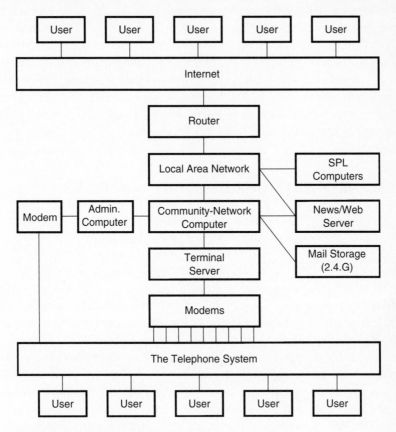

Figure 9.15 SCN System

drives to fail without loss of data. NPTN also recommends a terminal server to handle the communication between the modems and the host computer, as they "are relatively cheap and make life much easier" (1993b). They also recommend that you don't skimp on modems, as they will be in near constant use, or on a large tape drive to facilitate making the time-consuming daily backups with as little manual intervention as possible.

The modular approach to system architecture is sound for many reasons. The basic reason is that modularity is a simple way to take advantage of all available components and to spread the processing load among machines. This is often done by turning various machines into servers for different software services, like news reading, Web server, or e-mail. Another advantage is that older components can be replaced incrementally when needed. This architecture also can lead to the situation where a single component of failure will not crash the entire system.

For the extremely cost-conscious community-network developer it is possible to get 486 or Pentium PCs relatively cheaply and run the public domain Unix clone Linux (Welsh et al., 1994) on them. There are electronic distribution lists dedicated to Linux and other appropriate public domain software. Low-end work station pricing has also come way down as there are now machines available for under $3000. These machines can be grouped together in a cluster (where each machine performs a specialized task) and can provide acceptable performance on a small budget.

COMMUNITY-NETWORK DELIVERY CHANNELS

"Have you ever gotten a call on your television?
Have you ever bought concert tickets from a cash machine?
You will."

AT&T ad, *People Magazine,* November 27, 1993

Besides illustrating how commercial concerns are actively engaged in framing the possibilities of future network use, the advertisement above illustrates the impending uses of new and traditional delivery channels that could radically change some familiar patterns of information and communication in the home, workplace and community. In this section the term "delivery channel" is applied loosely to the physical medium, protocols, and the interfaces that allow information to pass back and forth between the community-network computer and users and services on computers. It is important to think of delivery channels in a general sense because the physical substrate, protocols, and policies are changing rapidly. Because of this rapid evolution, community-network proponents should be active participants in all decisions concerning public uses of delivery channels that might include voice-grade telephone, ISDN, cable television, or radio transmissions.

The term "infrastructure" refers to the base-level technology—both hardware and software—that is used to deliver information; it might be thought of as intelligent wiring or plumbing for information and communication. Currently infrastructure takes the form of telephone connections, cable television connections, and connections via invisible electromagnetic radiation for wireless telephones, radio and broadcast television. In the near future, there will be more types of "wire"—such as LEOS (low-level earth-orbiting satellite), direct broadcast, and other technologies. There will also be "smarter wire," including cable television retooling that would allow communication in both directions, ISDN telephone connections, and *integrated* technologies such as new set top boxes that can be used to control television sets and also to pull together several other types of communicating devices including the television and the telephone.

Telephone, wireless, cable, TV, and personal computer companies are beginning to compete in many services. One such service is broadcast television offered in conjunction with access to the Internet and, perhaps, thereby to community networks, through personal computers connected to cable networks with so-called cable modems. Soon, the services may encompass interactive video applications made available on computers, and eventually extend to data and video applications on television sets controlled by set top boxes.

The term "information superhighway" evokes many images of an ubiquitous high-speed network, providing information from all over the world to homes, schools, libraries, businesses, and government offices. One image identifies the information superhighway with the Internet, another with cable television networks having the oft-quoted capacity of 500 digitized and compressed video channels. The term originated in the United States as a metaphor for the National Information Infrastructure (NII), a government-sponsored network infrastructure. Though the use of the metaphor has increased with the growing availability of data and video networks, a community network considering becoming an "on-ramp to the information superhighway" should remember that there is no such specific entity as the "information superhighway," and consider carefully the specific nature of any network to which it might connect.

Dial-up

Connecting over existing telephone lines via a modem connected to a personal computer or terminal from home, work, or other locations is probably the simplest and most direct way to access the community network. This access method is open to anybody with a home computer, modem, telephone line, and telecommunications software. And, using SLIP, PPP, or TIA serial line protocols, someone with a home computer can effectively be "on" the Internet, allowing that person to use graphical Web browsers, for example. The variety of possible hardware and software at the user end presents challenges to the person using the community network as well as to the community-network developers who must try to accommodate as many users as possible. For one thing, a long-distance telephone call might be required to reach the community network, discouraging frequent and significant use for a large number of people. Also, modem speeds vary considerably, thus affecting the amount of data that can be sent across the telephone lines. If transmission is fast, then displaying a screenful of information that the user didn't absolutely require would not be terrible. If, however, transmission is slow, the user will not want to be subjected to *any* unnecessary information. Suppose graphics information is being transmitted over a telephone line, particularly a *slow* telephone line. Because graphics information is generally orders of magnitude greater in quantity and hence slower to transmit than textual information, it must be specifically needed by the user. If the graphic (or sound video or other large document) is merely decorative, then it is an unnecessary frill that detracts from the system's usefulness.

From the community-network side, it must be expected that users will use a wide variety of means by which to contact the community network. These include anything from a lowly dumb terminal that can only display characters to a powerful multimedia work station. Based on this wide variety of approaches, it is clear that the use of text-only is the lowest common denominator for all systems, and if *text only* is supported, then all users (that can read) will be able to use the system.

On the other hand, some information is inherently graphic. Maps and other geographic information, for example, cannot be translated into equivalent textual representations. Because of requirements for graphics and the desire on the part of users to take advantage of more advanced hardware, community-network developers are exploring the use of GUIs (graphical user inferfaces) and newer software tools like Mosaic in their systems. Steve Cisler's question "How are you going to keep them happy with VT100 emulation once they've seen Mosaic?" (1995a), reflecting the seemingly inexorable push towards graphical approaches, is very relevant.

Client-Server Architectures

Whether telephone-based or not, the fundamental issue with client-server architectures is, How does the receiving program know what is data and what is something else? With a strict text-only character-based system, this is not a problem: Everything is either viewed directly as text or downloaded for later viewing. Once out of that regime, it becomes important that the sending system (the community-network system) *knows* something about the receiving system (typically a home computer). They must "speak the same language."

This shared language can become very sophisticated. It can be used for all types of display screen control as well as more advanced capabilities like information compression (at the sending side) and decompression (at the receiving side). Sophisticated user interfaces can be developed with the right protocol and "intelligence" on both ends of the communications channel or pipe. When software on both ends of the pipe speak the same language, to accomplish fairly complex tasks by working together, this is a "client-server architecture." In the case of a community network, the system is the "server," while the terminals or computer at home, work, or in a public access location are the "clients." Typically a client can only communicate with a server of the same type.

Examples of these client-server architectures can be found in commercial BBS systems (like Coconut, Ripterm, or FirstClass) or in commercial network systems like America Online or Prodigy. The servers on these systems are often able to communicate both with character-based and with full-fledged "smart" clients that are capable of understanding the full language or protocol that the client and server use to communicate with each other. These protocols may, for example, enable a user to resize windows on the local (client) system without sending or receiving any information from the server. These systems are relatively portable across client platforms because the vendors have developed clients with software that runs on Macintoshes, PCs, and other computers.

The trouble with these commercial protocols is—of course—that they're all *secret* or proprietary. Each protocol is a carefully guarded, proprietary secret that doesn't understand other protocols and whose use in a public way would constitute a violation of copyright. Moreover, requiring the use of a proprietary system to access the system would be contrary to the spirit of a community network. Therefore, public domain protocols are needed. HTTP (HyperText Transfer Protocol) offers one such protocol for accessing multimedia information across the Internet. Unfortunately, Mosaic and other graphical Web browsers are not well-suited for users who use ordinary TTY telecomm programs and modems over telephone lines.

Another criticism of the World Wide Web is its emphasis on "publishing" rather than two-way communication. The Web allows people to "put their shingle up" on the Internet but it's currently less supportive of conversations (using e-mail, forums, or chat, for example). There are several efforts afoot however, to support conversational functionality using the Web (such as Hypermail—see Appendix D), and these should become increasingly common within a few years. There is ongoing work in at least two different languages—Java from Sun (Sun, 1995) and Tcl/Tk developed by John Ousterhout (1994) while at UC Berkeley—to provide "active content" within Web pages. The HotJava and Tcl-based Surfit! browsers are early attempts to extend beyond the Web's publish-only mode. In addition, some new browsers are using the new VRML (Virtual Reality Modeling Language) allowing 3D interactivity over the Web.

Tcl (pronounced "tickle") and Tk, a user-interface toolkit built on Tcl, could also be used as the basis of a high-level client-server system that could be used over ordinary telephone lines (the interface shown for the fictitious Erewhon Community Network in Figure 9-4 is a Tk object). It should be noted, however, that these approaches have the potential problem of executing commands on the user's local machine posing significant security challenges and could have potentially catastrophic results (erasing all files, for example). The safe-Tcl language (Borenstein, 1995) provides one way to address this problem; other approaches are also being investigated.

Internet

When people discuss on-line network communications, terms like "cyberspace," the "net," or "the Internet" are often used to describe the totality of the electronic web. The Internet is actually a collection of networks. All of the networks that comprise the Internet use a common language (or set of protocols) called TCP/IP to communicate with each other—to send and receive the bits of data that may be part of a love note, an ad hominem attack, executable software, graphic, video, or audio information. There are literally millions of computers connected together with satellites, high-speed telephone lines, fiber-optic cable, and other connections to form the Internet.

Individuals that use community networks and individuals that develop community networks often want the system to be "on the net." To be "on the net" generally means that you have access to the other computers on the net and can access their information and services with the full suite of available Internet tools, including electronic mail (e-mail), FTP (for transfering files back and forth between the local and remote computer), Telnet (for logging into other computers), IRC (for Internet Relay Chat, allowing multiple IRC users to "chat" together using text on a "channel"), and Mosaic (or Netscape or other Web browsers for Internet hypertext access).

Historically, many community networks have not had ready access to the Internet. There are many reasons for this barrier but it has been very vexing to those in the community-network community. They—very rightly—objected to the fact that their tax dollars had been used for many years subsidizing network use by the educational and technological elite. Many regional providers had contributed to the idea that "ordinary people" had no right to this technology, basically because they didn't have the intelligence to use it correctly or responsibly. Additionally, many people whose use had been subsidized for years strenuously object to subsidizing those in the technological backwater. To them, subsidy to the poor is "socialism," whereas subsidy to the privileged just seems natural.

There are three issues to be addressed in considering the relationship of community and networks to the Internet. The first is, What does it mean to be on the Internet? The second is, How conducive is the focus on the Internet to the principles and goals of community networking? The third is, How should a community network secure an Internet connection should it wish to do so?

Community Networks on the Internet

What does it mean for a community network to be "on" the Internet? There are various interpretations, and being "on" the Internet is not necessarily an unambiguous proposition. Traditionally, it has meant having a 24-hour-a-day direct connection using a router and a modem over a leased phone line. Minimally, being on the Internet means having an e-mail address that can be used by any other person on the Internet. Hence, my address of "douglas@scn.org" ("douglas" is my logon name to scn; "scn" is the Seattle Community Network's acronym and "org" means that scn is in the "org" domain, a nonprofit organizational designation) can be used to send me e-mail from anywhere in the world by anyone with access to Internet mail. In order for the routing of this mail to happen correctly, several things must have occurred. The first is that the "scn.org" domain name must be registered with the Network Information Center (NIC). The community-network organization must fill out a domain registration form containing domain name, contact information, and Internet provider (IP) address to be used. The NIC will check that the name has not already been taken. The community-network organization would have previously registered with the NIC for the IP address mentioned above or else would have arranged with their local Internet provider for the address to be used. An IP address is a four-part address (four numbers separated by periods) that will uniquely identify (at a low networking level) the machine to which it is attached. An IP address is required for direct attachment to the Internet.

Interestingly, having a name need not imply that the system is directly on the Internet. E-mail can be routed between the computer "on" the Internet and then exchanged over lower-speed telephone lines using any number of existing methods. Besides having a name (e.g., "scn.org") and an IP address, your machine's address must be placed in routing tables. These are used by the computers responsible for distributing data through the web of computers so that the right piece of information ends up in the right location. While Internet e-mail is fundamental to a community network (and available for little cost, especially for creative and enterprising developers), providing full Internet access for all users may be impractical. Fortunately, there is a wide range of mid-range approaches to be investigated.

Many community networks have not had to worry about their Internet connection because they are affiliated with a university, a library, or a local government with an Internet connection. Without that affiliation getting connected to the Internet may be more difficult. The first part of the job is to locate an Internet provider. If you think of the Internet as a huge network of information pipes, your community network won't be part of the plumbing if you can't find a tap to connect your (two-way) hose to. Finding an Internet provider is like locating a telephone company to "hook up" your telephone—only it's somewhat more mysterious.

Historically, there have been few providers of direct-connection Internet services and most access was through a handful of mid-level providers who were themselves connected to the top level of the Internet, the "backbone." Attaching to a mid-level provider was almost always priced in the same way: an annual fee for unlimited access, based on bandwidth. The cost usually ran between $30,000 and $35,000 for a T1 connection (MacKie-Mason and Varian, 1994). Mid-level providers were nearly all nonprofit corporations.

Nowadays, providers are more plentiful and they are far less likely to be nonprofit corporations. Access can be provided now over ISDN, fractional T1, T1, and T3 telephone lines. Mid-level providers are beginning to offer additional value-added services including e-mail, disk space, domain name service, and the like. Connecting directly to the Internet means paying for a fast, dedicated telephone line, a router (a special-purpose computer), and Ethernet interface cards for the community-network computer. Although I had no luck locating Internet providers with the Seattle "yellow pages" telephone directory, I did find relevant lists on-line on both the InterNIC and the Yahoo Web pages (see Appendix D).

Community Networks and the Internet—Made for Each Other?

Newspaper reporters and others often translate "community networks" as "Internet for the masses" or (worse yet) as an "on-ramp to the information superhighway." Both translations—popularity notwithstanding—are inaccurate and misleading. For one thing, both suggest that individuals and communities need to merge or become one with a global system, thus vaporizing the local community focus that community-network developers are striving to promote. The on-ramp analogy has several unfortunate connotations. One is that on-ramps to actual highways are, at best, necessary evils and, at worse, environmental blots. An on-ramp is generally used to get away from the local scene—usually at a high speed—towards a glittering destination several miles down the turnpike. To place the focus on the on-ramp is to place the focus on a retreat from the local community. In the words of Frank Odasz, this is the difference between the Internet and the "inner-net."

Beyond reporters' spins, what other issues are involved with integrating community networks with the Internet? While there is nothing intrinsically wrong with providing access to the Internet via the community network, there are several practical obstacles that community-network developers may need to face. The first obstacle may simply be a resource-allocation issue among the developers. Where should they be spending their time? Should they be developing local information, capacities and relationships or should they be developing services for accessing the Internet? Since commercial providers are springing up to offer these latter services, perhaps Internet access should not be the primary goal for community networks.

The second possible obstacle may be more intractable. While the "acceptable use" policies (forbidding commercial use of the Internet) are no longer a factor, other policies such as "bandwidth reselling" or the financial cost itself may be prohibitive. Let's assume that you're discussing prices with an Internet provider. That provider may want to know how many users you'll be supporting and charge you some amount per user. Since you are buying bandwidth to supply to your "customers" (users), you have now become an Internet provider of sorts, a "reseller" of Internet resources. Each "customer" of yours may translate—in their eyes—into one less customer for them. At any rate, you'll be asked to specify what type of "bandwidth" you'll need. (Bandwidth is the technical term for the size of the information "pipe." The fatter that pipe is, the more information can pass swiftly through it. And fatter pipes mean larger bills for the community network.) As the number of Internet providers increases, it should be relatively straightforward to negotiate a good price for some degree of intermediate service for your users.

Residential Broadband Access

Cable television started as a local entrepreneurial activity in rural areas of the United States in the 1960s, as community antennas were erected to distribute broadcast television signals over cable to homes that were unable to obtain a clear signal. Now, cable companies are extremely large commercial organizations that are searching for new sources of revenue by offering services such as telephone and data connections. To do this, they are investing heavily in market trials and in building cable networks capable of transmitting information not only from the cable "headend" to the home, but also in the reverse direction. At the same time, telephone companies are investigating ways to use their existing equipment to provide broadcast and interactive television, as well as high-speed data.

The networks that supply these cable services will provide higher performance than dial-up and many Internet connections. If the cable system headend is connected to the Internet, all users (scaling issues aside) of the cable system could, in theory, have access to the Internet as well as to cable television. The data will travel on separate channels in the upward and downward directions (from and to the computer, respectively). The relative capacity of these paths is under debate (see Barlow [1995] for example). A network that provides only a small upward path and a large downward path may be suitable for Internet browsing and "interactive" television, but will not facilitate the transmission of large quantities of information *from* the home. As new applications for computer and communications technology become available to the public, the architecture of the residential broadband network provided by the cable or telephone company may become an issue of concern to community networks.

Users could continue to use computers at home to access community-network data applications, such as e-mail, if residential broadband networks provide the delivery channel. The computers would connect to the network using a cable modem, which must be compatible with the data equipment installed in the headend. The cable modem would connect to a community network in a manner similar to an Internet connection, precluding the need for dial-up access. Data rates of between 1 and 10 Mbps—much faster than dial-up or ISDN—are expected, though this capacity may be shared among several residences in the same area.

Interactive set top boxes will take several years to become common, and when they do, they will probably lack keyboards at first. It is unclear whether the living areas of the home, where people normally watch television, will provide an environment suitable for the focused activity of network access. Until television displays become more sophisticated, their image quality may be insufficient for the kind of work people commonly carry out on home computers. While television *can* provide a social focus in living areas, computer use generally does not.

Residential broadband networks may provide up to 75 broadcast cable television channels, as well as extra capacity to transmit data and video in response to requests from the individual consumers. Communities, often through their local government, have negotiated access to broadcast channels for many years. In the near future, they will face new challenges—to present their existing community-network services (perhaps through an Internet connection) and to develop interactive video applications over the new two-way network capacity. It is currently unclear whether government regulation will require cable companies or telephone companies to provide access as "common carriers" to third parties who wish to present services over their networks. Mark Wheeler, an engineer with Apple Computer specializing in cable television applications recommends that community-network organizers find out who the cable contract administrator is for the community, and find out when the current cable contract expires. This information is invaluable for negotiating with cable television providers on PEG (public access, educational, governmental) access issues.

Langdon Winner has referred to applications such as "video on demand" and home shopping, where the upstream channel capacity is extremely constricted, as "interpassive"—rather than interactive—television. Some have suggested that the remote control for an interactive television system will need only one button labeled "Buy." Despite this concern, interest will probably increase in community-oriented interactive television applications. Network providers may wish to offer a local community focus in order to interest subscribers in their revenue-generating services, and community networks will probably need to respond to demands from their constituency for access—as users and information providers—to interactive video. Because the people who express this interest may or may not be actively involved with the data-oriented services of the community network, this may represent an opportunity for a community network to serve a larger constituency. Community networks may come to play an important role in working with network providers to provide interactive video services of value to the community.

To take advantage of residential broadband networks as they become available, community networks will need to consider a wide range of issues: a presence on the network for existing data applications; support of computer software to access existing data applications; access to the network for interactive video applications; production and compression of video content; interactive video application development, or "authoring"; and user-interface development for both computer and set top box. It is clear that community-network developers must broadly define their mission to not only provide access to existing technology but to stay abreast of technological trends. They must be alert to new challenges as well as opportunities for continuing community support.

Technological feasibility alone will not guarantee that community networks will be available on cable television. Cable television is *not* a common carrier. Compare phone service, where all providers are guaranteed that they can get "an account," that is, get telephone service. By contrast, cable television companies are not obligated to provide a channel for community-networking programming. Many communities have negotiated with cable companies to provide public service programming, educational services through local universities, and government-oriented services such as broadcasts of city council meetings. Because cable companies have been granted monopolies or partial monopolies, the federal government has granted the local franchising authority the power to negotiate with them for PEG access. The inclusion has often required prolonged public pressure. Without this pressure, cable companies are unlikely to surrender a channel for community networks and the local authority may be unwilling or unable to negotiate for appropriate access.

ISDN

ISDN—Integrated Services Digital Network—offers another approach to the delivery channel of the future. ISDN offers a unified method of bringing in a wide range of information to the home, office, factory, store, or public access location by means of the existing global telephone network. ISDN, for example, can handle voice or data (or both at the same time), making it a good candidate for computer-supported cooperative work (CSCW) applications. In these "groupware" applications, people in different locations can work on computer applications together while speaking to each other and seeing each other. ISDN is faster than character-based or PPP/SLIP connections over regular telephone lines but slower than T1 or T3 leased lines. ISDN service is now available in most urban locations in the United States, but its additional monthly cost and the ISDN interface costs make it an unlikely delivery channel in the near future for community networks, where universal access is important.

Configuration, or "Putting It All Together"

Although the community network should look like a single integrated system, in reality it is probably a *collection* of hardware and software working together as a coherent, unified system. The Cleveland Free-Net, for example, "is not a single computer. It is a collection of more than a dozen machines all operating in coordination with each other" (Neff, 1995). This state of affairs is inevitable. Over the years, it is quite natural that the project will accumulate additional computers. At the same time, the number of users will also have grown substantially. For those reasons, it is quite natural to seek a way to connect all of the machines together to take advantage of the cumulative processing power. Since there are a variety of *software* functions that also need lashing together, a straightforward strategy is to distribute these software functions to the various machines at your disposal. For example, machines can be turned into news servers, gopher servers, Web servers, mail servers,

Telnet servers, file servers, and so on. Usually these machines will all be connected via a local area network, and one or more of them are "on the Internet." Additionally, file-storage protocols such as NFS can be used to share disk storage with the other machines.

Community networks also need to be connected to other community networks and to other existing electronic resources, including BBSs. These connections can be invisible to end users, thus helping to create a seamless resource for users. Alternatively, the connections can be visible to users, thus providing users with *tools* for their own use. Electronic mail is an example of a seamless resource: Sending e-mail to somebody beyond the local community network shouldn't require any additional work of the user.

CONCLUSIONS

The question "What can technology do to help" is almost always the wrong question.

Donald Norman (1993)

While the six core values of the new community will no doubt persist as critical issues for humankind over the next ten, hundred, or thousand years, the state of computer technology is likely to change in ways that we can scarcely imagine today—and the change may occur in a short period of time. Forums, MUDs, chat programs, multimedia mail, Archie, gophers, and Mosaic, today are recognizable net denizens. These familiar services are likely to evolve and mutate into possibly unrecognizable new forms. Tomorrow infobots, knowbots, softbots, and others may stalk the net. The research community will need to concentrate on systems that scale up to accommodate extremely large numbers of users (Cisler, 1995b) and on interfaces that accommodate a wide variety of users, including those who don't use the Roman character set and those with special needs. The community-network community will need to keep abreast of the new technology, weaving it together in imaginative ways to serve the needs of evolving new communities. This will not be a trivial undertaking. However, as the Bagdikian quote at the beginning of this chapter asserts, technology should serve culture and society—not the other way around!

Chapter 10

Developing and Sustaining Community Networks

Are we going to design and build circumstances that enlarge possibilities for growth in human freedom, sociability, intelligence, creativity, and self-government? Or are we headed in an altogether different direction?

Langdon Winner (1986)

Community networking entrepreneurs face a formidable challenge: Are they part of a social phenomenon that is destined to stall or implode . . . or do they represent a vibrant force, capable of building on the knowledge they have accumulated, adapting to a rapidly changing world and community needs, and ultimately achieving positive, lasting social change in their communities?

Mario Morino (1994)

EVOLUTION OF A COMMUNITY NETWORK

The development of a community network corresponds strongly to the development of the community-network organization. Each organization will generally pass through eight fairly distinct stages of development. These stages—establishing an initial group, organizing and planning, inaugurating the network, running the network, implementing projects and programs, building strategic alliances, evaluating the network, and working toward long-term impact and sustainability—are discussed in the sections that follow.

ESTABLISHING A GROUP

If no group has already started a community network, the commercial firms will be able to write more of the ground rules and create a system designed primarily to achieve their business goals.

Steve Cisler (1993)

If an individual or a group of people have decided that they're interested in developing and supporting a community network they will be faced with one of three situations. The first is that there is no existing local community network nor is there any type of organized effort to establish one. This is becoming less common as projects are increasingly springing up in rural and suburban areas as well as in the larger cities. The second situation is that there is an organized project to develop a community network, a situation that is becoming more and more prevalent. While an individual may have fewer opportunities to stamp the project with a personal imprimatur in this scenario, there is a greater likelihood that a system will actually be developed when an organized effort gets underway. Finally, also with increasing prevalence, is the third situation, in which a community network or some type of public access computer network already exists. The intensifying activity in public networking, including efforts of nonprofits, for-profits, and government organizations, makes it very difficult to know how best to play a meaningful role in the process.

It is becoming increasingly likely that one or more community-network projects will already be underway in a community. For those actively interested in helping to develop community networks, it is a good idea to begin gathering information about the project. This can be done by attending the meetings, talking to the people, logging on to the system, and getting copies of brochures, policy statements, principles, and whatever else is available. You may decide that the project is worthwhile and that you would like to start volunteering on the project. In the worst case, you may feel that the project is so profoundly misguided that you want to devote your energies to defeating it! I would caution you, however, to give community-network developers some benefit of the doubt as you are assessing their project. Developing a system democratically with limited resources and a largely volunteer base is far from easy. If the system needs repair, maybe you can help fix it! I'd also caution against going into the first meeting and assuming that you know everything and that they know nothing. This most certainly won't be the case and the other people on the project (who have been working for months or years planning it) may not appreciate it. The fact is that you will have good thoughts and advice but that your input may be better informed and better received after you've spent more time with the project.

Here is a sample of possible questions to help you think about the project.

- Who's organizing it? Who's involved with it? Who makes the decisions? How are the decisions made?
- What are the goals? What are the principles?
- What is the process for attaining the goals?
- Who funds the project? Where will revenue come from?

- What type of organization is it? Nonprofit, for-profit, government? A partnership?

- Is the project democratically run? Is it well run? Are all members of the community welcome? Are diverse opinions respected? Do the organizers have a good idea of what they're doing?

If the project is sponsored by the government, you have more of a "right" to get involved than if it is a profit-making enterprise (although it may be difficult to exercise that right). If the system is designed to make a profit, you may try to work with others to develop a low-cost access method for people with low income or to develop policies that promote free speech as well as privacy.

Whether or not community-network projects are underway in your community and whether or not the community-network (and other public communication and information) projects help support the community and democratic technology, it is important to talk to others in your community who are involved in similar concerns and struggles. You will be better informed and more influential if you can get involved in a group—ad hoc or otherwise—that shares your concerns. This approach is discussed in more detail in the next chapter.

Developing a community network is by definition a *community* project: A single person may initiate the process, but a single person's vision must not dictate the goals of the project. Nor should the absence or presence of a single person determine its fate. The members of the organizing group should represent a wide range of constituencies, goals, and skills within the community. The members should share a commitment toward developing the community resources, and they must be willing to work with others—who likely come from strongly dissimilar backgrounds—patiently and honestly.

Launching a Community-Network Project

If you'd like to explore the idea of developing a community network in your area, there are several available options. Many individuals and groups start their project by contacting the National Public Telecomputing Network (NPTN) (see Appendix A) who will send two useful books (one on starting community networks or Free-Nets and the other on Academy One, their educational program discussed in Chapter 3) and "If It Plays in Peoria...," a videotape (NPTN, 1992) that describes the basic Free-Net philosophy based on the Heartland Free-Net in Peoria, Illinois. The NPTN "Blue Book" (Grundner, 1993b) suggests that an "organizing committee of approximately 10–12 people launch the project and that these people form five subcommittees—namely Hardware-Software, Ways and Means, System Design, Staff and Facilities, and Network Relations (for coordinating with NPTN)."

CapAccess, the civic networking system in Washington, DC, launched their project with a large public meeting at George Washington University. They advertised the meeting electronically and were surprised (and pleased) when over one hundred people showed up. At that meeting they laid out the objectives for the system and the challenges that they faced. They also chose a project chair and established several committees and a chair for each.

In Seattle, the Seattle chapter of Computer Professionals for Social Responsibility (CPSR), viewed the NPTN videotape mentioned above and decided to help launch a Seattle community network as a chapter project. For a year or more prior to that, chapter members had discussed ways in which they could play a part in the community-networking arena.

After deciding on the project, chapter members began making plans to introduce it to the Seattle community. We approached Kay Bullitt, a long-time Seattle activist, about hosting a kick-off meeting at her house. Several notable and influential projects in Seattle had been introduced in this way. Kay, who was familiar with CPSR's "Risk and Reliability" work regarding the dangers of computerized nuclear weapon systems like the "Star Wars" Strategic Defense Initiative (SDI), was agreeable, and a spring evening was chosen. Over 40 guests including representatives from the University of Washington, public television station KCTS/9, Seattle Public Library, educational community, business community, environmental community, minority communities, and the social services attended the initial gathering. We stressed that the project was just beginning and that we were seeking ideas and involvement. Some people who attended that meeting are now on our advisory board. We are also working with the public television station, and, most especially, with the Seattle Public Library.

CPSR/Seattle chapter members had familiarity with many issues, strong technical ability, and experience with networks and electronic communications. Since the chapter had never developed large, long-term projects, there were some gaps in organizational, political, and business skills. Meeting discussions would occasionally, and without warning, lurch suddenly from the topic at hand into a philosophical, political, or esoteric technical discussion. Fortunately, it was realized early on that the technology, policy, and processes should be driven by a set of principles rather than the reverse, and developing SCN principles (Fig. 10.1) was one of the first tasks of the project.

During this early phase, some criticism was leveled that there was no "needs assessment" of the project. Although at the time I secretly wished that I could have snapped my fingers and magically had a "needs assessment," I now feel that the project did not suffer unduly by not having it. For one thing, the group that was organizing the project was not experienced in producing this type of document. The job was too large, and the community itself or specific smaller communities within the larger community would have been bet-

Seattle Community Network Principles

The Seattle Community Network (SCN) is a free public-access computer network for exchanging and accessing information. Beyond that, however, it is a service conceived for community empowerment. Our principles are a series of commitments to help guide the ongoing development and management of the system for both the organizers and participating individuals and organizations.

Commitment to Access

Access to the SCN will be free to all.

We will provide access to all groups of people, particularly those without ready access to information technology.

We will provide access to people with diverse needs. This may include special-purpose interfaces.

We will make the SCN accessible from public places.

Commitment to Service

The SCN will offer reliable and responsive service.

We will provide information that is timely and useful to the community.

We will provide access to databases and other services.

Commitment to Democracy

The SCN will promote participation in government and public dialogue.

The community will be actively involved in the ongoing development of the SCN.

We will place high value in freedom of speech and expression and in the free exchange of ideas.

We will make every effort to ensure privacy of the system users.

We will support democratic use of electronic technology.

Figure 10.1

Commitment to the World Community

In addition to serving the local community, we will become part of the regional, national, and international community.

We will build a system that can serve as a model for other communities.

Commitment to the Future

We will continue to evolve and improve the SCN.

We will explore the use of innovative applications such as electronic town halls for community governance, or electronic encyclopedias for enhanced access to information.

We will work with information providers and with groups involved in similar projects using other media.

We will solicit feedback on the technology as it is used and make it as accessible and humane as possible.

Figure 10.1 (Cont.)

ter equipped to do that work. A set of principles is more likely to retain moral strength over the long run than a set of community needs that will undoubtedly change over time. Also, as noted in Chapter 1, a capacity-based approach, championed by Kretzmann, McKnight and their colleagues at Northwestern University (1993), is a more affirming approach to community problem-solving because those programs are developed by focusing on a community's strengths rather than its deficits.

ORGANIZING AND PLANNING

In all things that are purely social we can be as separate as the fingers, yet one as the hand in all things essential to mutual progress.
                                                                Booker T. Washington

After an initial group is established, its major responsibility is devising the largely social mechanisms that will enable people to come together and cooperatively conceive a community network and promote its general development. These mechanisms should describe the general decision-making, responsibility allocating, and communicating methods that will guide the group. The tasks faced at this point are as substantial and complex as those faced by a small company struggling to develop a new product. In community-network development the resources are generally fewer and the challenges are greater, however.

For one thing, a company or a government agency is dealing with paid employees, while the community-network organization is largely dealing (at least initially) with unpaid volunteers. In the company or agency, employees will have at least "minimal competency" as well as accountability in their job, can be relied upon to devote some established amount of time per week to their job, and often work together in central offices to communicate with each other and coordinate their actions. In addition, employees in companies or government agencies can be fired. These characteristics are not shared by community-network organizations that are run by volunteers who may work sporadically on the project.

Developing shared perspectives on both the vision and the process for attaining the vision is indispensable for success. Face-to-face group meetings provide a critical forum for addressing that objective which e-mail alone can not provide.

When the project first begins, it is tempting to jump right in and begin presenting the vision of community networks, deciding what software to buy, designing the user interface, or initiating any number of exciting and necessary activities. Since early decisions have a tendency to become "built-in" to the system, it is important that these decisions are sound.

When any community project is first launched, project participants will be highly enthusiastic and have a strong conception of what the project should be. Unfortunately, this strong conception may not be shared by others. Proceeding from this ambiguous and contradictory beginning may lead—among other problems—to division and hard feelings within the group, mistrust within the funding community, and confusion among potential network users. Developing a shared vision may be the single most important task that the group must accomplish at the onset. Moreover, this vision must be powerful enough to spark enthusiasm on the part of the developers, pragmatic enough to convince possible funders, and simple enough to be understood by the community at large.

To help support this process, Apple Librarian Steve Cisler describes the use of a spoked circle as a graphical decision aid (Fig. 10.2). The circle represents the "space" of decisions that must be made regarding the system, while the endpoints of the spokes represent the two possible ways in which the decision could be made. In his paper on "Community Networks: Past and Present Thoughts" (1994a), Cisler shows an example of the spoked-circle approach that was used by the Silicon Valley Public Access Link (SV-PAL) Project. The upright spoke, for example, might be labeled "architecture" and the location of the small circle on the spoke near the "distributed" endpoint

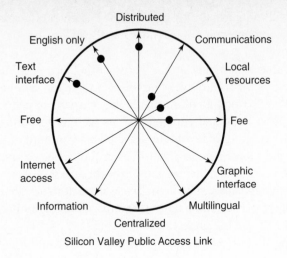

Figure 10.2

depicts the decision to use a distributed architecture instead of a centralized one. A point on the middle of a spoke would indicate an intermediate position between the views represented by the endpoints.

There are no stringent requirements as to how to use the tool. Simply identifying the spokes can be an important first step, as the spokes clearly show which decisions are to be made. It may not be critical to determine the exact location of the spot indicating a decision. In some cases, a group may decide to postpone a decision, but it is a *group* decision, nevertheless, that ultimately must be made with others in the group. If it hadn't been resolved, for example, whether the network should be free to use or whether there should be fees, the organizers could say, "We're still trying to resolve this. Which approach do *you* think is best?" The tool can be used as a way to explain compromises or transitional circumstances by showing the current point in relation to the direction along which the developers plan to proceed. For example, when the system is launched it might be deemed necessary to charge users a small fee, but ultimately the system would be expected to be free to use. It might also be necessary to begin with text-only displays, but with a commitment to move to more advanced graphical displays when certain conditions are met.

The integrative potential and inherent plasticity (as well as the potential for multiple and possibly conflicting perspectives) of community-network services are shown very clearly and effectively in the description of possible community-network services that Frank Hecker, CapAccess (Washington, D.C.) activist, first published on the communet electronic distribution list (1994). In Fig. 10.3 these services along with their respective "real-life" coun-

Possible Community-Network Services

Network provider	Providing a "raw" transmission facility over which people could send or receive any type of information and on which they could build higher-level services
Publisher or broadcaster	Collecting, generating, and disseminating information
Distributor or wholesaler	Taking information generated by others and redistributing it to others, whether end users or not
Library	Permanently storing information for later access
Salon	Sponsoring discussion forums on topics of both general and specialized interest
Public phone	Providing "gateway" access to remote systems and services
Post office	Enabling people to send and receive personal electronic mail
Personal office	Providing people with on-line work areas, and document-creation and manipulation tools
Group office	Providing groups of people with on-line shared spaces to support collaborative work
School	Training people to use on-line services and resources, including those associated with the Internet
Consultant	Assisting outside organizations in bringing in house the capabilities to provide on-line services and resources

Figure 10.3

terparts are described. Without agreement on which services the community network is supposed to provide to the community, there is a high likelihood that the project will suffer from miscommunication and conflict.

Along with trying to develop a shared image of what the community network will look like, the developers must create an organization and set of processes that can work *as a team* to realize the dream. It is during this phase that the design and realization of the organizational infrastructure—covered in more detail later in this chapter—must be initiated.

INAUGURATING THE COMMUNITY NETWORK

From: Governor Mike Lowry
To: "Seattle Community Network" <welcome@scn.org>
Subject: Welcome

Congratulations to Seattle Community Network on the creation of this electronic forum for the citizens of Seattle.

The Seattle Community Network will enable the exchange of information and ideas between people regardless of geographic, social or economic boundaries. This technology will support conversations and relationships within the local community and among citizens of our extended global community.

Members of Computer Professionals for Social Responsibility and the staff of Seattle Public Library are to be commended for their dedication to providing public access for all citizens.

From: "James A. Grant" <jag@cacs.usl.edu>
To: welcome@scn.org
Subject: Congratulations!

The Acadiana Chapter of Computer Professionals for Social Responsibility (CPSR) send you hearty congratulations on the inauguration of your local community network. We acknowledge your leadership role in the provision of networking capabilities to various underserved segments of the community. We look forward one day to following your example and profiting from your experience.

To: welcome@scn.org
From: hkorpine@vipunen.hut.fi (Heikki J Korpinen, Free-Net Finland)
Subject: Welcome Seattle!

As not being able to join your 7th June party in Seattle I'll virtually welcome you all to come along to the endless interaction with rest of us online.

Best wishes for your fine efforts.

From: welcome@scn.org (Welcome To SCN)
Subject: greetings, Earthling

Thank you for your welcome message!
We think SCN is really cool!
We hope SCN does great.

(Reed age 8)
(Barney age 11)
(Isabel age 9)

Just as the birth is a critical part of the development of a human, so too is the inauguration of the network, when the system is made available for the first time and community members can dial into the system or use it via public access terminals. It is critical to remember that this step is neither the first nor the last step. Essential preparations must be made *before* the system is established to help ensure that expectations are met, and a redoubled effort must be made *after* the system is established to help ensure that the system continues to grow in ways that meet the needs of the community. Inaugurating the system—like a birth—marks the turning point between an idea shared by a small group and a reality to be shared by the community.

Getting the network up and running is an important and exciting milestone in the evolution of the project. It is the moment that the community network becomes *real*—an entity that can be described in an actual, rather than in a virtual or future, sense. Also, as with any birth, the situation is irreversibly changed. Events that arise after the roll-out are more pressing than those that happened before.

SCN's Community Introduction

The announcement that SCN was operational was made in a "community introduction" at the downtown branch of the Seattle Public Library. The SCN group, wary of possible glitches, consciously avoided creating a major event with extravagant promises and the like. Two early SCN supporters, Liz Stroup, the head librarian at the SPL, and Jim Street, the president of the Seattle City Council, both spoke at the introduction. SCN members had also solicited welcome messages from people all over the world and various Washington State politicians. These greetings were placed on-line for inspection while selected ones were printed out and placed on the wall of the auditorium and included in a small press kit. There were two or three short speeches by SCN volunteers, a brief demo, and the community introduction was culminated by three children from a local school who sent a short thank-you e-mail message to a mailing list alias that expanded to include the electronic address of everybody who had sent a good luck message to SCN. (The thank-you message and a few welcome messages are included under the "Inaugurating the Community Network" heading.) Although other communities have launched their network with more fanfare (such as having the governor of the state or Vice President Al Gore cut a ribbon), the SCN community introduction was attended by nearly one hundred people and seemed perfectly appropriate for SCN.

RUNNING THE NETWORK

Many of the present community networks are labors of love; they draw on the volunteer spirit of both technical and non-technical citizens in a town or region . . . These are magic moments, but the day-to-day activities and the financial burden of growing a system to meet the demands of an ever-expanding base of new users can try the unity of even the most energetic and cooperative organizing groups.

Steve Cisler (1995b)

When the system is operational, community members can begin to put information on-line and start forums. Members of the community-network organization need to train the community members to use the system ("mentoring") and help them solve the problems that inevitably arise. The community members who have provided community information on the system and have started forums will begin their own marketing and outreach, communicating with individuals and groups on the possible uses of the system. When individuals and independent organizations perform these functions, the network begins to grow organically in the community. At the same time, it is also useful to provide introductory material and training to potential users. The "road shows" that SCN volunteer Jim Horton organized at Seattle City and King County libraries were, and continue to be, an excellent vehicle for these activities.

Behind the scenes there are a myriad of tasks that the community-network organization volunteers and staff members must accomplish. These include everyday duties such as registering users, answering the telephone (and/or voice mail and e-mail), registering new users and establishing new accounts, distributing brochures, logging donations and putting money in the bank, performing backups of user files and other data, adding or replacing modems and other devices, and many other activities.

There are also less frequent activities such as recommending hardware and software, negotiating with vendors (of all types) and potential strategic partners, giving presentations, fundraising, dealing with the press and other public relations duties, dealing with policy problems that arise, and short-term and long-term planning.

Running a community network is similar in many ways to running a business. Community networks need to perform valuable services for the community in an efficient and cost-effective manner. As noted, this requires a combination of everyday activities as well as other activities that help respond to exigencies and prepare for the future. Extensive discussion of these activities is beyond the scope of this book. Clark Rogers and Brian Vidic have produced a pragmatic guide (1995) to the management of community information services based on years of experience. Since a community network is also a business, it is useful to think in those terms. Paul Hawken's book on "Growing a Business" offers many good ideas (1987). Finally, since fundraising and proposal writing are generally critical to community network development, it would be useful to consult some of the excellent references on this (Hall, 1988).

It is important to plan carefully for running the network, but it is quite probable that there will still be surprises. In Seattle, SCN's particular bane was user registration. User registrations were picked up at the post office or fax machine. After these were retrieved, volunteers recorded donations, established network accounts and passwords, and mailed the account information to the new users. Volunteers also sent out registration information to people who requested it by telephone or by electronic mail. When the user registration process was taking six or more weeks to establish a new account, there were lots of rumblings. After two months of continued confusion, a more effective system was developed and the waiting period dropped to two weeks. Although some of the challenges will tax the limits of an organization, the Seattle experience shows that a motivated organization will rise to the occasion and meet the challenges.

IMPLEMENTING PROJECTS AND PROGRAMS

> *The real heart of the effectiveness of any community network . . . is the learned*
> *ability for any given group to work purposely together toward a productive end.*
>
> Frank Odasz (1995)

The purpose of the community network is to promote community participation. Participation in the community network can take two basic forms. One form involves directly using the network in activities such as on-line forums, including those specifically devoted to discussing the system and how well it meets community needs. Modifying and developing services and hosting forums are also included here. The second form involves working with community members and organizations to develop projects and programs, especially those that support the core values of the new community.

While providing information and forums is important, these activities only go so far. To truly develop community technology that helps meet community needs and builds technological literacy, network organizers and community organizations will need to develop *focused programs* that use the technology to meet their goals. In Seattle, for example, discussions have been underway with representatives of a coalition for the homeless to provide and improve services for the homeless, with the League of Women Voters to increase voter awareness and participation, and with the Evergreen Society to enhance the deliberative infrastructure of the state's nonprofit organizations.

Some types of projects may be more conducive to community network/ community action partnerships. Rogers and Vidic, for example, describe the "user responsive developmental models" including "community memory" or archives; technical assistance network; legislative connections; community training enhancement; and data access collaboration. The "participatory action research" (PAR) framework can be used to orient this second, strongly community-based approach to implementing projects and programs.

A discussion of PAR as employed in a "critical indicator" and a "social contract" project can be found in Appendix F. Each project is notable because it is participatory, long-term, and community-oriented. In addition, both projects have an orienting theme that is at once easy-to-understand, compelling, and action-oriented. Each project could also be well-served by an effective and ubiquitous community network.

BUILDING STRATEGIC ALLIANCES

To strengthen democracy, we need to integrate NII implementation with local organizational development. And not just any organizations, but specifically those that serve, advocate for, and are run by people from the parts of our society that are least likely to be able to buy their way into a market-driven NII that rations access according to personal income. We must think beyond the already daunting goal of providing service to large numbers of individuals through access points located in public buildings, libraries, and shopping malls. We need to adopt a strategy of working through and with grassroots organizations.

Steve Miller (1996)

Community networks must integrate as well as empower. They must become *woven* into the fabric of community—not patched or pieced. Thus community networks need to work strongly and strategically with other community institutions and organizations. After all, these organizations have been working with the community for many years. Organizations, as Steve Miller (1996) has pointed out, are "multipliers" that "leverage any available support services" and are more capable than individuals of creating long-lived community assets. When organizations become involved, they often will conduct training, help raise funds, and advertise the system to their members. Saul Alinsky realized the value of working with organizations and community organizations were a key ingredient in his organizing strategy (1969).

Forming strategic alliances is not without pitfalls, however. Some agencies may want a monopoly on information; some may want to manage the entire network—their way; some may have a closed process; some may believe in censoring some voices; some may want to make money; and some may impose unreasonable and insurmountable demands. Nevertheless, with principled partners, strategic alliances can make the difference between a marginal community network and an effective community network.

Why might organizations want to cooperate with an upstart community network project? The main reason is that the primary mission of the organization may implicitly call for such an alliance. For example, early this century when C. W. Smith, the city librarian of the Seattle Public Library stated that the public library should be a center of public comfort as well as public education, he hardly envisioned electronic community networks, yet were he alive today, he would advocate for them, as a natural consequence of the library's mission. Organizations falling into this category generally feel that they can reduce their costs and/or improve their service by providing electronic delivery or access via computer networks. Another reason is that it may be a legal requirement for an organization or agency to extend its traditional role electronically. In particular, a government agency may be required to provide information in electronic form to the public. This data could include the so-called "crown jewels" James Love of the Taxpayers Assets Program has identified (see Chapter 8) or community related information such as that made available by the Center for Neighborhood Technology in Chicago (see Chapter 5). Or perhaps public participation or comment is stipulated as a necessary part of the planning process. For example, the Washington State Growth Management Act requires procedures for "early and continuous public participation in the development and amendment of comprehensive land-use plans and development regulations implementing such plans" (Section 14, SHB 2929) and explicitly states the provision for ". . . broad dissemination of proposals and alternatives, opportunity for written comments, public meetings after effective notice, provision for open discussion, communication programs, information services, and consideration of and response to public comments. . . ." When such a requirement exists, it may be possible to force compliance through several means including legal action. Of course "cooperation" of this sort, however necessary in some cases, is too adversarial to be described as a strategic alliance.

When I first began looking at community networks, approximately half of the systems were associated with a university, a library, or both (Schuler, 1994). These percentages may be declining as more types of organizations become involved. There are surprisingly diverse types of community organizations with whom a strategic alliance may be desirable. Some of these possibilities are listed in Fig. 10.4. Any organization whose mission includes a strong degree of public participation is a potential partner. Any other corporation—communications, high technology, or otherwise—may also be supportive. This support may be based on a desire to build a market for its product or service or a commitment to support the community from which its labor force is drawn. Apart from merely using the network or supporting it on some level with equipment or dollars, the bottom line for an alliance or strong partnership is that both parties need to benefit from the partnership. Both need to be able to accomplish more of their mission with the alliance than they could accomplish without it. This benefit could mean involving more people in a dialogue with the organization, bringing more services to an organization (for example, introducing network services to a school), or simply generating positive publicity for the organization.

Approaches to cooperation will be as varied as the organizations themselves. Government networks can cooperate by making government information available on the public network, while community networks can sponsor forums on civic issues. Environmental and other advocacy groups can contribute information to the community network. Media organizations can work cooperatively on public journalism projects, while public access television advocates, League of Women Voters, and consumer groups may push information-technology goals on a political level. Libraries and community-network organizations make natural allies, of course, and some issues involving alliances of this sort are discussed in the next section.

SCN and SPL: A "Mini" Case Study of Successful Alliance

The Seattle Community Network (SCN) and the Seattle Public Library (SPL) are currently working together in a cooperative arrangement that benefits both parties. While the road to partnership may not be as smooth as this one was and the specifics of various community partnerships will undoubtedly vary, reviewing the stages in the SCN/SPL process will still provide a useful example.

People in the SCN project originally convened a meeting with about 40 people from the community, including representatives from the library. SCN representatives presented the early vision and asked for feedback. Reactions were mixed. Some people were not interested in the idea at all; others weren't interested in the particular vision that was presented. Yvonne Chen

Possible Strategic Partners

1. Other community networks

2. Public and public access broadcasting and cable stations

3. Community (nonprofit and for-profit) radio, television, and newspapers

4. Media and arts organizations—especially alternative and community-based

5. Educational institutions—including K–12, community colleges, training institutes, and universities

6. Libraries

7. "Peace dividend" locations including closed military bases

8. High-tech and telecommunications firms—Boeing, AT&T, or Microsoft, for example

9. Local, regional, state, federal government agencies—employment agencies, for example

10. Electronic bulletin-board systems

11. "Good government" groups—League of Women Voters, for example

12. Economic development and anti-poverty groups

13. Advocacy groups—ACLU, arts and media groups, environmental groups, fair information, toxics right-to-know organizations, for example

14. Social service providers—including crisis intervention and referral organizations

15. Hospitals and clinics

16. Community centers—YMCAs, YWCAs, Boys and Girls Clubs, for example

17. Ethnic organizations—El Centro de la Raza, for example

18. Other civic revitalization and activist groups

Figure 10.4

and Jim Taylor from the Seattle Public Library, however, were interested, and informal discussion about a collaborative effort began that night.

Randy Groves of SCN and I started meeting regularly with Yvonne and Jim. In retrospect it is clear that this portion of the process should not be hurried (the first "working agreement" took seven months to complete). It is important that all parties trust each other and that any working agreements are clear and well conceived. It is also important that the parties negotiate as peers. As the two parties are very likely to be vastly dissimilar in terms of budget, staff size, and length of service in the community, there may be a tendency for the more powerful party to exert its will over the fledgling community-network organization. If pressure tactics are used by any party, it's better to address this explicitly or back away from the negotiation, as it's a good indication of how the organization will operate in the future.

The negotiation period offered an opportunity to size up and evaluate the potential partners' goals and concerns. The Seattle Public Library, for example, had concerns about SCN's staying power as well as potential negative publicity that might be generated by racist or other unsavory postings that could appear on the network. People working with SCN, on the other hand, worried that the library might try to dominate or take undue credit for SCN.

Any major agreement with another organization should be a legal document whether it is a letter of agreement, memo of understanding, a contract, or other instrument. The initial letter of agreement between the Seattle Community Network and the Seattle Public Library specified one year, yet could be easily renewed. The library agreed to physically locate the SCN hardware in the SPL computer room. The library also agreed to provide a small workspace—desk, bookshelves, and so forth—for SCN use. Since the project was just starting, providing physical space for hardware and personnel saved SCN quite a bit of money that was subsequently spent on a computer upgrade and more telephone lines. The library also devoted several dial-in lines to SCN. Most importantly, from SCN's free, public-access point of view, the library installed SCN as a menu choice on its public access system that could be reached via modem and from each of its 23 neighborhood branches. This important step ensured that everybody in the Seattle area had free access to a community computer system, one of the SCN principles. It also meant that SCN became closely dependent on the library for physical access to its computers. Finally, in any alliance it is important to include an orderly procedure for withdrawing from the agreement. If SPL, for example, were to tell SCN that they had to clear out their computer the next day, it would be very disruptive. By the same token, if SCN were to withdraw from the agreement, it would be disruptive to SPL.

The SCN and SPL relationship has thus far been very productive, but it represents only a beginning. There are many possibilities for new joint projects that exist now and will arise in the near future (some of which are described in Chapter 11). Representatives of both SCN and the SPL will need to work together and with the community to craft the programs that are most effective in fulfilling their respective missions.

Additional Thoughts on Strategic Alliances

Strategic alliances are not without hazards for a beginning computer-network project. For one thing, a computer-network effort could be sidetracked from the goals that it has set for itself by a persuasive or more powerful organization. When time is at a premium, advancing one aspect of the project generally means setting others aside. The prospect of a strategic alliance could interfere with the development of a community network. The potential partner, for example, could insist on certain terms in a memo of understanding that were in conflict with the goals of the community network. The desire to join forces with an influential organization could convince the community-network developers to modify their principles, policies, or strategy. A potential partner could insist that the community network charge a fee for services or that some information providers should be denied network use.

Other problems could surface over the use of the names of other partners. On the one hand, an organization might want to invoke the name of another partner to imply that they have stronger affiliations with that organization than they actually have. On the other hand, an organization might not always give proper recognition to other organizations in the alliance. An example of this would be accepting kudos that rightfully belonged to another organization.

Another possible hazard of an alliance, lastly, is the danger of the community network fading from public view as it becomes increasingly seen as just a "part of" another organization. As a matter of fact, a community network organization, over time could begin to lose its own identity and *merge* into the larger organization—playing in *its* political arena, kowtowing to *its* bureaucracy, and generally assuming a subsidiary status.[1]

A good partnership will be synergistic, with each partner undertaking the activities for which they are best suited. Ideally, developing an effective community network will be a natural consequence of each partner's overall mission. Fighting over turf, control, or credit can be very damaging to any project. However tempting an alliance looks to the community-network de-

---

[1] There are positive sides to a merger, of course, including increased financial security. In September, 1995, WETA, a Washington, D.C. based public broadcaster, acquired CapAccess, the Washington, D.C. community network, in a move that was enthusiastically welcomed by both organizations.

velopers, they need to exercise caution and analyze the situation carefully. And if an existing alliance turns sour, it may be necessary to disassociate the network from the relationship.

EVALUATING COMMUNITY NETWORKS

Action-based initiatives are needed to explore the possibilities of community networking that will be primarily motivated by the imaginations of the participants. Non-obtrusive measures of the many levels of "success" need to be designed and implemented.

Frank Odasz (1994)

Comments from attendees at the first "Ties that Bind" (Cisler, 1994b) community-networking conference, sponsored by Apple Computer and the Morino Institute, reveal the wide range of well-intentioned and ambitious hopes, goals, and expectations for community networks. An almost random sample of expectations from the attendees[2] includes ". . . development of civil society in a post-apartheid South Africa" (Bowles, page 1); ". . . enable our community to plug into the great world" (Kimball, page 2); ". . . work with children and youth and are interested in how we can tap into and contribute to the resources of community networks to further our efforts" (Decrem, page 3); ". . . civic networking at the local community level" (Coffey, page 4); ". . . economic revitalization, environmental consensus building, and education." (Jackson, page 4); ". . . learning applications within the school, for the local community, and for larger virtual communities" (Newman, page 4); ". . . providing open forums where free speech is encouraged" (Figallo, page 5); ". . . bridge the gap that currently exists between people" (Bowman, page 5); ". . . helping K–12 teachers learn how to use the Internet" (Siegel, page 5); and ". . . ensure the participation of the neglected inner schools, to consolidate information in a one-stop electronic center, to create innovative applications of the community network to reduce social and environmental problems" (Marcus, page 6).

Without an effective evaluation process, developers and other interested parties won't know if progress is being made or if their goals are being met. An effective evaluation process will provide invaluable information that can be used as the basis to change or to maintain strategic directions of the project. It can also be useful externally. Being able to define, perform, and pre-

---

[2] This roster of attendees and accompanying comments was sent to all registered attendees. It was not part of the formal proceedings.

sent a meaningful evaluation can be useful in funding requests, press reports, public testimony, and community outreach.

Approaches to Evaluation

Kathleen Gygi, a graduate student in the Community and Regional Planning
Program at the University of New Mexico, has written a very good report on
the evaluation of community networks (1995). In her report she describes
two main types of evaluation: (1) the comparative analysis of computer-
network systems in which individual systems (or generic computer-network
models) are compared and (2) the individual-project assessment in which an
individual community-network system is evaluated according to the goals
or criteria that the organization or community itself has designated as important.

Gygi has suggested five dimensions for comparing community-network
systems and models. These are (1) services, (2) capacity, (3) accessibility, (4)
ownership, and (5) financing. Examining these—or other—dimensions is
useful in establishing initial goals and design approaches for a planned system. In this approach, one looks carefully at data from other systems. The
data would also provide a good basis for evaluating the progress (in number
of users, for example) that the community network had made as compared
with others that had been running for the same amount of time.

Gygi's second approach to evaluation, the individual-project assessment,
places the focus on individual community networks. Community-network
goals are often very high but the progress towards them is often reported in
terms of numbers of registered users (or other numeric values) or through a
small number of personal anecdotes. These methods are generally inadequate, however, as they insufficiently link objectives to results. If getting low-
income residents to use electronic resources is a goal, then the total number
of users reveals little or nothing about reaching that goal.

Ann Bishop of the Graduate School of Library and Information Science at
the University of Illinois, proposes a six-step approach to planning and evaluation (1994).

1. Choose objective(s) (e.g., increase Free-Net use by senior citizens)

2. Make it measurable (e.g., issue Free-Net user names to 100 people over
   65 in 1995)

3. Brainstorm alternative means of accomplishing objective(s) (e.g., marketing campaign for seniors, set up public access terminal in senior center,
   increase number of on-line resources geared to seniors)

4. Rank each alternative in terms of cost, feasibility, fit with organizational goals, other criteria

5. Calculate final rank to select best alternative

6. Plan for implementation of chosen alternative and measurement of its success.

Art Noble, an environmental activist in Seattle suggests creating five lists—needs, objectives, procedures, evaluation criteria, and budget—as still another way to link objectives to evaluation. With his approach, each individual need is linked to an objective, procedure, evaluation criteria, and budget, which, together, form a well-organized approach to proposal writing.

It is critical to be able to discern progress towards stated community-network goals. Although the goals will vary by community and by project, it is important that programs can be evaluated in some meaningful way. Focusing from the onset on evaluation methods that are well integrated with the rest of the project (such as those proposed by Bishop or Noble) will prove invaluable to the success of the project.

LONG-TERM IMPACT AND SUSTAINABILITY

> . . . if we are to keep our community-based computer networks and information servers from becoming the equivalent of an underfunded county or city hospital—an information source of last resort—then we must face these challenges now.
>
> Steve Cisler (1995a)

The aims and motivations of the community-networking movement are not new. They've been anticipated and rehearsed several times this century as people endeavored to build stronger communities. These earlier struggles were marked more frequently by failure than success and include the community-center movement, the battle for amateur (noncommercial) radio, and the fight for community public access television. Although each had their particular idiosyncrasies of history and personality, all examples offer valuable lessons for the community-networking movement. Success is not guaranteed. It is clearly possible that the community-network movement may implode, as Mario Morino has warned, or merely shrivel into oblivion.

As with any social and political institution, the shape of individual community networks will depend on many factors. Some are global and national in scope, but many are strictly local, such as competition from other services, funding availability, as well as the motivating principles, expectations, and interests of the developers and community members. Since the future is difficult to predict and even harder to influence, it is somewhat unlikely that the community-network movement will attain the high goals it has set for itself. Nevertheless we can sketch guidelines that increase the likelihood of success.

Network Organization Type—Nonprofit, For-Profit, or Government

Given the goals and underlying philosophy guiding the development of community networks, it is natural to ask what *type* of legal entity is the best vehicle for developing and maintaining them. As we will see, there are three main types—nonprofit, for-profit, and government—and a wide variety of hybrids as well. But before we consider what type of organization should run the community network, let's reconsider what sorts of things a community network must institutionalize. The short answer to this is that a community network must have principles, policies, and processes as described below.

- The principles of the organization must support the six core values. The mission and principles should be made explicit and be usable as a barometer to measure and evaluate the organization and the system.

- The policies should support free speech, privacy, and other important aspects of a democratic institution.

- The processes should be democratic, allow citizen input and *control* of the network.

While these guidelines don't necessarily rule out any type of organization, the current values and orientation of for-profit corporations seem to argue against this approach. For one thing, for-profit corporations are loathe to consider any outside influence, sometimes battling to ensure that their own stockholders can't place issues of social, ethical, or environmental concerns on annual meeting ballots. For-profit corporations rarely express a commitment to free speech or to forums for alternative voices. Many of the commercial networks censor on-line postings that don't meet certain standards. To be fair, until these networks can be protected from legal action resulting from postings, their approach will remain cautious. But traditional commercial media—newspapers, radio, television, and the like—have a long history of control, suppression of unpopular stories, censorship, propaganda, and manipulation. The cooperative model of a for-profit corporation where each "member" owns an equal share seems to have a better chance at meeting the requirements than the traditional for-profit model.

Government, likewise, has several factors working against it. The United States' propensity to spy on its citizens (historically and currently through modern technology like the "Clipper Chip") and its recent betrayal of first amendment rights makes it a somewhat unworthy recipient of public trust, although it remains more committed to free public information than many other types of organizations. Also, in the United States, the government is prohibited by law from *directly* funding public media, a curb that is intended to discourage state propaganda (but doesn't prevent the government from having thousands of public relations people, however). In both the case of the Corporation for Public Broadcasting (CPB) and the public library system, the government gives funds to an organization that is at least nominally independent from government. Of course, in the case of the CPB, originally intended to air alternative viewpoints, these funds are often held political hostage when "objectionable" material is aired (and where public stations' broadcasting bandwidth is coveted by well-heeled media conglomerates). If the American people decide that community networks are, like free public libraries, important enough to be universally available and at least partially funded with public funds, then it would be desirable to fund them in such a way to avoid some of the unproductive political wrangling that accompanies current funding approaches.

Most community networks in the United States have been developed by nonprofit organizations. That doesn't necessarily mean that nonprofit organizations are the best vehicle for community networks. A nonprofit organization, for example, can be as exclusive or as removed from the community as other types. Furthermore, a nonprofit organization whose focus lies outside the community-networking area may be unable or unwilling to give the project the necessary attention. The chances are very good, moreover, that a nonprofit organization will be starved for funds and will be run largely by volunteers—a source of energy that is not likely to be sustainable over the long run. Although nonprofits have generally served as the launching pad for community networks, there are now a multitude of options available to developers that include variants on older models, hybrids, or wholly new creations.

In short, there may be no one best organizational type for community networks. The community network (as previously mentioned) must meet three requirements: (1) principles that address core values, (2) open policies, and (3) open processes. A for-profit concern is likely—even obligated—to put profits above the community. A government concern may be overly controlling, exclusive, closed, or patronizing. A nonprofit may also be exclusive and self-serving, while being unable to obtain the necessary resources and skills to run a community network effectively. A nonprofit community network that abides by the three requirements, with adequate government funding and independence from government control, may be the best hope for a sustained, useful community network. Unfortunately, current political and economic realities may not allow such a network to develop in the United States in the near-term. Many of the sections that follow in this chapter (as in the section on funding, for example) will discuss issues that directly relate to the ways in which a community-network organization can be developed.

Structure of the Organization

How the organization is structured greatly influences the development and maintenance of a community network and how well the organization can respond to both opportunity and crisis. The organizational structure should suggest both the tasks that need doing as well as whose responsibility it is to do them. The structure should *support* the project—it shouldn't be a straitjacket imposing overly restrictive and bureaucratic procedures—nor should it impose a hierarchy where volunteers or information providers are denied an opportunity to participate in a variety of activities.

The remainder of this section assumes that the organization is nonprofit and may or may not have paid staff. A for-profit or government-run community network will have similar functions, but may organize itself differently. (It is unlikely, for example, that a for-profit community network would have many volunteers.) In the case of a nonprofit organization, the relationship of paid staff members to volunteers and to the decision-making capabilities within the community network are both important considerations. In general, the community network organization needs to develop a shared vision, a shared plan, and a shared voice. It also needs to establish how work will be organized, assigned, evaluated, and sanctioned. And it must effectively coordinate the work of paid staff and a variety of volunteers who will generally serve on a committee or a board of directors or advisory board.

SCN Structure

The SCN Project originally established five committees that corresponded to five major areas of responsibility. These are based loosely on NPTN recommendations in the "Blue Book" (NPTN, 1992):

1. Hardware/software for all technical aspects, including recommending, evaluating, installing, porting, debugging, and maintaining the system

2. Outreach, for general public relations, working with strategic partners, publicity, and fundraising

3. Policy, for determining policy and considering policy issues

4. Services, for working with information providers, and designing system-user interface (including menu arrangement)

5. Staff and facilities, for all considerations related to hiring, evaluating, remuneration, termination of staff, and facilities management.

In addition to the five committees, a Coordinating Council or steering committee, composed of an elected representative from each of the committees and two other members-at-large elected by the entire membership was established. Also, as negotiated in the formal agreement with the Seattle Public Library, an SPL representative was added to the Council. The role of this body is to respond quickly when necessary, to help determine strategic directions for the group, and to make recommendations. For example, the Coordinating Council may recommend that the group purchase a new computer, which is then voted on by the group. Although this group is not a board of directors in a legal sense (because the CPSR board is the controlling body until SCN becomes an independent organization), its functions are analogous to a directorial board. In fact, some members of this body may be among the first board members of Seattle Community Network once it becomes an independent nonprofit organization.

The advisory board is yet another body that assists with the community-network development. The advisory board is generally comprised of people in the community who are well-recognized for their contribution in one realm or another. For example, the SCN advisory board includes representatives from environmental, ethnic, Seattle city government, education, library, and citizen-activist communities. Although the role of advisory board members is often symbolic, advisory-board members who are enthusiastic about the project can actively assist it in many ways.

In addition to volunteers, paid staff members sometimes work on community networks. Although this usually has happened only when an institution like a university or library has allowed an employee to work on the network, the situation may be changing somewhat due to increased interest from foundations, government, and business. A time when people are actually paid to work on the system—a mythical and magical time in the utopian future for many community-network developers—may actually be arriving in many communities.

What positions would it be appropriate for paid staff to fill? In general, there are two categories: mission-critical and leadership. The mission-critical jobs include those that must be done on a regular basis or the project will fail. If funds existed and if volunteers were not available for registering several hundred new users per week, an employee might be hired to perform this role. Other mission-critical tasks might include rebooting the community network computer, performing regular back-ups, restoring user files, or any number of system-maintenance tasks. If the community-network machine were prone to crashing and if it couldn't be rebooted over the telephone and if the machine were miles away and it were 3:00 in the morning, then a volunteer might not be particularly easy to find.

A leadership role is qualitatively different than a mission-critical one, although many tasks (project-management, for example) require both roles. A person with the major responsibility for running the system—typically an "executive director" in the nonprofit world—assumes responsibilities for speaking for the group, developing strategic alliances, and obtaining funding through proposal writing and other means. The executive director is usually hired by the board of directors and generally is responsible for the staff and volunteer coordination as well as the day-to-day operations.

Communication and Coordination

Running a community-network project can be as complex and as demanding as running a business, with the critical difference being that many, if not most, of the participants in the network project are unpaid volunteers. For that reason, they don't necessarily work in the same location, nor at set times. For those reasons communication and coordination are vital to the success of the project.

Ongoing Communication at SCN

The most important lesson learned from the SCN experience in this area was alluded to earlier: It is critical for participants to agree on basic goals and processes before representing the project to outside people. The early—sometimes tempestuous—SCN planning sessions where major issues were discussed were ultimately very valuable. Hammering out the issues helped provide key insights for the project and helped construct a vision that was truly shared by the whole group. Having this shared vision helped the participants speak with the same voice and increased the solidarity of those who would be working together for the next several years.

A subsidiary issue arose, that of speaking for the project. Before a shared vision existed (and occasionally afterwards), an individual would disclose to others, give a statement to the press, make an agreement, or write an article or letter that purported to represent the views of the project. While this was never done maliciously, it was widely acknowledged to be potentially damaging to the project. Our approach to this problem had three thrusts. One, the Coordinating Council would review all written material (especially proposals) before it was distributed. Two, in meetings SCN representatives were encouraged to say, "I personally can't make decisions for the project—I'll take this issue back to the Coordinating Council." Three, people who were familiar with the SCN vision were encouraged to speak to the press and in formal presentations. Since SCN was not a closed organization, it was more susceptible to problems of mixed messages than smaller, more exclusive organizations. Yet after the shared vision was defined and some communication guidelines were agreed upon, these types of problems all but vanished.

The SCN project meets every month—on the third Wednesday—at a branch of the public library. Some community-network groups set aside half an hour before the actual working meeting begins. This is a good opportunity to talk about the general project, answer questions, and possibly view the Heartland Free-Net (NPTN, 1992), Naples Free-Net (1995) or other suitable videotape. After a brief welcome, attendees at the meeting introduce themselves and briefly describe their interests and affiliations. Each committee chair gives a report, and volunteer opportunities are discussed. This is followed by consideration of pressing business, such as discussion of new by-laws or a controversial proposal or event. At the end of the meeting, each committee meets briefly to discuss current issues and concerns, and new people often start working with a suitable committee. Committees usually meet at various times throughout the month. In Seattle, the Services committee meets two or more times every month, Hardware/Software meets formally once every one or two months, and the SCN Coordinating Council, which serves as a steering committee or executive body, meets once a month. Various electronic forums are employed, especially now that the system has become operational. There is an electronic mailing list for each committee, one for all project volunteers, and one for people who are interested in community networks whether or not they're working on the project. SCN also uses electronic forums for each committee. The medium allows a multitude of communication approaches among participants, a flexibility that can sometimes result in confusion. For this reason, it is critical that all appropriate participants share in each forum's information and expectations. Electronic forums, e-mail, and listserves can be very useful but they're not a panacea, nor are they a substitute for face-to-face meetings.

Documentation

Developing basic documents is another important responsibility that helps to ensure long-term impact and sustainability. Documents include FAQs (a list of answers to Frequently Asked Questions), a statement of purpose and principles, and a business plan and budget (see Appendix D and the Web site for this book for some sample documents). Another important document is the policy statement, which addresses a wide range of complex issues including censorship, privacy, dealing with grievances, and establishing forums. The organization's by-laws and articles of incorporation are legally required and form the basis for system governance over time. Other documentation includes brochures and registration forms to distribute to the general public.

Expenses and Funding

We shouldn't be surprised to learn that there are financial costs associated with the operation of a community network. As Tom Grundner has frequently noted, "Free-Nets are inexpensive to run, but they aren't free." Funding is needed for computer and communication equipment as well as office space and office expenses. Funding may also be needed to compensate people for performing system administration, outreach, software development, and maintenance tasks. As we've mentioned, it is unlikely that volunteers and donated space and equipment can meet the need for professional service over the long run. Unfortunately, funding for community networks thus far has been sporadic and unreliable. It is necessary to find funding for the short-term, but it's equally important to develop equitable, reliable, and replicable funding approaches for the long term.

There is wide variability in the costs of running community networks. Many current systems are "church-basement" operations with no paid staff and a handful of volunteers performing the necessary tasks, while other systems have state-of-the-art equipment, paid staff, and a relatively steady cash flow. Looking at the current crop of community-network systems, however, may not be indicative of what the next generation and succeeding generations of community networks will look like. Also, since the systems are still in their infancy, many have had to rely to a large degree on the largesse of others. Computer manufacturers like Sun Microcomputers of Canada have donated machines to several of the Canadian Free-Nets, while Ameritech, the regional telephone system in the midwestern United States, has given substantial support to NPTN. US West has helped fund the Big Sky Telegraph in Montana, while Hewlett-Packard and Meta Systems Design donated hardware and software to PEN in Santa Monica. In helping launch the Seattle Community Network, the Seattle Public Library donated the physical space for the computer and the nonexclusive use of some of their telephone lines; Washington Library Network (WLN) donated the Internet connection; BSDI donated the UNIX operating system; and PCN Computer, a local retailer, donated the original machine. IBM as well as local businesses and organizations donated substantial numbers of obsolete—though usable—terminals and modems that have been distributed without charge to information providers and other nonprofit organizations.

Just as public television stations vary in scale from shoestring operations to behemoths in some metropolitan areas, community networks also vary in scale. The size and role of the staff and the physical surroundings and the sophistication of the technological infrastructure including computer, disk drives, modems, and phone lines can also vary wildly from location to location. (SCN actually started operating with a budget in the *hundreds* of dollars!) A staff could run a minimal operation providing bare-bones support, or it could be a more dynamic and proactive operation deeply involved in a wide range of community activities. We may find that community networks are beginning to shift slightly from an all-volunteer base of information and service providers to one where professionals are employed to moderate or manage certain services, such as the homework services mentioned in Chapter 3. A community network might also pay staff to develop services that are shared ("cybercasted") with other community networks, much as PBS affiliates share television shows.

Community-network costs can be broken into three main categories (shown in Figs. 10.5, 10.6, and 10.7): staff costs, office and organizational costs, and technology and infrastructure costs. These categories are general and can vary tremendously. The Seattle Community Network, for example, is running (two years after initial launch) almost entirely with volunteer staff and a "virtual office" consisting of a post-office address, telephone voice mail, and e-mail contact, but essentially no physical office space of its own. (There is some available office space at the library, and the monthly meeting is conducted in a public meeting room at a Seattle branch library.) On the other extreme, office facilities could contain classrooms, meeting rooms, and even an auditorium. And technology costs, of course, can also vary. Factors include the number of people served and the availability of technology, which could include Internet capability in the near term as well as video, audio, or more extravagant capabilities in the longer term.

Estimating Costs

How much would it cost to run a community network for a municipal area of, say, half a million people? It's difficult to get a reliable figure for this as it would depend on technology costs, staffing (and number of volunteers), and user demand, all of which are difficult to quantify based on current data. User demand, for example, would depend on system accessibility, user in-

Staff Costs

Administration

    Establishing user accounts

    Maintaining financial records

Technical Support

    Bug fixing

    Integrating new services

    Backing up user data

Outreach

    Grant writing

    Presentations and article writing

    Developing newsletter and other publications

    Negotiating with other organizations

    Publicity, such as press releases

Services

    Coordinating volunteer activities

    Developing materials

    Training

    Policy development

    Developing and conducting user surveys

    Answering telephone, e-mail, and written queries

    Dispute resolution

Optional

    Software development

    Professional services, such as education

    Political work

Figure 10.5

Office and Organizational Costs

Facilities—Office

Telephone costs

Computer(s)

Printer

Fax machine

Copier

Paper

Filing cabinets

Rent

Utilities

Software

Printing costs

Postage

Book and magazine subscriptions

Miscellaneous office supplies

Other

NPTN affiliation

Legal

Insurance

Payroll service

Conference and other travel

Figure 10.6

Technology and
Infrastructure Costs

Computer(s)

   Modems

   Disk drives

   Telephone lines

   Internet connection

   Terminal servers

Figure 10.7

terest in services, and competition. Although it's impossible to precisely develop cost estimates, we can try to develop something that's not too far off, based on several assumptions.

Although neighborhood computing clusters connected to a central hub are a possibility, we'll use the general FreePort model of a single, central hub of Unix-based computers to which users can connect via telephone or Internet. (A connection via the Internet currently costs about one-hundredth of a telephone connection.) What about user demand? How many people who could use the community network at a given time would do so? Like our other guesstimates, this figure is difficult to pin down. The number of modems and telephone lines of community-network systems is currently the limiting factor on demand, according to Tom Grundner. For purposes of this analysis, let's say that one person in 200 people will want to use the system at a peak time. This works out to about 2500 users on-line at one time, or about six times the number of maximum users that the Cleveland Free-Net can handle.

A very rough analysis would include $150,000 for computer equipment, $50,000 for modems, another $200,000 for miscellaneous equipment and telephone lines. If salaries, rents and other expenses came out to $600,000, then $1,000,000 a year should be nearly adequate for a regionally based community network. Using a population figure of 500,000, the yearly cost per person would be $2.00 per person. (The National Capital Free-Net is worth noting here because of its extensive community use and professional administration and the fact that its budget is available on-line!) Note that the amount of money spent on salaries depends on how much of the work is done by volunteers. Obviously, if tasks done by volunteers were shifted to paid staff, the costs would quickly escalate. Of course, current data suggest that use may never approach these high levels. The Cleveland Free-Net, for example, has 40,000 registered users out of a metropolitan population of nearly three million. Santa Monica's PEN system has 7,000 registered users (with 4000 log-ins per month) and a population of 95,000. As Frank Odasz points out, no community has over 5 percent of the population on-line (although this figure may now be obsolete), and only a small percentage of registered users, say five to fifteen percent, are regular users. However, this percentage is likely to become much higher as the number of users increases, network use becomes cheaper, and network software becomes easier to use.

Funding Options

Developing an adequate, equitable, and sustainable funding stream is one of the major challenges facing community networks. There are two basic ways to look at the prospects for funding: funding by direct users or through indirect users (see Fig. 10.8). Individual users and organizational information providers that benefit directly from using the services (consuming and/or providing) on the network are *direct* users. (Note that this includes advertisers.) Foundations, government agencies, or businesses that benefit when other people use the network are *indirect* users. It is interesting to note how interrelated funding issues are to community-network policy and how subtle the arguments can be. It also is worth noting how strong the pressure becomes to *charge* for services when funding is difficult and sporadic.

Funding by Users—Donations

People who use the community network can help fund their community network in two ways. The first is through voluntary donations, much as public

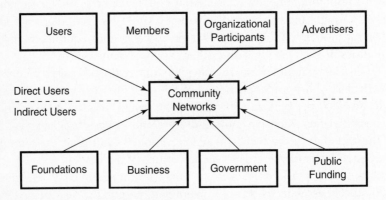

Figure 10.8 Funding Possibilities

television and radio stations in the United States hold regular "pledge drives" to exhort the faithful to ante up. Although these funding drives consume a lot of staff time and resources, this approach is relatively successful in many communities. "Viewers like you" supply much of the annual revenue for the average PBS television station. If this approach covered all expenses, then other issues would be largely irrelevant. In New York City, community radio station KBIA is funded solely by user donations—they won't accept money from foundations or businesses. The National Capital Free-Net in Ottawa has been regularly receiving over $3,000 a week in voluntary user donations in addition to over $110,000 (Canadian) in government funding. It has generally been demonstrated, however, that voluntary donations by users are insufficient for funding a community network. In the rare cases where voluntary funding does seem to work, moreover, there is often an accompanying doubt whether the trend will continue indefinitely.

Another approach to voluntary funding that an enterprising community-network organization may employ is selling network-related merchandise such as T-shirts or coffee cups. And, of course, there is the usual panoply of fundraising activities including spaghetti dinners (or other food easily prepared in mountainous quantities), auctions, bake sales, and car washes. Resorting to these prosaic approaches may mean the difference between survival and extinction—and they're all familiar, time-tested, and community-oriented.

Funding by Users—Paying for Services

The other approach to funding by users is through fees. This model, while presenting funding opportunities, diverges from the original motivation for community networks. A free model for *basic* services is conceptually simple and clean—it doesn't require complicated explanations like many pay-for services approaches. People immediately understand it just as they understand other public, universally available, civic institutions like free fire and police protection, public schools and public libraries.

People of fewer economic means will be discouraged from using a fee-based service. Since we are consciously trying to involve all members of the community, erecting economic barriers would be nonproductive. Even if poor people could afford the services, they are less likely to participate without the knowledge or expectation that the services will provide anything of value to them. Another funding possibility—offered by many developers—is to charge for "premium services" such as a SLIP connection (to the Internet) or FTP capabilities from the community network. Unfortunately, charging for premium service create a two-tiered user community, where the "paying customers" who pay the community-network bills may begin receiving more attention than those using "basic services."

There are also pragmatic considerations to charging users. When an organization charges people for services, it becomes a commercial establishment in the eyes of many people and leads to higher expectations (and higher costs, perhaps for customer services and marketing). If, for example, the system went down, users of a commercial system might complain vociferously whereas users of a noncommercial organization, although disappointed, might be more forgiving. Community networks must strive to deliver reliable service but users will need to have realistic expectations especially during the early phases of a community network's development. Finally, if users are charged for services there is a layer of administration—including usage monitoring, billing, and accounting—that must be added. Debt collection alone could become a major headache.

In spite of these reservations, some community networks will still institute fees for services. There are a variety of approaches to these charges, and some may be more effective as well as less harmful than others. The primary way to charge for a service is to establish what the services are and determine suitable fees. There could be "basic service" (the same for everybody) or "premium service," for example. There could also be fees for out-of-community users, user IDs (the Free-Nets often assign user names like BB142 or CZ881), or an original registration-processing fee.

These could be a basic flat rate or another rate based on actual, monitored usage. Actual usage could be based on amount of disk storage used, length of time logged on, or number of characters sent via e-mail. The possibilities here are nearly endless, and people have spent a lot of time trying to devise the "right" charging approach. The more complex the pricing scheme is the more difficult it will be for the user to understand. Moreover, these pricing schemes introduce an administrative layer that must calculate the rates, send out bills, and the like. Staff people must also be available to answer questions about bills and make changes if necessary. The bottom line is this: Charging for service is *not* a panacea for funding concerns.

The community-network community needs to promote—for as long as possible—the idea that a useful and effective, free community-oriented electronic commons is feasible. The best way to demonstrate this goal is with *actual working systems.* The existence of lively, highly reliable, free community networks will make it more difficult for fee proponents to make effective counterclaims.

Support by Members

If the community-network organization is a *membership-based* organization with an active dues-paying membership, then there will be *some* predictable revenue. In keeping with the principles of inclusivity, the organization should be inexpensive to join, and it should be possible to perform volunteer work in lieu of paying dues. Becoming a member is completely voluntary and is an institutionalized approach to supporting the community-network organization. Normally, only members could vote for board-member positions or be eligible for a board-member position, although nonmembers could perhaps serve in some capacity. Before we advocate such a suggestion, let's look at the implications of such an approach.

The first question to ask is whether there is a reason to become a *member* or if this is just a donation with a different name. Here we are making a distinction between users and members, although there could be a large overlap between the two categories. Also, membership is not a prerequisite for community-network use: That would be a fee-based approach going under a different name. If a community-network organization is an *advocacy* organization as well as a service, then a membership organization is not only plausible, but preferred. If a person uses the system but does not support the system's goals or advocacy stance, that person should not be coerced into being a member. However, if the community network is organized and operating following the suggestions in this book, the answer is clear: Community-network organizations are inherently advocacy organizations— hence, voluntary membership is desirable.

The question of membership raises anew a possible connection between service and funding. If some people are *users* and some are *members*, then wouldn't it be natural to give the members a little more disk space, a private telephone line, or other membership benefits? As tempting and obvious as that approach may appear, this division of people into two distinct castes would be counter to the goals of the community network.

The final question remains as to whether a membership-based approach to funding would be adequate. Initial experience has been encouraging in the Buffalo Free-Net case and with SCN. Although local conditions vary widely and the effectiveness of membership-based organizations varies accordingly, nevertheless, a membership-based organization raises important possibilities about community support as well as funding opportunities for those networks.

Funding by Indirect Users

If the funding source is not composed of people or organizations that use the network directly, then it is an *indirect user* of the community network. Indirect users might include businesses who would make donations for civic and community responsibility, recognition for good work in the community, or tax write-offs (by donating obsolete equipment or surplus inventory, for example). Other businesses, especially telecommunications or computer companies, may see the community network as a way to decrease their expenses or to increase the market for their services or products. (A community network may make it easier to pay bills electronically or to help increase long-distance telephone calls, for example, making it attractive to telephone companies.) Foundations may see certain community-network programs as within their purview, improving social services, education, or the quality of democracy, for example. Finally, government agencies—at all levels—may choose to support community networks through bonds or direct funding. Tom Grundner of NPTN has developed an intriguing proposal for a "Corporation for Public Cybercasting" (1993a), which would match federal funds up to a limit with local funds for community-network development and administration. Government has myriad responsibilities in the areas of information access and facilitation of communication, especially because delivery of government services is so important. Additionally, since government is under increasing pressure to reduce costs, a community network that reduced costs might be an effective government investment. Although currently not in vogue, government partnership with community organizations and activists may hold the key to long-term community-network survival.

Advertising on Community Networks

I believe the quickest way to kill broadcasting would be to use it for direct advertising.

Herbert Hoover (Fowler and Crawford, 1990)

For thousands of years commerce of some sort has been fundamental to the affairs of a community. Since commerce is inseparable from community affairs, it makes little sense to arbitrarily prevent it from being part of a community network. Community want ads seem indispensable for innumerable reasons: People have general announcements, are looking for a new baby stroller or a used car, or need to advertise a garage sale. People may want to provide living space in exchange for help with child care.

On the other hand, relying on advertising for a substantial percentage of community networks funding is problematic. The ill-effects, ranging from implicit control of the system (including content, policy, and board membership) to general "commodification" of information of the system. The network's basic nature could change to that of a newspaper's classified advertisement section or home shopping network rather than a library or inn. An over-reliance on advertising revenue carries the threat of redirecting the focus from the community to mass culture in general. Pepsi-Cola, General Motors, Reebok, Microsoft or other large companies advertising on a "community network" would qualitatively change it.

In the early days of radio, broadcasting was not the dominant mode (Czitrom, 1982). By 1922 there were approximately 15,000 licensed amateur transmitting stations in the United States and perhaps another quarter of a million people who could receive signals but not broadcast. Radio enthusiasts developed the ARRL (American Radio Relay League) and lobbied extensively for their rights. As the ARRL print advertisement in the 1920s beckoned, "After you grow tired of the broadcast stuff, come in with us and enjoy real radio." They viewed broadcasting as just one use of radio, just as community-network developers might view commercially oriented and controlled broadcasting over the information superhighway as just one type of access that should coexist with other noncommercial, community-oriented uses. Although well organized, the radio enthusiasts of the 1920s lost the fight. While the community-network developers of the 1990s prepare for the next incarnation of that fight, we would do well to reflect on the challenges (and failures) faced historically by other community media advocates (Felsenstein, 1992).

Clearly, if the intent is to develop a community network addressing the spectrum of community needs, including commerce, care must be taken to prevent the system from becoming just an electronic billboard and also prevent undue economic influence on the system, its organization, purpose, and directions. Since it is important to promote individual usage and influence over those of corporate interests, it will be necessary to level the playing field or even tilt it in the direction of the individuals. "Classified ads," if designed according to fairly strict criteria, could sidestep many of the dangers of asymmetric funding sources, commercial influence, and fee-based services that advertising poses to communications medium. Unfortunately, for those looking for a reliable and steady source of income, reliance on paid advertising—even limited paid "classified advertising"—is inconsistent with the principles of a community network. Simply put, allowing people to display their commercial messages *for a price* is a type of fee-based service and, as such, is a form of discrimination based on individuals' ability to pay. Although the distinction between it and advertisements can sometimes be fuzzy, a "public acknowledgement" of support that does not advertise products or services is generally acceptable.

Providing for the ability to place classified ads on the system without charge is, however, entirely consonant with the objectives of a community network and the economic needs of the community. For leveling purposes and for other practical reasons it may be necessary to limit the length of time that the posting will stay on the system (usually a week, two weeks, or a month), the size of the ad (usually one screen), and the number of ads that can be posted per week or month by one user. Seattle Community Network permits one free 14-line ad per week.

A more subtle issue arises if individuals or groups *sometimes pay.* This is the same issue that arises with the concept of fee-based services in libraries, where patrons with certain needs that are designated as being beyond the scope of ordinary needs, can elect to use those services for a fee. The first problem is that now a charging process must be introduced along with the entire administration of a new system, requiring staffing and funds to implement and operate. Nor is it obvious that the charging of fees for ads would bring enough revenue to compensate for the additional expenses. Moreover, this shift in focus changes the nature of the whole system. As in libraries with fee-based services, a danger exists that the world of users would be divided into those who pay for the services and those that don't pay for the services and that paying users would get a more favorable treatment than nonpayers.

Funding by Organizational Participants

If an organization saves $10,000 per year by using the community network (in reduced staff, computing costs, or mailing costs, for example), then investing $1000 per year (voluntarily) into the community network would be a very good investment. An alternative to this would be to actually charge the information providers (perhaps on a sliding scale, based on ability to pay) to include their information. On analysis, this approach makes the network organization beholden—or unequally beholden—to information providers, especially big account information providers. This approach can ultimately become a counterproductive advertising-based approach, as discussed above. The worst thing about this approach, however, is that it renews the bias of money and could act to squeeze alternative and unpopular voices from the network. On the other hand, donations by organizational participants should be encouraged—not as a quid pro quo, but as an investment in a community-wide resource that organizational participants use and enjoy. Joint development planning and joint proposals should also be encouraged, and these activities are very appropriate for strategic alliances.

Funding by Indirect Users

There are many organizations and individuals who are interested in successful community networks who may or may not be direct users of the systems. These *indirect users,* including foundations, government, or businesses, have a wide and diverse range of motivations, responsibilities, and resources to draw upon.

Foundations are often oriented toward advocacy or social change and may be interested in exploring new uses of community networks to further their mission. Unfortunately, many foundations are apprehensive and somewhat leery of new technology or may be loathe to explore new ideas.

Government, too, has a wide range of responsibilities in this area and is exploring many of them in some detail. These responsibilities include providing access to government information and services. In the United States, government historically has helped guide the development of transportation and communication technologies that are deemed to benefit the country, including the postal system, the highway system, and, more recently, the Internet. However, ideological articles of faith (including vague promises that the private sector will efficiently, inexpensively, and equitably provide many of the functions that government is expected to provide) are artificially constraining current discussions. These attitudes, along with a public policy that has been disproportionately influenced by large corporations and a relative lack of technological sophistication helps retard the development of creative and progressive initiatives from government.

Businesses represent a third type of indirect user of community networks. Businesses may want to encourage the development of civic institutions and to be positively associated with that development. In a more self-interested way, businesses may feel that providing another access route to their information, products, and services may benefit their bottom line.

Public Funding Possibilities

There are several other funding mechanisms that are also worth some discussion. In the public access television world, an approach has been found that is relatively stable and relatively free of political wrangling (especially when compared to the never ending legislative struggle over public broadcasting). With the public access television approach, cable providers have often been required by contract either to run their own public access facility or to remit a portion of their profits (via a tax) to a city government or other organization to run the facility. Information superhighway corporations (including communications, computer, and media companies) could all contribute in this way to support nonprofit, community networks. Miles Fidelman of the Center for Civic Networking has done a substantial amount of work in examining funding models—public and otherwise (1995)—including the airlines, the interstate highway system, electricity and other utilities, the telephone network, cable television, the Corporation for Public Broadcasting, and the Internet.

Bonds could also be a source of revenue for city- or county-run facilities, as could funding directly from existing budgets. A Community Development Corporation (CDC) is yet another option. CDCs are quasi-governmental bodies that have some public resources or capabilities open to them including, in some cases, the ability to tax.[3] Business Improvement Districts (BIDs) or Building Improvement Areas (BIAs) are established when a majority of business owners in a community vote to impose a tax on themselves. This tax is then used to fund projects for which the BID/BIA was established. Many BIDs/BIAs are for community beautification, for fresh paint or new shrubbery, for example. Others are more ambitious, perhaps working for refurbishing an entire community or business district, like the New York City BIDs. While CDCs or BIDs/BIAs offer intriguing possibilities for local initiative and control, they are not necessarily as democratic as they could be and can sometimes be unaccountable as a result.

The Funding Challenge

The multiplicity of benefiting groups and organizations and individuals spells a multiplicity of funding possibilities. Each source brings a different approach toward funding, outreach, bookkeeping, and so forth. The situation is fairly complicated—a jigsaw puzzle with scattered and dynamic pieces. The challenge that funding presents over the long term may prove to be one of the most perplexing community-network issues of all.

CONCLUSIONS

It's in our hands now, or, more specifically, it's in your *hands to make it all work.*

Tom Grundner (1993a)

Community networks go through distinct phases of evolution and each phase is marked with distinct opportunities and challenges. Nobody knows the precise formula for successfully developing and sustaining community networks. There are, however, several guidelines that should prove helpful. The first is that the community-network organization must itself be a *community*. This is a fundamental point of this book: A community is needed at

---

[3] Since local laws vary, developers are advised to check with municipal attorneys or law departments or with the state attorney general for precise guidelines.

the core of the effort. Developing a community network is not a business proposition, and a community-network organization is not a machine. When the project itself is a community, it is more likely that a shared vision will exist and that people will work together cooperatively. Since many people on the project are volunteers, a paycheck is not an issue. They will work together because they enjoy it.

Saying that the project is not a business project is not to say that the project shouldn't be run efficiently. In many ways, such as planning, budgeting, and managing, the financial affairs of a community-network organization need to be professional and "businesslike." In fact, in many ways, the organization is a business. Also, since time and money are likely to be scarce, it is important to recognize skills that exist within the project, including fundraising, communication, technical, or organizational skills. Communication and coordination within the project needs special attention, particularly as the project grows. Using electronic capabilities is, of course, a logical approach, but brochures, newsletters, and other printed material are also useful.

It is critical to involve the community in the development of the network. Community organizations are natural partners, and their work will help spread the word and increase the effectiveness and reach of the community network. The community network must be a part of the community. If it's detached from the community, it's not a *community* network. Local newspapers, radio, and television stations are community organizations, as well, and they should be kept up to date regarding the project and should also be considered as possible strategic partners.

Finally, it will be necessary to be diligent, patient, diplomatic, persevering, and, at times, cautious. People working on the project need to be able to listen to the viewpoints of others. They need to listen well to other people working on the project, to people in the community, and to people working on similar projects locally and around the world. As time goes on there will be pressure to water down your original principles. Establish high principles at the onset and stick with them.

Chapter 11

Directions and Implications

History is full of instances where people, against enormous odds, have come together to struggle for liberty and justice, and won—not often enough, of course, but enough to suggest how much more is possible. . . . The willingness to undertake such action cannot be based on certainties, but on those possibilities glimpsed in a reading of history different from the customary painful recounting of human cruelties. In such a reading, we can find not just war but resistance to war, not just injustice but rebellion against injustice, not just selfishness but self-sacrifice, not just silence in the face of tyranny but defiance, not just callousness but compassion.

Howard Zinn (1994)

We need a Charles Dickens today more than we need a computer specialist.

Herbert Schiller[1]

THE FUTURE OF DEMOCRATIC TECHNOLOGY

The world is emerging from a long cold war that has profoundly marked the thinking and behavior of its leaders and citizens over the last half-century. Indeed in the United States almost all decisions, including those related to science, technology, and society, were couched in cold-war rhetoric. The abrupt ending of the cold war has seemingly left Americans confused and without direction, similar to the mood in periods directly following this century's two World Wars. The ending of an era of profound global tension paradoxically has not brought relief but an uneasy unsureness of thought and of purpose (Chapman, 1994) that is preventing citizens and the institutions that ostensibly serve them from addressing critical social needs with the neces-

[1] Directions and Implications of Advanced Computing Symposium. Boston, MA. April 23, 1994.

sary compassion, confidence, and creativity. This chapter offers glimpses into some of these issues especially as they relate to the future of community and democratic technology.

CORPORATE AND GOVERNMENTAL IMPERATIVES

Every American will have a cellular phone, which will probably be a fax which will probably be a modem, which will probably in some way tie them into a world. Whether they want to or not, frankly every American will be competing in the world market with Germany and China and Japan.

Speaker of the House Newt Gingrich, in his opening speech to the Republican Congress, Dec. 11, 1994

Corporations are the chief form through which society's resources are marshalled and, consequently, are the most dominant force in American and global economic life. In everyday consciousness, the "market"—often ignoring evidence to the contrary and belying personal observation—is seen as an unchallenged fount of goodness and wisdom. Consequently, any criticism of corporations is considered to be misguided and heretical. The conquest has not been limited to a conquest of consciousness. In America, the two major political parties both accept the prevailing attitude that corporations—not citizens—are supreme. Not surprisingly, corporations now oversee the entire political process, including fundraising, legislation, campaigning, and regulating.

The commercial sector is currently conceptualizing and developing a wide variety of network applications that are now prominent in national media. This coverage routinely fails to mention, however, any public-interest, truly interactive, participatory, civic, or community-owned and operated networks or services. On top of that, large computer, telecommunications, and media companies are involved in formal and informal discussions with the government on the future of the National Information Infrastructure (NII), but there is virtually no effort to involve "ordinary" citizens in either education or consultation.

Sometimes this focus on the commercial appears to be largely accidental and based on ignorance or natural bias towards "experts" and "professionals." Newspaper and magazine reporters *may* be unaware of the profusion of community-network systems and increased interest within the nonprofit community when they run breathless accounts of the "Electronic Superhighway" (see, for example, *Time*, 1993) exalting a high-technology future for the medium that is controlled exclusively by giant corporations. Other incidents suggest less generous interpretations, however. One such incident involved a secret meeting between Republican congressional members and CEOs of the largest telecommunications companies in January of 1995. While the meeting may not have technically violated federal laws banning closed meetings, actions like this raise crucial questions as to the motivations of these major players and their interest in supporting the real needs of their constituents and customers.

The National Information Infrastructure (or NII) is the catch-all term that is used to describe the sum total of the technological systems that we rely on to communicate with and obtain information. When we examine what is meant by the term, we find (like the gentleman who discovered he had been speaking prose his whole life) that an NII is something that has existed since the invention of the telegraph. It simply names the complex of technological underpinnings that allow a person or organization in one location to share information or communicate with a person in another area. This information infrastructure has become increasingly faster, busier (accommodating more data), and more universally used in recent years. Furthermore this process shows no sign of stopping or slowing down. In fact, development is likely to accelerate as millions of additional users stream in and billions of dollars are invested in new programming, new services, and new technology.

The White House Agenda for Action

In 1993, the Clinton-Gore administration released "version 1.0" of "The National Information Infrastructure Agenda for Action," which rehashes many of the utopian claims for network technology such as "the best schools, teachers, and courses would be available to all students without regard to geography, distance, resources, or disability." While the report endorsed improving access to government information, extending the concept of "universal service" to electronic resources, and implementing an NII projects program for government, universities, libraries, school districts, health-care providers, and other nonprofits, it also unequivocally stated that "the private sector will lead the development of the NII." The government, in other words, is capitulating any leadership role to corporations, entities whose goals are unlikely to be driven by the public good.

In 1994, the U.S. National Telecommunications and Information Administration (NTIA) announced the first major federal support program for people and organizations using telecommunications in their communities. This program, the Telecommunications and Information Infrastructure Assistance Program (TIIAP), was established "for planning and demonstration projects to promote the goals of development and widespread availability of advanced telecommunications technologies; to enhance the delivery of social services and generally serve the public interest; to promote access to government information and increase civic participation; and to support the advancement of an advanced nationwide telecommunications and information infrastructure." Later that year, the NTIA made 91 awards totaling $170 million to recipients in nearly every state. Although nearly obliterated by the Republican-dominated Congress, the program was also repeated in 1995.

With several hundred proposals submitted each year, this program demonstrated as well as amplified a strong interest in using new communications technology in many areas (including government, educational, library, and public television and radio) by all manner of nonprofit organizations (including those working with ethnic groups, people with disabilities, people with low incomes, youth, civil rights, and child abuse prevention, among many others). The award winners also addressed an enormous range of technologies and represented a wide variety of organizations and organizational partnerships, including those involving government, nonprofit groups, and businesses.

The infusion of this first round of public funding has enabled over 90 projects to either get started or advance to the next phase of their work. The money—and the prospect of more to come—effectively turns up the heat on a number of projects, accelerating a process that may or may not have happened without the money. The petri dish of networking projects will be teeming—at least in the foreseeable future—with new and innovative networked organizational life forms.

While the program is positive in the main, there are several concerns. Although the focus was changed in 1995, the intention of the original request for proposals made it clear that the money was primarily for hardware and software expenditure. Unfortunately, this promoted an orientation around *technology;* less on information and data and even less on the connection to the community. When people place their focus on the technology, it is quite easy to lose sight on *why* one might want to use the systems. It also leads to a *Field of Dreams* naiveté—if we build it, they will come. The program also introduces another incipient concern, that of commercial—or private—profit versus the public good by promoting public-private collaboration. While current thinking suggests that "reinventing" government, business, and other institutions is desirable, it is not clear or generally acknowledged what principles should guide these increasingly common reinventions, nor is there a body of accumulated wisdom to guide the process. Reinventing often involves the development of relationships between people and organizations that historically had little or no contact; when contacts existed, they were likely to be formal, constrained, and bound by contract. Developing new relationships is commonly believed to be more efficient and more effective.

Presumably there will be less bureaucracy, more flexibility, and everybody will be more entrepreneurial. But new relationships will give rise to new responsibilities and new ethical issues. When the line gets blurred between profit-making by private corporations and acting in the public good by government or social agencies, the opportunities for inappropriate behavior both small and large increase dramatically.

Since an incredible amount of reinventing has taken place in a short period of time, new guidelines that could potentially help people recognize, avoid, and arrest undue influence of government by business interests, are not in place. Unfortunately, the TIIAP awards do little in the way of addressing these issues—except possibly to exacerbate them. For one thing, the TIIAP awards stipulated *matching* funds. In many cases the source of matching funds was a company such as a telephone company, and in some cases it was a foundation. In the case of the commercial support especially, the very real possibility of inappropriate influence on the course of the project must be anticipated and avoided. In the rush to reinvent and form new alliances, the government objective of serving the people could end up becoming secondary to serving corporate needs.

Building an Infrastructure for Democracy

The government is currently a key player in the area of network applications. It distributes vast amounts of information and services, and electronic distribution of information and services will become increasingly important in the future. Indeed, activity along these lines is increasing daily at all levels of government. Although this issue is currently receiving scant attention, government support and protection for an *infrastructure* for democracy is the most critical, basic, and pressing role of government in a democratic society.

As discussed in Chapter 4, democracy depends on several fundamental elements. Education is one of the most vital of these, as a democratic society will only be as effective as its citizens. This is one of the most important reasons why democratic countries need high-quality public education. Closely related to education is the need for access to information and communication. This second simple requirement has many important implications, as the information and communication infrastructure that people rely upon is undergoing fundamental changes, predicated in part by new computer and telecommunications technology. If corporations are allowed to become filters or for-profit purveyors of basic information then the democratic infrastructure will continue to degrade. If government abdicates its responsibilities in this area, corporate imperatives will become more influential and the "will of the people" will become increasingly meaningless.

To preserve, cultivate, and strengthen a democratic infrastructure requires the exercise of civic responsibility. A primary responsibility is to ensure that individuals and organizations—especially those with alternative or minority voices—can participate in democratic discourse. Meeting this responsibility also means discouraging monopolistic control of information (which, as we know from Chapter 7, is a very real danger), and it means ensuring common carrier status to distribution channels. (A cable television company shouldn't be able to deny access or charge higher rates to competing companies or to deny commercials that conflict with its legislative agenda, for example.)

In order to make the transition from the current "media monopoly" (Bagdikian, 1992) to a democratic infrastructure, the government needs to discourage excessive concentration of ownership. Unfortunately, the trend seems to be going in the opposite direction, as evidenced by the Communications Act of 1995, which eliminates many national and local ownership limits and bans on cross-ownership. Although these ideals are facing stiff opposition from an increasingly libertarian and religious-right-oriented Congress, the government needs to be proactive as well as reactive in fostering progressive, community-oriented, and participatory network projects. Although the government has initiated some innovative programs such as the TIIAP programs and virtual public conferences on topics such as "universal service and open access to the telecommunications network" (United States Department of Commerce, 1994), these represent a minimal beginning. Without strong citizen self-education and governmental consultation with citizens and citizen groups, large telecommunications corporations will determine the shape and direction of the next information and communication infrastructure.

SHAPING THE NEW TECHNOLOGY

With the cold war behind us, deep political and economic transformations are underway. We have an opportunity to remake technology into the servant of democracy and society. A better opportunity may not come again in our lifetime.

Richard Sclove (1994a)

Many people feel that technology is *autonomous*, independent, and beyond the control of society. As such, people read about it and talk about it and—like the weather—rarely do anything about it. Yet people could have more control over technology and its effects *if* they realized the power they could wield and assumed increased responsibility. Currently only a handful of people regularly attempt to influence the shape and direction of technology through its physical design, through policies surrounding its use, and through actively imagining and representing possible futures.

The idea of absolutely *controlling* technology—including community networks—is untenable. *Shaping* it iteratively and collaboratively, on the other hand, by reflecting, imagining, discussing, prescribing, designing, monitoring, and evaluating current and future technological systems is not only sensible but absolutely essential. Moreover, many of society's institutions need to extend their roles and responsibilities so they too can participate in this process.

The University as a Test-Bed for Community Research

The major universities that participated with big government and big business in the 40-year cold war are increasingly the targets of "political disenchantment" on the part of the public, in the words of Harvey Brooks (1993) from the Kennedy School of Government at Harvard. Universities—in the United States at least—have become large and impersonal—vast institutions with tenuous links to the community. With increasing public disenchantment and government support waning, the research opportunities offered by the coming of the interconnected community networks could help breathe life into the university, especially if these were conducted as partnerships with the community. Loka Institute executive director Richard Sclove, who has been studying ways to actively engage citizens democratically in the broader affairs of science and technology, has advocated the concept of "science shops" that have been launched in several places in Europe (Sclove, 1994a). These shops are essentially store-front research centers that work with community members to develop action plans in their community. Participation in a science shop movement could help rescue academia from the conflicting attractions of ivory tower isolation and marketplace prostitution to which it finds itself drawn (Barber, 1992). Some other new community-academia research opportunities are listed in Fig. 11.1.

In general, there are many ways in which universities and colleges can renew or build links with communities. A few recommendations—some of which are already in place—are listed below.

• Continually involve citizens, reassess responsibilities to citizens.

• Support strategic alliances and joint projects with community and advocacy groups and with other educational institutions.

• Take a proactive role in community-oriented and democratic policy creation, information, and dissemination.

New Research Opportunities

Business Schools: Developing flexible models of business that transcend the purely profit-taking model to include community and environmental responsibility.

Communications and Media Studies: Comparing community networks with "traditional" media. What functions do they supplant? Complement? Exploring how community networks alter traditional control over creation and distribution of news and other information.

Computer Science: Developing user interfaces and information-retrieval methods that promote effective access to a wide variety of information types (including text, graphics, voice, video, and datasets) from remote sites.

Economics: Analyzing new patterns of funding systems, analyzing costs and benefits of community-based information systems, systems for recompensing authors of electronic material. Developing equitable funding models for community enterprises.

Education: Developing collections of courseware, information, and services that can be made available electronically and effectively accessed and used by large numbers of community members especially those who have little access to existing educational programs. Developing and evaluating models for effective learning and collaboration over distances. Ensuring that appropriate in-person educational models are developed and not supplanted by electronic-only models.

Engineering: Developing a new ethic of engineering that acknowledges, understands, and embodies responsibility and purpose in technological design.

Environmental Studies: To study the effects and potential of telecommunications systems on the environment. To devise new ways in which environmental information can be presented electronically.

Geography: Studying the effects of information and communications technology on demographics, land use and population.

Information and Library Sciences: Exploiting existing wide area information servers for sharing of information over a wide area as well as working with prototypes and next-generation information sharing applications; Developing new approaches to information retrieval, distribution, and synthesis.

Medicine and Public Health: Exploring new community-based approaches to delivery of health care information and health care. Exploring the effects of participant-initiated conversation with health-care providers as well as other health-care system consumers. Effects of networking on community mental health.

Psychology: Exploring new phenomena arising from network use including addiction, lurking, posing. What needs are met through community network use? What psychological problems are initiated or exacerbated by network use?

Political Science: Studying and proposing new models of political participation. How do community networks change traditional political relationships and institutions such as the political party? What effects do community networks have on political discourse?

Public Affairs: Developing policy frameworks and analysis methodologies. Making policy recommendations and designing public projects.

Sociology: Conducting research on usage patterns and individual and collective on-line behavior. Studying effects of community networks on actual and virtual communities. How do virtual communities coalesce, behave, and manage themselves? How do community networks effect social roles, responsibilities, and overall social structures?

Urban Studies: Working with citizen groups to devise critical indicators and other tools for understanding and improving the urban condition. Analyze the effects of telecommunications policies on communities, particularly in regard to low income and minority populations.

Figure 11.1

- Develop new models of collaborative, community-oriented research.

- Encourage more community-oriented research and work as part of "ordinary" undergraduate and graduate education.

- Give college credit for "intern" positions in the community, which could last from several weeks to several years.

- Augment the institution's mission statement to include responsibility to community.

- Open up university resources to the community (including telecommunications, computers, and libraries).

- Establish a new class of student called "community student" through which a community member can—for a very small fee—take advantage of university resources, develop and undertake a course of study, and be awarded a certificate after completion.

- Lend support including technical, advisory, and scholarly resources to community-network development.

The Future of Libraries

Electronic information is taking on strange new shapes; it is a mix of content, communication, and services. It is not clear to libraries what part of the new kind of information is properly part of their responsibility.

Clifford Lynch (1993)

The need for libraries as free public institutions has been popularly acknowledged for about 150 years. Their broad role, facilitating access to useful information, is undergoing reexamination as information becomes increasingly digital (and nontextual) and increasingly electronically distributable. Moreover, the context of libraries, including their relationships with government, content providers, and the public is changing.

Libraries, traditionally, have been "buying collectives," using resources of a community to acquire a wide variety of information that is useful to the community libraries. They have necessarily been advocates for public access to information. In this role libraries facilitate access to information in various ways: They select, store, index, archive, arrange, and provide expert assistance in locating information. They also provide a free public (physical) space in the community for people to engage in a wide variety of community activities including studying, public meetings, story telling, and literacy training. Libraries, of necessity, filter information. Because they have limited money for purchasing and limited shelf space for storage, much information is not made available through libraries, and older information is often discarded to make way for the new. Libraries must routinely weigh quality, costs, and public needs when purchasing material.

Vickie Reich and Mark Weiser, researchers from Stanford and Xerox PARC (Palo Alto Research Center), have explored dimensions along which libraries can evolve as electronic communication becomes more widespread. One of their reports (1993) begins with the observation that a national information infrastructure already exists in the United States. This network consists of books, magazines, and newspapers and their distribution methods, broadcast radio and television, and the telephone system. Importantly—and this fact is often missed—the tens of thousands of school and public libraries constitute an important community nexus on the existing network. Reich and Weiser specifically focus on the "situational functions" of libraries that transcend the common conception of libraries as mere information repositories. The narrow view is sometimes used as a rationale for the planned extinction of libraries following necessarily the advent of new electronic information resources. Reich and Weiser, however, note that of the eight public library roles—community activities center, community information center, formal education support center, independent learning center, preschoolers' door to learning, popular materials library, reference library, and research center—only three are primarily informational. The other five roles are due, in part, to the *physical* and "situational" place in the community.

Karen Coyle, a specialist with the University of California Library System, points out several current deficiencies with the Internet as a comprehensive information resource. The information on the Internet is becoming increasingly varied, yet these are only pockets of knowledge with vast gaps. It has been characterized as being miles wide but an inch deep. As Coyle points out, the information is unindexed for the most part, and no overarching scheme is likely to be in widespread use in the near future. It may be the case that the amount of information on the Internet is growing faster than the capabilities of the automated searching tools that are currently used to navigate and locate information. If this is indeed the case, then information, while becoming more plentiful, is in some sense getting more difficult to obtain. Also accessing information over a network means that hardware, software, or network glitches could arbitrarily delay or prevent access to some material. Clifford Lynch, also of the California Library System, raises a number of additional concerns in his report to the Office of Technology Assessment (1993). One such concern is that network information providers will increasingly rely on *licensing* rather than *copyright* regulations in making information available, thus stressing the public library's ability to make information freely available through *lending*.

Although digital resources are currently qualitatively inferior in many ways to good libraries (that increasingly offer access to electronic resources in addition to other resources), it is clear that electronic resources will be assuming greater importance in the future. For this reason, librarians and the library institution will need to work hard to maintain the roles listed by Reich and Weiser in this new era. Some recommendations to the library community are as follows:

- Continually involve citizens in planning and decision-making and continually reassess responsibilities to citizens.
- Work with on-line content providers to help maintain inexpensive and equitable access to information.
- Maintain and explore new possibilities for physical presence in the community (branch libraries, pocket libraries, co-locations).
- Help educate community members and organizations on use of new information technologies and information policy issues.
- Experiment with electronic spaces and devices.
- Engage in strategic alliances and joint projects with other groups.
- Take a proactive role in policy creation, information, and dissemination.
- Work with the community-network community to help ensure that library meets its objectives.

Work, Technology, and Democracy

The workplace of today is no longer a location.

Elaine Bernard[2]

Work, a central and timeless aspect of human existence, is currently undergoing substantial redefinition. This change has largely resulted from increased global capitalism that is fueled in part by new communications technology. This redefinition is taking place within a very brief time historically, and represents yet another threat to the community that is occurring without public planning or discussion. Indeed, discounting the cheering section in the business media, there is very little substantive discussion of these changes in a widespread or public way. Although this is not the place for a

---

[2] Directions and Implications of Advanced Compatibility Symposium. Boston, MA. April 24, 1994.

lengthy discussion of the possible effects of the computer on the nature of work, a brief elicitation is necessary.

Starting at the most general level, the threats of unemployment due to computer automation that have been anticipated since the 1950s are finally beginning to become a reality. This has been noted by social critics such as Aronowitz and DiFazio (1994), and Rifkin (1994) as well as in business periodicals such as *Business Week* and *Fortune*. This should come as no surprise: Computer systems are invariably introduced as a way to reduce costs, and the general strategy is to have computers do the work that was previously done by people. Of course, computers also create new challenging and well-paid jobs, but these amount to a small fraction of the jobs they eliminate. Computers also change the nature of work in many other ways, some quite subtle. Some of the ways, discussed in much greater depth in *Computerization and Controversy: Value Conflict and Social Choices* edited by UC Irvine professor Rob Kling (1995), include deskilling (making jobs simpler and thus available for people with less skills and education, for lower pay), job reorganization (according to "rational" guidelines, often amounting to a new breed of Taylorism), computer monitoring (where computers are used to spy on workers, collecting statistics such as keystrokes per minute, length of conversation per telephone request for help, or bathroom visits per day), or telecomputing (where workers are "allowed" to work at home, saving office expenses for the company while setting up the possibility of what Barbara Garson [1989] calls an "Electronic Sweatshop").

The future of work is of interest to all of society. Unfortunately, this topic is incredibly diffuse, immensely challenging, and global in nature (and, as such, unlikely to be solved at a community level). Nevertheless, "work" could become a focus for community and democratic development and community networks can play a role in that discussion (also see Chapter 6). Some possible actions for community networks include the following:

- Develop ongoing community-wide discussions about work, employment issues, and workers' rights.

- Monitor local businesses for work and employment practices, both exemplary and objectionable, especially those receiving public funds or tax breaks (and corporate welfare!).

- Explore new community/labor opportunities and develop programs.

- Build community-investment programs.

- Develop meaningful work programs based on community needs.

Civic Renaissance

The decline of community life and the apparent inability of traditional institutions to ameliorate the situation has not gone unnoticed in the United
States and around the world. Amitai Etzioni (1993), Robert Bellah (Bellah et
al., 1985), and many others have launched several programs to reinvigorate
civic and community participation, including the communitarian political
movement (Etzioni, 1993). Largely in response to local problems, citizens
around the world have launched literally thousands of initiatives in the last
few years to address these civic problems. *Streets of Hope* (Medoff and Sklar,
1994) is an excellent explication of the ambitious Dudley Street Neighborhood Initiative in South Boston. *Against All Odds* (DeSilva, 1989) describes
a host of community-based projects in poor regions around the world. These
efforts are often unconnected to efforts in other cities or national institutions
but are local responses to local needs and circumstances. These efforts generally are not professionally initiated or controlled, nor do they employ "tried
and true" problem-solving approaches (that don't seem to work like they
used to). Instead their approach is often tentative and experimental and, as
such, is unlikely to be based on "scientific findings" or recommendations of
special panels. Often the focus is on "common-sense" values like the need for
discussion, the need to participate, or the need to volunteer.

The Millennium Communications Group, in a report prepared for the
Rockefeller Foundation, entitled "Communications as Engagement" (1995)
has highlighted community projects of this type and has identified 14 different descriptors for these "revitalization initiatives at the local level." The report arranges these descriptors—urban partnerships, visioning and strategic
planning, collaborative community problem-solving, dispute/conflict resolution, leadership development, religious institution initiatives, national/
community/voluntary service, deliberative discussion, citizen participation,
issue-driven initiatives, civic journalism, civic networking, media produc-
tion/distribution, neighborhood and community organizations—into an
"architecture" that describes the descriptor, lists some examples, and lists national or state organizations that are acting to help weave a stronger web of
consciousness and action. The report goes on to list 10 strategies for "supporting and accelerating revitalization" that resonate with themes in this
book, such as "create demand for civic journalism," "leverage the infrastructure of national nonprofits," "create new media," and help to create a "larger
picture" (see Appendix B for information on the Millennium Web site).

Community (or "civic") networking is clearly part of this larger Civic
Renaissance movement, but with a twist or two. One difference is that the
community-networking movement has communication *technology* as a cen-

tral focus. According to the Millennium report, the other types have very little experience with modern telecommunication technology. For this reason, the community-networking movement has much to offer the other groups who, according to the report, have a strong interest in learning how to use the technology. On the other hand, the other groups have more experience dealing with the types of problems that community-networking developers want to help address. Another difference is that with a focus on technology, community-network developers are in a good position to agitate for more democratic use of communications technology, and to educate and alert other groups to its importance.

The American Civic Forum is a national effort to encourage, organize and channel the development of citizenship towards addressing community problems. Their "Civic Declaration" (ACF, 1994), coordinated by Harry Boyte, Benjamin Barber, and Will Marshall, explains that their aim is "to re-assert the authority of civil society against both the encroachments of government, however well intended, and the disruptions of unfettered markets, however efficient." The declaration provides numerous examples of how community groups built issue-based agendas, started schools, trained people, and convened forums that work towards solutions of public problems with inclusive, public programs. The collaborative and nonpartisan Civic Practices Network (CPN) (Sirianni et al., 1995), is an out-growth of the American Civic Forum, coordinated by Carmen Sirianni of Brandeis University and Lew Friedland of the University of Wisconsin (with support of the Alliance for National Renewal), brings together a diverse array of organizations within the new citizenship movement. The CPN uses the World Wide Web as a new medium for "civic story telling" as well as for presenting their vision of new citizenship and helping to build a network-style coalitional framework.

An important aspect of the CPN is its broad coverage of nine critical topics—community; environment; families, gender, children; health; journalism; community networking; religion; work and empowerment; and youth and education (see Fig. 11.2). Each topic includes "Civic Perspectives" (background articles that provide good coverage of historic, philosophic and other important viewpoints on the topics) and "Stories and Case Studies" (containing abstracts and extensive reports on specific initiatives). The community topic, for example, has civic perspectives "Regenerating Community" by John McKnight (1987) and "Kernels of Democracy" by Ken Thomson (1995), while the case studies include "East Brooklyn Congregations Build Nehemiah Homes," "Dudley Street Neighborhood Initiative Revitalizes Community" (mentioned above), "Portland Neighborhood Associations Bring Local Voice to City Government," and "South Bronx Rebuilds from the Bottom Up." The stories in the community section (and in the others) are not

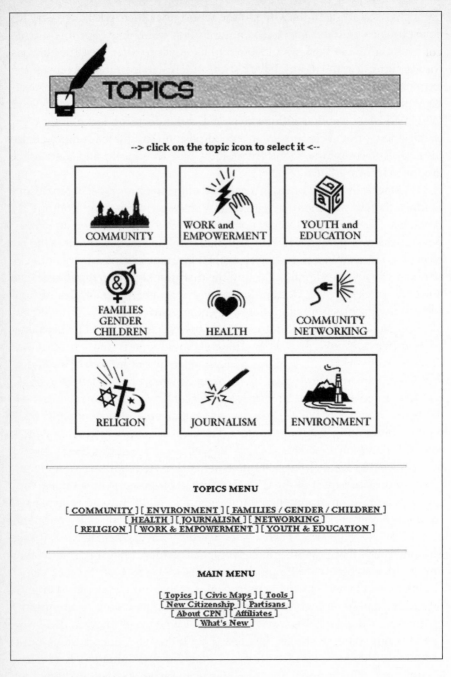

Figure 11.2   Civic Practices Network

sales pitches filled with glowing reports, but rich accounts that contain disappointments, mistakes, missed opportunities, as well as successful outcomes. Sirianni, Friedland, the topic editors, and other participants envision the Web pages as a focus for collaborative efforts as well as a tool for the next generation of community workers. In a similar vein, the Millenium group has launched the "Grass-roots Tool-Box" (1995) project; it incorporates the World Wide Web, faxes, and television into an integrated civic revitalization program. Both of these projects illustrate that the electronic medium provides the potential for widespread access, a methodology for distributed collaboration, and a test-bed for additional tools, such as those that search the case studies using various means in order to locate relevant ones.

The majority of people are unfamiliar with the telecommunications issues that their tax dollars helped engender. Moreover, critical decisions are being framed, debated, and made without their advice or consent. Since these decisions will shape the form of future modes of communication and, hence, of the nature of society, citizens have an immense stake in these proceedings. For this reason, government institutions at all levels should convene local and regional meetings before critical and potentially irreversible actions are taken. These meetings can take several forms including large conferences, neighborhood workshops, or on-going advisory boards that include community members. Unfortunately, the government may have to be pressured into participating and embarrassed into inviting noncorporate representatives into important advisory roles.

There would be several purposes of these proposed meetings. One purpose would be to educate people on the basic concepts of telecommunications technology and issues. In Seattle, Eric Rehm and Aki Namioka (1994) of the local chapter of Computer Professionals for Social Responsibility (CPSR) developed a presentation on the "National Information Infrastructure" that included a description of the technology in clear language. To raise local awareness and activism on the issues, Rehm, along with Parker Lindner and David Griffith of Electra, a Seattle "coalition for electronic democracy," developed a "20 Policy Questions for Public Debate" fact sheet (Fig. 11.3) that has been used to raise important concerns with a variety of community groups in Seattle. Besides playing an educational role, the government also needs to facilitate an exchange of ideas with the citizenry. Several criteria should guide this effort. The exchange must be open, iterative (building on multiple sessions that allow time for reflection and research), inclusive (involving a wide mix of people), and genuine (in other words, not just be a symbolic or obligatory ritual). The public needs to play a strong role in *public* policy development; without this it will continue to be created, in secret, by "experts" with little or no civic or community understanding or compassion.

---

20 Policy Questions for Public Debate

1. Who should own the information superhighway?

2. Who should build the information infrastructure?

3. Who should manage our information-delivery system?

4. How will we assure free speech?

5. How can we overcome obstacles and barriers that make some groups information rich and others information poor?

6. How can we reestablish diversity of content?

7. Should the information highway be regulated?

8. What is universal access?

9. How much does information cost?

10. How will we connect?

11. How will we learn to use this resource?

12. How about privacy?

13. When does private data become public information?

14. What information should be available on-line?

15. How could electronic networks improve access to government information?

16. How will individuals choose information services?

17. Competition or concentration?

18. What can citizens do?

19. What should government do?

20. What next?

Figure 11.3

Although citizen participation has enjoyed sporadic but generally luke-warm success in the United States, models of successful participation approaches do exist in other countries. In Denmark, for example, there is a process that has been used in a variety of issues including genetic engineering of animals (Sclove, 1994b). Using this model, citizens (housewives, office and factory workers, garbage collectors, teachers and so on) work together with subject-matter experts over a course of six months in several structured meetings in addition to doing some research and reflection at home. Models like these suggest that there is room for citizen participation in *all* manners of decisions, even those related to esoteric technical and scientific knowledge. If the government doesn't initiate these programs itself, it may need to be cajoled into it. These decisions are too important to be made without input from the citizenry.

Encouraging public education and debate at all levels is especially important now. This need may be addressed most easily by working with local or national organizations (see Chapter 8 and Appendix A) and by making concerns known via individual correspondence and testimony. Many organizations are currently developing vision statements and policy recommendations on these issues.

The development of independent and free on-line services and information effectively complements political efforts by providing a highly visible proof of concept. Developing such community-networking services not only benefits the community directly, but it also provides valuable public education and strengthens the civic renaissance movement. Also, the availability of high-quality free services will encourage commercial information and service providers to improve the quality of their services in order to be competitive.

Public Participation's Rocky Road

While public participation is a constant theme in this book, its practice is not without pitfalls. Long-time community activist, Harry Boyte warns the would-be do-gooder, that "public life is no love-in."[3] Citizens new on the community activism scene should expect some resistance and hostility from unexpected quarters (including from presumed allies), and some will come with surprising virulence. Moreover, those conflicts can assume a wide variety of forms. Although there is no one way to respond and my experience is limited, the topic is worth discussing briefly here.

There are some basic rules to dealing with conflict. The first rule is that it should be expected. Conflict—even attack—is inevitable. If you are trying to

[3] American Civic Forum meeting. Washington, D.C. December 9, 1994.

accomplish anything in the public sphere, you will probably accumulate critics and/or enemies. Another rule is that criticism should not be dismissed out of hand. It is important to discuss it with others in the organization and try to understand its motivation and its importance.

Although the criticism may be motivated by turf warring, resentment at not being consulted, everyday conspiracy weaving (some people do this as a full-time hobby), or just plain misanthropism, it should be analyzed and considered. Sometimes it will be necessary to change the way the organization goes about its business or to rethink how to present the community-network vision or to redefine how volunteers or staff work within the community. At other times you may hear criticism that is so diffuse and third-hand that it is impossible to deal with either conceptually or practically.

Another rule is to keep calm and to keep things in perspective. As most of us are unaccustomed to being attacked—personally or otherwise—it may be difficult to stay philosophical. It's important to realize that although the attacks seem personal and addressed directly at you, the attacker is going after a visible proponent of the system, which may be you today and someone else tomorrow. It is also important for the organization's members to stick together, to agree on shared goals and, in general, how to attain these. Problems may also arise from within the organization, especially in relation to responsibilities and duties. There are no easy answers to these issues, but open communication and a team-oriented approach are very important for preventing problems and for dealing with them when they arise.

Criticism and attacks can come in many flavors. I once received e-mail from somebody who was very enthusiastic about volunteering for the Seattle Community Network. In a postscript, he asked whether I thought it was "necessary" to have forums on gay issues. I wrote back, thanked him for his interest, and sent him the information he requested. I also told him that several people had expressed interest in a gay issues area, so one was established. That was the last we heard from that person. Other criticism came from a person in the BBS community, who accused SCN of trying to put them out of business because of the "one-stop shopping" metaphor we were using. In actuality, community networks and BBS systems need to interoperate synergistically. The BBS could be the home of special-purpose information and discussion (like a BBS in Seattle for opportunities for disabled people), some or all of which could be shared with the community network. For its part, the community network could offer a connection to the Internet so, for example, BBS users could send and receive e-mail from other people on the net.

Another criticism of SCN involved the openness of the process. Ironically, there appears to be some link between greater democratization and criticism. SCN meetings, for example, are open to all and everybody has a chance to speak. Anybody can also join a committee. If SCN didn't explicitly and publicly strive for a democratically run project, it might not even attract the relatively small amount of criticism that it does receive.

Another possible criticism is based on the company you keep. In other words, if you're associated with city government in any way, you may be deemed a tool of city government. If you're working with a public radio station, you may be accused of kowtowing to them. In general, working with any organization or institution does involve *some* risk. Community-network developers need to be cognizant of this risk, to anticipate possible problems (especially those of improper influence), to work to avoid them, and to deal with them if and when they arise. Community-network developers also must be aware that they are open to this criticism, criticism that couldn't legitimately be leveled without cooperative alliances.

Another criticism that one might encounter is that the organization is not truly community-based or that the community-network developers don't (or shouldn't try to) "speak for the community." This criticism invariably carries some validity. It doesn't mean, however, that the development of the system should be halted. The community-network organization *can not* speak *for* the community. (In communities over a certain size, there probably can never be a single spokesperson.) Care should be taken not to commit this sin of hubris. The community-network organization can, however, speak *in defense of* the community and offer opinions and suggestions for community participation and access, like any other organization within the community. To the criticism of not being truly community-based, the response can only be: "We recognize that we're only part of a very diverse community and we're working to involve others as well." Working closely with an ever expanding number of community organizations *is* the only real answer to this concern.

INFORMATION ISSUES FOR THE FUTURE

> At present our society persists in designing a great many technical artifacts in ways that make people feel passive, superfluous, stupid, and incapable of initiating action. Such systems bear the cultural embryos of tomorrow's citizenry. For as we invent new technical systems, we also invent the kinds of people who will use them and be affected by them. The structures and textures of future social and political life can be seen in the blueprints of technologies now on the drawing board.
>
> Langdon Winner (1991)

Information is the raw material of knowledge, experience, and communication. Over the millennia, human beings have developed a multitude of forms of information along with numerous conventions and policies regarding its use. New electronic forms and distribution patterns of information are now forcing community-network developers (and many others) to consider the implications of these changes. Many of these changes are critical to community networks and proponents will need to play a part in upcoming debates if these issues are to be resolved in a satisfactory manner.

Access, Barriers, and Use

Community-network developers speculate that community networks in the twenty-first century will be as common as public libraries are now. Currently they are available only in few locations and accessible to relatively few users. (Even after adding Internet users and commercial on-line users, the total on-line population in the United States is probably under 10 percent.) If the systems are to be used widely, they must be easy to use, easy to access, and free of structural barriers to their use. Among other things, the systems must be reliable and responsive; the user interface must be intuitive and unintimidating; and special-purpose interfaces must be developed for those with special needs.

While public terminals in numerous, diverse locations are critical, home availability is also important. People must be able to easily and inexpensively participate through various means. Telephone, cable television, wireless, and other approaches all represent possible delivery channels and a certain percentage of the bandwidth of each should be reserved for educational and community use.

A "barrier" is anything that acts to prevent or discourage access to community networks (Fig. 11.4). In the case of electronic information and services, a barrier may be lack of access to the hardware, telephone lines, or the Internet. A barrier may be the inability to read or write in the language being used, or to see the screen. A barrier may exist because the potential user is incarcerated or, in the opposite extreme, homeless. The person may actually be afraid of computers or just be unable to use them. The person may not have a need to use them (like the proverbial fish and the bicycle) because the available information and communication options are irrelevant to them. The barriers rarely occur singly; in the most common case, several barriers will stand in the way. Often these occur as a string of barriers and any one of them—like a link on a chain—can cause a break in access. A person may overcome several barriers only to be defeated by a telephone busy signal.

Barriers to Community Use

- Lack of convenient access to hardware, telephone lines
- Lack of convenient access to Internet (e.g., person is not a university student)
- Can't get software to work properly
- Cost barrier to telephone
- Cost barrier to Internet
- Cost barrier to services
- Useful services do not exist
- Services perceived to not exist
- Friends and people with similar interests and background don't use it
- No need perceived
- Can't type
- Can't write
- Can't read
- Vision-impaired or other physical challenge
- Non-English writer/reader
- Computer illiterate
- Doesn't want "extra burden"
- No "extra time" for use—too busy
- Just wants to relax after work
- Computer averse—don't like them, distrustful of technology
- Satisfied with life as-it-is

Figure 11.4

Bringing Down Barriers

There are strategies for surmounting each barrier described above. After having gathered some preliminary data on the barrier, one is ready to develop action plans along two fronts. The first is that of developing services and making available information that is based on individuals' specific needs and that helps address the new community core values. Basically this means that community-network developers must work with individuals and groups to co-develop projects and programs (such as those discussed in Appendix F). Note that developing those projects should not be narrowly and artificially constrained to be "a network project," but should encompass a spectrum of activities including training, providing terminals, hosting community meetings, and the like. In addition, it means helping to reduce the cost and ease of accessing the system. Moreover, any serious proposal to establish universal access to community networks should include a study that identifies links between barriers and various population groups within the community. The second type of action plan is that of changing the context within which the community network exists. This may encompass a wide range of educational and political activity including lobbying, legislation, and placing community networking and other public information policy issues on the agenda.

It is clear that some people do not want to use community networks. That is certainly their prerogative, and community-network developers should not presume that people need to or want to use these systems. Many people read books instead of watching television, for example. At the same time, however, developers should not presume that groups that aren't currently using the systems don't want to use them. Experiences with homeless people using the free public terminals at the Seattle Public Library suggest otherwise, as does the manifesto of the Los Angeles gangs, the Crips and the Bloods (discussed in Chapter 1). Clearly, however, different groups of people, as well as individuals within groups, have different habits, motives, wishes, needs, and attitudes that must be accommodated.

All of us start life helpless and, as Deborah Kaplan from the World Disabilities Council notes, many of us will ultimately become disabled in one way or another as we go through life. In other words, designing for this type of user is not a matter of supporting *them* but a method of supporting *us*. As discussed in Chapter 9, the design of the user interface can make a big difference for those users as well as for non-English speaking users. Getting the cost as low as possible is crucial for both rural users and for economically disadvantaged users. Free public terminals will help those without facilities at home and those without homes at all.

Community-network organizers in different cities will go about bringing down barriers in different ways. For example, the Seattle Community Network (SCN) has been working very closely with the Seattle Public Library, and with public television and radio stations. SCN is also working with neighborhood groups, youth groups, and environmental groups. Community-network groups in other cities are working with universities, K–12 schools, public access cable groups, or community centers. The trajectory of the efforts will depend on the needs, interests, and opportunities that exist in specific communities.

The idea of reducing barriers can be distilled to three major points. One, information and services must be interesting and useful. Two, the system must be usable by all people, including those who speak languages other than English, are blind, or are otherwise impeded from using the system effectively. Three, access must be ensured through low costs, public and private access points, and the ability to "get through" (with a minimum of telephone "busy signals," for example). Needless to say, this all presupposes a vital and equitable civic society in which high quality public education and other civic amenities are universally available.

Universal Access and Equitable Participation

Citizens of the new community must be vigilant to defend and advocate universal access and equitable participation (Miller, 1996). We cannot rely on commercial interests to make the necessary guarantees. Their overriding concern of profitability, responsibility to shareholders—not citizens—and a closed decision-making process argue strenuously against it. Furthermore, as Sandra Schickele has clearly demonstrated (1993), the requirements of the free market mechanism are not met in the case of the Internet. She concludes that public subsidy is essential if network resources are to be made widely available.

The need for accountability, public participation, and visibility clearly point to public ownership of some type. Increasing the role of government, however, is viewed skeptically by many. Government can be corrupt, beholden to special interests, inefficient, unresponsive, or antagonistic to citizen participation and oversight. Lack of funds, technological expertise, and experience further hamper government's effectiveness. Nevertheless, community networks in democratic societies must ultimately have a close relationship to a government, which in turn must be controlled by citizens. Community-network organizers will need to be creative and persistent in designing new collaborative relationships with government in this era of heightened skepticism of government. Osborne and Gaebler's prescriptions for "reinventing government" (1993) particularly those involving "community-owned government," "mission-driven government," and "decentralized government" are especially relevant in considering the role of government in community-network development and support.

Privacy Concerns

> *Protecting privacy in the electronic age is like trying changing the oil on a moving car.*
>
> Electronic "Signature" of Chris Hibbert

As Chris Hibbert's signature reminds us, the computer—especially the networked computer—has qualitatively changed the nature of privacy. More and more organizations both large and small are collecting information on individuals. With this vast collection of data, it is inevitable that much of the information contains errors or is out of date. A 1991 article in Consumer Reports described a study that analyzed 1,500 TRW, Trans Union, and Equifax reports that revealed that 43 percent of the files contained errors (Garfinkel, 1995). Since this information frequently resides on networked computers, it is no longer isolated in islands, but is part of a growing web of information that can be linked into larger "virtual databases" on individuals. These databases contain information of all types, including all medical, financial, and legal records. This, incidentally, is a critical reason why social security numbers should not be used as a "key" for use in databases (other than databases that are used to administer social security or other related government services). A database key is a unique number that is used to extract the other information that's associated with that key. If individuals' social security numbers are used as the key in numerous databases, it can be used as a master key; different databases can be matched together to form a composite virtual database that transcends the stated purpose for which the data was collected.

Information gathered from various points in a person's life can also be linked temporally into a revealing data portrait. This makes a vast corporate-government, collaborative, "cradle-to-grave" information-gathering program increasingly plausible. This linkage is not an idle fantasy. As CPSR/Seattle activists discovered, such a partnership could be ushered in through unlikely portals. The current educational reform approach depends on being able to establish and monitor performance goals for students. While this may be a laudable goal, assessing student progress also depends on collecting a wide range of student data (including psychological data) that would then be shared with educational institutions at various levels and with educational researchers (NEGP, 1993). Although this information would be very sensitive, there is little evidence that educational reformers at the federal, state, or local levels are giving privacy concerns enough thought.

Collecting vast amounts of data for any reason raises the specter of state surveillance and control. While control over individuals and communities is probably not an *explicit* aim, we must strenuously question the need for such intrusive, systematic, and sustained data collection. Educational reform literature explicitly states that collected information might be shared with prospective employers. A Department of Labor study (SCANS, 1992) suggests that a student might provide employers with an electronic resume that includes confidential ratings of that student's work-related behavior (including such values as self-esteem, responsibility, and integrity/honesty), all keyed to the student's social security number! Thus an employer might learn, for example, that a student had low "integrity/honesty" scores in second grade and decide not to hire him or her some 20 or 30 years later. The Fair Code of Information Practices (see Chapter 8) continues to provide solid guidelines even in such a situation, and community-network developers should abide by the code's guidelines in their own work while simultaneously fighting to protect privacy in other areas as well.

New Types of Information

Clifford Lynch, the Director of Library Automation at the University of California at Oakland, poses an important and generally unasked question related to free information (1993): "Whenever information is offered for free (or, indeed, even for what seems to be an unrealistically low cost), it is reasonable to ask: why?" Where did it come from? Who is offering it? Who paid for it and why?

As Lynch points out, much of this free or low-cost information is distributed by government agencies and its distribution is required by law. Other free information is provided by political parties, corporations, education organizations, lobbyists, activists, and so on, and these will generally represent the viewpoint of the organizations that developed the information. The other main source of free or very inexpensive information is *sponsored* in some way. A daily newspaper is largely supported by its advertisers; broadcast commercial television is supported exclusively through commercials.

Of course, neither type of information is free: Government publications are paid for by taxes, while information that is sponsored through advertising or other means result in significantly higher product costs. (Advertising, as Lynch points out, is very inefficient. Most people buy cars infrequently and need product information about cars at that time only, yet television viewers see several car ads every day!) There are also other problems with sponsorship including the direct and indirect effects it has on content. These issues are discussed in the information and communication chapter (Chapter 7) as well as in the social architecture chapter (Chapter 8).

Most of the e-mail I receive every day falls between the extremes of valuable mail and "junk" mail. As Lynch points out, this is part of the "new, ambiguous class of 'free' information appearing on the Internet." This information is vulnerable to a wide variety of limitations including inaccuracy, outdatedness, prejudices, errors in judgment, sloppy thinking, and can contain misquotes or out-of-context quotes. Moreover, there is often no commitment to the timeliness, reliability, or the maintenance of the data. Nor is there a regular and guaranteed feedback loop between information provider and consumer. Indeed, an expectation (of some people) that information found on the Internet is true has resulted in more than one false rumor endlessly bouncing around in cyberspace.

The information residing on community networks will often belong to the "new, ambiguous class" that Lynch describes. The amount of this type of information, at least in the short term, is not expected to shrink. In all likelihood it will continue to grow explosively. In addition to thinking about the best ways to cope with the limitations discussed above, we should remind ourselves of the *advantages* that this new information offers. The main one is that people will have new voices and new power, and people will be able to begin new conversations. We may begin to hear alternative voices—impassioned—untainted by party lines, orthodoxy, and corporate control.

Since a large amount of information on a community network does belong to this "ambiguous, new class," some responsibility for both maximizing benefits and minimizing limitations falls to the community-network organization. Part of this process involves network media literacy. People will need to get used to this new type of information. It may be important to be suspicious or skeptical of the information without being dismissive. And it will be important to understand the interfaces and searching techniques that will help people find what they need and new techniques of filtering to ignore what they don't need.

TECHNOLOGY DIRECTIONS

Why is it more fun to read about the new technologies than to use them? Because imagination is more agile than reality.

Donald Norman

New technologies including display devices, wireless, multimedia and the like, coupled with new applications and modes of interacting such as MUDs (Curtis, 1992), conversational e-mail (Borenstein, 1992; Shepherd et al., 1990), and software agents (Riecken, 1994) together have important implications for usability, service providing, and participatory democracy. Technical innovations should be introduced into community networks when they will increase the ability to meet user needs. At the same time, adopting new technology will necessarily introduce some changes and even resistance. This may translate into disruptions in the user community as prior conventions and patterns of interactions undergo modification. By being cognizant of these implications, network developers can be alert to the need for training, user preparation, usability testing, and participatory design.

New technology can also introduce or exacerbate gaps in quality of service by delivering a better or faster service to *some* of the users. The incorporation of new technology, however, shouldn't dilute universal access. Low-cost text-based terminals must not, for example, be made obsolete with the introduction of new graphics technology. The solution probably will require multiple user interfaces, resulting in an "interface gap" that does not sacrifice the basic level of universal access.

Media Convergence and Divergence

The intriguing possibility of "media convergence" (Pool, 1983) accompanies an unprecedented two-way use by tens of millions of people on a "net" that ultimately could connect all people. It also could intermingle many forms of media including television, radio, print, and telephones that are beginning to share characteristics while becoming accessible through a variety of end-devices. A future "net" that connects programmable devices over very fast, densely interconnected "wires" linking vast numbers of people becomes in essence a meta-medium, a plastic medium that is capable of replicating any of the traditional media (books, newspapers, broadcast radio, ham radio, and so on). Besides being capable of mimicking other media, the future net can give rise to any number of new forms, currently undreamt of, using a bewildering variety of new software clients, browsers, and agents.

Although this may sound a little like science fiction, consumers will likely be faced with many of these media "divergence" issues in the near future. For one thing, there will be profusion of services available through a variety of devices in the home. In all likelihood, the ubiquitous television set will still occupy a central—should I say hallowed—location in the home. But this will probably change from a passive purveyor of images to a coordinator of services. There will obviously be some modicum of two-way interaction available if plans for video-on-demand, home shopping, cyber-porn, or instant polling are carried out. If tomorrow's do-everything tube becomes the central collecting point for connecting to the net, then community networks need to be there.

A Global Network

Two of the nation's wealthiest entrepreneurs in communications and computers plan to disclose today the formation of a new company to develop a global satellite communications network far more ambitious than anything contemplated before.

The network would transport information ranging from ordinary telephone calls to high-resolution computerized medical images and two-way video conferences to and from virtually any spot on the planet.

As envisioned the system would be able to deliver almost as many services as the new fiber-optic networks being built by many telephone companies, but it would be able to reach underdeveloped and rural areas that are typically cut off from advanced communications.

The New York Times, March 21, 1994

Even while U.S. billionaires are busily announcing ambitious plans for interconnecting virtually every person on the planet, global communications are spreading rapidly. Twenty-two countries connected to the Internet for the first time in 1995; the Internet growth rate is faster outside the United States than it is within (Bournellis, 1995), and satellite broadcasting beams continuously into remote villages around the world. While the hoopla and media focus suggest that this process is inevitable, it would seem prudent—if a bit iconoclastic—to review some constraints, limitations, and cautions.

For one thing, the globalization of electronic networks might *allow* a person to step up to the device that permits the use of the system but *deny* him or her the use of the system based on an inability to pay. Since usage costs include infrastructure costs, there would be little economic justification for installing the "last mile" for *two-way* participation, especially in poor and/or sparsely populated areas.

Community-Based Global Networking

A global network is quickly becoming a reality. The Institute for Global Communications, presented with the Norbert Wiener award by CPSR for its work in developing network technology to empower previously disenfranchised individuals and groups working for progressive change, offers PeaceNet, EcoNet, ConflictNet, LaborNet, and access to several international partner organizations to subscribers in over 70 countries (see Appendix A). With truly global networks impending, it's not too early to begin considering the prospects of a global community of communities. National Public Tele-computing Network (NPTN) affiliates, for example, are active in Canada, Finland, New Zealand, and Germany and community networks are thriving in Italy. The community-network movement should welcome international partners, establish "sister networks," hold joint congresses, co-develop electronic services, and generously share information.

The very issues that we've been exploring from the perspective of a relatively technologically advanced country are also global issues. The gap between rich and poor is severe in the United States as well as in other countries, with virtually no middle class in many less-developed countries. There is also a huge chasm between the developed countries (that are home to 25 percent of the world's population but own 95 percent of the world's computers) and the developing countries (Frederick, 1993). The increasing globalization of corporations has apparently superceded the reach of the nation while concentrating immense power into a few commercial giants. NAFTA and other treaties have carved the world into gigantic trading blocs. The concentration of power and the accompanying commodification of information exacerbate the marginalization of peasants, workers, and low-income people throughout the world. With little or no access to communication technologies, these people will be passive consumers of images or information produced elsewhere. They will not be *included* in any images unless a factory explodes, a bus careens off a cliff, a famine develops, or a civil war erupts in their vicinity. They will not be included in a dialogue because there is no perceived economic benefit.

These trends have not gone entirely unnoticed by media producers and distributors, communications researchers, and activists around the world. In early 1994, representatives of the Fourth International Symposium on New Technologies of Audiovisual Communications met and produced a declaration addressing the increasing corporate and military domination of communications resources and the resulting disempowerment both materially and culturally of people throughout the world (Fig. 11.5).

The internationalization of corporate influence has also helped spur an internationalization of other concerns like the rights of indigenous people, workers, women, and peasants, as well as environmental concerns (although these efforts are often tightly limited). NAFTA and similar treaties have forced labor issues into the international arena. On the other hand, many NGOs such as CARE, Oxfam, or Amnesty International have been global in scope for years. Cheaper telecommunication prices and increas-

---

Portion of New Delhi Declaration

We believe in the pressing need for global democracy, not a global supermarket, and affirm our unity in support of the following:

1. All peoples and individuals shall have the right to communicate freely, to utilize the tools of communication and to inform themselves and others.

2. Airwaves and satellite paths are a global peoples' resource to be administered equitably, with a significant portion devoted to serving the public interest and for community use.

3. We oppose the militarisation of space and the exploitation of space for corporate interests. Any exploitation of airwaves transmission channels and earth orbits should be subject to a public levy to be used to support local community expression, facilitate non-commercial information exchange, and to contribute to equitable distribution of information technologies.

4. Communication and information technologies must be used to facilitate participatory democracy and the development of civic society, not to limit democratic rights.

5. Information systems exhibit great potential for real popular participation and should be organized according to the principles of decentralization in order to nurture and sustain cultural diversity and humanitarian values.

Figure 11.5

ing availability of networks like IGC are beginning to provide some small amount of relief from the consistent rising of the new global, corporate tide.

Community networks are being developed throughout the world. These include projects in Africa, Europe, Asia, the Americas, and other places. Other efforts—such as the MISANET project in Africa—have democratization of communications technology at their core. As corporate interests expand and information commodification continues, community-based efforts must also expand. Preserving and strengthening local, community efforts while expanding communications globally will present a major challenge to the community-network movement.

THE GREAT EXPERIMENT

It is one of the most beautiful compensations in life that no man can sincerely help another without helping himself.

Ralph Waldo Emerson

The United States as a nation has enjoyed almost every imaginable advantage: millions of fertile acres to farm; spectacular mineral, forest, and water resources; an unremitting inventive spirit; physical separation from potential enemies; a steady influx of motivated and intelligent immigrants; and a Constitution and a Bill of Rights that encourage participation and pluralism. Yet despite these advantages, the United States has very great economic disparity (with accompanying deleterious effects in education and health), high murder rates, high drug-use rates (especially of alcohol and cigarettes), and an impoverished public dialogue.

Denial of problems and trivialization of problems have a solid tradition in America. Even though 200,000 people lost jobs in just six months in 1930, President Hoover, the Congress, and the American press refused to acknowledge that a problem even existed. When the problem finally began to receive some attention, the press and many others (Hoover among them) were quick to label the displaced workers as *lazy* people who didn't want to work—as if a fifth of a million people simultaneously decided that they didn't want or need an income. American racism is another case in point. Although there is an unbroken history beginning with the genocidal treatment of native Americans and continuing through slavery days, lynchings, segregation, and selective use of the death penalty, these basic facts are often prevented from appearing in history text books.

An interesting—and life-critical—socio-historical experiment is taking place in present day America and around the world. Can democracy come to terms with its problems and address them? Or will nativism, simplistic thinking, pandering media, rampant consumerism, censorship, blind faith, and greed simply overwhelm these efforts?

Technological Inheritance

The human race displays a mix of both altruism and treachery. At times people will kill each other vigorously and happily. At other times, they will treat each other with respect and love. To a large degree, a person's actions and thoughts are framed by the thoughts, conventions, institutions, and other prevailing circumstances of the cultural milieu in which the person lives. If the person grows up in dangerous circumstances, the world, too, will look dangerous. If a person grows up without violence, the world will look safer and more secure. If a person has all the opportunities of life, he or she is more likely to succeed. When there are few opportunities, failure is more likely. Some people, stronger or weaker than the rest of us, will ignore society's invisible supports or restraints, but these are exceptions.

Although we all exist *within* a cultural milieu, we are also part of it. In some way, each of us makes a contribution—generally small—to the overall cultural milieu, the sea we all must swim in. Some people make large contributions, for good or for bad, while the rest of us generally have minor influences, over family, friends, or fellow workers. We can not afford to deny our interdependence on each other. We can no longer pretend that individuals have no responsibility for the community. At the same time, we cannot pretend that the community has no responsibility for the individual. The cultural milieu shapes us while we're shaping it. This ebb and flow is largely invisible, but it can't be ignored.

Each generation builds on the investment left by previous generations. This in effect is our *inheritance*. This inheritance includes the physical—freeways, parks, forests, art work—and the intellectual as well—laws, religions, science, customs, and ideas. Gar Alperowitz, the president of the National Center for Economic Alternatives, tells a fascinating story (1994) of the "technological inheritance" that helped prepare the ground for the ascendency of billionaire software developer Bill Gates of Microsoft. The story begins with the U.S. federal government which, having funded 18 of the 25 most significant advances in computer technology between 1950 and 1962, was one of the most steady and generous benefactors of the U.S. computer industry. This huge investment by the American government (funded obliviously by millions of American taxpayers) helped launch the Digital Equipment Corporation that developed the PDP line of computers. Using this as the springboard, Gates's colleague, Paul Allen, created a simulated PDP-10 chip, upon which Gates wrote a version of the BASIC programming language (which itself was originally funded by the U.S. National Science Foundation). Gates, though obviously an innovator and capable business person, obviously has greatly benefited from the technological inheritance bestowed upon him by the U.S. government and the U.S. people.

Beyond the technological inheritance, Microsoft and Bill Gates benefit from other aspects of inheritance not generally recognized. Of the squads of programmers employed by Microsoft, many attended state universities, or before that, public elementary and high schools. They drive to school on public roads, drink fresh water, and eat safe food ensured by government action and legislation that was enacted before they were born. Beyond these types of inheritance, the United States has offered to Gates and to others a "conceptual inheritance" that makes it even *possible* for him to create vast machineries of wealth. This inheritance is not a *natural* right. On the contrary, it is a right that has been granted by conscious decisions, through the Constitution, the Bill of Rights, and through countless pieces of legislation and court rulings.

The ubiquity of our social inheritance (which is often unacknowledged or conveniently forgotten) helps preserve the myth of independence. Our society is in fact a cultural and social ecosystem whose machinations are the product of human design. It is this ecosystem that profoundly affects each and every human on each and every day. The independence myth is used in two basic ways. In addition to denying the contribution (technical or otherwise) that other people have made, one can deny the effects that one has or *could* have on others. When one allows the myth to become the scripture for one's life, shirking responsibility is a natural by-product. Hence, this approach is useful for justifying maximal self-interest: hard to justify in objective terms, harder still in humanistic terms, but convenient as a rationale for self-indulgence and guilt-free overconsumption—and one conveniently supported by conventional wisdom and dominant ideology.

Why Get Involved?

The question of why people should help other people is of course a timeless one. It has been a central religious concern for centuries. For example, the Christian Bible asks "If a rich person sees his brother in need, yet closes his heart against his brother, how can he claim that he loves God?" (I John 3:17). Answering this question becomes more pressing in an era of increasing economic disparity coupled with the apparent ability and desire of the affluent to create fantasy land enclaves for themselves, isolated from any direct contact with the less fortunate and, in many cases, at the expense of the less fortunate.

The answer to the question of why people should get involved contains elements of both selfishness and altruism. The "selfish" side is best expressed by Seneca's warning, "When a neighbor's house is burning, your house is also at peril," which points out the obvious fact that absolute isolation or quarantine is not possible. Two short examples can be used to show this. The first has to do with health. Neglecting the health concerns of poor people can and will cause reverberations throughout all classes. Untreated diseases, for example, among the poor can spread to the rich. The general overuse and abuse of antibiotics in some areas of the world helps breed new resistant diseases that ignore national and economic class boundaries. Another example is from the area of crime in terms of both prevention and detention. Americans seem very eager to hire private security guards and build more prisons. Yet these all must be paid for, whether directly out of pocket or through taxes and increased insurance. Another somewhat less "selfish" reason is that a more equitable society with a less tenuous societal web would be safer, more convivial, and more enjoyable to all concerned. Also as Robert Putnam has observed, a society with strong social ties is in many ways more efficient economically as well as being better equipped for dealing with social issues.

Finally, there is an altruistic side to the challenge of "being part of the solution." The altruistic reason directly contradicts the model of humans as coldly calculating economic reasoners who would only expend resources if they *knew* that they'd receive back a reward that was at least equal in value to their expenditure. No such guarantee of a return on social investment exists. (Those people who are only working on the economic return-on-investment model are classic "free riders," taking advantage of a convivial system without contributing.) The "reward" of community-building will hopefully show up in obvious ways, like improved cultural or sustainability indicators. On the other hand, the benefits may not show up for many years. As Theodore Roosevelt said, "What we do for ourselves dies with us. What we do for our community lives long after we've gone" (Lavelle et al., 1995).

Conditions for Success

In this book we have focused on the development of community networks as one way to help anchor and ground "new communities." Of course, community networks are intended to be just one aspect of a new society, a new society that is more democratic, flexible, inclusive, equitable, and sustainable than our current one.

Like many other books, this ends with an exhortation for action. If ordinary people do not become involved, the vision described in this book has no chance to become realized, technology won't truly serve people, and the ordinary person will remain a passive and unimportant consumer of commodities, viewpoints, and identity. This book, however, does not end with specific injunctions. There is no ultimate destination, only some guidelines for charting the course. People must collectively determine that course, a course guided by principles, discourse, and humanity, not dogma, greed or hatred.

Self education—thinking, reading, and writing is important. We need to acknowledge problems in society and understand the legitimacy of people's positions. An unemployed steel worker or logger has legitimate and serious concerns. So do inner city dwellers whose plights have been largely disregarded. It is important to develop knowledge about the community and to increase the *capacity* of the community for learning and for self-knowledge. The knowledge about the community needs to contain information on community capacities and community indicators, especially how they relate to the six core values.

Dialogue is also critical. It is important to discuss these ideas with other people and attend meetings in communities. Contact the organizations listed in the appendixes. It is also very important to get involved with local community networks and with other information and communication infrastructure projects. Government and business projects are not sacrosanct! They're your business! Find out all you can about them—why are they doing what they're doing? Who will benefit? Who will lose? What services will become available—to whom and at what price? What services *aren't* becoming available? It is critical to get this information, analyze it, and distribute the findings to the media, local government, and non-profit organizations. Post them on public networks! It is important to work with other institutions and organizations in your community as well—churches, labor unions, community councils, and social service groups—to develop influential strategies employing both carrots and sticks.

One of the most important activities will be the development of projects and products, including neighborhood campaigns, workshops, articles, network services, software development, training sessions, and alternative media. Whenever possible, these projects should be collaborative (including people and organizations of varying philosophical approach and constituencies), additive (building successes on successes) and focused on democratic community-building (by addressing the six core values).

To participate in this endeavor, a basic time commitment must be made. The more time people choose to expend on a regular and sustained basis, the more likely that success will come. Since this challenge is so great, one shouldn't expect changes to occur at once. Nevertheless, there will be times when successes of small and great magnitudes will occur, and people should not be surprised when this happens. It will then become important to use that success as the foundation for another. It is not easy to allocate new portions of time for community projects. It generally means identifying some activity that you can forego or accomplish in less time. It is critical to identify this time and begin setting it aside and using that time for projects. The question of what to do with that time is important, of course, but there are no set answers to that question. People will gravitate to areas that they're interested in, but at the same time it is important to listen to the ideas and project descriptions of other people as well.

Ultimately, the new community will be supported with new community institutions, some brand new and some fashioned from older ones. These must be integrated into the community, not be independent or adversarial. Government agencies, political parties, corporations, media companies, social service agencies, and nonprofit organizations may all undergo change. These organizations and institutions need to write new community contracts that help institutionalize shared goals and aspirations and a willingness to work together for the common good.

It is probably time for the people in the community-network movement to begin to think about the advantages, if any, of stronger communication and collaboration between them. Some important strides have been made in that direction: There are several organizations devoted to community networking including NPTN, with which many community networks and Free-Nets are affiliated. There are lively conferences and electronic discussion groups. Beyond these important activities, the question needs to be asked if there are organizational arrangements, political campaigns, educational opportunities, or other means by which the interests, strengths, and enthusiasm can be brought together into a greater unity. In Canada, the Telecommunities Canada organization has been instituted to help "ensure that all Canadians are able to participate in community-based communications and electronic information services by promoting and supporting local community-network initiatives" and to "represent and promote Canadian community movement at the national and international level." And in December of 1995, Steve Snow of the Charlotte Web community-network system proposed the International Association of Community (or Civic) Networks (IACN), which would serve as a sort of trade association for community networks. At the same time any new organizations or working arrangements must preserve the local character and integrity of the individual efforts.

Perhaps human life on earth is an *experiment*. Perhaps human life on earth consists of millions and millions of experiments, some tiny, some gigantic, all being conducted simultaneously. But each experiment has actors or players and outside factors that cause changes. Guessing, theorizing, and hypothesizing about what these changes will be is the essence of science, and the scientist who devises the most elegant and most comprehensive theory that is validated experimentally is held in high esteem.

People (who are simultaneously experimenters and experimentees) make interesting objects of study, for they don't follow the same rules that inanimate objects follow. For one thing, their hypotheses can sometimes be self-fulfilling. In other words—the consequence is often *interpreted* according to the dictates of their hypotheses. What this means in general is that human beings construct their own perspectives, world views, that, in turn, help influence the future hypotheses. Currently we develop these perspectives from many sources—parents, neighbors, images on billboards or on television, words in a book or lessons from school, advice or admonishment from world leaders, the president, a rabbi, mullah, priest, or minister, or from labor, civil rights, or business leaders. Since we humans can shape the world through our perspectives and hypotheses, let us consciously develop ones that can lead to richer lives for all.

The world is in need of new hypotheses: new hypotheses that support the new community, new hypotheses that support the core values of society. And with these hypotheses as our new beginnings we must study, talk, reason, and act. It is possible to make the great experiment that we call life on earth a success, but it will take work.

A community revitalization "revolution"—of which community networks are just one part—can't be carried out by individuals nor can it be orchestrated by an institution or a company. It will be necessary for thousands, millions, of people and organizations with a strong and urgent sense of social responsibility to link together and push firmly in a forward direction, an *equitable* and *sustainable* direction. Community must be indeed be a web, a fabric of strong and interlocking elements, like foliage on a hilltop that entwines into a dense covering preventing the wind and the water from ripping apart the hilltop.

If there is no struggle, there is no progress.

Frederick Douglass (Bobo et al., 1991)

Appendix A

Organizations

This appendix contains a wide variety of organizations that would be sympathetic to some (if not all) of the goals outlined in this book. Some of these organizations are large and some are very small. Most of them would like to hear from you and all of them would like your support. This support could take several forms including acquiring their literature, volunteering for them, or joining their organization as a member. Many organizations also have electronic resources available such as Web pages, distribution lists, etc. Some of these are listed in Appendix B. Also be sure to check with various Web searching engines (like Lycos or WebCrawler) for sites not listed below. The classification scheme I've used seemed like a logical choice at the time!

Categories

Advocacy and Support
Arts and Cultural Organizations
Civic and Democratic Revitalization
Community and Civic Networking
Community Centers
Community Empowerment and
  Revitalization
Community Health
Community, Public, and Alternative
  Media
Cyber-Rights, Access, and Democracy
Economic Alternatives
Education
Environmental Justice

Foundations and Corporate
  Programs
Government Accountability and
  Advocacy
Government Agencies
International
Labor
Library Organizations
Referral Organizations
Sustainability
Telecommunications Forums
  (International, National, and
  Regional)
Other and Unclassified

ADVOCACY AND SUPPORT

ADA Vantage (ADA stands for the
  Americans with Disabilities Act)
Kathryn Shane McCarty
202-296-2328
fax 202-659-5234
1001 Connecticut Ave., NW, Suite 435
Washington, DC 20036

The Advocacy Institute
David L. Cohen
202-659-8475
fax 202-659-8484
1707 L St., NW, Suite 400
Washington, DC 20036

Alameda County War Memorial
Joe McDonald
WWW: http://www.ci.berkeley.ca.us/
  vvm/ (Berkeley Vietnam Veterans
  Memorial)
P.O. Box 9064
Berkeley, CA 94707

Center for Media Education
Kathryn Montgomery
202-628-2620
WWW: http://www.scn.org/ip/cti/
  home.html
fax 202-628-2554
jchester@cme.org
1511 K St., NW, #518
Washington, DC 20005

Community Technology Institute
Pat Barry
206-441-7872
cvm@avoice.com
P.O. Box 61385
Seattle, WA 98121

CompuMentor
Daniel Ben-Horin
415-512-7784
fax 415-512-9629
cmentor@compumentor.org
89 Stillman St.
San Francisco, CA 94107

Digital Queers
digiqueers@aol.com
584 Castro, #150
San Francisco, CA
http://www.dq.org/dq

Drum, Inc. (Internet connectivity to the
  African and African American
  community)
Carter E. Bing
919-382-3302
faq@drum.ncat.edu
WWW: http://drum.ncat.edu
P.O. Box 486
Durham, NC 27702-0486

HandsNet
Sue Dormanen
408-257-4500
fax 408-257-4560
HNOOO3@hansnet.org
20195 Stevens Creek Rd., Suite 120
Cupertino, CA 95014

International Institute for Interracial
  Interaction
Richard Little
612-339-0820
fax 612-339-3288
600 21st Ave. South
P.O. Box 212, Augsberg College
Minneapolis, MN 55454

Mexican American Legal Defense and
  Educational Fund
Robert Almanzan
213-629-2512
fax 213-629-8016
634 South Spring St., 11th Floor
Los Angeles, CA 90014

National Asian Pacific American Legal
  Consortium
Karen Narasaki
202-296-2300
fax 202-296-2318
1629 K St., NW, Suite 1010
Washington, DC 20006

National Association for the
Advancement of Colored People
(NAACP)
Wade Henderson
202-638-2269
fax 202-638-5936
Washington Bureau
1025 Vermont Ave., NW, 11th Floor
Washington, DC 20005

National Coalition on Black Voter
Participation
James Ferguson
202-659-4929
fax 202-659-5025
1629 K St., NW, Suite 801
Washington, DC 20006

The National Conference
Chris Bugbee
212-206-0006
fax 212-255-6177
71 Fifth Ave.
New York, NY 10003

National Congress of American
Indians
JoAnn Chase
202-546-9404
fax 202-546-3741
900 Pennsylvania Ave., SE
Washington, DC 20003

National Council of La Raza
Eric Rodriguez
202-785-1670
fax 202-785-0851
1111 19th St., NW, Suite 1000
Washington, DC 20036

National Urban League
Robert McAlpine
212-310-9000
fax 212-593-8250
500 East 62nd St.
New York, NY 10021

New York Youth Network
Ellen Meier
212-678-3829
fax 212-678-4048
ebm15@columbia.edu
Teachers College, Columbia
University, Box 8
New York, NY 10027

TASH (Disability advocacy/rights
organization)
410-828-8274
fax 410-828-6706
29 W. Susquehanna Ave., Suite 210
Baltimore, MD 21204

ARTS AND CULTURAL ORGANIZATIONS

American Documentary/P.O.V.
Ellen Schneider
212-989-8121
fax 212-989-8230
povpbs@pop.igc.apc.org
220 W. 19th St., 11th Floor
New York, NY 10011

Arts Wire
Gary Larson
202-682-5036
fax 202-682-5611
glarson@tmn.com
2514 K St., NW, #11
Washington, DC 20037

Cultural Environmental Movement
cem@asc.upenn.edu
P.O. Box 31847
Philadelphia, PA 19104
WWW:http://ccwf.cc.utexas.edu/
  ~cmbg/cem.html

Electra
David Keyes
206-722-4369
keyesd@u.washington.edu
P.O. Box 20369
Seattle, WA 98102

Electronic Cafe International™
Sherrie Rabinowitz and Kit Galloway
310-828-8732
ecafe@netcom.com
WWW:http://www.metawire.com/
  ecafe/
1649 18th St.
Santa Monica, CA 90404

National Alliance for Media Arts
  and Culture
Julian Low
510-451-2717
fax 510-451-2715
lowj@aol.com
655 13th St., Suite 201
Oakland, CA 94612

National Campaign for Freedom of
  Expression
David Mendoza
202-393-2787
fax 202-347-7376
dmendoza@tmn.com
918 F St., NW, Suite 609
Washington, DC 20004

National Organization of Artists'
  Organizations
Helen Brunner
202-347-6350
fax 202-347-7376
nao@tmn.com
National Union Building
918 F St., NW, Suite 611
Washington, DC 20004-1406

New York Foundation for the Arts
David Green
212-366-6900
fax 212-366-1778
155 Avenue of the Americas
New York, NY 10013

Northwest CyberArtists (NWCA)
Larry Berg
206-764-9371
NWsysLaw@netcom.com
WWW:http://nwlink.com/
  cyberartists/

CIVIC AND DEMOCRATIC REVITALIZATION

The Alliance for National Renewal
Sharon Helfant
800-223-6004
fax 303-571-4404
ncl@csn.net
WWW: http://www.csn.net/anr
1445 Market St., Suite 300
Denver, CO 80202-1728

America Speaks
Carolyn Lukensmeyer
202-783-4963
fax 202-347-2161
915 15th St., NW, Suite 600
Washington, DC 20005-2375

American Civic Forum
Carmen Sirianni
617-736-2652
fax 617-492-1949
sirianni@binah.cc.brandeis.edu
Pearlman Hall
Brandeis University
Waltham, MA 02254

American Civil Liberties Union
Ann Beeson
212-944-9800 Ext 788
fax 212-869-9065
beeson@aclu.org
132 West 43rd St.
New York, NY 10036

Campus Outreach Opportunity
  League (COOL)
Jennifer Bastress
202-637-7004
fax 202-637-7021
1511 K St., NW, Suite 307
Washington, DC 20005

Center for Community Change
Bruce Hanson
202-342-0519
fax 202-342-1132
1000 Wisconsin Ave., NW
Washington, DC 20007

Center for Democracy and Citizenship
Harry Boyte
612-625-0142
fax 612-625-3513
Hubert Humphrey Institute,
  University of Minnesota
301 19th Ave. South
Minneapolis, MN 55455

Center for Living Democracy
Annette Larson
802-254-1234
fax 802-254-1227
RR#1 Black Fox Rd.
Brattleboro, VT 05301

Center for Policy Alternatives
Linda Tarr-Whelan
202-387-6030
fax 202-986-2539
1875 Connecticut Ave., NW, Suite 710
Washington, DC 20009

Center for the Study of Community
Cheryl Charles
505-982-2752
fax 505-982-9201
4018 Old Santa Fe Trail
Santa Fe, NM 87505

Civic Network Television
Ralph Widner
800-746-6286
fax 202-887-5901
P.O. Box 63550
Washington, DC 20035-3550

Civic Practices Network
Carmen Sirianni
617-736-2652
fax 617-492-1949
sirianni@binah.cc.brandeis.edu
Pearlman Hall
Brandeis University
Waltham, MA 02254

The Common Enterprise
Juan Sepulveda
210-734-8809
fax 210-735-8761
311 Mistletoe, Apt. 1
San Antonio, TX 78212

The Communitarian Network
Amitai Etzioni
202-994-7997
fax 202-994-1606
comnet@unix1.circ.gwu.edu
2130 H St., NW, Suite 714-J
Washington, DC 20052

Community Resources Inc.
Mark Bourdon
701-293-6462
fax 701-237-0982
P.O. Box 447
Fargo, ND 58107

Corporation for National and
  Community Service
Eli Segal
202-606-5000
fax 202-565-2794
1201 Vermont Ave., NW
Washington, DC 20525

Independent Sector
Government Relations
David Arons
202-416-0554
fax 202-457-0609
1828 L St., NW, 12th Floor
Washington, DC 20036

Institute for Local Self-Government
Clark Goecker
916-658-8208
fax 916-658-8240
1400 K St., Suite 400
Sacramento, CA 95814

Institute for the Study of Civic Values
Edward Schwartz/Jo Anne Schneider
215-238-1434
fax 215-238-0530
edcivic@libertynet.org
1218 Chestnut St., Suite 702
Philadelphia, PA 19107

League of Women Voters of the US
Gracia Hillman
202-429-0854
fax 202-429-0854
1730 M St., NW, Suite 1000
Washington, DC 20036

Loka Institute
Richard Sclove
413-253-2828
fax 413-253-4942
loka@amherst.edu
WWW:http://amhux4.amherst.edu/
  ~loka/menu.html
P.O. Box 355
Amherst, MA 01004

National Civic League
Mike McGrath
800-223-6004
fax 303-571-4404
ncl@csn.net
WWW: http://www.csn.net/ncl
1445 Market St., Suite 300
Denver, CO 80202-1728

National Voting Rights Institute
617-441-8200
fax 617-441-6363
voting-rights@igc.apc.org
1130 Massachusetts Ave., Third Floor
Cambridge, MA 02138

Pew Partnership for Civic Change
Suzanne Morse
804-971-2073
fax 804-971-7042
145-C Ednam Dr.
Charlottesville, VA 22903

The 21st Century Project
Gary Chapman
512-471-8326
fax 512-471-1835
gary.chapman@mail.utexas.edu
LBJ School of Public Affairs
Drawer Y, University Station
University of Texas
Austin, TX 78713

The Urban Institute
James Gibson
202-833-7200
fax 202-429-0687
2100 M St., NW
Washington, DC 20237

Walt Whitman Center for the Culture
  and Politics of Democracy
Benjamin Barber
908-932-6861
fax 908-932-1922
Department of Political Science
409 Hickman Hall
Douglas Campus
Rutgers University
New Brunswick, NJ 08903

COMMUNITY AND CIVIC NETWORKING

American Civic Forum
Carmen Sirianni
617-736-2652
fax 617-492-1949
sirianni@binah.cc.brandeis.edu
Pearlman Hall
Brandeis University
Waltham, MA 02254

Center for Civic Networking
Richard Civille
202-362-3831
fax 202-986-2539
ccn-info@civicnet.org
gopher.civic.net:2400/
WWW: http://www.civic.net:2401/
  ccn.html
P.O. Box 53152
Washington, DC 20009

Community Memory Project
Lee Felsenstein
415-842-6144
felsenst@interval.com
Efrem Lipkin
510-845-3170
efrem@netcom.com

Computer Professionals for Social
  Responsibility
Audrie Krause
415-322-3778
fax 415-322-4748
cpsr@cpsr.org
WWW:http://www.cpsr.org/dox/
  home.html
P.O. Box 717
Palo Alto, CA 94301

Institute for Metropolitan Affairs
Richard Kreig
312-341-4335
rkeig@acfsysv.roosevelt.edu
Roosevelt University
430 S. Michigan Ave.
Chicago, IL 60605

Morino Institute
Mario Morino
703-620-8971
fax 703-620-4102
info@morino.org
WWW:http://www.morino.org/
1801 Robert Fulton Dr., Suite 550
Reston, VA 22091

National Public Telecomputing
  Network
nptn@nptn.org
WWW: http://www.nptn.org/
P.O. Box 1987
Cleveland, OH 44106

Nonprofit Organizations' New Media
  Center
Bruce Rosenthal
202-408-0008
fax 202-408-0111
itvguy@aol.com
1019 19th St., NW, 10th Floor
Washington, DC 20036

Public Netbase
Institut für Neue Kulturtechnologien—
  Institute for New Culture
  Technologies
Ministry for Science Research & Arts
Stella Rollig
+ 431 5226794
fax + 431 5226794
1070 Wien, Messeplatz 1
Messepalast/Museumsquartier
Vienna, Austria

The Technology Resource Consortium
  Chair
Marshall Mayer
406-442-3696
fax 406-442-3687
desktop@igc.apc.org
c/o Desktop Assistance, Inc.
324 Fuller Ave., Suite C2
Helena, MT 59601-5029

Telecommunities Canada
Lisa K. Donnelly
613-241-9554
fax 613-241-2477
am412@freenet.carleton.ca
National Capital FreeNet/Libertel de
  la Capitale nationale
gopher://gopher.ncf.carleton.ca:70/11
  /ncf/conference2
WWW: http://www.freenet.mb.ca/
  tc/index.html
375 Wilbrod St.
Ottawa, ON
Canada K1N 6M6

The 21st Century Project
Gary Chapman
512-471-8326
fax 512-471-1835
gary.chapman@mail.utexas.edu
LBJ School of Public Affairs
Drawer Y, University Station
University of Texas
Austin, TX 78713

XS4ALL ("Networking for the
  masses")
account@xsfall.nl
St. XS4ALL, P.O. Box 1848
1000 BV Amsterdam, The Netherlands

COMMUNITY CENTERS

Boys & Girls Clubs of America
James Cox
404-815-5700
fax 404-815-5727
1230 Peachtree St., NW
Atlanta, GA 30309-3494

Davis Community Network
Kari Peterson
916-750-0101
dcnadmin@dcn.davis.ca.us
P.O. Box 1563
Davis, CA 96517

Electronic Cafe International™
Sherrie Rabinowitz and Kit Galloway
310-828-8732
ecafe@netcom.com
WWW:http://www.metawire.com/
  ecafe/
1649 18th St.
Santa Monica, CA 90404

Old North End Community/Tech
  Center
Lauren-Glen Davitian
cctv@emba.uvm.edu
c/o CCTV
294 Winooski Ave.
Burlington, VT 05401

Playing to Win
Peter Miller
ptwadmin@igc.apc.org
Education Development Center
55 Chapel St.
Newton, MA 02158

Plugged In
Bart Decrem
415-322-1134
info@pluggedin.org
WWW:http://www.pluggedin.org/
1923 University Ave.
East Palo Alto, CA 94303

Technology Education Council of
  Somerville
Kate Snow
617-625-6600
fax 617-625-2519
ptwsccc@igc.org
167 Holland St.
Somerville, MA 02144

Virtually Wired Educational
  Foundation, Inc.
Coralee Whitcomb
617-542-5555
info@vw.org.
WWW: http://www.vw.org
55 Temple Pl.
Boston, MA 02111

YMCA
101 N. Wacker Dr.
Chicago, IL

COMMUNITY EMPOWERMENT AND REVITALIZATION

ACORN
501-376-7151
523 W. 15th St.
Little Rock, AR 72202

Center for Community Change
Julia Burgess
202-342-0519
fax 202-342-1132
1000 Wisconsin Ave., NW
Washington, DC 20007

Center for Neighborhood Technology
  (publishes "The Neighborhood
  Works")
312-278-4800
fax 312-278-3840
WWW:http://www.cnt.org/
2125 W. North Ave.
Chicago, IL 60647

Center for Policy Alternatives
Matthew Nelson
202-387-6030
fax 202-986-2539
1875 Connecticut Ave., NW, #710
Washington, DC 20009

Citizen Action
312-645-6010
225 W. Ohio St., #250
Chicago, IL 60622

Civic Practices Network
Carmen Sirianni
617-736-2652
fax 617-492-1949
sirianni@binah.cc.brandeis.edu
Pearlman Hall
Brandeis University
Waltham, MA 02254

Coalition of Community Foundations
  for Youth
Cindy Sesler Ballard
816-842-4246
fax 816-842-8079
1055 Broadway, Suite 130
Kansas City, MO 64105

Community Development Society
Lisa Betancourt
414-276-7106
75547.2561@compuserve.com
http://www.infoanalytic.com/cds/
1123 N. Water St.
Milwaukee, WI 53202

Community Information Exchange
Kathy Desmond
202-628-2981
fax 202-783-1485
1029 Vermont Ave., NW, Suite 710
Washington, DC 20005

Computers and Social Change
c/o Kallen Tsikalis
ktsikala@tristam.edc.org

Do Something
Mylan Denerstein
212-523-1175
fax 212-582-1307
423 West 55th St., 9th Floor
New York, NY 10019

Education Center for Community
  Organizing
Terry Mizrahi
212-452-7112
Hunter College, School of Social Work
129 East 79th St.
New York, NY 10021

The Enterprise Foundation
Ed Quinn
410-964-1230
fax 410-964-1918
American City Building
10227 Wincopin Circle, Suite 500
Columbia, MD 21044

Federation for Industrial Retention
  and Renewal (FIRR)
Jim Benn
312-252-7676
fax 312-278-5918
3411 W. Diversey, Suite 10
Chicago, IL 60647

Industrial Areas Foundation
516-354-1076
36 New Hyde Park Rd.
Franklin Sq.
New York, NY 11010

Institute for Metropolitan Affairs
Richard Kreig
312-341-4335
rkeig@acfsysv.roosevelt.edu
Roosevelt University
430 S. Michigan Ave.
Chicago, IL 60605

Loka Institute
Richard Sclove
413-253-2828
fax 413-253-4942
loka@amherst.edu
WWW:http://amhux4.amherst.edu/
  ~loka/menu.html
P.O. Box 355
Amherst, MA 01004

Millennium Communications Group,
  Inc.
WWW:http://www.cdinet.com/
  Millennium/
Ann Beaudry/Marcia Sharp
202-872-8800
fax 202-872-8845
mllninc@clark.net
1150 18th St., NW, 8th Floor
Washington, DC 20036

National Association of
  Neighborhoods
Althea Jackson
202-332-7766
fax 202-332-2314
1651 Fuller St., NW
Washington, DC 20009

National Community Building
  Network
Ed Ferran
510-893-2404
fax 510-893-6657
672 13th St.
Oakland, CA 94612

National Urban Coalition
Ramona Edelin
202-986-1460
fax 202-986-1468
1875 Connecticut Ave., NW, Suite 400
Washington, DC 20009

National Urban League, Inc.
Robert McAlpine
202-898-1604
fax: 202-682-0782
WWW:http://www.nul.org/index.html
1111 14th St., NW, 6th Floor
Washington, DC 20005

Neighborhood Innovations Network
John McKnight
708-491-3518
fax 708-491-9916
Center for Urban Affairs and Policy
  Research
Northwestern University
2040 Sheridan Rd.
Evanston, IL 60208

Program for Community Problem
  Solving
William Potapchuk
202-783-2961
fax 202-347-2161
915 15th St., NW, Suite 601
Washington, DC 20005

Public Allies
Vanessa Kirsch
202-638-3300
fax 202-638-3477
815 15th St., Suite 610
Washington, DC 20005

Red de Informacion Rural (REIR)
Scott Robinson
525-682-4687
fax 525-687-6030
ssr@xanum.uam.mx
WWW:http://tonatiuh.uam.mx:70/
  RIE
Louisiana 133-2
Colonia Napoles
Mexico, D.F. 03810
Mexico

Southern Empowerment Project
615-984-6500
323 Ellis Ave.
Maryville, TN 37801

Technology Education Council of
  Somerville
Kate Snow
617-625-6600
fax 617-625-2519
ptwsccc@igc.org
167 Holland St.
Somerville, MA 02144

Who Cares? A Journal of Service and
  Action
Heather McLeod
202-628-1691
fax 202-628-2063
1511 K St., NW, Suite 1042
Washington, DC 20005

COMMUNITY HEALTH

American Health Decisions
714-647-4920
fax 714-647-3610
505 Main St., Suite 400
Orange, CA 92668

American Public Health Association
Claude Hall
202-789-5618
fax 202-789-5661
1015 15th St., NW, Suite 300
Washington, DC 20005

American Self-Help Clearinghouse
Ed Madara
201-625-7101
fax 201-625-8848
St. Claves-Riverside Medical Center
Denville, NJ 07834

The Healthcare Forum
Kathryn Johnson
415-356-4300
fax 415-354-9300
425 Market St., 16th Floor
San Francisco, CA 94105

New York Youth Network
Ellen Meier
212-678-3829
fax 212-678-4048
ebm15@columbia.edu
Teachers College, Columbia
  University, Box 8
New York, NY 10027

Who Cares? A Journal of Service and
  Action
Heather McLeod
202-628-1691
fax 202-628-2063
1511 K St., NW, Suite 1042
Washington, DC 20005

COMMUNITY, PUBLIC, AND ALTERNATIVE MEDIA

Adbusters Media Foundation ("To
  detoxify your media environment")
Brenda Shaffer
604-736-9401
fax 604-737-6021
WWW: http://www.adbusters.org/
  adbusters
adbuster@wimsey.com
1243 West 7th Ave.
Vancouver, BC V6H 1B7

Alliance for Community Media
Barry Forbes
202-393-2650
fax 202-393-2653
alliancecm@col.com
666 11th St., NW, Suite 806
Washington, DC 20001-4542

AlterNet and the Institute for
  Alternative Journalism
415-284-1420
fax 415-284-1414
alternet@alternet.org
WWW:http//www.alternet.org/an
77 Federal St.
San Francisco, CA 94117

Center for Media Education
Jeff Chester
202-628-2620
fax 202-628-2554
jchester@cme.org
1511 K St., NW, #518
Washington, DC 20005

Corporation for Public Broadcasting
Scott Roberts
202-879-9600
fax 202-783-1036
WWW:http://www.cpb.org
901 E St., NW
Washington, DC 20004-2037

Cultural Environmental Movement
cem@asc.upenn.edu
WWW: http://ccwf.cc.utexas.edu/
~cmbg/cem.html
P.O. Box 31847
Philadelphia, PA 19104

Fairness and Accuracy in Reporting
Janine Jackson
212-633-6700
fax 212-727-7668
fair-info@fair.org
WWW:http://www.fair.org/fair/
130 West 25th St.
New York, NY 10001

Inter Press Service
212-286-0123
fax 212-818-9249
ipshre@gn.apc.org
WWW:http://wn.apc.org/ips/ips.htm
777 United Nations Plaza
New York, NY 10017

KPFA-FM
510-848-6767
fax 510-883-0311
kpfa@well.com
WWW:http://www.well.com/user/
kpfa/
1929 Martin Luther King, Jr. Way
Berkeley, CA 94704

National Federation of Community
Broadcasters (NFCB)
415-771-1160
NFCB@aol.com
WWW:http://soundprint.brandywine.
american.edu/~nfcb/
Fort Mason Center, Bldg. D
San Francisco, CA 94123

Pacifica Radio
ppspacific@igc.apc.org
WWW: http://open.igc.apc.org/
pacifica/
1929 Martin Luther King, Jr. Way
Berkeley, CA 94704

Paper Tiger Television
212-420-9045
fax 212-420-8223
WWW:http://www.papertiger.org
339 Lafayette St.
New York, NY 10012

Pew Center for Civic Journalism
Ed Fouhy
202-331-3200
fax 202-347-6440
601 13th St., NW, Suite 310 South
Washington, DC 20005

The Poynter Institute for Media Studies
813-821-9494
fax 813-821-0583
801 Third St. South
St. Petersburg, FL 33701

Project Censored
Carl Jensen
707-664-2500
project.censored@sonoma.edu
WWW:http://censored.sonoma.edu/
ProjectCensored/index.html
Sonoma State University
Rohnert Park, CA 94928

Project on Public Life and the Press
Jay Rosen
212-998-3793
New York University
Department of Journalism
10 Washington Pl.
New York, NY 10003

Project on Public Life and the Press
Lisa Austin, Research Director
Fax and Tel: 207-799-8918
AUSTINLA@ACFCLUSTER.NYU.EDU
37 Haven Rd.
South Portland, ME 04106-3177

Public Broadcasting System
703-739-5000
WWW:http://www.pbs.org/
1320 Braddock Pl.
Alexandria, VA 22314

UNPLUG
800-UNPLUG-1
360 Grand Ave.
P.O. Box 385
Oakland, CA 94610

Who Cares?: A Journal of Service and
  Action
Heather McLeod
202-628-1691
fax 202-628-2063
1511 K St., NW, Suite 1042
Washington, DC 20005

CYBER-RIGHTS, ACCESS, AND DEMOCRACY

ACM U.S. Public Policy Committee
Barbara Simons
202-298-0842
usacm-dc@acm.org
666 Pennsylvania Ave., SE
Washington, DC 20003

Alliance for Public Technology
Ruth Holder
202-408-1403
fax 202-408-1134
holder@apt.org
901 15th St., NW, #230
Washington, DC 20005

American Civil Liberties Union
Ann Beeson
212-944-9800, Ext. 788
fax 212-869-9065
132 West 43rd St.
New York, NY 10036

Americans Communicating
  Electronically
Judith Hellerstein
202-333-6517
fax 202-707-7000
judithh@tmn.com
WWW:http://www.sbaonline.sba.gov:
  80/ace/
2400 Virginia Ave., NW, #1005C
Washington, DC 20037

Center for Democracy and Technology
202-637-9800
fax 202-637-0968
info@cdt.org
WWW:http://www.cdt.org
ftp://ftp.cdt.org/pub/cdt/
1001 G St., NW, Suite 700 East
Washington, DC 20001

Chicago Coalition for Information
  Access
S. Kritikos
312-561-8153
napoli@wwa.com
WWW:http://cs-www.uchicago.
  edu:80/pub/discussions/cpsr/ccia/
  ccia.html
P.O. Box 25841
Chicago, IL 60640

Coalition for Networked Information
Craig Summerhill
202-296-5098
fax 202-872-0884
craig@cni.org
21 Dupont Circle, #800
Washington, DC 20036

Community Technology Institute
Pat Barry
206-441-7872
cvm@avoice.com
WWW:http://www.scn.org/ip/cti/
   home.html
P.O. Box 61385
Seattle, WA 98121

Computer Professionals for Social
   Responsibility (CPSR)
Audrie Krause
415-322-3778
fax 415-322-4748
info@cpsr.org
WWW:http://www.cpsr.org/dox/
   home.html
P.O. Box 717
Palo Alto, CA 94301

Electra
David Keyes
206-722-4369
keyesd@u.washington.edu
P.O. Box 20369
Seattle, WA 98102

Electronic Frontier Foundation
Andrew Taubman
415-668-7171
fax 415-668-7007
info@eff.org
WWW:http://www.eff.org
P.O. Box 170190
San Francisco, CA 94117

Electronic Privacy Information Center
   (EPIC)
202-547-9240
fax 202-547-5482
info@epic.org
WWW:http://epic.org
666 Pennsylvania Ave., SE, Suite 301
Washington, DC 20003

Internet Society
WWW: http://www.isoc.org
Washington, DC

National Campaign for Freedom of
   Expression
David Mendoza
202-393-2787
fax 202-347-7376
dmendoza@tmn.com
918 F St., NW, Suite 609
Washington, DC 20004

The Society for Electronic Access
212-592-3801
sea-member@sea.org
WWW:http://www.panix.com/sea/
P.O. Box 7081
New York, NY 10116-7081

Taxpayer Assets Project
James Love
202-387-8030
fax 202-234-5176
love@tap.org
WWW:http://www.essential.org/tap
   /tap.html
P.O. Box 19367
Washington, DC 20036

Universal Service Alliance
415-455-4575
fax 415-455-0654
2173 E. Francisco Blvd., Suite L
San Rafael, CA 94901

Voters Telecommunication Watch
Shabbir Safdar
718-596-2851 (last resort)
To join their mailing lists send mail to
   listproc@panix.com.
vtw@vtw.org
gopher://gopher.panix.com:70/11/vtw
WWW:http://www.vtw.org/

ECONOMIC ALTERNATIVES

Appalachian Center for Economic
  Network—ACENET
June Holley
614-592-3854
fax 614-593-5452
jholley@tmn.com
94 N. Columbus Rd.
Athens, OH 45701

Center for Community Economic
  Research
Anders Schneiderman
510-643-8293
ccer@garnet.berkeley.edu
WWW:http://garnet.berkeley.edu:
  3333/
2521 Channing Way, #5555
Berkeley, CA 94704-5555

Center for Policy Alternatives
John Wilcox
202-387-6030
fax 202-986-2539
cfpa@cap.gwu.edu
1875 Connecticut Ave., NW, Suite 710
Washington, DC 20009

Center for Popular Economics
413-545-0753
cpe@acad.umass.edu
P.O. Box 785
Amherst, MA 01004

Center for the Study of
  Commercialism
Susan Monaco
202-797-7080
fax 202-265-4954
1875 Connecticut Ave., NW, #300
Washington, DC 20009-5728

Committee on Strategies to Reduce
  Chronic Poverty
Greater Washington Research Center
Carrie Thornhill
202-466-6680
fax 202-466-7967
1129 20th St., NW, Suite 204
Washington, DC 20036

The Enterprise Foundation
Ed Quinn
410-964-1230
fax 410-964-1918
American City Building
10227 Wincopin Circle, Suite 500
Columbia, MD 21044

Highlander Research and Education
  Center
615-933-3443
fax 615-933-3424
hrec@igc.apc.org
1959 Highlander Way
New Market, TN 37820

National Community Building
  Network
Ed Ferran
510-893-2404
fax 510-893-6657
672 13th St.
Oakland, CA 94612

National Urban Coalition
Ramona Edelin
202-986-1460
fax 202-986-1468
1875 Connecticut Ave., NW, Suite 400
Washington, DC 20009

Neighborhood Reinvestment
  Corporation
Hubert Guest
202-376-2400
fax 202-376-2600
1325 G St., NW, Suite 800
Washington, DC 20005

Urban Strategies Council
Thornton House
Maria Campbell Casey
510-893-2404
fax 510-893-6657
672 13th St., Suite 200
Oakland, CA 94612

EDUCATION

Academy One
Linda Velzeit
714-527-5651
linda@academy.la.ca.us
7151 Lincoln Ave., Suite G
Buena Park, CA 90620

UNPLUG
800-UNPLUG-1
360 Grand Ave.
P.O. Box 385
Oakland, CA 94610

Campus Outreach Opportunity
  League (COOL)
Jennifer Bastress
202-637-7004
fax 202-637-7021
1511 K St., NW, Suite 307
Washington, DC 20005

Choices for the 21st Century Education
  Project
Susan Graseck
401-863-3155
fax 401-863-1247
choices@brown.edu
Thomas J. Watson Jr. Institute for
  International Studies
Brown University
Box 1948
195 Angell St., 2nd Floor
Providence, RI 02912-1948

Community Technology Institute
Pat Barry
206-441-7872
cvm@avoice.com
WWW:http://www.scn.org/ip/cti/
  home.html
P.O. Box 61385
Seattle, WA 98121

Education Development Center
212-807-4200
fax 212-633-8804
6 Morton St., 7th Floor
New York, NY 10014

Highlander Research and Education
  Center
615-933-3443
fax 615-933-3424
hrec@igc.apc.org
1959 Highlander Way
New Market, TN 37820

I*EARN
914-962-5864
fax 914-962-6472
info@copenfund.ig.apc.org
The Copen Family Fund
345 Kear St.
Yorktown Heights, NY 10598

Loka Institute
Richard Sclove
413-253-2828
fax 413-253-4942
loka@amherst.edu
WWW:http://amhux4.amherst.edu/
  ~loka/menu.html
P.O. Box 355
Amherst, MA 01004

National Center for Community
  Education
Duane Brown
810-238-0463
fax 810-238-9211
1017 Avon St.
Flint, MI 48503

National Community Education
  Association
Starla Jewell-Kelly
703-359-8973
fax 703-359-0972
3929 Old Lee Highway, Suite 91-A
Fairfax, VA 22030

National Education Association
Center for the Revitalization of Urban
  Education (CRUE)
E. LaMar Haynes
202-822-7015
fax 202-822-7997
1201 16th St., NW, Room 317
Washington, DC 20036

National Education Association
John Yrchik
202-822-7465
fax 202-822-7697
yrchik@lhc.nlmnih.gov
1201 16th St., NW
Washington, DC 20036

National Parent Teacher Association
Arnold Fege
202-331-1380
fax 202-331-1406
2000 L St., NW, Suite 600
Washington, DC 20036

Public Education Fund Network
Wendy Puriefoy
202-628-7460
fax 202-628-1893
601 13th St., NW, Suite 290 North
Washington, DC 20005

Student Pugwash USA
Greg Craven
202-393-6555
fax 202-393-6550
uspugwash@igc.apc.org
815 15th St., NW, Suite 814
Washington, DC 20005

The Union Institute
Mark Rosenman/Sharon Parker
202-496-1630
fax 202-496-1635
1710 Rhode Island Ave., NW,
  Suite 1100
Washington, DC 20036

ENVIRONMENTAL JUSTICE

Citizens' Clearinghouse for Hazardous
  Waste
P.O. Box 6806
Falls Church, VA 22040

Environmental Justice Resource Center
Robert D. Bullard
Clark Atlanta University
Atlanta, GA 30314

Environmental Working Group
WWW:http://www.ewg.org

Highlander Research and Education
  Center
615-933-3443
fax 615-933-3424
hrec@igc.apc.org
1959 Highlander Way
New Market, TN 37820

Los Angeles Community / Labor
  Center
Eric Mann
213-387-2800
fax 213-387-3500
The Wiltern Center
3780 Wilshire Blvd, Suite 1200
Los Angeles, CA 90010

National Toxics Campaign Fund
1168 Commonwealth Ave., 3rd Floor
Boston, MA 02134

Project for Public Spaces, Inc.
Fred Kent
212-620-5660
fax 212-620-3821
153 Waverly Place
New York, NY 10014

Renew America
Deborah Sliter
202-232-2252
fax 202-232-2617
1400 16th St., NW
Washington, DC 20036

The Trust for Public Land
Noelle Collins
415-495-4014
fax 415-495-4103
WWW:http://www.tpl.org/tpl
116 New Montgomery, 4th Floor
San Francisco, CA 94105

FOUNDATIONS AND CORPORATE PROGRAMS

Apple Library of Tomorrow
Steve Cisler
sac@apple.com
WWW:http://www.apple.com/alot/
  alotsites.html
One Infinite Loop
Cupertino, CA 95014

Benton Foundation
Andrew Blau
202-638-5770
fax 202-638-5771
ablau@benton.org
WWW:http://www.cdinet.com/
  benton/
1634 Eye St., NW, 12th Floor
Washington, DC 20006

The Boston Foundation
Charlotte Kahn
617-723-7415
fax 617-589-3616
One Boston Pl., 24th Floor
Boston, MA 02108

Coalition of Community Foundations
  for Youth
Cindy Sesler Ballard
816-842-4246
fax 816-842-8079
1055 Broadway, Suite 130
Kansas City, MO 64105

Council on Foundations
Lauren Cook
202-466-6512
fax 202-466-5722
1828 L St., NW
Washington, DC 20036

Funds for the Community's Future
David Milner
202-331-0592
fax 202-331-0594
1133 15th St., NW, Suite 605
Washington, DC 20005

Independent Sector
Sandra T. Gray
202-223-8100
fax 202-416-0580
1828 L St., NW, Suite 1200
Washington, DC 20036

International Healthy Cities
  Foundation
Leonard Duhl
510-271-2660
fax 510-643-6981
One Kaiser Plaza, Suite 1930
Oakland, CA 94612

John D. and Catherine T. MacArthur
  Foundation
312-726-8000
4answers@macfdn.org
gopher://gopher.macfdn.org/
WWW: http://www.macfdn.org/
140 S. Dearborn St., Suite 1100
Chicago, IL 60603-5285

Kettering Foundation
David Mathews
513-434-7300
fax 513-439-9804
200 Commons Rd.
Dayton, OH 45459

The Markle Foundation
212-489-6655
fax 212-765-9690
info@markle.org
75 Rockefeller Plaza, Suite 1800
New York, NY 10019-6908

Murray and Agnes Seasongood Good
  Government Foundation
David Altman
513-721-2180
fax 513-721-2299
414 Walnut, Suite 1006
Cincinnati, OH 45202

National AIDS Fund
Patricia Mathews
202-408-4848
fax 202-408-1818
1400 I St., NW, Suite 1220
Washington, DC 20005

NYSERNet
Jean Polly
315-453-2912
jpolly@nysernet.org

Pew Partnership for Civic Change
Suzanne Morse
804-971-2073
fax 804-971-7042
145-C Ednam Dr.
Charlottesville, VA 22903

Public Education Fund Network
Wendy Puriefoy
202-628-7460
fax 202-628-1893
601 13th St., NW, Suite 290 North
Washington, DC 20005

Robert Wood Johnson Community
  Health Leadership Program
Susan Bumagin
617-426-9772
fax 617-451-5838
30 Winter St., Suite 1005
Boston, MA 02108

GOVERNMENT ACCOUNTABILITY AND ADVOCACY

Center for Responsive Politics
Ellen Miller
202-857-0044
WWW:gopher://gopher.igc.apc.org:
  5050/1
1320 19th St., NW, Suite 700
Washington, DC 20036

Center for Policy Alternatives
Burck Smith
202-387-6030
fax 202-986-2539
1875 Connecticut Ave., NW, Suite 710
Washington, DC 20009

Common Cause
Ed Davis
202-736-5724
fax 202-659-3716
72212.1111@compuserve.com
2030 M St., NW, 3rd Floor
Washington, DC 20036

Government Accountability Project
Congressional Accountability Project
Gary Ruskin
202-296-2787
gary@essential.org
fax 202-408-9855
810 First St., NE, #630
Washington, DC 20002

Institute for Local Self-Government
Clark Goecker
916-658-8208
fax 916-658-8240
1400 K St., Suite 400
Sacramento, CA 95814

OMB Watch
Patrice McDermott
202-234-8494
fax 202-234-8584
patricem@cap.gwu.edu
1742 Connecticut Ave., NW
Washington, DC 20009-1171

People for the American Way
Jim Halpert
202-467-4999
fax 202-293-2672
pfaw@tmm.com
2000 M St., NW, #400
Washington, DC 20036

Taxpayer Assets Project
James Love
202-387-8030
fax 202-234-5176
love@tap.org
WWW:http://www.essential.org/tap
  /tap.html
P.O. Box 19367
Washington, DC 20036

GOVERNMENT AGENCIES

Federal Communications Commission
Chris Wright
WWW:http://WWW.fcc.gov/
1919 M St., NW
Washington, DC 20554

Industrial Extension Service Network
Ted Maher
202-720-7185
tmaher@esusda.gov

National Science Foundation
703-306-1234
fax 703-306-0202
firstop@nsf.gov
WWW:http://stis.nsf.gov/
4201 Wilson Blvd.
Arlington, VA 22230

National Telecommunications and
  Information Administration (NTIA)
202-482-3999
fax 202-501-6198
tiiap@ntia.doc.gov or info@iitf.doc.gov
WWW:http://www.ntia.doc.gov
gopher.ntia.doc.gov/
14th St. and Pennsylvania Ave., NW,
  Room 1609
Washington, DC 20230

Office of Technology Assessment
202-224-8996
WWW:http://www.ota.gov/index.html
U.S. Congress
Washington, DC 20510-8025

State Cooperative Research, Education,
  and Extension Service
Thomas Tate
202-720-2727
ttate@reeusda.gov
U.S. Department of Agriculture
Room 3901—South Building
Washington, DC 20250-0915

U.S. Environmental Protection Agency
Henry Topper
202-260-6750
fax 202-260-2219
Office of Pollution Prevention and
  Toxics
401 M St., SW, #7408
Washington, DC 20460

VISTA (Volunteers In Service To
  America)
WWW:http://libertynet.org/~zelson/
  vweb.html (Unofficial)

INTERNATIONAL

The information in this section was obtained from the Web site of the
Institute for Global Communication (IGC) (http://www.igc.org/). The
following networks are all member organizations of the Association for
Progressive Communication (APC). There are APC partner networks in
other countries not listed here who may be able to provide inexpensive connections. Contact IGC or consult their Web site for additional information.

Argentina
  Wamani
  CCI
  Talcahuano 325-3F
  1013 Buenos Aires, Argentina
  Tel: +54 (1) 382-6842
  apoyo@wamani.apc.org

**Australia, Pacific Islands,
Southeast Asia**
  Pegasus Networks
  P.O. Box 3220
  South Brisbane Qld 4101
  Australia
  Tel: +61 7 3255 0255
  Fax: +61 7 3255 0555
  pegasus@peg.apc.org

Brazil, South America

AlterNex IBASE
Rua Vicente de Souza 29
22251-070 Rio de Janeiro, Brazil
Tel: +55 (21) 286-0348
Fax: +55 (21) 286-0541
suporte@ax.apc.org

Canada

Web
NirvCentre
401 Richmond St. West
Suite 104
Toronto, Ontario M5V 3A8
Canada
Tel: +1 (416) 596-0212
Fax: +1 (416) 596-1374
outreach@web.apc.org

Colombia

ColNodo
Avenida 39 No. 14-75
Santafe de Bogota, Colombia
Tel: 57-1-3381277
Fax: 57-1-2861941
Access numbers: 57-1-2871806 /
    2324246
soporte@colnodo.apc.org

Ecuador

Ecuanex
Casilla 17-12-566
Calle Ulpiano Paez #118 y Av. Patria
Edificio FLACSO, 4to piso
Casilla 17-12-566
Quito, Ecuador
Tel: +593 (2) 227-014 or 508-277
Fax: +593 (2) 227-014
intercom@ecuanex.apc.org

Germany, Switzerland, Turkey

ComLink e.v.
An der Lutherkirche 6
D-30167 Hannover, Germany
Tel: +49 (511) 161 78 11 (Voice)
Fax: +49 (511) 165 26 11
Modems: +49 (511) 165 22 11 (5 lines)
support@oln.comlink.apc.org

Great Britain

GreenNet
393-395 City Rd., 4th Floor
London EC1V INE UK
Tel: +44 1 (71) 713 1941
Fax: +44 1 (71) 833 1169
support@gn.apc.org

Mexico

LaNeta
Insurgentes Sur 1228-204,
D.F., Mexico, C.P. 03210
Fax (525) 5755335
soporte@laneta.apc.org

Netherlands

Antenna
Box 1513
NL-6501 BM Nijmegen, Netherlands
Tel: +31(80) 235-372
Fax: +31(80) 236-798
support@antenna.nl

New Zealand

PlaNet
78 Straven Rd.
Christchurch, Canterbury 8001
New Zealand
Tel: +64 3 343-2633
support@planet.apc.org

Nicaragua, Central America

Nicarao
Apartado 3516 Iglesia Carmen
1 cuadra al lago
Managua, Nicaragua
Tel: +505 (2) 283-188/283-092
Fax: +505 (2) 281-244
ayuda@nicarao.apc.org

The Nordic, Baltic States

NordNet
Huvudskaersvaegen 13, nb
S-12154 Johanneshov, Sweden
Tel: +46 (8) 600 03 31
Fax: +46 (8) 600 04 43
support@nn.apc.org

Russia, Commonwealth of Independent States

GlasNet
Ulitsa Sadovaya-Chernograizskaya,
4, Suite 16a
107078 Moscow, Russia
Tel: +7 (095) 207-0704
Fax: +7 (095) 207-0889
support@glas.apc.org

Slovenja

Histria & Zamir Transnational Net (ZTN)
HISTRIA, ABM d.o.o.
Resljeva 1
61000 Ljubljana
Slovenja
Tel: + 386 61 133-1402 (office), +386 61
125-0325 (comm. center)
Fax: + 386 61 133-1406 (office), +386
61 125-2107 (comm. center)
support@histria.apc.org

ZTN systems can be reached at:

Belgrade
ZAMIR-BG
Tel: +381 11 632 566
Voice support at tel: +381 11 635
813 / 626 623
support@ZAMIR-BG.ztn.apc.org

Ljubljana
ZAMIR-LJ
Tel: +386 61 126 3281
(Di and Do 12:00-14:00)
support@ZAMIR-LJ.ztn.apc.org

Pristina
ZANA-PR
Tel: +381 38 31276
Voice support at tel: +381 38 31031 /
31036
support@ZANA-PR.ztn.apc.org

Sarajevo
ZAMIR-SA
Tel: +387 71 444-200
Voice support at tel: +387 71 444 337
support@ZAMIR-SA.ztn.apc.org

Tuzla
ZAMIR-TZ
Tel: +387 75 239-146 (3 lines)
Voice support at tel: +387 75 239-147
support@ZAMIR-TZ.ztn.apc.org

Zagreb
ZAMIR-ZG
Tel: +385 41 271 927. (Node 1), +385
41 423 044 (Node 2)
Voice support at tel: +385 41 422 495
support@ZAMIR-ZG.ztn.apc.org

South Africa

SangoNet
P.O. Box 31
Longsbank Building, 13th Floor
187 Bree St.
Johannesberg 2000, South Africa
Tel: +27 (11) 838-6944
Fax: +27 (11) 492 1058
support@wn.apc.org

Ukraine

GLUK—GlasNet-Ukraine
14b Metrologicheskaya Str.
Kiev, 252143 Ukraine
Tel: +7 (044) 266 9481
Fax: +7 (044) 266 9475
support@gluk.apc.org

United States, China

PeaceNet/EcoNet/ConflictNet/
LaborNet/WomensNet
Institute for Global Communications
(IGC)
18 De Boom Street
San Francisco, CA 94107
Tel: +1 (415) 442-0220
Fax: +1 (415) 546-1794
igc-info@igc.apc.org
Gopher: gopher.igc.apc.org
WWW: http://www.igc.apc.org

Uruguay, Paraguay

Chasque
Casilla Correo 1539
Montevideo 11000, Uruguay
Tel: +598 (2) 496-192
Fax: +598 (2) 419-222
apoyo@chasque.apc.org

LABOR

Communications Workers of America
cwao1@aol.com
501 Third St., NW
Washington, DC 20001-2797

Communications Workers of America
  Local 6143
Gary Woitena
210-224-6143
fax 210-224-0052
71363.320@compuserve.com
WWW:http://www.igc.apc.org/cwatx
  /cwa6143.html

Los Angeles Community / Labor Center
Eric Mann
213-387-2800
fax 213-287-3500
The Wiltern Center
3780 Wilshire Blvd., Suite 1200
Los Angeles, CA 90010

National Writers Union
Alec Dubro
202-466-0079
fax 202-543-2462
72614.1375@compuserve.com
521 10th St., SE
Washington, DC 20003

LIBRARY ORGANIZATIONS

American Library Association
Peggy Barber
312-280-3217
fax 312-280-3224
50 East Huron St.
Chicago, IL 60611-2795

American Society for Information
  Science
Lois Lunin
202-965-3924
922 24th St., NW
Washington, DC 20037-2229

Association for Research Libraries
Prue Adler
202-296-2296
fax 202-872-0884
21 Dupont Circle, NW
Washington, DC 20036

Libraries for the Future
Diantha Schull
800-542-1918
fax 212-682-7657
WWW:http://www.inch.com/~lff
521 Fifth Ave., Suite 1612
New York NY 10175-1699

REFERRAL ORGANIZATIONS

Alliance of Information and Referral
  Systems
Peter Aberg
206-523-6296
fax 206-524-7341
pkaairs@aol.com
2753 N.E. 92nd St.
Seattle, WA 98115

SUSTAINABILITY

Context Institute (Publishes *In Context*
  magazine)
Robert Gilman
206-842-0216
P.O. Box 11470
Bainbridge Island, WA 98110

Sustainable Development Network
Raoul Zambrano
zambrano@undp.org

Sustainable Seattle
Richard Conlin
206-382-5013
sustnble@sch.org
WWW:http://www.scn.org/
  sustainable/susthome.html
c/o Metrocenter YMCA
909 Fourth Ave.
Seattle, WA 98104

TELECOMMUNICATIONS FORUMS
(INTERNATIONAL, NATIONAL, AND REGIONAL)

Access For All (New York City)
David Green
green@artswire.org
Barry Lasky
212-366-6900
blasky@artswire.org
c/o NY Foundation for the Arts
155 Avenue of the Americas
New York, NY 10013

Ad-hoc Coalition for Seattle's
  Information Infrastructure
c/o Eric Rehm (CPSR/Seattle)
206-865-8904
eric@scn.org
c/o David Keyes (Electra)
206-722-4369
keyesd@u.washington.edu
P.O. Box 20369
Seattle, WA 98102

Chicago Coalition for Information
Access
S. Kritikos
312-561-8153
napoli@wwa.com
WWW:http://cs-www.uchicago.
edu:80/pub/discussions/cpsr/ccia/
ccia.html
P.O. Box 25841
Chicago, IL 60640

Chicago Community Information
Consortium
Philippa Gamse
312-341-4335
fax 312-341-3608
WWW:http://www.cnt.org/ccic.html
pgamse@interaccess.com
Institute for Metropolitan Affairs
430 S. Michigan Ave., Rm. 846
Chicago, IL 60605

Citizens' Coalition on Austin's
Networking Future
c/o Gary Chapman, The 21st Century
Project
512-471-8326
fax 512-471-1835
gary.chapman@mail.utexas.edu
gopher.tpoint.net:40007/00s/
community/ccanfmission.txt
LBJ School of Public Affairs, Drawer Y,
University Station
University of Texas
Austin, TX 78713

Telecommunications Policy
Roundtable
Emily Littleton
cme@cme.org
1511 K St., Suite 518
Washington, DC 20005

TPR-NE
c/o Coralee Whitcomb
617-542-5555
cwhitcom@bentley.edu
55 Temple Pl.
Boston, MA 02111

Appendix B

Community-Network Electronic Resources

This list contains a wide variety of electronic resources. The classification scheme used in Appendix A is also used here. This list is far from comprehensive, as there are new electronic resources appearing every day. If you can't find what you're looking for here, you may want to check with organizations listed in Appendix A.

This appendix and other information from this book can be found in the Web pages that have graciously been provided by the Morino Institute (http://www.morino.org/schuler/ncn.htm). If for any reason you can't access this URL, try the Community Network Movement URL (http://www.scn.org/ip/commnet/home.html).

ADVOCACY AND SUPPORT

AIDS Info BBS
Modem: 415-626-1246
WWW: http:itsa.ucsf.edu/~beng/
  aidsbbs.html

Archimedes Project ("Leverage for
  individuals with disabilities through
  information technology")
WWW: http://csli-www.stanford.
  edu/arch/arch.html

Berkeley Vietnam Veterans Memorial
WWW: http://www.ci.berkeley.ca.us/
  vvm/

Black/African Resources (Art McGee's
  List)
WWW: http://www.sas.upenn.edu/
  African_Studies/Home_Page/mcgee.
  html

Center for Information Technology
  Accommodation
http://www.gsa.gov/coca

Child/Family Interactive Network
Eileen Traylor
info@cfin.org
WWW: http://www.cfin.org

Computer Network Services, Internet,
  and Information Resources for
  Women
WWW: http://www.igc.apc.org/
  womensnet/

CyberQueers FAQ
WWW: http://cyberzine.org/html/
  GLAIDS/Faqs/queersfaq.html

CyberQueer Lounge
WWW: http://www.cyberzine.org/
  html/GLAIDS/glaidshomepage.html

Hands Off Washington/Washington
  Citizens for Fairness
Kelly Evans
206-323-5191
HandsOff_Washington@eor.com
WWW: http://www.eor.com/
  howhtml/how.htm

Hawaiian Language Center
WWW: http://www.olelo.hawaii.
edu/

Hawaiian Language Immersion
WWW: http://maui.com/~mauilink/
  PLOM/PLOMHome.html

Homeless List
Gopher://csf.colorado.edu/00/psn/
  homeless/

Homelessness in America
WWW: http://www.teleport.com/
  ~cool/homeless.html

National Coalition for the Homeless
WWW: http://nch.ari.net

Oneida Nation
WWW: http://nyser.org/oneida

OTA's Native American Resource Page
WWW: http://www.ota.gov/
  nativea.html

Rainbow Pages (Voice-based,
  telephone-access community-
  information services)
For more information contact Paul
  Resnick, presnick@research.att.com

Sistah Space
WWW:http://carmen.artsci.
  washington.edu/Sisterhood/
  Welcome.htm

Streetlife Gallery
WWW: http://internetcafe.allyn.com/
  slg/slg.html

UK Homeless
WWW: http://sl.cxwms.ac.uk/
  Academic/AGPU/staffpag/
  robinson/interest/homeless/
  homepage.html

ARTS AND CULTURE

Cultural Environment Movement
  Distribution List
Send requesting e-mail to
  cmbg@ccwf.cc.utexas.edu (Cynthia
  Bock-Goodner).

A Day in the Life
For more information contact NTPN or
  Academy One (see Appendix A).

Northwest CyberArtists Distribution
  List
Send "subscribe cyberartists firstname
  lastname" to listproc@u.washington.
  edu.

CIVIC AND DEMOCRATIC REVITALIZATION

Civic Practices Network
WWW: http://cpn.journalism.wisc.
edu/

Communications as Engagement
WWW: http://www.cdinet.com/
Millennium/

Community Network Movement
WWW: http://www.scn.org/ip/
commnet/home.html

Community Stories
WWW: http://www.csn.net/anr/
comindex.html

Contact Center Network—Directory of
Nonprofit Resources
WWW: http://www.contact.org

Institute for the Study of Values
WWW: http://libertynet.org/
~edcivic/iscvhome.html
Gopher://gopher.civic.net:2400/11/
cdiscv

Neighborhood Early Warning System
(NEWS)
WWW:http://www.cnt.org/news.html

Neighborhoods Online
WWW: http://libertynet.org/
community/phila/natl.html

The Neighborhood Works
WWW: http://www.cnt.org/tnw/
tnwhome.htm

Resources for Non-Profits
WWW: http://www.eskimo.com/
~pbarber

What's New In Activism Online
WWW: http://www.wnia.org/
WNIA/

COMMUNITY AND CIVIC NETWORKING

American Communities
WWW: http://www.aspensys.com:85
gopher://amcom.aspensys.com:75

City.Net
WWW: http://www.city.net

Civic Nets (Reti Civiche e Freenets)
WWW: http://vega.unive.it/contrib/
audies/civicnet.html

Communet Distribution List
Send mail to listproc@list.uvm.edu
with message "subscribe communet
firstname lastname."

Community Computer Networks &
Free-Net Web Sites
WWW:http://freenet.victoria.bc.ca/
freenets.html

Community Network Movement
WWW: http://www.scn.org/ip/
commnet/home.html

Community Networking Resources
WWW: http://sils/umich/
Community/Community.html

Community Networking Documents
and Resources
WWW: http://www.nlc-bnc.ca/
ifla/services/commun.htm

Community Networks Surveys
FTP: ftp://cs.washington.edu/
research/community-networks/
WWW: http://www.cs.washington.
edu/research/community-
networks/

Creation, Organization and
Management of Public-Access
Nonprofit Networks Distribution List
Send mail to listserv@cespivm2.unlp.
edu.ar with "subscribe FREENET
firstname lastname" message.

De digitale Stad
WWW: http://www.dds.nl/

Freenet-admin Distribution List
Must be an NPTN affiliate to
participate. Contact NPTN
(Appendix A) for more information.

Free-Nets & Community Networks
WWW: http://hearld.usask.ca/
~scottp/free.html

Intentional Community Page
WWW: http://www.well.com/www/
cmty/

Millennium Communications
WWW: http://cdinet.com/Millennium

NPTN Cybercasting Catalog
WWW: http://www.nptn.org/
about.nptn/whois/jmk/catalog.html

NCF Survey
WWW: http://debra.dgbt.doc.ca/
~andrew/survey.html

PACS-L—Public-Access Computer
Systems
Send e-mail to listserv@UHUPVM1.
UH.EDU with "subscribe PACS-1
firstname lastname" message

Public Access Networks
WWW: http://www.morino.org/

Success Stories
WWW: http://bcn.boulder.co.us/
community/resources/why/helped.
html

USA CityLink
WWW: http://www.NeoSoft.com:80/
citylink/

Virtual Communities Forum
WWW: http://www.emedia.net/feed

WWW Guide to Community
Networking
WWW: http://http2.sils.umich.edu/
ILS/community.html

COMMUNITY CENTERS

Cyber Café Guide Version 12.1 (Cyber
Cafés around the world!)
WWW: http://www.easynet.co.uk/
pages/cafe/ccafe.htm/usa_west

Playing to Win
Gopher: gopher.igc.apc.org" and then
select "Organizations on the IGC
Networks Gopher" and scroll down
to "Playing to Win."

Speakeasy Cafe
206-728-9770
cafe@speakeasy.org
WWW: http://speakeasy.org
2304 2nd Ave.
Seattle, WA 98121

COMMUNITY EMPOWERMENT AND REVITALIZATION

Civic Practices Network
WWW: http://cpn.journalism.
  wisc.edu/

Essential Information
WWW: http://www.essential.org/
  EI.html

Geographic Information Systems
  Distribution List (gis-l)
Send mail to listserv@urisa.org with
  "subscribe gis-l" message.

Neighborhood Early Warning System
  (NEWS)
WWW: http://www.cnt.org/news.
  html

The Neighborhood Works
WWW: http://www.cnt.org/tnw/
  tnwhome.htm

PAR-Talk (Participatory Action
  Research) Distribution List
Send mail to listproc@cornell.edu with
  message "subscribe par-talk
  firstname lastname."

PARNet: Participatory Action Research
  Network
WWW: http://munex.arme.cornell.
  edu/parnet/home.htm

Red de Informacion Rural
WWW: http://tonatiuh.uam.mx:70/
  RIE

Information for Non-Profits
WWW: http://www.eskimo.com/
  ~pbarber

Trust for Public Land
WWW: http://www.tpl.org/tpl

What's New In Activism Online
WWW: http://www.wnia.org/
  WNIA/

COMMUNITY HEALTH

AIDS Info BBS
Ben Gardiner
415-626-1245
ben@QueerNet.ORG
Modem: 415-626-1246
WWW: http://itsa.ucsf.edu/~beng
  /aidsbbs.html

CHESS
For more information contact Robert
  Hawkins, rphawk@macc.wisc.edu.

Computer Link
For more information contact Patricia
  Brennan, pfb@po.cwru.edu.

The NPTN Health and Wellness Center
WWW: http://www.nptn.org:80/
cyber.serv/hwp/

MADNESS Distribution List
Send mail to LISTSERV@sjuvm.stjohns.
edu with "subscribe madness firstname lastname" message.

RTK Net
info@rtk.net
202-234-8494
WWW: http://rtk.net/
SCARCnet

WWW: http://www.gii-
awards.com/nicampgn/3912.htm

Tobacco Control Archives
WWW: http://www.library.ucsf.edu/
tobacco

COMMUNITY, PUBLIC, AND ALTERNATIVE MEDIA

Boulder Vocal Point
WWW: http://bvsd.k12.co.us/
schools/cent/Newspaper/
Newspaper.html

Cultural Environment Movement
Distribution List
Send requesting e-mail to
cmbg@ccwf.cc.utexas.edu (Cynthia
Bock-Goodner).

Detroit Journal—Striking Journalists
WWW: http://www.rust.net/
~workers/union/union.html

MISANET Welcome Directory
WWW: ftp://ftp.misanet.org/

San Francisco Free Press
WWW: http://www.ccnet.com/
SF_Free_Press/

Shred of Dignity, ca. 1989
WWW:http://www.wps.com/Shipley
/shipley.html

Washington Free Press
WWW: http://www.cyberspace.com/
~mrobesch/wfp2.html

CYBER-ACCESS AND CYBER-RIGHTS

California Electronic Government
Information
WWW: http://www.cpsr.org/cpr/
states/california/govaccess

Cyber-Rights Working Group
See Computer Professionals for Social
Responsibility in "Other" section (see
Appendix B).

Electronic Democracy Information
Network (EDIN)
WWW: http://garnet.berkeley.edu:
3333/

GovAccess
Send mail to Majordomo@well.com
with "subscribe GovAccess
YourEmailAddress" message.

Privacy International
WWW: http://www.privacy.org/

Seattle Rally Against Internet
  Censorship (RealAudio)
WWW: http://www.wnia.org/
  WNIA/hap/rally.html

U.S. Public Policy Committee of ACM
  (USACM)
WWW: http://www.acm.org/usacm/

ECONOMIC ALTERNATIVES

Foundation for Enterprise
  Development
WWW: http://www.fed.org/fed/

FUTUREWORK Distribution list
Send to listproc@csf.colorado.edu
  message "subscribe futurework
  firstname lastname."

Global Solidarity
Access is through WWW:
  http://uts.cc.utexas.edu/~jdrew

HungerWeb: Fifty Facts About Poverty
WWW: http://garnet.berkeley.
  edu:3333/faststats/povertystats.html

Technology, Employment &
  Community Conference
WWW: http://www.cs.uchicago.edu/
  discussions/cpsr/jobtech/job-
  tech.html

EDUCATION

Academy One Program
WWW: http://www.nptn.org/cyber.
  serv/AOneP

AskERIC—Department of Education
  (Collection of educational
  information)
WWW: http://ericir.syr.edu/
Gopher: ericir.syr.edu
Email: askeric@ericir.syr.edu

Collaboratory
Contact NPTN or Academy One (see
  Appendix A).

EdWeb—Educational Computing and
  Networking
WWW: http://k12.cnidr.org:90/
  resource.cntnts.html

The Electronic School
WWW: http://www.access.digex.net/
  ~nsbamags/e-school.html

Exploratorium
WWW: http:/www.exploratorium.
  edu/default.html

Homework Assistance Hotline
Ellen Bialo
212-769-0909
Interactive Educational Systems
  Design, Inc.
310 W. 106th St.
New York, NY 10025

KidLink
WWW: http://www1.snunit.k12.il/
snunit_e/kidlink.htm

OERI—Department of Education's
Office of Education Research and
Improvement
Gopher: gopher.ed.gov
WWW: http://www.ed.gov

Star Trek RPG
Contact NPTN or Academy One (see
Appendix A).

Virtual High
WWW: http://www.wimsey.com/
~larryds/VH/

ENVIRONMENTAL JUSTICE

EnviroLink Network
WWW: http://envirolink.org

RTK Net
info@rtk.net
202-234-8494
WWW: http://rtk.net/

SCARCnet
WWW: http:www.gii-awards.com/
nicampgn/3912.htm

Tobacco Control Archives
WWW: http://www.library.ucsf.edu/
tobacco

What's New In Activism Online
WWW: http://www.wnia.org/
WNIA/

FOUNDATIONS, NONPROFITS, AND CORPORATE PROGRAMS

Select Nonprofit Organizations on the
Internet
WWW: http://www.ai.mit.edu/
people/ellens/non.html

GOVERNMENT ACCOUNTABILITY

Congressional Reform Briefings
Send e-mail to listproc@essential.org.
with "subscribe CONG-REFORM
firstname lastname" message.

GOVERNMENT AGENCIES

Fedworld
Telnet: fedworld.gov
Modem: 703-321-8020
WWW: http://www.fedworld.gov

HUDUSER
WWW: http://huduser.aspensys.
  com:84/huduser.html
Gopher://huduser.aspensys.com:73

NTIA HOME PAGE
WWW:http://www.ntia.doc.gov/

Seattle Public Access Network (PAN)
Modem: 206-233-7100
Telnet: pan.ci.seattle.wa.us
Login: "new" or "guest"
WWW: http://www.pan.ci.seattle.
  wa.us/

Thomas (Access to national legislation
  and other information)
WWW: http://thomas.loc.gov/

INTERNATIONAL

Institute for Global Communications
  (IGC)
Gopher: gopher.igc.apc.org
WWW: http://www.igc.apc.org

LABOR

AFL-CIO
WWW: http://www.aflcio.org/

Cornell Industrial Labor Relations
  School
WWW: http://www.ilr.cornell.edu/

Industrial Workers of the World
  Resource Directory
www@sf.iww.org
WWW: http://iww.org/

LABNEWS
Send mail to listserv@cmsa.Berkeley.
  EDU with "subscribe labnews"
  message.

LaborNet (IGC)
WWW: http://www.igc.org/labornet

The Sheet Metal Workers International
  Association
WWW: http://www.smwia.org/

Strike Page
WWW: http://www.igc.apc.org/
  strike/

UnionWeb Home Page
WWW: http://www.unionweb.org/

Union-D Discussion List
Send e-mail to listproc@wolfnet.com
 with the message: "subscribe
 UNION-D firstname lastname"

Usenet Newsgroups
clari.news.labor
misc.jobs.contract

LIBRARY

ALAWON-ALA Washington Office
 Newsline
Send e-mail to listserv@uicvm.uic.edu
 with "subscribe ALA-WO firstname
 lastname" message.
.
IFREEDOM-Censorship and
 Intellectual Freedom
Send e-mail to
 listserv@SNOOPY.UCIS.DAL.CA
 with "subscribe IFREEDOM
 firstname lastname" message.

PACS-L-Public-Access Computer
 Systems
Send e-mail to listserv@UHUPVM1.
 UH.EDU with "suscribe pacs-1
 firstname lastname" message.

PUBLIB-Public Libraries
Send e-mail to listserv@nysernet.org
 with "subscribe publib firstname
 lastname" message.

PUBLIB-NET-Internet Use in Public
 Libraries
Send e-mail to listserv@nysernet.org
 with "subscribe publib-net firstname
 lastname" message.

SUSTAINABILITY

EnviroLink Network
WWW: http://envirolink.org

Sustainable Seattle—Critical Indicators
WWW: http://www.scn.org/ip/
 sustainable/Indicators/indicators95/
 indicators95.html

TELECOMMUNICATIONS FORUMS
(INTERNATIONAL, NATIONAL, AND REGIONAL)

TPR-NE Distribution List
tpr-ne@mitvma.mit.edu

OTHER

Activ-l (Peace, social justice, environment, and community activism)
Send e-mail to listserv@umcvmb.missouri.edu with message "sub activ-l."

Centre for Computing and Social Responsibility
WWW: http://www.cms.dmu.ac.uk/CCSR

Computer Professionals for Social Responsibility Distribution Lists
Send mail to listserv@cpsr.org with "LIST" message.

Computer Professionals for Social Responsibility On-Line Archives/Resources
WWW: http://www.cpsr.org/
FTP, WAIS, and Gopher: cpsr.org:/cpsr

FASTnet Subscription (moderated)
Send e-mail to majordomo@igc.apc.org with "subscribe FASTnet" message.

Impact Online
WWW: http://www.webcom.com/~iol

Loka Alert Subscription
Send e-mail to loka@amherst.edu (subscription isn't automated).

Loka Institute
WWW: http://www.amherst.edu/~loka/

The Network Observer
Send mail to rre-request@weber.ucsd.edu with "subscribe firstname lastname" subject.

Nonprofit Support Site
http://www.uwm.edu/People/mbarndt/mindex.htm
"Internet Tour on Enhancing Planning and Participation"
http://www.uwm.edu/People/mbarndt/planpart.htm

Pol-sci-tech (the international sibling list to FASTnet) Subscription (nonmoderated)
Follow same instructions as for FASTnet subscribing (above), except the message text changes to "subscribe pol-sci-tech."

Science Shop Distribution List (Loka Institute)
Send e-mail to listserv@ncsu.edu with "subscribe scishops firstname lastname" message.

Sci-Tech Studies Distribution List
Send mail to listserv@kasey.umkc.edu with "subscribe sci-tech-studies firstname lastname" message.

Tech-Society Distribution List
Send mail to majordomo@mail.ieee.org with "subscribe tech-society" message.

Appendix C

Community Networks

This appendix contains a list of community networks in the United States and around the world. It is not comprehensive, so don't assume that a system doesn't exist just because it's not listed here. I have not listed organizing efforts; it is quite likely that an organizing effort is going on in your community even if there is no community network listed below. If you're interested in starting a community network or working on an existing effort, I suggest that you contact National Public Telecomputing Network (NPTN, listed in Appendix A) to see if there is an organizing committee in place. You may also want to check with your local library or the computer science department of a local university. Sending a note to the Communet Listserve or to various community network Web sites (see Appendix B) may also be a reasonable approach if you can't locate any project through other sources.

Although I have tried to make these listings as accurate as possible, there are bound to be some errors. Please feel free to send updates or corrections to me, as I will make an effort to keep the *New Community Network* Web site current. If community networks continue to grow as fast as they have been in recent years, maintaining the site could be a full-time job. For that reason I cannot guarantee the accuracy of the information in the site.

There are a great many types of systems listed below. Some charge a small fee for usage. Most do not. Many of the systems listed below are NPTN affiliates (and I thank NPTN for providing the information). A few systems listed are NPTN educational affiliates and are therefore not community networks in a strict sense, but the contact names that are listed here will likely be quite useful. The chances are good that the projects need volunteers, but since this will vary from project-to-project, your best approach is to contact the project you're interested in for further information on the next meeting.

Finally, please note that the projects listed here don't necessarily subscribe to the guidelines, philosophy, or motivation that I've presented in this book. Nor do I necessarily subscribe to theirs. Each system is listed geographically. U.S. community networks are listed by states and Canadian systems are listed by provinces.

UNITED STATES

ALABAMA

Mobile Area Free-Net, Inc.—SW
  Alabama
Geoff Peacock
334-405-4600
geoff@maf.mobile.al.us
P.O. Box 40894
Mobile, AL 36640-0894
Login: visitor
Password: visitor
Modem: 334-405-4636
Telnet: maf.mobile.al.us
WWW: http://www.maf.mobile.al.us

ARIZONA

AzTeC Computing—Tempe
Joseph A. Askins
602-965-5985
joe.askins@asu.edu
Login: guest
Password: visitor
Modem: 602-965-4151
Telnet: aztec.asu.edu

CALIFORNIA

Access Sacramento—Sacramento
  county only
Wes Doak
916-456-8600, Ext. 132
fax 916-451-9601 telefax
access@sna.com (w) or
  onramp1@netcom.com (h)
4623 T St., Suite A, Sacramento, CA
  96819-4743
Login: "Guest" login optional
Gopher: N/A (Several G-sites and FTP
  sites under construction for larger
  community-based datafiles)
  WWW: http://www.sna.com/access
(Will be linked to multicounty area
  network entitled "Net at Two Rivers"
  when that network comes online
  sometime in the next few months.)

CORE—Seal Beach
Keith Vogt
1-800-272-8743
kvogt@eis.calstate.edu
Telnet: eis.calstate.edu

Davis Community Network—Davis,
  CA and Yolo county
916-750-0101
dcnadmin@dcn.davis.ca.us
P.O. Box 1563
Davis, CA 96517
Modem: guests please use Web URL
WWW: http://www.dcn.davis.ca.us
(Davis Community Network has a
  basic membership fee of $15/month
  for 50 hours of modem access per
  month and 2mb of disk storage.)

Los Angeles Free-Net—Los Angeles
Phil Mittelman
310-476-4307
philm@lafn.org
257 S. Barrington Ave.
Los Angeles, CA 90049
Login: See menu
Password: See menu
Modem: 818-776-5000
Telnet: lafn.org
WWW: http://lafn.org

Public Electronic Network (PEN)—
  Santa Monica residents only
Keith A. Kurtz, PEN Project Manager
310-458-8383
fax 310-395-2343
kkurtz@pen.ci.santa-monica.ca.us
Modem: 310-458-8989
Telnet: pen.ci.santa-monica.ca.us
WWW: http://pen.ci.santa-
  monica.ca.us
The City of Santa Monica, 1685 Main St.
Santa Monica, CA 90401

Redwood Free-Net—Mendocino
  county
Pat Hunt
707-463-4154
Administrator@RedwoodFN.org
105 N. Main St.
Ukiah, CA 95482
Login: Blank login will bring up
  registration screen
Password: your choice
Modem: 707-463-6527

SLONET Regional Information
  Network—San Luis Obispo and
  northern Santa Barbara counties in
  California
Mark Porczak
mporczak@slonet.org
P.O. Box 15818, San Luis Obispo, CA
  93406
Login: sloguest
Modem: 805-781-3666
Telnet: slonet.org
WWW: http://www.slonet.org/
  slonet.html

solano.community.net, napa.
  community.net,
  coco.community.net.—Napa, Solano,
  Contra Costa counties, Northern
  California
707-422-1034
info@community.net
AIS Community Network
1955 W. Texas #7-299
Fairfield, CA 94533
Login: guest
Password: guest
Modem: 707-422-1250, 707-258-3300,
  415-372-4280
Telnet: community.net
WWW: http://community.net

Tahoe-Truckee Community Network—
  Lake Tahoe Basin / Truckee (CA,
  Nevada)
916-587-1128
sass@sierra.net

Box 10150
Truckee, CA 96162
Login: Create your own
Password: Create your own
Modem: 916-546-4003

COLORADO

Boulder Community Network—
  Boulder county
Catherine Weldon
303-492-8176
weldon@bcn.boulder.co.us
3645 Marine St.
Campus Box 455- University of
  Colorado, Boulder
Boulder CO 80309-0455
Login: bcn (need Internet access to
  reach us unless caller is a local
  human-service provider)
Telnet: bcn.boulder.co.us
WWW: http://bcn.boulder.co.us

Denver Free-Net—Denver
Drew Mirque
303-270-4300
drew@freenet.hsc.colorado.edu
Login: guest
Modem: 303-270-4865
Telnet: freenet.hsc.colorado.edu

InfoZone—regional community (5000
  sq. mi. local calling area) around
  Telluride
Richard Lowenberg
970-728-6960
fax 970-728-4638
rl@infozone.org
Login: WinGuest or MacGuest
Modem: 970-728-5553
Telnet:198.147.224.4 (InfoZone
  CommunityNet)
WWW: http://infozone.telluride.
  co.us/InfoZone.html
Telluride Institute, InfoZone, Box 1770
Telluride, CO 81435

Southwest Colorado Access
  Network—6500 sq. miles of SW
  Colorado
Bill Ball
970-749-2495
bill@scan.org
P.O. Box 5371, Durango, CO 81301
Modem: 970-259-9350
Telnet: 199.45.222.2
WWW: http://web.frontier.net/
  SCAN/r9/swcolo.html

CONNECTICUT

Bridgeport On-Line—Bridgeport, CT
Gary Koos
203-366-3921
fax: 203-366-3921
Login: Sign-up on-line
Modem: 203-367-4013
P.O. Box 3710
Bridgeport, CT 06605

FLORIDA

Alachua Free-Net—Gainesville
Bruce Brashear
904-372-8401
76314.352@compuserve.com
Login: visitor
Modem: 904-334-0200
Telnet: freenet.ufl.edu

SEFLIN Free-Net—Broward county
Elizabeth Curry
305-357-7318
currye@mail.seflin.lib.fl.us
Login: visitor
Modem: 305-765-4332
Telnet: bcfreenet.seflin.lib.fl.us

Suncoast Free-Net—Florida Central
  West Coast area (Tampa/
  St. Petersburg)
813-273-3711
infodesk@scfn.thpl.lib.fl.us
Suncoast Free-Net
900 N. Ashley Drive, Tampa, FL 33602
Login: visitor
Modem: 813-273-3755 or 813-298-1653
Telnet: scfn.thpl.lib.fl.us

Suncoast Free-Net—Tampa
Marilyn Mulla
813-273-3714
mullam@firnvx.firn.edu
Visitor login: visitor
Modem: 813-273-3755
Telnet: ns1.thpl.lib.fl.us

Tallahassee Free-Net—Leon county
904-487-2665
rousem@freenet.fsu.edu
Tallahassee Free-Net 200
W. Park Ave, Tallahassee, FL 32301
Login: visitor (lowercase)
Modem: 904-488-5056
Telnet: freenet.fsu.edu
WWW: http://www.freenet.scri.fsu.
  edu

GEORGIA

Worth County-Sylvester, GA Free-
  Net—Lee, Dougherty, and Worth
  counties
Kent Guske
912-776-7718
Kent_Guske@peanut.org
P.O. Box 768, Sylvester, GA 31791
Login: Guest
Modem: 912-776-1255

IDAHO

Panhandle Free-Net—Idaho
  Panhandle (covering region north of
  Coeur d'Alene, ID, to Canadian
  border, east to Montana, west to WA)
James Murray
Melody Martz
208-263-5400
c/o emoryg@iea.com
Panhandle Free-Net 201 N. 4th
Suite 101, Sandpoint, ID 83864
Login: auto-register
Modem: 208-263-6336

ILLINOIS

Prairienet—Urbana and East-Central
  Illinois
217-244-1962
info@prairienet.org
c/o GSLIS
501 E. Daniel St.
Champaign, IL 61820
Login: visitor
Gopher: gopher.prairienet.org
Modem: 217-255-9000
Telnet: prairienet.org
WWW: http://www.prairienet.org/

INDIANA

HoosierNet—Bloomington
812-349-4638
webmaster@www.bloomington.in.us
303 E. Kirkwood, Bloomington, IN
  47402
Modem: (812) 349-3282
WWW: http://www.bloomington.
  in.us

LOUISIANA

BRAIN-Baton Rouge Area Interactive
  Network, Inc.—Baton Rouge and
  surrounding parishes
Ann McMahon
504-346-0707
anniemac@acm.org
1646 Belmont Ave., Baton Rouge, LA
  70808

Greater New Orleans Free-Net—Nine-
  parish metro New Orleans
504-539-9242
johnv@gnofn.org
1600 Canal St. 527
New Orleans, LA 70112
Login: visitor
Modem: (504) 529-5576
Telnet: gnofn.org
WWW: http://www.gnofn.org

MASSACHUSETTS

UMASSK12—Amherst, Massachusetts
Morton Sternheim
413-545-1908
mms@k12.oit.umass.edu
Login: guest
Modem: 413-572-5583 or
  413-572-5268
Telnet: k12.oit.umass.edu

MICHIGAN

Almont Expression—Almont
George Pratt
810-798-8150
gpratt@expression.org
Login: Visitor
Password: Visitor
Modem: 810-798-8290

Education Central—Mount Pleasant
Hal Crawley
517-774-3975
hcrawley@edcen.ehhs.cmich.edu
Login: visitor
Modem: 517-774-3790
Telnet: edcen.ehhs.cmich.edu

Genesee Free-Net—Flint and Genesee
  counties
Mike Mosher
810-232-3667
mmosher@genesee.freenet.org
P.O. Box 3605, Flint, MI 48502-3605
Login: guest
Gopher: genesee.freenet.org:70
Modem: (810) 232-9905
Telnet: genesee.freenet.org
WWW: http://genesee.freenet.org

Greater Detroit Free-Net—Detroit
Paul Raine
810-574-8549
info@detroit.freenet.org
Login: visitor
Telnet: detroit.freenet.org

Great Lakes Free-Net—Battle Creek
Merritt W. Tumanis
616-961-4166
merritt_tumanis@fc1.glfn.org
Login: visitor
Modem: 616-969-4536
Telnet: fc2.glfn.org

Macatawa Area Free-Net—
  Holland/Zeeland
616-355-1770
Jipping@Macatawa.Org
Macatawa Area Coordinating Council
400 136th Ave., Suite 416
Holland, MI 49424
Modem: 616-355-1083
WWW: http://www.macatawa.org

Walden III—Dickinson county
Tim Sipes
906-774-6081
sipest@walden3.org
424 S. Stephenson Ave.
Iron Mountain, MI 49801
WWW: http://www.walden3.org

MINNESOTA

The River Project—Minneapolis/St.
  Paul and surrounding suburbs
612-331-8575
mtn@mtn.org
125 SE Main St., Minneapolis, MN 55414
Login: Need an account
WWW: http://www.mtn.org

Twin Cities Free-Net—Minneapolis/
  St. Paul metro area
612-379-9144
info@freenet.msp.mn.us
P.O. Box 581338, Minneapolis, MN
  55458-1338
Login: guest
Password: guest
Gopher: host: freenet.msp.mn.us,
  port: 70
Modem: 612/827.2711
Telnet: freenet.msp.mn.us
WWW: http://freenet.msp.mn.us/

MISSOURI

COIN—The Columbia Online
  Information Network—Boone,
  Callaway, Howard
314-642-2398; 816-248-1670; 314-386-
  2646; 314-499-9474
helpdesk@mail.coin.missouri.edu
P.O. Box 1267, Columbia, MO 65205-
  1267
Login: guest
Gopher: gopher.coin.missouri.edu
Modem: (314) 884-7000
Telnet: telnet.coin.missouri.edu
WWW: http://www.coin.missouri.edu

Ozarks Regional Information Online
  Network (ORION)—Southwest
  Missouri
417-837-5050, Ext. 15
helpdesk@mail.orion.org
P.O. Box 760, Springfield, MO 65801
Login: guest
Gopher: gopher://gopher.orion.org
  (not currently being updated)
Modem: (417) 864-6100
Telnet: telnet://telnet.orion.org
WWW: http://www.orion.org

Show-Me Net—Southeast Missouri
Larry Loos
314-243-8141
Loos@mail.mac.cc.mo.us
c/o Riverside Regional Library, 204 S.
  Union, Jackson, MO 63755
Login: Web Access
Modem: Not available yet
Note: May not be operational.

MONTANA

Big Sky Telegraph—Dillon
Frank Odasz
406-683-7338
franko@bigsky.dillon.mt.us
Visitor login: bbs
Modem: 406-683-7680
Telnet: 192.231.192.1

NEW MEXICO

La Plaza Telecommunity—Taos
Patrick Finn
505-758-1836
fax 505-751-1812 (May change)
info@laplaza.taos.nm.us
Login: None available
Modem: 505-758-2345
Gopher: gopher://laplaza.taos.nm.us
Telnet: laplaza.taos.nm.us
WWW: http://www.laplaza.taos.nm.us
La Plaza Telecommunity Foundation
224 Cruz Alta
Taos, NM 87571

Santa Fe Free-Net—Santa Fe
Valentine Riddell
(505) 466-4552
orenda@rt66.com
HC75 Box 141, Galisteo NM 87540

NEW YORK

Buffalo Free-Net—Eight counties of
  Western New York (Allegheny, Erie,
  Cattauragus, Chautauqua, Genessee,
  Niagara, Orleans, and Wyoming)
Dr. Neil Yerkey/Jim Gerland
716-645-3069
bfn@freenet.buffalo.edu
The Buffalo Free-Net Project-State
  University of New York at Buffalo,
  School of Information and Library
  Studies, 381 Baldy Hall, Buffalo, NY
  14260
Login: freeport (to apply for an
  account)
Gopher: freenet.buffalo.edu (May not
  be operational)
Modem: 716-645-3085
Telnet: freenet.buffalo.edu
WWW: http://freenet.buffalo.edu

Capital Region Information Service of
  New York (CRISNY)—Capital region
  in Upstate New York

Norman D. Kurland
518-442-3728
nkurland@crisny.org
www.crisny.albany.edu

Rochester Free-Net, Inc.—Rochester,
  New York, and the Finger Lakes area
Jerry Seward
716-594-5414
jerry@vivanet.com
5 Spicewood Lane, Rochester, New
  York 14624-3717
WWW: http://www.vivanet.com/
  freenet

NORTH CAROLINA

Charlotte's Web—Charlotte and
  vicinity
Steve Snow
shsnow@charweb.org
704-336-8533
c/o Public Library of Charlotte and
  Mecklenburg County
310 N. Tryon St.
Charlotte, NC 28202
Login: webguest
Modem: 704-336-8013
gopher: gopher.charweb.org
Telnet: wilbur.charweb.org
WWW: http://www.charweb.org

RTP net—(previously known as
  Triangle Free-Net) Research Triangle
  Park area including Raleigh,
  Durham, Chapel Hill, and Cary
Judy Hallman
919-962-5277
judy_hallman@unc.edu
Office of Information Technology
310A Wilson Library, UNC-CH
Chapel Hill, NC 27599-3460
Login: freenet
Password:None
Telnet: RTPnet.org
WWW: http://WWW.RTPnet.org

NORTH DAKOTA

SENDIT—Fargo
Gleason Sackman
701-237-8109
sackman@sendit.nodak.edu
Login: bbs
Password: sendit2me
Modem: 701-237-3283
Telnet: sendit.nodak.edu

OHIO

Akron Regional Free-Net—Summit,
  Portage counties
216-643-9145
info@freenet.akron.oh.us
c/o Akron-Summit County Public
  Library
55 S. Main St.
Akron, OH 44326-0001
Login: hit enter until password request
  appears
Password: visitor
Modem: 216/434-ARFN
Telnet: freenet.akron.oh.us

Cleveland Free-Net—Cleveland
Jeff Gumpf
216-368-2982
jag@po.cwru.edu
Visitor login: Select #2 at first menu
Modem: 216-368-3888
Telnet: freenet-in-a.cwru.edu

Dayton Free-Net—Dayton
Patricia Vendt
513-873-4035
pvendt@desire.wright.edu
Login: visitor
Modem: 513-229-4373
Telnet: 130.108.128.174

Greater Columbus Free-Net—Franklin
  and surrounding counties of Ohio
Steve Gordon
614-292-4132
sgordon@freenet.columbus.oh.us
1224 Kinnear Road, Columbus, OH
  43212

Login: Only dial-in guest logins
  allowed—login as guest
Gopher: gopher.freenet.columbus.
  oh.us
Modem: 613-292-7501
Telnet: No guest telnets allowed
www.freenet.columbus.oh.us

Learning Village Cleveland—
  Cleveland
John Kurilec
216-498-4050
jmk@nptn.org
Login: visitor
Modem: 216-498-4070
Telnet: nptn.org

Lorain County Free-Net—Elyria
Thom Gould
1-800-227-7113, Ext. 2451 or 216-277-
  2451
aa003@freenet.lorain.oberlin.edu
Login: guest
Modem: 216-366-9721
Telnet: freenet.lorain.oberlin.edu

Medina County Free-Net—Medina
Gary Linden
216-725-1000, Ext 2550
gfl@freenet.medina.edu
Login: visitor
Modem: 216-723-6732

Richland Free-Net—Mansfield
Ed Rebmann
419-521-3112
earmrcpl@class.org
Login: visitor
Modem: 419-526-0144

SEORF—Athens
Damien O. Bawn
614-662-3211
bawn@oucsace.cs.ohiou.edu
Login: guest
Telnet: seorf.ohiou.edu

TriState Online—SW Ohio, N
  Kentucky, SE Indiana
sysadmin@TSO.Cin.IX.net
P.O. Box 54067, Cincinnati, OH 45254-
  0067
Login: visitor
Modem: (513) 579-1990
Telnet: TSO.Cin.IX.net
WWW: http://WWW.TSO.Cin.IX.net

Youngstown Free-Net—Youngstown
Lou Anschuetz
216-742-3075
lou@yfn.ysu.edu
Login: visitor
Modem: 216-742-3072
Telnet: yfn2.ysu.edu

OREGON

Eugene Free Community Network
  (Oregon Public Networking)—Lane
  county
503-484-1446
sbrenner@efn.org
P.O. Box 1914, Eugene, OR 97440
Login: guest
Gopher: gopher.efn.org
Modem: (503) 687-2996
Telnet: haus.efn.org
www.efn.org

Oregon Public Electronic Network
  (OPEN)—City of Salem/Marion
  county
Ken Phillips
503-588-6355
fax 503-588-6369
kphillips@open.org
690 Ferry St., SE
Salem, OR 97301
WWW: http://www.open.org

Oregon Public Networking—Lane
  county
Penny Cass
503-484-9637
office@efn.org
P.O. Box 1914
Eugene, OR 97440
Login: guest
Gopher: gopher.efn.org
Modem: 503-687-2996
Telnet: efn.org
www.efn.org

PENNSYLVANIA

Chester County InterLink—Chester
  county
Chuck Peters
610-431-2673
director@ccil.org
Chester County InterLink
c/o Chester County Hospital
701 East Marshall Street
West Chester, PA 19380
Login: tourist
Password: tourist
Modem: 610-431-2839
Telnet: locke.ccil.org
WWW: http://www.ccil.org

Hill House Community Access
  Network—Hill District and
  Pittsburgh
Carl Redwood
Chrishelle Thomas—Eugene
412-392-3136
redwood@hillhouse.ckp.edu
1835 Centre Avenue, Pittsburgh, PA
  15219
Modem: Not available yet
Telnet: hillhouse.ckp.edu
WWW: http://hillhouse.ckp.edu/
  hhcan/hhcan.html

RHODE ISLAND

Ocean State Free-Net—Providence
Howard Boksenbaum
401-277-2726
howardbm@dsl.rhilinet.gov
Modem: 401-831-4640
Telnet: 192.207.24.10

TENNESSEE

Jackson Area FreeNet—Jackson
Don Lewis
901-425-2640
dlewis@jackson.freenet.org
Jackson State Community College
2046 North Parkway
Jackson, TN 38301
Login: visitor
Gopher: gopher.jackson.freenet.org
Modem: 901-427-4435
Telnet: jackson.freenet.org
WWW: http://www.jackson.freenet.
org

TEXAS

Austin Free-Net
Sue Beckwith
1711 S. Congress Ave., 3rd Floor
Austin, TX 78704
512-326-9084
sue@austinfree.net
WWW: http://www.austinfree.net/

Rio Grande Free-Net—El Paso
Don Furth
915-775-6077
donf@laguna.epcc.edu
Visitor login: visitor
Modem: 915-775-5600
Telnet: rgfn.epcc.edu

VIRGINIA

Blacksburg Electronic Village—
Montgomery county and the Virginia
Tech community
Cortney Martin
540-231-4423
fax 540-231-7413
bev.office@bev.net
1700 Pratt Dr., Blacksburg, VA 24060-
6361
Gopher: gopher.bev.net
WWW: http://www.bev.net/

Central Virginia's Free-Net—Central
Virginia
Daniel Arkin
804-320-3424
darkin@freenet.vcu.edu
23 Sesame Street
Richmond, VA 23235
Login: visitor
Password: guest
Modem: (804) 828-8694
Telnet: freenet.vcu.edu
WWW: http://freenet.vcu.edu/
cvanet.html
VaPEN—Richmond
Joe Aulino
804-225-2099
jaulino@pen.k12.va.us
Telnet: vdoe386.vak12ed.edu

WASHINGTON

Kitsap Free-Net—Bremerton
Michael Schuyler
206-377-7601
michael@kitsap.lib.wa.us
Modem: 360-698-4737
Telnet: 198.187.135.22

LinkNet—Kitsap county
Michael Schuyler
360-405-9139
michael@linknet.kitsap.lib.wa.us
Kitsap Regional Library
1301 Sylvam Way
Bremerton, WA 98310
Login: guest
Gopher: linknet.kitsap.lib.wa.us/70
Modem: (360) 698-4737

Seattle Community Network—
Seattle
Randy Groves
206-365-4528
info@scn.org
Login: visitor
Modem: 206-386-4140
Telnet: scn.org
WWW: http://www.scn.org/

Tri-Cities Free-Net—SE Washington
Bruce McComb
509-586-6481
sysop@tcfn.org
RECA Foundation
605 S. Olympia, #74
Kennewick, WA 99336
Login: guest
Password: visit
Modem: 509-375-1111
Telnet: tcfn.org

WASHINGTON, DC

WETA/CapAccess—Washington DC
  and vicinity
703-824-7300, fax 703-824-7350
info@weta.capaccess.org
P.O. Box 2626
Washington, DC 20013
Login: guest
Password: visitor
Gopher: gopher.capaccess.org
Modem: 202-785-1523
Telnet: capaccess.org
WWW: http://www.capaccess.org
Note: Upcoming system changes will
  affect modem number.

WISCONSIN

Chippewa Valley Free-Net—Eau
  Claire
Steve Marquardt
715-836-4827
smarquar@uwec.edu
Login: guest
Modem: 715-834-1450
Telnet: cvfn.org

DANEnet—Dane county
Bob Horn
608-262-7730
P.O. Box 5284
Madison, WI 53705
Login: guest
Modem: 608-265-8444
Telnet: danenet.wicip.org
WWW: http://danenet.wicip.org

Omnifest—Milwaukee
Neil A. Trilling
414-229-4041
neil@csd.uwm.edu
Center for Community Computing
P.O. Box 413
Milwaukee, WI 53201
Login: visitor
Gopher: Via Univ of WI-Milwaukee
  gopher
Modem: 414-229-OMNI
Telnet: omnifest.uwm.edu

CANADA

ALBERTA

Calgary Free-Net—Calgary
Shawn Henry
403-220-8914
henry@freenet.calgary.ab.ca
Suite 810
400 Third Avenue, SW
Calgary, Alberta, T2P 4H2
Login: guest
Password: guest
Modem: (403) 282-4075 and (403) 282-
  3707
Telnet: freenet.calgary.ab.ca
WWW: http://freenet.calgary.ab.ca/

BRITISH COLUMBIA

CIAO!—Trail, B.C.
Ken McClean
604-368-2233
kmcclean@ciao.trail.bc.ca
2279 Columbia Ave.
Trail, B.C., V1R 1K7
Login: guest
Modem: 604-368-5764
Telnet: 142.231.5.1

Prince George Free-Net—Prince
  George
Lynda Williams
604-562-9281
lynda@freenet.unbc.edu
210 N. Quinn St.
Prince George, B.C. V2M 3J5
Login: guest
Modem: 604-563-3977
Telnet: freenet.unbc.edu

Victoria Free-Net—Greater Victoria
  region (all toll-free dialing areas
  served by BC TELECOM)
604-727-7057
hq@freenet.victoria.bc.ca
4252 Commerce Circle
Victoria, BC, CANADA V8Z 4M2
Login: guest
Gopher: gopher.freenet.victoria.bc.ca
Modem: 604-479-6500
Telnet: freenet.victoria.bc.ca
WWW: http://www.freenet.victoria.
  bc.ca/vifa.html

NEWFOUNDLAND

St. John's InfoNET—St. John's,
  Newfoundland
Louise McGillis
St. John's InfoNET Association
mcgillis@morgan.ucs.mun.ca
Login: guest
Telnet: infonet.st-johns.nf.ca
WWW: http://www.infonet.
  st-johns.nf.ca
P.O. Box 23222
Churchill Square P.O.
St. John's, Newfoundland, Canada
  A1B 4J9

NOVA SCOTIA

Chebucto Community Net—Halifax
902-494-2449
c/o Dept. Math Stats & CS, Dalhousie
  University, Halifax, Nova Scotia,
  Canada B3H 3J5
Login: guest
Modem: 902-494-8006
Telnet: ccn.cs.dal.ca
WWW: http://www.ccn.cs.dal.ca

Niagara Peninsula Free-Net—Niagara
  region
905-684-7200, Ext 304
bev@freenet.niagara.com
3340 Schmon Parkway, Unit 2
Login: guest
Gopher: freenet.npiec.on.ca
Modem: 905-684-6736
Telnet: 205.211.3.2

ONTARIO

National Capital Free-Net—Ottawa
David Sutherland
613-788-2600, Ext 3701
aa001@freenet.carleton.ca
Visitor login: guest
Modem: 613-564-3600
Telnet: freenet.carleton.ca

Prince Edward County Community
  Development Corporation
Randy Ellis
613-476-7901
fax 613-476-7235
peccdc@loyalistc.on.ca
WWW: http://www.reach.net
43 Main St., P.O. Box 2559
Picton, Ontario, Canada K0K 2T0

Toronto Free-Net—Toronto
Registrar 416-979-9242
registrar@freenet.toronto.on.ca
c/o Ryerson Polytechnical University
  Library
350 Victoria Street, Suite #766
Toronto, Ontario, Canada M5B 2K3
Login: Guest
Modem: 416-780-2010
Telnet: freenet.toronto.on.ca

SASKATCHEWAN

Saskatoon Free-Net—Saskatoon,
  Saskatchewan
306-374-8288
helpdesk@sfn.saskatoon.sk.ca
Box 339, RPO University
Saskatoon, SK
S7N 4J8
Login: guest
Modem: 306-946-3700
Telnet: freenet.sfn.saskatoon.sk.ca
WWW: http://www.sfn.saskatoon.
  sk.ca/

AROUND THE WORLD

AUSTRALIA

Victoria's Network: VICNET—
  Victoria, Australia
Adrian Bates
OZ-03-9669 9714
adrianb@vicnet.net.au
State Library of Victoria
328 Swanston Street
Victoria 3000, Australia
Login: No guest yet but free access in
  some public libraries
Modem: (03) 9669 9714
Telnet: not yet
WWW: http://www.vicnet.net.au

AUSTRIA

Public Netbase
WWW: http://www.t0.or.at/

FINLAND

Free-Net Finland—Finland's K-12
  school (whole nation)
Heikki Korpinen
358-0-4514007
korpinen@freenet.hut.fi
Free-Net Finland, Helsinki
University of Technology
02150 Espoo
Finland, Europe
Login: visitor
Gopher: gopher.freenet.hut.fi
Modem: N/A (by Finnish Telecom)
Telnet: freenet.hut.fi
WWW: http://www.freenet.hut.fi/

GERMANY

Bayreuth Free-Net—Bayreuth
Wolfgang Kiessling
0921/553134
Wolfgang.Kiessling@Uni-Bayreuth.de
Telnet: freenet.uni-bayreuth.de

Bremer InfoThek—Bremen
Heiderose Wagner
49-421-218-2674
rose@informatik.uni-bremen.de
Universitaet Bremen,
Forschungsgruppe
  Telekommunikation
Bibliothekstrasse 1
28359 Bremen, Germany
WWW: http://infothek.informatik.
  uni-bremen.de

Free-Net Erlangen-Nuernburg—
  Erlangen
Dr. Walter F. Kugemann
+49-9131-85-4735
Walter.Kugemann@fim.uni-erlangen.de
Visitor login: gast
Modem: +49-9131-85-8111
Telnet: 131.188.192.11

GREAT BRITAIN

Milton Keynes Community Network—
Milton Keynes (55 miles north of
London)
44 (0)1908 652183
P.G.Davis@open.ac.uk
IET.Open University.Walton
Hall.Milton Keynes.Bucks.MK7
6AA.UK
Modem: 44 (0)1908 271188
Telnet: 137.108.103.22 with FC Client
http://www-emrg.open.ac.uk/mkcn/
mkcn1.html

HUNGARY

Koz-Hely Project
WWW: http://caesar.elte.hu/Koz-
Hely/index.html (in English)

ITALY

RCM—Rete Civica Milanese
+39 2 55006332
fiorella_de_cindio@rcm.dsi.unimi.it
MILANO, Italy
Login: curioso
Modem: +39 2 55182133
Telnet: rcme.usr.dsi.unimi.it 3003
WWW: http://wrcm.usr.dsi.unimi.it

Rete Civica di VENEZIA—"Milione"
(Multi Internet LInked Open
NEtwork)
City, State, Country: VENEZIA, Italy
martin@unive.it ;
luigi@cidoc.iuav.unive.it
WWW: http://alexcube.iuav.unive.it/
milione/milione.html

Rete Civica di ROMA
ROMA, Italy
HTML url: WWW: http://www.
comune.roma.it/COMUNE

Rete Civica di BOLOGNA—Progetto
IPERBOLE
(Internet PER BOlogna e l'Emilia-
Romagna)
+39 51 203184
Bologna, Italy
WWW: http://www.bologna.
nettuno.it/bologna and
http://www.comune.bologna.it
(Bologna was the first Italian city with
a Civic Net.)

Rete Civica di TORINO
Torino, Italy
WWW: http://www.comune.torino.it

Rete Civica di LIVORNO
LIVORNO, Italy
WWW: http://www.comune.livorno.it

Rete Civica di LUCCA
LIVORNO, Italy
WWW: http://www.lunet.it/
SERVIZI/RETE_CIVICA/hmecitt.htm
(This civic net is maintained by an
Internet provider, not by the
community.)

Rete Civica di PISA
PISA, Italy
WWW: http://www.cpr.it/civ_txt/
pisa.html

Rete Civica di CUNEO
CUNEO, Italy
WWW: http://www.cuneo.alpcom.it
(This civic net is maintained by an
Internet provider, not by the
community.)

ICELAND

Reykjavik Homepage
http://www.rvk.is/www/enska

NETHERLANDS

XS4ALL—Amsterdam
WWW: http://www.dds.nl/

NEW ZEALAND

Wellington Citynet—Wellington
Richard Naylor
+64-4-801-3303
rich@tosh.wcc.govt.nz
Modem: +64-4-801-3060
Telnet: kosmos.wcc.govt.nz

RUSSIA

St. Petersburg
WWW: http://www.spb.su/index.
  html

SWEDEN

Swedish East Coast FreeNet
WWW: http://www.lp.se/gerrie-
  warner/freenet.htm

UKRAINE

Kyiv FreeNet
Tel: 228-63-93
webmaster@freenet.kiev.ua
WWW: http://freelunch.freenet.
  kiev.ua/Project/freehome.html
1 Klovskii Uzviz, Kyiv, 252010

Appendix D

Seattle Community Network Documents

A community-network organization will need to produce many different kinds of documents. These include legal documents, marketing brochures, proposals, registration forms, newsletters, and press releases, just to name a few. Space does not permit a comprehensive listing of documents, so just a few examples (all from the Seattle Community Network project) have been included. There are more examples on the *New Community Networks* Web Site (see Appendix B), including pointers to documents from other community networks. (The National Capital Free-Net has many good examples.) The SCN principles and the SCN disclaimer have been reproduced at other places in this book and have not been included here.

Welcome to the Seattle Community Network

Seattle Community Network is a free, public computer network run by volunteers. Founded by the Seattle chapter of Computer Professionals for Social Responsibility, SCN went online serving the Greater Seattle area in the Spring of 1994.

SCN is committed to providing equal access to information for all users, and thanks to the support of the Seattle Public Library and a number of other generous benefactors, we are able to offer accounts to everyone. Please feel free to request registration materials.

SCN uses the Freeport menu software. You can browse with your Web browser. If you also want to contribute to the forums, the bulletin boards within the SCN system, you will need to telnet to scn.org, and be a registered user.

SCN Freeport Menus

SCN Information Providers' Homepages

SCN Links to Other Free-nets and Community Resources

SCN's Internet Free Speech Page

Contributing to Seattle Community Network

Comments? Volunteers? If your browser has 'mailto' capability, you can click here—or send mail to webadm@scn.org.
FAQ I Registration I SCN Policy I Telnet to SCN

Figure D.1   Seattle Community Network Home Page

Seattle Community Network
Frequently Asked Questions (FAQ) List

e-mail: help@scn.org   voice-mail: (206) 365-4528
Revision: October 4, 1995

Q. What is the Seattle Community Network (SCN)?

A. Seattle Community Network is a free-access, community information system (Free-Net) for the greater Seattle area. SCN is a project of the Seattle chapter of Computer Professionals for Social Responsibility (CPSR).

Q. What's a Free-Net?

A. Free-Net systems are community network systems that are affiliated with the National Public Telecomputing Network (NPTN). These systems are now on-line, actively serving millions of users in about three dozen communities worldwide. There are "Free-Net" systems in North America, Iceland, Germany, Finland, Norway, Australia, and elsewhere. For more information about Free-Nets, contact: info@nptn.org.

Q. How does one log-on to the system?

A. You can access SCN one of seven ways:

1. Dial-up SCN phone lines: (206) 386-4199.

2. Dial-up Seattle Public Library system: (206) 386-4140. Then type "visitor" at the first log-in prompt.

3. Dial-up King County Library system: Seattle: (206) 382-2116, Covington: (206) 630-2898, Issaquah: (206) 313-9159.

4. Dial-up (PAN) Seattle's Public Access Network: (206) 233-7100. SCN can be accessed from the Community, Social, Health menu. You will need to be a registered PAN user for this access to work.

5. Internet: Telnet to scn.org.

6. In-library access from Internet-capable patron terminals in the Seattle Public Library or the King County Public Library, from the Internet menu page.

7. From a Web browser: http://www.scn.org.

Q. What communication settings work for dial-up access?

A. Use 300–14.4K bits per second (bps), no parity, 8 data bits, one stop bit (2400-8-N-1).

Q. Is TDD dial-up access available?

A. Not yet. Please send e-mail to let us know if TDD access would be helpful to you or someone you know.

Q. How much will using SCN cost me?

A. There are no charges to use this system. However, since SCN costs money to run, donations are encouraged.

Q. Why do I want to be a registered user?

A. Everybody can use SCN. However, if you want to receive electronic mail (e-mail), or contribute to on-line discussion groups, we need to know how to contact you; therefore, you need to register. If you don't register, you are always welcome to use the network as a visitor and read all the information that is available.

Q. How do I become a registered user right now?

A. You can request a registration packet on-line as a visitor to SCN. You will be registered after you read the Policy Statement, Disclaimer, and Code of Etiquette, and return the signed user agreement. If you cannot log-in as a visitor to enter your contact information on-line, call (206) 365-4528 and leave your name and address to request a registration packet.

Q. Will SCN sell or release my name and address to any other organization?

A. No. It is against the policy of the Seattle Community Network to release the registered-user list to any other organization.

Q. Is SCN run by the Seattle Public Library?

A. No. The Seattle Public Library may provide information or facilitate discussion on topics such as public process through the Seattle Community Network. The Library is interested in exploring different means for bringing information to the community. SCN and SPL have signed a working agreement through November 1996.

Q. What is the relationship of SCN to the City of Seattle Public Access Network (PAN) project?

A. PAN is a project initiated by Seattle's Department of Administrative Services. The PAN project is designed to provide access to government information. We at SCN are very interested in working closely with the city to make these capabilities widely available.

Q. What hardware is SCN using?

A. We currently are using a SUN SPARC 5 and SUN SPARC SLC with 3.5 GB of disk storage, both running SUNOS 4.1.3.

Q. What software are you using?

A. We are running the FreePort community networking software that is used in many Free-Net sites around the world. It was written by a team at Case Western Reserve University in Cleveland, Ohio.

Q. What access to the Internet do you provide?

A. SCN provides Internet electronic mail (e-mail) services to all registered users, and access to the World Wide Web (WWW) via Lynx.

Q. When can I use e-mail?

A. You can use e-mail as soon as you become a registered user (see above).

Q. What volunteer opportunities are available?

A. We're glad you asked that question! Please take a moment to read the Volunteers section under Visitors and Information on SCN (go vols).

Q. My organization would like to provide information to the system. How can we make this happen?

A. Send e-mail to Nancy Kunitsugu, our SCN information-provider focal point (nancyk@scn.org) and tell us about your organization and the person we should contact. You may also call (206) 365-4528 and leave a voice message.

Q. We'd like to use this system but we don't have access to computers. What should we do?

A. You can use SCN in any Seattle Public Library branch. SCN is on menus on at least one patron terminal at every Seattle Public Library branch. We are also available in all the King County Library System branches. Also, if you are part of a nonprofit group that could benefit from SCN access and have no computers, let us know—we may be able to help.

Q. I may have some hardware to donate. What does SCN need?

A. We need async terminals, large capacity SCSI disk drives (>500 MB), memory (16MB of 60ns SIMMS—for SUN SPARC or 3/486), modems (2400—14.4kbps), recent technology Unix machines.

We also need donations of computers, printers, and modems for community organizations that want to be information providers. If you have equipment to donate, please send e-mail to Kevin Higgins (wheels@scn.org), or call (206) 365-4528 to leave a message.

Q. I'd like to donate money to SCN. Is my contribution tax-deductible?

A. Yes! As Free-Net founder, Tom Grundner, said, "Free-Nets are inexpensive but they aren't free." We rely on donations from individuals and businesses. A donation of any size is welcome. SCN is a project of the Seattle chapter of Computer Professionals for Social Responsibility (CPSR), a tax-exempt, educational, 501(c)(3) organization; thus all contributions are tax-deductible.

Q. Do you have public project meetings? Where and when are they held?

A. SCN volunteers meet monthly on the fourth Wednesday at 7:00 P.M. We meet in the basement-level meeting room of the Seattle Public Library, University branch (on the corner of Roosevelt Way NE at NE 50th St., in the University district of Seattle). Please enter by the south side door, on the 50th St. side of the building.

Q. How can I contact people at SCN?

A.

General Info	help@scn.org	Help, Info, Bug reports
Nancy Kunitsugu	nancyk@scn.org	Services
Bob Mascott	mascott@scn.org	Fundraising, Hardware/Software
Aki Namioka	aki@scn.org	Policy
Kevin Higgins	wheels@scn.org	Outreach, Equipment donations

Seattle Community Network Policy Statement

Revision: June 21, 1994

I. GUIDELINES

SCN is committed to the following guidelines for network users:

+ FREE SPEECH
SCN is committed to maintaining free speech rights for all participants.

+ FREE ACCESS
SCN is committed to providing free access to information for the community at large.

+ RIGHT TO PRIVACY
SCN is committed to maintaining the privacy of individuals.

+ DUE PROCESS
SCN is committed to maintaining the right to due process of individual users of the network.

SCN does not and will not have any agreements with individuals or organizations that require restrictions to its policies, the code of etiquette, or the disclaimer.

SCN will not sell or give its list of registered users to other organizations. Computer Professionals for Social Responsibility, Seattle chapter (CPSR/Seattle), the nonprofit organization providing SCN, may contact users, via U.S. Mail, for fundraising purposes. If SCN becomes independent of CPSR/Seattle, CPSR will respect the new organization's nondistribution policy.

SCN will not disclose any information about individual users without a court mandate and approval of the governing board. Before disclosing information we will attempt to notify affected users.

II. USER REGISTRATION

SCN has both nonregistered and registered users.

+ NONREGISTERED USER
As a nonregistered user, you can browse freely on the network. If you want to have additional network privileges, you need to become a registered user.

+ REGISTERED USER
As a registered user, you can browse anywhere in the network and have access to all its materials and services. You can post your own materials and information, contribute to on-line discussions, and send and receive electronic mail (e-mail).

To become a registered user:

1. Complete a registration form, which includes the Code of Etiquette.
2. Read and agree to follow the Seattle Community Network Policy Statement and the Code of Etiquette.
3. Read and acknowledge your understanding of the Seattle Community Network "Disclaimer."

Registered user accounts are for individuals only. Organizations must also sign up under an individual user account.

III. SERVICES

SCN offers the following services for network users:

+ INFORMATION ACCESS
All information on SCN is private, except information published in forums and other public areas.

+ FORUMS
Definition: A forum is a "place" on the network devoted to the interactive discussion of a specific topic. All users can read and registered users can post messages that fit the stated purpose of the forum.

SCN does not support or allow exclusionary forums.

SCN supports community and open access to information.

Registered users may request the creation of a new forum.

Active forums will be kept on the network. Inactive forums will be deleted after a period of time set by the governing board.

A description of the purpose and nature of each forum and its criteria for message posting can be found on the network.

If you have a complaint about a forum, you can petition the governing board to investigate your complaint and the conduct of the forum.

There are two types of forums: moderated and unmoderated.

> *Moderated forums*
> Messages to moderated forums are reviewed by a person, or group of people, to determine if they are in keeping with the stated theme and purpose of the forum. Moderators have the right to reject your message and not allow it to be posted.

Unmoderated forums

Messages to unmoderated forums are not reviewed prior to posting.

+ INFORMATION PUBLICATION

Definition: Information publication is a service allowing information providers to post material for all users to read. Information providers are users or associations of users, including businesses and organizations. Information providers communicate information through a designated individual user or users.

+ CLASSIFIED ADS

If you are a registered user, you can post classified ads in the classifieds area. Ads are limited to a certain number of words and can be posted for a limited period of time. Businesses and organizations must identify themselves as such.

+ ELECTRONIC MAIL (e-mail)

Electronic mail (e-mail) is a service to facilitate private communication between two or more people.

SCN supports e-mail distribution lists for groups of users who wish to send messages to a select set of people.

Unsolicited advertising via e-mail is not permitted on SCN. This rule prohibits both commercial and nonprofit advertisements or requests.

+ INFORMATION "FILTER"

If you are a registered user, you can use a "filter" facility provided by the network to screen out unwanted postings or mail.

IV. GOVERNANCE

Until such time as by-laws have been written, the SCN governing board will consist of the members of the Coordinating Council.

The Coordinating Council is responsible for maintaining policy documents (e.g., Code of Etiquette, Disclaimer) and settling disputes.

Known violations of the Code of Etiquette will result in warnings from the governing board and may lead to revocation of registered status for an indefinite amount of time. Any warnings or revocations can be appealed to the governing board. Governing board decisions are final. Of course, individuals can still use the system as nonregistered users.

If an individual would like to challenge any items in the Code of Etiquette, the governing board will listen to the challenge and make a decision.

Users have the right to appeal any decision made by the governing board.

Appendix E

Community-Network Technological Components

SOFTWARE

Community Networking

Community Information Exchange, Inc. (CIX)
info@ix.net
513-321-7463
Cincinnati, OH
WWW: http://www.ix.net/cix

FreePort
Many Free-Net systems use the FreePort software, which is available from Case Western University, Cleveland, for $850 for NPTN affiliates. There is fairly general agreement that this software—as it exists—is inadequate. Many community networks use FreePort software that has been modified with code developed by the National Capital Free-Net organization in Ottawa. Contact NPTN for more information.

Metasystems Design Group, Inc.
703-243-6622
fax 703-841-9798
info@tmn.com
WWW: http://www.tmn.com/
2000 North 15th Street, Suite 103
Arlington, VA 22201

InterLink (Also see Chester County [Pennsylvania] Interlink in Appendix C)
Eric S. Raymond
esr@locke.ccil.org
WWW: http://www.ccil.org/~esr/home.html

Bulletin-Board Systems

FirstClass
SoftArc, Inc.
905-415-7000
sales@softarc.com
100 Allstate Parkway
Markham, Ontario, Canada

Galacticomm
The Major BBS, Worldgroup
(954) 583-5990
sales: (800) 328-1128
fax: (954) 583-7846
online Service: (954) 583-7808
WWW: http://www.gcomm.com
sales@gcomm.com
4101 SW 47th Ave., Suite 101
Ft. Lauderdale, FL 33314

World Wide Web Browsers

Browser	Platform	FTP Site	Directory Location
Lynx	VT100	ftp2.cc.ukans.edu	/pub/WWW/lynx
	DOS		/pub/WWW/DosLynx
Cello	DOS, Windows	fatty.law.cornell.edu	/pub/LII/Cello
Mosaic	DOS, Windows	ftp.ncsa.uiuc.edu	/Web/Mosaic/Windows
	Macintosh		/Web/Mosaic/Mac
	X Windows		/Web/Mosaic/Unix
MacWeb	Macintosh	bitsy.mit.edu	/pub/mac/web/macweb
WinWeb	MS-Windows		/pub/dos/web/winweb
Netscape	MS-Win, Mac	ftp.netscape.com	/netscape1.1
Web Explorer	OS/2	ftp.ibm.net	/pub/WebExplorer

About Java
http://www.javasoft.com/about.html

The HotJava Browser
http://www.javasoft.com/hotjava.html

Shareware, Public Domain, or Copyleft Software

GNU Software
Send mail to info-gnu-request@prep.ai.mit.edu.

I-COMM (Graphical Browser For Shell, VAX, and FreeNet Account)
icomm@talentcom.com
WWW: http://www.talentcom.com/icomm.htm

Linux Archive
WWW: http://sunsite.unc.edu/pub/Linux/welcome.html

Linux Journal Web Site
WWW: http://www.ssc.com/

MUD Software
Essentially all MUD server software is freely available for FTP, although it is not technically in the public domain; usually the authors retain a copyright. For example, here's a URL for the latest release of the LambdaMOO server software:

  ftp://ftp.parc.xerox.com/pub/MOO/LambdaMOO.tar.Z

MUD Resources
WWW: http://www.cis.upenn.edu/~lwl/mres/mfaq.html

DELIVERY CHANNELS

CableLabs, Inc.
WWW:http://www.cablelabs.com/

Internet Service Providers
WWW:http://www.yahoo.com/Business_and_Economy/Companies/
  Internet_Service_Providers/Internet_Access_Providers/Regional/

@Home Home Page (TCI and Kleiner/Perkins/Caulfield collaboration)
WWW:http://www.home.net

The Glenview/Northbrook Community Model
WWW:http://www.ncook.k12.il.us/

Papers from MIT (both by S. E. Gillett)
WWW:http://www.tns.lcs.mit.edu/publications/
  1. Connecting Homes to the Internet: An Engineering Cost Model of Cable vs. ISDN
  2. Public Policies to Encourage Cable and ISDN Internet Access

Wireless Technologies and the National Information Infrastructure
WWW: http://otabbs.ota.gov/T218

OTHER SOFTWARE

eVote: Frontier Systems
415-493-3631
e-mail: eVote@netcom.com
HyperMail
WWW: http://www.eit.com/software/hypermail/hypermail.html
3790 El Camino Real, #147
Palo Alto, CA 94306

Safe-Tcl Specifications (Documentation, working implementation, and examples)
WWW: ftp://ftp.fv.com/pub/code/other/safe-tcl.tar

Safe-Tcl Overview Paper
ftp://ftp.fv.com/pub/nsb/safe-tcl-ulpaa-94.{txt,ps}

Safe-Tcl Distribution List
Send mail to safe-tcl-request@cs.utk.edu.

World Wide Web Robots, Wanderers, and Spiders
WWW:http://info.webcrawler.com/mak/projects/robots/robots.html

Appendix F

Notes on Community-Wide Projects

It is not enough for a handful of experts to attempt the solution of a problem, to solve it and then to apply it. The restriction of knowledge to an elite group destroys the spirit of society and leads to its intellectual impoverishment.

Albert Einstein

PARTICIPATORY ACTION RESEARCH

Community networks provide important areas of research for traditional academic research (see Chapter 11), but research need not be confined to universities. Community members themselves can propose and conduct meaningful research that community networks can help support in many ways.

Some social scientists apparently feel compelled to squeeze the relevance *out* of their discipline by attempting to emulate their colleagues in the "hard sciences" like physics and chemistry who generally enjoy greater funding levels. Although social scientists do not brand their enterprise as *irrelevant*, there is often very little relationship between social *science* and social *action* and many social scientists feel that this relationship must be explored and strengthened. William Foote Whyte, an eminent sociologist who wrote the influential *Street Corner Society* (1993), notes that, "It is important, both for the advancement of science and for the improvement of human welfare, to devise strategies in which research and action are closely linked."

Participatory Action Research (PAR) is an approach to scientific inquiry in which the scientific method is employed to conduct research while *simultaneously* bringing about desired social change, thus *linking* research and activism (Whyte, 1991). Each word in PAR's title carries an important meaning. "Participatory" implies that the people affected have a critical role in each phase of the process; "action" implies that *action* (as opposed to passive inquiry alone) is both desired and necessary; while "research" implies that research is conducted, hypotheses posed, experiments planned and conducted, and—most importantly—learning occurs.

PAR differs from "normal science" in several important ways. For one thing, PAR advocates stress that the dictates of "standard science" such as repeatability, control variables, and closed-world assumptions are largely irrelevant in real-world situations involving people. Whereas a lump of clay may act like a lump of clay year-in and year-out, knowledge about the beliefs and actions of people and communities is far less static. Findings, for example, that are related to current community networks may not be applicable to future community networks. Findings relevant in Seattle might not apply to situations in San Diego, Tokyo, Little Rock, or Johannesburg. Furthermore, PAR—as distinct from "normal science"—imposes less orthodoxy on its practitioners. According to Whyte, Greenwood, and Lazes (1991), "The complexity of the world around us demands the deployment of a variety of techniques and strong intellectual and methodological discipline, not a commitment to the hegemony of a single research modality." Thus PAR techniques are adaptable to new developments and new contexts, making it at once liberating and challenging.

PAR is a hybrid methodology in which "research" (basically, a systematic approach to learning) is coupled with the objective of improving a social situation or problem. The nursing community maintains, for example, both perspectives. Society needs nursing to attain and maintain health. At the same time, the nursing community needs to continually improve its perspective, approach, techniques, and store of knowledge. If nurses only ministered—and neglected research—their expertise and usefulness would stagnate over time. On the other hand, if nurses only conducted research and ignored their everyday business, people who depend on nursing would suffer. Similar arguments can be made in the context of community networks. For example, it is important to host on-line political discussions between community members using community networks. At the same time, however, it is worthwhile to explore ways in which the quality and effectiveness of the discourse can be improved over time.

It is important that community members actively participate in the research process. Besides having a stake in the results of the research, participants offer critical insight not available elsewhere. In Whyte's words, "We always encounter one or more individuals who are especially knowledgeable, insightful, and perceptive regarding the dynamics of their organization or community" (1991). Since users are full partners in PAR, this approach fosters community involvement in community-network development.

Richard Baskerville and Trevor Wood-Harper (1993) describe PAR as a circular process (Fig. F.1). The process consists of several steps in which both consultant and client work together to diagnose, plan and take action, evaluate results, determine what was learned, and then start again with new or revised diagnoses. The efforts of Sustainable Seattle (described in the next section) illustrate how a community group can use these concepts.

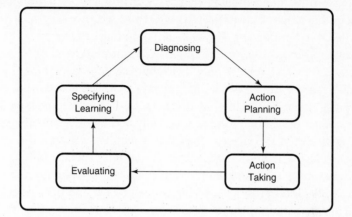

Figure F.1   The Participatory Action Research Cycle [after Baskerville and Wood-Harper]

SUSTAINABLE SEATTLE: COMMUNITY PAR

We view the process and product as interwoven and equally valuable. Part of our task is to practice and develop the skills of civic democracy and volunteer participation.

Richard Conlin, Sustainable Seattle co-founder

In 1991, following a conference hosted by the Global Tomorrow Coalition, a group of social activists in Seattle launched an ambitious multiyear project to develop a community network and civic forum centering around the idea of sustainability. Though many people today view sustainability as largely an environmental paradigm, it is one that can capture the long-term cultural, economic, civic, and educational health and vitality of a region as well. Because sustainability is a complex term and difficult to define and comprehend, the first goal was the development of a set of "critical indicators of sustainability" that would assist in defining the term and defining Seattle's current status. Since that time the project has matured into a community-wide program divided evenly into research and community action. One commendable aspect of their effort has been the patient, evolving, consensus-driven manner in which the project has taken shape and unfolded over time without being driven by set agendas.

Using Indicators of Sustainability

When the project was launched, the "indicators of sustainability" were designed to form its intellectual as well as motivational foundation. *Indicators* are measurable values that accurately reflect and coalesce several factors that are deemed to be important. The selection of indicators as core constructs of the endeavor demonstrates the founders' commitment to a long-term rather than a quick-fix effort, for it is only by examining how the values of the indicators change over time that an understanding of trends can arise. Examining changes over time may also bring to light relationships *between* indicators. Two indicators, for example, may actually bear inverse relationships to each other. If this were the case, it would be more difficult to use those particular variables to undergird the notion of sustainability.

When people in the community identify indicators that are important to them, the indicators are more liable to carry personal and operational meaning than when social scientists in an ivory tower identify theoretical constructs that are significant only to an academic community. The indicators aren't meant to be abstract values whose chief virtue is their measurability or their relationship to other abstract measurable values. The indicators are carefully chosen to reflect activity within a community that is desired or not desired by that community. Furthermore, because the community identified the indicators, there is a feeling of ownership and confidence in them.

Forty indicators from four areas—environment, population and resources, economy, and culture and society—were initially selected. In order for these indicators to be useful, they must pass several tests. The first test is whether they represent the general trend that they are intended to. For example, Sustainable Seattle wanted to assess overall environmental quality and wanted to capture that assessment with a small number of indicators. The population of wild salmon was eventually chosen as a useful indicator. The number of returning salmon is directly influenced by such factors as forestry practices, development patterns, and water quality.

The second test is whether the indicator *can* be measured accurately at all, and if so, whether the data can be easily obtained. Since the number of volunteers was relatively small, Sustainable Seattle determined that indicators whose values could be derived from existing reliable data were to be given priority over indicators whose values could not be attained readily. Additionally, indicators for which historical as well as current data exist are more useful in terms of identifying trends. Although sending teams of activists out into the community, like China's "barefoot doctors," to gather data may be undertaken in the future (and would make a very good focus for a television or newspaper story), Sustainable Seattle is not currently doing that.

Activists must think carefully about how to gather the data, how big the sample should be, how to avoid biased samples, and other aspects of scientific research. The pursuit is also inherently educational, and community goals and values motivate the learning. In other words, the educational community program is developed based on an actual community need, not from love of learning per se.

Disseminating Information

The description of Sustainable Seattle's indicators was published in a simple form and made available for a nominal charge. Each indicator along with its data was shown graphically on a separate page. For example, the data on the "wild salmon population" indicator are shown in Fig. F.2. Realizing that the indicators are not independent, the group also illustrated how the indicators related to each other (Fig. F.3). The document depicting the indicators, their

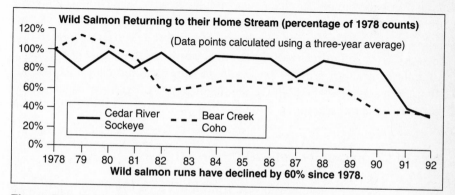

Figure F.2   Critical Indicator: Wild Salmon Population

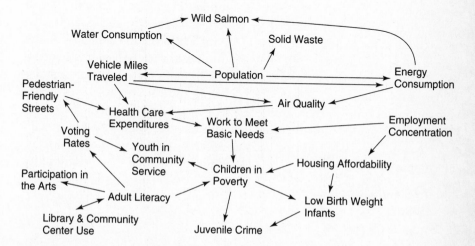

Figure F.3   Linkages Between Critical Indicators

values and relationships, has been quite popular and over 1000 copies of the document were distributed within just a few months of its release. A second printing was required and the Local Agenda 21 organization in the UK reprinted the document for distribution there.

Positive Change in the Community

While Sustainable Seattle's report on Seattle's critical indicators presents a useful snapshot of several important aspects on the community's agenda, it does not by itself create a sustainable society. According to their newsletter (Sustainable Seattle, 1994), ". . . understanding trends in our community is only the first step in the journey towards sustainability. The next step is to *change* the community." To that end, Sustainable Seattle initiated a Communities Outreach Project "to create measurable improvements in the behaviors and practices that drive the indicators, both on large and small scales, as a result of homes and organizations changing their behavior in response to this project." Their ambitious goal "is to enable and inspire people in the many different communities in greater Seattle to transform the values of sustainability into actions that will move Seattle, the region, and the planet towards long-term cultural, economic, and environmental health and vitality."

Role of a Community Network

People from Sustainable Seattle and from the Seattle Community Network have been exploring ways to use SCN in their indicators project. In early 1994, Sustainable Seattle put its "Sustainability Data Base" and the indicators document on-line using the Seattle Community Network. In mid-1994, a moderated forum was initiated in which sustainability issues were discussed. Sustainable Seattle also has made their information available on the World Wide Web and uses e-mail to communicate with people in other sustainability projects around the world in planning a conference on sustainability and computer networks. A critical indicators project provides substantial leverage of community resources. A project at a university which identified, measured, and analyzed 20 indicators and used a staff of, say, 20 people would be a large and expensive project. A critical indicators project is, by comparison, quite modest and decentralized, and one that a community network could help hold together.

NEW COMMUNITY SOCIAL CONTRACTS

> *We the people...*
>
> Opening words of the Constitution of the United States

Jean-Jacques Rousseau's book, "Of the Social Contract" (1984), first published in 1762, was intended to develop the basic principles of a free society. In the book Rousseau championed many now-accepted views, such as universal education. The basic notion of his book, of course, is the idea of the "social contract," the implicit and explicit agreements that people make among themselves that bind society into a cohesive whole.

Ed Schwartz, a long-time community activist from Philadelphia, Pennsylvania, has developed a fascinating program for revitalizing communities using Rousseau's insight as the foundation. Schwartz heads up the Institute for the Study of Civic Values which initiated the Social Contract Project in 1993. The project arose from Schwartz's observations that there were three necessary "ingredients" that communities need to help reverse the decline in community and civic values.

> *We need a renewed understanding that our civic values—the principles articulated in the Declaration of Independence, the Constitution, and the Bill of Rights—define the values that we share and provide a powerful framework for promoting cooperation among our people.*
>
> *We need a procedure for relating civic values to contemporary problems that can be used by community organizations throughout the country in establishing their own goals.*
>
> *We need a process that defines the mutual responsibility of individuals, business, and government to achieve the goals that we hope to achieve for ourselves and the country.*

The wisdom of Schwartz's approach is the use of the "social contract" idea as an explicit method by which to negotiate goals among a truly diverse group of people and use those goals to bring about social change in the community. The idea of a "contract" or pact between groups of people is simple but compelling. And the contract captures the spirit of cooperation and dedication for the greater good in a form that can be shared by the whole community.

The Queen Village neighborhood in South Philadelphia was the first community to work with the Institute using this model. Initially, representatives from a wide range of groups—leaders of civic groups, business representatives, homeowners, tenants, and residents of a large public housing development—were selected. These representatives then participated in a social contract leadership seminar (the "procedure" alluded to in the quotation above) facilitated by the Institute. The length of the seminars varies based upon several factors including the number of participants and the complexity of the neighborhood's concerns. The result of this phase is a draft "social contract," a written document (the "process" from the above quotation) which the key groups of people have agreed to support. The contract (reprinted in full below in Figure F.4) is consciously modeled after the Preamble to the Constitution of the United States. Since the Preamble describes who constitutes "the people," how they can "promote the general welfare," and what is "a more perfect union," it guides participants in a natural way into considering these key questions in their own communities.

Although the Queen City effort does not currently use a community network, there are many ways in which a community network could help the project. The social contract itself, for example, could be put on-line, where community members could refer to it. Electronic forums could be started on all relevant aspects of the contract. Additionally, any aspect of the contract that had an action component could use electronic support. Notices of the "job readiness workshops" (in point three, the economic opportunity section) could go out electronically in addition to more traditional means, for example. A project coordinator working on point four could use the commu-

---

We the people of Queen Village—homeowners, tenants, residents of Southwark Plaza, and others who serve the Queen Village neighborhood between the River and 6th Street from Lombard Street to Washington Avenue—endorse and pledge to implement the following social contract among all those with responsibility "to promote the general welfare" of the neighborhood:

To Preserve Neighborhood Security:

We will work to establish an ongoing partnership with law enforcement authorities to eliminate drug dealing, public drinking, and other behavior destructive to the neighborhood from all parts of Queen Village. As part of this effort, we will work to preserve the South Street mini-station and to determine the best strategy for full staffing of the Southwark mini-station. Citizen groups and the police will work together to achieve effective community participation in neighborhood anti-crime efforts.

To Promote the Physical Revitalization of Queen Village:

1. We will work together to insure that all homeowners, landlords, tenants, and the Philadelphia Housing Authority maintain their properties and respect one another's rights as neighbors.
2. We join with the Southwark Tenants' Council in demanding enforcement of a lease with the same standards of rent payment, maintenance, and security that tenants and homeowners throughout the neighborhood are expected to uphold. We support the enforcement of the Southwark Tenants' Council Good Neighbor Policy.
3. We will work to initiate a comprehensive plan for securing full occupancy of all vacant residential and commercial buildings within the community.

To Improve the Appearance of Queen Village:

1. We will work with the South Street and 4th Street Business Associations to end trash dumping on the neighborhood's major commercial corridors.
2. We will cooperate fully with the City's Clean Blocks Program and Recycling Programs.
3. We will work with the volunteer organizations which maintain the parks, open spaces, and street trees.

To "Secure the Blessings of Liberty"
to Young People in the Neighborhood:

1. We will work in partnership with the schools serving Queen Village to insure quality education for our children. The schools will work with the community to preserve the highest standards of educational performance. All organizations serving Queen Village will promote parent involvement in Home and School Councils and recruit tutors and mentors to assist the students.

2. We will work to expand indoor recreation through the Boys' and Girls' Club and to extend scholarships to neighborhood young people to participate in the summer camp sponsored by United Communities of South Philadelphia.

(Continued)

3. We will seek participation of area young people and businesses in the Mayor's Youth Employment Program.

To Promote Economic Opportunity for All Queen Village residents:

1. We pledge our support and cooperation with the proposed Special Services District on South Street to preserve a decent business climate on a major commercial corridor.
2. We will work to establish adult literacy programs in the neighborhood and to recruit neighborhood volunteers to teach in them.
3. We will introduce job readiness workshops for all those seeking opportunities for employment.
4. We will work with area businesses to identify qualified residents for jobs in the neighborhood and to disseminate information from the Private Industry Council and the County Board of Assistance's "New Directions" concerning city-wide job placement and training programs.

   We pledge to cooperate in achieving these goals as an expression of our continuing commitment to build a "more perfect union" in Queen Village among all those who live and work in our community.

Figure F.4   Queen Village Social Contract

nity network to communicate with area businesses, the Private Industry Council, and the County Board of Assistance.

Both Sustainable Seattle and the Queen City Social Contract offer a coherent and compelling framework for community wide projects. Either approach, especially coupled with a PAR orientation, could work synergistically with a local community network effort. The simplicity of both programs, moreover, increases the likelihood of widespread community adoption and activism.

Bibliography

ACF (1994). *Civic Declaration: A Call for a New Citizenship*. Dayton, OH: Kettering Foundation.

Adams, F., and Hansen, G. (1992). *Putting Democracy to Work: A Practical Guide for Starting and Managing Worker-Owned Businesses*. San Francisco, CA: Berret-Koehler Publishers, Inc.

Agee, P. (1976). *Inside the Company: CIA Diary*. New York, NY: Bantam Books.

Agre, P., and Schuler, D. (1996). *Reinventing Technology, Rediscovering Community: Critical Explorations of Computing as a Social Practice*. Norwood, NJ: Ablex Publishing Co. (Forthcoming.)

Alexander, C., Ishikawa, S., and Silverstein, M. (1977). *A Pattern Language: Towns, Buildings, Construction*. New York, NY: Oxford University Press.

Alexander, R., and Gilmore, P. (1994, July/Aug.). The emergence of cross-border labor solidarity. *NACLA Report on the Americas*.

Alinsky, S. (1969). *Reveille for Radicals*. New York, NY: Vintage.

Alkalimat, A., Gills, D., and Williams, K. (Eds.) (1995). *Job-Tech: The Technological Revolution and Its Impact on Society*. Chicago, IL: Twenty-First Century Books.

Alperovitz, G. (1994, Oct.). Distributing our technological inheritance. *Technology Review*.

Anderson, R., Bikson, T., Law, S., and Mitchell, B. (1995). *Universal Email: Feasibility and Societal Implications*. Santa Monica, CA: RAND Corp.

Aronowitz, S., and DiFazio, W. (1994). *The Jobless Future: Sci-Tech and the Dogma of Work*. Minneapolis, MN: University of Minnesota Press.

Asp, E., and James G. (1983). Social support networks and the schools. In Whittaker and Garbarino (1983).

Austin, L. (1994, Summer). *Public Life and the Press: A Progress Report*. Department of Journalism. New York, NY: New York University.

Bagdikian, B. (1992). *The Media Monopoly*. Boston, MA: Beacon Press.

Bailie, M., and Winseck, D. (Eds.) (1996) *Democratizing Communication: Comparative Perspectives on Information and Power*. Cresskill, NJ: Hampton Press.

Bainbridge Island Arts and Humanities Council (1995). *Bainbridge Island Community Cultural Plan.* Bainbridge Island, WA: Arts and Humanities Council.

Barber, B. (1992). *An Aristocracy of Everyone: The Politics of Education and the Future of America.* New York, NY: Ballantine Books.

Barber, B. (1984). *Strong Democracy: Participatory Politics for a New Age.* Berkeley, CA: University of California Press.

Barber, P. (1994). *Non-Profits in Washington.* Seattle, WA: The Evergreen State Society.

Barlow, J. (1995, May). Death from above. *The Communications of the ACM.*

Baskerville, R., and Wood-Harper, T. (1993). A critical perspective on action research as a method for information systems research. Technical Report. Binghamton, NY: State University of New York.

Beasley, W. (1994). The OTA/NPTN Teleforum Project: The Second Multi-City "Electronic Town Hall." Cleveland, OH: National Public Telecomputing Network. Also available from the Office of Technology Assessment, Washington, DC.

Bellah, R., Madsen, R., Sullivan, W., Swidler, A., and Tipton, S. (1985). *Habits of the Heart: Individualism and Commitment in American Life.* New York, NY: Harper and Row.

Belson, D. (1994). *The Network Nation Revisited.* Electronic document. http://www.stevens-tech.edu/~dbelson/thesis/thesis.html. Bachelor's thesis. Stevens Institute of Technology.

Berry, W. (1990). *What Are People For?* Berkeley, CA: North Point Press.

Bishop, A. (1994). *What Does Your Community Need? Measuring Community Information Needs and Outcomes.* Report. Champaign-Urbana, IL: University of Illinois, Graduate School of Library and Information Science.

Bishop, A. (Ed.) (1993). *Emerging Communities: Integrating Networked Information into Library Services.* Champaign-Urbana, IL: University of Illinois Press.

Bizzel, P. (1982, Fall). Cognition, convention and certainty: What we need to know about writing. *PRE/TEXT* 3. In Graff (1992).

Bloods and Crips. (July/Aug., 1992). Bloods and Crips program to rebuild Los Angeles. *Z Magazine.*

Boal, I. (1995). A flow of monsters: Luddism and virtual technologies. In Brook and Boal (1995).

Bobo, K., Kendall, J., and Max, S. (1991). *Organize! Organizing for Social Change.* Washington, DC: Seven Locks Press.

Borenstein, N. (1995). *E-mail with a Mind of Its Own: The Safe-Tcl for Enabled Mail.* Morristown, NJ: First Virtual Holdings, Inc.

Borenstein, N. (1992). Computational mail as network infrastructure for computer-supported cooperative work. *Proceedings of CSCW '92.* New York, NY: The Association for Computing Machinery.

Borenstein, N., and Freed, N. (1993). MIME (Multipurpose Internet Mail

Extensions). Electronic document. ftp://nic.merit.edu/documents/rfc/rfc1521.txt.

Bournellis, C. (1995, Nov.). Internet '95. *Internet World.*

Boyte, H. (1989). *CommonWealth: A Return to Citizen Politics.* New York, NY: Free Press.

Boyte, H. (1984) *Community Is Possible.* New York, NY: Harper.

Branscomb, L. (Ed.) (1994). *Empowering Technology.* Cambridge, MA: MIT Press.

Brennan, P. (1992). Computer networks promote caregiving collaboration: the ComputerLink project. In Frisse (1992).

Brook, J., and Boal, I. (Eds.) (1995). *Resisting the Virtual Life: The Culture and Politics of Information.* San Francisco, CA: City Lights Books.

Brooks, H. (1993). Research universities and the social contract for science. In Branscomb (1994).

Browne, H., and Sims, B. (1993, Winter). Global capitalism, global unionism. *Resource Center Bulletin.*

Bruckman, A. (1994a). "Serious" uses of MUDs? In Klein and Whitcomb (1994).

Bruckman, A. (1994b). Democracy in MUDs. In Klein and Whitcomb (1994).

Bruckman, A. (1994c). *Moose Crossing: Creating a Learning Culture.* Thesis Proposal. Cambridge, MA: MIT.

BST (1993). *Homesteading the Educational Frontier.* Dillon, MT: Big Sky Telegraph.

Calhoun, C. (1986, Dec.). Computer technology, large-scale social integration, and the local community. *Urban Affairs Quarterly.*

Calhoun, C. (1980, Jan.). Community: toward a variable conceptualization for comparative research. *Social History.*

CCN (1993). *A Vision of Change: Civic Promise and the National Information Infrastructure.* Cambridge, MA: The Center for Civic Networking.

CEM (1995). *Cultural Environmental Movement Prospectus.* Philadelphia, PA: Cultural Environmental Movement.

Chamberlin, J. (1994, June 21). The Right To Be Wrong. Speech. Choice and Responsibility: Legal and Ethical Dilemmas in Serving Persons with Mental Disabilities Conference. Albany, NY.

Chang, E., and Leong, R. (Eds.) (1994). *Los Angeles—Struggles toward Multiethnic Community.* Seattle, WA: University of Washington Press.

Chapman, D. (1994, Jan.). The national forum on science and technology goals. *Communications of the ACM.*

Cheswick, W., and Bellovin, S. (1994). *Firewalls and Internet Security.* Reading, MA: Addison-Wesley.

Cisler, S. (1995a, Jan.). Can we keep community networks running? *Computer-Mediated Communication Magazine.* Also in Cisler (1995b).

Cisler, S. (1995b). (Ed.) *Ties that Bind: Converging Communities.* Cupertino, CA: Apple Computer Corp. Library.

Cisler, S. (1994a). Community networks: past and present thoughts. In Cisler (1994b).

Cisler, S. (1994b). (Ed.) *Ties that Bind: Building Community Networks.* Cupertino, CA: Apple Computer Corp. Library.

Cisler, S. (1993). Community computer networks: building electronic greenbelts. In Bishop (1994).

Cisler, S. (1992). *Call for proposals: Apple library of tomorrow.* Cupertino, CA: Apple Computer Corp.

Civille, R. (1995). The Internet and the poor. In Kahin and Keller (1995).

CNT (1995). NEWS—The Neighborhood Early Warning System. Chicago, IL: Center for Neighborhood Technology.

CNT (1992). *Working Neighborhoods: Taking Charge of Your Local Economy.* Chicago, IL: Center for Neighborhood Technology.

Coate, J. (1992). Innkeeping in cyberspace. In Agre and Schuler (1996).

Cohen, B. (1994). MISANET project proposal. Available from cohene-misanet.org.

Conklin, J. (1988). gIBIS: A hypertext tool for exploratory policy discussion. In Tatar (1988).

CPSR (1993). Serving the Community: A Public Interest Vision of the National Information Infrastructure. Palo Alto, CA: Computer Professionals for Social Responsibility.

Curtis, P. (1992). Mudding: social phenomena in text-based virtual realities. In Agre and Schuler (1996).

Curtis, P., and Nichols, D. (1993). *MUDs Grow Up: Social Virtual Reality in the Real World.* Palo Alto, CA: Xerox Palo Alto Research Center.

CWA. (1995). Changing information services. Washington, DC: Communication Workers of America.

Czitrom, D. (1982). *Media and the American Mind.* Chapel Hill, NC: University of North Carolina Press.

Dahl, R. (1989). *Democracy and Its Critics.* New Haven, CT: Yale University Press.

D'Antonio, M. (1994). I or we? In Cisler (1994b).

Davis, J. (1993, Fall). Focus on computers and the poor: a brand new poverty. *The CPSR Newsletter.* Palo Alto, CA: Computer Professionals for Social Responsibility.

Davis, M. (1994). *eVote Manual.* Palo Alto, CA: Frontier Systems.

Davis, M. (1992). *City of Quartz.* New York, NY: Vintage.

Delzeit, L. (1995). Academy One introduces classrooms to the Internet. Available electronically from a-1 @nptn.org. National Public Telecomputing Network.

DeSilva, D. (Ed.) (1989). *Against All Odds: Breaking the Poverty Track*. Alexandria, VA: Panos Institute.

de Toqueville, A. (1945). *Democracy in America*. New York, NY: Alfred A. Knopf.

Dibbell, J. (1993, Dec.). A rape in cyberspace or how an evil clown, a Haitian trickster spirit, two wizards, and a cast of dozens turned a database into a society. *The Village Voice*.

Dickinson, D. (1988, Winter). New horizons. *In Context*.

Dieberger, A. (1993). The Information City—A Step Merging of Hypertext and Virtual Reality. Poster at Hypertext '93. Seattle, WA.

Doctor, R. (1994, Oct.). Seeking Equity in the National Information Infrastructure. Internet Research, 4 (3).

Doctor, R. and Ankem, K. (1995). *A Directory of Computerized Community Information Systems*. Unpublished report. Tuscaloosa, AL: School of Library and Information Studies, University of Alabama.

Donaghy, K. (1994). 'Enehana Kamepiula: Technology for a Hawaiian Speaking Generation. In Cisler (1994b).

Drake, W., and Schiller, H. (1994). Policy for the Global Information Infrastructure, DIAC-94.

Drew, J. (1995). The Global Solidarity and Cross Border Labor Project Web. Accessible through http://uts.utexas.edu/~jdrew.

Dumont, M. (1994, Mar./Apr.). Deep in the Heart of Chelsea. *Mother Jones*.

eCE (1994 Nov.). Engagierte Computer Expert Innen (eCE), eCE-gram 5. Press release. Amsterdam: The Netherlands.

Ede, L., and Lunsford, A. (1990). *Collaborative Writing—Singular Texts/ Plural Authors: Perspectives on Collaborative Writing*. Carbondale, IL: S. Illinois University Press.

Engst, A. (1994). *Internet Start Kit*. Indianapolis, IN: Hayden Books.

Etzioni, A. (1993). *The Spirit of Community*. New York, NY: Crown Books.

Farb, P. (1974). *Word Play: What Happens When People Talk*. New York, NY: Alfred A. Knopf.

Farrington, C., and Pine, E. (1992). Commmunity memory: A case study in community communication. In Agre and Schuler (1996).

Felsenstein, L. (1995). Untitled paper on the "Perception of equality on the net" and other topics. Distributed at Ties That Bind Conference. May, 1995. See Cisler (1994b).

Felsenstein, L. (1993, May). The commons of information. *Doctor Dobbs Journal.*

Felsenstein, L. (1992). The hacker's league. In Schuler (1992).

Feuer, A. (1993). The Seattle People's Internet Cooperative. *Community Television Review,* V. 16, N. 6.

Fidelman, M. (1993, Oct. 14). Regulatory reform for convergent media. Communet electronic distribution list posting.

Fisher, R. (1981). From grass-roots organizing to community service: community organization practice in the community center movement, 1907–1930. In Fisher and Romanofsky (1981).

Fisher, R., and Romanofsky, P. (Eds.) (1981). *Community Organization for Urban Social Change.* Westport, CT: Greenwood Press.

Fisher, R., and Ury, W. (1981). *Getting to Yes.* Boston, MA: Houghton Mifflin.

Fiske, E. (1991). *Smart Schools, Smart Kids.* New York, NY: Simon and Schuster.

Flower, J. (1994, Jan.). The other revolution in health care. *Wired.*

Fowler, G., and Crawford, B. (1990). *Border Radio.* New York, NY: Limelight Editions.

Frederick, H. (1996). Mexican NGO computer networking and cross-border coalition-building. In Bailie and Winseck (1996).

Frederick, H. (1993). *Global Communication and International Relations.* Belmont, CA: Wadsworth.

Friedman, L. (1996). Electronic democracy and the new citizenship. *Media, Culture, and Society.* (Forthcoming.)

Friedman, M. (1962). *Capitalism and Freedom.* Chicago, IL: University of Chicago Press.

Friere, P. (1993). *Pedagogy of the Oppressed.* New York, NY: Continuum.

Frisse, M. (Ed.) (1992). *Proceedings, 16th Annual Symposium on Computer Applications in Medical Care.* New York, NY: McGraw-Hill.

Fuchs, V. (1983). *Who Shall Live? Health, Economics and Social Choice.* New York, NY: Basic Books.

Gablik, S. (1991). *The Reenchantment of Art.* New York, NY: Thames and Hudson.

Gallagher, A. Jr., and Padfield, H. (Eds.) (1980). *The Dying Community.* Albuquerque, NM: University of New Mexico Press.

Galloway, K., and Rabinowitz, S. (1992). Welcome to Electronic Cafe International, a nice place for hot coffee, iced tea & virtual space. In Jacobson (1992).

Garbarino, J. (1983). Social support networks: Rx for the helping professions. In Whittaker and Garbarino (1983).

Gardner, L., and Paul, R. (1993). Developing a hypertext geographic information system for the Norfolk and Suffolk Boards Authority. *Hypermedia* 5:2.

Garfinkel, S. (1995, Sep.). Separating Equifax from fiction. *Wired.*

Garrett, J. (1993). The world we want: emerging communities, emerging information. In Bishop (1993).

Garson, B. (1989). *The Electronic Sweatshop,* New York, NY: Penguin.

Geoghegan, T. (1992). *Which Side Are You On: Trying to Be for Labor When It's Flat on Its Back.* New York, NY: Plume.

Gerbner, G. (1994, July). Television violence: the art of asking the wrong question. *The World and I.*

Godwin, M. (1994, Oct.). Meme, counter-meme. *Wired.*

Godwin, M. (1994, June). Nine principles for making virtual communities work. *Wired.*

Goel, M. (1980). Conventional political participation. In Smith et al. (1980).

Goodman, P. (1960). *Growing Up Absurd.* New York, NY: Vintage.

Gore, A. (1991, Sept.). Infrastructure for the global village. *Scientific American.*

Graff, G. (1992). *Beyond the Culture Wars: How Teaching the Conflicts Can Revitalize American Education.* New York, NY: Norton.

Graham, H., and Gurr, T. (1969). *The History of Violence in America.* New York, NY: Bantam Books.

Greider, W. (1993). *Who Will Tell the People?* New York, NY: Simon and Schuster.

Greif, I. (Ed.) (1988). *Computer-supported Cooperative Work: A Book of Readings.* San Mateo, CA: Morgan Kaufmann Publishers, Inc.

Grudin, J. (1990). Interface. In *Proceedings of the 3rd Conference on Computer-Supported Cooperative Work.* New York, NY: The Association for Computing Machinery.

Grundner, T. (1993a). Seizing the infosphere: an alternative vision for national computer networking. In Bishop (1993).

Grundner, T. (1993b). *Organizing Committee Manual* (The "Blue Book"). Moreland Heights, OH: National Public Telecommunication Network. (Available only for NPTN affiliates organizing committees).

Gustafson, D., Hawkins, R., Boberg, E., Bricher, E., Pihgree, S., and Chan, C. (1994). The use and impact of a computer-based support system for people living with AIDS and HIV infection. *Proceedings of the 17th Annual Symposium on Computer Applications in Medical Care.* Philadelphia, PA: American Medical Informatics Association.

Gustafson, D., Bosworth, K., Hawkins, R., Boberg, E., and Bricher, E. (1992). CHESS: A computer-based system for providing information, referrals decision support and social support to people facing medical and other health related crises. *Proceedings of the 16th Annual Symposium on Computer Applications in Medical Care.* Philadelphia, PA: American Medical Informatics Association.

Gygi, K. (1995). *Developing an Evaluation Framework for Community Computer*

Networks. Unpublished report. Community and Regional Planning Program, University of New Mexico.

Hall, M. (1988). *Getting Funded. A Complete Guide to Proposal Writing.* Portland, OR: Continuing Education Publications, Portland State University.

Hatch, J., and Eng, E. (1983). Community participation and control or control of community participation. In Sidel (1984).

Hawken, P. (1987). *Growing a Business.* New York, NY: Simon and Schuster.

Hawkins, R. (1995, May 8). Personal correspondence.

Hecker, F. (1994, September 21). Community Network Services. Electronic document. ftp://ftp.digex.net/pub/access/hecker/draft/services.txt.

Herman, E., and Chomsky, N. (1988). *Manufacturing Consent.* New York, NY: Pantheon.

Highlander Center (1993). *Environment and Development in the USA: A Grassroots Report.* New Market, TN: Highlander Center.

Highlander Center (1991). *Community Environmental Health Program Report.* New Market, TN: Highlander Center.

Hiltz, S., and Turoff, M. (1993). *The Network Nation* (2nd Ed.). Cambridge, MA: MIT Press.

Hinds, C. (1992, Spring). From the front lines of the movement for environmental justice. *Social Policy.* Also in Highlander Center (1991).

Hollender, J. (1990). *How to Make the World a Better Place.* New York, NY: William Morrow and Co.

Holley, J. (1994). *Growing Sustainable Communities.* Athens, OH: Appalachian Center for Economic Networks.

Holley, J. (1993). *A Market-Niche Approach to Microenterprise Development: The Food Ventures Project.* Athens, OH: Appalachian Center for Economic Networks.

Homer-Dixon, T., Boutwell, J., and Rathjens, G. (1993, Feb.). Environmental change and violent conflict. *Scientific American.*

Howard, R. (1985). *Brave New Workplace.* New York, NY: Viking.

Illich, I. (1973). *Tools for Conviviality.* New York, NY: Harper and Row.

Illich, I. (1972). *Deschooling Society.* New York, NY: Harper and Row.

Invisible Seattle. (1985). IN.S.OMNIA Number 1. Seattle, WA: Function Industries Press.

Ivins, Molly (1995, May/June). Lyin' bully. *Mother Jones.*

Jackson, J. (1993, Apr./May). Talk radio: who gets to talk? *EXTRA!*

Jackson, K. (1985). *Crabgrass Frontier.* New York, NY: Oxford University Press.

Jacky, J., and Schuler, D. (Eds.) (1980). *Directions and Implications of Advanced Computing.* Norwood, NJ: Ablex Publishing Company.

Jacobson, L. (Ed.) (1992). *Cyberarts: Exploring Art and Technology.* San Francisco, CA: Miller Freeman.

Jensen, C. (1993). *Censored! The News That Didn't Make the News—And Why.* Chapel Hill, NC: Shelburne Press.

Jobtech (1995). Jobs and Technology. Electronic document. http://cs-www. uchicago.edu/discussions/cpsr/jobtech/job-tech.html.

Johnson, R., and Johnson, D. (1988, Winter). Cooperative learning. *In Context.*

Jorgensen, L. (1995, Mar./Apr.). AM armies. *EXTRA!*

Judis, J. (1994, Mar./Apr.). What's the deal? *Mother Jones.*

Kahin, B., and Keller, J. (Eds.) (1995). *Public Access to the Internet.* Cambridge, MA: MIT Press.

Kamber, M. (1990, May). Signs of life, signs of death. *Z Magazine.*

Kapor, M. (1991, Sept.). Civil liberties in cyberspace. *Scientific American.*

Karp, S. (1994, Apr.). The politics of education: an interview with Herbert Kohl. *Z Magazine.*

Katz, M. (1990). *The Undeserving Poor: From the War on Poverty to the War on Welfare.* New York, NY: Pantheon.

Kerwin, A. (1993, Jan. 6). Advertiser pressure on newspapers is common; survey: more than 90% have been pressured but only one-third have caved in. *Editor and Publisher.*

Klein, H. (1995, June). Grassroots Democracy and the Internet: The Telecommunications Policy Roundtable—Northeast USA (TPR-NE). *Proceedings of INET '95.* Washington, DC: The Internet Society.

Klein, H. and Whitcomb, C. (Eds.) (1994) Directions and Implications of Advanced Computing. *Proceedings of DIAC-94.* Palo Alto, CA: Computer Professionals for Social Responsibility.

Kling, R. (Ed.) (1995). *Computerization and Controversy: Value Conflict and Social Choices* (2nd Ed.). San Diego, CA: Academic Press.

Kollock, P., and Smith, M. (1995) *The Sociology of Cyberspace: Social Interaction and Order in Computer Communities.* Thousand Oaks, CA: Pine Forge Press.

Kollock, P. and Smith, M. (1994). Managing the virtual commons: cooperation and conflict in computer communities. Electronic document. http:// www.sscnet.ucla.edu/soc/csoc/vcommons.htm. Sociology Department, University of California at Los Angeles.

Kosinski, J. (1971). *Being There.* New York, NY: Harcourt Brace Jovanovich.

Kozol, J. (1991). *Savage Inequalities.* New York, NY: HarperCollins.

Kramer, R. (1969). *Participation of the Poor: Comparative Community Case Studies in the War on Poverty.* Englewood Cliffs, NJ: Prentice-Hall.

Kranich, N. (1994). Staking a Claim in Cyberspace: Ensuring a Public Place on the Info. Highway. Westfield, NJ: *Open Magazine.*

Krasny, M. (1994, May/June). What is community? *Mother Jones.*

Kretzmann, J., and McKnight, J. (1993). *Building Communities from the Inside Out.* Evanston, IL: Center for Urban Affairs and Policy Research, Northwestern University.

Kunstler, J. (1993). *The Geography of Nowhere.* New York, NY: Touchstone.

Labor/Community Strategy Center (1992). Reconstructing Los Angeles from the bottom up. Los Angeles: The Labor/Community Strategy Center.

Lappé, F., and Du Bois, P. (1994). *The Quickening of America.* San Francisco, CA: Jossey-Bass, Inc.

Laurel, B. (1991). *Computers as Theater.* Reading, MA: Addison-Wesley.

Lavelle, R. and the staff of Blackside. (Eds.) (1995). *America's New War on Poverty.* San Francisco, CA: KQED Books.

Lavender, C., Blythe, G., Montulli, L., Grabe, M., and Ware, S. (1995). *Lynx Users Guide Versions 2.3.7 Beta.* Electronic document. http://kufacts.cc.ukans.edu/lynx-help/Lynx_users_guide237.html.

Lerner, S. (1994) The future of work in North America: good jobs, bad jobs, beyond jobs. Electronic document. http://www.cs.uchicago.edu/discussions/cpsr/jobtech/future-of-work.html. (Originally published as The future of work. In *Futures,* Mar., 1994.)

Leslie, J. (1995, Winter). The high tech future of social change. *Who cares.*

Levin, H. (1980). The struggle for community can create community. In Gallaher, Jr. and Padfield (1980).

Levy, S. (1984). *Hackers: Heroes of the Computer Revolution.* New York, NY: Dell.

Lindsay, P. (1982). The effect of high school size on student participation, satisfaction and attendance. *Educational Evolution and Policy Analysis,* 4.

Liu, C., Peck, J., Jones, R., Buus, B., and Nye, A. (1994). *Managing Internet Information Resources.* Sebastopol, CA: O'Reilly & Associates.

Love, J. (1995). Internet community KO's anti-FOIA provision. Electronic document. http://www.essential.org/listproc/tap.info/0138.html.

Love, J. (1993). Access to government information. In Bishop (1993).

Love, J. (1992). Crown jewels: congressional legis. Electronic document. http://www.essential.org/listproc/tap-infor/0002.html. Washington, DC: Taxpayer Assets Project.

Lowenberg, R. (1995). *Information Ecology 101.* Telluride, CO: Telluride Institute.

Lynch, C. (1993). The roles of libraries in access to networked information: cautionary tales from the era of broadcasting. In Bishop (1993).

Machanick, P., Apteker, R., Green, P., and McWalter, T. (1994). MISANET: The Southern African press on the net. In Klein and Whitcomb (1994).

MacIver, R. (1970). *On Community, Society and Power.* Chicago, IL: University of Chicago Press.

MacKie-Mason, J., and Varian, H. (1994, Feb. 17). Some economics of the Internet. Tenth Michigan Public Utility Conference.

Madara, E. (1993). *Tapping Mutual Aid Self-Help Opportunities On-Line.* Denville, NJ: American Self-Help Clearinghouse.

Mann, E. (1991). *LA's Lethal Air: New Strategies for Policy, Organizing, and Action.* Los Angeles, CA: Labor/Community Strategy Center.

Maser, M. (1994). Curriculum emerging: re-inventing learning communities. Electronic document available from the author. See Virtual High entry in Education section of Appendix B.

Masinter, L. (1994). Collaborative information retrieval: combining talking and searching. In Klein and Whitcomb (1994).

Masinter, L., and Ostrom, E. (1993). Collaborative information retrieval: gopher from MOO. *Proceedings of INET '93.* Washington, DC: The Internet Society.

Mathews, D. (1994). *Politics for People: Finding a Responsible Public Voice.* Champaign, IL: University of Illinois Press.

McClelland, B., and Donovan, T. (Eds.) (1985). *Collaborative Learning and Teaching Writing, Perspectives on Research and Scholarship in Composition.* New York, NY: Modern Language Association.

McCord, C., and Freeman, H. (1990, May 31). Excess mortality in Harlem. *New England Journal of Medicine.*

McKnight, J. (1987, Winter). Regenerating community. *Social Policy.*

McKnight J. (1994, Feb.). Community as client: a challenge for nursing education. *Public Health Nursing.*

McKnight, L. (1994). Public services for the global information infrastructure. In Klein and Whitcomb (1994).

McMillen, N. (1981). The Citizens Council in New Orleans: organized resistance to social change in a deep south city. In Fisher and Romanofsky (1981).

Medoff, P., and Sklar, H. (1994). *Streets of Hope: The Fall and Rise of an Urban Neighborhood.* Boston, MA: South End Press.

Meinke, J. (1995). Eratosthenes experiment—call for participation. Electronic document. Available from the author. Lakewood, OH: Lakewood School District.

Melvin, P. (1981). A cluster of interlacing communities: the Cincinnati social unit plan and neighborhood organization, 1900-1920. In Fisher and Romanofsky (1981).

Mercy, J., Rosenberg, M., Powell, K., Broome, C., and Roper, W. (1993, Winter). Public health policy for preventing violence. *Health Affairs.*

Millennium Communications Group (1995). *Communications as Engagement.* Washington, DC: Millennium Communications Group.

Miller, E. (1994). The Charlotte project: helping citizens take back democracy. Poynter Papers: No.4. Petersburg, FL: Poynter Institute.

Miller, H. (1973). *Medicine and Society.* Oxford, UK: Oxford University Press.

Miller, P. (1993, Fall). The community computing center movement. *CPSR Newsletter.*

Miller, S. (1996). *Civilizing Cyberspace: Policy, Power, and the Information Superhighway.* Reading, MA: Addison-Wesley.

Morgan, E. (1995). Ties that bind: converging communities—a travel log. Electronic document. http://www.lib.ncsu.edu/staff/morgan/ties-that-bind-95/index.html.

Morino Institute (1995a). *Directory of Public Access Networks.* Reston, VA: The Morino Institute.

Morino Institute (1995b). *The Promise and Challenge of a New Communications Age.* Reston, VA: The Morino Institute.

Morino, M. (1994). *Assessment and Evolution of Community Networking.* Washington, DC: The Morino Institute.

Morris, D., and Hess, K. (1975). *Neighborhood Power.* Boston, MA: Beacon Press.

Morriset, L. (1993). Annual Report. New York, NY: Markle Foundation.

Naisbitt, J., and Aburdene, P. (1991). *Megatrends 2000.* New York, NY: Avon.

Nakano, E. (1994). Building common ground: the liquor store controversy. In Chang and Leong (1994).

Namioka, A., and Schuler, D. (1996). Developing community networks. Workshop handouts. http://www.scn.org/ip/commnet/workshop.html.

National Center for Injury Prevention and Control (1993). The Prevention of Youth Violence: A Framework for Community Action. Atlanta, GA: Centers for Disease Control and Prevention.

Nauer, K. (1994, Feb./Mar.). The loss of the neighborhood grocer. *The Neighborhood Works.*

Navarro, A. (1993). The South Central Los Angeles eruption: a Latino perspective. In Chang and Leong (1994).

Neff, R. (1995). The Cleveland Free-Net: status as of June 1995. On-line document. Cleveland Free-Net.

NEGP (1993). Goal to technical planning subgroup on core data elements. Washington, DC: national Education Goals Panel.

NFN (1995). Naples Free-Net. Naples, FL: Naples Free-Net Organizing Committee.

Nilsson, E. (1988). A bucket of worms: computerized vote counting in the United States. In Schuler (1988).

NIST (1994). The information infrastructure: reaching society's goals. NIST Special Publication 868. Gaithersburg, MD: National Institute of Standards and Technology.

Norman, D. (1993). *Things That Make Us Smart: Defending Human Attributes in the Age of the Machine.* Reading, MA: Addison-Wesley.

NPTN (1993a). *Cybercasting Services.* Moreland Hills, OH: National Public Telecomputing Network.

NPTN (1993b). *Organizing Committee Manual.* Moreland Hills, OH: National Public Telecomputing Network.

NPTN (1992). Community computing. Videotape. Moreland Hills, OH: National Public Telecomputing Network.

NVRI (1995). *Challenging the Wealth Primary: Continuing the Struggle for the Right to Vote.* Cambridge, MA: National Voting Rights Institute.

Odasz, F. (1995). Community networks: an implementation planning guide. Electronic document. telnet://bigsky.bigsky.dillon.mt.us/pub/franko/ Guide. Dillon, MT: Big Sky Telegraph.

Odasz, F. (1994). The need for rigorous evaluation of community networks. In Cisler (1994b).

Odasz, F. (1991, Summer). Big Sky Telegraph. *Whole Earth Review.*

Oldenberg, R. (1991). *The Great Good Place: Cafés, Coffee Shops, Community Centers, Beauty Parlors, General Stores, Bars, Hangouts, and How They Get You Through the Day.* New York, NY: Paragon House.

Ornstein, A. (1991). Does school size influence school effectiveness? *American Secondary Education,* 20 (1).

Orwell, G. (1961). *1984.* New York, NY: New American Library.

Osborne, D., and Gaebler, T. (1993). *Reinventing Government: How the Entrepreneurial Spirit Is Transforming the Public Sector.* New York, NY: Plume.

Ostrom, E. (1990). *Governing the Commons: The Evolution of Institutions for Collective Action.* New York, NY: Cambridge University Press.

OTA (1995). OTA's Native American Resource Page. Electronic document. http://www.ota.gov/nativea.html. Washington, DC: Office of Technology Assessment.

OTA (1993). *Making Government Work: Electronic Delivery of Federal Services.* Washington, DC: Office of Technology Assessment.

Oulette, L. (1994, Summer). The video revolution. *Media Culture Review.*

Ousterhout, J. (1994). *The Tcl Language and the Tk Toolkit.* Reading, MA: Addison-Wesley.

Paper Tiger Collective. (1991). *ROAR! The Paper Tiger Television Guide to Media Activism.* New York, NY: The Paper Tiger Television Collective.

Pascarelli, E., and Quilter, D. (1994) *Repetitive Strain Injury: A Computer User's Guide.* New York, NY: Wiley.

Pateman, C. (1970). *Participation and Democratic Theory.* Cambridge, England: Cambridge University Press.

Phillips, K. (1990). *Politics of Rich and Poor.* New York, NY: Random House.

Piller, C. (1994, Oct.). Dream net. *Macworld.*

Piller, C. (1993, July). Bosses with x-ray eyes. *Macworld.*

Piven, F., and Cloward, R. (1979). *People's Movements: Why They Succeed, How They Fail.* New York, NY: Vintage.

Pool, I. (1983). *Technologies of Freedom.* Cambridge, MA: Harvard University Press.

Postman, N. (1986). *Amusing Ourselves to Death: Public Discourse in the Age of Show Business.* New York, NY: Penguin.

Postman, N., and Weingartner, C. (1969). *Teaching as a Subversive Activity.* New York, NY: Dell.

Powledge, T. (1995, Jan.). The Maryland net: almost free, almost good. *Wired.*

Putnam, R. (1995, Jan.). Bowling alone: America's declining social capital. *Journal of Democracy.*

Putnam, R. (1993, Spring). The prosperous community—social capital and public life. *The American Prospect.*

Quitner, J. (1994, Oct.). Billions registered. *Wired.*

Raymond, E. (1994, Mar.). InterLink Prospectus. Electronic document available from the author. See InterLink information in Appendix E.

Rehm, E., and Namioka, A. (1994). *Developing an Open and Equitable Information Infrastructure.* Palo Alto, CA: Computer Professionals for Social Responsibility.

Reibel, J. (1994). The Institute for Learning Technologies: pedagogy for the 21st century. Electronic document. http://www.ilt.columbia.edu. Institute for Learning Technologies.

Reich, R. (1995). *Secession of the Successful.* In Lavelle et al. (1995).

Reich, R. (1992). *The Work of Nations.* New York, NY: Vintage Books.

Reich, V., and Weiser, M. (1993). *Libraries Are More Than Information: Situational Aspects of Electronic Libraries.* Palo Alto, CA: Palo Alto Research Center, Xerox Corp.

Reid, E. (1991). Communication and community on Internet relay chat. Master's thesis. Melbourne, Australia: University of Melbourne.

Rendell, S., Naureckas, J., and Cohen, J. (1995). *The Way Things Aren't: Rush Limbaugh's Reign of Errors.* New York, NY: The New Press.

Rheingold, H. (1993). *The Virtual Community.* Reading, MA: Addison-Wesley.

Rice, R., and Atkin, C. (Eds.) (1989). *Public Communication Campaigns* (2nd ed.). Thousand Oaks, CA: Sage.

Riecken, D. (1994, July). Intelligent Agents. Special issue. *Communications of the ACM.*

Rifkin, J. (1994). *The End of Work: The Decline of the Global Labor Force and the Dawn of the Post-Market Era.* New York, NY: G.P. Putnam's Sons.

Rittel, H., and Kunz, W. (1970). Issues as elements of information systems. Working Paper #131. Institut fur Grundlagen der Planung I.A., University of Stuttgart.

Robert, H. (1971). *Robert's Rules of Order, Revised 1971.* New York, NY: William Morrow and Co., 1971.

Rogers, C., and Vidic, B. (1995). Community information service management guidelines. Pittsburgh, PA: The InfoWorks Partnership.

Rosen, J., and Merritt, D. (1994). Public journalism: theory and practice. Dayton, OH: Kettering Foundation.

Rottenberg, A. (1985). *Elements of Argument: A Text and a Reader.* New York, NY: St. Martin's Press.

"Rough Writer" (1994). Economic Opportunities Afforded by Telecommunication Technology. Electronic document. telnet://bigsky.bigsky.dillon.mt.us. Dillon, MT: Big Sky Telegraph.

Rousseau, J. (1984). *Of the Social Contract.* New York, NY: Harper & Row.

SCANS. (1992). *Learning a Living: A Blueprint for High Performance.* Washington, DC: U.S. Department of Labor.

Schickele, S. (1993). The economic case for public subsidy of the Internet. ftp://cpsr.org/cpsr/nii/harvard.pubaccess.symposium/economics/economic.case.txt

Schiller, H. (1994) NII—Public Good or Corporate Monorail? Westfield, NJ: *Open Magazine.*

Schiller, H. (1989). *Culture, Inc., The Corporate Takeover of Public Expression.* New York, NY: Oxford University Press.

Schor, D. (1995). Forward. In Lavelle et al. (1995).

Schor, J. (1991). *The Overworked American: The Unexpected Decline in Leisure.* New York, NY: Basic Books.

Schuler, D. (1994, Jan.). Community networks: building a new participatory medium. *Communications of the ACM.*

Schuler, D. (Ed.) (1992). Directions and Implications of Advanced Computing. *Proceedings of DIAC-92.* Palo Alto, CA: Computer Professionals for Social Responsibility.

Schuler, D. (Ed.) (1990). Directions and Implications of Advanced Computing. *Proceedings of DIAC-90.* Palo Alto, CA: Computer Professionals for Social Responsibility.

Schuler, D. (Ed.) (1988). Directions and Implications of Advanced Computing. *Proceedings of DIAC-88.* Palo Alto, CA: Computer Professionals for Social Responsibility.

Schuler, D., and Namioka, A. (Eds.) (1993). *Participatory Design: Principles and Practices.* Hillsdale, NJ: Lawrence Erlbaum Assoc.

Schwartz, E. (1994a). Telecommunications and economic development: creating the relationships. Reston, VA: The Morino Institute.

Schwartz, E. (1994b). Telecommunications and economic development: the Philadelphia story. Reston, VA: The Morino Institute.

Schwartz, E. (1991). Building community. Philadelphia, PA: The Institute for the Study of Civic Values.

Sclove, R. (1994a, Jan. 12). Democratizing technology. *The Chronicle of Higher Education.*

Sclove, R. (1994b, Nov. 17). Citizen-based technology assessment. *Loka Alert* 1-12. Amherst, MA: The Loka Institute.

Sclove, R. (1993). Technological politics as if people really mattered: Choices confronting progressives. In Shuman (1993).

Sclove, R., and Scheuer, J. (1994). On the road again? If information highways are anything like interstate highways, watch out! In Kling (1995).

Sedgwick, H. (1930). *The Art of Happiness.* New York, NY: Bobbs-Merrill.

SFC (1995). Society and the future of computing. Electronic document. http://www.lanl.gov/SFC.

Shaffer, C., and Anundsen, K. (1993). *Creating Community Anywhere.* New York, NY: Putnam Publishing Group.

Shepherd, A., Mayer, N., and Kuchinsky, A. (1990). Strudel—An extensible electronic toolkit. *Proceedings of CSCW/90.* New York, NY: The Association for Computing Machinery.

Shuman, M., and Schweig, J. (Eds.) (1993). *Technology for the Common Good.* Washington, DC: IPS Books.

Sidel, V. (Ed.) (1991). *Health Care for a Nation in Need.* New York, NY: The Institute for Democratic Socialism.

Sidel, V., and Sidel, R. (1984). *Reforming Medicine.* New York, NY: Pantheon Books.

Sidel, V., and Sidel, R. (1983). *A Healthy State.* New York, NY: Pantheon Books.

Sirianni, C., Friedland, L., and Schuler, D. (1995). The new citizenship and the Civic Practices Network (CPN). In Cisler (1995b).

Sivin-Kachala, J., and Bialo, E. (1992). *Using Computer-Based, Telecommunica-*

tions Services to Serve Educational Purposes at Home. New York, NY: Interactive Educational Systems Design, Inc.

Smith, D., Macaulay, J., et al. (Eds.) (1980). *Participation in Social and Political Activities.* San Francisco, CA: Jossey-Bass.

Smith, L. (1995, Mar./Apr.). Hate talk: talk radio that's all right, all the time. *EXTRA!*

Snellen, I., and Wyatt, S. (1993). Blurred partitions but thicker walls involving citizens in computer supported cooperative work. *Computer Supported Cooperative Work,* 1:277-293.

Soloway, E. (Ed.) (1993, May). Technology in Education. Special issue. *Communications of the ACM.*

Stephens, M. (1989). *A History of the News.* New York, NY: Penguin.

Stone, A. (1991). *Keystrokes to Literacy.* Lincolnwood, IL: National Textbook Co.

Sustainable Seattle (1994, Spring). Sustainable Seattle Newsletter. Seattle, WA: MetroCenter YMCA.

Tatar, D. (Ed.) (1988). *Proceedings of the 2nd Conference on Computer-Supported Cooperative Work.* New York, NY: The Association for Computing Machinery.

Templeton, R. (1994, Summer). Zero tolerance for Channel One. *Media Culture Review.*

Thoman, E. (1989, Fall). A new media agenda. *In Context.*

Thomson, K. (1995). *Kernels of Democracy.* Medford, MA: Lincoln-Filene Center, Tufts University.

Toffler, A., and Toffler, H. (1980). *The Third Wave.* New York, NY: William Morrow and Co.

TPR (1994, Jan.). Renewing the commitment to a public interest telecommunications policy. *Communications of the ACM.*

Umstead, D. (1995). The Oneida Indian Nation on the World Wide Web. In Cisler (1995b).

United States (1994). *Statistical Abstract of the United States.* U.S. Census Bureau. Washington, DC: US Government Printing Office.

Varley, P. (1991, Nov./Dec.). What is really happening in Santa Monica? *Technology Review.*

Waters, H. (1982, Dec. 6). Life according to TV. *Newsweek.*

Welsh, J., et al. (1994). *The Linux Bible.* San Jose, CA: Yggdrosil Computing Inc.

Weiser, M. (1993, July). Some Computer Science Problems in Ubiquitous Computing. *Communications of the ACM.*

Whittaker, J., and Garbarino, J. (1933). *Social Support Networks: Informal Helping in the Human Services.* Hawthorne, NY: Aldine De Gruyter.

WHO (1986). Ottawa charter for health promotion. An International Conference on Health Promotion. Ottawa: World Health Organization, Health and Welfare Canada and Canadian Public Health Association.

Whyte, W. (1993) *Street Corner Society: The Social Structure of an Italian Slum* (4th Ed.). Chicago IL: University of Chicago Press.

Whyte, W. (Ed.) (1991). *Participatory Action Research.* Newbury Park, CA: Sage.

Whyte, W., Greenwood, D., and Lazes, P. (1991). Participatory action research: Through practice to science in social research. In Whyte (1991).

Winner, L. (1986). *The Whale and Reactor.* Chicago, IL: University of Chicago Press.

Winner, L. (1991, Winter). Artifact/ideas and political culture. *Whole Earth Review.*

Wittig, M. (1991, Summer). Electronic city hall. *Whole Earth Review.*

Wittig, R. (1994). *Invisible Rendezvous: Connection and Collaboration in the New Landscape of Electronic Writing.* Wesleyan, CT: Wesleyan University Press.

Wohlstetter, P. (1985). Art A to Z. In Invisible Seattle (1985).

WSJ (1994, Sept. 15). Internet—companies go on-line to chat, spy, and rebut. *Wall Street Journal.*

Zinn, H. (1994). *You Can't Be Neutral on a Moving Train: A Personal History of Our Times.* Boston, MA: Beacon Press.

Index

Note: Page numbers followed by n indicate footnotes.

A

Abdo, Judy, 124
Academia
  influence on community networks,
    280
  as test-bed for community research,
    383–386
Academy One, 84–86, 109
  Co-Laboratory program of, 91
  sonnet-writing contest conducted by, 85
Access, 47–48, 134, 398
  equity of, 91, 94
  to health-care information and
    communication, 151
  special-purpose user interfaces for,
    288–295
  universal, 401–402
Access networks, 450–451
Access organizations, 430–431
Accommodation, by community networks,
  47–48
Accountability, of government, 141–142
  government accountability networks and,
    452
  government accountability organizations
    and, 437
ACF (American Civic Forum), 391
Actions, 17–22
  capacity building, 17–18
  citizen-led projects/citizen action, 19–20
  citizen participation, 18
  for conviviality and culture, 70–71
  for economic equity, opportunity, and
    sustainability, 212–214
  for education, 107–110
  government and business roles in,
    20–21
  for health and well-being, 174–175
  intercommunity cooperation, 21–22
  for media, 249–252
  as orientation of new community, 9–10
  for strong democracy, 142–143
Adams, Frank, 205
Adaptive technologies, 47–48
Administration, decentralization of,
  286–287

Advertising
  for alcohol and cigarettes, 169–170
  censorship and, 241–242
  as funding source, 370–372
Advocacy organizations, 418–419, 437
  influence on community networks, 280
Advocacy resources, 445–446
Agenda control, as criterion for democratic
  process, 115
Agents, 309–310, 323, 324
AIDS Info BBS, 163–166
Alabama, community networks in, 458
Alberta, community networks in, 468–
  469
Alcohol advertising, 169–170
Allen, Paul, 410
Alliance for Community Media, 283
Alliances, strategic, 271–272, 346–352
Alternative media organizations, 428–430
Alternative media resources, 450
Alzheimer's disease, ComputerLink and,
  155–156
American Civic Forum (ACF), 391
American Civil Liberties Union, 283
American Council of the Blind, 283
American Library Association, 283
American Radio Relay League (ARRL), 371
American Society of Information Scientists,
  283
America Online, 300, 306
Ameritech, 361
Anonymity, 266
  freedom conferred by, 58
  of health-care information and
    communication, 152
Antisocial behavior, 125
  precluding, 258–260
  responding to, 268–269
Appalachian Center for Economic
  Networks (ACEnet), 199–202
Apple Computer, 243
Archie, 311
Arizona, community networks in, 458
Armed forces, impact on public opinion,
  237–238
ARRL (American Radio Relay League),
  371